BE...
BE...
1900 BELMONT...
NASHVILLE, TN 37212

Constructing American Lives

Biography and Culture in Nineteenth-Century America

SCOTT E. CASPER

Constructing American Lives

Constructing

American Lives

Biography & Culture in Nineteenth-Century America

SCOTT E. CASPER

The University of North Carolina Press

Chapel Hill & London

© 1999
The University of North Carolina Press
All rights reserved
Designed by Richard Hendel
Set in Monotype Garamond
by Tseng Information Systems, Inc.
Manufactured in the United States of America
The paper in this book meets the guidelines for
permanence and durability of the Committee on
Production Guidelines for Book Longevity of the
Council on Library Resources.
Library of Congress Cataloging-in-Publication Data
Casper, Scott E.
Constructing American lives: biography and culture in
nineteenth-century America / Scott E. Casper
    p.   cm.
Originally presented as the author's thesis (Ph.D.)—
Yale University.
Includes bibliographical references and index.
ISBN 0-8078-2462-3 (cloth: alk. paper).—
ISBN 0-8078-4765-8 (pbk.: alk. paper)
1. Biography as a literary form.   2. United States—
Biography—History and criticism.   3. United States—
Social life and customs—19th century.   I. Title.
CT34.U6C37   1999
808'.06692—dc21   98-22056
                 CIP
03 02 01 00 99   5   4   3   2   1

The publication of this book has been aided
by generous support from the L. J. Skaggs
and Mary C. Skaggs Foundation.

203068

BELMONT UNIVERSITY LIBRARY

CT
34
.46
C37
1999

ABC-2036

for

Frances Carr Casper

and

Muriel Gutman

CONTENTS

ILLUSTRATIONS

ACKNOWLEDGMENTS

This book is no more self-made than its author, and it is a pleasure to thank those who have helped shape both. Richard Oberdorfer first inspired me to envision history as a profession; he and many other teachers at Norfolk Academy set standards for writing and teaching that remain with me. At Princeton, Lee Clark Mitchell and James McPherson encouraged me to probe the connections and test the boundaries between history, literature, and culture.

Constructing American Lives began as a dissertation in Yale's American Studies Program, where my director Richard Brodhead offered unfailing support and advice that made all the difference. I benefited also from readings by Bryan Wolf, David Brion Davis, and Nancy Cott. Jon Butler, who read the dissertation with a humanely critical eye, taught me the value of ruthless revision. Every graduate student should have a teacher like Ann Fabian, whose friendship and intellectual vitality and imagination I continue to cherish. Many friends in graduate school provided advice, citations, and camaraderie; I am particularly grateful to Jonathan Cowden, Leah Dilworth, Karin Gedge, Stephen and Barbara Lassonde, Stephen Rachman, Kristin Robinson, Christopher Shannon, Glenn Wallach, Elizabeth White, and Susan Williams. Christopher Grasso has read every draft of every part of this project ever since we began our dissertations. Chris has been its toughest, most constructive critic at every level, from large arguments to choices of words.

My debt to the American Antiquarian Society is similarly large. As a research fellow at AAS in 1990–91 and in many visits since, I became acquainted with the history of the book—and with the most remarkable research staff I have been privileged to know. Joanne Chaison, research librarian extraordinaire, has shared the excitement of my archival discoveries, many of which were as much hers as mine. Marie Lamoureux, Dennis Laurie, Tom Knoles, and many others located obscure books, articles, and manuscripts; they often brought materials to my attention that I would not have thought to look for. The other side of AAS is its unparalleled community of visiting researchers, whose stay and scholarship John Hench facilitates with unflappable hospitality. I have benefited immeasurably from conversations with and perceptive readings by a number of scholars whom I first met at AAS, notably Norma Basch, Steve Bullock, William Gilmore-Lehne, Jeffrey Groves, Mary Kelley, Carolyn Lawes, Barbara and Ron Meldrum, Rosalind Remer, Amy Thomas, Michael Winship, and Ronald and Mary Zboray. Thanks also to Richard Brown and Charles Monaghan for sharing useful citations.

As I presented portions of this project at conferences and seminars, numerous commentators, fellow panelists, and listeners offered ideas, citations, and advice. I would like to thank them all. In particular, I was fortunate to participate in a 1993 National Endowment for the Humanities Summer Institute at Vassar College, where Daniel Peck, Wayne Franklin, Margaretta Lovell, Angela Miller, Nancy Cook, and many other scholars responded generously to a presentation about the project as a whole.

Numerous other libraries and archives have made research possible and pleasant. The reference staffs of Sterling Memorial Library, the Beinecke Library, and Manuscripts and Archives at Yale assisted me in finding many sources easily and efficiently. The Houghton Library at Harvard University, and especially curator of manuscripts Leslie Morris, welcomed me into its collection of literary and publishing manuscripts, including uncatalogued material. I also enjoyed working in the Alderman Library and Special Collections at the University of Virginia, the Connecticut Historical Society, the Watkinson Library at Trinity College, Hartford (where Alesandra Schmidt helped me get through the Charles Dudley Warner collection at breakneck pace), the New York Public Library, the Southern Historical Collection at the University of North Carolina, Chapel Hill, the Huntington Library, and the Library of Congress. For permissions to quote from materials in their collections, I am grateful to the following: the American Antiquarian Society; the Boston Public Library; the Connecticut Historical Society, Hartford; the Houghton Library, Harvard University; the Huntington Library; the Maryland Historical Society; the New-York Historical Society; Special Collections and Archives, University of Kentucky; the Southern Historical Collection, Wilson Library, University of North Carolina at Chapel Hill; Manuscripts Division, South Caroliniana Library, University of South Carolina; Special Collections, Alderman Library, University of Virginia; the Watkinson Library, Trinity College; and the Yale Collection of American Literature, Beinecke Rare Book and Manuscript Library, Yale University. Earlier versions of portions of this book previously appeared in *American Literary History,* the *Journal of Women's History,*

Nineteenth-Century Prose, and in *Reading Books: Essays on the Material Text and Literature in America,* edited by Michele Moylan and Lane Stiles.

Without financial assistance, this book (and my graduate education) would have been only a dream unfulfilled. My research was generously supported by a Mellon Fellowship in the Humanities from the Woodrow Wilson Foundation, a University Fellowship at Yale, a Kate B. and Hall J. Peterson Fellowship at AAS, the Stanley J. Kahrl Fellowship in Literary Manuscripts at the Houghton Library, and a Junior Faculty Research Award from the University of Nevada, Reno.

The University of Nevada, Reno, has sustained this project in countless ways over the past six years. The UNR Libraries have been superb, answering many questions, tracking down the obscurest interlibrary loan requests, and purchasing reference sources that assisted me enormously. Millie Syring and Mike Simons deserve special thanks for enabling me to find elusive materials. Scott Lupo provided valuable research assistance. My deepest gratitude is to the Department of History, unusual among history departments in its deliberate emphasis on cultural history. This book is richer for my conversations with all of my colleagues, notably Martha Hildreth, Bruce Moran, Eric Rauchway, and Hugh Shapiro. Several deserve particular thanks: department chair Jerome Edwards, for important moral and administrative support for my research and writing; Jen Huntley-Smith, for reading several chapters perceptively and sharing my enthusiasm for book history; Elizabeth Raymond, for sage advice about this book's organization and ideas and for a splash of cold water when speculation outpaced evidence; and Dennis Dworkin, for always encouraging me to imagine the broader implications of my work—and to address them clearly and directly. Dennis and his family, Amelia Currier and Sam Dworkin, are also the warmest friends I could have wished for in my adopted western home.

The publishing process, smooth and pleasurable throughout, has been a wonderful education for a historian of the book. Everyone at the University of North Carolina Press has been marvelous. Ever since I first met Lewis Bateman in the summer of 1992, he has championed this project and explained the intricacies of moving it from manuscript to book. Pam Upton has managed its production with great care, good humor, and wonderfully thorough explanations of process and style. Suzanne Comer Bell copyedited the manuscript with similar precision and sensitivity. Lawrence Buell and Anne Rose, the press's once-anonymous readers, each read the manuscript at two different stages and offered smart advice that has enhanced it in myriad ways. At UNR, David Parsons tackled the monumental task of preparing the index with insight and gusto, as well as proofreading in the final stages. Creating a book requires far more than its author's words, and I am grateful to them all.

Above all, I am fortunate to have a wonderful, supportive family. Elliot, Carol, Jonathan, and Matthew Agin helped make New Haven my home for six years. Dean Casper always encouraged my education unconditionally. My sister Tracy Casper Lang, brother Andrew Casper, and brother-in-law Eric Lang have watched and listened as this project took shape, and have shared with me many good times away from it. My grandmother Muriel Gutman rightly calls herself my biggest fan; the feeling is mutual, and I couldn't ask for any better. Through everything, my mother Frances Carr Casper has been my greatest teacher and my best friend. Her love, support, and example have made all of this possible.

Constructing American Lives

Biographical Mania

Toward a Cultural History of Genre

Great however as has been its influence from the earliest times, Biography has obtained within the last half century a degree of attention and importance it never before enjoyed. Lives of men eminent in art, distinguished for achievements, or notorious for misfortunes or wickedness, have, during this period, been more than quadrupled. The public look with impatience for the memorials of departed greatness; the press groans under the un-usual burden; our libraries are filling up with amazing rapidity; in fact, Biography is the rage of the day. —Yale Literary Magazine, *June 1845*

Woody and Mia, Charles, Camilla, and Diana (also known as Squidgy), Joey and Amy, O. J. and Nicole, Hillary and Bill, John and Lorena, Oprah and Roseanne, Tonya and Nancy: a list like this shucks and adds every fifteen minutes. We enjoy a non-stop transitory first-name intimacy with a great deal of secondhand experience. We blur the difference between news, entertainment, scandal, and trivia. The broadsheet New York Times *and the tabloid* Weekly World News *often serve up the same dish, al-though the presentation differs. Issues and ideas don't shape daily discourse —celebrity, personality, and anecdote do. We've become a culture of biography.* —Justin Kaplan, The Yale Review, *October 1994*

Groaning presses, overstocked libraries, an impatient public: in nine-teenth-century America, biography could be found nearly everywhere a reader looked, and readers were enthusiastically looking. Commercial publishers and religious tract societies produced hundreds of book-length biographies every year from the 1830s on. Periodicals included sections of "Biography." Newspapers ran reverent obituaries and sensationalistic lives of felons. Collective biographies and biographical dictionaries sketched in brief the lives of many who never received full-length biographies. And biographies turned up almost every place where Americans read: in homes and schools and libraries, to be sure, but also in political clubs, ladies' sewing circles, young men's mutual improvement societies, Civil War camps, even prisons. Biography was not simply a genre of writing. In an age before radio and television, it was *the* medium that allowed people to learn about public figures and peer into the lives of strangers. Twice in midcentury, periodicals summed up the situation; Americans had a "Biographical Mania."[1] More than this, biographers and critics and readers alike believed that biography had power: the power to shape individuals' lives and character and to help define America's national character.

This belief in biography's cultural power explains why Americans wrote so much, and wrote so much about, biography throughout the century — and it is at the heart of this book. The nineteenth-century Biographical Mania was not the same thing as the "culture of biography" that Justin Kaplan contends we have become. Today, popular biography (including forms besides the written, such as the "Biography" program on the cable A&E network) trades heavily in curiosity about famous figures, not on the deeper purpose of building readers', viewers', or a nation's character. Most biographies that seek to shape character fall neatly into the realm of juvenile schoolbook tales, unworthy of critics' attention. Critics write about biography largely in literary and ethical terms: the best way to portray a subject's life, the appropriate use of his or her private papers. Moreover, most of the biographies they write about appeal to the same rarefied audience as their criticism. When those critics discuss mass-market biography, they do so from a distance. Woody and Mia and Hillary and Bill provide a catchy introductory hook, but Kaplan's point is that our "culture of biography" has contributed to the corruption of our public discourse — and his article winds up discussing the "true" biographer's more arduous, less transitory, and altogether more literary endeavors. In the nineteenth century, biography meant something different. American magazines published myriad articles on the *purposes* of biography. In their diaries, women and men in all regions of the nation described reading biographies and taking useful lessons from them. Certainly nineteenth-century biographers, readers, and critics thought about form, and certainly they considered how subjects ought best to be portrayed. But execution and portrayal served larger objectives. Biography did not simply reflect culture, nor was it primarily a vehicle for meeting the insatiable demands of a public that made and dropped celebrities, Andy Warhol–style, every fifteen minutes. When it succeeded, it did so by influencing people's lives, not just stimulating their imaginations literary or otherwise. Biography had constructive, cultural purposes.

This book is about biographies and ideas about biography in America from the 1790s to the turn of the twentieth century. It examines how Americans wrote, published, and read these texts, and how their conceptions of the genre changed throughout the century. Biography helped Americans understand themselves and their national identity as they manufactured a new culture to match their new polity, wrote national and local histories, debated the merits of literary romanticism and realism, explained their democratic culture with the frontier thesis, and professionalized the academy. Biography, of course, was not written or read in isolation from the transatlantic literary world. In this larger sense, this book looks at biography in America between Samuel Johnson's late-eighteenth-century theory of portraying "domestic privacies" and the emergence of Freudian psychology as a powerful new model for biographers. I am concerned with how biographies worked: their purposes and the rhetorical, narrative, and documentary means they employed to achieve those objectives. I am equally interested in how Americans understood, discussed, debated, and reshaped the meanings of biography over a century. As a cultural historian, I do not begin with a definition of "good" biography and test works against it. Rather, I ask two large questions. How did nineteenth-century Americans conceive of the genre? And what can studying nineteenth-century American biography tell us about nineteenth-century literature and culture?

"Biography" for Nineteenth-Century Americans

One answer to the first question may seem hopelessly (or delightfully) atomistic. "Biography" did not simply exist throughout place and time, some monolithic literary ideal to be used or abused. To a religious tract society in the 1830s, biography was a vehicle for encouraging conversion or offering examples of active Christian engagement in the world, and the texts it published reflected this basic fact. To Espy Williams, a twenty-two-year-old New Orleans playwright and biography reader in the 1870s, however, biography was emphatically not a source of models to imitate, but instead a communion with other literary minds. The cultural history of a genre should involve texts, ideas, and experiences. It should include authors, publishers, critics, and readers. And it should interweave literary, institutional, and social history. Therefore my treatment is of a wide range of works: campaign biographies, memoirs of pious women, patriotic and analytical lives of American statesmen, mug books filled with brief sketches of midwestern farmers. All were labeled "biography," however disparate their contents and the circumstances of their creation, publication, and dissemination. This book seeks to decipher what the people who wrote, sold, or read these different kinds of books meant when they called them biographies. Further, it explores what these people's distinct conceptions of "biography" reveal about cultural production and reception in nineteenth-century America.

Despite the diversity encompassed by the label "biography," the story of the genre's development illuminates the ways Americans understood the relationship between individual character and the broader meaning of America's history. In the first decades of the new republic, the predominant message of American-written biographies was didactic and nationalistic. Biographers and critics sought to proclaim America's glory and virtue to the world (and to America itself) and to instill the Revolutionary fathers' virtues in sons imperiled by their temporal and cultural distance from the founding. But another strand existed in biographical criticism: an emphasis on "domestic privacies" drawn from Johnson's essays. The disjuncture between nationalistic biography and Johnsonian criticism reflected a larger conflict over where character lay. Republican theory made the public preeminent. Civic virtue (displayed in public) was essential to individual character, and biography should record this virtue and recommend it to readers. Although no less didactic than the republican nationalists, Johnson located character in the interior, private realm and exhorted biographers to explore that realm and get behind glorious public deeds. Between 1820 and 1860, didacticism and nationalism remained the two dominant paradigms for biography. Each, however, developed along its own, new course. Biographies of self-made men and memoirs of pious women aimed to inculcate particular virtues that were increasingly private and interior, unlike the civic virtue of earlier biographies. Nationalism continued most fully in the development of historical biography as pioneered by Jared Sparks. Sparks considered biography a branch of history, with a mission akin to the state historical societies founded in these years: preserving America's fast-fading past, separating documentary "truth" from unreliable "tradition" or lore before it was too late. By the 1840s, this biographical nationalism came to be expressed localistically. American history could emerge through the accumulation of local histories and biographies. Soon, however, historical biographers like Sparks were challenged by writers who argued that the insistence on documentary evidence left out too much of the story, the emphasis on the "great" excluded too many potential subjects, and the centrality of New England ignored the rest of America.

Also around midcentury, a growing number of critics reevaluated the meaning of biography itself—and argued that biography, as currently practiced, was being done all wrong. They condemned the didactic tendencies to whitewash flaws and make subjects into cookie-cutter models of specific virtues. They decried the historical biographers' proclivity to substitute documented facts for truths about a unique human character. And they directed that biography focus on the "inner man," a concept not unlike Johnson's "domestic privacies" but different in its distinction between the "private" and the "inner." In this new vision of biography, derived from contemporary English notions, the critics also sought to create hierarchy within the genre. Some types of biography, written by certain sorts of writers for certain sorts of readers, were better than others. It was no coincidence that this criticism emerged in the wake of the mass expansion of book production and reading after 1830, when hack biographers allegedly degraded the genre by pandering to masses of readers. As the critics came to define biography as a self-consciously literary endeavor, the former newspaperman James Parton self-consciously defined his identity as America's first professional biographer. In the process, he negotiated between the levels of biography that critics and publishers had come to distinguish by the 1860s: the "high" world of biography as literature and the "middle" realm of didacticism, each associated with different sorts of publishers and readers.

Notwithstanding the critics' strictures, biography remained the essential genre for creating American pantheons: collections of lives that represented the nation's history, aimed to promote values and virtues, or both. Two varieties of pantheons developed in the century's closing decades. Biographical series, produced by literary publishers like Houghton Mifflin, offered select individual biographies as parts of a larger American history centered in the Northeast. "Mug books" of local biography published by subscription firms in Chicago and San Francisco added thousands of local farmers, businessmen, and town officials to America's biographical history, in the process challenging both the historical hegemony of New England and the idea that biography should tell of just the "choice and charmed" political and literary elites. At the same time, academic historians influenced by evolutionary theory began to question the value of biography itself. If larger forces, not individuals, had shaped history, did not biography preserve an archaic, romantic emphasis on great men? This view could not stem the popularity of biographies, however—thanks to the enduring sense that individual lives provided an unparalleled human window into the past, the continuing notion that contemporary youth could benefit from the examples of illustrious forebears, and the advent of psychology and celebrity in the twentieth century.

Three arguments underpin my narrative about biography in nineteenth-century America. First, debates over biography were microcosms of larger debates over *character:* what it was, where to find it, and how to portray it. Second, biography had a double-edged relationship with *history.* As a branch of history it could reinforce larger master narratives about the American past, but by adding neglected individuals and groups it could also challenge those narratives and suggest alternative interpretations. Third, by century's end several key seeds of our modern "culture of biography" had been sown, notably a new critical vocabulary that defined biography as *literature* and distinguished "good" biography from almost all the *biographies* actually being written and read. Given that biography deals with lives lived in the past, it is ironic that American biography's own nineteenth-century past has been effaced by subsequent biographers and scholars alike. The literary redefinition of biography, begun in the 1850s and completed in the 1920s, accounts for this neglect. As these issues intermingle throughout my chronological narrative, let me explain each one briefly here.

Although authors and readers saw biography as an agent of character formation throughout the century, "character" had no static or unanimously shared definition. In the eighteenth century and into the post-Revolutionary period (1790–1820), the term was widely equated with "reputation," the way one was perceived in the eyes of the world. To be more precise, it meant two things at once. One's performance or actions on the public stage *revealed* one's character (true self), and at the same time they *fixed* one's character (reputation) in others' eyes. In emphasizing the revelation of character in public, these definitions coincided with the essential tenet of post-Revolutionary American republicanism: that a republic's survival depended on its citizens' civic virtue, their commitment to participate in public life and place the public good before private interest.[2] Hence American biographers of these years focused on their subjects' public lives and deeds—because that was where they perceived character, and because that was how they could help mold the next generation of citizens. Johnson's theory of biography made little headway in American biographical practice before 1820 largely because most Americans did not share his notion of character.

The development of liberal individualism and evangelical Christianity helped redefine character in several ways. The term increasingly referred to what one did habitually: *habits* of industry, temperance, piety, and so on. As such, character would no longer necessarily be displayed or seen in one's actions on the public stage. At the same time that habits—increasingly, private habits—came to define one's character (true self), they were also seen to determine one's success or failure in public, at least in the rhetoric of character formation preached by ministers, advice manuals, and biographies. Cultivating the right character, it seemed, was a prerequisite to becoming a self-made man or a true Christian. Character also now denoted a cluster of characteristics that could be defined, described, and presumably inculcated, especially through biographies. This new notion of character, in turn, helped redefine the self as something that could be formed over time. The diaries of American readers reveal that many used biographies as examples and encouragement in forming those selves, religious and secular.[3]

From roughly midcentury on, romantic critics took issue with didactic and utilitarian notions of character and with the biographies that promoted them, and they reconceived biography as an antidote. These critics emphasized *individuality,* defining character (or the true self) as that which made an individual unique. In their view, the myriad lives of self-made men and pious Christians replaced individuality with formulaic bundles of characteristics, labeled "individualism" or "piety." The traits that didactic biographies promoted did not constitute the subjects' true selves, and reading such books could not help readers cultivate their own characters in a romantic sense. Biography, the romantic critics believed, should influence a reader's character through inspiration, not imitation: the example of a truly individual subject could encourage the reader to develop his or her own "genius." Again, American readers' responses suggest that they used biography this way even before American critics embraced romantic ideas in the 1850s. However, it was not uncommon for readers, unlike the critics, to read biographies both didactically and romantically, finding models for emulation and sources of inspiration. By 1886, the Episcopal bishop Phillips Brooks recommended biography to the young men of Exeter for its examples of individuality—now as a buffer against an emergent culture of professionalism, specialization, and standardization where forming "professional" character meant creating another sort of homogenized self.[4]

As a historical endeavor, biography had the power to reinforce *or* challenge prevailing narratives of the American past. Those narratives emanated from the Northeast. The leading historians were New Englanders, and their work usually issued from publishers in Boston and New York. Most of them shared a "great man" approach (in which both parts of the phrase applied). Implicitly or explicitly, they espoused a vision of American history with New England at the center, from the seventeenth-century Puritans to the nineteenth-century flowering of American literature. Myriad biographies confirmed all of these tendencies, for New Englanders far outpaced citizens of other regions in writing about their forebears. The preeminent biographical series of the century, Jared Sparks's Library of American Biography in the 1830s and Houghton Mifflin's American Statesmen and American Men of Letters in the 1880s and 1890s, similarly focused on New England's eminent men. But these key works neither monopolized the field nor precluded alternative historical visions. Biography could be a useful vehicle for other visions precisely because it lacked the sweep of history: through biography, neglected figures could be added to the national picture. If enough such figures could be collected, new notions of the larger history became possible. Writing brief lives of scores of Revolutionary women, Elizabeth Ellet argued in the 1840s for the importance of women's influence in the struggle for independence. In thousands of biographical sketches, midwestern mug books implied that the frontier experience, not the Puritan past, had defined the American character. Most such works never directly rejected dominant historical interpretations, but they all suggested that America's story lay in the lives of ordinary men and women, people ignored and forgotten by traditional historical narratives.

These works also reconceived how "history" could be done, not just what it emphasized. The nineteenth century witnessed the enshrinement of historical "objectivity," beginning in America with Sparks and his cohort and climaxing in the academic profession of history. Fundamental to the objective ideal was the distinction between the "professional" and the "amateur," for the emerging cadre of historians suspected history written by or for its subjects' descendants (unless those descendants belonged to their own professional ranks). Equally fundamental was evidence: verifiable documents of the past, distinct from oral lore and fuzzy sentiment. This epistemology, as much as the great-man ideology, rendered whole categories of subjects historically invisible. Genres not associated with documentary "truth" could be used to tell their stories. Novels could make protagonists of ordinary soldiers and farmers, and cheap narrative autobiographies could give marginal characters a voice. But biography, because it was identified with "truth," provided a better way to place little-known figures in the *historical* record. To do so, authors reframed Sparks's rules of evidence to incorporate oral lore. They argued that corroborated memory should be counted authentic where documents were lacking, or went to the subjects themselves for information and stories. As the academic profession of history became entrenched toward 1900, these approaches could not pass its muster. Nonetheless, they retained the claim of truth and created history for subjects who otherwise would have been forgotten.

As "literature," biographies were always part of a constellation of genres with overlapping conventions, goals, and markets. The standard definitions of biography in nineteenth-century dictionaries — "a history of lives, a writing of lives" or "the history of the life and character of a particular person" — suggested that biography as a genre shared something with history (its "truth," at least in dealing with someone who had actually lived) and with many novels (its focus on an individual subject).[5] The purposes of biographies linked them also to numerous forms of writing not usually considered literary (religious tracts, partisan newspapers, advice manuals), as well as to plays, novels, and histories with similar messages and themes. Readers and certainly critics understood biography as a distinct literary form, but many readers simultaneously elided its purposes and effects with those of other genres. A biography like a religious manual could inculcate right habits; a biography like a novel could "thrill." Moreover, biographies existed in America's multiple literary cultures alongside works of other sorts. The political-communications network that produced antebellum campaign biographies also published party songbooks. Religious memoirs constituted just one category in the American Tract Society's catalog. James Parton published biographical stories next to sentimental fiction in the *New York Ledger,* beside local-color writing in the *Atlantic Monthly,* and near essays on public affairs in the *North American Review.*

By century's end, however, it was clear that biography did not constitute part of "literature." Although critics from midcentury on sought to invest biography with specific properties usually associated with the best in poetry and fiction, their efforts essentially failed. Critics applied the phrase "*con amore,*" which described the poet's or novelist's unique affinity with a subject, to the relationship between biographers and their subjects. They dismissed biographies written for overt political, moral, or eulogistic reasons. They encouraged biographers to write more like novelists, to enthrall readers with well-written stories instead of deluging them with innumerable facts. Biographies overwhelmingly fell short of the critics' standards — perhaps not surprisingly, since those standards emerged in large measure as a reaction against the popular literary market. Beginning with Houghton Mifflin's American Men of Letters series, biography and literature became linked in two other ways. Like much English literary biography since Johnson's *Lives of the Poets,* American literary biography served as a vehicle of criticism: knowing an author's life could presumably shed light on his or her works. Like its contemporary model, the English Men of Letters series, the American series also used biography to shape the concept of a national literature. But critics did not classify these new biographies *as* literature.

Moreover, readers preferred other biographies, frustrating the critics' desire to create a more enlightened reading public. In 1885 Parton noted with some concern the public's rising interest in the "trifling" private details of famous people's lives. At the same time, he observed this in a book called *Some Noted Princes, Authors, and Statesmen of Our Time*—which, no less than the works he found potentially troublesome, took contemporary, mostly living personalities as its subjects. Parton hedged his bets by assuring readers that his book contained nothing to violate "the reasonable privacy of public individuals," but even the word "reasonable" suggested that some privacies had now become unreasonable.[6] Moreover, books like this one and the increasing number of newspaper and magazine biographies of famous people appealed primarily to readers' curiosity, not their desire for moral improvement, romantic inspiration, or historical understanding. These divisions persist. Few literary critics today would place any biography—let alone an American one—on a list of a hundred, or even five hundred, major literary works. Equally few literary biographies make their way onto best-seller lists, even though biography retains the popularity it has enjoyed since well before the *Yale Literary Magazine* diagnosed America's biographical mania in 1845.

Biography and the Cultural History of Nineteenth-Century America

Beyond these arguments about biography itself, the development of and debates over biography are worth studying for several larger reasons. First and simplest, biography was phenomenally popular in nineteenth-century America—and we know virtually nothing about it. Paradoxically, our lack of knowledge stems in part from the assumption that we know all about it. In the century between James Boswell and Lytton Strachey, "good" biographies were few, and few of those were American. Most American biographies served to inculcate morality and patriotism, eulogized their subjects, and promulgated historically inaccurate legends about our noted men. Biographies were not good literature and they were bad history; what more is there to know? In answering this question as a cultural historian, I am among the many recent scholars who study long-neglected or long-derided literature, recovering works that had meaning for nineteenth-century readers. These scholars ask how popular literature sought to shape its readers' conceptions of themselves and their world, rather than whether it was any good by modern standards. This book seeks to recover not simply "noncanonical" works but an entire genre that lies outside our literary canon, and to suggest historically how it got there.[7]

It is striking that the modern scholarship of literary recovery has focused on practically everything except biography: sensational dime novels, sentimental fiction written by women, exotic travel literature, even pornography. Much of this scholarship has sought to recover or locate the subversive within nineteenth-century American writing: to find literature that challenged prevailing ideologies of capitalism, middle-class morality, patriarchy, or white supremacy and to find similar challenges within long-familiar texts. Biography has remained in shadow, I think, because nothing about it seems subversive. It seems the paramount genre of dominant liberal individualism and self-made manhood, the genre *against* which women's or working-class fiction protested. If we are looking for a subversive imagination or ideological alternatives in nineteenth-century America, biography is not the place to find them. This is not to say, however, that Americans agreed about the definition or uses of biography. Ideas about biography always engendered debate. At every point in the century, influential authors and critics in America's literary metropolises, usually influenced by English ideas of biography, aimed to direct the ways Americans thought about the genre. Nationalistic biographies clashed with cosmopolitan literary ideals; written lives championing a particular region or locale countered supposedly national narratives; and biographies about ordinary people challenged tomes about great men as the makers of American history. Certainly biographers' stories and messages promoted particular ideologies, more often than not the ones that predominated in their times. The form of biography did emphasize the individual, and the subjects of biographies tended to be those who had succeeded, even if success meant owning an eighty-acre farm outside Lincoln, Nebraska. It is nonetheless a mistake to dismiss biography as monolithic.

Beyond the debates within biography, alternatives to and arguments about biography emerged in other genres. These are not central to my story: I do not, for instance, dissect how working-class fiction responded to the middle-class vision of entrepreneurial *and* artisanal biography. At several points, I do allude to the ways familiar works in other genres responded to the limits of biography. These discussions remain brief and few given the constraints of length and focus, but they serve as an essential reminder that debates over biography never existed in a literary vacuum. Consider this poem:

> When I read the book, the biography famous,
> And is this then (said I) what the author calls a man's life?
> And so will some one when I am dead and gone write my life?
> (As if any man really knew aught of my life,
> Why even I myself I often think know little or nothing of my real life,
> Only a few hints, a few diffused faint clews and indirections
> I seek for my own use to trace out here.)

Walt Whitman rejected "the biography famous" for the same reasons romantic critics disdained the bulk of contemporary biographies: the failure to understand a subject's "real life," the inner man behind the external facts and scattered surviving letters. Whitman went two steps further. To critics who argued for better biographers, he responded that no man can know "my life." And to those, including Longfellow, who called autobiography the truest form of biography ("What is autobiography? / It is what a biography ought to be."), Whitman wondered whether even he could truly know himself. With this poem added to its prefatory material in 1867, *Leaves of Grass* became autobiography composed as poetry and counterposed explicitly against biography.[8] Understanding biography can enhance our analysis of works in other genres that tried to address the gaps biography could not or would not fill.

Ultimately, though, now-obscure biographers and ordinary readers outnumber familiar authors in this book. Discussing relatively unknown writers is necessary for exploring the history of an unfamiliar genre. The need to enter readers' thoughts and worlds is less obvious. Most comprehensive histories of genres contain no evidence from readers, only reference to "the reader" constructed, addressed, or implied by the texts. However, arguing that biographies had constructive, cultural purposes seems incomplete without some consideration of whether and how real readers responded to those texts and purposes. The history of readers is exceedingly difficult to adduce. Who would have guessed that future president James A. Garfield recorded three decades of biography reading in his diary, or that early-nineteenth-century library records would reveal people waiting to borrow the volumes of John Marshall's *Life of George Washington?* Moreover, every evidence of readership comes with interpretive pitfalls. Library records, particularly circulation registers, provide glimpses into local reading communities. But checking out a library book is not the same thing as reading it: some people probably returned books unread. Equally likely, some borrowings indicate multiple readers within a household.[9] More leisured Americans had far greater opportunity not just to read but also to leave evidence of their reading—diaries, journals, letters—than those with fewer resources (including slaves and members of the working classes). No single reader, nor even a few dozen readers, represented the range of responses to any text, let alone a whole genre. Further, writing diaries and letters was itself an act of literary construction. Ordinary diarists modeled their entries and writing styles on those they read in memoirs and novels, and described biographies in language learned from biographical prefaces and criticism. Many a young man's college commonplace book was designed for his father's scrutiny or his own "improvement." But once we understand readers' responses as cultural constructions, we can seek connections between ostensibly unmediated diary entries and seemingly lofty periodical criticism.

I am interested in recovering the American experience of biography, not simply a neglected genre. This book's subtitle, *Biography and Culture in Nineteenth-Century America,* denotes two key distinctions. First, "American biographies" were not the same as "American biography." The phrase "American biographies," meaning books in the genre produced in America, could encompass American-written works (on Napoleon as well as Washington), lives of American subjects (by English as well as American authors), or simply books published in the United States (including American imprints of European works). "American biography," as discussed by nineteenth-century authors and critics, had national connotations. It became a rallying cry at various points in the century, for instance when early-national leaders sought to establish a uniquely American culture. It also described American-written lives of figures associated with the nation: the life of a Revolutionary hero in Sparks's Library of American Biography, but not the religious memoir of a pious Connecticut woman written by her minister. Second, neither the texts called "American biographies" nor the concept of "American biography" was synonymous with the American experience of biography. A reader seeks a lock of Aaron Burr's hair and autographed letters by Burr and James Parton to paste into his copy of Parton's biography of Burr. The daughter of one of Elizabeth Ellet's subjects objects to Ellet's portrayal of her mother, and Ellet includes a new sketch of the woman in her next volume. A prospective author emphatically tells Houghton Mifflin why he will not write a volume for its American Men of Letters series. Each of these episodes reveals something beyond the biography involved, something about what American readers and writers thought biography to be—and what they made it.

The fragmentary evidence of Americans' biography reading suggests this hypothesis: Even though they often blurred the lines between biography and other genres, and even though they often read biography for historical knowledge, many American readers also possessed a biographical imagination. By this I mean a proclivity to see individual lives as stories: not merely sequences of events or episodes, but totalities with a certain coherence. Several cultural historians have recently suggested as much and identified the sources of this imagination. Novels, especially the bildungsromans and sentimental fiction that were extremely popular from the late eighteenth century on, presented just such stories of lives. So did several widely read autobiographies, like Benjamin Franklin's. The next step was for these readers to conceive of their own lives as stories, with themselves as author and protagonist. As authors, they could first model their habits, actions, and lives on those of the characters they encountered in fiction. Eventually more and more Americans authored their life stories literally, writing autobiographical accounts. Despite great variations in details, many of these accounts shared an ethos broadly defined as entrepreneurial or romantic. Their author-protagonists had left homes and families, often traveling far away to seek new occupations in the transforming economy and society of the early republic. Or they had left the spiritual roots of their upbringing to seek their own answers to cultural and religious questions. A market economy, evangelical religion, and romanticism all encouraged people to think of themselves as free agents, characters in the making (and on the make) on stages of their own devising. New experiences, success, a desire to tell their stories, and maybe their children's and grandchildren's entreaties help explain why these accounts came to exist. The narrative conventions found in novels and other autobiographies like Franklin's helped shape *how* these autobiographers told their life stories. In other words, as scholars have begun to delineate it, the biographical imagination sprang from novel reading and experience and culminated for some successful Americans in autobiographical production.[10]

Imaginatively and concretely, biographies played a pivotal role in shaping the American biographical imagination. No less than novels, they modeled right feelings and proper behavior, and readers took the lessons. In dozens of diaries, readers expressed their desires to live like the people they encountered in biographies. If the search for life's meaning could take people away from the homes and ideas of their youth, it could also prompt a search for new models that biography could provide, even to so-called self-made men. Some readers (including James A. Garfield) went further in mature years, comparing the entire trajectories of their life *stories* to those they read about. By late in the century, various biographical institutions promoted Americans' sense that their own lives were stories. Prominent figures increasingly told their life histories to journalists. Thousands of less-prominent citizens sat for interviews or answered questionnaires for the companies that published mug books. Even when the questions remained rudimentary, they encouraged subjects to consider their lives as wholes, to connect the circumstances of their youth to their hard-won success. Just as nineteenth-century Americans (unlike contemporary literary critics) saw autobiography as a subset of biography, not a separate genre, this autobiographical impulse comprised only part of the larger desire to commit people's life stories to print. This desire led family members to write—or solicit others, from local ministers to the nation's preeminent biographer James Parton, to write—the lives of deceased relatives. The ever-rising number of biographies and the expanding diversity of biographical subjects encouraged more and more people to believe that they and their kin had life stories, indeed life stories worth telling. America's biographical mania and Americans' biographical imagination fueled each other.

Beyond tracing the interplay between biography and culture in nineteenth-century America, this book proposes what a cultural history of genre might look like. In this I bring together two movements within recent scholarship. One, which has become known as the new historicism, argues that texts can be understood only in relation to the material and ideological circumstances of their production. New historicism is fundamentally a way of reading texts, a movement within literary criticism. This form of analysis presupposes that texts do not simply reflect "context" but that the division between texts and contexts is far more problematic, perhaps even artificial. The other, the history of the book or *histoire du livre,* delineates the mechanisms of print culture, to explore the conditions in which books are produced, distributed, and consumed at a given historical moment. Its sources tend to be archival records rather than literary works: the inventories of booksellers and libraries, the papers of publishing houses, the diaries of readers. Historians of the book argue that context includes not just political or cultural ideologies and economic conditions, but the specific conditions of publishing, authorship, and reading—a constellation that Richard Brodhead has called a "culture of letters."[11]

Several recent analyses of long-neglected genres, notably Cathy Davidson's work on American novels of the early republic and Michael Denning's study of nineteenth-century American dime novels, fuse elements of these approaches, grounding textual interpretations in carefully described contexts of production and reception. Davidson and Denning both attend closely to debates over genre: moralists' and political leaders' critique of the novel around 1800, magazines' and librarians' objections to cheap fiction late in the century. Both argue that the fiction they examine had subversive potential, offering visions of empowerment to politically, legally, or economically disfranchised members of the body politic. But although Davidson and Denning adduce some evidence of actual readers—marginalia in surviving copies of *Charlotte Temple,* autobiographical reminiscences of working-class readers—neither introduces readers as commentators on genre. Critics of early fiction or the dime novel speak to and about readers, but readers seem to respond simply by the act of reading the works the critics proscribe. Direct answers to critics come not from readers but from the texts: *The Coquette* is made to speak both for and to women readers of the early republic, and *Larry Locke: Man of Iron* does the same for laborers of the Gilded Age. "The reader" replaces readers, and models of oppositional response stand in for actual responses.[12]

This book differs by introducing actual readers into the discourse of genre. It tries to get closer to readers themselves, and always to distinguish "the reader" whom authors, critics, and publishers envisioned from the Americans who read biographies. In doing so, it addresses a gap recently identified by James L. Machor. Historians of the book have told us much about "who read, what they read, and why they read" but little about "how people read." Reader-response critics have generally supplied the "how" only through theoretical models, and new historicists have tended to locate "the reader" within the text. The few close analyses of historical readers' responses have focused mostly on how particular individuals read within the contexts of their personal lives.[13] My goal is different. I hope to demonstrate that individual readers participated in the discourse of genre, that they construed "biography" for themselves, and that their constructions were connected to those occurring in biographies and criticism. Thus readers appear throughout this book (rather than in a distinct grounding chapter at the beginning), as do discussions of the contours of book production and consumption at various points in the century.

This book's scope also sets it apart from most recent cultural analyses of genre: it traces the discussion of a genre over a full century, exploring change over time as well as the cultural situation of biography at several particular moments. This extended span complicates still further any notion of "the reader." It is difficult to identify a model biography reader at any single point in time. A campaign biography of Martin Van Buren and a religious memoir of a pious woman, both written and read in 1836, sought different audiences and elicited different responses. It is more difficult to describe a model reader in the context of change in the culture and in the genre. It would be tempting, for instance, to construct a middle-class "reader" for biography, a reader interested in rising within the dominant culture (economically like the self-made man, or spiritually like the evangelical Christian). Such an interpretation would take biographies as middle-class handbooks and would counterpose them against genres like subversive, working-class dime novels. However, the diaries and memoirs of actual readers complicate this picture. If biography was part of middle-class culture, over a century "biography," "middle-class culture," and the relationship between the two underwent profound transformations.[14] Readers construct meaning within particular cultural situations, which might include (among other things) religious beliefs and activities, political leanings, place of residence, gender, and stage of life. It should not be surprising that a devout Methodist during the Awakening of the 1830s read biographies differently than did a cosmopolitan politician or a romantic playwright four decades later. Nor should it be surprising that the same politician had read differently when he was a twenty-five-year-old collegian. Equally important, readers construct the meaning of a genre within the cultural situation of the genre itself. Readers could decide for themselves whether biographies were good or bad, but their standards owed much to the discourse about biography in their times.

One note on the structure of this book: Between the five main chapters, which develop the story of biography through the nineteenth century, are interludes designed to capture moments in Americans' biographical experience. Two of these interludes (on Parson Weems and on Nathaniel Hawthorne and Jared Sparks) concern the production and critical reception of biographies. The other two (on two readers of the 1830s and 1840s, and on James A. Garfield's experience as reader and subject of biographies) concern the meanings of biography in individuals' lives. Individually, these interludes offer snapshots of the relationship between Americans, biographies, and concepts of the genre. Taken together, they mark in microcosm many of the changes over time that the chapters explore at greater length.

Biographers in their works, critics in their reviews, editors in their correspondence, and readers through their diaries and letters all participated in a discourse that persisted and changed throughout the nineteenth century—and that continues to persist and change in our own day. As Justin

Kaplan reminds us, biography is no less ubiquitous or interesting today than it was when the *Yale Literary Magazine* described groaning presses, overstocked libraries, and eager readers a century and a half ago. The meaning of biography is no less diverse and contested: scandalous exposés of celebrities compete (usually successfully) for best-seller status with archivally researched lives of historical figures and psychological portraits of the powerful and famous. Biographers, critics, and readers still argue whether subjects have been portrayed accurately and fairly. The rest of this book attempts to restore a similar complexity to the past. As it complicates our picture of biography in nineteenth-century America, it also deepens our view of nineteenth-century American culture itself, adding richness and flux to generalities like "individualism" and "middle-class culture." Most important, it explores how the specific economic, institutional, and social dimensions of print and reading intersected with particular and changing aesthetic values, political ideologies, and moral beliefs to shape the ways people experienced texts.

CHAPTER

I

Didactic Nationalism
versus Johnsonian Theory,
1790–1830

I have been reading Johnson's lives of poets and famous men, till I have contracted an itch for Biography; do not be astonished, therefore, if you see me come out, with a very material and splendid life of some departed Virginia worthy—for I meddle no more with the living. Virginia has lost some great men, whose names ought not to perish. If I were a Plutarch, I would collect their lives for the honor of the state, and the advantage of posterity.—William Wirt to Dabney Carr, June 8, 1804

With these words the Virginia attorney and author William Wirt unwittingly revealed much about the understanding of biography in the early republic. Inspired by Samuel Johnson's *Lives of the English Poets* to write biographies himself, Wirt suggested that the American biographical impulse derived from English models. It also grew out of peculiarly American circumstances—the honor of Virginia—as much as any desire to emulate Johnson or Plutarch. Moreover, his concern with "posterity" reflected a common theme in the new nation: implanting the virtues of the Revolutionary fathers in the rising generation. Critics called for "American biography," the lives of subjects specifically identified with the founding of the country. At least as early as 1788, when David Humphreys billed his *Life of Israel Putnam* as the first such work, biographers of American subjects offered the same message. Lives of Americans could teach and inspire the young, commemorate those who had won American independence, and proclaim the new nation's place beside—or superiority to—European monarchies. Biography writing became part of the multifaceted effort to create a national identity and culture.

But what sort of national identity and culture? Multiple worlds of readers, critics, and biographers existed in the early republic, as three events of 1817 show. In February, sixty citizens of Washington County, New York, founded a social library. Over the summer, the second volume of Joseph Delaplaine's *Repository of the Lives and Portraits of Distinguished Americans* appeared, which rekindled a battle between critics over the nature of biography. While this fight was raging, William Wirt's biography of Patrick Henry appeared. The Washington County library patrons, the critics who argued over Delaplaine's work, and the Virginia men of affairs whose approval Wirt wanted belonged to different social worlds.

In all three, the picture of "American biography" was complex, for American readers, critics, and writers were attempting to assert cultural independence while British biographies and British theories of biography continued to dominate the transatlantic literary landscape. Although American-written lives of American subjects made up a growing part of library patrons' biographical fare, many of the nation's most heavily circulated biographies were American reprints of European works. Samuel Johnson's theory of biography, which permeated almost every American critical discussion of the genre, stood at odds with most American biographers' practice. Johnson and many American critics argued that private habits, not public deeds, gave the truest measure of character, and that biography should emphasize individual character over national history. Biographies of American patriots in these years concentrated on their subjects' public careers and deeds, finding the truest signs of republican character on the battlefield and in the legislative chamber. Johnsonian theory and nationalistic practice rarely came into open conflict. But their infrequent collisions, like the one over Delaplaine's *Repository,* suggested the tensions between British-derived criticism and American nationalism. William Wirt's thirteen-year struggle to write the biography of Patrick Henry, the book he ultimately produced, and its critical reception revealed the depth of these tensions. By the time his *Sketches of the Life and Character of Patrick Henry* appeared in the fall of 1817, the Revolution was forty years distant and Wirt had modified his original, Johnsonian plans significantly. And he had learned that helping to create "American biography"— his own work and the genre itself—involved questions of truth, character, and his own authorial role that he did not imagine when he contracted his "itch for Biography."

Biographical Production and Biographical Reading

The opening of a new century provides a capital opportunity to look back at the one just concluded. Or so the New York minister Samuel Miller believed: in 1803, his *A Brief Retrospect of the Eighteenth Century* appeared, containing "a sketch of the revolutions and improvements in science, arts, and literature during that period." Among those improvements Miller numbered the proliferation of biographies. Since 1700, "every literary country of Europe has produced a greater number of biographical works than at any former period. There certainly never was an age in which *Memoirs, Lives,* collections of *Anecdotes,* &c. respecting the dead, were so numerous, and had such a general circulation." Miller then described the various forms of biography that had multiplied: biographical dictionaries, collective biographies about "particular classes of eminent persons" such as naval officers or physicians, book-length lives of individual figures, and most recently *"Accounts of distinguished Living Characters."* Only in the notes in the back of his second volume, where Miller added items he had omitted, did he mention an American book: "The *American Biography,* by the late Rev. Dr. Belknap, . . . is a work honourable to the compiler, and highly useful to the student of American history."[1]

Between 1790 and 1820, American periodicals repeatedly called for biographies of illustrious Americans, which could announce the new nation's place alongside Europe. The *American Law Journal* sought "memoirs of the eminent men of this nation, who have challenged a place on the rolls of fame, and taught an envious world that *America* is not less the nurse of liberty than the cradle of glory." The *Portico* wrote that no other nation had produced so many deserving subjects of biography in its first forty years. American lives of American subjects had long included works of local interest, often published in pamphlet form and circulated only locally or regionally, ranging from sermons and orations on the life of a departed minister to sensationalistic, confessional lives of condemned criminals. When critics talked of "American biography," however, they meant something different: lives of individuals clearly associated with the history of what had become the United States. Biographers responded to these entreaties, echoing the magazines' rhetoric of national assertion. The introductory message in John Maxwell's 1795 memoir of George Washington was typical: "Gratitude obliges every nation to transmit to posterity the memory of these personages, who by their patriotic and heroic virtues, have distinguished themselves from the rest of their countrymen and fellow-citizens, that their name and fame may be perpetuated from one generation to another, and that others may be animated and excited to imitate them in their virtues. And . . . no nation in the world has more reason to perpetuate the memory of their patriots and heroes, than the United States of America has to perpetuate theirs, especially their amiable and beloved Gen. Washington."[2]

Many of these American biographies were collective in form: magazine series, volumes of collective biography, and biographical dictionaries. The *Columbian,* one of the earliest magazines in the new republic, ran Jeremy Belknap's biographical essays as the "American Plutarch" in 1788 and 1789. After 1800, such series multiplied. Only book reviews and poetry appeared more frequently than biographies in magazines of the 1810s. The best known were the naval biographies in the *Analectic Magazine,* written initially by Washington Irving, which proved so popular that the editors renamed their product the *Analectic Magazine and Naval Chronicle.* James Jones Wilmer's *American Nepos* (1805) and Thomas Woodward's *Columbian Plutarch* (1819) offered essay-length sketches of American figures, much as the ancient biographers of their titles had sketched the deeds of classical worthies. The most ambitious collective biography, Delaplaine's two-volume *Repository of the Lives and Portraits of Distinguished Americans* (1816–17), contained engraved portraits and brief biographies of recent American subjects. At least three biographical dictionaries composed solely of American entries appeared between 1809 and 1815. Their entries suggested the dual motivation of New England Congregational religion and American patriotism. William Allen's *An American Biographical and Historical Dictionary* (1809) included sketches of almost seven hundred figures: nearly three hundred had achieved prominence in religion, including the first ministers of every town in New England, and over two hundred more had won political or military fame in the colonial or early national years. Most of the rest were physicians or educators; scattered entries described travelers, writers, and citizens noted for longevity.[3]

Only George Washington stood above the spate of collective biographies, earning numerous book-length biographies of himself alone. The historian and geographer Jedidiah Morse's "A True and Authentic History of His Excellency George Washington" (1790) also included biographical sketches of Generals Montgomery and Greene, but at least five biographies devoted solely to Washington appeared in the decade after his death in December 1799. Mason Locke Weems's became the most famous and almost certainly the best seller. Perhaps because no copyright laws prevented its piracy, the biography by the English author John Corry was printed in the widest variety of places: not just Philadelphia, New York, and Boston but also Poughkeepsie, Baltimore, New Haven, Trenton, Pittsburgh, Wilmington (Delaware), Bridgeport (Connecticut), Barnard (Vermont), and even a German edition in Lebanon (Pennsylvania). The two most widely circulated lives of Washington, Weems's *Life and Memorable Actions of George Washington* and Chief Justice John Marshall's five-volume *Life of*

George Washington, had more centralized printing histories. Printers in several locations produced early editions of Weems's work, first published as a memorial volume just months after the first president's death. But once Weems expanded his book in 1806, adding for the first time a dedication to "my young countrymen" and the story of young George and the unfortunate cherry tree, all of its editions were the product of Mathew Carey's Philadelphia firm. Marshall's work, a more ambitious undertaking because of its length and consequent expense to publisher and buyer alike, was also the product of one publisher, Caleb P. Wayne of Philadelphia. Sold by subscription, Marshall's *Life of Washington* had more than 7,000 subscribers who hailed from every state and territory, from over 650 cities, towns, and counties. Entire communities whose members had not subscribed individually had access to the volumes: libraries purchased forty-three subscriptions, and firms (perhaps booksellers operating circulating libraries) another forty-eight.[4]

Still, Wayne found that the work's sales could not make up its expense: they were so disappointing that, according to Weems, he was unlikely to "do much more at the printing business." In the early American book trade, every new biographical project involved some form of financial risk; the more ambitious the endeavor, the greater the chance of financial catastrophe. If even a life of Washington could ruin its publisher, other works were even riskier. The distribution history of Belknap's *American Biography* (1794) was probably typical: sales were slow in Charleston and presumably even slower in less metropolitan areas of the South. The biographical dictionaries, heavily weighted toward New England subjects, probably had largely regional circulation. The *American Quarterly Review,* published in Philadelphia, criticized Allen's dictionary as "attractive only to the New-England race: — the book abounds with clergymen, whose labours and qualities were either trite or jejune." Subject matter alone does not explain these works' limited circulation. Book distribution in the early republic divided markedly along regional lines. Carey and Weems twice tried and failed to cultivate the book trade in the South through networks of incipient booksellers. Selling books in the South involved difficulties in transportation and credit that even the most enterprising Philadelphia publisher could not overcome, and no comparable publisher emerged in any southern state. When an 1825 American edition of Lempriere's *Universal Biography* sold 1,344 (87 percent) of its 1,548 subscriptions in New York and New England (and 520 in two cities, New York and Boston), its concentration may tell us as much about the nature of the book market as about regional tastes.[5] The truly national distribution of the lives of Washington—Weems's and, even in commercial failure, Marshall's—was the exception, not the rule.

The risks associated with new publishing ventures help explain why American imprints of European biographies, many of them originally written decades earlier, remained far more numerous than American-written lives of American subjects. The book trade in the early-national United States was in transition between the colonial predominance of European-imported books and the indigenous, centralized publishing industry that would develop by midcentury. The American Revolution had encouraged domestic publishing in several ways. Publicizing and promoting the Revolution had given printers a new prominence and expanded the number of printers in the states and the number of towns with print shops. The suspension of Anglo-American trade, too, provided an impetus for domestic industries, including printing. Nonetheless, as the nineteenth century opened, printers still bought most of their equipment from abroad, and many of the books they printed were new editions of European works. In the absence of international copyright protection, American printers could republish even the most recent London books with impunity. The origins of Americans' reading fare, which varied for numerous reasons of access and interest, fell into three large categories: books actually imported from Europe, American imprints of European works, and American-written works, virtually all of which were the products of American printers and publishers. The third category, which had long included almanacs, sermons and other religious works, newspapers, and governmental publications, expanded during the early republic to include an increasing diversity of literary, historical, didactic, and scientific productions. But in these latter genres, American imprints of European standards continued to outnumber American-written works throughout the first quarter of the century. When the English critic Sydney Smith caustically asked, "In the four quarters of the globe, who reads an American book?" he might as well have been referring to the relatively small number —not just what he perceived as the inferior quality—of American works.[6]

Because local printers generally made their money in job printing (stationery, legal forms) and steady sellers (like almanacs) and had limited distribution networks, most American editions of belles-lettres appeared from the presses of urban printer-publishers like Mathew Carey in Philadelphia and Isaiah Thomas in Worcester, who worked with other printers, agents, or booksellers inside and outside their own cities. There were exceptions: the most popular American novel, Susannah Rowson's *Charlotte Temple,* competed successfully with European works, and numerous printers outside the large cities produced their own imprints of it. But most of the best-selling fiction in the United States was European-written, and most American editions came from the major print centers, Boston and Philadelphia (and increasingly New York after 1810).[7] American imprints of European biographies followed the same pattern. No European-written biography in the early republic promised enough profit for numerous local printers to attempt editions. The standard works, which appeared in libraries around the nation, included Plutarch's *Lives,* Johnson's *Lives of the Poets,* Philip Doddridge's *Some Remarkable Passages in the Life of Col. James Gardiner* ("the Christian soldier"), and John Aikin's *A View of the Life, Travels, and Philanthropic Labors of the Late John Howard.* Many of these books, as well as Henry Hunter's *Sacred Biography,* owed their American circulation to their connection with the transatlantic growth in evangelical religion through the eighteenth and early nineteenth centuries. Though these works seem to have been widely read, none sold steadily enough to justify a local imprint. With very few exceptions, their American editions were the products of printer-publishers in Boston, Philadelphia, and New York.

Biographies produced outside these primary print centers were more likely to tell the lives of locally prominent figures, from ministers to murderers. At least one such volume offers evidence of the audience it sought to reach. In 1802 the Bennington, Vermont, printer Anthony Haswell compiled the *Memoirs and Adventures of Captain Matthew Phelps,* a traveler who had descended the Mississippi River to New Orleans but now lived in the Vermont town of New Haven about eighty miles north of Bennington. The list of 627 subscribers in the back of the book reveals that more than half lived within forty miles of Bennington, and that fewer than fifty hailed from outside Vermont. (Most of those came from nearby counties in New York and Massachusetts that were closer to Bennington than Phelps's own New Haven.) A few subscribers, perhaps local storekeepers or booksellers, ordered six or more copies, bringing the total number of copies ordered to 686. This subscription list gives clues about the distribution networks of secondary print centers like Bennington: even a strong seller like Phelps's memoirs, which Haswell reprinted in 1804, had largely regional circulation. At the same time, its preface—written by Haswell— suggested a connection to a wider world of biographical writing. Haswell employed the same language about the utility and enjoyment of biography that could be found in imported steady sellers and lives of prominent

Americans alike. In short, Vermont readers could enjoy and profit from Phelps's life both because he was a local worthy and because biography itself afforded useful amusement.[8]

But did they? Our understanding of readers in the early republic remains sketchier than surviving records of the book trade. Three types of American readers existed before the Revolution: an "educated male elite," who were "aggressive buyers of books" produced largely in Europe; urban readers, including women, who "patronized bookstores or subscription libraries in populous areas in search of the current fashionable productions of London publishers"; and rural and working-class urban Americans, those "most isolated from European culture and removed from a sense of participating in a shared British heritage," with access to far smaller numbers of books. In the thirty years after the Revolution ended, these types underwent slight modifications. The proliferation of American imprints meant that both the educated elite and the circulating-library patrons were increasingly likely to read American-made (if not American-written) books. And the ideology of the Revolution encouraged the concept of a "republican literature" that crossed occupational and economic lines; the subscribers to at least one New York magazine, though on average wealthier and more professional than the population at large, included artisan carpenters, printers, and sea captains as well as attorneys, physicians, and wealthy merchants. Nonetheless, literacy levels, physical connection with the commercial centers of the book trade, and economic means all helped to define what books were available to different readers. Variations in taste also shaped readers' experiences: Carey and Weems's foray into the southern book trade foundered in part because Carey failed to heed Weems's admonitions about what rural southerners would and would not read.[9]

The contents of personal and social libraries suggest how access to biographies could vary. Wealthy individuals with large personal libraries often bought lives of a wide range of subjects. Thomas Posey, a politician who owned the largest personal collection in Indiana before 1820, owned lives of Washington, Philip II, Louis XIV, and Charles V; a set of Plutarch; and seven volumes of the *British Plutarch,* a biographical compendium. Thomas Jefferson, who purchased scores of books from Europe, owned approximately forty volumes of classical, European, and British biography, many of them produced abroad, and another twelve lives of American figures, including Washington, Franklin, the scientist David Rittenhouse, and General Charles Lee. Similarly, members of prosperous urban social libraries like the Library Company of Philadelphia and the

Charleston Library Society could borrow dozens of biographies published in London, Paris, and other European cities as well as those printed in the United States. Less wealthy and less cosmopolitan Americans owned far fewer biographies, although many had access to American imprints of European works through local social libraries. In Indiana, families with small personal libraries of three to five books tended to own a Bible, hymnbook, and almanac, and perhaps "a biography of Washington or Bonaparte or a religious leader." For readers—particularly in the Northeast—outside the large cities or without extensive personal libraries, membership in a library association widened their choices. By one estimate 266 social libraries were founded in the United States during the 1790s, a far cry from the 110 established between 1731 (when the first was formed) and 1790. Small, rural social libraries in the new nation frequently stocked lives of religious figures and histories of European monarchs, as well as Plutarch and a few other biographies. These collections paled in comparison with the personal libraries of men like Jefferson, but they offered rural American readers a broader selection than they would have enjoyed before the Revolution, when libraries scarcely existed outside the metropolitan centers.[10]

The circulation records of one such library offer suggestive evidence about early American readers' interests. The Washington County Farmers and Mechanicks Library, a shareholder library in the northeastern New York town of Cambridge, numbered approximately sixty members when founded in 1817.[11] The patrons included multiple members of several families and farmers of relatively little wealth as well as town leaders. Some almost certainly had access to books outside the library's collection, for in these years the nearby Salem printers Dodd and Stevenson occasionally advertised new additions to their bookstore and circulating library in their newspaper, the *Washington County Post*.[12] Because no complete catalog remains, our knowledge of the library's holdings consists only of books borrowed by at least one member at some point; thus we cannot know what books remained on the shelves, never checked out. The borrowed books included approximately 150 titles, ranging from fiction and religious literature to history, travel narratives, and biographies. Historical romances appear to have been especially popular: six of Sir Walter Scott's novels, the most works by any single author, and three more by the English author Jane Porter constituted the heart of the fiction. The eighteen biographies included a few American-written lives (Marshall's five-volume *Washington,* Weems's *Life of Francis Marion,* and lives of Franklin and Lafayette) and several familiar European biographies available in American imprints (Robert Watson's *Philip II,* Voltaire's life of King Charles XII of Sweden, and lives of Wellington, Napoleon, and John Knox). Hunter's *Sacred Biography,* Leonard Woods's life of the missionary Harriet Newell, Plutarch's *Lives,* and a work called "American Biography" (which could have been Belknap's *American Biography* or one of the biographical dictionaries) rounded out the biographies. All of these works were typical of the small collections in early-nineteenth-century rural libraries.

The biographies that circulated most heavily were those of American subjects. Thirty-eight members checked out at least one volume of Marshall's *Life of Washington;* the lives of Franklin (borrowed by thirty members) and Marion (twenty-seven) were the next most popular. As a comparison, thirty-seven members charged out Jane Porter's *Scottish Chiefs,* the library's most popular novel. Among the lives of Americans, works that might have been considered scholarly like Marshall's heavily footnoted *Washington* and those more clearly directed toward a wider audience like Weems's romantic *Life of Marion* both possessed wide appeal. Contemporary military men were the most popular non-American subjects. Nineteen members checked out the lives of Napoleon and Wellington, and fifteen that of Lafayette, whose role in the Revolution made him virtually an American figure. The scarcity of books may have accounted for another feature of the Washington County circulation: multiple borrowings of the same works. Some members checked out Weems's *Life of Marion* and the *Life of Franklin* (which may have been some version of Franklin's autobiography, or a biography by Weems or another author) repeatedly over the thirty-year life of the library. These multiple borrowings may suggest the "intensive" reading that historians have identified in preindustrial American communities where books were scarce — and among people who place particular value on or gain repeated meaning from rereading specific books (like the Bible).[13] Significantly, virtually no member ever checked out the biography of a European figure more than once. Only the lives of the Americans Washington, Marion, and Franklin enjoyed this intensive use in Washington County.

The method in which members read Marshall's *Life of Washington* is particularly intriguing. Some read just the first two volumes, but sixteen members read at least four, and nine read all five. Moreover, several people checked out the same volumes repeatedly. Peter C. Hill read all five volumes in order in the 1820s, soon borrowed the first four again, and read them again in the mid-1830s. Other readers seem to have favored particular volumes. It is equally clear that Marshall's *Washington* was in constant demand when the library opened in 1817. Volume 1 was checked out during all but five weeks between February 1817 and July 1818, and the other volumes were almost as popular. Fortenatus Sherman's circulation record suggests the consequences of this popularity. In April and May 1822, Sherman checked out Volumes 1 and 2 in order. But when he returned the second volume on June 3, he could not check out the next one, because John Austin had had it since April 3. So Sherman borrowed Volume 4 instead, presumably hoping the third volume would be available when he returned the fourth. It was not; Thomas Hill had borrowed it in the meantime, and Sherman had to wait until October 19 to get it. When Sherman returned Volume 3 on December 6, Volume 5 was on the shelves, and he could complete Marshall's massive work. Alexander Skelly was luckier: he began with the first volume on April 4, 1821, and borrowed each subsequent volume the day he returned the previous one, returning the fifth on January 23, 1822. Clearly, a work that had ruined its publisher found new life within this reading community.

What do the circulation records of Fortenatus Sherman, Alexander Skelly, and the other members of their reading community reveal? It is easy to list all that they do not reveal: whether the person who checked out a book was in fact the household member who read it, what reading materials these library patrons obtained from other sources like Dodd and Stevenson's bookstore, and especially *how* they read and whether their purposes and interpretations coincided with those prescribed by biographers and critics. The sequential borrowing of Marshall's *Washington* and the repeat borrowings of Marshall's and Weems's works strongly indicate that these books were in fact read, by the members or by someone else within their households. And in this interest, the Washington County readers echoed what critics and biographers alike argued in these years: that American citizens wanted to read the lives of American worthies. But many contemporary reviewers criticized Marshall's *Life of Washington* because it was not truly the biography it claimed to be. Its first volume rarely even mentioned Washington, and subsequent volumes subordinated Washington's life to the general history. Perhaps the readers of Washington County appreciated Marshall's work for precisely what it was — a history of America. Maybe, too, Marshall's focus on the wider history helps explain why Fortenatus Sherman was willing to read the volumes out of order. Had the work traced Washington's personal and political maturation in the style of a bildungsroman, Sherman might have been more inclined to wait for the third volume in June 1822. Critics also found fault with Parson Weems's life of Francis Marion, the next most popular biography in the Washington County library. Weems had drawn his narrative from material written by Brigadier General Peter Horry, a member of Marion's regiment, and had embellished Horry's statements significantly. As Weems explained it, he had written a biography in accord with the popular "passion" for novels; as Horry and many critics saw it, Weems had compromised truth unforgivably.[14] But perhaps the Washington County readers, fond of the English historical romances of Sir Walter Scott and Jane Porter, found exactly what they wanted in Weems's rendition of Marion's life: a historical romance on American soil.

Considered in the wider context of their other reading, the biographical choices of the Washington County library patrons might imply a fundamental difference from the critics who discussed the purposes of biography reading and from the biographers who prefaced their works with essays on the utility of biography. Possibly these readers thought about the lives of Washington and Marion not as part of a discrete genre called "biography," but as parts of other overlapping genres or interests, such as American history and historical romance. The secondary biographical interest in the Farmers and Mechanicks Library, contemporary events, suggests the same point. The most-borrowed biographies of Europeans dealt with the lives and deeds of Napoleon and Wellington, and many of the popular works in other genres also treated recent occurrences, such as the War of 1812 and Captain James Riley's 1815 shipwreck and captivity in Africa. For the readers of Washington County, these works might all have belonged to the same category, distinguished not by literary genre but by similarly contemporary subject matter. In describing the purposes of biography and prescribing how biographers should treat their subjects, critics and biographers may have sought to create an awareness of genre among readers like these, who drew boundaries between their reading far differently. Just as likely, however, the critics and biographers—based predominantly in cosmopolitan Boston, Philadelphia, and New York—inhabited a very different literary world, linked more closely to each other and to their English counterparts than to rural American readers.

Critics, Biographers, and the Problem of Republican Biography

Readers in the early republic may not have thought about biographies in terms of genre, but contemporary critics certainly did. In dozens of articles and book reviews, American periodicals explained the differences between biography and other literary forms—defining biography, in large part, by what it was not. Most biographers also devoted some attention to defining biography: in a preface, at the beginning of a first chapter, or occasionally within their main narratives. At first glance, these two sets of discussions seem to share a fundamental understanding of the genre and a common language for describing it. Critics and biographers alike argued that biography's chief virtue was its extraordinary combination of "instruction and amusement." More thorough examination, however, reveals not one shared language about biography, but two potentially contradictory ones. One, drawn from the essays of Samuel Johnson, appeared in the United States almost exclusively in the periodical criticism. The other, founded on American patriotism and republican ideas of citizenship, appeared in most of the biographies as well as in some of the critical literature. Taken to their logical conclusions—which rarely occurred—these two visions of biography represented opposing concepts of the biographer's task and of the very meaning of character.

Numerous biographers and almost every critic who discussed the genre applauded the instructive value of biography. The biographers' self-consciousness about genre can seem foreign to today's reader: an early-nineteenth-century preface was as likely to describe the edifying power of biography as to introduce the subject of the book. Such statements were not new; they appeared in many of the eighteenth-century English biographies reprinted in America and found in dozens of American libraries.[15] James Jones Wilmer wrote in his 1805 collection *The American Nepos* that "We trace the progress of good men with pleasure, and we behold the crimes of bad men with detestation. Biography is therefore not only the most entertaining, but is also the most instructive kind of history." Critics agreed. Biography entertained by creating relationships between subject and reader. Reading a great man's life "ennobled" readers, "as though we were actively admitted to participate in his friendship." Together, man's "curiosity to know" about the wise and eminent and his "imitative propensity" made biography a "rational and unfailing" pleasure, a "decisive and emphatical" lesson. Because "men are influenced more by example than precept," biographies could stir the reader "to the performance of great and generous deeds" more powerfully than abstract moral principles could.[16]

As these descriptions suggest, biography could "improve" the reader in several ways. The most mechanical was "imitation." Biographies provided specific steps that the reader could follow and virtues that he could emulate in order to become a republican citizen (or, later, a "self-made man"). Biographies might also "stimulate" or "inspire" by depicting the nobility of great men: reading Washington's life would not offer lessons in how to lead a revolution, but it would stir the reader's own patriotism and hatred of tyranny. The critic who wrote that biography "ennobled" the reader implied this less imitative use of the genre. As we will see, later critics would draw on romantic ideas about the self to argue that the biography of great men could encourage the reader to develop his own individuality, not follow socially prescribed models of virtue and action. In the early republic, however, the virtues and feelings that biography was supposed to inspire were clear: American patriotism, disinterested republican citizenship, the use of reason. Inculcating these virtues was hardly the province of biography alone. All branches of literature and the arts in the early republic claimed to instruct as well as to amuse, in order to deflect critics who would call them useless, perhaps even dangerously aristocratic luxuries in a land of republican simplicity. In stating that Washington's "virtuous simplicity [in] private life . . . though less known than the dazzling splendour of his military achievements, is not less edifying in example or worthy the attention of his countrymen," Jedidiah Morse also strengthened the case for biography as edifying and worthy of readers' attention, much as the dramatist Royall Tyler's portrayal of the simply dressed Colonel Manly made *The Contrast* into an argument for republican theater as well as republicanism.[17]

The idea that biography served an instructive function was hardly an American creation, even if an emphasis on *republican* instruction was specific to the American context. It dated back at least as far as Plutarch's *Lives,* standard reading fare for young gentlemen in Revolutionary and post-Revolutionary America (and probably many others who did not record their reading). Moral instruction also loomed large in the three types of character sketch most common in seventeenth-century England: the biographical "character," the historical miniature, and the Theophrastan character. Many English biographers of the 1600s and 1700s adopted a bipartite structure known as the "life and character." The "life" traced incidents and events chronologically from the subject's birth to his death. The "character," generally a final chapter found most frequently in religious biographies, interpreted the inner workings of his mind and personality or summarized his signal traits. The historical miniature had classical roots. Following Tacitus, many historians in the seventeenth and eighteenth centuries included brief lives of notable individual figures. According to one scholar, these sketches "made the most important advances in the description of complex human beings in English prose before the eighteenth-century novelists." They also, however, limited themselves to the subjects' public, political lives and deeds, which served as lessons to the reader. The Theophrastan character was the most overtly didactic of the three. Like the allegorical figures in John Bunyan's *Pilgrim's Progress,* Theophrastan characters exemplified a single virtue or vice, offering one-dimensional models of traits to be emulated or avoided.[18]

Puritan spiritual biographers in colonial America drew especially on the "life and character" and historical miniature forms, even as they advanced a notion of "American biography" different from what would appear in the early republic. Seventeenth-century English Puritans had already transformed religious biography from the medieval, hagiographic recounting of miracles to a narrative of the subject's journey through "stages of spiritual growth." This new model, which owed much to Augustine's *Confessions* and John Foxe's *Book of Martyrs,* at once testified to God's redemptive power and offered a guide for the Puritan reader concerned with the state of his own soul. Because the journey toward salvation had an established path, these biographies tended to subordinate individual idiosyncrasies and personal characteristics to conventions of narrative and language. The best-known Puritan history, Cotton Mather's *Magnalia Christi Americana* (1702), included extended life-and-character biographies of New England's founders and leaders and brief biographical miniatures of little-known ministers. In the full-length biographies Mather adopted many Plutarchan techniques: revealing public heroes' "character" in their actions, even mimicking Plutarch's penchant for dramatic introductions. In the miniatures he related the archetypal spiritual journeys of "more typical representatives" of Puritanism, who exemplified "the Christian virtues of faith, service, humility, and redemptive suffering." Mather and other Puritan historians in America employed Puritan typology to suggest the parallels between individuals' path to salvation and the history of the New England community itself, and between recent Puritan figures and their scriptural correlatives (for instance, John Winthrop was Mather's "American Nehemiah"). By extension, America became the new Israel, with its own place in Christian history. Although this notion would become prevalent again in mid-nineteenth-century religious biographies, biographers and historians in the new republic identified the "Americanness" of American biography with republican ideology.[19]

For American critics of the early 1800s, more important than Puritan antecedents was the work of the eighteenth-century titan of biography, Samuel Johnson. Johnson was no less a moralist than the other biographers and critics of his age, but he sought to render "character" more complex. By the time he started writing biographies, writers in other genres — notably the novelists, but also essayists like Addison and Steele — were seeking to portray individualities of life and manners. Johnson wanted to get deeper than manners, which often masked rather than revealed the essence of a subject. His *Lives of the English Poets* sought to capture the complexities of their subjects, for verisimilitude *and* moral effect. After all, readers could presumably learn more from characters they could recognize as human than from oversimplified caricatures. In his essays on biography, *Rambler* No. 60 and *Idler* No. 84, Johnson recommended that biographers lead readers "into the private lodgings of the hero" and portray the subject in his "domestick privacies" rather than in the "vulgar greatness" of public life. Too many biographers, he thought, omitted the "invisible circumstances" that would be most useful to readers who sought "natural and moral knowledge" or enhanced "virtue." Since men were all "prompted by the same motives, all deceived by the same fallacies, all animated by hope, obstructed by danger, entangled by desire, and seduced by pleasure," a reader could derive more instruction from "a judicious and faithful narrative" of even the most obscure person than from archetypal or eulogistic presentations of the most prominent.[20] American critics generally accepted and repeated Johnson's logic.[21]

When these critics contrasted biography with other genres, they were drawing on Johnson. The glorification of biography as "a real and rational pleasure, and . . . a powerful stimulus to every virtuous action" went hand in hand with the contemporary critique of the novel, whose stories were not "real" and whose effects were not "rational." The *Literary and Philosophical Repertory* advised young novel readers "to exchange these idle dreams of a heated imagination, for the bright examples and the solid instruction contained in Biography." Biographies, the real "tales of truth" that novels falsely claimed to be, appealed to the reasonable curiosity about human nature while novels excited unhealthy passions and "idle dreams" that led only to disappointment or moral ruin.[22] The critics were fighting a rising tide. Fiction achieved new levels of popularity in the first quarter century of the republic, led by Sir Walter Scott's works, which helped lend legitimacy to the genre. Ironically, sentimental novels—many of them biographical in form, centered on the experiences of one central (and often female) character—may have resembled the critics' vision of biography more than most biographies of the period. *Charlotte Temple* and *The Coquette* both admitted readers into intimate scenes of their protagonists' lives, as critics argued biographies should. However, intimacy made novels even more pernicious: it could lead readers to believe that these books' narratives, full of seduction and glittering scenes, were indeed tales of truth.

Eulogy, the second genre often contrasted with biography, did not pose the same danger. Critics' complaints about eulogy stemmed, rather, from its inferior instructive power. Eulogy (or panegyric) taught less effectively than did biography because it made its subjects too perfect. Because eulogy commemorated real lives, it was preferable to fiction, but its subjects were "cultural ideals," not recognizable individuals. Critics complained when biography became too much like eulogy. All too often, said critics, biographers eulogized their subjects, out of "friendship," "national pride, party spirit, and love or hatred to the character," or even "the sordid purpose of gaining patronage and swelling subscription lists." No matter what the cause, the effect was the same: in its abstract praise, panegyric obscured the real person with whom readers could sympathize and sacrificed "naked truth, divested of all hyperbole." Critics and reviewers believed that biographers should praise virtues but also censure vices, particularly those of famous men whom readers were likely to imitate. Also unlike eulogists, biographers were expected to reveal the foibles and individualizing qualities that made their subjects more human, less grand, and more believably emulable.[23]

If biography surpassed fiction in its "truth" and eulogy in its balance, it was a more effective teacher than history because it showed readers the private man behind the glorious public deeds. Following Johnson, critics argued that readers felt closer to a great man "in the bosom of his family" and "in all the undress of life" than in the councils of state. More important, ordinary readers would find useful examples for their own conduct in his daily life, not in public events and extraordinary situations and actions.[24] Marshall's *Life of Washington,* which barely introduced Washington until the second volume and covered his entire early life in a page and a half, was frequently faulted for its excessive concentration on history, even if "the history of the life of Washington is that of American independence." The *Monthly Anthology* complained of "too little biography" in the work, and the *New-England Galaxy and Masonic Magazine* wondered if Marshall's volumes could even be called biography rather than history. Marshall's work was hardly alone. The *American Quarterly Review* summed up the shortcomings of much American biography in 1827: "Your modern biographer . . . rarely leads you into the private lodgings of the hero — never places you before the poor reasonable animal, as naked as nature made him; but represents him uniformly as a demi-god."[25]

Demigods, however, were precisely what assertive nationalism — the other hallmark of early American biographical criticism and especially of biographies themselves — tended to produce. At the same time many critics espoused standards drawn from British (usually Johnsonian) commentary on biography, they and other critics also called for American biography to assert the nation's place beside European monarchies. Even as they argued that biography should avoid eulogy, tell the truth, and seek the private man, they also wanted American biographies that would glorify the nation and its early heroes. Unless the Revolutionary fathers received biographical attention soon, their reputations would fall from memory. The *New-England Galaxy* lamented in 1817 that "the name and bodies of half our distinguished men perish together" for lack of biography. Before Delaplaine's *Repository of the Lives and Portraits of Distinguished Americans,* wrote the *Portico,* "we have had nothing like a regular system of American Biography: nothing to which we could refer, either for the gratification of a laudable curiosity, or for evidence of national distinction." Moreover, American biography had a duty to instill republican values in the rising generation, as the *American Gleaner* explained in its first issue.[26] Critics who combined British-derived criticism and American assertiveness resembled other cultural nationalists of the early republic. In his self-portrait *The Artist in His Museum* (1822) Charles Willson Peale employed European painting conventions to portray his museum of American species and heroes. Similarly, Tyler's play *The Contrast* was a drawing-room comedy, modeled on the popular British genre, that contrasted American manners and beliefs favorably against English ones.

Biographers seconded the critics' call for American biographies. Thomas Woodward's *Columbian Plutarch* yoked biographical tradition to American nationalism. Its title echoed both Plutarch's *Lives* and the well-known *British Plutarch,* a compendium of English biography. Its preface began with the typical comment that biography "has ever been esteemed as one of the most useful branches of literature," mentioned its classical origins, and quoted "a late writer" on the threefold purpose of biography, "to delight, to instruct, and to stimulate." After this paragraph, derived directly from contemporary British criticism, Woodward quoted Johnson himself. But then he turned to America's "full share" of "truly illustrious characters": "The people of the land of Washington, Franklin, Rittenhouse, Rush, and Hamilton, may dispute the palm of philosophy, and patriotism, with any other nation of the globe." Nearly every biographical dictionary and work of collective biography, and many of the lives of single individuals, contained such a sentiment, as well as the concept that the post-Revolutionary generation had particular lessons to learn from American biography.[27]

This assertiveness mingled with insecurity: American critics worried that the defects in domestic biographies would invite European ridicule. One reviewer predicted that William Dunlap's *Life of the Late Charles Brockden Brown* (1815) would receive "the sneers, the censure, and the contempt of European criticks" because it failed to present Brown's character and contained numerous errors in style. "The literary character of the nation, is endangered by every crude production of the kind." Delaplaine's *Repository* received a similar complaint for its "employment of phraseology. A foreign critic would condemn a whole volume on account of a single delinquency. Give him but the least spot to rest the fulcrum of his criticism upon, and he will overthrow a much more ponderous quarto than the one before us."[28] American biography at once sought and trembled before the eyes of the world.

Indeed, it had reason to tremble, for nationalism could easily conflict with the critical standards derived from British biography. Much as American biographers claimed to avoid eulogy, they remained too close to the Revolution in time and sentiment to assume an impartial air. David Humphreys reflected on this dilemma in one of the earliest post-Revolutionary biographies: to "treat of recent transactions and persons still living" was "always a delicate and frequently a thankless office," but "so transient and indistinguishable are the traits of character, so various and inexplicable the springs of action, so obscure and perishable the remembrance of human affairs, that, unless attempts are made to sketch the picture, while the present generation is living, the likeness will be forever lost, or only preserved by a vague recollection." At the same time, Humphreys's own life of Putnam brimmed with the sort of effusive praise that concerned some critics. In his *Memoirs of General Lafayette,* Samuel L. Knapp at once denied and excused eulogy: "in this case, a plain statement of facts may be construed, by those ignorant of the life of La Fayette, into a disposition to bestow extravagant praise." Despite such disclaimers, American biographers were often criticized for "adulation to the living, and extravagant eulogy of the dead." As Thomas Wilson wrote in 1817, nearly thirty years after Humphreys, "The difficulty of faithfully delineating" American heroes lessened as their era receded, but "the age of adulation and detraction yet exists" because "each Commander is yet living in the affection of surviving relatives and friends."[29]

Lives of American worthies invariably espoused republican simplicity and devotion to the nation, but many contained other ideological messages, too. The biographical sketches in several leading American magazines gave readers "Idols of Order," professional men of the wealthier classes who represented republican stability, not revolutionary change in the social order. Like many other projects of cultural nationalism, such as Noah Webster's dictionary, these sketches sought to provide unity for a far-flung people divided by ethnicity, economic status, and custom. All

Americans, contended these cultural promoters, could now share a set of beliefs, traditions, and founders; the magazine biographies promoted that unity through an image of social hierarchy. Jeremy Belknap's *American Biography,* the first important biographical collection, more ambivalently reflected the conflicting visions of the 1790s. While his sketches of John Winthrop and other Puritan leaders contained elements of republican ideology (notably the fear that faction and self-interest could destroy an organic community), other sketches like those of John Smith and Christopher Columbus reflected a more liberal sensibility that praised the "enterprising individual." Even early biographical dictionaries served competing theological ends, when the orthodox Calvinist William Allen and the liberal John Eliot offered opposing views of the Puritan fathers. The dictionaries became an early vehicle for "the rivalry between Arminian and Calvinist historians" that was also taking shape in the rivalry between the liberal *Monthly Anthology, and Boston Review* and the orthodox *Panoplist Magazine.*[30]

Moreover, while many biographies of Washington praised the Father of His Country for standing above and against political parties, other lives served partisan ends. Henry James Pye's *The Democrat: Or, Intrigues and Adventures of Jean Le Noir* (1795), a fictionalized life of "a Democratic Missionary, sent from the Metropolitan See of Sedition and Murder at Paris," was a diatribe against the Jeffersonian "Democratic Clubs" of the 1790s and the egalitarianism of the French Revolution. James Cheetham's 1809 biography of Thomas Paine, dedicated to Vice President George Clinton, claimed that James Madison's election to the presidency represented a Virginia monarchy that had stolen Clinton's rightful place. Cheetham, a controversial and much-sued New York newspaper publisher, and a former admirer of Paine and Jeffersonian Republican who had turned virulently against the Jeffersonians and Paine, introduced new stories of Paine's drunkenness and illicit relationship with Marguerite de Bonneville. The biography that received the most partisan response was Marshall's *Life of Washington,* whose fifth volume (on the post-Revolutionary years) presented the Washington administration from the Federalist point of view. Incensed, Jefferson asked Joel Barlow to write an opposing history. When Barlow refused, Jefferson considered writing a refutation himself or releasing his public correspondence and private memoranda of the 1790s to set the record straight.[31]

The one thing that almost every biography in the new republic *failed* to accomplish was the one thing that many critics wanted: the revelation of character through the subject's "domestic privacies," his private life and thoughts. One notable exception was Cheetham's life of Paine. In its preface, Cheetham described in Boswellian fashion how he had known Paine and often listened to him discuss his ideas. This acquaintance allowed Cheetham to see "his want of good manners, his dogmatism, the tyranny of his opinions, his peevishness, his intemperance, and the low company he kept"—but also to acquire "a knowledge of the man." In this case, the Johnsonian language about biography clearly cloaked personal and partisan animosity. And Cheetham's deepest glimpse into Paine's domestic life, his imputation that Paine had fathered one of Madame de Bonneville's children, cost the biographer $150 in a much-publicized lawsuit.[32] However, critics rarely discussed the dissonance between Johnsonian expectations and nationalistic biographical practice, the carping at Marshall's *Life of Washington* notwithstanding. These facts raise two questions. First, why did few biographers share many critics' Johnsonian vision of the genre? Second, why did critics fail to hold American biographies to Johnsonian standards?

To post-Revolutionary biographers who sought to imbue their readers with republican civic virtue, battlefields and councils of state were precisely the appropriate grounds for biography. These biographers did not "fail" to record their subjects' domestic privacies, because they did not seek to do so. If they intended to inspire civic virtue—commitment to the common good over individual self-interest, manifested in traits of simplicity and patriotism—their proper emphasis lay on public actions and characteristics. Certainly military and naval figures left more evidence of public deeds than of domestic life, but even figures to whom Johnson's strictures might apply often appeared almost exclusively in public dress. James Jones Wilmer's extended sketch of David Rittenhouse might seem an exception: after describing Rittenhouse's scientific accomplishments and public virtues, Wilmer (who knew Rittenhouse for twenty-six years) turned toward "the more limited circles of private life." But he hoped "it will not be thought that I tread too closely upon his footsteps, when I presume to lift the latch of his door, and to exhibit him in the domestic relations of a husband and father." Utterly at odds with Johnson's concept of biography, which required no such apology for perceived presumption, Wilmer's statement hinted at a doctrine of privacy that would emerge fully only several decades later. Ultimately Wilmer revealed only that Rittenhouse's "domestic" life "exhibited the taste of a Philosopher, the simplicity of a Republican, and the temper of a Christian." Even the slightest glimpse of domestic privacies, in republican biography, accomplished the opposite of what Johnsonian critics intended. Rather than reveal individualizing qualities, it reinforced the larger lessons about republican (and Christian) character found in myriad other biographies. For similar reasons, collective lives were the preferred form of "American biography" in the early republic. Collective biographies (and their visual analogues, portrait pantheons) implied that founding a republic required a group of men devoted to a common good larger than themselves, not just an individual.[33]

Critics did not often take biographers to task for leaving out domestic privacies because they shared the biographers' larger cultural objectives. Particularly in magazines that ran their own series of "American biographies," the rhetoric of American assertion was more prominent than the language of Johnsonian theory from the beginning. These magazines shared the biographers' goals: preserving American worthies from oblivion, announcing American glory to the world, and inculcating the Revolutionary fathers' virtues in the next generation. Periodicals that championed the Johnsonian concept of biography most forcefully often did so in a general article about the genre, but not in reviews of specific books (if they reviewed books).[34]

Moreover, the dissonance between republican biographical practice and Johnsonian biographical theory often went unquestioned because these two discourses existed, for the most part, in different realms of American literary culture. Samuel Johnson's theory of biography flourished in magazines connected to a transatlantic literary culture, like the *Floriad,* produced by a literary society of young men in Schenectady, New York, or the *Monthly Anthology, and Boston Review.* Such magazines were the least likely to publish reviews of American biographies unless those biographies sought critical attention as "national" works. (Most biographical reviews in the *Monthly Anthology* treated English, not American, books.) This helps explain which works did receive opprobrium. Marshall's *Life of Washington* had all the elements of a national, critically reviewable work: the foremost American subject, an author who was chief justice of the Supreme Court and possessed access to Washington's papers through his nephew Bushrod Washington, and a claim to be the definitive biography of Washington. This was no ephemeral production best adapted for schoolroom use; it sought literary as well as didactic or commemorative status, and therefore represented the nation's literary products. As such, some critics judged it on literary as well as on nationalistic standards. Indeed, it is more appropriate to say that in such cases the literary standards *became* the national standards, for these American biographical works had to hold their own with comparable European productions. Their authors—at least in the opinion of cosmopolitan critics—had to adhere to recognized literary standards, even as their subjects displayed the very different greatness associated with the American republic. This was the paradox of early-republican biography.

At least once, the two concepts of biography came into open conflict, revealing the multiple layers of this paradox. In 1814, Philadelphia publisher and printseller Joseph Delaplaine began planning his multivolume *Repository of the Lives and Portraits of Distinguished Americans.* Delaplaine, a prodigious promoter with a knack for imagining new projects, had already published Latin schoolbooks, an American edition of the *New Edinburgh Encyclopedia,* and a monthly magazine. Like other engravers and printers, he had sought to capitalize on the War of 1812, producing a series of prints of the major American naval victories. When this project failed to reach completion, he devised the *Repository:* a series of biographical sketches of distinguished Americans, each accompanied by an engraved portrait. Combining American patriotism with an elegance of production comparable to that found in similar European works, the *Repository* was to be a definitive national biography and an example of American artistic prowess. Charles Caldwell, an editor of the *Port Folio,* would write the biographies, which were to include living as well as deceased American worthies (a decision that the *Analectic Magazine* questioned).[35] When the first half-volume appeared in July 1816, at a cost of four dollars to subscribers, several newspapers greeted it with enthusiasm. *Poulson's American Daily Advertiser,* in fact, praised the inclusion of living subjects, for all too often "the meed of Patriotism [had been] restricted to posthumous applause." A letter to the editor of the *Philadelphia True American,* reprinted in Charleston, could not recall another work "more entirely American" or one "the execution of which could reflect more credit on the national character."[36]

Within a few months, however, three of the nation's foremost literary quarterlies—the *Analectic,* the *Port Folio,* and the *Portico*—all pronounced the opposite judgment. Disparaging the newspapers' praise, the *Port Folio* denied that the *Repository* was "a most magnificent work" or "a national undertaking." The *Portico* encouraged Delaplaine "for his own profit, as well as for the credit of our country, to recall the whole edition of this first volume, and commence anew." The biographies were overly embellished, full of metaphors and incongruous juxtapositions and "high wrought, hyperbolical *eulogies* which, *mutato nomine,* are the same, for every subject." (The engraved portraits were called mediocre, too.)[37] Above all, the *Portico* and especially the *Analectic* damned the *Repository* for neglecting the domestic privacies of its subjects. Samuel Stanhope Smith, moral philosopher, president of Princeton, and longtime antagonist of Charles

Caldwell, wrote the *Analectic*'s review. Signed simply "S.," this review expressed disappointment in the much-heralded *Repository,* especially because the work was "professedly national." Smith explained what constituted the proper material for a biography: the subject's actions "with his friends in the private circle, and with his family by the fire-side," which distinguished biography from history. The author of the *Repository,* claimed Smith, was "too much of a historian for a biographer," too often neglected "the duty of a biographer, a strict and scrupulous impartiality towards [his] subjects," and frequently lapsed into eulogy. The *Repository* dismayed Smith because it omitted the domestic anecdotes and "little parts and peculiarities of character" that revealed subjects more completely than catalogs of public actions ever could.[38]

Just weeks later, Caldwell fired back. On September 23 his pamphlet, "The Author Turned Critic: Or, the Reviewer Reviewed, Being a Reply to a Feeble and Unfounded Attack on Delaplaine's Repository," appeared from Delaplaine's presses (with five pages of advertisement for the *Repository*). In large measure a personal assault on Smith, Caldwell's pamphlet also answered the critique. Smith had forgotten to note, said Caldwell, that "every public, as well as every professional man possesses a twofold character; a public and a private, — one which is the property of his family and friends; and another which belongs to his fellow-citizens and his country." A biographer's purposes should dictate which of "these two characters" to depict. In a work designed to inspire the emulation of impressionable readers, the public character was more important, Caldwell argued. "You cannot imitate private peculiarities, simply because they are *private* and *peculiar.* As well you might think of imitating, by your own, the peculiar form of an individual's nose, the shape of his forehead, or the colour of his eyes or his hair. . . . Give me, then, I repeat, the materials of public character, and *I* will cheerfully resign to yourself and your friends, the anecdotes of the kitchen, the dressing room and the parlour." According to Caldwell, everyday private actions did not constitute the "real man," whose "moral powers and intellectual faculties" distinguished him from the inferior animals. Only petty minds could wish for "the mere peculiarities of character": "That man whose curiosity is to know the cut and quality of Caesar's robe or Cicero's cloak, is not very likely to become himself a Cicero or a Caesar." And "too curiously to pry into the secret histories" of living or recently deceased subjects would be indelicate and unacceptable. "*Public* traits of character," in contrast, provided "objects of imitation, and springs of action" and showed the subject when he was "most himself." So went Caldwell's legitimation of public biography.[39]

Smith and Caldwell shared a set of basic premises about the *purpose* of biography, even if they disagreed about its methods. Both were overtly didactic: biography provided models for emulation. Both were nationalistic: *American* biography proclaimed the new nation's glory to its own citizens and to the world. Smith worried about Caldwell's biographies precisely because they would be read by European critics inclined to carp at any flaw; Caldwell asserted that the biographer should "hold up to the gratitude and admiration of his country" the actions of its eminent individuals.[40] They disagreed over how to present the character of the biographical subject, and ultimately over what character was. Smith agreed with Johnson that public actions were not the character, but a veil that had to be lifted to reveal the "real" workings within. Caldwell admitted a possible disjuncture between public and private actions and traits, but unlike the Johnsonians he located character in *both* realms and gave primacy to the public, thereby justifying prevailing American biographical practice. Caldwell never suggested that his vision of biography was a peculiarly American response to a British body of criticism. Indeed, he cited British forerunners of the *Repository* in order to legitimate his effort. But Caldwell's concept of biography, unlike most contemporary criticism, squared with the overwhelming mass of biographies in the early republic.

Another defender of the *Repository* linked the Johnsonian concept of biography to something positively pernicious: the novel. Two months after its scathing review, the *Portico* published an anonymous contributor's dissent. This response, like Caldwell's pamphlet, defended the value of public biography against those who would emphasize the details of personal life and habits:

> With these minutiae in relation to great men, we are gratified much in the same way that we are with the love speeches and little events that befall the love sick hero of a novel. We are just as much instructed in the one case as in the other. No wise reader thinks of imitating either the one or the other, in these common place trifles. He who does, makes himself ridiculous. We are aware that those whose models of biography are taken from the novels of the day, the petits maitres and little misses will think differently. They will ask whether General Washington combed his hair backward or forward, whether he drank his tea hot or tepid, whether he sat erect at table, like the duke of Marlborough, or Edgar Mandlebert, or leaned forward, like Dr. Johnson, or Commodore Trunnion. Well enough for a circulating library, but very unfit for aid in forming the character of a nation.[41]

Early American (and British) novels had won readers' devotion, in large part, because they had depicted characters in the familiar surroundings of daily life—precisely the approach Johnson had commended to biographers. Now this emphasis itself became a novelistic conceit inappropriate to the instructive mission of biography. (Commodore Trunnion was a character in Tobias Smollett's 1751 novel *The Adventures of Peregrine Pickle*.) With a series of telling contrasts, this reviewer also implied a literary hierarchy: biography above the novel, the "wise reader" above "petits maitres and little misses," and "forming the character of a nation" over "a circulating library." The last two of these, especially, alluded to the fact that circulating libraries' contents (as opposed to the contents of social libraries like the Washington County Farmers and Mechanicks Library in New York) consisted primarily of novels *and* that their membership (also unlike social libraries') was heavily female. The contemporary critique of the novel— and of the effeminate, decidedly unrepublican citizens that novel reading would produce—was now deployed in defense of Delaplaine's *Repository,* with its sketches of the public lives of public men, against the Johnsonian vision of biography.

When the second half-volume of the *Repository* appeared in summer 1817, newspapers entered the debate, and the terms of debate shifted. This time, the *Analectic* criticized the biographies in the *Repository* for their anonymous authorship, which made them as unreliable as the "innumerable sketches of lives and characters, eulogistic and detractory, with which our periodical publications and daily papers, from Maine to Georgia, are constantly teeming." Except for the *Repository*'s elegant packaging and corresponding high price, there was no difference between these biographies and "the assertions of anonymous paragraphists in the daily prints." Consequently the future historian, reader of the next generation, or foreign reader could not trust their accuracy or impartiality.[42] Now the "daily prints" struck back. Almost every newspaper commentary lauded Delaplaine for his patriotism and "indefatigable industry and unwearied assiduity." Several answered specific charges that magazines had leveled at the *Repository:* including living subjects made the work more useful and interesting; adding anecdotes about private occurrences would have either made the work too long (and thus expensive) or forced Delaplaine to reduce the number of subjects; publishing authors' names would have produced "political heart-burnings and bickering."[43]

Equally important, several newspaper writers attacked the *Analectic* or the quarterly literary magazines directly. A correspondent to the *New-York Evening Post* attacked the *Analectic*'s unprovoked and paltry hostility which, from the shades of secrecy, sends forth the shafts of groundless censure against so splendid and national an undertaking as that of Mr. Delaplaine[.] That work, sir, is conducted by talents that reflect honour on the American name, and has nothing to fear from the puny criticism of this small gentleman. Why then should he, who is but a wren, aim his beak at the eagle? The plumage he would pluck he cannot hope to wear, and on the pinion he would maim he can never expect to soar.

Defending Delaplaine's *Repository* against the shafts of magazine critics, these newspaper writers also placed themselves on the American side of a larger cultural contest. Delaplaine's work (and by extension its newspaper champions) was "the eagle." The quarterlies, with their "blind and obstinate veneration for the English style of reviewing," represented another version of the attack on the United States—this time cultural, not military—that the nation had recently vanquished in the War of 1812. Even after the king's troops had withdrawn from American territory, "native criticks" with English cultural tastes remained to carp at American artistic progress.[44]

The debate over Delaplaine's *Repository* illustrated how conflicts over biographical theory and practice could become intertwined with broader social and cultural conflicts. Cultural nationalism was at issue throughout. In its admirers' eyes, the *Repository* announced America's literary and artistic accomplishments (as well as its great men) to the world. Its detractors replied that although such a demonstration of American achievement was desirable, the *Repository* did not fulfill this purpose because of its flaws as biography, art, or both. But the issue of whether biography should treat the subject in his domestic privacies (the Johnsonian vision) or in his public deeds and character (the republican vision) was central only in 1816. At that point, the debate was still confined to the same literary-social circle as the sales of the *Repository* itself: in metropolitan magazines that catered to an American audience for culture along European lines, and in Charles Caldwell's pamphlet. The *Repository,* after all, was a luxury book, at four dollars a half-volume affordable to only a limited segment of American readers. When the battle resumed in September 1817, the circle widened. Newspapers accused the magazines, which had deprecated the literary judgments of the "daily prints," of European-inspired elitist criticism (and defended the *Repository,* which may have been more "American" in content but was no less "elitist" in its potential audience). But at this point, the theoretical arguments over public and private biography gave way to a different set of issues, less centered on the nature of biography. Even then, the discussions occurred in urban newspapers—which, if they reached rural readers at all, reached rural readers who were unlikely ever to see Joseph Delaplaine's *Repository*.

These distinctions are significant, for they remind us finally of the different literary cultures in which biographies moved in the early republic. Like John Marshall's *Life of George Washington,* Joseph Delaplaine's *Repository of the Lives and Portraits of Distinguished Americans* engendered conflict because it proclaimed itself a national work. But Delaplaine never developed even the kind of marketing network that C. P. Wayne had used to sell subscriptions nationwide for Marshall's *Life of Washington,* much less the network through which Mathew Carey and Mason Locke Weems had made Weems's far-cheaper life of Washington a truly national bestseller. Calling a book "national" meant, in this case, only that the *Repository* aimed to display American worthies and American artistic accomplishment and to offer members of the rising generation lessons in their fathers' virtues. In another sénse, the debate over the book exposed several ways in which a "national" biography did not exist at all, no matter how biographers, critics, and cultural entrepreneurs sought to promote a shared ideology at home and a reputation for America abroad.[45]

Writing Biography in the Early Republic: The Trials of William Wirt

The story of William Wirt and his *Sketches of the Life and Character of Patrick Henry* raises many of the issues we have already encountered, especially the relationship between Johnsonian and republican notions about biography. But here we can examine those issues not as arguments between opposing critics or between biographers and critics, but as tensions within the experience of one biographer. Although he knew that public affairs not domestic privacies would be at the center of his story, Wirt began his project with a Johnsonian idea: he wanted to capture what was unique, not archetypal, about Henry. By the 1810s, his conception of the project changed. Gone was the Johnsonian language that sought to make the biographical subject familiar, replaced by a preservationist, historical tone and rhetoric that accentuated the distance between present and past. Writing historical biography introduced new issues. Henry was dead, but Wirt's sources of information were not. Searching for "truth" thus involved weighing the often-conflicting memories of Henry's aging colleagues against each other and against what Wirt found in documentary sources. At the same time, Wirt sought to bridge generational and re-

Shortly after completing his biography of Patrick Henry, William Wirt declined to be included
in a portrait gallery of distinguished Americans that the enterprising Joseph Delaplaine envisioned as his *Repository* was failing. Paying to appear in Delaplaine's "Panzographia," Wirt
wrote, would "indicate a sickly and over-weening anxiety for the public gaze." Nonetheless,
Wirt did sit for this 1820 portrait by Charles Bird King. (Courtesy Redwood Library and Athenaeum, Newport, Rhode Island)

gional chasms. He wrote for an older generation that had lived through the Revolution and for a rising generation that had not, for a Virginia audience familiar with the outlines of Henry's life and for a national readership unversed in the Old Dominion's past or unwilling to admit Virginia's primacy in the Revolution. Differing ideas of genre and truth, multiple and often distinct audiences: these shaped the ways he constructed Henry's life and his own role as Henry's biographer.

So did his hard-won position within Virginia's professional and intellectual elite. William Wirt had not joined the Virginia aristocracy at birth: he was born in Maryland, of Swiss-German descent, and his early years were marked by straitened circumstances. As we shall see, writing Henry's biography became part of Wirt's strategy to solidify his elite status, in two senses. By telling the life of a "Virginia worthy," Wirt could assert his own loyalty to the Old Dominion. In this sense, writing the biography of Henry could enhance Wirt's own biography, his lasting fame. It could also damage his reputation if done poorly. Therefore, he was especially solicitous of leading Virginians' opinions throughout the dozen years he composed the book. Moreover, in choosing the life of *Henry,* a statesman who had similarly begun life in financial hardship and joined the governing class only later, Wirt could justify his own rise by analogy. After all, Henry's trajectory demonstrated that the elite was not a closed circle. In this sense, the biography of Henry contained traces of Wirt's own autobiography.

William Wirt envisioned himself as a classically educated gentleman and a defender of Virginia's Jeffersonian republican traditions against the declension of the rising generation—even though he, born in 1772, must have seemed part of that generation to men like Jefferson.[46] When his foray into biography began, Wirt was an attorney and author who had made his way from modest beginnings to education and incipient legal prominence. Orphaned at eight, he attended academies intermittently throughout his childhood and youth when his family's finances allowed. At twenty he moved to Virginia to establish a legal practice, and soon thereafter married into the prominent and wealthy Gilmer family of Albemarle, Thomas Jefferson's county. Jefferson's recommendation launched him into public service as clerk of the House of Delegates in 1799. Over the next two decades, he alternated between public office, almost always appointive, and legal work. He remarried after his first wife's death in 1799; in 1803, when his second wife was expecting their first child, he produced his first literary effort. This series of familiar essays, "The Letters of the British Spy," appeared first in the Virginia *Argus* and shortly thereafter in book form and made him something of a literary celebrity. The essays, which included sketches of prominent Virginians such as John Marshall and James Monroe, displayed Wirt's vision of declension: the present generation was neither as patriotic nor as well educated as its predecessor, and classical oratory was giving way to an excessively ornamented, insufficiently disciplined style.[47]

These concerns were not Wirt's alone. They were a hallmark of his professional and literary circle, which included Jefferson's nephew Dabney Carr, St. George Tucker, and other men of wealth and social standing. The social world Wirt inhabited by 1805 (thanks to his marriages and legal career) shared neoclassical literary tastes, a belief in the importance of oratory, and for the most part Jeffersonian Republican political views. Assertive champions of Virginia and collectors of Virginiana, these men wrote extensively about the state and owned numerous volumes written by Virginians or dealing with the Old Dominion's history and celebrated men. By the early nineteenth century, many among this elite wrote to each other and to a wider public that Virginia was entering a period of decline from its Revolutionary glory days. In poetry and in fiction as well as in Wirt's "British Spy" and later essays, these men exhorted the rising generation to apply itself to study so that the Commonwealth might maintain its pre-eminence. Wirt himself organized two series of essays, *The Rainbow* and *The Old Bachelor,* in which he and his friends expounded on these issues. The theme of declension was not unique to Virginians in the early republic, but for men of Wirt's social and intellectual circle it assumed particularly local meaning as they watched other states gain economic and political primacy.[48]

When in 1804 Wirt stated his objectives — "preserving the memory of our illustrious men" and "perpetuating to Virginia the honour of having given them birth" — he meant several things. His goals seemed to emphasize the state's reputation more than the nation's and thus to express the concerns of his circle. But asserting a state's role in the national history and writing national history were not disconnected endeavors in these years. Wirt's words, as well as his desire that the work be useful to "the rising generation," paralleled the assertive nationalism of numerous contemporary histories, plays, paintings, portrait pantheons, and collective biographies. Other objectives were more personal. By describing "our" illustrious men, Wirt may also have been reinforcing his Virginian identity at a point when he was still solidifying his professional and social position in the state. In letters to his wife, Wirt wrote that this biography could earn him money and increase his reputation. Husband and father of a growing family, ambitious lawyer who remembered the financial hardships of his youth, he justified long absences from home, during which he solicited materials for the book, on the grounds that its publication could dispel future monetary worries and provide inheritances for his children. (No previous American author had been so fortunate—which might lead one to suspect that he wrote these letters to justify his project in domestic terms his wife would appreciate.) Just as important, the book could ensure "my own immortality as well as that of Mr. Henry." With others of the Revolutionary and post-Revolutionary generations, Wirt shared the republican idea that "the passion for fame" was "not only innocent, but laudable and even noble." Wirt meant the kind of fame that welded the public good to private interest. As long as the fame derived from "virtuous and useful actions," desiring it served to encourage civic endeavors like commemorating republican heroes and providing models for the next generation. Only when a man wanted "that kind of fame which Bonaparte has" was the passion for it dangerous.[49]

Wirt's conception of the biography reflected republican ideas about character at a moment when new political alignments, social transformations, and democratic visions were redefining and reshaping "republicanism." Historians of the past thirty years have debated what republicanism meant at different times and to different people, and whether it was ever the central ideological element in the Revolutionary struggle and post-Revolutionary period. Notwithstanding these debates, it is possible to sketch several elements of the ideal republican "character" as late-eighteenth-century contemporaries portrayed it. Above all, the republican patriot placed the public good above his private or partisan interests. This quality assumed additional (and often partisan) meaning as political parties emerged: each party claimed that its leading men were the true "republicans" while its opponents' were motivated by petty partisanship.[50] By the late 1790s, party was part of the political process in Virginia. Patrick Henry lamented this development and attempted to remain above party, even as Federalists encouraged him to run for governor under their banner. William Wirt, who would hail Henry's nonpartisanship in his biography and who sought the same reputation for himself, received his first public office when the victorious Republicans ousted Federalist officials and replaced them with men of their own.[51] Other elements of republican character reinforced one's attention to the public good. Simplicity of habits and tastes, for instance, prevented the good republican from succumbing to the twin temptations of avarice and an aristocratic style of living (and thus to those who would divert his attention from the public interest).

It is significant that many elements of the "republican" character applied particularly to men of independent means, because by the early republic the meaning of Revolutionary republicanism came to be extended by people outside traditional elites. The image of simplicity had been donned by society's leading men (and extolled by their biographers) to suggest their incorruptibility and their continuing attachment to agrarian pursuits — but most ordinary American farmers had no need to adopt such poses. As early as the Revolution itself, however, some leading men became concerned about the potentially democratic implications of their republicanism. Virginia's evangelicals offered models of authority and language that challenged the gentry; Patrick Henry had been the foremost practitioner of new models of public expression. By the 1790s and early 1800s, several American writers created paired sets of characters — one representing the republican statesman of the earlier era, the other representing the new American democrat. Royall Tyler's play *The Contrast* depicted not just Colonel Manly, the veteran in faded uniform (not fashionable clothing) who seeks pensions for his comrades, but also Jonathan, his manservant who sees the potential of the Revolution to make him an independent farmer. Hugh Henry Brackenridge's picaresque novel *Modern Chivalry* took the contrast further, making Captain Farrago a republican statesman akin to Colonel Manly but his servant Teague O'Regan more explicitly an enterprising climber of the emergent, democratic variety. By the time Wirt came to write Patrick Henry's biography, several models of "republican" character, which were not necessarily reconcilable, were available for presenting his subject — one whose life and career could be interpreted in various ways, given his humble origins and populist following.[52]

Wirt's conception of biography in 1805 included more than glorifying Henry's public deeds, describing his political and social milieu, and fitting him into republican archetypes; it also included revealing Henry's unique character to the reader. Old Williamsburg newspapers and information about Henry's legal and political colleagues did not bring Wirt "near to the character of Mr. Henry or . . . enable me to bring my reader so." Here was the Johnsonian idea that biography brought the reader close to the subject through its portrayal of specific traits and habits. (It is worth recalling that Wirt contracted his "itch for Biography" as he read Johnson's *Lives of the Poets*.) But Wirt had never met or seen Henry, a disadvantage that made writing a biography along the Johnsonian model virtually impossible. To remedy this deficiency, he asked men who had known Henry to describe him as minutely as possible: "even to the color of his eyes, a portrait of his person, attitudes, gestures, manners; a description of his voice, its tone, energy, and modulations; his delivery, whether slow, grave and solemn, or rapid, sprightly and animated; his pronunciation, whether studiously plain, homely, and sometimes vulgar, or accurate, courtly and ornate,—with an analysis of his mind, the variety, order and predominance of its powers; his information as a lawyer, a politician, a scholar; the peculiar character of his eloquence, &c., &c." Wirt considered such information "the most interesting part of biography," which could emerge not from "any archives or records," but best of all from the memory of an acute observer.[53]

By "character" Wirt meant Henry's distinctive traits and habits, but not his domestic privacies. Indeed, his friend Tucker explained to him in 1813 that describing private character was both impracticable and inappropriate for biographies of Virginia's worthies. Few anecdotes of great men's private lives survived in Virginia, wrote Tucker, because these men "have all glided down the current of life so smoothly, (except as public men,) that nobody ever thought of noticing how they lived, or what they did; for, to live and act *like gentlemen,* was a thing once so common in Virginia, that nobody thought of noticing it."[54] Further, using language much like Charles Caldwell's defense of Delaplaine's *Repository,* Tucker argued that such anecdotes (even if they did exist) were not what readers wanted. Essentially rejecting Johnson's argument about what made biography fascinating, Tucker suggested that American biography gained its importance and appeal from its accounts of public deeds, which were fast fading from memory as Revolutionary figures and their acquaintances died. Whether because he agreed with Tucker or because he lacked the intimate acquaintance necessary to describe Henry's domestic privacies (the Johnsonian method), Wirt emphasized his subject's public character as early as his initial planning in 1805—even as he sought to paint a portrait of Henry's "genuine life." The details of gesture, pronunciation, and mental powers that Wirt sought from Henry's associates all concerned Henry's public appearance and gifts.

The product of Wirt's early labors, an 1807 unpublished draft of Henry's life from his birth in 1736 to his first great legal success in 1763, demonstrates his early attempt to paint a Johnsonian portrait of Henry's unique character, though it would be seen almost entirely on the public stage. He wanted to capture the essence of a particular human being, not just reproduce a flat republican type, even as he adhered to the republican vision of biography as instructor to the rising generation. Written as a first letter "to a young gentleman at William and Mary College," this sketch echoed the form he had employed successfully in *The Letters of the British Spy:* the educated, republican elder instructing the younger reader through the example of a famous subject. However, Wirt quickly turned from republican patriotism to Johnsonian language about biography. Wirt could not, he explained, give the young collegian "all those strokes which discriminate the character and which can be collected by personal acquaintance and observation only." Only the biographer with "the fire-side confidence" of his subject—like Tacitus with Agricola, Johnson with Richard Savage, or Boswell with Johnson—could hope "to unfold the whole character; . . . to charge the narrative with those private and domestic incidents which give to biography its deepest interest; in short to write the genuine life from the best and highest evidence instead of writing a general panegyric or a satire." Without this personal acquaintance, Wirt had turned to the next best sources: "respectable gentlemen" who *had* known Henry and "public records." Not only did the Johnsonian model avoid panegyric and satire; it also differed from history. Wirt explained to his young gentleman that he was writing Henry's life, not the history of Virginia or of the United States. (He knew that Marshall's recently published *Life of Washington* had been criticized on this score.) Most important, he warned his addressee to "discard those romantic prepossessions in favor of Mr. Henry," because this was biography, not fiction. The novelist Samuel Richardson might create perfect heroes, but in real life "perfection belongs to no man." [55]

Having said this, Wirt went on to portray an imperfect yet heroic Patrick Henry. Wirt's Henry, despite several renowned ancestors, was born into a poor family; as a young man he worked briefly as a barkeeper. Indolence was his chief flaw: he avoided intellectual pursuits and failed twice at mercantile endeavors. To the argument that Henry's lack of book learning made him a more natural orator and man, Wirt replied that Henry would have gained intellectual energy, not been "enfeebled or debased by a communion with books." Even when he turned to law, his aversion to book training hampered his rise. His leap to fame occurred not through hard work, but on "one of those rare occasions . . . which untrammel argument at the bar, give scope to general information and afford a range for genius": the 1763 Virginia controversy over parsons' compensation. Wirt told the story as high drama. Henry's father was the presiding judge in the case, and Henry's uncle was among the leading clergymen whom the young lawyer "assailed" in the name of the people. After Henry's speech, his "father burst into tears of rapture" and the people carried him on their shoulders like a victorious political candidate. This event established his reputation as lawyer, orator, politician, and "man of the people."[56]

This depiction of the early Henry, much of which Wirt preserved in the finished book published a decade later, reflected the author's own early life and his view of intellectual culture. After all, Wirt, too, had started life inauspiciously, and his father had run a tavern—an occupation whose stigma he could dispel by attaching the role to Patrick Henry as well.[57] Unlike Henry, Wirt had sought classical education from youth, and in *The Letters of the British Spy* he argued that modern American orators did not possess sufficient classical training. Wirt's refusal to excuse Henry's intellectual laziness may have stemmed from a comparison between himself (also a lawyer, orator, and politician, though distinctly not a man of the people) and his subject. It also resulted from his didactic aims: to countenance Henry's indolence, given his genius, could encourage rising Virginians similarly to ignore their studies. At the same time, Wirt's description of Henry's central flaw served a Johnsonian biographical purpose. Narrated in scenes from his youth and early manhood, it admitted readers into acquaintance with an element of Henry's character distinct from archetypal republican virtue.

Within this 1807 manuscript, Wirt moved from one sort of biography to another. The first half, describing Henry's inattention to study and numerous early failures, captured a young man whose success was not assured from the start and suggested a multifaceted character. Lurking throughout this portrayal was the implication that Henry always possessed a native genius waiting to burst forth. Once it did, the biographer became one of the multitude celebrating the young lawyer's victory. Wirt's language became increasingly dramatic, and he compared Henry's oratory and origins with those of Demosthenes. The human Henry became a classical figure— a model consonant with portrayals of statesmen in the new nation (and more indicative of Wirt's own education in the classics than of Henry's inattention to literature), but hardly consistent with the biographical practices of Johnson and Boswell cited at the beginning of the piece. After completing this "letter," Wirt seems to have dropped the project for the next three years.

When he resumed it in 1810, "regard to truth" superseded his earlier Johnsonian emphasis on individual character.[58] Although the didactic objective remained, the route to didacticism now ran almost exclusively through collecting facts about Henry's public world, not delving into his character. Wirt's methods now consisted largely of verifying historical information. Quite possibly Wirt believed that he had already done the part of the biography where character had greatest prominence: the section on Henry's youth and early adulthood, which would appear in the finished book much as it had in the unpublished 1807 manuscript. Now he was writing about Henry's involvement in the Revolutionary crisis, which called for authentic narration of public events. Possibly, too, by the mid-1810s with the Revolution ten years more distant, the desire to record the public facts accurately assumed increasing importance for Wirt.[59] He spent increasing effort asking about when things had happened and trying to reconcile conflicting accounts.

Wirt's concern for reputations—Patrick Henry's, other historical figures', his sources', and ultimately his own—made his task more difficult. One episode particularly troubled him. Under disputed circumstances, Henry resigned his colonelcy of the first Virginia regiment and command of all Virginia forces in February 1776. Henry's admirers argued that Henry resigned as a matter of honor, after repeated insults from his second-in-command and the colony's governing bodies. His detractors suggested that cowardice and military inexperience made Henry an unsuitable commander who seized an excuse to resign. Depending on one's point of view, Edmund Pendleton, the chairman of the Virginia conventions, either envied Henry's popularity (and thus wanted to diminish his military authority) or recognized Henry's limited military abilities (and thus desired to shift responsibility elsewhere). Jefferson reported that Henry's acquaintances had believed he "wanted personal courage," since after all "his brother William, and half brother Syme were notorious cowards." But since Jefferson had heard only one such anecdote and since the rumor had been neither proven nor disproven, he recommended that Wirt simply "bury the question . . . in oblivion." It could only diminish Henry's reputation in the fields where he excelled (as "Orator & Statesman"), and the whole story "would die away if not excited." Jefferson shared the detractors' view, but why press the point?[60]

The biographer's sympathies (unlike Jefferson's) lay with Henry, and Wirt removed neither the episode nor the impression that Henry had been slighted. When he sent the manuscript for Jefferson's comments, Wirt wrote that dealing unfavorably with Pendleton "has given me pain—but truth, and the justice due to Mr. Henry, seemed to require it."[61] Recounting the episode, he explained in the book, was difficult but unavoidable. Truth, as determined by "the evidence in my possession"—Wirt cited newspaper articles, correspondence, and legislative acts—forced him to relate an incident unflattering to Pendleton; whether contemporaries had treated Pendleton justly was not the biographer's affair. But the republican biographer owed Pendleton, "too virtuous a man, and too faithful a patriot, to have yielded consciously to any other motive of action than the public good," the most generous reading of motives (even if the word "consciously" hinted at deeper motives than Pendleton himself perceived).[62] Henry could appear as the beloved leader of his troops, Pendleton as a patriot committed to military success, and Wirt as simultaneously the faithful biographer and the republican commemorator of *both* American worthies.

Such balancing acts only increased Wirt's anxiety about how this biography would affect his own reputation. He could omit his sources' names if mentioning them would produce or exacerbate animosities—but his own name was to appear on the cover and title page of the book, for the first time. (His *Letters of the British Spy* had appeared anonymously, although Wirt's identity had quickly become an open secret.) Fully two years before the book appeared, Wirt's Philadelphia publisher James Webster announced it as forthcoming and magazines speculated about how Wirt would accomplish the task. By now Wirt occupied a different social position from that of 1805. Then he had been working to establish himself among Virginia's professional elite, hoping the book would make money, and building his legal practice. By 1815 he was "securely established as a member of the upper class," thanks to his own efforts and especially his wife's substantial inheritance. He had a houseful of relatives, friends, servants, and slaves; he was an authority on Virginia's legal code; he had written a second series of essays, *The Old Bachelor* (1811), that helped spur him to resume the Henry biography.[63] In 1805 his literary efforts served to make his reputation; a decade later, the biography seemed to him more likely to damage what he had built than to add to his lustre.

Anonymous authorship was never a consideration, not only because his project was public knowledge at least as early as 1815 but also because the trustworthiness of his narrative depended upon the public identification of its author. Anonymous or pseudonymous authorship might be acceptable for works that clearly represented an individual's sentiments (like familiar essays) or partisan views, or for works of imagination that laid no claim to truth. However, in a partisan era when "anonymous paragraphists" in the newspapers might harbor interests that colored their statements, claims of historical or biographical truth possessed little weight without their authors' names. As long as one could assume that disinterested, educated men were writing the biographies, anonymity could be trustworthy. At the point when this assumption collapsed—and by the 1810s, as several magazines' responses to Delaplaine's *Repository* indicated, it had—anonymity became merely a cloak for unknown interests. Once uncertainty crept in, the trustworthy had to make their names known in their works, so as not to be confused with the anonymous paragraphists. Wirt's reputation as a Virginian who had access to the materials for a biography, as an orator who could write about Henry's oratory, and as an accomplished writer was precisely the basis for his book's "authenticity"—and all the more reason for anxiety.[64]

The preface to *Sketches of the Life and Character of Patrick Henry* reflected this concern with reputation and illustrated how Wirt's concept of his project had changed in the dozen years since 1805. The first sentence set the tone: "The reader has a right to know what degree of credit is due to the following narrative; and it is the object of the preface to give him that satisfaction."[65] In the next ten pages Wirt described each eminent Virginian who had shared recollections and information, and explained how each had known Henry. This testimony to his informants' reliability supported Wirt's own claim to biographical "authenticity." Gone from the prefatory matter was all trace of the letter to the "young gentleman at William and Mary College" that had framed his 1807 draft. Gone, too, was the Johnsonian discourse about the nature of biography, with its parallels between Wirt's life of Henry, Johnson's life of Savage, and Boswell's life of Johnson. The quest for historical accuracy was now paramount. As a result, the preface suggested a different role for the biographer. No longer the republican elder teaching a young gentleman through Henry's example, Wirt now presented himself as an interlocutor between his older informants and the rising generation.

The structure of the book echoed this change. *Sketches of the Life and Character of Patrick Henry* was aptly titled, for it was a "life and character" that resembled many English biographies in this form (including some of Johnson's lives of poets). After the preface, Wirt's book contained ten "sections" and a conclusion. The sections (the "life") told Henry's story chronologically, with footnotes indicating where Wirt had obtained information and quotations. Only Section 1, a revised version of Wirt's 1807 draft on Henry's early years, dealt significantly with Henry's life outside the public sphere. Moreover, only here did the didacticism prominent in that early draft survive. Here Wirt presented Henry as a model for emulation and warned "the youthful reader" not to imitate Henry's indolence. Each of the succeeding nine sections, on Henry's political life, took its focus from a public event or sequence of public events—Henry's service in the Continental Congress in 1774–75, for example, or the ratification debate in Virginia. Several sections contained long extracts from contemporary letters and published documents, including forty pages quoting Henry's speech in a 1791 circuit-court case. As in English "lives and characters," the conclusion or "character" synthesized the recurring themes of Henry's life, summarized his leading virtues and vices, and presented the details of personal appearance, manner, and oratory that Wirt had sought from the start. Here Wirt also defended Henry against those who labeled him a demagogue or a follower rather than leader of popular opinion. As a series of epistolary essays to a young reader, a structure Wirt was still considering as late as 1815, Henry's biography would have emphasized the formation of character.[66] In recasting the biography, Wirt revised his larger aim: replete with footnotes, *Sketches of the Life and Character of Patrick Henry* was foremost a historical biography.

No matter how copious Wirt's citation of authorities, his portrayal of Henry was nonetheless overwhelmingly sympathetic and heroic. Wirt proudly claimed to have included every charge ever leveled against Henry. He also dismissed all but one of those charges. The exception, Henry's support for the Alien and Sedition Acts in the last years of his life (1798–99), presented a trickier problem. This stand, widely unpopular in Virginia, had severely damaged Henry's reputation in his home state. Wirt had written to Jefferson that this section of the book would be short, for "He did as much good in his better days; and no evils resulted from his later aberrations. Will not his Biographer, then, be excusable in drawing the veil over them, and holding up the brighter side of his character, only, to imitation?" In sketching his subject's character, Wirt described faults: intellectual indolence, "love of money," and overweening "passion for fame." However, the catalog of Henry's virtues—especially his innate understanding of human nature—dwarfed these three flaws. If slightly imperfect, he was "one of those perfect prodigies of nature, of whom very few have been produced since the foundations of the earth were laid."[67] Wirt's rhetorical flourishes and elaborate metaphors reinforced the heroic portrayal, even if they contrasted with the simplicity Wirt described as central to Henry's character and oratory. Young Henry was "a plant of slow growth"; Henry's speeches shook the "pillars of the temple" and "burst" the "cords of argument . . . as the unshorn Samson did the bands of the Philistines"; his oratory was like a mountain stream.[68]

Wirt's Henry fused the two visions of "republican character" prominent in the early republic: the common representative of a less-exalted citizenry, and the elite representative of order. Throughout the biography, Wirt emphasized Henry's simplicity of dress and habits. Henry "belonged to the body of the people," who believed that he had been "sent to them expressly for the very purpose of humbling the mighty, and exalting the honour of his own class." Partly because of his origins, partly because he knew where his support lay, Henry shared their manners, plain dress, simple food and drink, and even "their own vicious and depraved pronunciation." Men of higher station considered these manners "a premeditated artifice" to win popular favor, but Henry needed no such affectations: he already had the people's allegiance. Most of the charges against Henry, Wirt argued, came from aristocratic Virginians resentful or jealous of the "plebeian" Henry's popularity and status. Moreover, Wirt's Henry was more revolutionary than the men around him: he prodded wealthier Virginians toward revolt. "[I]t was he alone, who, by his single power moved the mighty mass of stagnant waters, and changed the silent lake into a roaring torrent."[69] At the same time, Wirt described Henry through comparison with classical analogues, a rhetorical strategy often used in the early republic to suggest stability. If Washington was the American Cincinnatus, Wirt labeled Henry the "American Demosthenes." Early American magazines favored this approach in their biographical sketches, which endorsed harmonious social hierarchy by likening subjects to classical "idols of order." Wirt went so far as to point out that Henry and Demosthenes both achieved oratorical fame at the age of twenty-seven, a coincidence one reviewer ridiculed as meaningless.[70] Simplicity of habits marked the figure of republican stability no less than that of democratic unrest. Depictions of Washington often described his eschewal of finery, and *The Contrast*'s Colonel Manly distinguished himself from the foppish Billy Dimple by wearing his faded Revolutionary uniform rather than the latest fashion. This recurring detail in Wirt's presentation of Henry thus fit the images of both the classical figure (as interpreted in republican America) and the Revolutionary firebrand from outside the elite.

Wirt took care, however, to place Henry's incendiary potential safely in the past—and to suggest that any resemblance between Henry and new, grasping democrats like Brackenridge's character Teague O'Regan was troubling, not virtuous. The "want of literary discipline" that characterized Henry's oratory and that kept him from becoming one of the Revolution's great writers may have been suitable for his times and mission. Perhaps the ordinary people "admired him the more for his want of discipline."[71] But Wirt did not commend this model to young men of 1817. Nor did he commend Henry's love of money. One characteristic that Wirt did praise as an example to his own contemporaries flew against an emergent liberal politics: Henry's refusal to align himself with either of the nascent parties of the 1790s. Political partisanship remained suspect in the 1810s, and Wirt took care to place both his Henry and himself above it. Supporting the Alien and Sedition Acts did not make Henry a Federalist; it placed him in league with Washington, who presumably stood above party. Wirt, who knew the rancor over Marshall's unabashedly Federalist *Life of Washington*, determined to avoid such difficulty: "It is not my function to decide between these parties; nor do I feel myself qualified for such an office. I have lived too near the times, and am conscious of having been too strongly excited by the feelings of the day, to place myself in the chair of the arbiter. . . . Let us, then, remit the question to the historian of future ages; who . . . will probably decide, that, as in most family quarrels, both parties have been somewhat in the wrong." In the 1790s, partisans on each side had argued that the other side endangered the very existence of the republic. Now, in the aftermath of the War of 1812, Wirt softened those battles into reconcilable domestic squabbles.[72]

Sketches of the Life and Character of Patrick Henry thus contained multiple visions of republican character and several different forms of biography writing. Although Wirt hoped to present Henry's "genuine life," an individualized portrait like those Johnson had sketched of his poets, he never adopted Johnson's method of revealing the subject in his "domestic privacies." Indeed, Henry's entire "domestic" life appeared in three passages—including just a single page for the deaths of Henry's wife, father, and uncle, the survival of his mother, the sale of his farm and his purchase of another, and his remarriage and removal to "his newly acquired estate."[73] Similarly faint in Wirt's book were traces of the republican didacticism central to his objectives a decade earlier. Despite the dedication to "the young men of Virginia," Wirt no longer concentrated on offering a model for the rising generation. He did recommend patriotism and simplicity and warn against laziness. But following these suggestions could not make young men into new Patrick Henrys, because Henry's importance sprang from his unique characteristic: the God-given, extraordinary perception of human character that made him "a prodigy of nature" and suited him for the equally extraordinary task of leading a revolution. Wirt's book offered two other kinds of lessons instead. One was inspirational. Even if a young reader could not become Henry, Henry's biography could motivate him to patriotic endeavors. This concept, pivotal to Wirt's 1807 "letter to a young gentleman at William and Mary College," was peripheral within the book as published in 1817.

The other, more important kind of lesson was historical—because Wirt's book was a historical biography above all: an attempt to inscribe the record of the past while some who remembered it still survived. Biography writing in early-national America involved bridging past and present, and Wirt's *Sketches of the Life and Character of Patrick Henry* reveals that even by 1817 the nature of the bridge was changing. By capturing Henry's life in print, Wirt could tell the history of the Revolutionary era, especially in Virginia, to the present generation. Wirt's position in the 1810s—too young to have heard Henry in his prime, too embedded in the politics of the early republic to make judgments—constrained his work. So did the fact that some of the statesmen at the 1788 Virginia ratifying convention were still alive, for "therefore, delicacy forbids us to speak as they deserve." But timing also required that he write the life of Henry now, before the sources for an "authentic" life died. Rather than provide the present with emulable models from the past, the bridge of historical biography emphasized the lengthening distance between present and past.[74]

Wirt was not the only biographer in the 1810s to imply such a bridge. Charles Caldwell, who wrote the short biographies in Delaplaine's *Repository* and defended American biographers' focus on subjects' public deeds, also wrote a book-length life of General Nathaniel Greene, published two years after Wirt's life of Henry. Caldwell was more explicitly nationalistic and commemorative than Wirt: he sought "to aid in the defence of the American character" against foreign "imputations" and dedicated his book not to young men but to "the surviving officers of the revolutionary army." However, the two biographers' purposes were similar. Both wanted to preserve for the historical record the deeds of an often-neglected Revolutionary hero and to awaken readers' admiration (but not imitation, which was impossible). Like Wirt, Caldwell emphasized his research, including both printed works and participants' recollections. Also like Wirt, Caldwell gave primacy to public deeds—in effect, getting the last word in the debate over Delaplaine's *Repository*.

Private character is much more an object of individual curiosity, than of general interest, or public importance. A representation of it may amuse and entertain; but it is rarely calculated to instruct or improve. . . . But this is not all. It is impossible to give a full and faithful representation of the private character of an individual, without a personal and intimate acquaintance with him. Neither an inspection of his familiar letters, nor the minutest narratives of those who knew him, can qualify a writer for so delicate a task. He who trusts to such materials, may compose a pleasing fancy-picture, but can never succeed in giving a faithful portrait.[75]

A Johnsonian approach would not serve the American biographer's purposes, nor was it practicable in this instance. Historical instruction—the primary form of improvement that resulted from reading biographies like Wirt's and Caldwell's—differed from the more inspirational objectives of collective biographies like Delaplaine's *Repository* or Woodward's *Columbian Plutarch*. But they all agreed, explicitly or implicitly, about what facets of "character" belonged in American biography.

If Wirt sought through historical biography to connect present to past, what readers did he envision for his work? As he wrote the book, Wirt considered the different literary worlds in which it might be read. The *Analectic* warned of three types of readers when it anticipated the book in 1815: "The grave man will read it for instruction, the frivolous for amusement, and the critic according to his disposition, either to detect faults, or to display its beauties. The first will require fidelity in the narrative, the second variety in the incidents, and the third, a watchful attention to the rules of good writing. Although I doubt not the last of these classes will be gratified with Mr. Wirt's Life of Patrick Henry, yet it will hardly be possible to please both of the former." Wirt knew, and Jefferson reminded him, that "European critics" were likely to "tomahawk away" at whatever he produced. American critics might do the same, but none had "sufficient weight of character to destroy it." But what of ordinary readers, asked Wirt. "Does not Fame depend upon the *multitude* of readers and approvers?" The "candid and sensible reader" might allow for the monotony of much of Henry's life, but "the thousands of readers on whom fame depends" preferred poetry and novels to histories and biographies. Even if the "grade and quality" of the novelist's fame were inferior to those of the biographer, the "spread, the propagation and continuity" of the novelist's were far greater. Wirt doubted whether the life of Patrick Henry, concerned largely with "speaking, speaking, speaking" and limited in its imaginative possibilities by the adherence to facts, would attract a wide readership.[76]

Responses to the book, which came from across the United States, revealed how generation and geography affected people's perceptions of it. Richard Morris Jr., an acquaintance of Wirt who read the near-final draft, effused that "it treated of the age of glory in Virginia, it gave me a delightful acquaintance with those men who made it the age of Glory, it elevated 'my own, my native' State to a proud equality with Athens and Rome, and with all my Virginianism about me I knew not how to part with it." Moreover, Morris reported that his uncles were delighted with the book. "It carried them back to the times and scenes of their youth; 'they fought all their battles o'er again'; and interrupted me so often with their exclamations, that I could with difficulty proceed. They made some remarks in relation to certain parts of the narrative, which it is necessary that you should know, and which I will communicate on my next visit to Richmond." Although all of these Virginia Morrises loved the book, they reacted differently to it. The younger Morris saw an unbridgeable distance between present and past. Too young to remember the Revolutionary years, he made "acquaintance" with the leading figures of that era through Wirt's book. If those days were the "age of Glory," the very phrase implied that that age was now gone, accessible only through books and uncles. Those uncles, in contrast, responded to the book in much the way that some of Wirt's sources had when they supplied him with information: it provided an opportunity for recollection, a real bridge of memory. Also like Wirt's sources, they had stories of their own to tell Wirt, perhaps to correct his narrative. Other Virginians responded equally enthusiastically, predicting success across the nation and even with "some of the politicians & many of the Literati of Britain." Wirt himself was less sanguine, responding grumpily to Morris that the book was boring and that nobody outside Virginia would read it.[77]

In fact, the book did reach a wider audience. *Sketches of the Life and Character of Patrick Henry,* like many other works by southern authors in the early republic, was published in Philadelphia. Perhaps for this reason several Philadelphia newspapers noticed the book. *Poulson's American Daily Advertiser* published glowing letters from two subscribers. One described the book as a "literary Comet . . . shot forth to the enraptured contemplation of the republic of letters" and argued that its dedication to the young men of Virginia was too modest: "Every American should read this Book." This reader elided the historical and the commemorative uses of biography: a biography could be drawn from "the best possible authorities" *and* serve as a monument to Henry—while at the same time providing more enjoyment than any novel or romance he had ever read. The book circulated well outside Henry's state and the publisher's city. By January 1818, just two months after publication, it was in the catalog of the small social library in rural Charlestown, New Hampshire. As it went through subsequent editions over the next thirty years, it came to appear in libraries from Charleston, South Carolina, to Chittenden City, Vermont. Newspapers in Charleston, New York, Albany, and Boston reviewed it or printed extracts from it. And although several newspaper reviewers hinted darkly about what American magazine critics with European tastes would do to an American work (echoing the battle over Delaplaine's *Repository*), several magazines including the *Portico* praised Wirt's book highly.[78]

But the reputation that mattered most to Wirt depended on the authenticity, not the popularity, of his work—a judgment that rested in the minds of men like Jefferson and St. George Tucker, Virginia worthies of the Revolutionary generation. Jefferson became Wirt's toughest Virginian critic. He had written Wirt several long letters full of reminiscences and information about Henry and Revolutionary Virginia, much of which Wirt incorporated into the book. Nevertheless, after reading the manuscript, Jefferson expressed ambivalence: "Those who take up your book will find they cannot lay it down," but Wirt's celebration of Henry "presents a very difficult question, whether one only, or both sides of the medal should be presented. It constitutes perhaps the distinction between panegyric and history." Two months earlier, Jefferson had complained about Wirt's "flowery" style, suggesting that "It will please young readers in its present form, but to the older it would give more pleasure and confidence to have some exuberances lightly pruned." Apparently Jefferson condemned the book more harshly to others. When Daniel Webster and George Ticknor visited Charlottesville in 1824, Jefferson called it "a poor book, written in bad taste, and . . . written less to show Mr. Henry than Mr. Wirt."[79] Jefferson's criticisms troubled Wirt, for they touched the issues he had worried about from the start. His ornamented writing style, he had told numerous correspondents, was better suited to literary essays than to "sober" biography writing, "fettered by a scrupulous regard to real facts."[80] After all Wirt's efforts to collect materials, to have Jefferson call the book a "panegyric" was a severe indictment indeed. Jefferson had his own biases, and had at times encouraged Wirt to omit events and charges from his story. His disappointment surely stemmed in part from the fact that Wirt had presented Henry far more favorably than Jefferson liked. Even so, his opinion, not only as Virginia's foremost living statesman and man of letters but also as one of the leading "authorities" on whom Wirt had based his own biographical authority, mattered greatly to Wirt. (Carping from John Taylor of Caroline, who called the book "a splendid novel," meant less.[81]) Jefferson's suggestion that the book would "gratify the young" but "shake the confidence of the aged in the truth of my story" challenged the generational balance that Wirt had sought to achieve. If the book were solely a prettily written biography for "young people," it would belong to the same category as Parson Weems's lives of Washington and Marion—charming schoolbooks but suspect histories in the estimation of those Wirt most wanted to please.[82]

Another set of critiques, from Massachusetts, illustrated anew the difficulties biographers faced in the early republic and foreshadowed debates that would take center stage in later years. On January 13, 1818, Wirt asked his publisher to send a copy of the book to John Adams. (By this time Wirt was attorney general of the United States, having accepted President Monroe's appointment just when the book appeared in November.) Wirt's gesture was prompted by a letter eight days earlier from Adams, who had borrowed the book from a friend and read much of it already. Adams wrote that "Your Sketches of the Life of Mr. Henry have given me rich entertainment," but went on to say that if he "could go back to the age of thirty-five, I would endeavor to become your rival,—not in elegance of composition, but in a simple narration of facts, supported by records, histories, and testimonies of irrefragable authority." What would Adams produce? "Sketches of the Life and Writings of James Otis, of Boston," on one of the dozens of Massachusetts luminaries as bright as Henry. Wirt disclaimed any desire to place Virginia's heroes above the Bay State's, an unconvincing assertion from an author who had asserted the Old Dominion's preeminence in the Revolution. Adams responded with another letter describing one of Otis's pamphlets, which appeared a year before Henry's first Revolutionary resolutions. In sum, Adams did not begrudge proper due to "the well merited glories of Virginia, or any of her sages or heroes, but I am jealous, very jealous, of the honor of Massachusetts." Like Jefferson, Adams was less kind to Wirt's book when discussing it with others. He wrote that Wirt "knows nothing of the real origin of the American Revolution." He also encouraged William Tudor, an editor of the new *North American Review*, to write a life of Otis that would counter Wirt's claims for Henry.[83]

Another of Adams's comments to Tudor was equally revealing. "Your judgment of Mr. Wirt's biography of my friend Mr. Henry, is in exact unison with my own. I have read it with more delight than Scott's Romances in verse and prose, or Miss Porter's Scottish Chiefs and other novels."[84] Walter Scott and Jane Porter were, of course, two of the most popular novelists of the 1810s; their books circulated more often than almost any others in the Farmers and Mechanicks Library in Washington County, New York. But to compare a biography to them suggested that it was exactly what it was not supposed to be: a novel. It might seem that Adams was complimenting Wirt for making biography more enjoyable than the best novel. Yet we know from his other remarks that he doubted Wirt's understanding of the Revolution. Admiration for Wirt's "elegance of composition" was a double-edged sword: it implied that Wirt had substituted style for substance, the novelist's tools for the biographer's. Wirt, as several modern scholars have noted, was not simply Henry's first biographer but also one of Virginia's first mythmakers, sketching scenes of striking oratory and a noble aristocratic culture besieged by equally compelling Revolutionary forces. This image may have resonated most deeply with younger Virginia men like Richard Morris Jr., who had not lived through the Revolution. For such men, living in an Old Dominion where increasingly economic success was proving difficult and genteel families were turning inward, away from the public sphere, the earlier period may indeed have seemed an "age of glory."[85] In urging Tudor to write Otis's biography, Adams suggested that Massachusetts needed to produce its own story of America's Revolutionary origins, so that Virginia mythmaking would not become national history.

The severest commentary on *Sketches of the Life and Character of Patrick Henry,* which appeared in Tudor's *North American Review,* anticipated two issues that would come to dominate debates over biography in the next forty years. The first was the relationship between "truth" and "tradition." According to the *North American's* reviewer, Wirt had relied too heavily on "tradition," or unsubstantiable reminiscences. Wirt had constantly complained of a dearth of written sources as he composed the book and had relied upon Henry's acquaintances to fill in much of the story. For this reviewer, such a method sacrificed reliable "truth." The other issue concerned the relationship between state, section, and nation. Like Adams, this reviewer took issue with Wirt's assertions for Henry and Virginia. In the name of "the truth," not "to weaken the claims of one state, and strengthen those of another," this critic listed a variety of ways Massachusetts, not Virginia, had instigated the American Revolution.[86] This 1818 struggle, between two states' literary elites over the initiation of the Revolution, would by the 1850s broaden into a sectional debate over the writing of American history. At the center of both issues would be the man who reviewed Wirt's work for the *North American Review:* Jared Sparks.

But 1817 was not 1850. Adams's, Tudor's, and Sparks's complaints about Wirt's book were not the cultural analogue of the Missouri Compromise debate of two years later. Between the end of the War of 1812 and the Webster-Hayne debate of the 1830s, a New England version of American history would develop, nurtured especially by old Federalists and new National Republicans at odds with Jeffersonian and Jacksonian political supremacy. However, when Massachusetts men argued with Wirt's claims, the central issue was state pride. Although southerners (and some twentieth-century scholars) would later read Wirt's book as "Southern" biography, Wirt himself conceived of it as Virginian and American. His vision was firmly rooted in his own context, not in the sectional divisions of later decades. Ever conscious of the status he had attained in his adopted Virginia, Wirt grappled with models of biography and tenets of contemporary criticism imbibed from his classical education and cosmopolitan reading tastes, hoped to satisfy the Old Dominion's intellectual elite that he had produced an "authentic" life of Henry, and wanted his book to appeal to a wider audience that was far more abstract for him than for the bookselling Parson Weems. William Wirt sought to delineate Patrick Henry's character at a time when Americans were debating whether public or private life was the stage on which virtuous character appeared. He sought to immortalize Virginia's role in the Revolution at a time when regional writers worked to mold national history in their own image. And he sought to write for Revolutionary veterans and the rising generation alike at a time when those groups were growing ever more distant from each other—and when the truths and myths of the Revolution were becoming increasingly inextricable.

Fables of Parson Weems

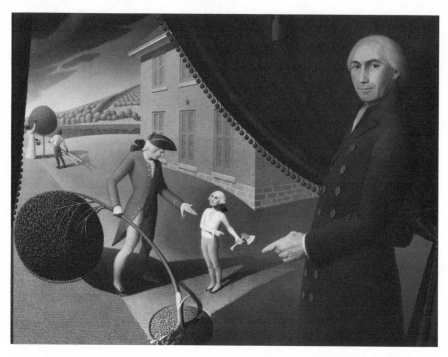

Grant Wood, *Parson Weems' Fable,* 1939, oil on canvas. Perhaps the only American painting of a biographer "at work." (Courtesy Amon Carter Museum, Fort Worth, Texas [accession #1970.43])

The twentieth century has not been kind to Mason Locke Weems. Historians have derided his biographies as moralistic fables full of fabricated anecdotes. Some have depicted him as the prototypical American huckster, using sermons to peddle his books across rural America. Most devastating, perhaps, was *Parson Weems' Fable,* the Iowa painter Grant Wood's satirical recreation of Weems's most famous anecdote. In Wood's painting, Weems draws back a cherry-red curtain, complete with red tassels that bear unmistakable resemblance to cherries, to reveal little George Washington—hatchet in one hand, other hand pointing at the nicked cherry tree, head taken from Gilbert Stuart's portrait—confessing his transgression to his father. Weems was not Grant Wood's only target: he at once satirized the parson's storytelling *and* Stuart's granite portrait. Both Weems and Stuart, the painting seems to suggest, created enduring myths that rendered the "real" Washington (if such a person existed at all) doubly difficult to reconstruct. Fables alone remained.

Even during his own lifetime Weems received considerable abuse. St. George Tucker, the Virginia jurist and writer who advised William Wirt on the biography of Henry, equated Weems's popular success with the poverty of American biography writing in the new republic:

> American biography, at least since the conclusion of the peace of 1783, is a subject which promises as little entertainment as any other in the literary world. Our scene of action is so perfectly domestic, as to afford neither novelty nor variety. Even the biographer of Washington [Marshall] has been reproached with imposing upon his readers the history of a nation, instead of the life of an individual. Parson Weems has, indeed, tried to supply the defect; but I never got further than half the first paragraph:— "George Washington, (says that most renowned biographer,) the illustrious founder of the American Nation, was the first son of —— Washington, by a *second* marriage: a circumstance, (says this profound divine, moralist, and biographer,) of

itself sufficient to reconcile the scruples of tender consciences upon that subject." I do not pretend that I have given you a literal transcript of the passage; but, I believe the substance is correct. I shut the book as soon as I had read it, and have no desire to see any more of it.[1]

The *Monthly Magazine and American Review* called Weems's original edition "eighty pages of as entertaining and edifying matter as can be found in the annals of fanaticism and absurdity." A Dr. Bigelow of Boston read his review before the Anthology Society, which published it in the *Monthly Anthology, and Boston Review* in 1810: "The reverend author of this book before us, which we are at a loss whether to denominate a biography, or a novel, founded on fact, has presented a specimen of writing, which for variety and oddity is almost an unique in the annals of literature."[2]

Despite such opprobrium Weems's biographies, especially his lives of Washington and Marion, were certainly the widest-selling and probably the most widely read biographies written by an American in the half century after independence. Few of the literary quarterlies reviewed Weems's works, but newspapers from Georgia to New England carried notices of them, no doubt often planted by Weems and his enterprising publisher Mathew

Carey. Price likely contributed to these works' circulation, for Weems and Carey recognized early the economic benefits of combining heavy volume with low profit margin. In fact, its low price may help explain why Weems's life of George Washington appears in relatively few social libraries' catalogs. It was so cheap, and Washington was so dear, that families of even modest means could and did buy their own copies. Carey's network of traveling book salesmen (including Weems himself) also contributed to the nationwide success of the book. Crafty marketing, low cost, and effective distribution methods alone cannot explain the popularity of Weems's books, however.

Weems's biographies sold prodigiously because he knew his audience better than any other biographer in the early republic. His knowledge came from experience selling books across rural America, especially in the South, Pennsylvania, and New York. Even more than the publishers for whom he worked, Weems understood what sold. He told Carey what to send for the widest southern sale and chided Carey when he sent the wrong kinds of books. He also warned C. P. Wayne about the potential problems of John Marshall's *Life of George Washington:* it would fail if "prostituted to party purposes" or if the volumes failed to appear in steady succession. Fully aware of his ability,

he sold himself to publishers even as he sold their work to readers. To Carey he wrote, "I am sure — very sure — *morally* & *positively* sure that I have it in my power (from my universal acquaintance, Industry & Health) to make you the most Thriving Book-seller in America. I can secure to you almost *exclusively* the whole of the business in the middle & western parts of all these Southern states from Maryland to Georgia inclusive. I can push your books not only into many of the Colleges, & most of the smaller seminaries of learning, but into almost every Congregation of Christians, whether Baptist, Presbyterian, Episcopalian, as also into the private libraries of Doct^{rs}. Lawyers & Divines."[3]

Never one to miss an opportunity, Weems wrote to Carey just weeks after George Washington died on December 14, 1799. "Washington, you know is gone! Millions are gaping to read something about him. I am very nearly prim^d & cock^d for 'em. 6 months ago I set myself to collect anecdotes of him. You know I live conveniently for that work. My plan! I give his history, sufficiently minute — I accompany him from his start, thro the French & Indian & British or Revolutionary wars, to the Presidents chair, to the throne in the hearts of 5,000000 of People." The book would describe Washington's great virtues for "the imitation of Our Youth"; several clergymen and "Classical Scholars" had read and commended it; at twenty-five or thirty-seven cents a copy it could be immensely profitable. In its first incarnation, the eighty-page version published within weeks of this letter (and dated February 22, Washington's birthday), Weems wrote a memorial volume akin to the hundreds of sermons preached and published after Washington died. He had actually begun the book well before December 1799, but Washington's death led to several changes. Dedicated to Martha Washington, the book promised "a feast of true *Washington Entertainment and Improvement,* Both to ourselves and our children." In several ways, this was a book calculated for the moment. It argued that Washington's death provided an occasion for national unity during the coming presidential contest between Adams and Jefferson and consoled Mrs. Washington on her loss of "that *best* of husbands." In early 1800 Weems's preface recommended biography for its concrete examples of virtues, but the book was hardly less ephemeral than dozens of other biographical sermons.[4]

It was in the sixth edition, published in 1808, that Weems's life of Washington achieved its enduring form. Weems had introduced many of the now-famous anecdotes, including the story of young George and the cherry tree, in an 1806 edition published in Augusta, Georgia. But that edition apparently had lim-

ited circulation, and it remained eighty pages long like the preceding versions. The Philadelphia edition of 1808, written after Weems had finished selling Marshall's *Life of Washington* for C. P. Wayne, was nearly three times as long. It had a new title: *The Life of George Washington: With Curious Anecdotes, Equally Honorable to Himself, and Exemplary to His Young Countrymen.* It added the story of Mary Washington's dream, in which her five-year-old son extinguishes a fire on the family's roof by means that become metaphors for the Revolution and the establishment of the new republic (a new roof). Its title page also identified Weems, for the first time, as "formerly rector of Mount-Vernon Parish." Carey bought the copyright from Weems for $1,000 later that year, a bargain the author soon regretted. Despite Weems's occasional complaints that he wanted to add more material, Carey kept printing the book in the same 228-page form for the next two decades. With minor modifications, this version of the biography remained in print through the nineteenth century, going through dozens of editions and numerous publishers.

Weems's *Life of George Washington* has also in the last two decades received the attention of various historians and literary critics, who find in its pages corroboration for their interpretations of early national culture. Perhaps Weems's *Washington* was a conservative attempt to re-place revolutionary passion with plain-spoken, patriarchal social control, a precursor to James Feni-more Cooper's novels. In contrast, Weems's story of Washington and the cherry tree might exemplify the *antipatriarchal* impulse of the post-Revolutionary years. Unlike the prevailing early-eighteenth-century view of fathers as absolute rulers and children as inherent disobeyers tarred with original sin, Weems's depiction of young George's en-counter with his father reenacts a post-Lockean vision. "The republi-can child is at once excused for his age, never obliged to dissemble his feelings, and comforted with bound-less parental solicitude." In this formulation, Weems helps set the stage for nineteenth-century paren-tal relationships based on sentiment and love rather than filial obedience. Or was Weems a different sort of transitional figure, "a captain in the swelling moral militia of bourgeois culture in early-nineteenth-century America"? In his own life as well as his work, the bookselling par-son sought to reconcile religion and profit-seeking, nowhere so visibly as in the biography of Washington. Weems certainly played down Wash-ington's aristocratic upbringing and turned the book into a story of self-made manhood, "a success manual for young Americans."[5]

Few scholars, however, have con-sidered what Weems and numerous reviews and advertisements called this expanded edition: the "private life" of Washington. In part Weems adopted this language to distin-guish his work from Marshall's *Life of Washington,* whose difficulties he knew firsthand. In letters to Carey he extended the comparison. Hawk-ing Marshall's work gave Weems limited pleasure, for "I am not in my element, tis chiefly the best Reli-gious Work Moral & Political (i.e. Republican) Books that I wish to circulate. [E]rgo in this History of Washington I *feel* no great interest. It is not half so moralizing & Re-publican as my own of which by the by I publish'd here this winter and have nearly sold off the whole im-pression 1500 copies."[6] Public versus private, Federalist versus Republi-can, poor seller versus bestseller: Weems clearly envisioned his biogra-phy of Washington as the antithesis of Marshall's.

Weems's emphasis on the value of private biography placed him squarely within the debate over biog-raphy in the early republic—even if he and his books traveled in a world apart from the English-inspired literary magazines that ridiculed his work and repeated Johnsonian theory. In the opening pages Weems explained that all Americans knew Washington's deeds as general and president, but that these showed only "the greatness of public charac-ter, which is no evidence of *true great-ness;* for a public character is often an artificial one." Weems's subsequent description of his project echoed Johnson even more forcefully (and prefigured Samuel Stanhope Smith's attack on Delaplaine's *Repository* a decade later): "It is not then in the glare of *public,* but in the shade of *private life,* that we are to look for the man. Private life is always *real* life. Behind the curtain, where the eyes of the million are not upon him, and where a man can have no motive but *inclination,* no excitement but *honest nature,* there he will always be sure to act *himself;* consequently, if he act greatly, he must be great indeed." (Grant Wood was thus not the first to depict Weems lifting a curtain to reveal Washington's life.) Nobody had heretofore told of Washington's private life as "the *dutiful son*—the affectionate brother—the cheerful school-boy—the diligent surveyor—the neat draftsman—the laborious farmer—and widow's husband—the orphan's father—the poor man's friend." All that anybody had seen was Washington the "Demigod." If Washington's life held any utility for youthful American readers, it lay in his private virtues. Young Americans could emulate those, even if they would not lead revolutions.[7]

Like William Wirt, Weems cited the people who had shared anecdotes with him. He identified some by name and place of residence: "John Fitzhugh of Stafford" was his source for Mary Washington's

manners; "Col. Lewis Willis," Washington's "play-mate and kinsman," had told him about Washington throwing a stone across the Rappahannock. Other sources were more oblique: "an aged lady, who was a distant relative, and when a girl spent much of her time in the family," or a "very aged gentleman, formerly a school-mate of his."[8] These citations, however spurious, represented another attempt to identify the book as biography—whose "authenticity" separated it from the novel.

If Weems understood what "biography" required, he also understood how permeable the boundaries between genres could be. Unlike most contemporary critics, he relished that permeability. He envisioned different genres as complementary, not oppositional. Perhaps because he knew rural American audiences so well (and made his living selling books to them), he was not inclined to condemn novels. He wanted to sell them "moralizing & Republican" books but never recoiled from adding a dash of romance to make moral books more appealing. This impulse led to his conflict with Brigadier General Peter Horry in 1809. Horry, a member of Francis Marion's regiment in the Revolution, had tried in vain to write a biography of his former commander. He therefore sent his reminiscences to Weems, who promised to "immortalize" Marion in biography, to "polish and colour it in a style that will, I hope, sometimes excite a smile, and sometimes call forth the tear." After finishing the manuscript, Weems reminded Horry that "I told you I must write it in my own way, and knowing the passion of the times for novels, I have endeavoured to throw your facts and ideas about Gen. Marion into the garb and dress of a military romance." Horry was infuriated. "A history of realities turned into a romance! The idea alone, militates against the work. The one as a history of real performance, would be always read with pleasure. The other as a fictitious invention of the brain, once read would suffice. . . . You have carved and mutilated it with so many erroneous statements, [that] your embellishments, observations and remarks, must necessarily be erroneous as proceeding from false grounds. Most certainly 'tis not MY history, but YOUR romance." Horry's name appeared before Weems's on the title page nonetheless, perhaps to suggest the authenticity of the facts within. No matter how he embellished the "facts" — and at least one reader of Horry's manuscript believed that Weems was less guilty than Horry claimed — Weems never strayed from the central principle of early-national biography writing: that the paramount function of biography was didactic. Indeed, he hoped that his lives of Washington and Marion would be used

as schoolbooks (which would also increase their sale).[9]

Even as he echoed the didactic arguments for biography, Weems moved toward a new sort of didacticism. The familiar Johnsonian and nationalistic arguments both divided public from private character. For Johnson and his disciples, "character" consisted of the private habits and traits, unique to the individual biographical subject, that could be glimpsed only when the veil of public appearance was lifted. For republican biographers and critics like Charles Caldwell, public actions and virtues provided the truer measure of "character" or the "real man." In either case, life's two realms were essentially distinct. Weems united them in a new way — one that prefigured the next generation's apostles of self-made manhood. A direct relationship existed between the public and the private: the character that Washington cultivated in private life made his public successes possible. That character combined the public virtue of patriotism with industry, benevolence, and religion, traits associated with the rising ethic of liberal self-making and the growth of evangelicalism.

Weems also foreshadowed an emerging distinction within the idea of the "private." For him, private character differed from "domestic privacies" in the Johnsonian sense. Private character meant a constellation of traits displayed outside the political and military arenas. Discussing this was the biographer's obligation—but discussing details of Washington's marriage or of Martha Washington's life was not. Weems could, he wrote, tell of Mrs. Washington, but explained that it was "contrary to the rules of biography, to begin with the husband and end with the wife." What did he mean? Examining the life of a subject's wife, on the pretense of writing her husband's biography, crossed the boundaries of propriety. Herein lay the emerging argument that would eliminate women's presence from most biographies of male subjects for the next half century. Even if his private *virtues* belonged in the biography, the subject's *privacy*—embodied by his wife—became sacrosanct. Leaving wives out was nothing new in American biographies: almost none of the nationalistic biographies of the new republic gave their subjects' wives more than a few sentences. But this omission squared with republican theory, which defined public virtues as masculine ones, much as the word "virtue" itself derived from the Latin word for "man." Weems helped to reshape the concept of "virtue" inward, toward traits like benevolence and piety increasingly associated with women. To write women out of biographies would now require a different rationale—one based on a new conception that glorified privacy.

Mason Locke Weems thus did more than pioneer new, liberal concepts of the self-made man or new, Lockean notions of patriarchal authority. He represented and helped effect a transformation in the concept and nature of American biography. Over the next two generations, distinctly gendered versions of biographical didacticism would develop, the masculine version taking Weems's work as a seminal antecedent. And Weems would continue to find a wide audience among Americans. On the eve of civil war, President-elect Abraham Lincoln addressed the New Jersey state senate and reminisced about his early years. "[A]way back in my childhood, the earliest days of my being able to read, I got hold of a small book, such a one as few of the younger members have ever seen, Weem's Life of Washington." Weems's descriptions of the battles in New Jersey had fixed themselves in young Lincoln's mind, and "I recollect thinking then, boy even though I was, that there must have been something more than common that those men struggled for."[10]

The familiarity of Weems's work was best illustrated in the first best-selling American novel of the 1850s. Susan Warner's *The Wide, Wide World* (1850), a female bildungsroman about young Ellen Montgomery's struggle to become a pious, self-abnegating Christian as successive maternal figures passed away, became the most popular American novel before *Uncle Tom's Cabin*. In it, John Humphreys gives Ellen a book for Christmas. " 'What is this? Wime's—Wiem's—Life of Washington—Washington? he was—May I look at it?' " she asks. The book, of course, is Weems's *Life and Memorable Actions of George Washington,* and Ellen quite literally cannot put it down: "An hour passed. Ellen had not spoken or moved except to turn over leaves." All this Christmas day, *"the book* was in her head." If the popularity of *The Wide, Wide World* provides evidence of an American audience for novels in the mid-nineteenth century, its text suggests something else: that Weems was so familiar that readers would recognize him from Ellen's mispronunciations—for Warner never does spell his name correctly.[11]

The Wide, Wide World also complicates any strictly gendered notions of who read Weems in antebellum America. Weems provided more than just patriotic military stories for young men like Lincoln. Upon first reading the book, Ellen becomes completely enraptured by the father of her country. "Whatever she had found within the leaves of the book, she had certainly lost herself." Ellen's sheer fascination with the father of her country parallels her desire to lose her "self"—her rebellious spirit and willful urges—to her heavenly Father. Biography also pro-vides civic education to the young American, male or female: Ellen becomes as thoroughly patriotic as she is submissively pious and can assert the legitimacy of the Revolution because of the biographies she has read. (Later in the novel, when Ellen must defend the United States in the face of her Scottish relatives' criticisms, she mentions that she has read "two lives of Washington," as well as other historical works.) In addition, the biography offers moral instruction. Discussing the defects of Nelson—whose biography has nonetheless absorbed her—Ellen argues that Washington is the better model. " 'I don't think, sir, I ought to like a man [such as Nelson] merely for being great unless he was good. Washington was great and good both.' "[12] Ellen has gained exactly what critics, her benefactor John, and Weems himself hoped that readers would: entertainment and instruction. Fully fifty years after Weems's book first appeared, it became enshrined anew in popular culture. Perhaps fittingly, given Weems's own understanding of the permeability between genres, that enshrinement occurred in a sentimental novel—a fable of self-making that could become for young women like Ellen what Weems's work had been for Abraham Lincoln.

Representative
Men and Women,
1820–1860

I finished Weld's Life of Franklin, containing his autobiography, this morning . . . I have thus read successively Biographies of Henry and Franklin. I know of no two lives that can be more profitably perused. . . . They were the very antipodes of early American success. . . . The one was prudent, methodical, and expedient; the other careless and prodigal. — George Anderson Mercer, August 8, 1858

Mary. —Are there no histories of good and great women, mother? I should very much like to read them; perhaps they would do me as much good as the life of Dr. Franklin did Mr. Mordaunt; for you often tell me that I want industry and application.
—Sketches of the Lives of Distinguished Females, *1833*

To peruse biographies profitably took on new meanings in the second quarter of the century. As concepts of virtue were transformed in the wake of economic, political, and social change, so too were the predominant lessons that biographies taught. George Anderson Mercer, a young southerner, suggested as much in the traits he culled from Horatio Hastings Weld's *Life of Benjamin Franklin* and Wirt's *Life of Patrick Henry*. Prudence, method, expedience, carelessness, and prodigality might represent the keys to success or failure as a "self-made man," but they were not the civic virtues enshrined in early republican lives of Revolutionary heroes. Wirt's description of Henry's indolence and even Weems's account of Washington's industry presaged this shift; between 1820 and 1860 lives of male subjects combined, often uneasily, the virtues associated with civic life and with self-made success. These biographies at once reflected and helped define new concepts of the public and of character. New notions of female character also emerged in these years, grounded in the social experience and the cultural ideas of the northern, Protestant middle class. And the number of "female biographies," lives of women subjects, increased exponentially. This high rate of increase stemmed partly from the relative paucity of female biography before 1830. It also resulted partly from transformations in publishing that made increased production possible in many genres besides biography. But the most important reasons for the expansion of female biography and the specific forms it took were the increase in women's reading and writing associated with the evangelical revivalism of the 1830s and new, middle-class forms of activity that offered women new avenues into prominence as agents of reform and as subjects of biography.

Contrary to promoting a single ideology of gender roles and expectations, American biographies from the 1820s to the 1850s displayed many of the tensions that accompanied social and cultural change. The central tenet of early-national biography, that biographies should instruct as well as amuse, remained—but what should they teach? Lives of eminent merchants, ostensibly the self-assured captains of a new capitalist order, carefully balanced their subjects' economic accomplishments with their public services, while biographies of artisans sought a middle ground between asserting working-class identity and using the same language of self-made success found in the merchants' lives. Campaign lives of presidential candidates, whose overt lessons were partisan ones, also promoted a concept of the public sphere that fused earlier republican notions with newer ideas of liberal democracy. Biographies of European queens, lives of women renowned for charitable and religious activities, and memoirs of largely unknown Christian women each suggested visions of women's realm, ranging from the most constricted "woman's sphere" to an expansive Christian womanhood with the power to reform society. And all of these works—implicitly in their didacticism and explicitly in their statements about the genre—attested to the power of biography itself to shape individual character and, by extension, the larger society.

"National" Production and American Readers' Experiences

In September 1862, the *Christian Examiner* surveyed the recent proliferation of biographies and concluded that "In these days of book-making and of publishing, there is scarcely a life lived that does not stand some chance of being written about." Indeed, between the *New-York Mirror*'s 1830 description of an American "biographical mania" and the *Christian Examiner*'s comment, a massive expansion occurred in the production of biographies in the United States. According to one bibliography, more than ten times as many biographies written by Americans appeared from 1840 to 1860 as had appeared from 1800 to 1820. When multiple editions of individual works and American editions of European-authored biographies are taken into account, the rate of growth becomes even greater. The *North American Review* hardly exaggerated when it argued in 1857 that "In our own day . . . there are more 'Lives' written in proportion to the bulk of literature than ever before." Some cultural historians have linked this expansion to the rise of American individualism and to surging interest in the nation's history.[1] But these developments had begun before 1830, and much of the proliferation lay in the lives of European subjects and in religious biographies of pious subjects—neither of which can be explained in nationalistic terms.

The *Christian Examiner* identified a more important factor when it described "these days of book-making and publishing," for both technological and organizational changes revolutionized publishing in the middle third of the century. Advances in technology included the Hoe cylinder press and the techniques of stereotyping and electrotyping, which produced plates used for repeated editions of the same works. At the same time, the book trade underwent a profound transition. Large firms in New York and Philadelphia, and to a lesser extent Boston and Cincinnati, came to dominate the publishing market, although local presses continued to produce books. Firms such as Harper and Brothers consolidated printing, publishing, and distribution, which in the early republic had been the province of distinct entrepreneurs—witness Mason Locke Weems's activity as distribution agent for C. P. Wayne and Mathew Carey. The two seven-story buildings that housed the Harper operation in New York strikingly illustrated the centralization and capitalization of the book trade.[2]

Another measure of that centralization appears in the catalogs of dozens of libraries, large and small, from Providence to New Orleans to San Francisco. In the attempt to expand their reach, firms like Harper created "library series" of books beginning in the 1830s. Originally developed in Great Britain, library series were collections of diverse books sold as a set by the publisher. These series often combined history, biography, travel narrative, philosophy, and popular science. Individuals could buy the series or particular volumes, but the series were especially suited for schools, libraries, and other institutions that could purchase large numbers of books. The most famous and most widely disseminated was Harper's Family Library, 51 of whose 187 volumes were biographies, ranging from Alexander the Great to Peter the Great, Mohammed to Washington, Napoleon and Josephine to DeWitt Clinton.[3] Library catalogs around the United States reveal the importance of the Harper's Family Library for the dissemination of biography. Of forty-eight libraries in twenty states between

1834 and 1862, thirty-five possessed the series. A second series, the Library of American Biography (all American subjects) edited by Jared Sparks beginning in 1834, found similarly wide distribution: thirty-three of the same libraries owned its volumes. More than half of these libraries held both. For new or small libraries, these series could become the cornerstone of a biography section. The Mercantile Library of San Francisco listed two hundred biographies in its first catalog (1854), eighty-eight from these two series. The far smaller Calais Circulating Library in Vermont opened in 1832 with fifteen volumes of biography—fourteen from Harper's Family Library. Combined with Plutarch, individual lives of Washington, and Washington Irving's omnipresent *Life and Voyages of Christopher Columbus,* these two series provided the patrons of a small library with lives of the major figures of ancient, European, and American history. At the same time, larger, more established libraries such as the Library Company of Philadelphia also purchased these series. As dozens of libraries acquired Harper's Family Library and the Library of American Biography, a national base of American-produced biographies was developing.[4]

At the same time, other organizations on the periphery of the capitalized book trade also contributed to the proliferation of print—and of biographies. As itinerant ministers traversed the countryside speaking to camp meetings and gatherings of potential converts, denominations organized American religious life: increasingly centralized denominational councils and synods sent out preachers with schedules of assignments and published tracts that colporteurs distributed throughout the nation. Along with the denominational publishers, religious publishing concerns like the American Tract Society and the American Sunday-School Union created a second national network of bookmaking and distribution, largely detached from the commercial publishing houses. These worlds could intersect, for instance when commercial firms became the publishers for a religious organization's literary output. The tract societies' catalogs included scores of biographies of clergymen, pious women, and children. The development of religious publishing illustrates, too, a continuing symbiosis between the local and the national. Memoirs of ministers and pious citizens appeared not just from the major tract societies, but also from presses in Greensborough, North Carolina, Springfield, Ohio, Irvington, New Jersey, and New Albany, Indiana. Many of these works partook of the same conventions as the nationally distributed ones; conversely, many tract biographies began as local memoirs, especially the lives of devoted women written by ministers or loving spouses. Far from developing separately, national networks and local biography influenced each other's growth.[5]

A similar relationship emerged in political publishing. Like the development of nationally organized religious denominations and tract societies, the rise of organized political parties in the 1830s generated enormous amounts of published material. Partisan newspapering dated back to the Federalist-Republican battles of the 1790s, but in the 1830s the literature of political campaigns—broadsides, songsters, and especially lives of the candidates—multiplied as Democrats and Whigs competed for voters' loyalty. Political publishing, like religious publishing, tended to occur in its own universe, a political-communications network that reached from national and state party committees to local newspaper editors to town and district partisan clubs and individual voters. Until 1852, most political publishing took place outside the world of the major capitalistic firms. Even though an occasional campaign newspaper, like Horace Greeley's 1840 *Log Cabin,* circulated around the nation and became an important source of information for other papers, politics came home to voters in the local papers that announced rallies and gatherings. The national party might commission a biography like Richard Hildreth's *Life of William Henry Harrison,* but local editors sold it, printed pamphlet versions of the candidate's life, and ran excerpts from it in their papers. An advertisement in the Steubenville, Ohio, *Log Cabin Farmer* indicated the importance of the local printer: "The Life of General Harrison, In pamphlet form—32 pages—just published and for sale at this office. Price $2 00 per hundred." In the realm of political publishing, then, the connections with the world of commercial print were predominantly local.[6]

The wide availability of biographies after 1830 was thus replete with paradoxes. "American" biography included Napoleon and Washington, felons and saints, local ministers and internationally renowned divines, shoemakers and statesmen. Rather than creating a homogeneous national reading population, new networks of publication and distribution offered biographies for a multitude of tastes. As readers of both genders and in diverse settings demonstrated, the Harper's Family Library and other products of the metropolitan publishers nationalized access to European and American works, but did not control how individuals or communities of readers read. In the aggregate, the "biographical mania" meant numerical proliferation; for American readers, it meant the increasing availability of biographies to suit specific interests.

The circulation records of two New England libraries of the 1830s reveal how this diversity afforded individual readers and reading communities a variety of choices previously unavailable. The Worcester Atheneum, founded in 1830 in Massachusetts' second-largest city, drew its forty-five members from the legal, theological, and economic elite. The members included a future governor, a future mayor, several lawyers and ministers, two prominent authors (Aaron Bancroft and John S. C. Abbott, both also ministers), and the wealthiest men in Worcester, Stephen Salisbury and Daniel Waldo.[7] The Benson Female Lending Library, established four years later in rural Windsor County, Vermont, existed for only four years, during which forty-six women borrowed books. Far less is known about these women than about the patrons of the Worcester Atheneum: surnames suggest that several families were represented by multiple library members (four women named Kellogg and three Barbers, Goodriches, Griswolds, and Dickinsons).[8] Although both of these libraries possessed numerous volumes of Harper's Family Library, they possessed different volumes and supplemented them quite differently. The Atheneum's biographies resembled those in many other middle-sized, urban libraries after 1830, which combined the Family Library with individual works also produced by national publishers. Its seventy-eight biographies included the entire Family Library and diverse other new works: Jared Sparks's life of Gouverneur Morris, James Austin's life of Elbridge Gerry, and European subjects ranging from Byron to Queen Elizabeth. Established with a mandate to select "the most approved modern books," the Benson Female Lending Library was far smaller. Its entire collection at its outset consisted of fewer than seventy books, and it added just thirty more during its existence. Its fifteen biographies included seven from Harper's Family Library—but not the entire series. The members clearly selected some volumes and chose not to purchase others. The lives of Josephine, Mary Queen of Scots, and Female Sovereigns, as well as *The Court and Camp of Bonaparte* and biographies of Charlemagne, George IV, and Celebrated Travellers appeared in the library's holdings, but ten other Family Library biographies, all of men, did not. Moreover, these women augmented their biographical holdings differently than did their male counterparts in Worcester. Whereas most libraries bought lives of Washington, Columbus, and Franklin to accompany the publishers' series, these women added James D. Knowles's memoir of the missionary Ann Judson, Hannah More's memoirs, Lydia Maria Child's *Good Wives,* and a few more biographies of pious women.

In two ways, the patrons of these libraries displayed common interests. Most dramatically, books connected to Napoleon and Josephine dominated biographical circulation in both libraries. In Worcester, Bourrienne's *Private Memoirs of Napoleon Bonaparte* was the most popular biography, followed closely by the Family Library's *The Court and Camp of Bonaparte* and *Memoirs of the Empress Josephine*. In the Benson women's library, the

Memoirs of Josephine headed the list of most-borrowed biographies. This fascination was widespread in 1830s America. In addition, Harper's Family Library volumes were popular in both the Worcester Atheneum and the Benson Female Lending Library. These books' novelty, as much as a particular interest in their contents, may have enhanced their appeal. In both libraries, Family Library biographies made up the majority of recently published lives. In the Worcester Atheneum, which owned roughly equal numbers of biographies published before and after 1825 (thirty-eight before, thirty-four after), the readers clearly preferred new books. Only five borrowed Marshall's *Life of Washington,* and just one checked out more than two volumes of it. Of course, Marshall's work was now three decades old—a fact that might account for its apparent lack of appeal. Of the Atheneum's eighteen most popular biographies, all but three had appeared since 1825. Older biographies languished on the shelves, while newer works —most of them products of the emerging national publishers—received considerable use. (Such a comparison is impossible for the Benson Female Library, almost all of whose biographies were new.)

Within these similarities, however, lay equally significant differences. Both sets of patrons, clearly, wanted to read about the central event in recent European history—the Napoleonic reign—and its key figures. But where the men of the Worcester Atheneum favored the life of Napoleon, the women of the Benson library checked out the memoirs of Josephine. Of the eighteen most popular biographies in the Atheneum's collection, fourteen were biographies of men, including Columbus, Byron, Mohammed, and George IV as well as Napoleon; four were lives of women, all queens or empresses (including Josephine). In the Benson Female Lending Library, Hannah More's poetry was far more popular than any biography, a fact that may help explain why nine women checked out More's *Memoirs.* The only lives of men among these women's favorite biographies appeared in J. A. St. John's *Lives of Celebrated Travellers,* which possessed the appeal of travel narrative as well as of biography. On some level, then, biographical reading (or at least the borrowing of biographies) in these two libraries— one composed entirely of men, the other entirely of women—seems to have been linked to gender.

As always when examining library circulation records, we must be careful not to overstate their implications. Both sets of patrons may have had other sources of books. There were certainly other library associations in Worcester, and the members of the Atheneum possessed the financial means to acquire books for personal collections. Christopher Columbus Baldwin, a member of the Atheneum who kept a diary, recorded reading a variety of books, not all borrowed from the Atheneum. Less is known about the Benson community, but other libraries may have existed, and by the 1830s most parts of the Windsor district of Vermont had access to a wide variety of reading matter. This very variety, however, may increase the possibility that the Benson Female Lending Library was established with a specific, gendered purpose. (Its name certainly suggests so.) Both the biographical collection and the biographical borrowing in the Benson Library exhibited a greater degree of gender-specificity than their Worcester counterparts: although most of the biographies in the Atheneum were of men, lives of women comprised a significant minority of the Atheneum's biographies, and several received considerable use. Even a patron who checked out biographies only of men, such as Christopher Baldwin, did not necessarily read those books with conscious reference to gender. He enjoyed Moore's *Life of Byron* but complained that its author "is about as selfish in making it as Boswell was in writing the life of Johnson"—a fault presumably not unique to male biographers. After reading the lives of Byron and Johnson, Baldwin wrote, "I like a minute biography of a famous man as everybody does the minute geography of a famous city or battle ground"—a comment that referred to famous *men* but described a reason for reading biographies that might be applied to male or female subjects.[9]

Gender-conscious biographical reading may have occurred most frequently when gender was the defining characteristic of a setting. Whereas the rural Benson Female Lending Library may have been such a setting, the Worcester Atheneum's members may have been linked primarily by a sense of cosmopolitanism and class status in an increasingly stratified city. In 1816 the Female Reading Class of Colchester, Connecticut, met almost weekly from February 14 to October 23. Starting with *Priestley's Historical Lectures,* these women discussed the value of history in terms that male or female readers might have used: "History by displaying to us the characters of truly great men . . . tends to inspire us with a taste for true greatness & solid glory. . . ." But on May 22, "Clarissa Bigelow read the memoirs of Lady Jane Grey"—beginning twelve weeks on the lives of famous women.[10] Twenty-seven years later, the Centre Missionary Sewing Circle met regularly in Worcester to raise money for the missionary enterprise. As the women sewed, one of them read aloud to the others, often from works of female biography: the "Memoirs of Mrs. Rumpf," the "Memoirs of Mrs. Eli Smith," and the *Life of Isabella Graham.* This last book, the biography of a woman who had founded various charitable institutions through successful fund-raising, may have provided a model for the sewing circle's labors.[11] Read in another setting, the same life could assume different meaning. The mother of young Virginian Launcelot Minor Blackford read the *Life of Isabella Graham* and other biographies aloud to her children on Sunday mornings. Here biography became a vehicle of religious instruction, and apparently an effective one, for Blackford wrote that Mrs. Graham's memoir was "admirably suited for Sunday exercises."[12] A model directly applicable to the Worcester women's charitable work served as a general, perhaps less gender-specific, example of active piety in a Sunday family circle.

Many individual readers saw biographical subjects as models for emulation—a constant theme of the works themselves. The lives of Benjamin Franklin and Patrick Henry were common reading for young men, North and South. In Franklin's life and writings, Silas Felton of Worcester "found many valuable precepts, which I endeavoured to treasure up and follow." After reading both men's lives, George Anderson Mercer compared Franklin's prudence and method with Henry's carelessness and prodigality. Twenty-five-year-old Virginian John Montgomery Gordon, who read a biography of the English leader William Pitt in 1835, described Pitt in language that resembled Mercer's. "I know no work better calculated to rouse the latent or stimulate the active ambition of a young man. At 24 he met and defeated in argument, Lord North, Fox, Burke, Sheridan and a host of inferior orators." Such remarks were not uncommon in contemporary reviews, which often focused on the subject rather than on the biographer.[13]

The lives of celebrated women, though less numerous than those of heroic men, could also serve as models—but responses to such works were far more mixed than comments on male subjects' lives. Harriet Cooke, who taught school and took in boarders when her husband went to debtor's prison, applied Isabella Graham's biography directly to her own venture beyond the bounds of domesticity: if Graham could subsist on "potatoes and salt" and assume financial responsibility for her family, so could she. When twenty-four-year-old Louisa May Alcott read Charlotte Brontë's "very interesting, but sad" life in June 1857, the aspring writer wondered "if I shall ever be famous enough for people to care to read my story and struggles. I can't be a C. B., but I may do a little something yet." In contrast, David Schenck, a southerner, found Margaret Fuller's life interesting but detected in it "a display, an unnecessary array of her acquirements amounting to fulsome egotism." In at least one instance, a woman objected to a male biographer's life of a female subject. Maria Mitchell, the renowned astronomer at Vassar College, read Edward Brooke Hall's *Memoir of Mary Ware, Wife of Henry Ware* in 1853 and objected to Hall's attempt "to encourage the use of the *needle*. It seems to me that the needle is the chain of woman, and has fettered her more than the laws of the country." Here a reader rejected a biographer's didactic message, even if Mitchell did not describe her opinion of Mary Ware's life. Most readers whose recorded comments survive echoed Silas Felton and George Anderson Mercer, seconding rather than rejecting the lessons that biographers advanced.[14]

Religious biographies provided women and men with sources of inspiration. Martha Foster Crawford longed to imitate her fellow missionary George Dana Boardman: "If I could feel his humility—his utter distrust of self—and supreme confidence in our Heavenly parent!" George Gilman Smith of Georgia wrote in his diary on April 3, 1856, of the impact of a single biography: "I had broken every law Divine and was almost tempted to despair to give up hope for this life or for the future, when providence directed that my eye should fall upon the Life of Dr. A. Clarke. I read a few of the first pages of the book, and became again convinced that it was my duty to God to Earth to the injunction of my dying mother, to seek the Lord." Smith's account is significant for linking his conversion not just with the character of Dr. Clarke but with the act of biography reading itself. Samuel Rodman of New Bedford, Massachusetts, who participated actively in temperance and abolitionist societies and kept a diary for nearly forty years, read biographies often and attended biographical lectures. After an evening at home reading the life of the English abolitionist William Wilberforce, "who was as eminent for his religious watchfulness in the midst of his public and social duties as for his social and forensic talents," Rodman wrote, "May his example strengthen my endeavors to live up to the dictates of my conscience."[15]

Not all readers responded to biographies as didactic works, because not all biographies possessed didactic aims. Lives of Napoleon and Josephine, for instance, drew much of their appeal from their elements of romance; comparing the experience of Josephine with that of Germaine de Staël's fictional heroine Corinne, Hannah Gale explained that "Josephine's receives an additional charm, from the fact that we know it to be true." Other biographies appealed to readers' curiosity, extending earlier traditions of eccentric and criminal biography. The "Lives of the Felons" published in the *National Police Gazette,* for example, were adventure stories for the mass audience of the penny press; the excitement of the criminals' lives and the police's pursuit far overshadowed any moral messages they might possess. William Johnson, a free black man in antebellum Mississippi, dismissed Lewis L. Allen's *Thrilling Sketch of the Life of the Distinguished Chief*

Okah Tubbee—an escaped Mississippi slave who gained fame in the North for his stage performances as an Indian and whose memoirs claimed him to be the illegitimate son of a Choctaw chief—as "a tisue [*sic*] of Lies from beginning to Ending." The lives of contemporary political figures, often written for partisan purposes, equally often drew partisan responses, as two readers' reactions to biographies of Andrew Jackson attest. In 1832 Christopher Baldwin of Worcester complained that John Eaton's *Life of Andrew Jackson* did not tell "the whole story"; nearly thirty years later Benjamin L. C. Wailes of Mississippi praised James Parton's life of Jackson for laying "all of old Hickory's sin and imperfections bare." Other readers commented on biographies as might literary critics, distinguishing the subject from the biographer and praising or censuring the biographer's style. Launcelot Blackford praised Joseph G. Baldwin's *Party Leaders* for a "racy, spirited, and pleasing style (combined with a dash of humor . . .)," Marshall's *Life of Washington* for its "very plain and easy style," and Weems's *Life of Washington* for "a pleasant and in some places beautiful style." Alexander Beaufort Meek of Alabama preferred less intrusive authorship, praising John Gibson Lockhart's *Life of Sir Walter Scott* because "There is no attempt on the part of the author to *show off* himself, but to present a fair and correct biography."[16]

Given the diverse ways Americans commented on the biographies they read, it might seem strange to explore didactic biographies along gendered lines. However, many of these biographies sought to construct the meanings of manhood and womanhood for those who read them, and even those that did not explicitly do so defined masculine and feminine spheres of activity implicitly. And didacticism was unquestionably the most common purpose of biography between 1820 and 1860. Educational reformers considered biography appropriate reading for children; indeed, Horace Mann wrote to his fellow school reformer Henry Barnard in 1852 that "Biography *of the right sort of lives*" was better children's fare than history, whose tales of crime and war depicted "too terrible a world to make children acquainted with."[17] Yet children were not the only readers whom biographers sought to instruct. Young men and women in their teens and twenties about to enter adult roles, as well as religious strivers of all ages, could also find examples of action and virtue in biography. The surviving commentaries of just such readers reveal that many of them did.

*Merchants, Artisans, and Candidates: Biographical Manhood
and the Construction of the "Public"*

The popular lives and collective biographies of eminent merchants, "mechanics," and other "self-taught men" that proliferated between 1830 and 1860 were products of a cultural mission. Writing in the *American Annals of Education and Instruction* in June 1831, "Civis" recommended biography that "presents the lives of *self made men,* and points out with clearness the several steps by which they arrived at eminent usefulness. . . . The rising youth of this hemisphere need to be told, and told *often,* that usefulness of incalculable amount, character of eternal value, are within their reach." Contemporary conduct manuals agreed: youth should study biography for examples of character and its formation, and for the inspiration provided by the lives of those who had risen from obscurity and poverty to fame and fortune. The concept of character that underlay this advice differed from both of the earlier definitions, Johnsonian and republican. Beginning particularly in the late 1820s, advice manuals for young men articulated a direct relationship between public and private: the character one cultivated in private life placed one on the permanent path to fortune or ruin, especially in urban society and a market economy. Industry, persistence, and temperance kept young men out of the clutches of "confidence men and painted women," while indolence, gambling, and drink rendered them easy prey for these unscrupulous characters as well as fallen men in their own right. Moralists painted graphic pictures of the contrasting fates that could befall their impressionistic young readers.[18]

The cultural emphasis on character formation and the direct correlation between public and private character arose in large measure from a rising social concern about "moral free agents." The Second Great Awakening, an amorphous but spectacular series of revivals that began in Kentucky in the late 1790s and peaked around the nation in the 1820s and early 1830s, helped transform religious doctrine as ministers like Charles Grandison Finney rejected the Calvinist emphasis on original sin and suggested the perfectibility of the individual. This concept rendered human beings religious free agents, responsible for the salvation or damnation of their souls. At the same time, the migration of young men from tightly knit families and organic communities to newly developing large cities released them from relationships that had circumscribed their autonomy but also ensured their proper progression to manhood. Moreover, the increasingly impersonal market economy allowed, indeed encouraged, hypocrisy and duplicity among strangers. Faced with the difficulty of knowing private motives and habits in this society of strangers, moralists devised ways for their readers to see others' true "character," from phrenology (the science that linked cranial and facial structures with inner character) to codes of "sincere" dress. Conduct manuals and the entire constellation of "self-education" sought to build and protect young men's own characters: lyceums, lectures, even sports became part of the obsession with character formation.[19]

The central text for the biography of self-made men was Benjamin Franklin's *Autobiography,* available to Americans in a multitude of sources: full-length editions, magazine profiles, collective biographies, sketches in schoolbooks and almanacs. This Franklin was not the Enlightenment scientist or the toast of Paris, and certainly not the trickster who valued the appearance of industry as highly as its reality. Biographers of the mid-nineteenth century adopted the Franklin who had entered Philadelphia nearly penniless and pulled himself up through reading, mutual improvement societies, and a systematic routine of character formation. In a collection of *Memoirs of the Most Eminent American Mechanics* published in 1842, Henry Howe drew liberally on Franklin's life for "its value as an example and lesson, perhaps the most instructive to be anywhere found, for all who have to be either the architects of their own fortunes, or their own guides in the pursuit of knowledge."[20] Other self-made men—merchants who had begun as farm boys, inventors whose genius had flowered in adversity, or presidential candidates who had been barefooted orphans—followed the Franklinian path, at least in their biographers' narratives.

Collections like Howe's book and the "mercantile biographies" in Freeman Hunt's popular New York monthly, *The Merchant's Magazine and Commercial Review,* offered aspiring young men examples of success. Biographies of successful businessmen and eminent men who had engaged in mercantile pursuits appeared approximately every other month in the first three years of Hunt's magazine (1839–41), three or four times a year through 1846, and sporadically thereafter. Announcing the first biographical sketch in August 1839, Hunt wrote that "Mercantile biography properly claims a place" in a magazine "where everything that can excite the young to an honorable emulation, should be set forth." Hunt's biographies also aimed to glorify the commercial professions against those who would denigrate them. Merchants had established and nourished "the temples of religion, the halls of benevolence, the marts of commerce, and the noble literary institutions which adorn and distinguish our cities." From their biographies young men would learn that they were entering a noble profession and find practical models to help them surmount obstacles to success.[21] Just as the previous generation's biographies of Revolutionary heroes tended to subordinate personal habits to grand, archetypal virtues, the lives of self-made men usually offered stories of poor lads elevated by persistence and industry. Indeed, the archetype was itself the message: the moralists who wrote these biographies championed adherence to this set of virtues and habits, not the quirky individuality of Boswell's Johnson.

Yet these new biographies differed significantly from their nationalistic predecessors. First, the terms of success were different. In the early national biographies the result of virtuous republican character was national glory; the character of Washington mattered because he had achieved national independence. In contrast, the character of a mechanic or merchant led to individual, and often economic, success. Biography as a genre had always narrated individual lives, but this new biography championed *individualism,* the entrepreneurial ethos of the new middle class, in a way that early republican lives had not. In addition, the very idea of the "self-made man" implied independence from the republican community whose service had been the hallmark of the early heroes.[22] As if to answer critics who decried such autonomy, the authors of these biographies took care to combine individual gain and public good. The sketches in Hunt's magazine routinely detailed their subjects' contributions to their cities and nation. John Frost, a prolific author of biographical collections, wrote in his *Lives of American Merchants, Eminent for Integrity, Enterprise, and Public Spirit* (1844) that "The merchants of this country, though often thoughtlessly charged with a disposition to regard nothing but their own interests, or at most the general interests of commerce, have always shown themselves, in great public emergencies, among the devoted of our illustrious band of patriots." Frost sought to inspire young men and to defend merchants to those "engaged in other pursuits."[23] While biographers of self-made men promoted the values of liberal individualism, they also demonstrated that concern for the public good remained, at least rhetorically, an integral characteristic of the great and good subject. Franklin was again the archetype, a bridge between republican civic virtue and liberal self-made manhood.

The second difference between the biographies of self-made men and their predecessors lay in the later works' emphasis on the formation, rather than simply the display, of character. Earlier biographies had adopted the Lockean premise that youthful character was malleable: their nearly ubiquitous prefatory professions of instructive purpose implied an impressionable reader. But these books usually did not show the development of their *subjects'* characters. In most cases a subject's childhood and youth occupied only a few paragraphs or pages of his biography. Weems's Washington was an exception, but although the reader saw him as a child and young man, he never saw him *becoming*; Washington was always perfectly honest, industrious, devoted to his mother. Franklin's *Autobiography,* which traced its protagonist from youth to manhood *and* from anonymity and penury to acclaim and worldly success, and suggested the means that had sped his progress, provided the model for many later biographies. Not only did the mercantile and mechanic biographies follow Franklin in portraying the path to success; many of them also emphasized their subjects' commitment to helping younger men. Gideon Lee, the former New York mayor and merchant whom Hunt's *Merchants' Magazine* profiled in January 1843, extended a "liberal and sustaining" hand to aspiring businessmen. John Grigg, a Philadelphia merchant whose biography appeared in the magazine eight years later, always offered "young beginners . . . words of encouragement." Those words—echoed throughout mercantile biography—included persistence and industry, to be sure, but also moderation and aversion to speculation.[24]

At the same time that lives of Franklinesque self-made men celebrated the virtues of an emerging commercial order, books like *Lives of Distinguished Shoemakers* responded, "Let us begin to regard MANUAL TOIL as the true discipline of a man." Artisanal biographies—written ostensibly for and by artisans—were far fewer than mercantile ones. Most biographies of "mechanics" were really the lives of inventors; and while self-made men might begin on the farm or in a trade, they always ended up in the countinghouse or the statehouse. The preface to the anonymously authored *Lives of Distinguished Shoemakers*—published in 1849 in Portland, Maine, outside the large publishing centers—revealed artisanal biographies' different and ambiguous position. In the first paragraph, the author bridged the worlds of literature and shoemaking: "Coleridge has said, that the Shoemakers' trade has been followed by a greater number of eminent men than any other branch of mechanical employment. . . . We have descended into the labyrinths of biographic lore, and brought up whatever of value we could find; and, of course, acknowledge our deep indebtedness to the literary world, generally; but the cutting out, stitching together, and fitting for use, are ours." Although the very first clause looked to Coleridge for shoemakers' significance, the deference to literary authority soon became perfunctory; that we, "of course, acknowledge our deep indebtedness" suggested convention rather than sincerity. As "the cutting out, stitching together, and fitting for use" became "ours," two changes occurred. First, artisanal biography was taken from the realm of literature by its presumably artisan authors. More strikingly, literary endeavor was recast as manual craft, in the terms of shoemaking itself.[25]

The preface then stitched the book squarely within the genre of biography, and fitted that genre to its readers. "Our object has not been to create, but to collect what has been widely scattered, and condense what has been greatly expanded, into a compact and available form, for the benefit of readers whose access to extensive libraries, as well as opportunities for reading, are necessarily limited." The mission suggested here was almost scholarly: collecting the widely scattered "truth" and avoiding "imagination" at the possible expense of "flowery or poetic" composition. The appeal to readers with little money and time echoed similar statements in other contemporary collective biographies. Later paragraphs identified the twofold purpose and audience: to assert the dignity and value of shoemaking to wealthier classes, and to encourage shoemakers themselves to cultivate their intellectual faculties.

> We have made shoes—we hope to make many more—and are aware that the craft is looked down upon by many, who, did they know the state of the case, would be compelled to look up. We hope the following pages will disabuse their innocent minds of the foolish prejudice, and lead all to judge more as men and brothers—less as artisans—less as inferiors. . . .
>
> We have written to do good—to elevate the aims and aspirations of a great and influential class, who have powers, if developed and wielded aright, for incalculable benefit in their day and generation. . . . should [our endeavors] lead but one individual to view himself as something nobler and better than a "digesting machine"—to feel that the *man* is superior to the workman—that to enlarge, instruct and develop the mind, to labor for the benefit and advancement of the race, to do something for the future, in order to cancel our debt to the past, is more important than carving leather neatly and making money fast;—the writer will be abundantly satisfied.

This statement suggested a divergence between self-education and material advancement; the value of artisans' learning lay not in "making money fast" but in something "nobler and better." In its vision of education for the sake of spiritual and intellectual advancement alone, this preface directly countered the message that many lives of self-made men helped to popularize, that the importance of mental culture lay primarily in its instrumental value.[26]

For all this assertiveness, the biographical sketches that comprised this

Lives of Distinguished Shoemakers were remarkably similar to the entrepreneurial biographies. They trumpeted self-education and omitted any descriptions of the artisans at work. All but one of these "shoemakers" achieved their eminence in other work; most of them were apprenticed to shoemakers in their youth but did not follow the trade. The subjects in the book included Quaker founder George Fox, bookseller James Lackington, and philosopher Jacob Behmen. Revolutionary patriot Roger Sherman "commenced business as a shoemaker, but did not continue in it long," instead going into commerce with his brother in order to make more money and gain "more time to read and improve his mind." The message of this volume, in fact, was familiar to readers of other biographies: that intellectual self-education was the key to happiness and social mobility, the element that made the "workman" or "digesting machine" into the "man." As in mercantile lives, the trade remained a path—a noble path, to be sure— to higher intellectual and material attainments. James Woodhouse, the one subject in the book who remained a "village shoemaker," received one of the shortest biographies, because so little was known of his life apart from his occasional poetry. Shoemakers might *deserve* biographies, but writing them could prove nearly impossible unless the subjects had done something *besides* shoemaking.[27]

Indeed, even in their assertiveness artisanal biographies echoed their mercantile contemporaries. Lives of merchants, as one scholar has argued, sought Americans' "social sanction" of commercial pursuits. To declare those occupations' "moral and cultural worth," the authors of these biographies used an earlier language of social value, describing merchants in quasi-religious or even feudal language (as lords of trade, men of honor, and the like).[28] The *Lives of Distinguished Shoemakers* ultimately underscored the ways biographical convention blunted artisanal assertion. To demonstrate shoemakers' worth to a wider readership, the biographer had to present achievements that were not intrinsically related to shoemaking at all. And to shoemakers themselves the biographer relayed the same message that Freeman Hunt's magazine gave to its readers. With hard work and self-education, even the humblest man could rise, indeed rise out of shoemaking. Starting humbly was no embarrassment, but these lives emphasized what shoemakers could become, not what they were. This focus stemmed in part from the problem of materials (the only reliable evidence of shoemakers being the records of those who had made their mark elsewhere). But it also reflected the prevailing ideology of the mercantile lives. Perhaps biography, focused on individual accomplishment, was not the ideal genre to promote an "artisan republicanism" based on mutuality and opposed to an individualist ethos. More likely, the anonymous author of the *Lives of Distinguished Shoemakers* shared the philosophy of individualism, at the very moment when New England shoemaking was being industrialized. While merchants sought cultural legitimacy through a language of an earlier cultural elite, shoemakers—at least in biography—sought recognition of their worth on the basis of middle-class self-making, not artisanal shoemaking.

The biographies of presidential candidates that appeared in 1824 and every fourth year afterward presented a more complex vision of self-making than did either the mercantile or the artisanal biographies. Upon first reading, campaign lives seem anything but complex. They promoted a party's candidate and programs, linked individual nominees with nationally shared ideals, and presented partisan ideologies in politically attractive forms. But campaign biographies were more than a tool of electoral politics. Like other narratives of masculine self-formation in the young republic, they sought to define American citizenship, the relationship between past and present, and the nature of the public sphere. The didactic purpose of this partisan literature extended beyond instructing the reader to vote for a William Henry Harrison or a Franklin Pierce. Lives of presidential candidates became primers of participation in family, society, and polity. Although primarily affiliated with the party newspapers and broadsides that excerpted and advertised them, campaign biographies were never fully distinct from the larger literary culture or from the broadly defined political culture that included schools and families as well as party organizations.[29] Their complexity resulted from their mixed messages. On the one hand, they sketched an organic society where fathers and hierarchical social institutions like the army and apprenticeship instilled republican civic virtue in future candidates. On the other, they claimed that candidates were the architects of their own fortunes, "self-made men" who had achieved success solely by their own efforts, and exemplars of the liberal vision that William Makepeace Thayer would later glorify in his "Log Cabin to White House" biographies. Moreover, the democratic elements of candidates' "self-making," such as mutual improvement societies where young men gathered to educate themselves, partook of the same ideals that animated aspiring middle-class men in an increasingly rootless society. Finally, campaign biography helped to define the public sphere in liberal society as male—and to place the genre of biography itself within that sphere, parallel to the domestic novel and the feminized home.

The earliest campaign biographies responded to a lack of clear ideological distinction between candidates. As James Monroe completed his second term in 1824, the presidency became seriously contested for the first time in twelve years. Monroe's cabinet included several presidential hopefuls, among them Secretary of State John Quincy Adams, Secretary of the Treasury William H. Crawford, and Secretary of War John C. Calhoun. Speaker of the House Henry Clay and Andrew Jackson, hero of New Orleans, also sought the office. All identified themselves with the Jeffersonian Republican party. In the absence of partisan difference, individuals' character and qualifications became a central issue, and the presentation of character assumed new importance. Federalists in 1796 and especially 1800 had assailed Thomas Jefferson's character, but behind the attacks had lain real ideological differences. Now the contrasts lay in the candidates themselves, particularly in their experiences (military, diplomatic, legislative) and regional affiliations. Campaign biographies emphasized these contrasts. John Eaton's *Life of Andrew Jackson* popularized anecdotes like the young Jackson's defiance to a British officer and presented Old Hickory as a man outside politics, the Cincinnatus who had retired after his military service ended and who could sweep corruption from Washington. Biographies of Jackson's opponents, all of whom held governmental office during the campaign, stressed their experience, nationalism, and high character.[30]

As the development of the Democratic and Whig parties in the 1830s added an ideological debate to the biographies, campaign biographers faced a central problem: how could they promote clearly partisan causes without opening themselves to charges of bias and their subjects to accusations of opportunism? To solve this problem, they invoked the tenets of contemporary biographical theory—adherence to truth and didactic purpose. Indeed, parties attempted to emphasize the "biography" over the "campaign." When the *Baltimore Republican and Commercial Advertiser* reviewed William Holland's biography of its 1836 candidate, it did so in the language of genre, not politics: "Of the several branches of polite literature, none perhaps, presents more captivations to the well-balanced mind, than general biography. Its usefulness extends to the right cultivation of the moral feeling, as well as to the mere acquisition of knowledge. . . . We rejoice, therefore, at this publication of the *Life of Martin Van Buren*." The concept that campaign biographies were impartial narratives of fact was clearly a fiction, because candidates' images were always contested territory, shaped oppositely by the different parties. Yet biography as a genre asserted the truth of its narratives, and campaign lives drew on this assertion. Biographers routinely claimed no partisan motives for writing, only admiration for their subjects. Moreover, they professed to give only the "facts, substantially as they were," widely available in published speeches and sketches. The biographer was here a compiler, not an inventor.[31] It was as if biography by its very nature defied mere partisan bias, even if a work of biography could serve a party's ends by presenting the life of a shining figure.

However specious, the assertion that the campaign biography served no partisan interest depended on the biographer's effacement of creative authorship. The campaign biography, at least rhetorically, consisted of facts; authors claimed never to have created anecdotes. In this formulaic literature, authors did create by fitting candidates to national ideals and partisan values, particularly when writing about obscure candidates like James Polk and Franklin Pierce. But that invention succeeded to the extent that it fit the candidate *into* the archetypes, not to the extent that it displayed originality of authorial vision. Like the sentimental novels whose power lay in their evocation of familiar cultural images, campaign biographies worked in their very adherence to formula.[32] And biographers succeeded if they remained invisible, preserving the illusion of biographical truth even as they aligned candidates with standard values and virtues. The campaign biography's mode of production and distribution enhanced authorial invisibility: because the most widely available biographies were probably the short, usually anonymous pamphlets printed and sold at newspaper offices, the authors of the book-length biographies tended to receive little attention.

The other tenet of biography, that the life of a great man provided an example for the young reader, similarly sought to deter accusations of petty politicking: by offering models for emulation, biographers raised the Polks and Clays above the hurly-burly of the transient political campaign. The paradox of campaign biography was that both creative authorship and politicking had to be denied. Because tradition barred candidates themselves from electoral maneuvering, biographers took pains to assert that their subjects had not authorized or had only reluctantly consented to the works. George D. Prentice, for example, reported that Henry Clay had "frankly acknowledge[d] the repugnance of his own private feelings to the contemplated publication." The candidate was "the architect of his own fortunes" but emphatically *not* the author or authorizer of his own biography, and the biographer was a compiler or reporter but not a creative author. Both needed to appear above the fray. By offering the reader an example to emulate, the biographer derived an alternative source of authority to write the candidate's life. "The biography of our country's most distinguished and honored statesmen is eminently fraught with encouragement and hope for her aspiring youth," began one life of Clay; the statement might have easily begun a life of Washington or Patrick Henry. Democracy offered a second justification. As citizens of a republic, "to whose intelligence are confided not only their own rights and those of their children, but, in a great degree, the future of humanity," Americans were obligated to study the lives and characters of the men who would lead them—and those lives became "the property of the people." Biographers claimed to serve not their parties or their subjects (for the candidates' sterling character needed no service) but their readers.[33]

Of course, they served all three. As Van Buren's biographer wrote, the campaign life sought "to exhibit by the history of an individual, the nature of the relation which that party sustains to its public men." Once the party system of Whigs and Democrats took shape, candidates embodied their parties' distinct principles, not merely the images of Cincinnatus or the experienced statesman (the prominent depictions of Jackson and Adams in 1824). Biographers offered copious extracts from candidates' speeches and writings to demonstrate their fidelity to partisan values and doctrines: the Democrats' strict construction of the Constitution, the Whigs' support for internal improvements. More than this, the narratives of candidates' lives implicitly evoked the same principles. The Democrats, who viewed the political party as a democratic institution in which any man could rise to leadership through hard work and loyalty to Jeffersonian and Jacksonian principles, portrayed their candidates as relatively ordinary men whose industry, rather than natural superiority, had elevated them to candidacy. George Hickman wrote in 1844 that in college James K. Polk had "never missed a recitation, nor omitted the punctilious performance of any duty." William Holland articulated the Democratic concept of leadership most clearly in his 1836 life of Van Buren: "It is only as a faithful representative of the pervading feelings and principles of his fellow men, their interests and their wants, that [the candidate] is invested with distinction and entrusted with the exercise of power."[34] Echoing the antiparty stance of the early republic, Whigs argued that political parties forced their members to sacrifice their own independent views and created artificial divisions in an organic society. Whig candidates, as depicted by their biographers, stood above partisan servility. Natural leaders loyal only to nation and principle, they rose to prominence by their innate brilliance and superiority. No common men, they were identified with the preservation and expansion of the republic in war and peace: Harrison at Tippecanoe, Clay in Congress, Taylor and Scott in Mexico. Biographers also linked Whig candidates to the evangelical reform movements whose adherents constituted an important segment of the party. Harrison had eschewed "the vice of intemperance" as a young soldier and closed a distillery on his farm, and Clay (a former duelist) had come to oppose dueling and favored the gradual abolition of slavery. And in the words of Caleb Cushing, Clay was "the chosen instrument of Providence" to save a republic corrupted by luxury and partisan spoils and weakened by depression. Democratic biographers generally did not depict their candidates in such providential terms. The models with whom biographers compared their candidates were especially revealing: Democrats were the heirs of Jackson, man of the people and founder of the party, while Whigs inherited the mantle of Washington, nonpartisan statesman and savior of the nation.[35]

For all these differences, it is possible to overstate the divergences between Democratic and Whig portrayals, which were often ones of emphasis. All candidates, Whig or Democrat, achieved success largely through hard work. William Harrison's determination proved that a frail-looking scion of a comfortable Virginia family could excel as a soldier in the western territories; only through assiduous application did Henry Clay develop his oratorical skills. Conversely, Democrats were not solely products of industry. Polk's biographer criticized those who derided hard work in favor of brilliance alone, but not those who combined some measure of extraordinary talent with industry. As depicted by Henry Rowe Schoolcraft, the 1848 Democratic candidate Lewis Cass more nearly fit William Holland's description of the quintessential Whig candidate: "no ordinary man—a man gifted by no common powers of mind, improved by no common degree of study, experience, reflection and cultivation." Cass might possess Jacksonian principles, but here too the biographer blurred the partisan distinctions. Schoolcraft devoted an entire section to Cass's benevolence and wrote that Cass "never tasted ardent spirits in any of its forms" and attempted to reform the Indians of their proclivity to alcohol. The biographical portrayal of Cass—extraordinary man, exemplar and advocate of reform—suggested the limits of cultural difference between Whig and Democratic "presidential images." So did the fact that all biographers, Democrat and Whig, portrayed their subjects as liberty loving and devoted to the Union. Every candidate had a patriotic ancestry, a less-than-comfortable childhood from which he rose to prominence, a connection to farming, and some military service. These experiences identified the candidate with the Revolution, the civilization of the frontier, and the protection of the ever-fragile republic. Because candidates after Jackson were too young to have fought in the Revolution themselves, their biographies often began with their fathers in order to demonstrate the connection.[36]

The characteristics that both parties' candidates and both parties' biographies shared were as important as partisan differences—for in the similarities we can observe the underlying and unifying cultural values beneath the entire structure of party politics. Here, too, we can examine not only how campaign biographies shaped candidates' life stories within contemporary political culture, but also how they helped define the contours of that culture itself. Defined broadly, political culture includes social visions that transcend party lines and the narrow realm of electoral politics, as well as the institutions that transmit those visions.[37] Campaign biography became such an institution in the Jacksonian era. It related most directly to two ideological elements of its political culture: the division of society into gendered spheres of activity, and the uneasy combination of a "republican" vision identified with the organic society of the founding generations and a "liberal" vision connected with the mid-nineteenth-century development of commercial, urban society.

In order to explore the cultural function of campaign biographies, it is necessary first to consider where women, especially the candidates' mothers and wives, fit into them. In the 1830s and 1840s Whigs adopted "feminine political symbols," in large measure due to their "particularly strong base in the Yankee middle classes," the heart of domestic ideology. Democrats, less tied to this constituency and to the reform movements that afforded women a realm of public participation, "remained relatively indifferent to feminine symbolism." The Whigs' "Log Cabin and Hard Cider" campaign of 1840 appealed to women and ran stories of women's participation in its newspapers. In one oft-reprinted anecdote, a young woman refuses to marry her fiancé until he pledges to vote for Harrison. A dialogue between a mechanic and his wife offered a more substantive political role for women: although the wife claims to "know nothing about politics," she brings her husband to see that the Democrats have "blindfolded you"—and the working class—with demagoguery. This dialogue concluded by asking, "Who will say that the wife, whose happiness is directly, and perhaps fatally influenced by political measures, has no right to use her influence in relation to this subject?" Whig papers also described women's actual efforts sewing banners for Harrison and attending parades and speeches, all defined as acceptable participation within the bounds of "influence." In contrast, Democratic papers generally ignored women, except when warning men against Whig harridans: "*Young men and Bachelors look out!* unless you want to wear ragged stockings, cook your own victuals, and tend your own children, have a care how you connect yourself with a brawling, female politician. If you would have your house a hell, and your home a curse, marry a 'feminine Tippecanoe,' one who is aiding and exciting the animosities, and participating in the political strife of the day." Given these partisan differences, one might expect Democratic and Whig biographers to portray candidates' wives and families differently. Perhaps Whig biographers might depict their candidates as first the products and later the fathers and husbands of families like those in domestic literature; at the very least Whig biographers would discuss candidates' domestic relationships. Conversely, perhaps Democratic biographers would leave wives and families out entirely.[38]

In fact, however, both parties wrote women out of their candidates' biographies. Many candidates seemed to have been born to single fathers: Harrison, Polk, and Cass learned their patriotism from their fathers but ostensibly had no mothers. Two exceptions, Andrew Jackson and Henry Clay, were raised by widowed mothers, but these pious women hardly exemplified a "republican motherhood" that instilled patriotism in their sons. Their principal role in the biographies consisted of leaving their sons to make themselves: Jackson's mother, devastated by the loss of two sons in the Revolution, sank into an early grave, and Clay's remarried and moved east with her new husband, leaving Henry alone in Kentucky. Nathan Sargent, one of Clay's biographers, described this latter event in particularly revealing terms: "He came to the State fatherless, penniless, and, with the exception of the few he had left behind him, friendless. She proved to him a parent, friend, and benefactor: has he not repaid her with more than filial attachment?" Here Clay replaced a real mother with a figurative one: the state of Kentucky nurtured "her" young "son," removing the candidate from a literal family and making the polity and society themselves a new family.[39] Wives, too, appeared only in passing, if at all, and little distinguished the Democratic from the Whig wife. A voter in 1844 could read Polk's and Clay's biographies without learning that either man was married (or that Clay had eleven children!). Wives who did appear entered briefly as kind domestics and quickly exited. Hannah Van Buren, who had died before her husband's candidacy, received a footnote; other marriages merited just a sentence or short paragraph. Anna Harrison was merely the "faithful companion of this distinguished patriot" and "daughter of John Cleves Symmes, the founder of the Miami settlements," with no mention of her own activity. Harrison's marriage became a transaction between men: the young soldier asked the old general for his daughter's hand, pointed to his sword as a means of support, and received Symmes's consent.[40]

Some campaign biographers justified the near-total omission of women and family life on the grounds of propriety. William Holland explained in his 1836 preface that he had collected and arranged materials on Van

Buren's political views, "together with such details of his personal history, as may be published with a due respect for private feelings." In his conclusion, Holland returned to this theme: Van Buren's familial feelings "are attractive traits in his character, on which, did propriety admit, the writer would gladly dwell." Eight years later, James B. Swain offered a similar rationale for leaving Henry Clay's "personal biography . . . untouched" and referring to Clay's wife and children only by implication: "it will be readily seen that those noble qualities of mind and heart which have made so glorious his public life, must have invested his domestic relations with the highest charms." Another of Clay's biographers, arguing that "the boy who works barefooted for his mother, will be very likely . . . to serve his country well," remarked that "The two spheres are kindred to each other." Yet the kinship was at most metaphorical: this boy would graduate from working for his mother to serving "his country, the mother of us all."[41] But the absence of the female and domestic as a real influence in the candidate's life resulted from more than propriety.

The underlying cultural story of campaign biographies, the definition of self-made manhood, occurred in a masculine public universe of education and action that *paralleled* the feminized domestic sphere. Although not bildungsromans whose protagonists seemed to develop or mature over time, campaign lives narrated a story of masculine self-formation that took place through a series of symbolic steps, each representing a stage of life, all building to the expected conclusions of heroism, statesmanship, and ultimately presidential nomination. That process happened in a series of "schools," each populated by men. The candidate's father, his first teacher, educated by lore and example. The fathers of Cass and Harrison had been prominent figures in the Revolution, a fact that biographers never failed to mention. The Revolutionary father did not simply lend inherited glory to his son; "the purest school of democracy," he taught the boy about the early days and their lessons. Thus Cass's "earliest memory was baptised, as it were, in the reminiscences of the Revolution." Fathers bequeathed their sons patriotism and love of liberty, but not wealth; even less prominent fathers than Benjamin Harrison and Jonathan Cass taught their sons "sound sense" and "republican simplicity."[42]

In subsequent stages the young man stood between surrogate father figures and the companionship and leadership of his peers. The second step in the future candidate's "education" took place in one of three larger schools: apprenticeship, academy or college, and the military. Henry Clay began young adulthood as a chancery clerk and later as amanuensis to George Wythe; in the drudgery of transcribing Wythe's opinions the young man learned "the great lesson of patient labor." With the sanction of Washington himself, Harrison joined the army and demonstrated his fortitude despite a frail body and privileged upbringing. At Exeter, Cass cultivated the "classical attainments" and "fondness for the military life" that would make him an accomplished literary figure and frontier governor.[43] As they reached adulthood, the candidates also joined groups of young men in mutual education. Soon after arriving in Kentucky, Clay joined a village debating club and overcame initial nervousness to become the accomplished orator who would lead the Congress. Cass enlisted in a volunteer corps of students at Exeter and quickly became its leader. Each of these settings — the apprenticeship in a frontier community, the academy, and the army — combined a hierarchical structure of authority with a more egalitarian relationship among young men. In each, the future candidate developed his industrious habits, offered glimpses of his future sphere of activity, and exhibited the first stirrings of leadership.

Unlike other narratives of young manhood, campaign biographies did not suggest anxiety about the relationships between sons and their real and figurative fathers. Several scholars have argued that ambivalence about filial legacies, exhibited in a tension between assertion of masculine independence and reverence for fathers and grandfathers, pervaded the generations of 1776, 1812, and the 1840s. The most influential life story of the period, Franklin's *Autobiography,* exemplified this tension. Franklin "made" himself in a series of revolts against oppressive or duplicitous father figures: his own father, his brother, the master printer Keimer, the untrustworthy Governor Keith. In place of filial relationships, Franklin created egalitarian sites of masculine education, notably the Junto and the Library Company of Philadelphia, where young men congregated for mutual self-improvement. His narrative also displayed the cleverness and even hypocrisy of self-manufacture: leaving a light burning late into the night gave the appearance of industry and "earned" others' trust. Campaign biographies, by contrast, harmoniously integrated reverence for fathers with education among peers, and suggested that the process of self-making included both, as well as the institutions in which they occurred.[44] Moreover, future candidates did not display Franklin's self-consciousness about their elevation. Character and industry, not machinations, occasioned their rise.

Once educated, candidates became "fathers" in the same masculine, public world in which they had been sons. "Like a father," wrote James Hall of Harrison's relationship with his soldiers, "he often gave in private the affectionate admonition, which precluded the necessity of a public exposure, and produced the desired end." Harrison here appeared as the disciplinary figure of the new middle class, which replaced "public exposure" with "affectionate admonition," but the setting was the military company. Another biographer sketched the scene of Lewis Cass's return from the French ambassadorship: "At Detroit, the Governor, legislature, city authorities, and people came out to welcome him home, as children welcome the return of a long absent father." The domestic sphere, so often absent literally from the campaign biography, was reconstituted outside the home and in a new, public, masculine "family." [45]

At the same time they existed in the "public sphere" of electoral politics, campaign biographies also defined the "public." In these biographies, "private life" did not mean domestic life. Private life, rather, was a zone that included community, neighbors, and profession, the realm *between* governmental service (the "public services," civil and military, so often in the titles) and the domestic sphere. This distinction between "public services" and "private life," both masculine realms existing outside the home, was the explicit dichotomy that campaign biographies drew. But in their very omission of domestic life, these works offered a second definition of the "public," through what they did and did not make public for the reader's consumption. This implicit definition of public and private placed everything in the biographies—public services and community life—on one side of a divide, and the domestic realm on the other, private in the sense of being off limits. Campaign biographies were not alone in this division: biographies of "self-made" men in the early republic routinely wrote out women and the domestic, creating a "dichotomy between a man's 'real' life—the life of private virtue and public accomplishment—and that segment of his life which was shared with his wife and children." [46]

In suggesting that the self-made man was in fact made in a series of masculine schools or institutions, campaign biographies paralleled the contemporary domestic fiction that gave a similarly gendered view of the female educational process. *The Wide, Wide World,* Susan Warner's best-selling 1850 novel whose protagonist read Weems's life of Washington, illustrated this parallel. Warner wrote men out of *The Wide, Wide World* nearly as completely as women vanished from campaign biographies. The novel's vantage point lay entirely within the domestic realm; women dominated young Ellen Montgomery's environments and activities. Here the "public" world of market and politics was the alien universe, tearing Ellen from her beloved mother and terrifying her when she must enter it (on a traumatic shopping trip). Her lessons were not those of independence, but of piety and submission to God's will, which she achieved after eight hundred pages and countless tears. We should beware of overstating the parallel. Men affected Ellen's enclosed domestic world, usually as malevo-lent forces, far more than women affected any candidate's life. (Her father's financial reverses occasioned Ellen's separation from her mother, for in-stance.) More substantially, many other domestic novels, especially those of the 1820s and 1830s, portrayed the home as a domain governed by men and women companionately.[47] But what emerges from the comparison is a contrast between two archetypal, gendered narratives of self-formation, with different teachers, different sites of learning, and different lessons.

The comparison suggests, finally, that campaign biographies—like the mercantile biographies in Freeman Hunt's *Merchant's Magazine*—offered one more institution of public, masculine education: the biography itself. Numerous campaign lives presented themselves as teachers, especially for young men without wealth or access to more formal schooling. One bi-ographer noted that "The career of Henry Clay is rich in instruction and encouragement to all upon whom fortune has laid her depressing hand."[48] Like the other institutions of masculine education, the reading of biog-raphy mixed hierarchy with egalitarianism. Just as fathers and surrogate fathers taught future candidates the lessons of patriotism and industry, the candidates' lives provided examples for the reader. The irony of campaign biographies' democratic rhetoric (that any man could rise as had the can-didate) lay in the connections that helped candidates to succeed. Not every reader could have a Revolutionary statesman like Benjamin Harrison for a father, or become amanuensis to a leading lawyer like George Wythe. But by offering new fathers for a generation without direct links to the Revolution—and by arguing that *reading* about these fathers constituted an inheritance as valuable as sitting at their feet—campaign biographies re-stored democracy, at least rhetorically.

Because any literate young man could read a biography, this "school" was in fact more democratic than an academy or college. William Holland's description of Van Buren's early education made this point explicitly:

> The example of Mr. Van Buren is dwelt upon more at length, in this connection, for the encouragement of the youth of our country who may believe themselves to be cut off by their poverty from aspiring to distinction. So numerous are the instances of success in public life, at-tained by men of imperfect education, as to raise a doubt whether, after all, their exclusion from a regular routine of study may not have been, in some respects, a benefit. Many instances of this kind appear in the brief history of our country. The names of Patrick Henry and Franklin

will occur to every one, and the early education of Washington himself was by no means complete.

At the present moment, the facilities for self education are so great that no person who can read is of necessity cut off from them.[49]

Holland's discussion revealed the layers of biography presumably embedded in the American reader's consciousness. In referring to Henry, Franklin, and Washington, Holland evoked the central biographical subjects of the early republic, the three men whose lives had been written most prominently. The stories of their "self-making"—and Van Buren's similarity to them—would "occur to every one" who had read Weems's *Life of Washington*, Franklin's *Autobiography*, and Wirt's *Sketches of the Life and Character of Patrick Henry*. Van Buren's lack of formal education served a political end: he became at once a man of the people unspoiled by aristocratic schooling and a logical successor to these Revolutionary heroes. But Holland moved a step further, linking these generations of "self-made" men to "the youth of our country," even the poverty-stricken, whose literacy was a tool for self-education presumably independent of wealth or heredity. In his campaign life of Abraham Lincoln a quarter century later, William Dean Howells made the same point by portraying the young Lincoln as a voracious, self-educated reader of newspapers, Shakespeare, Burns, Poe, and Blackstone's common law and offering Lincoln as an example to "the young student, climbing unaided up the steep ascent" and to "the rustic boy, who is to be President in 1900."[50]

The campaign biographies thus suggested a cultural ideology that fused republicanism, liberalism, and democracy. In presenting candidates as the products of hierarchical social relationships in their youth and as society's fathers in their adulthood, biographers echoed an earlier rhetoric that envisioned an organic society. Their emphasis on citizen virtue—the candidate's and the reader's—was a central part of republican ideology. But in arguing that candidates were self-made men, they also implied the increasing fluidity of such hierarchies. Moreover, in promoting literacy itself as the foremost teacher for the rising generation, campaign lives were newly democratic: they took the place of the real Revolutionary fathers whom most midcentury Americans did not have. Campaign biographers did not probe the contradictions between these values. For example, while the biographies' rhetoric emphasized the democracy of the reading experience, their narratives told of candidates who had sat at the feet of Revolutionary generals. (By 1860, Howells could twit this part of the campaign-life formula: ".It is necessary that every American should have an indisputable grandfather, in order to be represented in the Revolutionary period by actual ancestral service, or connected with it by ancestral reminiscence."[51]) Instead, biographers reconciled such potential conflicts, substituting biography reading for experience.

Even if this first generation of campaign biographies all too often mixed "truth" with what we now recognize as apocryphal and formulaic tales, the lessons they sought to impart carried cultural significance. As popular politics and the "public sphere" were being redefined and contested, campaign biography defined these realms as male and offered its (presumably male) readers examples of how to "make themselves" in them. Paradoxically, the self-made man was in these narratives made in institutions: the patriarchal family, school, military hierarchy, and debating club. Although by midcentury middle-class mothers played crucial roles in the "self-making" of their sons, and although the ideology of republican motherhood had long prescribed such roles for women, campaign biographies offered an older and completely masculine vision of the process.[52] However distant a Revolutionary father or a military career was from the young reader's actual experience, campaign biographies offered biography itself, the life of the exemplary candidate, as the ultimate masculine school. As Van Buren's biographer wrote in 1836, any young man who could read could rise.

Monarchs, Missionaries, and Memoirs: Biographical Womanhood and the Possibilities of the Public

Young women who read the lives of self-made men did not find lessons about how they too could rise by reading biographies and emulating their subjects. Perhaps, like Ellen Montgomery in *The Wide, Wide World,* they renewed their American patriotism by reading the life of Washington. But they may well have asked, as did the fictional child Mary Grenville in an 1833 book called *Sketches of the Lives of Distinguished Females,* "Are there no histories of good and great women, mother?" Mary explained to her mother that a Mr. Mordaunt had recently given her brother Henry a biography of Benjamin Franklin, which his own mother had read to him as a child and which had changed his habits from indolence to industry. Lives of prominent women, Mary imagined, "would do me as much good as the life of Dr. Franklin did Mr. Mordaunt, for you often tell me that I want industry and application." Mrs. Grenville responded, "Yes, my dear, there are many biographies of eminent women written and published," and proceeded to gather Mary and her young cousins and friends for six "evenings" of biographical instruction, each focused on a famous woman and narrated for didactic effect. Beginning and quickly dispensing with female sovereigns of antiquity and famed European queens, Mrs. Grenville devoted her greatest attention to five women known for their literary, benevolent, or religious activity—closing the book with the life of Ann Judson, the most famous American missionary.[53]

While the lives of eminent men attempted to reconcile the older vision of civic virtue and an organic society with the emerging concept of the self-made man, the bulk of female biography taught different precepts. Most lives of women written between 1820 and 1860 were linked directly or indirectly to the evangelical and reform crusades of the era, which were greatly responsible for both an expanded population of women readers and a growing number of documents that recorded women's experiences. And biographies of women multiplied rapidly in these years. Compared to the myriad lives of Revolutionary heroes, self-made men, and ministers, the stock of female biography remained scanty indeed: Arabella Stuart Wilson lamented in 1851, "How few of the memoirs and biographical sketches which load the shelves of our libraries, record the lives of women!"[54] But lives of eminent women were proliferating as were lives of eminent men, for many of the same reasons, notably the publishing revolution of the early republic. Not only did book-length biographies of women appear from the major publishing houses and especially the tract societies; magazines such as the *Albion* and the *New-York Mirror, and Ladies' Literary Gazette* ran sections of "Female Biography." Female biographies told of three sorts of women: those who had lived religious lives in obscurity, those who had achieved public renown for their religious, charitable, or literary activities, and European queens—whose biographies were among the most popular with nineteenth-century American readers, male as well as female. Their messages, while all connected with evangelical Christianity, ranged from the narrowest definition of "women's sphere" to the suggestion that women had active roles to play in the wide, wide world.

Those who discussed women's education in the early republic focused on the dangers of novel reading, but they also considered how biography could educate women readers. Some writers contended that cultivating women's intellect meant teaching them in many of the same subjects and ways that men were educated. This view had appeared in a 1766 London biographical dictionary of women called *The Female Worthies,* which included "the Most Illustrious Ladies, of All Ages and Nations, . . . Eminently Distinguished for their Magnanimity, Learning, Genius, Virtue,

Piety, and other excellent Endowments, conspicuous in all the various Stations and Relations of Life, public and private." The compiler of this work contended that nature had not granted women lesser intellect than men, but that women's intellectual deficiency arose only from a want of education and an overemphasis on luxury and dissipated amusements. By displaying the accomplishments of earlier women to young ladies of the 1760s, the author hoped to awaken contemporary women to their own rational capacities. Samuel Lorenzo Knapp, a New England writer and critic who produced several volumes of collective biography in the 1820s and 1830s, agreed. In his *Female Biography* (1834), a dictionary of noted women, Knapp wrote that "The learning of the females of this country has not been sufficiently masculine." By this he meant that women should learn not just history and biography but also the rules of philosophy and logic. Many female authors, he asserted, had not been taken seriously because they lacked this formal training. Knapp at once defined education in terms of a masculine standard *and* sought to broaden women's education, arguing for a more advanced course of female study at the same time he implied that men like himself were women's appropriate teachers. Like early-national educators such as Benjamin Rush and Judith Sargent Murray, Knapp advocated educating American women along the lines of Enlightenment rationalism. His subjects included women writers, mathematicians, and teachers, as well as pious wives and mothers of the great.[55]

Other writers argued that women and men read differently, and that this difference made biography particularly useful for women. The English writer Mary Hays, whose *Female Biography* appeared in an 1807 Philadelphia edition four years after its original London publication, claimed to write "for women, and not for scholars," seeking to benefit "my own sex," especially "the rising generation." To do so, she argued, biography had to be reshaped for female readers: "Women, unsophisticated by the pedantry of the schools, read not for dry information, to load their memories with uninteresting facts, or to make a display of a vain erudition. A skeleton biography would afford them but little gratification; they expect pleasure to be mingled with instruction, lively images, the graces of sentiment, and the polish of language. Their understandings are principally accessible through their affections: they delight in minute delineation of character; nor must the truths which impress them be either cold or unadorned." The Reverend John Bennet, whose "Letters to a Young Lady" appeared in the *American Museum* in the 1790s, suggested that biography would appeal to women readers precisely because it was as "familiar" as the domestic novel. "Instead of wars, sieges, victories, or great achievements," the subjects of history, biography "presents those domestic anecdotes and events, which come more forcibly home to her bosom and her curiosity." Here was the Johnsonian argument for "domestick privacies" applied specifically to the female reader: if biography's charm lay in its glimpses into the private moments of its subjects, how much more charming it was for readers whose own activity lay in the domestic sphere.[56]

Sketches of the Lives of Distinguished Females, the little volume in which "Mary Grenville" asked her mother whether biographies of women existed, implied the same thing. Published the year before Knapp's *Female Biography* as part of Harper's "Boy's and Girl's Library of Useful and Entertaining Knowledge," this anonymous book (its title page identified "An American Lady" as the author) literally placed biography within the domestic sphere. In a preface, the American Lady quoted a male biographer ("Mr. Sampson") on the value of biographical models for young men, then applied the principle to "the youthful female, whose character is capable of being moulded almost at will, and upon whom the influence of example acts still more powerfully than on the other sex." Arguing that girls were more malleable than boys, this author drew on the same philosophical concept that led critics to warn against the deleterious effects of novels on female readers—and she defined female biography squarely in terms of male biography, as a genre borrowed from "Mr. Sampson." A similar borrowing occurred when Mary Grenville took her interest in biography from her brother's conversation with Mr. Mordaunt. But then the book redefined biography as part of a wholly female sphere. In order to prepare for the "evenings" of biography, Mrs. Grenville "procured the best female biographies she could get, and some engraved portraits of celebrated women." For her part, Mary arranged the parlor just so: watering her plants, filling vases with fresh flowers, "carefully arranging" the books and portraits, placing "her mother's work-table and chair in the most pleasant part of the room, near the flower-stand, so that she might feel the soft wind which came through the window." In this middle-class home, created by a consumer culture (the books and engravings, "the muslin curtains," and presumably the furniture and flower stand had all been "purchased"), feminine influence reigned, symbolized by the flowers (suggesting both nurturing and beauty) and the worktable (female industry). This environment was just becoming a staple of sentimental fiction, which was moving away from the seduction tales of the early republic and toward the domestic novels that proliferated from the 1820s on.[57]

The sketches themselves emphasized how sentimental connections between subject and reader could become the most effective teachers. As

Mrs. Grenville read from the lives of women like the young poet Lucretia Maria Davidson and the missionary Ann Judson, she noted their feelings and sufferings; the girls responded with exclamations like "Poor Mrs. Judson! how glad I am that her sufferings are over. How few women could have borne up as she did, under such continued misfortunes!" This remark led Mrs. Grenville to remind the girls that Mrs. Judson endured because of her fortitude and piety. Mrs. Grenville closed the volume with a larger lesson: women's "conduct and character" influenced brothers and sisters, husbands and children "to press forward in the path which leads to excellence on earth, and a final, blessed home in heaven."[58] Here was not Enlightenment rationalism but sentimental evangelicalism, presented not by a male scholar but by an "American Lady" and an educated mother. If Samuel Knapp's *Female Biography* was the product of the educational theory that produced enlightened "republican mothers," *Sketches of the Lives of Distinguished Females,* subtitled "Written for Girls, with a View to Their Mental and Moral Improvement," looked toward the sentimental literature and culture of midcentury.

Didacticism lay at the heart of that culture, and even the lives of European queens could offer lessons in female behavior. English authors' biographies of queens achieved extraordinary popularity in midcentury America. The women of the Benson Female Library Society read Anna Jameson's *Lives of the Female Sovereigns* (part of Harper's Family Library) more than any other biographies. Agnes Strickland's *Lives of the Queens of England* were the most popular books among women readers in the New York Society Library, perhaps the largest social library in the nation— and in the ten most popular among men. The *Christian Examiner* elaborated that "No book is more borrowed from the circulating libraries than Mrs. Strickland's Queens of England and Scotland."[59] These tales of a bygone time possessed an appeal similar to that of Sir Walter Scott's historical novels. Strickland particularly emphasized the customs and costumes of Tudor-Stuart England in order to add color and romance. As *Godey's* (which promoted Strickland's work relentlessly) explained, "The amount of curious antiquarian lore respecting the toilettes and jewels of the queens, their domestic arrangements, their lives, misfortunes, and intrigues, hitherto unnoticed by history or biography, and now first developed and published by Mrs. Strickland, is truly wonderful. It renders her work unique, piquant, and exceedingly entertaining. The lives of queens, to us Americans, are like the annals of fairyland. They belong to another world— to the regions of poetry and romance." Strickland's work possessed the charms normally associated with fiction *and* the ultimate advantage of truth: reviewers took pains to praise the author's indefatigable research, not just "her glow of feeling." The fascination with Mary Queen of Scots and Elizabeth I was part of a larger American interest in the Tudor-Stuart period. Articles about the queens, most derived from Strickland's volumes, appeared in dozens of magazines between 1835 and 1865. By the 1850s some magazines even bemoaned the number of these works: the *Christian Examiner* asked, "When will the reading public get tired of royal and noble biographies?"[60]

In the hands of American writers, those biographies showed the incompatibility of political power and femininity. The three most popular stories, of Lady Jane Grey, Elizabeth I, and Mary Queen of Scots, provided variations on this theme. Lady Jane was the young innocent victimized by political opportunists. Married at sixteen to the young son of the duke of Northumberland, Jane had no desire to become queen and recognized Mary Tudor's superior claim. But once Northumberland's machinations placed Jane on the throne, her fate was sealed: imprisonment and ultimately execution. Moreover, Jane was the pious Protestant victim of the Catholic queen Mary, and thus a martyr for her faith as well as a young woman destroyed by the political maneuverings of men. In *Sketches of the Lives of Distinguished Females,* Mrs. Grenville summed up the contemporary image of Jane: "it was her misfortunes which showed her character in all its beauty and superiority," especially the piety that led her to accept her fate willingly. In contrast, Queen Elizabeth was the political adept whose very skill as monarch undermined her womanhood. Vain, power-hungry, and vindictive, Elizabeth represented the antithesis of the "true woman." Although a Protestant, she treated religion as a matter of expediency rather than true faith. Some American biographers condemned Elizabeth for abandoning all feminine traits to succeed as queen, while others (such as Sarah Josepha Hale) urged that her political ability be acknowledged and praised even as her personal traits should be censured. Politics victimized the true woman like Jane Grey—to whose virtues the amorality of political life was alien—and subverted the femininity of those women who entered it skillfully. Mary Queen of Scots presented a slightly more complicated case. Mary's various romantic liaisons made it difficult for writers to present her as a model of piety like Jane Grey, and her Catholicism made her an improbable religious martyr for Protestant America. Mary came to represent a third type: the romantic heroine whose passions (rather than innocence) caused her to become the victim of unscrupulous men. Like the protagonists of earlier seduction novels such as *Charlotte Temple* and *The Coquette,* Mary was undone by her excessive sensibility. But also like these fictional characters, sensibility made Mary all the more sympathetic. In addition, Mary's beauty and feminine charms earned her the enmity of her mannish cousin Elizabeth. When biographers juxtaposed these "rival queens," as they often did, Mary's history and fate sought to provoke a far more emotional response from readers than Elizabeth's harsh displays of power ever could.[61]

The biographical portrayals of these queens, taken together, suggest the ideology that historians have called the "cult of true womanhood," encompassing piety, purity, submissiveness, and domesticity.[62] Lady Jane Grey was heroic precisely because she possessed the first three of these. Elizabeth was an example to be avoided because she possessed none of them. Mary offered an odd combination. Although her indulgence of her passions offered a cautionary tale for young readers, her natural contrast with Elizabeth and her position late in life, as a pious woman bedeviled by religious fanatics in Scotland and resigned to her fate at Elizabeth's hands, brought her closer to the attributes of Lady Jane. Absent from all of these portrayals, however, was a favorable picture of female activity or authority. In the lives of the queens, authority and femininity were in inverse relationship, with little middle ground.

Memoirs of women like Ann Hasseltine Judson presented an alternative to this stark dichotomy: a heroic womanhood that was *not* passive, that achieved authority in the public world. Ann Judson and her husband Adoniram were well known in American religious circles long before Ann's death in 1826. Their missionary work was widely publicized in Baptist magazines and newspapers, which printed the Judsons' own letters from India and Burma. Three years after Ann Judson died, a Boston pastor named James D. Knowles composed a biography of her; his *Memoir of Mrs. Ann H. Judson, Late Missionary to Burmah* quickly became a best-seller in the annals of American evangelical literature. It also helped to make Ann Judson into a symbol of Christian womanhood. After all, she had died in the mission of saving heathen souls, after saving her heroic husband from death in a Burmese prison. Her legend endured over the next thirty years, thanks to continuous new editions of Knowles's book and a plethora of other biographies. She was joined by Adoniram's two succeeding wives, Sarah Hall Boardman Judson (who also died in Burma) and Emily Chubbuck Judson (better known as the writer Fanny Forester); the story of the "three Mrs. Judsons" became the best-known saga of American missionary work—and the most prominent literary promoter of missionary activity—before the Civil War.[63]

Female memoirs like the lives of the Mrs. Judsons demonstrated the public, active roles that women could play within the boundaries of evangelical Christianity and without losing their femininity. While all religious biography stressed accepting God's dominion, many memoirs also emphasized actively spreading that message, as Ann Judson had done. To be sure, many lives of pious women did not go far beyond conversion and death, but many others concerned women who had participated in the works of the evangelical empire. Sarah Sleeper devoted many pages to Martha Hazeltine Smith's work in establishing and running the New Hampton Female Seminary. Francis Wayland discussed how Harriet Ware founded the Providence Children's Friend Society, entering into public to raise money. The stories of these women could broaden the bounds of the "domestic" sphere, by encouraging middle-class women's activity in benevolent work, teaching, or missionary enterprises. Biographers carefully qualified their descriptions of women's public activity, to avoid the unseemly impression that their subjects possessed personal ambition. As if to balance the fact that "Miss Hazeltine acted independently, and in efficiency and strength exhibited masculine abilities," Sleeper wrote that "she was a woman in her affections." Wayland wrote that "Miss Ware's taste and disposition, strongly inclined her to the walks and enjoyments of private life. She acted in a public capacity only from a sense of duty. Worldly honor and renown had few attractions for her." Nonetheless, Wayland concluded the memoir with the lesson for readers that "a great power for good is placed in the hands of all of us, if we had but the energy and self-sacrifice to use it." Clearly, the life of a pious woman could encourage readers to be more than submissive, homebound servants of God.[64]

On rare occasions a biography could betray its female subject's ambivalence about trading public involvement for domestic life. Sleeper's *Memoir of the Late Martha Hazeltine Smith* explored Smith's decision to take teaching as her "sphere" and her difficulties in founding her seminary, as well as her "Labor for unconverted souls" among her students. At points a teacher's manual, the biography detailed her teaching methods, reading, and successes with students. Then the memoir took a strange turn. The young schoolmistress became acquainted with and engaged to the minister Joseph Smith, but then doubted her willingness to "resign public celebrity" for marriage. Simply put, Martha Hazeltine could not imagine "the thought of a quiet, unimportant existence." She broke the engagement, expanded her school, and plunged her energies into her own study. Several years later, she resumed correspondence with Smith and finally resolved "to close her public career" and make "her transition to domestic life." According to Sleeper, Martha now believed that breaking the engagement had been "decidedly *wrong*."[65] Sleeper presented the long episode of Martha's broken engagement as something of a cautionary tale, but the detail with which she told the story suggested a deeper ambivalence. The expansion of women's potential activities to include schoolteaching and school-founding—an expansion based, in the rhetoric of many of its advocates, on women's abilities in raising children—could work at cross purposes with their roles as private, domestic figures.

Whatever ambivalence they might imply about "domesticity," memoirs of pious, active women demonstrated no inclination to support changes in women's political status. The evangelical ideology located female suffering abroad in places like Burma, not in American women's political inequality. Most female memoirs avoided the issue of women's political rights, concentrating instead on the work of women like Ann Judson abroad and Harriet Ware in Providence. This ideology coincided with the mission espoused by Sarah Josepha Hale in *Godey's* and in her biographical compendium *Woman's Record* (1853) and by Catharine Beecher in her *Treatise on Domestic Economy* (1841): expanding women's educational opportunities and widening their "sphere" to include teaching, charitable work, and authorship. This belief united republicanism and evangelicalism. Educated women would spread their influence as Christians and Americans, teaching a heathen population abroad and a rising generation at home. Given women's separate realm of influence, woman suffrage was unnecessary, and (to some) even pernicious in abandoning women's distinctive mission.[66] After the Seneca Falls convention in 1848, at least one biographer made the contrast between evangelical ideology and political feminism explicit. Introducing yet another life of the Mrs. Judsons in 1851, Arabella Stuart Wilson employed the ideology of evangelicalism to answer those who decried the boundaries of women's opportunities: "Among the many benefits which modern missions have conferred upon the world, not the least, perhaps, is the field they have afforded for the highest development of female character. The limited range of avocations allotted to women, and her consequent inability to gain an elevated rank in the higher walks of life, has been a theme of complaint with many modern reformers, especially with the party who are loud in their advocacy of women's rights."[67] But if this last group of women would glance at female missionary work, continued Wilson, they would see a vast arena in which women could develop and display their unique capacities—capacities that women's-rights advocates, who presumably wanted women to imitate men, would abolish.

Lives of European queens and of Ann Judson may have been the most popular biographies of women in mid-nineteenth-century America;

memoirs of obscure Christian women distinguished for piety but not for worldly accomplishments were by far the most numerous. Though the tract societies published some of these works, many were local productions. The subject's friends, relatives, and ministers collected the diaries and letters of the departed one, interspersed these documents with a narrative of his or her life, and concluded with their own reminiscences. Ministers had long been popular subjects for such memoirs, in which sentimental language and themes increasingly displaced doctrinal and theological argument in the mid-nineteenth century. The greatest change in the composition of religious biography, however, was the increase in female memoirs. The biographies of pious women that proliferated after 1820 reflected women's centrality to antebellum religious revivals and church membership, as well as the breadth of experiences that the evangelical empire opened to women. By the 1850s perhaps as many lives of women as of ministers were being produced by the tract societies and in local communities. Female memoirs treated a variety of "humble believers" whose lives had been predominantly domestic and who had, in the words of one author, "possessed nothing more than ordinary endowments of intellect, but whose piety was of the brightest and holiest stamp."[68]

In order best to inculcate religious values, memoirs of the pious—both men and women—inverted the usual mission of biography. "The proposed object of a memoir usually is to portray the excellencies, and record the incidents connected with the life of some *distinguished individual,*" wrote the Rev. John Clark in 1837. Religious biographers, in contrast, stressed the very typicality of their subjects. These memoirs contended that their subjects offered the most inspiring examples—and therefore served God most effectively—precisely because they had *not* done great deeds or possessed striking intellects. Clark introduced his subject, the "young disciple" Anzonetta R. Peters, as "*so like* the rest of her species" that the reader who sought "something singularly striking, strange, or uncommon, will probably close the book in disappointment." In writing of his sister Martha, the Rev. Andrew Reed wrote similarly that "the history is entirely of a *domestic class.* The author has no splendid incidents, no improbable reverses, no extraordinary circumstances to excite curiosity and hold attention. The life he records, if interesting at all, must be so, not from its dissimilarity, but from its resemblance, to our own." Similarity to the reader's daily occupations was exactly the point. As another biographer wrote, "Few readers . . . will be able to rise up from the perusal of this book, and say that it does not reach their case."[69]

In subordinating temporal facts and dates to "organic markers" like conversion and death, the memoirs conceived of the crucial facts of "life" differently from secular biographies and suggested a different kind of source to document those facts. The subject's solitary, interior struggle toward conversion and acceptance of death as a spiritual victory over earthly existence was the most important part of her biography, dwarfing facts of where she was born or when she married. As one biographer wrote, "The true life of a Christian" was "*hidden*" from public view, from those who looked for striking events. In writing out "history" as contemporary historians saw it, the compilers of memoirs offered the core of personal experience as another kind of history. The greatest practical problem in writing this history was the dearth of materials recording the experiences of those women, undistinguished for public action or intellect, who would provide the best examples for the ordinary reader. Part of this problem was intrinsic to all religious biography: the most important "event" to record, the experience of religious awakening, occurred within one's own mind and soul. "No biographer has access to this Holy of Holies." The compiler of a memoir needed either action or the written remains of his subject; "Where these are both wanting, biography is not practicable."[70] Unfortunately, for women's and children's lives alike, such actions and materials were relatively scanty. These memoirs were usually written from the subject's letters to relatives and friends, her journal or diary, and her conversations with the author of the memoir, often a minister.

Both the typicality of the subjects and the materials used to write their lives reinforced the intimacy of female biography. That intimacy was evident from the books' titles. Whereas most biographies of men were called the "Life" or "Biography" of their subjects, women's lives were overwhelmingly entitled "Memoir" or "Memoirs," denoting both the more personal nature of their contents and their authorship or compilation by those who had known the subject well.[71] Unlike biographies of ministers, which usually included sermons and narratives of public deeds, female memoirs often took place in the home and recorded exchanges between close relatives and friends and (through diary entries) the innermost reflections of the individual soul. The reader was invited into the familial circle of the subject, to view her example as her own family and friends had. Andrew Reed began his sister's memoir with a letter to the reader, "welcoming you as an inmate of his humble family, and placing you before whatever in the character and life of a beloved relative may contribute to gratify or to benefit." More telling, the letters that compilers included in memoirs could as easily have been written to the unconverted reader as to the actual friends who had received them. Sarah Louisa Taylor's letters to her "intimate friend" Catharine, for example, prescribed methods of accepting God's dominion, including even reading biographies of other pious women: "You ask my opinion of religious biography, and of the emulation it excites. It certainly has a powerful effect. I think the perusal of well written narratives, and especially memoirs of females, has a happy influence, and is calculated to inspire with confidence, on the one hand, and humility, on the other."[72]

Female memoirs, in other words, dealt with the "private" sphere in multiple senses. Most clearly, their central action occurred inside the home *and* inside the solitary soul. It might be argued, too, that these works also defined the private sphere by the literary documents that were a part of it: personal letters, diaries, and ultimately the very religious memoirs that contained them. Several women's memoirs discussed their subjects' own reading of religious biographies. Sarah Louisa Taylor wrote to "Catharine" of reading the biographies of Ann Judson and of Mrs. Huntington. More generally, Charles Lester wrote of Mary Ann Bise that "Religious biographies were her favorite books" (though "her literary ardor" led her also to Boswell's *Life of Johnson*). For these women, the intimacy of religious biography worked; readers indeed felt spiritually akin to the pious subjects. After mentioning that she had read "the life and religious experience of Mrs. Ramsay, of S.C.," Mary Lyon continued: "She mentions, in terms of great self-abasement, the prevalence of her besetting sin; and sometimes appears almost in despair under its workings. I can easily comprehend her feelings." Presumably Mary Lyon's memoir would evoke the same response in a reader as "ordinary" as she.[73]

This relation between text and reader bore much in common with what one literary critic has called the "disciplinary intimacy" of sentimental novels, which taught readers the virtues of submission through cloying domestic settings and ever-multiplying prescriptions for behavior and thought. Readers could peruse not only Sarah Louisa Taylor's private journal but also letters that admitted them into the confidence of the deceased woman—who lived again in such exchanges and whose example could exert influence even after her death. The relatives, friends, and ministers who wrote memoirs like Sarah Taylor's justified their labors with precisely the argument that a memoir could extend the force of example to a readership wider than the subject's own circle of intimates—and that the example became effective through the reader's intimate acquaintance with the subject. In this way, female memoirs both employed the techniques and altered the message of the sentimental novels of the 1790s and early nineteenth century. Through exchanges between author, characters, and reader that can best be described as collusive, those novels challenged male-given standards of behavior and ideas about education.[74] Memoirs of pious women shared (and may indeed have borrowed) the novel's strategy of reaching the reader through emotional connection, but their explicit messages were far from subversive. Instead, they echoed one of the most potent pieties of evangelical culture, the virtue of accepting God's sovereignty and grace even (and especially) in death.

However, these memoirs could also serve in another capacity, one with complex possibilities: they helped teach readers how to *express* the experiences that were central to the process of religious conversion. First, they taught the feelings that one was *supposed* to have. Second, they showed readers the forms in which those feelings could be conveyed—not just the words and phrases, but also the vehicles (letters and journals). Female religious memoirs could well have become manuals of how to write a diary or letter and what sentiments to express. Ultimately, they might suggest exactly how a young woman could leave the necessary materials for her *own* memoir.[75] After all, the women who became the subjects of memoirs were not as "typical" as their memoirists claimed them to be. They were extraordinary, not only in the extent of their Christian virtue, but also in the very fact that they were the subjects of memoirs. They had achieved a form of secular immortality available to relatively few "ordinary" women.

It may seem cynical to argue that women left written remains in the hope of being memorialized as Sarah Louisa Taylor had been. But at least some evidence exists to suggest that the proliferation of female memoirs could encourage the writing of more. The preface to John Clark's *The Young Disciple* was unusual in that it explained just how the book came to be written. After the usual statements about Anzonetta Peters's lack of extraordinary talents and her consequent value as a model for emulation, Clark described how one of her friends wrote to him after her death, requesting that he compose the memoir: "The friends of Anzonetta R. Peters, are of the opinion that there are materials to form a memoir no less interesting and profitable than that of her cousin, Caroline Smelt. Mrs. P— requests me to say, that it is the desire of all, that a biography should be written of her." (Moses Waddell had written Caroline Smelt's memoir in 1818.) Next Anzonetta's mother wrote to Clark with a similar request, informing him that she was collecting the materials necessary for the memoir. Anzonetta's friend and mother stressed the instructive power of her example—and implied that *without* a memoir "'Anzonetta's holy example, devoted life, victorious faith, and triumph over death, must be entombed with her, or the remembrance of them cherished only by the few who knew her.'" Each of these phrases had become a convention by 1837 — a convention learned from other memoirs (like Caroline Smelt's) and thousands of tracts. Other memoirs probably came to be written much the same way *The Young Disciple* did: friends or relatives of a deceased woman prevailed upon a minister to write (and thus preserve) her life, supplying the documents and exerting whatever moral pressure they could.[76] In placing the interior lives of supposedly "private" women into public as the subjects of biography, then, these memoirs went well beyond their stated mission of doing God's work. If their archetypal narratives subordinated subjects' individuality to formulaic characteristics and experiences, their willingness to discuss the lives of real women — and the active role of subjects' families and friends in collecting materials and having these memoirs published — could belie the message of self-abnegation that the narratives preached.

Like campaign lives of presidential candidates, then, these memoirs of obscure women offered the reader an opportunity to "rise" that stemmed from biography-reading itself. The circumstances of that elevation, of course, differed significantly. Campaign biographies based their promise of opportunity on the nexus between literacy and American democracy, while pious memoirs saw opportunity in the link between literacy and the equality of all believers. Christian salvation always required redemptive grace — one could be a "self-made" Christian only so far. And where young men's opportunities lay in the public world of politics, young women's chance to emerge in "public" as subjects of memoirs occurred only after the end of pious lives, lived privately. These differences notwithstanding, both campaign biographies and pious memoirs went one step beyond the biographies of male merchants and female missionaries. Mercantile and missionary lives, as readers attested in their diaries, certainly offered examples of public activity. They also represented the two sides of the middle-class cultural crusade: the celebration of a liberal, capitalist society and ethic and the rise of evangelical Protestantism and social reform. Campaign lives and pious memoirs went further not in their social visions but in their emphasis on biography reading itself as a source of individual opportunity. When Van Buren's biographer referred to the lives of Washington, Franklin, and Henry that readers would (or should) know from having read other biographies, and when Sarah Louisa Taylor's biographer quoted her comments on reading the life of Ann Judson, they suggested the power of the genre.

That power was nowhere more apparent than in the work of William Makepeace Thayer, the preacher and editor who enjoyed a forty-year career

The spines of William Makepeace Thayer's books suggested their contents. The title of *The Bobbin Boy* appears within the ladder of success that leads Nathaniel Banks to the Massachusetts governor's mansion, while *The Printer Boy,* Benjamin Franklin, appears at his press, complete with kite, key, and lightning overhead. (Books in author's collection; photograph by Ted Cook)

writing biographies for young readers. Beginning in the late 1850s, Thayer's biographies of successful men and women built upon both the middle-class ideology of the merchants' and missionaries' lives and the self-reflexiveness about biography found in the campaign biographies and the pious memoirs. Born in 1820 to a merchant-manufacturer father and a mother of "limited education and unsatisfied literary longings," Thayer craved education from childhood. After completing his degree at Brown University, he studied theology and began teaching; from 1849 until 1857 he was pastor of the Congregational Church in Ashland, Massachusetts. He redirected his work toward the literary when throat trouble forced him to resign his pastorate. In 1857 he produced *The Poor Boy and Merchant Prince,* a guide to success for young men (particularly those "from twelve to twenty years of age" and those "who are serving in the capacity of employees, or are engaged in business for themselves") that drew its lessons from the life of the Massachusetts manufacturing magnate Amos Lawrence. Two years later he wrote a companion volume ("designed for girls from ten to eighteen years of age," though "persons of any age" could learn from it), *The Poor Girl and True Woman,* whose central character was Mary Lyon, founder of Mount Holyoke Female Seminary. Thayer organized these books topically, different chapters describing various virtues and keys to success. For instance, the thirty-two chapters of *The Poor Girl and True Woman* included "Female Influence," "A True Sister," "Amiability," "Mental Culture," "Industry," "Self-Reliance," "Decision," and finally "Piety." These were not so much biographies as advice manuals whose lessons came from the lives of successful men and women.[77]

With *The Bobbin Boy,* his 1860 biography of Massachusetts governor Nathaniel Banks, Thayer hit upon the formula he would employ for almost four decades. Here he narrated the life of one subject from early childhood to adulthood, with numerous references to other historical figures who shared similar attributes. The objective, as Thayer would repeat in preface after preface, was to show "how it was done" — "it" being the rise from humble beginnings to economic or political success. The "how" was always the same: perseverance, industry, and especially self-education, all themes he had emphasized in *The Poor Boy and Merchant Prince* and *The Poor Girl and True Woman,* now organized into biographical narratives. In his early works Thayer celebrated New England manufacturing and reform as the source of self-making. The success of Lawrence and Banks began in the environment of the mills, and Lyon's importance lay in her role as school founder. During the 1860s Thayer's focus would broaden. Rewriting Lincoln's life (originally called *The Pioneer Boy*) as "From Pioneer Home to White House," he inaugurated the "Log Cabin to White House" theme he would subsequently use in lives of Washington, Garfield, and Grant. In all his biographies Thayer gave the reader what he claimed to have desired in his own boyhood: lives replete with anecdote and written in a "colloquial style," including conversation.[78]

What made Thayer's biographies extraordinary was the layers of biography they contained: the subjects read biographies, and Thayer interspersed the central narratives with biographical anecdotes of other figures, from ancient times to modern America. *The Bobbin Boy,* meaningfully subtitled "How Nat Got His Learning," provides a useful example. In this book young Nat (who is never identified by last name, although the steps of his career make his identity clear) is "almost overcome" when he must leave school to work in the factory for his family's support. His mother reassures him, however, that "the manufacturing company have a good library for the operatives." To Nat's complaint that he will have little time to read after working a fourteen-hour day, his mother responds, "You will find as much time to acquire knowledge as ever Dr. Franklin did, and many other men who have been distinguished." Nat immediately gains encouragement, asking his mother, "Do you suppose that the life of Dr. Franklin or the life of Patrick Henry will be in the library at the factory?" Both are, of course, and Nat's biographical education begins. In addition to these lives, he reads a biography of Jefferson, and models his own actions on all three. Like Franklin, Nat organizes self-improvement societies and reading clubs; like Henry, he develops his oratorical skills; from Jefferson, he draws the ardent democratic and egalitarian spirit that will make him a Jacksonian and eventually a Republican by 1860. As a factory boy Nat also attends a lecture on the life of Count Rumford, "a self-made man, of the stamp of Dr. Franklin and others, whose biographies our young hearer had read with the deepest interest."[79]

Throughout Nat's biographical education, Thayer inserts additional anecdotes of other men to provide parallels to Nat's virtues and additional evidence of their efficacy. For instance, to buttress the claim that "no man ever accomplished much who was afraid of doing work beneath his dignity," Thayer adduces no fewer than nine examples, from Franklin and Washington to the portraitist John Opie (who sawed wood as a boy) and the physiologist John Hunter (who began as a carpenter). Nine examples similarly illustrate "distinguished men, who were very backward scholars in youth." Most important here, Thayer mentions four men who were, like

Nat, influenced by the biographies they read: the painter Guido by the life of Michelangelo, Franklin by Cotton Mather's life, Alfieri by Plutarch's *Lives,* and Loyola by the *Lives of the Saints.* Biographies pile upon biographies in Thayer's books. The final sentence of *The Bobbin Boy*—"Imitate it [Nat's success], then, by cultivating those traits of character which proved the elements of his success"—may be advising youthful readers to imitate Nat's habit of reading biographies as surely as it commends the virtues of industry and patience.[80]

Forty years later, Thayer discussed a success story that stemmed from his work. Apparently *The Bobbin Boy,* which described the Young Men's Debating Society of Boston, "fell into the hands of a young man nineteen years old, who was learning the wheelwright's trade. He was captured by the account of the debating society contained therein, and wondered if he and other youths in the village could not organize [a debating society] for mutual improvement." The young man's brothers and friends joined him, and the society succeeded. The results "changed the whole current of affairs in the family." The young man, who now aspired to "something higher and nobler, . . . dropped his trade, fitted for college, and became a popular preacher; another became a superintendent of schools in Massachusetts; and three became successful merchants, one of the three first becoming a graduate of Amherst College. The debating society did it." The language in which Thayer described this young man's inspiration was revealing: that Nat's story "captured" him suggested the potency Thayer attributed to biography.[81]

Thayer's project was twofold: he sought at once to instill the virtues and ideology associated with the northern middle class in young men (after *The Poor Girl and True Woman,* it would be thirty-seven years before he returned to female subjects in *Women Who Win*) and to celebrate that ideology itself as a route to individual success and social order and progress. Through industry, honesty, and biography reading, a young man like Nat or Thayer's dutiful reader could rise from a poor background to the professional ranks. If young men followed Thayer's precepts, the scourges that moralists like Thayer perceived in midcentury society (such as intemperance and hypocrisy) could be eliminated. The success story of Nathaniel Banks at once testified to the power of middle-class values and legitimated them. Yet Thayer's work was descriptive as well as prescriptive. As we have seen, young men like George Anderson Mercer and Launcelot Minor Blackford actually did read the lives of Henry and Franklin as models for their own conduct before Thayer began writing his biographies. Thayer's Nat, however exemplary, was thus not unique. Herein lay the definition of "character" at the heart of midcentury didactic biography: not the unique talents and traits of a celebrated figure, but precisely that bundle of characteristics that a reader could emulate.

Two Readers' Worlds

Nobody was ever just a reader. Nineteenth-century authors and critics knew as much: they prescribed biography reading (and reading in general) for its utility in the larger business of life, spiritual or secular. It is easily possible to imagine how that larger business helped shape what and how people read. When they left rich diaries, we can do more than imagine: we can begin to reconstruct the connections between biographical reading and larger worlds of experience. We now turn briefly to two such worlds from the decade between 1833 and 1843. Michael Floy, a devout Methodist and junior partner in his family's nursery business, lived in New York City's Bowery Village and began a diary in 1833, when he was twenty-five. In it he recorded the business of everyday life: producing new dahlias at the Floy nursery, teaching in a Sunday school, courting and eventually marrying. Julia Parker, the well-educated daughter of a Vermont physician, left home in June 1841 to teach at a girls' academy in Germantown, Pennsylvania. She was twenty-three. While she lived far from home, her diary recorded new experiences: visiting attractions in Philadelphia, preparing lessons for her students, unexpectedly finding her Episcopalian faith renewed. Floy and Parker both read widely and enthusiastically. Floy detailed where he bought books, what he read, what he thought of authors' literary styles and moral purposes. In the four years he kept his diary— he wrote the last entry in January 1837 and died four months later— he read and commented on more than twenty biographies. Parker's diary survives only in fragments (the parts published in an 1871 memorial volume), but it too contains lively descriptions of books, including nine biographies. In her case, biography served more than herself, for she read from biographies in her classroom. Personal circumstances—where they lived, what they considered important, what part reading played in the fabric of their lives—helped shape these young adults' biographical reading. At the same time, what they read and how they read depended upon the books available to them and the critical apparatus they brought to their reading.[1]

In the four years he kept his diary, Michael Floy recorded purchasing over two hundred books and reading more than a hundred.[2] A quarter of the books he read were biographies, ranging in topic from George Washington to Miss Mary Tooker (a pious Christian who had died young) and in original publication date from the seventeenth century to the year Floy read them. Floy did not simply read biographies; he wrote about their charms and defects *as* biographies. In October 1833, three weeks into the diary, he wrote that "I intend now to confine myself to reading biographies," a resolution he seems to have kept for the next four months. Even after this, when his reading broadened, he continued to read biographies often. Floy also echoed the critique of novels that had been especially prevalent around the turn of the century and persisted in Methodist teaching: he wrote in March 1835 that "I fully believe the novels and romances have made a greater part of the prostitutes in the world, to say nothing of the many miserable matches." Floy, in other words, thought about his reading in terms of genre, embracing some genres while rejecting others.[3]

Three factors predominantly shaped Michael Floy's biographical reading: the religious revivalism of the "Second Great Awakening" that spurred both individual commitment and denominational organization, the revolution in publishing that made a new world of books available to readers like him, and prevailing ideas about biography that encouraged (but did not force) him to read in particular ways. Floy had been born again at the Allen Street revival of 1828. When he began the diary he was an active church member, Sunday school teacher, and regular participant in various reform societies, including an antislavery society. Among the twenty-five biographies Floy recorded reading, sixteen were religious in nature. Several were British works that had sold steadily in America since the colonial period and been reissued by countless American printers and publishers: Philip Doddridge's *Life of Col. James Gardiner* (the "Christian soldier"), Aikin's *Life of John Howard,* the life of Harriet Newell, and Gilbert Burnet's lives of Sir Matthew Hale, John Wilmot (earl of Rochester), and Bishop William Bedell.[4] Others were more recent productions, most of them published originally in London and reprinted in the United States shortly before Floy read them. Significantly, most of Floy's religious biographies treated subjects who had devoted their piety to public endeavors like philanthropy and religious service, such as John Howard's work in prison reform and Harriet Newell's missionary work in India. Perhaps because he had already experienced conversion, Floy did not generally read biographies that focused primarily on their subjects' conversion experiences; rather, he read works that might provide patterns for a religious life after being reborn.

Floy's reading was connected materially and intellectually to his membership in the Methodist Church during its years of denominational organization. By the 1830s Methodism, which had begun as a dissenting belief, had become one of the fastest-growing, most populous denominations in the United States. An increasingly centralized denominational authority fostered and rationalized that growth, sending preachers to new districts and supervising an active program of publishing.[5] It is significant that at least four of the religious lives Floy read, plus another he mentioned buying but did not speak of reading, were reprinted in the United States by B. Waugh and T. Mason, the New York printers for the Methodist Episcopal Church. Beverly Waugh, whom Floy heard preach at least twice, was the principal book agent of New York's Methodist Book Concern in the 1830s; he would become bishop of the Methodist Episcopal Church in 1836.[6] Floy may have bought these works through a local bookseller or at the offices of Waugh and Mason, but in either case he may have considered the Methodist Episcopal imprimatur a sign of their value. His religious biographical reading included leaders of the church as well as exemplars of general piety: two of the Waugh and Mason vol-

umes were Richard Watson's *The Life of the Reverend John Wesley . . . Founder of the Methodist Societies* (1832) and Thomas Jackson's *Memoirs of the Life and Writings of the Rev. Richard Watson, Late Secretary to the Wesleyan Missionary Society* (1834), published just after Watson died. Moreover, Floy read Methodist biography through a Methodist lens. Robert Southey's biography of Wesley—not printed by Waugh and Mason, and attacked by Richard Watson in a pamphlet defending Wesley against Southey's "misrepresentations"—might be the work of "a fine writer, possessing much shrewdness and wit," but Floy, "shocked at Mr. Southey's impiety," refused to finish it. He clearly preferred Watson's biography of Wesley. Floy's praise was not confined to Methodist publications or subjects; about the subject of another biography he wrote, "I do not mind his Calvinism; he was a very pious useful man, that is enough for me."[7] But he was clearly sensitive to denominational lines in an era of rising denominationalism.

The rise of religious publishing in the 1830s was part of a larger revolution in print whose benefits Floy reaped. In April 1836, Floy's biographical reading took a secular turn. He read lives of Napoleon, Charlemagne, Nelson, Washington, Charles XII, and several noted explorers, and wrote that "History now engages me more than anything else." Specifically, all but one of the secular biographies Floy read belonged to a single publisher's series, the Harper's Family Library. Like the Waugh and Mason imprint for a Methodist reader, the Harper's Family Library name promised something: entertaining works that might improve the reader— in other words, no novels. Series like the Family Library depended on recognition from readers like Floy, who would buy future volumes on the basis of the series' name if they recognized them as part of an ever-expanding whole. And Michael Floy was just the sort of reader Harper's envisioned. When he spotted a young man reading a Family Library volume on a railway car, procured new volumes as they appeared, and complained about the Harpers' attempt to make more money by splitting the biography of Washington into two volumes, Floy demonstrated his understanding of the series as a publisher's device. He understood the mechanisms of the literary market that was emerging in his own day (in fact, he submitted a manuscript of his own, a mathematical treatise, to a Philadelphia publisher)—but he also participated in that market enthusiastically, grateful for "such privileges of reading as I now have."[8]

In judging biographies, Floy applied standards of moral and literary value that fused several concepts about the genre. One response reveals this combination: "Finished reading the Life of Bramwell (a pretty name). He was a holy, useful man, but his biographers did not understand the nature of a biography. They deal in general characteristics without particularizing. This is very unfortunate for Bramwell, as we learn that he was very popular and useful, and do not know how to do to imitate him, and consequently not much practical benefit is to be derived from the book." Biographer, subject, and reader all entered into Floy's consideration. The biographer's job was to deal in particulars rather than generalities; having failed to do so, Bramwell's biographers violated Floy's idea of the genre. On the one hand, the biographers' failure was "very unfortunate for Bramwell," the subject: justice had not been done him, and Floy could report only that he was holy, popular, and useful. On the other hand, the failure was one of poor didacticism. Because excessive generality made readerly emulation impossible, the book had no "practical benefit." Floy's commentary echoed two related ideas of biography prevalent in the early republic— that only through specificity could a subject receive just treatment and become known to the reader, and that the ultimate purpose of specificity was didactic, offering something for the reader to imitate or aspire to. When Floy liked a biography, he occasionally commented on its specifics. He read Aikin's *Life of Howard* because "I did not know precisely the nature of his benevolence," and finished the book "highly edified."[9]

Incipient romanticism mingled with this largely religious didacticism. Floy's interest in "genius" suggested contact with romantic ideas, even before Carlyle's *On Heroes and Hero-Worship* (1840) codified romantic hero-worship most popularly. Floy wrote that he loved geniuses, who were "a particular race of beings," and he often judged whether a biographical subject had been of this caliber. This fascination with genius in America had developed during and immediately after the Napoleonic era, as Americans attempted to make sense of Bonaparte's larger-than-life personality and actions within moral and political codes that condemned his militarism and autocracy. Lives of Napoleon were among the most heavily borrowed biographies in American libraries, and the Harper's Family Library included two works on him (John Gibson Lockhart's two-volume biography and *The Court and Camp of Bonaparte*) and another on Josephine. Floy shared this fascination. In a lengthy description of Lockhart's two volumes, he weighed his admiration of Napoleon's "astonishing vigor and ardor of soul" against his belief that Napoleon was "an in-grain bad man." Floy resolved this dilemma by returning to his own religious frame of reference: "I think I have derived instruction from the

work. Let me use as much exertion to secure a heavenly as Napoleon did to secure an earthly crown. I do admire an ardent soul."[10] Edging toward romanticism, Michael Floy's response to this biography nonetheless remained rooted in his personal piety and the didactic vision of the genre.

What made a "good" biography for Michael Floy, besides specificity? Like many critics of the period, Floy argued that biographers should be transparent, allowing the subjects to speak for themselves whenever possible and their actions to dominate the stage. He criticized biographers for "flashy" or "gaudy" prose and especially faulted James K. Paulding's *Life of Washington,* a two-volume work in Harper's Family Library. He compared Paulding's "high sounding sentences" and trite, "pretty similes" unfavorably with the "manly, austere, Thucydidean style of Lockhart, or the sweet, fascinating style of Southey, or the sprightly style of James's Charlemagne." The contrast pitted the authorial self-indulgence of Paulding's phraseology against three styles that accentuated the subject rather than the biographer. In this comparison Floy also raised the issue of nationality: not only was Paulding the only American among these biographers, but his florid style reminded Floy of "all the American authors" he had read. In his case, "American biography" was not necessarily a literary form to be desired or admired—no matter what contemporary critics were calling for.[11]

Michael Floy's biographical reading suggests several hypotheses about biographical experience in the 1830s. First, at least in Floy's case the American experience of biography was quite different from "American biography." Washington was the only subject whose life was associated with the nation, and almost all the biographies he read were republications of English works. In this, Floy was not alone. Thanks to the lack of international copyright laws and the relative paucity of American-written lives of Americans in the 1830s, both religious publishers and secular firms produced more biographies of European than of American origin. Second, at least two worlds of biography existed, produced in different parts of the publishing universe, and neither was a discrete genre of literature. Religious biography was part of the larger constellation of evangelical literature that included myriad sorts of moral tracts. Secular lives of Charlemagne and Napoleon were part of a larger category, "history," that intrigued Floy in 1836. Indeed, the pattern of Floy's reading indicated this distinction: all the biographies he read from 1833 until January 1836 were religious lives, and all after May 1836 were secular. So did the ways he discussed the works: his comments on religious biographies related almost entirely to the subjects' writings and examples, while his remarks about historical lives dealt far more with the biographers' styles. Perhaps this difference reflected the texts themselves. Religious lives tended to contain numerous extracts from their subjects' own writings, whereas Southey's, Lockhart's, and Paulding's works were dominated by their authors' narratives—and hence contained far more "style" to praise or condemn. But the difference also stemmed from the categories into which Floy placed them, and the purposes of those categories. Religious literature (including Christian biography) was explicitly didactic, while history (including secular biography) belonged to belles-lettres and was thus more conducive to literary (as opposed to moral) readings. Finally, the ways Floy read biographies—religious and secular, as his comments on Napoleon suggested—tended to echo the ways that contemporary biographers prefaced them and contemporary critics commented on the genre: as pleasurable instructions, sources of knowledge about particular individuals, and sources of examples and inspiration for readers' lives.

Julia Parker never swore off novels and never resolved to confine her reading to a particular genre. Her tastes were more catholic than Michael Floy's, too. She read novels, biographies, literary magazines, scientific treatises, religious history, and the *Episcopal Manual*. When a friend criticized fiction "on the ground of its utility, as well as that of its moral tendency," Parker disagreed. She had just finished Theodore S. Fay's "beautiful and instructive" novel *Norman Leslie,* which she recommended for several reasons: its hero was not "entirely enveloped in the mantle of perfection" but was still admirable; it contained "fine description of natural scenery," and it illustrated "some striking traits of American character." Not only did she relish a good novel; she also noted and praised Americanness (even if she did not elaborate what strikingly American traits *Norman Leslie* revealed). Except for acknowledging that her friend had "mentioned the Memoirs of Josephine published by the Harpers," Parker rarely wrote about the publication details of her books.[12] Perhaps she was less conscious of them than Floy, a New Yorker who might have procured many of his books directly from their publishers. However, she too benefited from the "privileges of reading" in an era of expanding book production and distribution. *Norman Leslie,* the *Memoirs of Josephine,* and several other works Parker mentioned were Harper and Brothers publications, and she read at least five books published by the leading Philadelphia firm, Carey, Lea, and Blanchard. Some of this reading occurred before she left Vermont

for Philadelphia, suggesting that a variety of metropolitan productions circulated well outside the metropolis. If their tastes differed, Floy and Parker shared the ability to choose books that accorded with those tastes—easy access that the publishing revolution had made possible.

Romantic literary tastes and intellectual ambition, not religious revivalism, influenced Julia Parker's biographical reading most emphatically. By her late teens Parker had read Milton, Cowper, Shakespeare, Byron, Mrs. Hemans, Scott, and Burns. In August 1840 (when she was twenty-two) she entered an academy in Keene, New Hampshire, "for the prosecution of my literary schemes especially." There she hoped to "review some particular branches of study, and to practice the colloquial use of the French and Italian languages," which she already knew how to read. An admirer of literary "genius" and "lover of a purely intellectual feast," she read Hayley's *Life of Cowper,* Boswell's *Life of Johnson,* and Carlyle's *Life of Schiller.* The *Life of Schiller* inspired her to learn German, "the vehicle of such transcendent elevation and originality of thought." Geographically distant from Emerson's and Fuller's Boston and Concord, Parker nonetheless expressed Transcendentalist sentiments. When the liberal Unitarian minister William Ellery Channing died two years later, Parker—now teaching in Philadelphia—wrote a memorial essay to the man who had inspired several of the Transcendentalists. Channing's thoughts, she claimed, "fan the spark of divinity within; kindle into a holy flame the generous emotions of the soul; reveal to it a consciousness of its wondrous capabilities, and the great end of being and action, and incite it, by the highest and purest motives, to the fulfilment of its sublime destiny."[13]

In the lives of literary figures, especially women, Parker found inspirations for the "spark of divinity" within herself. Reading the life of Germaine de Staël shortly after moving to Germantown in June 1841, Parker declared, "I love to read of the splendid qualities that made up her character. What a compliment, that Bonaparte dared not have her in his dominions by reason of her powerful influence." Four weeks later, after reading extracts from de Staël's life to her students, the young schoolteacher went further: "I cannot contemplate a mind like hers without the most ardent longing to turn aside from the beaten track of life, and explore those rich fields of observation, those secret recesses of thought, that the gifted *few* alone may enter. I feel immortal longings rise within me. I would consecrate my life, yea, my whole life, to improvement, — to the perfection of my whole nature. Would that I were the favored child of knowledge,

placed in the midst of her treasures, initiated into her deep mysteries. Surely I would be what I am not." Parker started reading the memoirs of Hannah More the next day, for "I love to read the biography of those gifted ones whose deep and penetrating minds were sanctified by holiness and illuminated by light from heaven." When she came to the "base ingratitude" and "malignant barbarity" that More had received for her "noble and disinterested efforts," Parker drew a lesson for herself. Even if kindness and humanity were little rewarded, "may I ever persevere in my aims, to benefit my fellow-creatures, and leave the result to God. Would that I could imitate her in her *humility* and practise her non-conformity to this deluding world." For Julia Parker, religion and romanticism were two sides of the same coin—not, as for Floy, potential opposites, with religious precepts providing shelter from the romantic uncertainties aroused by men like Napoleon. For Parker, minds like de Staël's, Johnson's, and Milton's were rays from heaven, "a spark of the Infinite and Eternal Spirit." Then again, her Napoleon was hardly the titan whose contradictions Floy tried to reconcile; he was the powerful ruler awed by Madame de Staël's greater influence. The women of genius whom Parker admired possessed no contradictions to be reconciled, at least not for a reader who prized female intellect.[14]

Parker used biographies in her Germantown classroom for two distinct reasons: to provide her students with female models of intellect and goodness, and to instill American patriotism in them. In her first months as a teacher, Parker was experiencing a spiritual rebirth. She started attending Episcopal services, read in William H. Wilmer's *Episcopal Manual,* and "most earnestly desire[d] to be a member of some church." Far from home and family, she found herself reflecting on the state of her soul. Perhaps spiritual introspection occurred as she considered her own influence over her students. When she "gave our pupils portions of the Biography of Hannah More," Parker wanted "to present to their consideration those traits in the character of this excellent woman, that the emulation of them may conduce to their present and eternal good. . . . Oh! when I stand at the judgment-seat, may it be my happiness to know that some *one,* at least, may have been led in the path to virtue and Heaven, by my instrumentality!" Parker had already told her class about Margaret Miller Davidson, the teenaged, recently deceased poet whose memoir Washington Irving had written. Parker called Davidson "all that was lovely, as well as intellectually great"—in other words, a perfect specimen of young womanhood to recommend to students—*and* "A sparkling gem in the constellation of American Literature." For patriotic education, however, biographies of men worked best. On October 23, 1841, she "gave to the young ladies of the school a biography of Patrick Henry." Quoting William Wirt's book almost verbatim into her diary, Parker called Henry "a masterpiece from the hand of nature, and so perfect, as the author remarks, that she would not allow art to touch him." Parker picked up on precisely the passage that Thomas Jefferson had criticized as too "flowery": Henry's oratory "was like the mountain torrent, carrying with it the flowers and the verdure of the soil over which it forced its irresistible course." Even if her students would not become political leaders or orators, the lives of Henry and Washington could benefit them. For Parker agreed with *Godey's* editor Sarah Josepha Hale, another woman of intellect whom she admired, that woman was "the guide and director of mind from its first opening." Her students had to be patriotic Americans for their own sake and for their future children's.[15]

Neither Michael Floy nor Julia Parker was the typical American biography reader. Both read more widely than most Americans probably did, and both commented at length upon their reading in diaries that have somehow survived into the twentieth century. Indeed, the differences between their biographical experiences illustrate how illusory the very notion of a "typical" reader is. Floy and Parker were roughly contemporaries (Floy was born ten years earlier, but both kept diaries in their early to middle twenties). Both were modestly well-educated, avid readers. But they read biographies differently, and not only because of the obvious matter of gender. Acutely sensitive to genre, Floy noted frequently how well a biographer had performed his role. Parker almost never did; she focused entirely on the subject, not the biographer. Despite these differences, Floy and Parker and numerous other Americans of their generation brought common critical languages to biographical reading: the long-familiar language of emulation, in which the lives of famous men and women could provide models of virtue and deed for the impressionable reader to follow; and the newer romantic language that Floy edged toward and Parker embraced, the philosophy epitomized by the poetry Parker copied into her diary the day she described Margaret Miller Davidson's biography. Actually, Parker misquoted Longfellow, unwittingly fusing romanticism and moral didacticism (and removing his reference to "men"). Where the seventh stanza of "A Psalm of Life" began "Lives of great men all remind us," the young schoolteacher wrote, "Lives of goodness must remind us / We can make our lives sublime." [16]

CHAPTER 3

Truth and Tradition, Nation and Section, 1820–1860

Accept my thanks for the two interesting volumes, in which you have commemorated the Women of the Revolution. . . . You ask my opinion, and desire me to express it frankly and plainly. In the first place then, my opinion is, that you have manfully resisted a temptation, which I feared would prove your greatest stumbling block: the mass of traditions, with which you could not fail to be encumbered. . . . Traditions have generally a foundation in truth, but they derive numerous accessions in a little time from ignorance, credulity, and a love of the marvellous. —Jared Sparks to Elizabeth F. Ellet, November 16, 1848

Commemorating America's worthies remained a foremost impulse to biography in the four decades after Joseph Delaplaine's *Repository of the Lives and Portraits of Distinguished Americans.* But that impulse took a new form, presaged in the late 1810s by Wirt's life of Patrick Henry. Wirt had paid tribute to a prominent American and sought to contribute to writing the national history—intertwined but potentially conflicting objectives. After all, those who would place figures into the narrative of the nation's past generally wanted to place them there in the most positive light. To resolve the conflict, historical biographers from the 1820s on sought to distinguish unsubstantiated lore ("tradition") from verifiable fact ("truth"). Their biographical method had more in common with history writing than with Johnsonian visions of portraying character. If a subject's "character" was to emerge, it came out of the documents that the biographer amassed and presented. As a result, these books emphasized subjects' public lives, deeds, and characters. However different from earlier portrait pantheons or contemporaneous campaign biographies, these historical biographies nonetheless extended the dominance of the public sphere in biography writing, through the kind of evidence they took to be central as much as through decisions not to discuss the private.

Jared Sparks was at the center of the new, historical biography. Harvard-educated historian and editor, Sparks first wrote about biography in 1818 when American historical biography was in its infancy. Its subjects were recently deceased, their lives belonged to the recent past, and their acquaintances and relatives remained to share stories with the biographer. Sparks criticized such reliance on "tradition" and began collecting documents of the American Revolution and its central figures in order to preserve the "true" or "authentic" history of the American past. From the late 1820s through the 1840s, he remained America's foremost documentary historian. Sparks's efforts coincided with those of the state historical societies founded in these same years for similar purposes. His biographical work reached its apogee in the 1830s when he edited the Library of American Biography, the first attempt at a definitive national biography based upon the principle of documentary evidence. Sparks and his work encouraged numerous others to write biographies along his model. Many of these writers corresponded with him, asked him about potential sources of evidence, and sent their work for his approbation.

Among the most ambitious correspondents in Sparks's network was Elizabeth F. Ellet. In *The Women of the American Revolution* (1848–50), Ellet drew upon Sparks's expertise and methods but questioned how well those methods could reveal women's lives. Ellet sought Sparks's guidance and encouragement when she decided to search for Revolutionary women, but she also sought information—anecdotal as well as documentary—from her subjects' relatives and friends, the very individuals whom Sparks considered the root of suspect "tradition." In several ways Ellet attempted to marry sentiment to scholarship, the world of women's writing and literary magazines to the realm of Sparksian history writing. She sought an audience of women readers and of historians like Sparks. She explained her project as both an addition to American historical literature and a tribute to women whose virtues and actions had helped win independence. She drew on the archive, citing written documents and published histories, and on the home, relating her "heroines' " family stories as part of national history. And she couched it all in Sparksian rhetoric—describing how she had tested family traditions against documentary evidence and risked alienating her subjects' descendants by her faithfulness to "truth." Beneath that rhetoric, however, lay a challenge to Sparks's focus on the public sphere: how could his methods be applied to the biographies of those who had left little written evidence of their lives and deeds?

Ellet's work was part of a larger movement within American historical biography by the 1840s. In the twenty years before civil war split the union, writers increasingly used the historians' methods to add previously neglected figures or whole categories of figures to the national history. This trend, visible even in the "second series" of Sparks's own Library of American Biography, implied a more inclusive notion of the American past and its worthy biographical subjects. Books like Griffith McRee's life of a North Carolinian patriot of the Revolution and William Cooper Nell's *The Colored Patriots of the American Revolution* aimed, through research in primary documents, to create a broader vision of who had won American independence. Conversely, biographers could use the scholarly methods in order to challenge the very idea of a shared national history. Leading southern intellectuals challenged the dominance of New Englanders in American history writing and of New England in the story of America's past. William Gilmore Simms, the foremost of these southerners, wrote biographies to evoke the spirit of his region and biographical criticism to exhort other southerners to do the same. Sparks downplayed the biographer's emotional connection to his subject, even if his immediate circle used his method to promote their own ideologies and New England's preeminence in the American past. Simms like Ellet suggested that attachment — sentimental, political, or regional — could combine with documentary truth to create a more accurate American history.

Defining Historical Biography

When Jared Sparks began his historical and biographical work in the 1820s, American history writing was in the midst of change. On the one hand, the *Atlantic Magazine* catalogued the problems that faced the American biographer: "The sources of information are scattered and imperfect; . . . funeral discourses are, with very few exceptions, extravagantly panegyrical, acrimoniously sectarian, or disgustingly fanaticall." Unlike European biographers, whose job had been made easier by previous compilers of papers, American biographers encountered great difficulty "collecting authentic materials."[1] On the other hand, the decade witnessed the flowering of the historical-society movement in the United States. Before 1820, only a handful of historical societies existed in America, all in the Northeast. In the 1820s, bibliophiles, writers, and professional men established societies in ten more states throughout New England and the Old Northwest. Southerners would follow suit in the 1830s, and by the 1840s numerous towns as well as states would have historical societies. In all, over a hundred societies existed in the United States before 1860, many of them the creations of a few men who collected papers, documents, and books pertaining to state or local history. Historical societies addressed precisely the problem the *Atlantic Magazine* lamented: the dearth of "authentic" materials for writing American history. They aimed above all to preserve the histories of their states or towns, by collecting documents and, if they could afford to, publishing them in volumes called collections or proceedings.[2]

The movement had begun in Massachusetts, and one key impetus for founding societies elsewhere was the concern that Massachusetts writers would distort the nation's history by placing Bay State men and events firmly in the foreground. When Jeremy Belknap and his associates founded the Massachusetts Historical Society in the 1790s, they envisioned it as the hub of a network of allied societies, all forwarding their findings to Boston. Local societies did form elsewhere in New England but maintained independence from the MHS. Indeed, one historian has called the historical-society movement and the rush to collect documents "a national movement, locally inspired" — a fitting phrase, given the proliferation of societies dedicated to gathering the surviving fragments of a particular state's or town's history.[3] Nonetheless, if any single place remained central to American history writing, it was Massachusetts. The Bay State claimed two of the premier historical societies, the MHS and the American Antiquarian Society (which had an explicitly national, not local, focus from its founding in 1812); Massachusetts men like George Bancroft, William Hickling Prescott, and Francis Parkman were at work by the 1830s on massive histories of the United States and other nations; Massachusetts was in the forefront of the movement to save and commemorate historic places like Bunker Hill. Some participants in the Massachusetts crusade to preserve and write American history belonged to the Federalist elite that had gone into political eclipse by the 1820s and redirected its efforts toward placing its conservative, hierarchical, New England–centered stamp on American history. Others wrote history (or, like Nathaniel Hawthorne, historical fiction) in order to interpret the Puritan past and its legacy: history writing became a major weapon in the arsenals of those who would condemn Puritan hypocrisy or defend Puritan idealism. Most of the prominent Massachusetts historians were Harvard educated; many were Unitarians.[4]

Jared Sparks attended Harvard, began professional life as a Unitarian minister, and belonged to this circle of historians — but did not make his historical reputation either as a proponent of New England's primacy or as a warrior in the battles over Puritanism. In his review of Wirt's *Sketches of the Life and Character of Patrick Henry,* written while he was editor of the *North American Review* in 1818, Sparks certainly allied himself with his fellow editor William Tudor and former president John Adams in attacking Wirt's claims for Virginian primacy in the Revolution. At this early date (Sparks was twenty-nine and had not written any historical works or begun collecting historical documents), the review was part of the New England Federalists' drive for cultural authority, of which the *North American* was fast becoming the chief literary exponent. But the review was also Sparks's first published statement about the genre of biography, significant in light of his future career. While he invoked familiar pieties about biography's instructive purpose, Sparks also worried whether "the taste, which has become so prevalent, for biographical sketches, notices, and anecdotes" was "favourable . . . to the interests of truth and letters." He disputed the Johnsonian notion that any man could deservedly become the subject of biography. The biographer of an ordinary person could lapse all too easily into fiction, for "his materials are few—he is obliged to resort to his invention for incidents, and to his fancy for embellishments." Beyond the conventional contrast between biography and novel, Sparks suggested that the same divisions between fact and fiction existed within biography itself. Even a figure as nationally prominent as Patrick Henry had left too few materials for a successful biography, Sparks concluded: "We have scarcely any thing but tradition to tell us, that such a man [as Wirt's version of Henry] existed."[5] The opposition here was between verifiable, documented fact and "tradition"—unsupported (and unsupportable) anecdotal reminiscence or orally transmitted lore. Sparks distinguished truth not just from the products of the imagination, but from the knowledge derived from an older oral culture as well. "Truth" emerged from the assiduous collection of documented facts.

Within a decade, Sparks devoted his life to that collection. He lost interest in the ministry by 1823 and burned his sermon notes the following year. Two financial transactions in 1824 symbolized his change of career: he sold his theological library and bought the *North American Review* (with the assistance of several backers). He also embarked upon two historical projects. One, collecting and publishing George Washington's papers, began with journeys to Mount Vernon and Europe and forays into governmental archives and family papers. Sparks was not alone in his search; historical writers and compilers crossed paths in American and European archives throughout the 1820s and 1830s, looking for state papers and correspondence. Sparks's other project, a biography of the American traveler John Ledyard (1828), followed the "life and letters" model of several other biographies of the period such as James T. Austin's *Life of Elbridge Gerry* (published the same year). Hilliard and Brown, his publishers, advertised that the author's research had uncovered enough "materials for a full and

Jared Sparks was forty-two when Thomas Sully painted this romantic portrait in 1831. At work on his biography of Gouverneur Morris, Sparks would envision the Library of American Biography the following year. (Courtesy Reynolda House, Museum of American Art, Winston-Salem, North Carolina)

authentic biography." Sparks's preface reinforced this: "All the papers that have been used are entitled to the credit of unquestionable authority."[6] The central terms here were "authentic" and "authority," and authenticity came from the trustworthiness ("credit") of the original document.

Biography, to Sparks, was always a branch of history. Even if biography had its own characteristics (for instance, recording the life of an individual), its paramount rule was the same as history's: to seek "truth" through documentary evidence. Anything not in the documents could be relegated to the subordinate status of "tradition." For Sparks, this included most incidents of private life and dispute. As Sparks prepared to write the life of Gouverneur Morris, he declared privately to Morris's widow that he would not discuss family "dissensions" and partisan "feuds"—"with which the public has so little concern." After all, "Mr. Morris was a public man, and . . . his life is to be written for the nation and for posterity." (Since Mrs. Morris controlled Sparks's access to family papers, documents recording family discord might not come into his view anyway.) Sparks collapsed Samuel Johnson's distinction between biography and history. For Johnson and the American critics who echoed him in the early republic, biography possessed instructive value because it *differed* from history: its narratives allowed readers to view subjects' unique, personal characteristics apart from the public stage. Sparks distinguished three kinds of biography. "Historical biography," or the life and letters, contained "copious selections from letters and other original papers" that dealt with the subject's involvement in public affairs and historical events. "Personal narrative," a life and letters with the letters left out, flowed from event to event without straying into general historical discussion or getting overwhelmed by extracts. Memoirs, which were "more rambling," could treat "affairs of a private nature." Sparks pursued the first two of these but never wrote or discussed memoirs. For him—as for most American biographers of the previous generation—the public stage remained the setting for biography, even if his means of substantiating public events were more rigorous. Only one reviewer criticized Sparks on this score, contending that too many biographers of "public men" were reluctant "to admit the fact, that they ever had any private life." However, the general critical acclaim for Sparks's work suggested that his objective was widely shared.[7] By 1832, Sparks had won a reputation for writing the "authentic" history of public men.

That year, Sparks embarked upon what would become his most ambitious biographical project: the Library of American Biography. As he explained it in his journal on July 28, "The purpose is to select some of the most prominent lives, from the first settlement of the country down to the present time . . . The series will thus serve as in some degree a connected history of the country, as well as to illustrate the character and acts of some of the most illustrious men of the nation. The lives are to be written by the most competent hands that can be engaged."[8] The term "Library" came from similar publishing projects on both sides of the Atlantic, such as Harper's Family Library. The vision came from Sparks's experience as editor of the *North American Review*. Like that quarterly, his library would be a collection of biographical "articles" written by various authors, with himself as editor. Most contributors would understand this conception, having written for the *North American* themselves. Taken together, the lives would comprise a national biography in two senses. They would create a history of the nation, told through biographies of its important characters. They would also make a compendium of "authentic" biographies of major American subjects, whose lives would be lost to posterity or clouded in traditions if not preserved soon. "Literary execution" and "accuracy of facts" were the key principles: these together would provide "both authority & attraction for readers." This was not to be "a biographic dictionary." Lives without "historical value" had no place in it, and the biographies should be products of their authors' research in documentary materials, not simply compilations of facts from previous lives and funeral orations (as many biographical dictionaries were).[9]

Audience weighed heavily on Sparks's conception of the project. The library "should have a popular aspect," he wrote. Neither the authors' scholarship nor long extracts from the subjects' writings should get in the way of "a spirited narrative." "Brief & pointed notes" and "frequent references to original authorities" were "a proof of research, & a guide to further inquiry, which many readers will prize & none will dislike." But discussions of arcane details should be kept to a minimum, lest the books appeal only to the "antiquarian" (and not the general reader). Sparks explained his view of American audiences for biography several years later: personal narratives that read briskly and avoided cumbersome quotation sold well, but lives and letters "found a dull market." He knew: his life and letters of Morris had sold poorly despite favorable reviews. In requesting John McVickar to write on the Protestant Episcopal bishop John Henry Hobart, Sparks assured McVickar that the biography he wanted would not "interfere" with the forthcoming (and presumably far bulkier) edition of the bishop's "life and works." Biographies for the library would "be rather in a popular vein, & suited to readers of every description," not just the readers of clergymen's lives and sermons who would be likely to read the other work. Sparks desired broad appeal not just to instruct "all classes of readers" about the nation's past, but also to make money. Like magazines, the Library of American Biography could not continue if it did not pay, and Sparks wrote tentatively about its existence and duration in 1832 and 1833.[10]

The Library of American Biography did pay—well enough that Sparks edited ten volumes between 1834 and 1838 and another fifteen in the mid-1840s — and it won wide circulation around the nation. An Indiana lawyer and bank officer named Calvin Fletcher read from four library volumes between 1843 and 1845, admiring "the interest [Sparks] preserves throughout the brief narrative" of Benedict Arnold. A transplanted Vermonter, Fletcher especially appreciated the life of Ethan Allen, which left him "better informed about the history of my native state." Fletcher seems to have enjoyed the series' variety, too: he read the biographies of William Phips, Israel Putnam, and Lucretia Maria Davidson (all in volume 7), John Stark and Richard Montgomery as well as Allen in volume 1, and Timothy Dwight and Count Pulaski in volume 14. The *Knickerbocker* noted "that the series receives a wide diffusion," and clearly numerous library associations agreed with the *American Whig Review* that the series "should have a place in every library."[11] A survey of forty-eight contemporary published library catalogs reveals Sparks's series in thirty-three, from Keene, New Hampshire (1834), to San Francisco (1854). The Ladies' Library of Lebanon, Connecticut (1844), the Public School Library of New Orleans (1848), and the Young Men's Association of Milwaukee (1855) all owned the series, a testament to its dissemination across the nation and to different groups of potential readers.[12] Reviewers overwhelmingly praised the series, too. In 1848 the *Methodist Quarterly Review* doubted whether Sparks "will leave anything behind him which will interest the great mass of posterity more deeply than this series of biographies." This comment suggested the popular appeal that Sparks had desired from the beginning.[13]

Although most reviewers did not make this distinction, the Library of American Biography actually appeared in two "series" — the first ten volumes in the 1830s, the next fifteen in the 1840s, with two different publishers and with a six-year hiatus between them. These two installments differed from each other in significant ways. If the Library of American Biography was to be a "national biography" or create "a connected history of the country," it did so differently in the 1840s than it had in the 1830s. What began as a product of Sparks's Massachusetts, Unitarian world and an expression of that world's version of "national" history ultimately became something more truly national. We can see this change in three ways: through the people who wrote for the series, through the subjects they wrote about, and through the larger narrative of American history that the series offered.

Sparks initially wanted well-known authors, educators, and statesmen, "the best writers in every part of the country," to write for the library: George Bancroft, William Hickling Prescott, Edward Everett, former

President John Quincy Adams. These writers were predominantly Sparks's fellow Harvard graduates, many of whom had attended college with him (including three, John Gorham Palfrey and twin brothers William B. O. and Oliver W. B. Peabody, who had attended Exeter with him, too). Even the man whom Sparks sought to write lives of southern figures—Samuel Gilman, minister of the Second Independent Church of Charleston and a prominent South Carolina author—came from Massachusetts (born in Gloucester) and Harvard (class of 1811). To enlist the most prominent men, Sparks offered the broadest choice of subjects. "It is a wide field," he explained to Bancroft, and "each one may for the most part pluck the flower of his choice." Other writers—especially men outside Sparks's Harvard circle—received specific requests, based on their areas of interest or expertise. John McVickar had studied theology under Bishop Hobart and become the bishop's close friend; New York politician and man of letters Gulian C. Verplanck was slated to write on Chancellor Robert Livingston, also a political leader and scion of a prominent New York family. Regional considerations also played a role, in large part because writers needed access to their subjects' papers in order to do the expected research. Hence Sparks asked Gilman to write on Francis Marion and to inform him "to whom in Carolina I can write" for lives of other prominent Carolinians, and he asked Timothy Flint of Cincinnati to write the life of Daniel Boone. But even though he told Verplanck that the success of the series depended on enlisting authors "of known reputation in different parts of the country," Sparks relied primarily on men closer to home: only six of the nineteen library authors in the 1830s had no Harvard credentials.[14]

The twenty-six biographies in the first ten volumes of the Library of American Biography (1834–38) represented northeastern Revolutionary figures and early Massachusetts worthies most heavily. The subjects ranged from the earliest period of exploration (John Smith, Sebastian Cabot, Father Marquette) to Puritan New England (Cotton Mather, William Phips) to the Revolution (particularly military figures like Anthony Wayne, Baron Steuben, and Israel Putnam). They also included notable post-Revolutionary figures in a variety of fields: scientist David Rittenhouse and inventor Robert Fulton, novelist Charles Brockden Brown and teenaged poet Lucretia Maria Davidson, diplomat William Pinkney, ornithologist Alexander Wilson. Two volumes contained a single, book-length biography, Sparks's life of Benedict Arnold (volume 3) and Convers Francis's life of John Eliot (volume 5). The others contained two, three, or four shorter lives. Significantly, many of the most prominent figures—Washington, the Adamses, Franklin—were absent. John Quincy Adams declined to write

Samuel Adams's life, and John Adams's papers were unavailable at that moment (Bancroft had them, in order to write a life and letters of the second president, and was under obligation not to loan them to other historians or biographers). Sparks intended to write Washington's and Franklin's lives himself, but only after he had completed his editions of their papers. Indeed, procuring the necessary materials was many authors' greatest problem. Charles Wentworth Upham originally planned to write the life of Roger Williams, but the "literati" of Rhode Island's historical society were reluctant to allow "a stranger & particularly a clergyman [to] write the biography of Williams" and had previously refused access to other biographers. Upham asked Sparks to intercede with them on his behalf. By June, another obstacle emerged. James Knowles, author of the best-selling life of missionary Ann Judson, was already working on a life of Williams and refused to relinquish either the project or the materials to Upham. So Upham instead wrote the life of Sir Henry Vane, which he had proposed to Sparks from the start.[15] For now, Sparks hoped the library would commemorate and preserve from oblivion the lives of men who might not otherwise receive their biographical due. Given the authors he had enlisted, and the documents to which they possessed access, those subjects tended to be New Englanders.[16]

The most common recurring themes in the Library's first ten volumes reflected the concerns of Massachusetts, Unitarian Whigs. The critique of Puritanism loomed large, because many lives of seventeenth-century Massachusetts leaders were written by liberal Unitarians with a dim view of Puritan theology and practice. Cotton Mather received the harshest treatment. William Peabody accused him of self-delusion, particularly in the witchcraft hysteria: his times "were credulous, and he even more than the times. Hence the marvellous was often quite as welcome to him as the true." Moreover, his filiopietistic biography of his father Increase would have been better left to another writer, since the younger Mather did not address "all those peculiarities of habit, character, feeling, and domestic life, which his relation to the subject of the memoir gave him the best opportunity to know." (Apparently Peabody wished Cotton Mather had been a Boswell—or at least a Johnsonian biographer—a century before Boswell and Johnson.) Other biographers also criticized Mather: Francis Bowen blamed him for Governor William Phips's susceptibility to the witchcraft scare, and both he and Convers Francis (in the biography of John Eliot) ridiculed elements of the *Magnalia*.[17] By the 1830s, Mather had become the focal point of the dispute between liberal Unitarians and orthodox trinitarians over the legacy of the Puritan past, and the liberal side found its way into Sparks's library, predictably, given the men who wrote for it. These writers appreciated the Puritans' idealism but little else about them. The *North American Review,* which shared the Unitarian bent, generally praised the library's treatment of Puritan fathers, while the orthodox Massachusetts Sabbath School Society produced a rival set of biographies to counter the ones in Sparks's series.[18] The *Methodist Quarterly Review,* too, noted that Unitarian clergymen had not written about Puritan leaders *"con amore."* Writers and critics who used this phrase generally meant "with sympathy," or in the words of the Methodist magazine, with "full appreciation of the character" of the subject. It would have been better, argued this magazine, if "more orthodox" men had written the lives of Eliot, Mather, and Edwards.[19]

Other cultural messages also appeared, although none as frequently as the critique of Puritanism. In an era when Andrew Jackson's Indian-removal policy met its fiercest opposition (at least among Euro-Americans) in Whig New England, several authors used their contributions to the series to attack the predominant, Democratic view of Indians as savages. Even Oliver Peabody, who devoted eight pages to Israel Putnam's "dark and bloody" Indian captivity during the French and Indian War, would not allow "our fathers" an easy "pardon." After all, "the most enlightened nations" had used those very Indians as their own "instruments of war," giving an ironic twist to the notion of "modern civilization." George Hillard (in the life of John Smith) and Convers Francis both took issue with any monolithic depiction of Indians. Hillard wrote pointedly that the Virginia Indians were "equally removed from the romantic *beau-ideal,* which modern writers of fiction have painted, and the monstrous caricature, drawn by those, who, from interested motives, have represented them, as 'all compact' of cruelty, treachery, indolence, and cowardice." Hillard made Smith and the early Virginians seem at least as morally questionable as the "noble being" Powhatan and his tribe. The history of Anglo-Indian relations, in this telling, consisted of "acts of cruelty, treachery, and oppression, that generally mark the conduct of both whites and Indians toward each other." These authors certainly shared some contemporary, stereotyped views: Francis called the Indian "simply a man, in whom the animal nature predominates," while Hillard sentimentalized the story of Pocahontas. And Francis implied that the Indians' "feeble" intellect had placed them against the path of inevitable progress. However, by challenging some stereotypes and emphasizing the cruelties of whites and Indians alike, these writers challenged the Jacksonian rhetoric of removal.[20]

Several biographies emphasized the practicality and hardiness that had been critical in settling frontier places and winning the Revolution. Edward Everett wrote that John Stark was the child of Scotch emigrants to Ireland, the "pioneers of civilization in New Hampshire, Vermont, and Maine"; Sparks described the "bold and hardy enterprise" of Ethan Allen and his fellow early Vermonters; Oliver Peabody wrote the life of Israel Putnam as pacan to the rough virtues of early freedom fighters who lacked the refinements of modern education. This theme evoked comparison between the eighteenth-century settler past and the mid-nineteenth-century present. Sparks prefaced his life of Allen by describing the differences between the eighteenth-century Vermont wilderness and contemporary towns, villages, and culture and between the early spirit of enterprise and the modern "steady perseverance of an enlightened and industrious population." The underlying story was the civilization of New England's frontier, decidedly not the trans-Appalachian West.[21] Beyond this, Sparks made the Green Mountain Boys' struggle against New Yorkers' claims to Vermont into a microcosm of the American Revolution itself—suggesting links between state experience and national experience and between frontier settlement and the Revolution.

One issue *not* often mentioned or alluded to was sectionalism, perhaps because only two of the twenty-six subjects (John Smith and Marylander William Pinkney) were associated with the South. The authors of those two biographies took pains to note the possibility for sectional harmony. Hillard argued that Smith's 1614 exploration of the New England coast created a connection between Virginia and Massachusetts, and by extension the regions in which they were preeminent; Henry Wheaton concluded his narrative of Pinkney's role in the Missouri Compromise debate with a plea for calm over the slavery issue in the name of national stability.[22] If the library mirrored sectional concerns, it did so only in that its northeastern editor and authors virtually ignored the South.

In what sense, then, was the Library of American Biography "American" in the 1830s? Certainly not in geographical or regional coverage: these ten volumes barely admitted the existence of regions south or west of New York, and their authors came predominantly from the same regions as the subjects. (Although Sparks had hoped to include lives of South Carolinians and Daniel Boone, the prospective authors never wrote them.) The library was "American" in that all the subjects had been distinguished for activity in America, of course. More broadly, the library did offer a version of American national history as Sparks sought to do from the beginning (complete with an index of subjects at the back of volume 10, so that readers could easily find historical events in the biographies where they appeared).[23] This national history contained four main periods: the scattered European discoveries in North America, Puritan New England with its idealism and its hypocrisies, the Revolution as a military event fueled by farmer-patriots like Israel Putnam, and finally the post-Revolutionary flowering of arts and sciences (which explains the lives of Brown, Davidson, Fulton, and Wilson). Although Sparks made no discernible effort to link the biographies together into a larger narrative, the theme of progress underlay many of them: the distance between Puritan intolerance and modern-day religious freedom and diversity, the development of a democratic revolutionary movement, the rise of cultural accomplishment in a nation of rougher frontier beginnings. In this implicit narrative, the Library of American Biography was not alone. It recapitulated the national history as New Englanders like Sparks envisioned it in these years.

It is worth noting that in *form* the biographies ranged beyond Sparks's preferred approach. For the most part, Sparks got what he wanted: well-written narratives without digressions from their subjects, with a minimum of extracts from subjects' writings, and based on research in original, "authentic" documents (as opposed to "tradition").[24] Within those parameters was room for variety. Some biographies, notably James Armstrong's lives of Montgomery and Wayne, were simple, straightforward accounts of events in which their subjects had played a part. Others interwove interpretation into their narratives. Sparks's *The Life and Treason of Benedict Arnold* sought to identify the causes as well as tell the story of Arnold's treason. Accordingly, he included anecdotes of young Benedict killing baby birds in front of their parents and strewing broken glass along the path where other children walked to school. Contrary to Sparks's wishes, Prescott's life of Brown and Upham's biography of Vane quoted extensively from their subjects' works. However, these subjects were literary men. Upham argued to Sparks that such biographies could not be complete without allowing the subjects to speak for themselves: Vane's words conveyed his character. Prescott quoted at length from Brown's novels for a different purpose. Prescott, who had long reviewed books for the *North American Review*, wrote this biography along the lines defined by Samuel Johnson's *Lives of the English Poets:* as a piece of literary criticism, in which the reader could sample the work and understand the critic's analysis of it. (Prescott unsuccessfully implored Sparks to relieve him of the task, because he could not write it *con amore*—with any feeling for Brown or Brown's work.) The title of Catharine Sedgwick's piece—*A Memoir of Lucretia Maria Davidson*—identified yet another approach. Like the myriad memoirs of pious Christian women, this biography took place within the subject's intimate world of home and thoughts. A popular domestic novelist (*Hope Leslie*), Sedgwick professed an explicitly didactic motive, "to set in a clear light before her young country-women the attractive model of Lucretia Davidson's character." Sedgwick's contribution connected Sparks's realm of history writing to the very different world of the Christian memoir and sentimental novel.[25] The Library of American Biography was thus a library of biographical forms, too: narratives of events, analytical biographies, lives and letters, even a female memoir.

In 1843, Sparks contracted with new publishers to resume the library —and over the next five years and fifteen volumes, it became a truly encompassing collection of American biographies, a testament to how the document-collecting historical impulse had spread nationwide.[26] The thirty-nine biographies in this "second series" displayed a regional breadth missing from the first series. To be sure, more Massachusetts lives appeared: Anne Hutchinson, Benjamin Lincoln, James Otis. But the New England subjects now included several Rhode Islanders (Samuel Gorton, Samuel Ward), Connecticut's Ezra Stiles and Timothy Dwight, and Edward Preble of Maine. More noteworthy, the new volumes reached well beyond New England: seventeenth-century insurrectionists Nathaniel Bacon of Virginia and Jacob Leisler of New York; colonial founders James Oglethorpe (Georgia), Leonard Calvert (Maryland), and William Penn (Pennsylvania); Revolutionary leaders Patrick Henry, William Richardson Davie (North Carolina), and Joseph Reed (Pennsylvania); and three figures associated with the trans-Appalachian West—Daniel Boone, Zebulon Montgomery Pike, and Thomas Posey (an early governor of Indiana). Similarly, Sparks now reached farther beyond his Massachusetts/Harvard circle for authors. Just ten of the twenty-six authors in the second series were Harvard men, seven of whom had written for the first series. These new authors' qualifications came not from their educational background but from their access to books and documents necessary to write those subjects' lives—and perhaps too from their ability to write *con amore*. William Gammell, a professor at Brown, wrote the life of Roger Williams that had eluded the non–Rhode Islander Upham. Even the new Harvard authors had local connections: George Burnap, who wrote the life of Calvert, had succeeded Sparks as pastor of the First Unitarian Church in Baltimore. Several authors had been instrumental in founding historical societies and collecting documents outside Massachusetts. Fordyce Hubbard, a transplanted son of Massachusetts who moved to North Carolina and became active in writing that state's history, wrote the life of Davie. Burnap was a founder of the Maryland Historical Society. Some had made their names in popular periodicals, not Unitarian ministry or the *North American*. Novelist Charles Fenno Hoffman was the first editor of the *Knickerbocker* magazine and part of the New York circle of William Cullen Bryant and James Fenimore Cooper—and the *Knickerbocker* applauded him for having written the life of Leisler "in the spirit . . . of a genuine Knickerbocker."[27] James Hall had edited the *Western Monthly Magazine* and written a campaign biography of William Henry Harrison.

Because many of the authors in this second series were connected to their subjects by family or state affiliation, filiopiety and state chauvinism were likely to assume a greater presence than they had in the initial ten volumes—raising the question of how the library's commemorative and historical purposes would coexist. George W. Greene, Samuel K. Lothrop, and Henry Reed all wrote on their grandfathers (Nathaniel Greene, Samuel Kirkland, and Joseph Reed). But these grandsons generally avoided eulogy, explaining that the very existence of the biography would commemorate a worthy ancestor and fulfill "both a public and a personal duty."[28] State loyalties could cause larger problems. For instance, in planning the life of Williams, Gammell referred to his subject as the "Rhode Island Romulus." Conversely Burnap, the Baltimore minister, read Gammell's work in order to determine whether Rhode Island could really claim the origins of religious freedom or whether his own Maryland deserved that distinction. After reading Burnap's work, Gammell expressed his disappointment about it to Sparks: Burnap "had told me that Calvert rivalled Roger Williams & though I knew he did not yet I imagined there was more ground for the opinion than there really is."[29] Several biographies criticized New England–centered history in the course of claiming their own states' place. Hoffman pointedly argued that Leisler's rebellion for New Yorkers' freedom in the 1680s sprang not from transplanted Puritanism but from local character, and he called Leisler "the first really republican ruler" in American history.[30] Once state historians became central in writing the library's biographies, would interstate rivalries over the past overwhelm Sparks's desire to create a national biographical project—and define the "nation" as a collection of states squabbling over reputation?

In the end, the new volumes generally did not create a cacophony of state voices vying for preeminence. Rather, the second series displayed an increasing sense that American history was localistic. Several authors admitted that their subjects were state, not national, figures—whose lives and locales belonged in the "national history" as parts of a multifaceted whole.[31] State historians most often claimed their subjects' right of inclusion in the larger history, not a place at the expense of other states' eminent men. By this definition, commemoration and historical accuracy remained compatible. To commemorate a state's leading figure or one's own grandfather meant not to eulogize him but to include him so that his memory would survive. Of course, biographers presented their subjects in a positive light, but they adhered to the Sparksian principle that their work be based on authentic materials, not unsubstantiated traditions. Many of them acknowledged the relatively new historical societies outside New England that had assisted their research.[32] Indeed, like the historical-society movement, Sparks's method offered historians and biographers outside New England a method of legitimating their states' contributions to American history.

Indicative of the ways the Library of American Biography had changed since its inception—as well as the reputation it had developed by the mid-1840s—was Sparks's correspondence with John Mason Peck, who wrote the life of Daniel Boone that Sparks had wanted from the beginning. Like many authors of the library's second series, Peck was neither a Harvard man nor a Unitarian. Born in Litchfield, Connecticut, in 1789, he left Congregationalism for the Baptist Church in 1810 and became a traveling preacher. He established a western Baptist mission at St. Louis in 1817, and for the next four decades established Bible societies and Sunday schools around the West and acted as an agent for Baptist publishing societies. At the same time, he became known for his publications on the West. Peck was not the first potential author to offer a biography to Sparks, and the fact that authors did so suggests that the library had become a desirable site of publication even by the late 1830s.[33] (Perhaps, too, these writers knew or suspected that writing for the library paid.) Peck introduced himself to Sparks as a collector of "materials of History & Biography in the Western Valley." He asked whether Sparks wanted an article on Boone for the Library—and enclosed another biographical sketch he had written, so that Sparks might "judge of my manner & style in sketching biography." Peck was auditioning his biographical skills for Sparks. By proposing to write on Boone, Peck suggested the inclusion of the western pioneers (and not just the Vermont ones) in a biographical project recognized by 1845 as a national venture. He offered it on Sparks's terms, making a point of his "examination of every document & authority" and ridiculing previous works, including Timothy Flint's, for their inattention to historical "truth." At the same time, Peck realized that his was "the only biography of a real frontier, or backwoods man in your series," and included "sketches of real *western* manners & incidents as to make it unique & characteristic."[34] In short, adding frontier biography to the Library of American Biography meant both following the Sparksian rules *and* showing western manners to the library's presumably eastern readers (who were not exclusively eastern, if Americans checked the volumes out of libraries from New Orleans to San Francisco).

Peck's correspondence with Sparks underscored how central Sparks himself was to the project of American historical biography in the 1830s and 1840s. Other aspiring biographers and historians asked Sparks for information about sources, sought his encouragement for their projects, and sent their work for his review. Henry Whiting, who wrote the life of Zebulon Pike for the Library of American Biography, wrote admiringly to Sparks that "You have ransacked the world for facts, and the occupation of research, after your day, respecting U.S. history, is likely to be gone." Lorenzo Sabine, a merchant and lyceum lecturer from Maine who wrote on Edward Preble for the library, treated Sparks as a mentor: "As Paul sat at the feet of *his* master, so have I had a place at yours, though personally strangers." Sabine, who had been "revolution-mad" ever since reading Weems's *Life of Washington* as a boy, had read nearly all of Sparks's works. When he decided to write about the American Loyalists, Sabine extended the Sparksian vision of biography writing—based on documentary evidence, eschewing "tradition"—to a group heretofore neglected or maligned, and he sought Sparks's counsel. After *American Loyalists* appeared in 1848, Sparks told Sabine not to worry about those who would accuse him of "toryism," for they had either not read the book or read it too quickly to understand it. All "competent judges" would appreciate it and use it in their own subsequent work, even if Sparks wished Sabine had cited his authorities more often for the reference of future researchers. Here was Sparks as "the master spirit of our historical & biographical literature" (Sabine's words): consulting with authors about potential projects, encouraging new contributions to the national history and biography, and sharing his standards for scholarship.[35]

Other biographers of the 1840s and 1850s repeated Sparks's objective of distinguishing truth from tradition. I. W. Stuart believed that he had "explored every pertinent and authentic record within his reach" in writing Jonathan Trumbull's life, while William Cutter "endeavored as far as possible" to reconcile conflicting accounts of Israel Putnam. Ashbel Steele explained most directly the relationship between fact and tradition, past and present in contemporary biography. Up to this point, the business of forming a nation and settling the frontier had been a worthy excuse for neglecting faded documents, and in earlier generations oral traditions had been "fresh and credible." By the 1850s, however, "Tradition has long since become deceptive. . . . Historic facts and incidents, as far as they can be obtained, are now demanded. Records are searched, libraries are ransacked, remains of long neglected, worm-eaten scripts, and registers in time-honored Bibles, as well as oldest cemetery inscriptions, are now sought for with an avidity in this country before unknown."[36] As Sparks (and other historical-society promoters) had argued since the 1820s, tradition could no longer be accepted as fact. Reviewers and critics agreed, routinely praising works "composed from original research" and authors who "neglected no available source of information."[37] The search for "authentic" materials was, it seemed, an advance for biography.

Alternatives to Sparks: Subjects, Methods, Genres

For some subjects, that search led nowhere. Moreover, Sparks and his network of biographers tended not to search for subjects who had not succeeded, who had not won prominence, whose accomplishments did not make the history books, and whose deeds had not been documented. Perhaps the efforts of ordinary soldiers, African slaves, and others had made possible the glory of the Washingtons and Jeffersons, but these subjects rarely got their due in historical biographies. Their biographical preservation took several forms, if it occurred at all. Some won the attention of historians, who searched for their written remains as assiduously as the most ardent Sparksian. Others wrote their own autobiographical accounts, replacing documentary "authenticity" with a truth founded in personal experience. At least one caught the notice of the prominent novelist Herman Melville, who used fiction to tell his story and note the ideological and methodological limits of Sparksian biography.

"Preservation" assumed special poignancy when biographers aimed to preserve not just documents but an entire people they thought was vanishing into oblivion. A variety of motives led several American writers to "Indian biography" in the 1830s. B. B. Thatcher's *Indian Biography* was published as part of the Harper's Family Library in 1832, the year the Supreme Court decided *Worcester v. Georgia* and President Jackson defied Chief Justice Marshall. Thatcher claimed three grounds for writing Indian biographies. Historically, it was "an act of mere justice to the fame and the memories of many wise, brilliant, brave and generous men,—patriots, orators, warriors and statesmen." Philosophically, because the Indians were "governed by impulse and guided by native sense," their biographies revealed "the true constitution of man." Morally, "We owe, and our Fathers owed, too much to the Indians,—too much from man to man,—too much from race to race,—to deny them the poor restitution of historical justice." Another project in Indian biography was more mercenary. Thomas McKenney, superintendent of Indian trade in the War Department and advocate of the Jeffersonian policy of "civilizing" Indians, made his office into a storage house of Native American documents, portraits, and relics in the 1820s. When President Jackson fired him in 1830, McKenney spirited materials out of his office and planned to make his fortune by creating a portfolio of Native American biographies and portraits. He approached his old friend Jared Sparks about writing the biographies. Sparks declined but introduced McKenney to the Ohio writer and editor James Hall. Hall welcomed McKenney's interest and unsuccessfully sought to corner the market by combining George Catlin's Indian portraits, McKenney's archive, and his own biographies. (Catlin declined to participate.) Although the first volume of McKenney and Hall's *History of the Indian Tribes of North America* did appear in 1836, the Panic of 1837 crushed their dreams of wealth. By the mid-1840s McKenney was asking a different kind of assistance from Sparks: loans to keep himself solvent.[38]

More than Thatcher or McKenney and Hall, the New York historian William Leete Stone wrote Native American biography in the Sparksian mode. In the mid-1830s Stone gathered manuscripts and books in order to write a history of the Iroquois in his native New York. That research led to two biographies, *Life of Joseph Brant-Thayendanegea* (1838) and its sequel *The Life and Times of Red-Jacket, or Sa-Go-Ye-Wat-Ha* (1841). Perhaps because he was writing about the New York Iroquois, displaced from their ancestral lands long before Jackson's removal policy, Stone used the rhetoric of vanishing cultures heavily: "that brave and ill-used race of men" were "now melting away before the Anglo-Saxons like the snow beneath a vertical sun." Even more than any author in the Library of American Biography, and certainly more than Thatcher, McKenney, or Hall, Stone condemned Euro-American treachery and cruelty. Christians in Massachusetts had killed Indians "as the agents and familiars of Azazel." Puritans in Connecticut had sold Indians into West Indian slavery. The Spanish American conquest had been far bloodier than anything the native peoples had practiced. But the Indians had had no historian of their own. Thus customs that made sense within their own culture (like scalping) had been distorted by American writers. Worse, even the American governmental records that a historian would ordinarily use distorted the truth, for "the public writers, and those in authority," had resorted to "their imaginations for accounts of such deeds of ferocity and blood, as might best serve to keep alive the strongest feelings of indignation" against England during the Revolution. Personal-hearsay evidence, of course, was inadmissible.[39]

Therefore Stone undertook documentary research more arduous than even the average Sparksian biographer. He had lived in the Mohawk valley of New York and grown up when the Revolution remained "fresh in the recollections of the people" as "traditionary treasures." But the documents of Revolutionary history then remained "ungathered." Stone went to Montreal and Quebec for materials, as well as various places in New York. His books contained a great deal of what twentieth-century scholars call ethnography—descriptions of Iroquois customs, family structures, and the like—because he, like the painter Catlin who had refused James Hall's mercenary offer, wanted to preserve a record of Native American life as it was. Stone found a cache of Joseph Brant's own manuscripts, including speeches, letters to the chief, and copies of Brant's responses. He published these and various other documents in his book, thus writing the sort of work Sparks called "historical biography" (and that other writers called "life and letters" or "life, letters, and speeches"). To those who would complain about the mass of materials, Stone replied that these documents had never before been published; he was doing for Native American history what historical societies did for local and state history. He also argued that this sort of biography, which allowed "the actors in the scenes described to tell their own stories," was now in vogue: Marshall had used it in the *Life of Washington,* Moore in his *Life of Byron,* and especially Lockhart in his *Life of Walter Scott.* Stone thus placed Indian leaders' lives into the Anglo-American biographical tradition. Moreover, he suggested that telling the life through a subject's own "authentic" documents became particularly important when the most accessible evidence, American official records and American observers' narratives (usually written from second-hand information), was mostly "deliberate fictions" with pernicious motives.[40]

Other subjects possessed little but their own stories, and staked a claim to memory by telling them in forms that somehow made it into print. These forms of autobiography derived from an oral culture (and would have been derided by Sparksians as tradition). Seeking Revolutionary war pensions, many penurious men and women told their Revolutionary experiences for the public record. Others wrote or else dictated their narratives in autobiographical, sometimes self-published pamphlets or chapbooks. Stories comprised much or all of these Americans' capital, one of their few marketable possessions. Some had started by telling their stories aloud in public places, escaping the label of beggary because they offered something in exchange for whatever money listeners gave. Such a figure was Israel Potter, a veteran of Bunker Hill who became a chair mender in London and later dictated his story to the Providence printer Henry Trumbull. Published in 1824, the *Life and Remarkable Adventures of Israel R. Potter* belonged to a class of works called "narratives." These ephemeral tales of true-life adventures often consisted of episodes from a person's experience, not an entire life "story." They focused on marginal figures who otherwise would not have survived in print: Indian captives, victims of shipwreck, eccentrics. And they were not considered biographies. Akin to picaresque fiction as well as to biography, narrative inhabited a separate genre because of its first-person narration, its emphasis on adventures rather than lives, and its publication in cheap, easily disposable form.[41] Israel Potter's chapbook story avoided oblivion only because Herman Melville made a novel of it thirty years later, published first serially in *Putnam's Magazine* and then by G. P. Putnam and Company in a cloth-covered volume.

Loosely based on the 1824 narrative, Melville's *Israel Potter: His Fifty Years of Exile* criticized Sparksian biography for its failure to include men like Potter—and responded with fiction. Melville had already commented on biography in his most famous story, published in *Putnam's* the year before *Israel Potter*. In "Bartleby," the narrator noted that although he might write "the complete life" of other law clerks, "no materials exist for a full and satisfactory biography of" Bartleby. Virtually no "original sources" existed, only the narrator's own mysterious experience with the pale scrivener. Here was a character beyond even autobiographical narrative, for Bartleby refused to relate his own story. Israel Potter had left more for the teller. Melville dedicated the book to "His Highness the Bunker-Hill Monument," the first major manifestation in landscape of New Englanders' preservationist inclinations. In this dedication he explained why Potter deserved the "tribute" of "biography, in its purer form." This "private of Bunker Hill" had long ago been "promoted to a still deeper privacy under the ground," his only pension the mosses that grew annually around his grave. Potter's life had not "appeared in the volumes of Sparks." The aegis of the Bunker Hill Monument mattered more than the imprimatur of the Library of American Biography because the obelisk was really America's "Great Biographer: the national commemorator of such of the anonymous privates of June 17, 1775, who may never have received other requital than the solid reward of your granite."[42]

Both Potter's 1824 *Life and Adventures* and Melville's 1855 *Israel Potter* used alternative genres to tell the story of a man ignored by "biography" in its contemporary, recognizable sense. Each of these alternative genres had alternative standards of truth and modes of truth telling. In the narrative, first-person experience testified to the tale's truth, not historical documentation. Melville replaced Potter's first-person narration with the third-person common to biography, having supposedly preserved the "autobiographical story" almost verbatim from the "tattered" 1824 chapbook on "sleazy gray paper" that he had "rescued by the merest chance from the rag-pickers." Even though Melville claimed only to expand on Potter's narrative as someone might retouch a "dilapidated old tombstone," he actually invented much of the story. His truth was the novelist's: the power to tell the story as he chose, despite its original basis in an actual life. By borrowing the biographical form, he may have implied that all biography too was the biographer's invention, much as "great men" were both the beneficiaries of the toil of all the Israel Potters and the creations of biographers. The fact remains, however, that Melville looked to a genre other than biography—or Sparksian biography, at least—to tell Potter's story.[43]

Contemporary biographical accounts of African Americans followed a similar distinction between narrative testimony and biographical history. Slave narratives, by far the most common such accounts, shared many of the characteristics of first-person "lives and adventures," like the 1824 version of Israel Potter's story. Usually told in the first person, these narratives relied on experience—the testimony of those who had lived under slavery—as the source of truth. Many of them also began with another kind of verification, the testimonials of leading abolitionists to the reliability of the stories within. Neither eyewitness testimony nor second-hand affirmation resembled historical documentation, however. In *The Colored Patriots of the American Revolution* (1855) William Cooper Nell, the first African-American historian, sought to add African-American achievement to the historical record on a scholarly basis. Nell's book did not claim to be biography. Each chapter told biographical anecdotes of a particular state's heroic African Americans, and no individual received more than a few paragraphs. Nell did cite a variety of sources: "journeys have been made to confer with the living, and even pilgrimages to grave-yards, to save all that may still be gained from their fast disappearing records." William Wells Brown's *The Black Man, His Antecedents, His Genius, and His Achievements* (1863), more than Nell's book, claimed the mantle of scholarly biography. It consisted of a series of biographical sketches ranging from Benjamin Banneker to Toussaint L'Ouverture, and Brown cited his research "amid the archives of England and France" and in the West Indies. Like slave narratives, *The Colored Patriots of the American Revolution* and *The Black Man* came into existence to promote racial equality and were published by abolitionist presses. No less than Frederick Douglass's *Narrative,* these books aimed to show that African Americans could become as American as anybody else. At the same time, Nell and Brown aimed to do in scholarly form what Melville accomplished fictionally: restore historical biography's omissions.[44]

Before the Civil War, Elizabeth Ellet's *The Women of the American Revolution* attempted most ambitiously to add neglected subjects to America's national history in terms Sparksians would accept. Like Herman Melville and William Cooper Nell, Ellet believed that American history writing and Sparksian biography writing had ignored a large group of Americans. To rectify the omission of women she relied on sources that Sparks and his disciples might question. Unlike Melville, she never abandoned the Sparksian notion of truth.

Marrying Sentiment to Scholarship

In researching and writing *The Women of the American Revolution,* Elizabeth Ellet offered a new definition of the methods and purposes of female biography. Whereas the ministers and relatives who wrote women's memoirs made no claims to scholarship and did not place their subjects in historical context, Ellet used biography to claim the American past for American women—as subjects, readers, and authors. She asserted that women, even unlettered Georgia farm wives and poor New England girls, had helped win American independence. She argued that contemporary women could look to Revolutionary heroines, not just to the Christian wives and missionaries depicted in memoirs, for models of character, just as contemporary self-made men could strive to emulate Washington and Franklin. Most innovative, she demonstrated through her own writing that women could step into public as preservers of the past, intermediaries between a vanishing generation and its descendants. Ellet sought to redefine how the past was told and who told it. Her work contributed to and prospered in the antebellum enthusiasm for things Revolutionary, which also inspired such endeavors as the restoration of Mount Vernon. At the same time, her painstaking research and determination to win Sparks's approval indicated her commitment to making a place for women in the scholarly history of the Revolution. Ellet's work lay at the border between the emerging profession of American history and the sentimental tradition that celebrated "woman's place."[45]

If *The Women of the American Revolution* aimed to unite the languages of woman's influence and biographical scholarship, it also suggested a disjuncture between the two.[46] Like other biographers, Ellet sought to describe a relationship between the present and the Revolutionary past. But that relationship was a complex mix of didacticism and antiquarianism. Domestic fiction and sentimental biography taught readers through archetypal characters, exemplars to be emulated. The historian's approach was more likely to depict the past as a bygone era to be revered for its difference from the present. When Ellet explained her project, she described two sets of materials for two discrete purposes. Some anecdotes would indeed have been "preserved" in authoritative "books, journals, or the papers of the day"—and Ellet, like Sparks, publicly rejected "tradition" in favor of "strict authenticity." But strict adherence to corroborated accounts and written documents of public deeds would reduce her work to a catalog of women's heroic acts, obscuring the *private* sphere where Ellet hoped to find the female "spirit" behind the male "history." For "details of personal history" she went to "the family and relatives of the heroines," precisely the sources Sparks criticized as tradition, because little documentary evidence survived from women's pens and about women's lives.[47] Attempting to recover forgotten women and educate the generation that had forgotten them, Elizabeth Ellet questioned whether Sparksian methods could tell women's lives fully.

Ellet's work involved personal tensions, too. Numerous women novelists of her day balanced their public presence against their recognition of (and often commitment to) the notion of women's private sphere. Like them, Ellet evidenced these conflicts in her writing and her encounters with publishers and public. Ellet's intellectual ambition led her further. Intellectual women of her generation lived in a United States where educational opportunities for women were expanding *and* where fears lingered that too much learning would "unsex" women. Novels, short stories, and poetry—the genres in which the most famous women writers prospered—were by the 1840s acceptable literary pursuits for women. So was translation, which constituted most of Ellet's early work, because the study of foreign languages had long formed part of female education. In moving from translation to scholarly biography, however, Ellet stepped into a new public role dominated and defined by male historians and critics. As she redefined that realm to include women as fit subjects of inquiry as well as inquirers, she sought assistance and support from prominent male historians by presenting herself in the established feminine role of "protégée," while she wrote more boldly and independently to less-known correspon-

After Edgar Allan Poe had excluded Elizabeth Ellet from his sketches of "The Literati of New York" in *Godey's Lady's Book,* the magazine printed a separate biographical sketch of her, accompanied by this portrait. (*Godey's Lady's Book,* February 1847; courtesy American Antiquarian Society)

dents. Ellet at once carefully crafted her own public persona and unwittingly expressed its unresolved tensions.[48]

Elizabeth Ellet had occupied the public world of authorship for more than a decade before she turned to women's history.[49] Born in 1812, she was the daughter of a physician who had helped settle the Sodus Point region of New York, near Lake Ontario, and his second wife, the daughter of a Revolutionary officer. Educated by a Quaker woman near her family's home, she came to think of herself as an intellectual; significantly, in later descriptions of her background she stressed her father's training with prominent Philadelphia physician Benjamin Rush, although William Lummis had largely given up medicine for commercial pursuits in Sodus Point. Ellet began to see her poetry and translations in print in the early 1830s. By 1840 she had mastered Italian, German, and French and written dramas as well as poetry. Her work appeared continuously in gift books and popular magazines, including *Godey's Lady's Book* and the *Democratic Review* (where her stories sometimes ran beside Hawthorne's). If not as popular as Catharine Sedgwick or Lydia Sigourney, Ellet certainly must have been familiar to middle-class magazine readers.[50]

Early on, she adopted several strategies for literary success. Seeking the approval of better-known literary figures, usually men, was one — even if it did not always turn out as she planned. In 1835 she and her new husband moved south when William Henry Ellet became professor at the College of South Carolina, but Elizabeth soon grew restless in Columbia. She visited New York frequently to see her family and participate in the literary world — especially the coterie of Edgar Allan Poe in the mid-forties. Her competition with the poet Frances Sargent Osgood to flatter Poe ended, it seems, in Ellet's helping to circulate the rumor of a Poe-Osgood affair and earning Poe's enduring enmity. Professing innocence in matters of financing and publishing while (in her own words) "manufacturing" her own image was another strategy. Even while haggling for money and offering to write reviews of her own work, she appealed to the conventional female posture that "we ladies know nothing, of course, of the usual methods of transacting such business." Although by 1847 she had become successful in periodical publishing and *Godey's* had run an effusive biographical sketch of her, the falling out with Poe had left her estranged from much of New York's literary world of women and men. Poe's partner in the *Broadway Journal* skewered her in a satirical novel, using her as the model for a character of literary pretensions who repeatedly corrected others' facts in order to display her own knowledge. Ellet may have believed it necessary to find a new field, with a new set of critics, if she was to regain the critical acclaim she had enjoyed in 1845.[51]

In 1846, the year Ellet began *The Women of the American Revolution,* she also began another project. *Evenings at Woodlawn,* a collection of legends she had previously translated for magazines, revealed much about her conception of herself as she began her work on the Revolutionary women. *Evenings* took place on an idyllic estate, where a professor recently returned from Europe assumed his place within "the appropriate sphere of the family circle." At the group's urging, the professor replaced the accustomed evening activities with the narration of popular European legends, relating "genuine traditions" of superstition and otherworldly beings. By compiling these tales and framing them into Woodlawn evenings, Ellet imagined herself in two roles: as the relatively passive, presumably female (although the company is mixed) listener *and* as the professional, learned, male teller/translator, endowed with knowledge and skills beyond those of her listeners. On the one hand, she referred to the Woodlawn group before Professor Azêle's arrival as "we" — suggesting that she was part of the group listening to his legends. On the other, Ellet herself was the scholar-translator who had brought legends "never . . . presented before in English dress" to American audiences for over a decade. This double conception is especially significant because Ellet was simultaneously planning *The Women of the American Revolution,* when she would again play the roles of listener (to Revolutionary women's stories) and professional teller (to her midcentury readers). Her new project would be no less a project of translation, only here the American past would become the foreign world to be assimilated into nineteenth-century, middle-class parlors.[52]

Ellet began collecting materials for *The Women of the American Revolution* in late 1846 or early 1847, following the trail of other peripatetic historians and biographers. In 1847 she gathered materials around her home in South Carolina, where early attempts "met with no success." Between November 1847 and May 1848 she read Revolutionary manuscripts and letters at historical societies in New York and Boston, Mercy Otis Warren's papers in Plymouth, and numerous published histories of the Revolution. Descendants and acquaintances of the Revolutionary women, however, supplied Ellet with the most material, through personal visits and correspondence. Almost every request for information contained this description of her project: "I am engaged in preparing a work on the Women of the Revolution to include biographical notices of ladies distinguished by eminent position or influence, heroic conduct or sacrifices, humanity to the suffering, &c."[53] These categories could include a great man's wife, a female soldier, or a woman who gave her food to the army — and the "&c" in every letter invited correspondents to furnish any story of an ancestor or acquaintance.

Ellet also sought the approval of male, "professional" historians by emphasizing her search for fact and authenticity. She told James Fenimore Cooper that "History says little about [the Revolutionary women], and that little is sometimes so contradictory in the different books — that it becomes important to separate truth from error—before it is too late." With her book in press, Ellet told him that "tradition I find cannot at all be depended upon" and that she had rejected some descendants' anecdotes "because they cannot be substantiated, and in some cases conflict with historical facts." Ellet seems to have reserved this stress on truth and reliability for male fellow scholars, to whom she was demonstrating her own rigor. Especially to Jared Sparks, Ellet positioned herself as a novice seeking his wider knowledge. When she first wrote to Sparks in December 1847, Ellet asked him to refer her to "documents that might furnish information" or "persons who would be able and willing to assist me." Over time, she developed a sense that she was joining a scholarly circle separate from filiopietistic or amateur interest in the past. She never ceased to treat Sparks with deference. She implored him after *The Women of the American Revolution* was published to point out the "errors or defects" in the work, which "no doubt, are more abundant than I am now aware of." She asked his appraisal of the finished work as "judicious criticism from an impartial and competent judge" (more reliable than flattering praise from her friends) and as "consolation for much uneasiness caused by the complaints of discontented descendants." But her list of those complaints resembled a series of war stories, exchanged between fellow historians amused at the "wild and wonderful traditions" provided by descendants who could not distinguish what true history was.[54] Ellet suggested a new collegiality with historians who had endured the barbs of those outside the scholarly circle.

To women and descendants of her Revolutionary subjects, Ellet employed a different language, of patriotic preservation and emotional attachment to the past. As she explained, the Revolutionary women would soon fade from memory. Only half-jokingly, Ellet wrote that "it seems that few people in Charleston even know the names of their grandmothers!" This exclamation identified both sides of her mission: to secure the grandmothers' rightful place in the history of "those trying times" and to teach their forgetful descendants "what the *women* did and suffered." Ellet wrote that remembering one's foremothers (and giving their stories to her) was itself a patriotic act, a contemporary parallel to the Revolutionary women's own patriotism.[55] Not unlike Sparks in the Library of American Biography, she also played on correspondents' loyalties to their own states. After informing Thomas Robbins that she had "collected quite a body of material from different States of the Union" but nothing from Connecticut, Ellet asked him for "some account of the heroines of your State." These requests all had sentiment at their core: love of one's ancestors, nation, or state. Another sentimental rhetoric emerged when Ellet asked the popular author and poet Lydia Huntley Sigourney for information on Connecticut women. She approached Sigourney modestly, inviting the better-known author to write these sketches herself and hoping Sigourney would "excuse the liberty I take in addressing you." Then she took a different turn. "I cannot feel as a stranger in addressing you—whom I have so long known by name and *heart*—and to whom I owe so much pleasure, in reading the productions of your pen." If Ellet addressed Cooper and Sparks with what might be called scholarly deference, she treated Sigourney with sentimental deference, linking herself with Sigourney in the language of "heart" rather than of historical fact. And it was in this language that Ellet invited descendants to supply anything "of interest enough to be a matter of family tradition"—a request that could conflict with the desire for authenticity she expressed to Cooper and Sparks.[56] The scholarly rigor that would satisfy the historian and the fond remembrance that would please the descendant could conflict in a finished book, even if Ellet could stress just one side of the dilemma to each correspondent.

Ellet attended to every aspect of her book's production: the illustration, the margins, the season in which it would appear. She exhibited the same combination of shrewd financial bargaining and professed naivete that she had displayed earlier in her career. She did "not wish to part with the copyright, but to make a bargain as advantageous as I possibly can," and she suggested the royalty figure of 15 percent and threatened to take the book elsewhere if her demands were not met—all the while describing herself as "entirely inexperienced in making bargains." Moreover, she invoked the same patriotism with publishers that she did to elicit information from descendants: "If I do not hear in some time, I shall fear that you are indisposed to join me in the work of immortalizing the heroines of the Revolution." Enlisting her subjects themselves in her own financial pursuits, Ellet revealed the developing symbiosis between herself and the Revolutionary women. Without them, she would remain a moderately known translator and popularizer of European legend, little different from various other contributors to the women's magazines and annuals. Without Ellet, the women of the Revolution would pass from memory as their children and acquaintances died, leaving only vague and diminishing lore as their "history." The Revolutionary women offered Ellet her own place in the literary culture; she offered them a place in the nation's history.[57]

Appealing to different correspondents in different ways was not merely a calculated strategy for obtaining information and making financial bargains. Each appeal was part of her own vision of the project, as *The Women of the American Revolution* demonstrated when it appeared in September 1848. Its dedication provided the first published signal of her multiple intentions:

TO

MY MOTHER,

SARAH MAXWELL LUMMIS,

THE DAUGHTER OF A REVOLUTIONARY OFFICER,

THIS WORK

IS RESPECTFULLY AND AFFECTIONATELY INSCRIBED.[58]

This dedication asserted the importance of female influence; Ellet's mother presumably inspired her efforts or her interest in the women of the Revolution. Yet Sarah Lummis existed here within a double frame. Her name, her individuality, was first linked to the two roles of "mother" and "daughter." (The married name Lummis itself implied a third role, wife, but Ellet never mentioned her own father.) These roles, in turn, appeared between two moments in time. As "my" mother and daughter of "a Revolutionary officer," Sarah Lummis connected the present to the past. The past was masculine, defined by the "officer" (Ellet's grandfather James Maxwell), not by Ellet's grandmother who was truly a "woman of the Revolution." The dedication thus implied three critical relationships in the nineteenth-century writing of women's historical biography: between women's individuality and culturally sanctioned, male-centered roles, between a feminine domestic ideology and a masculine vision of history, and between past and present.

The fifty chapters of *The Women of the American Revolution* included sketches of more than 120 women, both full biographies and single anecdotes. The subjects hailed from almost every state, as well as frontier Kentucky. The Carolinas were represented most fully, probably because Ellet's residence in South Carolina enabled her to collect sketches and anecdotes there herself. The subjects also varied in fame, from the nationally prominent Martha Washington and Abigail Adams to the locally notorious Nancy Hart of Georgia, "a honey of a patriot—but the devil of a wife!"[59]

Amid this diversity, two characteristics united Ellet's subjects—patriotism and domesticity. The patriotism of the Revolutionary women took numerous forms, from Rebecca Motte's consent to the burning of her house to Deborah Samson's service as a soldier in full male costume. Between these extremes were women who resisted British marauders and encouraged American husbands and sons. Teenaged Dicey Langston spied for the patriots. The Martin sisters dressed as soldiers to intercept notes intended for a British general, then returned home and resumed female attire to greet the British officers they had waylaid. Other women exercised their "influence" on male relatives. Mrs. Berry of New Jersey, for example, sent her husband to battle with the cry, " 'Remember, Sidney, do your duty! I would rather hear that you were left a corpse on the field, than that you had played the part of a coward!' "[60] "Homely heroism," the exertion of "influence" (a word Ellet used throughout the two volumes) "wrought quietly and unmarked" within the family, supported weary husbands and nurtured patriotism in children. Equally "homely" was the extension of household responsibilities to a greater number of people: cooking for regiments of soldiers, showing benevolence to the suffering, or affording hospitality and kindness—all of which made recipients of women's influence into a larger family.[61] The narrative structure of many sketches also reinforced cultural ideas about women's "appropriate sphere of home." Chapters often began not with their female subjects but with the subjects' fathers, husbands, or sons. ("THE MOTHER OF WASHINGTON!" exclaimed the first sketch.)[62] Ellet thus situated women's patriotism ideally within the domestic realm and the family. The cumulative effect of repeating traits such as "benevolence," "kindness," and "influence," and of defining women by their male relatives, was to strip many of the subjects of individuality. Even if their particular actions differed, these women appeared less as individuals than as "types": the plucky and resourceful southern farm wife, the hospitable northern gentlewoman, the generous and supportive general's lady.

Deborah Samson, who enlisted in the army in male disguise and fought undetected for three years, exemplified *improper* connections between patriotism, domesticity, and individuality. A "self-made" woman in exactly the way that male biographical subjects of the period were self-made men, Deborah was an individual as most of Ellet's heroines were not. Removed as a child from poor and dissolute parents, Deborah gained her education solely through her own "industry and attainment." Upon the outbreak of the Revolution, she regretted "that she had not the privilege of a man, of shedding her blood for her country." Soon she sewed a man's costume and enlisted as "Robert Shirtliffe." Her secret discovered only by the doctor who treated her near-mortal wound, Deborah feared exposure more than death.[63] Far more than in any other sketch, Ellet sought to explain Deborah's motives—to get at the inner motives behind the public deeds. However, Deborah required explanation precisely because she was abnormal. Ellet admired Deborah's patriotism and courage and compared her to Joan of Arc, but she also wrote that "the ignorance and error mingled with this enthusiasm, should increase our sympathy without diminishing the share of admiration we would bestow, had it been evinced in a more becoming manner." Deborah's individuality needed extenuating circumstances. Ellet found those circumstances in Deborah's "isolation from ordinary domestic and social ties": "She felt herself accountable to no human being." Put another way, Ellet had to explain Deborah Samson because she ventured outside the proper realm of female action, and she blamed Deborah's actions on the fact that this woman was "self-made." Deborah's assumption of masculine dress and activity implied almost literally, in Ellet's telling, that being "self-made" led naturally to being a man. Deborah's final absorption into the domestic, through marriage and motherhood after the war, reaffirmed the value of combining patriotism with the social and cultural roles deemed "appropriate" for a woman. Ellet concluded that Deborah's misdirected patriotism "cannot be commended as an example." [64]

Other Revolutionary "heroines" could be commended as models for contemporary women. Ellet transformed the era's most prominent woman into a paragon of domesticity. Although acclaimed as a beautiful young widow and a leader of fashionable society, Martha Washington took her greatest pleasure in "the duties of a Virginia housewife, which in those days were not merely nominal." She raised the children of her dead son (who "expired in the arms of his mother," in classic sentimental fashion), managed meals, supervised Mount Vernon's production of clothing, and shopped for George's handkerchiefs, even in "advanced age." By recounting Martha's conversation with a younger woman about "housekeeping and her domestic affairs," Ellet made literal the passage of domesticity across generations.[65] In one sense, making Martha Washington into a model of housewifery served to humanize a potentially dignified and distant character. But humanizing Martha did not so much eliminate distance as change its nature. Although the language and substance of domesticity narrowed the temporal gulf between Revolutionary subject and nineteenth-century reader, the presentation of Martha as exemplary housewife created a different distance, between the ideal heroine of "those days" and the real, somehow inferior modern woman. Elsewhere, too, Ellet compared women of the Revolution favorably with those of the present day. Philadelphia women collected clothing for the soldiers out of genuine charity, "not stimulated by the excitements of our day—neither fancy fairs, nor bazaars"—and in Revolutionary days "matrons of condition disdained not labor with their hands." The contrast between "our day" and "those days" suggested that Revolutionary women combined industry, benevolence, and dignity more successfully than did modern women.[66]

Beyond patriotism and domesticity, a third characteristic appeared prominently in many of Ellet's biographies: intellectual ability. Ellet described the well-known histories and dramas of Mercy Otis Warren and the unpublished writings of South Carolinian Sarah Reeve Gibbes, who left "Volumes . . . filled with well-selected extracts from the many books she read, accompanied by her own comments; with essays on various subjects, copies of letters to her friends, and poetry." Like patriotism, intellect won Ellet's highest praise when yoked to domestic duties and feminine traits. Elizabeth Shaw Peabody, the sister of Abigail Adams, read widely and recited literary passages to cultivate young people. "Attentive to her domestic duties, and economical from Christian principle, to purity of heart and highly cultivated intellectual powers she united the most winning feminine grace." Even Mercy Warren, whom Ellet obviously admired, "never permitted [scholarly pursuits] to interfere with household duties, or the attention of a devoted mother to her children." These were not bluestockings. Intellect, patriotism, domestic ability, and "feminine graces" like benevolence and kindness together composed the hallmarks of a woman of "influence." Ellet's presentation of the Revolutionary women at once preserved *and* created her own foremothers, giving her own combination of womanhood and intellect a past. Her description of Behethland Butler— "a superior mind . . . may belong to a woman without the development of any harsh or unfeminine lineaments"—had the defensive stance of an author whose intellect had raised questions about her femininity.[67]

Ellet's "packaging" of the Revolutionary women as exemplars for contemporary women shared much with the literary culture in which she had long written. Domestic literature abounded in the 1830s and 1840s, from mothers' manuals by Lydia Sigourney and Lydia Maria Child to novels such as Catharine Sedgwick's *Home* (1835). The most widely circulated and influential publication of this literary culture, *Godey's Lady's Book,* published Ellet's work throughout the 1840s. Ellet's ideology resembled that of Sarah Josepha Hale: Hale made *Godey's* the premier exponent of women's education and active use of that education (as teachers as well as mothers) for the improvement of the nation. In offering American women a past in which women had gained influence through patriotism, domestic ability, and intellect, *The Women of the American Revolution* similarly promoted an educated American womanhood whose influence—like their foremothers' influence during the Revolution, and like Ellet's own in telling their stories — would extend beyond a passive "cult of true womanhood."[68]

At the same time, Ellet described her work in Sparksian terms. She had eschewed all "fanciful embellishment," she told her readers, because the Revolutionary women's true stories were affecting enough to require only "simple narrative." More important, she kept her research constantly visible. In the preface she acknowledged the assistance of various male historians and the librarian of the New-York Historical Society and claimed to have consulted "many authorities, including all the books upon the Revolution." She cited letters and historical books in numerous footnotes. And she commented upon other historians' anecdotes about women — sometimes to confirm their truth, sometimes to quarrel with their interpretations.[69] Above all, Ellet described the hard work of distinguishing mere "traditionary information" from "responsible personal testimony" and "established historical facts." "Tradition," for Ellet as for Sparks, meant unsubstantiated legend; substantiation might come from subjects' letters or from the recollections of relatives and acquaintances if other sources corroborated them. Again and again Ellet contrasted tradition with authenticity. About Lucia Knox's personal character, she wrote that "Tradition speaks much of her, but little of what is said is sufficiently well-authenticated to relate"; several anecdotes of Dorothy Hancock "unfortunately cannot be obtained in a form sufficiently authentic for this sketch"; another "traditional anecdote is communicated by a relative of the family, who believe it entirely authentic."[70] Like her letters to Sparks, Ellet's footnotes and her distinctions between truth and tradition were an effort to join the community of historians — and to suggest a specific place for herself within that community. This place was below Sparks's: she never disputed his facts or interpretations.[71] Her criticism of other historians, however, implied that she placed herself above them on the subject of women's experiences and lives. Claiming her own place in scholarly circles was not her sole aim. Illustrating the symbiosis between herself and her subjects, she employed the historian's methods in order to place women in the "scholarly" history or "enduring record" of the Revolution.

In doing so, Ellet faced an additional problem that Sparks and his circle did not: the lack of women's records and the privacy of their lives. Giving women's influence a past involved criticizing the dominant portrayals of the Revolutionary period, with their great battles and heroic men. By 1848 "political history" offered few glimpses of women's lives. Only Abigail Adams's and Eliza Wilkinson's letters had appeared in print. Unpublished letters were few, since "letter-writing was far less usual among our ancestors than it is at the present day" and the dangers of wartime led correspondents to avoid "the all-absorbing subjects of the time." Worse, history as Ellet found it *could not* discuss women's central contribution because it focused on public deeds and actions, "the workings of the head, rather than the heart":

> Female character . . . impresses itself on the memory of those who have known the individual by delicate traits, that may be felt but not described. The actions of men stand out in prominent relief, and are a safe guide in forming a judgment of them; a woman's sphere, on the other hand, is secluded, and in very few instances does her personal history, even though she may fill a conspicuous position, afford sufficient incident to throw a strong light upon her character. This want of salient points for description must be felt by all who have attempted a faithful portraiture of some beloved female relative. How much is the difficulty increased when a stranger essays a tribute to those who are no longer among the living, and whose existence was passed for the most part in a quiet round of domestic duties!

The nature of female experience, "too quiet and secluded to furnish material for the chronicler of mere events," posed the most fundamental challenge.[72]

Ellet met that challenge by emphasizing biography over history and by tapping a source of information—descendants' memory—separate from public documents. Because "[w]e can only dwell on individual instances of magnanimity, fortitude, self-sacrifice, and heroism, bearing the impress of the feeling of Revolutionary days," biography suited the telling of women's lives better than history ("mere events") could. If women's influence in the home helped forge the nation, the best way to illustrate that influence historically was to narrate incidents about particular women in particular homes.[73] The failure of history also explained Ellet's reliance on subjects' descendants and acquaintances. If one accepted the early republican and Sparksian definition of "character," the character of public men could be revealed through public actions, chronicled in government documents, newspapers, and correspondence. Telling women's lives required different sources: the memories of those who had seen the character in private. Recollections constituted a prominent part of contemporary, ahistorical female religious memoirs, but Ellet used them in conjunction with the printed record to place her women *within* history. When discussing women's actions, printed sources were paramount: a Connecticut family might believe that its foremother sewed the state's first flag from her own garments, but Ellet discarded the account if published records opposed or would not support it. On women's character, though, descendants' memory possessed the presumption of truth. With information from Lorenzo Sabine, Ellet wrote in the first volume that Lucia Knox had "preferred the society of men to that of her own sex" and had regretted late in life "that her interest in political men and measures had engrossed her mind to the exclusion of aspirations and associations more befitting a woman's sphere." Too late, Ellet received a contradictory letter from Mrs. Knox's daughter—which she used to write a new, much expanded sketch for her third volume of *The Women of the American Revolution,* published in 1850. Now Mrs. Knox became a strong-minded but benevolent woman with the "strength of domestic attachments" and "all the deep and tender feelings which belong to feminine nature."[74] In depicting women's domestic abilities and character, descendants like Mrs. Knox's daughter provided more "authentic" evidence than historians like Sabine. Applying the scholarly historian's language to a source identified largely with the sentimental memoir, Ellet asserted the factuality of feeling: not only the significance of Revolutionary women's "home-sentiment" but also the reliability of familial attachment as an historical source.

The problem in combining male history and female biography, public documents and private recollections, ideologies of "fact" and "feeling," was that each of these realms or modes envisioned the past differently. Within *The Women of the American Revolution,* Ellet implied three different relationships between past and present. The first, associated with the domestic tradition, made the past into an exemplar for the present. Central to the pious memoirs that constituted the bulk of female biography in Ellet's day, this concept led the historian to describe the past in the terms of the present and to become a moralist creating models worthy of emulation.[75] The second, which appeared only infrequently in *The Women of the American Revolution,* valued the past for its role in creating the present. Past and present differed, but learning about the past could lead to a better understanding of national origins. While the first vision took feminine virtues and domestic duties to be constant over time, the second emphasized the linear and changeable: "Such were the matrons of the nation's early day. Had they been otherwise, America would not have been what now she is."[76] In this vision, the present's debt to the past had to be repaid through memory, not emulation. Building upon this notion, the third vision—the historian's—took the past as something to be preserved from oblivion. From her opening salvo against the current "manuscript-destroying generation," Ellet suggested that neglect and active destruction, of "hallowed" relics and buildings as well as manuscripts, shared responsibility for the loss of the past. In response, Ellet often wrote of "preserving" anecdotes. The brocade Martha Wilson had worn on July 4, 1776, had "become a victim to the modern taste for turning the antique dresses of grandmammas into eiderdown bed-spreads, and drawing-room chair-covers," but Ellet could preserve it by describing it in her book. Her language was revealing: leveling the "house in which General Putnam had his headquarters" to erect "a new and elegant mansion" was a "sacrilegious destruction." The past was sacred—and essentially different from the present, inaccessible even as an exemplar. As Ellet explained, "we, contented citizens of a peaceful nation, can form little conception of the horrors and desolation of those ancient times of trial."[77]

Ellet's role, as she imagined it, emerged from this inability. The *historical* biographer did not make Revolutionary women into nineteenth-century exemplars. She translated *memory* into *history* by describing bygone individuals and character types, as well as customs and relics. Memory, for Ellet, was the oral lore passed down from the Revolutionary women themselves to their descendants, who created "traditions" as they embellished the original. Ellet's correspondents might tell her anything "of interest enough to be a matter of family tradition," and without those traditions she would have little evidence at all of many subjects. But Ellet herself had to judge what was "authentic."[78] Because the reliability of the teller was paramount, Ellet often cited the person who had supplied the information. Best were the stories that came directly from the Revolutionary women. The image of the Revolutionary woman herself as "a living chronicle of days gone by," telling her stories to her children, appeared in several sketches and was central to Ellet's project of mediating between her subjects and her readers, between the past and the present. As in *Evenings at Woodlawn,* Ellet—the woman who had felt the spirit of the Revolutionary woman *and* the scholar who had seen material that "has never before been published"—was creating written history from oral lore. "Memory" could fade, but "a palpable form" or "an enduring record" would not.[79]

Collecting anecdotes and materials from all the states, Ellet translated not just memory into history, but local memory into national history. Ellet's national vision was evident in how she opened the volumes: the first with Mary Washington, the second with Martha Washington. Just as George Washington was the foremost symbol of the nation and just as Mount Vernon would become in the next decade a national shrine in the midst of sectional division, Washington's mother and wife served here to unify the sketches that followed. Many of those sketches told of women known only within their own communities. Several chapters, especially those about lesser-known women of the Carolinas, ended with statements like "her memory is still cherished in that locality" or "Her character is well appreciated throughout North Carolina, and the memory of her excellence is not likely soon to pass away."[80] Ellet's Revolution was a national event because it encompassed episodes and individuals of myriad localities, as well as figures of national unity like the Washington women. In this sense, *The Women of the American Revolution* was a female version of the Library of American Biography, as Sparks transformed his series in the 1840s. By the time Ellet wrote in 1848, Sparks's series contained lives of North Carolinians and westerners as well as New Englanders, mirroring the growth of historical societies and publications in every region of the United States. Ellet's work further expanded historical biography to new classes of subjects—all in the language of Sparksian "authenticity," and all in the name of adding to the national history.

Ultimately Ellet sought to accomplish something more: to bridge the languages and literary worlds of the domestic and the scholarly. Did this union of didacticism and preservation, sentiment and scholarship, succeed? For Ellet herself, *The Women of the American Revolution* certainly succeeded. Hailed as the foremost authority on America's "domestic history," she capitalized on her new prominence by writing similar works until her death in 1877. On first glance, the positive, even enthusiastic response to *The Women of the American Revolution* suggested that she had indeed brought together the increasingly divergent elements of her literary culture. Closer examination reveals that the reviews emphasized different facets of Ellet's work. *Godey's* examined Ellet's work as a production about, by, and for women. Comparing the Revolutionary women to "precious" but elusive "pearls in dark waters," the review enshrined these foremothers. Ellet had "proved herself an accomplished historian, the most difficult task in literature for a woman to perform." And Ellet's book would do for contemporary women what the women of the Revolution had done in their era. Its "influence" would "be wide and salutary as its merits and beauties are original and true." (However unwittingly, the review also identified the key difference between these two "influences": Ellet's was a market commodity whose publishers had "done their part well" and made it a valuable "present for the season of gifts.") The *North American Review*, in an unsigned review by the travel writer and historian Caroline Kirkland, approached Ellet's volumes from the world of "scholarly" biography that Ellet sought to enter. While *Godey's* wrote that the Revolutionary women "should be hallowed in the heart of their country," the *North American* said only that Ellet's "care and patience . . . deserve to be called pious," suggesting that Ellet revered the subjects but not that Americans should revere them, too. More important for the *North American* (as for Sparksian scholars) was the prospect of historical loss: "unless some one had conceived the happy thought of committing to enduring print, *just now,* all we know" of the Revolutionary mothers, our ancestresses would be consigned "to hopeless oblivion." Specific magazines' responses reflected their own places and standards within the literary and cultural world.[81]

Ellet won praise from virtually every major American periodical, from the "domestic" to the "scholarly," largely because of the nature of American literary culture and historical writing at midcentury. Above all, these periodicals shared the underlying belief that the mission of American literature was to instruct as well as to entertain. American magazines universally subordinated particular criticisms to enthusiasm for national history and reverence for the Revolution, even if they espoused different literary-critical standards. The *North American* suggested in its reviews and by its selection of books for review that history ranked above fiction in usefulness and worth; *Godey's* implied in its more eclectic book notices that many forms of literature could possess merit. However, no rigid hierarchy yet ranked "domestic" or "sentimental" works near the bottom—possibly because so many authors moved freely between genres. Elizabeth Ellet was far from alone in coming to history after a career in other fields. Many domestic writers and prominent historians of the 1830s and 1840s had achieved varied literary successes, and numerous women best known for fiction or poetry also wrote historical works (although not about American women). Similarly, although the 1830s and 1840s witnessed the grand, sweeping narratives of American romantic history, the desire to rescue the minutiae of the past from oblivion constituted another respected historical endeavor.[82]

Unlike many antiquarians, however, Ellet aspired to the status of "historian" and offered a larger argument about women's centrality that went beyond preserving near-forgotten facts. *Godey's* seconded that argument. Introducing a poem dedicated to Ellet, its editor wrote that Ellet had "by her late popular work, won 'golden' rewards, as well as the warm heart-blessings of her countrywomen," again yoking finance to feeling. The poem, celebrating *The Women of the American Revolution,* compared the familiar "proud glare" and "many torrents" of male history to the unheralded "soft light" and "small streams" of female influence. Here the revisionary potential of Ellet's history reached its logical conclusion, with woman,

"A star undimmed by Time's encroaching finger," at the center of history, standing behind and enduring beyond "the prouder sun." Exclaiming *"we have a past*—our glory comes from thence!" the poet celebrated Ellet's historicization of the domestic, giving women a history. And in emphasizing the "small streams" the poet affirmed the domestication of history, the rewriting of history from a female point of view, more explicitly than Ellet ever had. The only truly negative response to *The Women of the American Revolution,* in *Chambers' Edinburgh Journal,* explicitly denied what *Godey's* affirmed: the potential of Ellet's work and her subjects' lives not merely to "adorn war" but to reinterpret "regular history." *Chambers'* called her volumes "a storehouse of small materials," consigned her subjects to the "sub-historical" or "romantic," and argued that Ellet—whose work was not history and who was not "the historian"—had little talent for romance either. But this review appeared in a British periodical (which also objected to how Ellet had portrayed England's side of the war).[83]

To press her argument, Ellet played her own part in shaping the work's reception. Just after *The Women of the American Revolution* was published, she wrote an article for *Godey's* about "how I came to write a book." She described for her middle-class readers the choices she made between descendants' remembrances and substantiated testimony, the duty she felt to present her subjects as "true women," and the criticism she had received. Two items in this "Letter to M.D.S." (and to *Godey's* readers) were strikingly new. First, Ellet acknowledged the assistance of both men and women, in contrast to mentioning only men and libraries in her preface. Ellet now gave "credit where it is best deserved—to women—whose sympathy with the deeds and daring and suffering of their own sex in those ancient times of trial, has been most productive of knowledge."[84] However, while Ellet named the men who assisted her ("[T]he distinguished southern author, Mr. Simms," "that Prince of liberal and enterprising publishers, MR. GODEY," and "the great American biographer, Mr. Jared Sparks"), the women who supplied her with information remained nameless and collective. Ironically, Ellet recreated in the present what she sought to challenge in the past: the identification of women as a group rather than as individuals. Second, Ellet made a special point of showing the readers of *Godey's* the "rules" of biography that she followed, while remaining a woman in heart and spirit. She apologized "to those who find the anecdotes they have sent not included in the memoirs," but "traditions, however entertaining, should have no place in an authentic record, if they are unsupported by indisputable testimony, or if they are at variance with history, or with probability." Like her reference to "the great American biographer," this stress on authenticity was directed to those outside the circle of scholars, those who might not know who Jared Sparks was and why their family stories might not be "history." (Ellet sent a manuscript copy of the "Letter to M.D.S." to Sparks in November 1848, as a trifle to amuse the "serious" historian.) Encouraging readers to send their own anecdotes, Ellet concluded by rejoining the circle of women who wrote for and read *Godey's*. "Most gratefully will information be received from all who may be able or willing to send it; for dear to my heart are the Revolutionary women, and no task is so pleasing as that of paying them the tribute of praise."[85] Ellet was still negotiating among her various publics and objectives.

In *The Women of the American Revolution* itself, however, the balances were more precarious. Descendants complained precisely because Ellet had to make choices in her volumes that she had been able to avoid in her initial letters. Back in March 1848, Ellet could invite descendants to share all their memories while she denigrated "tradition" to Cooper and Sparks. But the published volumes had to balance between narrating family lore and ascertaining its authenticity. This balance could not fail to upset the descendant, the historian, or both. The volumes also had to place the Revolutionary women's stories within the larger narrative of the Revolution — and, if successful, to demonstrate how women affected the war, not just how they were affected by it. Ellet's biography of Esther Reed, the British-born wife of Pennsylvania's Revolutionary president, demonstrated the limits of her vision. Although the product of scholarly research and the recovery of a precious and exemplary foremother, the sketch ultimately echoed the *Chambers'* reviewer's charge that Ellet's women "humanised" war but did not truly influence its outcome. Reed's was one of Ellet's most successful biographies. By using Reed's letters and describing the historical situation in Revolutionary Pennsylvania, Ellet made this woman a distinct individual, fixed in time and place, as well as a model of motherhood, patriotism, and sacrifice (her young son dies; her charitable efforts drain her health and contribute to her early death). Yet Reed's biography never entirely united the domestic and the historical. After describing the colonies' rupture with England and the military situation around Philadelphia, Ellet broke for "a moment's meditation to pause and think of the sharp contrasts in our heroine's life." This two-page "meditation" on Esther's personal transformations (girl to woman, Englishwoman to American, scenes of luxury to ones of anxiety) ended, "But to return to the narrative — interrupted, naturally, by thoughts like these" — suggesting that the internal, private struggles of her female subject somehow "interrupted"

the public "narrative," the military events that controlled where Esther re-
sided and when she saw her husband.[86]

This sense of interruption pointed to Ellet's larger ambivalence about
where her Revolutionary women fit in the history of the Revolution.
The Women of the American Revolution had the potential to challenge the
Sparksian emphasis on public deeds and documents, and to reshape history itself from the vantage point of "home-sentiment." But Esther Reed's
"thoughts, and hopes, and wishes," the center of her biography, were not
the center of the Revolution, only a break in the narrative. Even if Ellet
placed her subjects into historical context, and even if her subjects did
more than merely "adorn war," neither did they change it. Like Esther's
personal struggles in the midst of the "narrative," these Revolutionary
women were essentially stuck in history, affected by "events" but unable to
affect them. Ellet was similarly confined by the genre she had chosen; she
had taken the radical (in literary terms) step into the masculine community of historical scholars, but her biographies supplemented rather than
rewrote the historical narrative. Esther Reed's enclosure illustrated the narrative limits of "domesticating history" through biography.

The political limits of Ellet's vision can be seen when we compare her
work with a contemporary use of the American past by a different group
of women. The Seneca Falls convention adopted its "Declaration of Sentiments" in July 1848, precisely when *The Women of the American Revolution* was
in press. The title of the women's-rights manifesto was ironic, for its advocates rejected the ideology of "sentiment" as an acquiescence to power-
lessness. This declaration employed the ideology of the Revolution and the
language and structure of the forefathers' political testament to indict the
"history of mankind" as a "history of repeated injuries and usurpations
on the part of man toward woman," a legacy discordant with the original declaration's rhetoric of rights and equality. In one sense, Ellet's work
paralleled that of the Seneca Falls convention: Ellet asserted women's right
to a place in the masculine preserve of the Revolutionary past. But innovative as she was in restoring women to the historical record and claiming
a public role for women as scholarly historians, Ellet never challenged the
political, legal, or social structure of her day. Rather, she ultimately argued
for national unity on grounds that could support and strengthen the political bonds of the union, the "home-sentiment" or "spirit which animated
all" in Revolutionary days.[87]

Ellet's work more closely paralleled the Mount Vernon Ladies' Association of the Union, the organization of women founded in 1853 to purchase

and restore the dilapidated home of the first president. The association, too, recognized that the prevailing conception of American "history" neglected the domestic. Just as histories had celebrated men and battles but not (until Ellet) women and homes, so monuments had commemorated battlefields and great men while disrepair had befallen historic houses. As we have seen, Ellet herself decried this neglect of the physical past in *The Women of the American Revolution*. The Mount Vernon Ladies' Association explicitly defined its mission as one of historic preservation *and* national unification amid the sectional crisis. Sentiment—Americans' shared commitment to the values of home—was the glue that had bound the colonies together in their first trial, that bound the present to the past, and that would now reinforce the bonds of union in the 1850s. And women applied the glue: not merely republican mothers teaching sons within the home, but republican mothers to the nation, stepping into public as the preservers of the past. Ellet and the ladies' association envisioned their projects as patriotic struggles. Their "heroism" involved saving the national past through writing and fund-raising rather than saving the nation through fighting. Their enemies were neglect and death rather than British invaders. To save Mount Vernon, the association solicited donations from men and women throughout the nation and competed with men who sought to buy Washington's home for less lofty purposes. To recover the Revolutionary women, Ellet solicited the aid of male historians and descendants of the Revolution and worked intricately with publishers. The past, in these women's hands, became an avenue for women to move into public space—in the name of the nation.[88]

Southern Biography and the Problem of Literary "Backwardness"

William Gilmore Simms, the foremost writer in the antebellum South, reviewed Ellet's *The Women of the American Revolution* in his *Southern Quarterly Review* in July 1850. Like every other American reviewer, Simms praised Ellet's work. Also like every other American reviewer, Simms approached *The Women of the American Revolution* from his own literary and ideological perspective. First he emphasized understanding the colonies' social and cultural character. The "spirit" of the colonies, he agreed with Ellet, helped explain the nature of their struggle for independence. Distinct national and regional characteristics existed and shaped historical events, a romantic concept that Simms shared with northern historians like George Bancroft. As adopted by Simms's own southern intellectual circle around midcentury, this belief reflected a desire that southerners understand and appreciate their own region's character. Then Simms lauded Ellet, "a Northern lady by birth, and education, and residence," for including numerous southern women. (He did not mention that she had lived in South Carolina for nearly fifteen years.) Simms took the occasion to chide other northern historians for their "large pretensions." They might believe that the entire revolution was "the work of 'the Saints' of Yankeedom purely," but two-thirds of Ellet's sketches told of southern ladies. In the future, Simms hoped, historians of each section of the United States would do for their own heroic women what Ellet had—including southerners, for many women's stories remained to be recovered.[89] This perspective on *The Women of the American Revolution* was among American reviewers uniquely a southern one.

Simms's review also revealed two critical facts about biography in the antebellum South. First, William Gilmore Simms himself was its central figure. He wrote four book-length biographies and numerous shorter biographical articles.[90] He reviewed a variety of biographies in his role as a magazine editor, notably for the *Southern Quarterly Review* from 1849 to 1854. And more than any other person, he argued that the South needed lives of its distinguished men. Second, beyond Simms, "Southern biography"— biographies of southern subjects written with an eye to distinguishing them *as* southern—barely existed at all. The two leading, longest-lived southern literary magazines (the *Southern Literary Messenger* and the *Southern Quarterly Review*) reviewed fewer than a dozen biographies of or by southerners between 1834 and 1861. Several of the biographies of southerners that they did review were the handiwork of northern authors. As the *Messenger* noted of Fordyce M. Hubbard, the transplanted New Englander who wrote on William Richardson Davie for the Library of American Biography, North Carolina could "claim no credit" for this biography, "as it was written by a stranger who has recently taken up his abode within her borders, and who has thus assumed the duty of teaching Carolina's sons the history of their fathers." John Pendleton Kennedy's *Life of William Wirt*, Hugh A. Garland's *Life of John Randolph of Roanoke*, a few lives of John C. Calhoun, and Simms's books paled in number against the myriad lives of northern subjects written in these decades. Southern periodicals hardly supplied the deficit: they ran very few biographical articles about southerners (or about anybody, for that matter).[91]

Critics like Simms encouraged Southerners to write the lives of their eminent figures for the sake of regional character. They echoed the arguments used three decades earlier to call for American biography: the commemoration of worthy founders and patriots, the education of the rising generation, the perpetuation of the South's unique character (reminiscent of earlier discussions of America's unique republicanism). Southerners had either "forgotten that the actions of the gifted and the noble should be commemorated in order to encourage an imitation of their example among future generations" or been too lazy to write their ancestors' biographies, complained the *Messenger*. "Ask a New Englander" for the names of his region's patriots, and he would "overwhelm you with an all-but countless catalogue"; ask a southerner the same question, and the answer would be stammering or silence. Simms used his review of Kennedy's *Life of Wirt* to encourage more southern-written lives of southern statesmen. "The people who show themselves indifferent to the deeds and glory of their ancestors," he explained, "are not likely, in this day of exigency, to produce sons worthy of their fathers."[92]

Furthermore, failure to commemorate its fathers in biography placed the South in danger "at this moment when its individuality is threatened." As Simms saw it, the South was "paying the penalty" for its historical indifference. "Our histories are slurred over by Yankee historians, the most important truths suppressed; our heroes receive but cold applause. Shall the warm and generous nature owe the record of its virtues, its uncalculating patriotism, its noble self-sacrifice, its oratory or its valor to the cold and frigid biographies of the unsympathising bigot of another and a too hostile region? Shall the story of the lion be written only by baser beasts?"[93] The moment when Simms reviewed Ellet's and Kennedy's books was critical politically as well as culturally: southerners in Congress were debating the admission of California, the Fugitive Slave Law, and what eventually became the Compromise of 1850. Simms's rhetorical questions conjured up the southern vision, expressed particularly at such points of sectional tension, that associated southerners with the warmth of passion and valor and northerners with the chilliness of market culture. Equally important, Simms suggested that biography could not be written by the "unsympathising." Only those with sympathy for their subjects—those who could write *con amore*, to use the phrase that was the opposite of Simms's "cold and frigid"—could produce biographies that recorded character as faithfully as fact. By extension, this meant that northerners could not write "true" lives of southern subjects.

This belief helps to explain why and how Simms wrote a variety of southerners' lives. As early as 1840 he was collecting notes on "worthies of Carolina Revolutionary History" including Francis Marion, Thomas Sumter, Andrew Pickens, Nathanael Greene, and William Moultrie.[94] At this point, his project was similar to William Wirt's in 1805: a biographical pantheon of figures eminent in his state's history (a history he wrote and had published in Charleston in 1840). Simms never wrote biographies of Sumter, Pickens, or Moultrie, but he did produce lives of Marion, Greene, Captain John Smith, and Chevalier Bayard in the 1840s. In them, he went further than Wirt—whose concern was always Virginia—to suggest the importance of southern, not just South Carolinian, contributions to the Revolution. As he explained in the *Life of Francis Marion,* "Our southern chronicles are meagre and unsatisfactory." This problem helped persuade him to write the book, but it also made it hard to separate "the vague tributes of unquestioning tradition" from "adequate authorities for the biographer." Like Sparks and Ellet, Simms often noted when "tradition" could not be trusted, and he included much of Weems's life of Marion ("a delightful book for the young") in the category of tradition.[95] His objective resembled that of many other historians working in the 1840s: to chronicle history that had not yet been written, to distinguish truth from faulty memory. He also hoped to commemorate the South as a region, a desire different from but not incompatible with national history (such as Sparks's) or particular states' histories (the concern of numerous contributors to the Library of American Biography in the 1840s).

Within his *Life of Marion,* Simms interwove the national, the regional, and the local. By likening Marion to George Washington—because of their parallel circumstances in youth, similar military glories, common virtues of simplicity and republican spirit—Simms argued that Marion belonged in the pantheon of America's national heroes. In some cases, though, these men's shared virtues belonged to their southern heritage. After the war, Marion returned to his farm and came to love its "manly industry[,] . . . that repose in action, which the agricultural life in the South so certainly secures." In a larger sense, the entire *Life of Marion* was southern biography. Set almost entirely in the southern military theater from Indian wars to the Revolution, it implied that here occurred the true revolution—the civil war among American colonists between loyalism and patriotism. It emphasized the chivalric, honor-bound nature of southern military life. And it omitted all the events that northern historians (and most biographers in Sparks's Library of American Biography) accepted as central: the Stamp Act crisis and subsequent resistance to king and parliament, the continental congresses, the ratification of the Constitution. Marion's importance was national, but his life reflected the history of his region. His life also embodied the distinctive culture of South Carolina. Simms's entire first chapter described the Huguenots' migration to America, love of liberty, commitment to principle, and success amid privations. By emphasizing the Huguenots, "a much better sort of people than those who usually constituted the mass of European emigrants," Simms gave South Carolinians a European heritage distinct from the English, Puritan roots celebrated by historians of other regions. When Simms wrote the *Life of Marion* and his other biographies in the 1840s, championing southern history and character meant adding neglected scenes to the national picture, not separating the South from the United States.[96] Simms's reviews of Ellet and Kennedy came later, in 1850 when sectional disputes had become more heated. Only then did he directly criticize northern historians for their "pretensions" and southerners for neglecting their own heroes' biographies.[97]

On another occasion Simms concerned himself more directly with how biographers should present a southern subject. He had serious misgivings about Hugh A. Garland's *Life of John Randolph of Roanoke,* which he believed had not captured Randolph's true nature. Voicing an emerging romantic view of biography more than the Sparksian historical approach, he wrote to his friend Nathaniel Beverly Tucker that Garland had failed in the "*personal* delineation" of Randolph. "Of J.R. the man we see but little." This was not the Johnsonian vision; Simms was not asking for details of Randolph's domestic habits. Rather, he wanted a biography that got to "the depths of his nature, his philosophy, his heart." Simms implored Tucker, in the name of Virginia and the South, to write a competing life of Randolph. A member of Simms's own intellectual circle, Tucker would presumably be able to see Randolph as a southern exemplar of "genius," not just an eccentric. Simms so wanted his friend to assume this responsibility that he explained how many subscribers the book could expect, offered to "distribute a goodly number of your circulars myself in most of the Southern states," recommended stereotyping despite its initial expense, and estimated exactly how much printing and binding would cost. Tucker would have to move quickly: only by announcing his "claim as the true biographer of J.R." could he head off sales of Garland's book. Tucker never wrote the book, but he did contribute a harsh review of Garland's to the *Southern Quarterly Review,* prompting an equally harsh response from Garland.[98]

If Tucker had written a life of Randolph, he might have encountered what Simms admitted even as he encouraged the project: "Our people, as a whole, are illiterate—by no means a reading people." Simms exaggerated; he was expressing the southern intellectual's frustration that his region failed to appreciate intellectual activity properly. Yet he was also identifying a central reason for the dearth of southern biography. Getting the right men to write southern lives would solve only half the problem. Whether the objective of biography was to educate readers in history or to develop their individual or civic character (state, regional, or national), readers were required. So were publishers, and few southern firms had the resources to publish a work of potentially low sales. Hence Simms encouraged Tucker to consider subscription sales, a familiar southern approach to book-selling that allowed a publisher and author to gauge demand before producing the work, produce only the number of copies demanded, or abandon the project if demand was nonexistent.[99] For a major biographical work, a life and letters that could run to two volumes as did Kennedy's *Life of Wirt,* a southern author might have to find a northern publisher with greater resources than any firm in Charleston. (Most of the books reviewed in southern literary magazines came from northern presses.)

If Simms's biographies and biographical criticism illustrated the central issues for "southern biography," Griffith J. McRee's experience helps reveal why so little southern biography existed beyond Simms.[100] In the mid-1850s, McRee decided to write a life of the North Carolina patriot and Supreme Court justice James Iredell. Himself a North Carolinian, McRee had access to Iredell's correspondence because his wife was Iredell's granddaughter. He thus had the qualifications to write a life that was "sympathising" by Simms's standards and "authentic" by Sparks's. He prepared to write the way Ellet, Sparks, and the contributors to the Library of American Biography had: by collecting materials. He engaged in a long correspondence with David Lowry Swain, president of the University of North Carolina and founder of the state's historical society. He described the "great mass of matter in my hands" and the tortuous process of discovering it. He took "great pains to be *accurate.*" He also sought to establish the place of North Carolina in the history of the American Revolution. As McRee explained in an early letter about his plans, his determination "to publish the greater part" of Iredell's letters might hinder the flow of his narrative and the sales of his book, but "in this way I can contribute most to the honor of North Carolina." The state needed such works, argued McRee, because "there has been on the part of most American historians a studied & disingenuous effort to discredit the South & especially NC."[101]

McRee's philosophy was southern sectionalism, but not southern nationalism: he aimed to secure North Carolina's place in American history, not to suggest the need for a separate southern nation. "I honor the illustrious men of New England," he wrote, "and can even admire the genius and the enterprise that can dignify trifles, and exalt mediocrity. As a southern man, I simply demand admission into the National Pantheon for those who have vindicated their right by ability, virtue, and patriotism." McRee was squarely within the tradition of midcentury historical biography. He sought to preserve from oblivion a figure who might otherwise be forgotten, and he wrote about his quest for historical truth: despite his "tender regard to the reputation of the State," he had "spoken the truth & the whole truth in me."[102] Also like other authors in the 1840s and 1850s, McRee employed the techniques of historical biography in order to balance the historical record, to compensate for the gaps left by the preeminent historians of the Revolutionary era (such as Sparks himself). For McRee, the neglected area was North Carolina and more broadly the South.

When he prepared to publish the *Life of Iredell*, McRee came to believe that northerners, and in particular northern publishers, maligned southern readers and maltreated southern authors. To his chagrin, northerners seemed to consider southerners (and especially North Carolinians) "the most non-intellectual people in the Union—cultivating turpentine rather than letters—neither bookmakers, or book readers." Northern firms offered credit to northern authors but required southern writers "to pay cash down as soon as the work is printed."[103] McRee, who planned to sell the *Life of Iredell* by subscription, had to find the money to pay his publisher D. Appleton, and abandoned his early plan to write three volumes on Iredell, settling for two. The publisher might well have wanted McRee to pay his production costs in advance because it foresaw limited appeal for his work. Iredell, by 1857 largely forgotten, had never been well known outside North Carolina, and the bulk of McRee's volumes consisted of the judge's letters. But McRee saw the issue as sectional: northern publishers held a dim view of southern, or at least North Carolinian, readers and writers.

Back home, McRee found that the publishers may have been right. He tried to sell subscriptions for the *Life of Iredell* across the state, enlisting friends and local editors to assist him. But potential readers insisted on seeing the book before they subscribed, and interest was meager. The Reverend Eli W. Caruthers, a fellow historian of North Carolina and friend of McRee, explained the problem in language that revealed these literary men's perceptions of North Carolina society and of subscription salesmen. "The people of my congregation are very plain country people" who, like most other Carolina farmers, would not be able to afford the work, and who "have been so often imposed upon by subscriptions that they have got a prejudice against them." McRee would thus have to rely "on the educated and liberal few" for his sales. Equally revealing was Caruthers's explanation of what it would take to sell McRee's book: "a *cute* Yankee who will go from house to house among the plain country people & stay all night or take dinner, as it happens, & talk pleasantly to the daughters & kiss the children & then take no denial until he gets a subscription. A drudgery & a condescension this to which I would not submit & therefore made no attempt to get subscribers for my own little volumes." This image of sharp Yankee book peddlers invading the North Carolina countryside—and of North Carolinian authors like Caruthers refusing to stoop to such machinations—echoed Simms's references in the *Southern Quarterly Review* to the cultural gulf between North and South.[104] Whether because North Carolinians were wary of subscriptions or because booksellers made little effort, McRee found few buyers. He finally came to the "painful . . . reflection" that "our people are not a reading people, care little for literature & have but little disposition to encourage *home production*."[105] Simms had addressed only half the problem when he called for southerners to write southern biography. Even if provided with lives of their notable ancestors, North Carolinian readers might not fulfill their end of the bargain.[106]

When members of the "educated and liberal few" shared their impressions of the *Life of Iredell* with McRee, they evidenced more than just "sectional" reading. Some North Carolina readers praised it as what McRee had intended: a vindication of North Carolina's importance in the Revolution and a long-overdue contribution to the literature and history of their state. Such readers took biography to be a branch of history, as did authors like Jared Sparks; several of them corrected specific facts in the volumes. A reader in Murfreesboro, whose grandfather figured in Iredell's life and in the biography, wrote that McRee had made a worthy "contribution to the mass of revolutionary documents" and had published some correspondence that would cause a "*sensation*." (He was likely referring to McRee's decidedly unromantic depictions of several North Carolinian Revolutionary heroes.) In contrast, others read the *Life of Iredell* distinctly as biography and described their impressions of Iredell's character. A Bostonian, who assured McRee that New Englanders' hostility to the South applied only to politics and not to literature, effused about Iredell's "strength of mind & principle coupled with his strong affections." For some, McRee's mode of presenting that character—through Iredell's own letters, often connected by very little of McRee's own prose—was worth comment. Cadwallader Jones of Hillsboro compared the *Life of Iredell* with Boswell's *Life of Johnson*. Just as Boswell's conversations with Johnson displayed the great man's character, so Iredell's letters provided "an unmistakable portrait of a character which every one must admire and love." In Jones's opinion, those letters also created the best history of Revolutionary North Carolina yet written.[107] If works like McRee's took biography largely as a branch of history, readers could also seek in them the delineation of individual character.

Given the increasingly sectional uses of historical biography, it should come as no surprise that a major scholarly life of Thomas Jefferson became the greatest lightning rod for antebellum critics' political divisions. This biography of the South's favorite son was the work of a New Yorker. Although he considered himself "decidedly *national,* i.e. opposed to sectionality," Henry Stephens Randall possessed great sympathy for Jefferson. A lifelong Democrat and sometime Democratic officeholder, he admitted his "decided preference for the early Republican party over the Federal party." He resented how pro-Federalist biographers had piled "mountains of attack" on Jefferson politically and personally for fifty years: John Marshall, Richard Hildreth, and most recently John Hamilton in the biography of his father, Alexander. A gentleman farmer (who specialized in raising sheep) and educational reformer (who superintended public schools at the county and state levels), Randall shared much with his subject. If these similarities predisposed him to admire Jefferson, they also helped him understand Jefferson's multifarious spheres of activity—a biographical sympathy that could lead him "deeper" than authors who looked only at politics. Randall described Jefferson's horsemanship, violin playing, conversational style, and farming practices.[108]

Randall knew from the start what kind of biography he did not want to write. "I would rather be a dog & bay at the moon than write in that sickly, silly, adulatory, mutual-admiration-Society, mutual scratch-back, tickle-me Billy-&-I'll tickle-you-billy spirit in which most of our American biographies have been written," he exclaimed to his friend, the Virginia historian Hugh Blair Grigsby. More temperate, he explained in the book that "Mutual Admiration Society" biographers, who made America's Revolutionary heroes into "Goody-two-Shoes" without the least fault or foible, defeated their own purpose: "Nobody puts actual faith in human impersonations of the perfect, either in intellect or character." Echoing Samuel Johnson and citing Boswell as a model, he distinguished between reverence, the intended effect of eulogistic biographies, and love, an emotion stirred only by truth to life. If "faithfully delineated," Revolutionary heroes "would in most instances be equally revered, and vastly better loved than now. A few admitted faults or foibles—a few piquant individualities—a few of the lackings of common humanity—would show them to be human, to be real." While impossibly perfect images were one problem, exclusively public ones were another. Jefferson's previous biographer George Tucker had told only of Jefferson's public life. "My work," Randall explained to Jared Sparks, "will enter vastly more into *personal* details (biography proper)." Although Tucker was "usually accurate to the letter in facts," he "did not enter into Jefferson's *feelings*"; he never got "below the *middle* of his subject . . . to the *bottom*." Randall wanted to get to the bottom of Thomas Jefferson.[109]

Doing so required a combination not unlike the one Elizabeth Ellet had employed. On the one hand, he ransacked documents and books and requested information from noted historians. "I think I have blood hound stauchness in *running down* game. . . . I will wager that for every page I have written of Jefferson I have Consulted *ten* authorities." He treated Sparks deferentially, asking the elder historian to settle several questions authoritatively. On the other, he won the authorization of Jefferson's descendants and relied upon their assistance more than anyone else's. He spent weeks at Monticello, read family papers, and listened to countless anecdotes from people who had known Jefferson in his old age. What Sparks called "tradition" became an essential source for Randall. As a result Randall described Jefferson's domestic life at length, but the line between truth and tradition blurred as it had for Ellet. He declined to reignite forgotten scandal and declared that the personal recollections of *"Respectable* families" were "as good authority as any other peoples traditions can be on that Subject . . . it is ungraceful to dispute *family* traditions, about themselves when there is no object in it." Among the family traditions that Randall disdained to "rake up" was the true paternity of Sally Hemings's children—which, he boasted privately to Sparks, he had learned from the family. (According to Randall, Jefferson's grandson T. J. Randolph had identified Jefferson's beloved nephew Peter Carr as the true father, a fact that accounted for the children's resemblance to Jefferson.) Becoming an authorized biographer had two sides: Randall had far more material at his disposal than any previous biographer of Jefferson (and perhaps any previous biographer of *any* major American subject), but that material came with strings attached.[110]

Those strings became apparent at several points in his *Life of Thomas Jefferson* (1857–58). "A seasoning of piquant faults" might make biographical subjects human, but Randall quickly denied that Jefferson possessed any. Even when evidence existed of seemingly minor lapses, Randall found ways to challenge it. For instance, Daniel Webster had visited Monticello in 1824 and remembered Jefferson describing Wirt's life of Patrick Henry this way: "It is a poor book, written in bad taste, . . . intended to show off the writer more than the subject of the work." Unwilling to credit

Webster's version entirely because it lacked "those gradations and quali- fications . . . essential to convey accurate impressions," Randall wrote to someone who had known Jefferson's "views and modes of expression" as well as anyone had: Jefferson's grandson. Thomas Jefferson Randolph had never heard Jefferson speak of Wirt's book so severely and concluded that Webster had "put down only those parts of Mr. Jefferson's remarks which accorded with his own views." Jefferson's letters to Wirt, of course, re- vealed a much *more* critical view of the book and of Henry—but Randall endorsed the grandson's view. This choice revealed much about Randall's approach. He conducted vast research, he questioned one-dimensional ac- counts in the name of truth to life, and ultimately he relied on testimony from Jefferson's family.[111]

As reviews of Randall's work attested, Jefferson remained nearly as con- troversial as he had been sixty years before. In 1860–61 two northern magazines—the Harvard-centered, liberal Unitarian *North American Review* and the Yale-based, conservative Congregationalist *New Englander*—revis- ited their internecine squabbles on Randall's *Life of Jefferson*. Writing in the *North American,* Thomas Bulfinch praised Randall for exhibiting Jefferson's "true character," thanks to the testimony of Jefferson's descendants. Bul- finch apologized for how "this part of the country" had maligned Jefferson in his day: "the usual bitterness of political animosity was increased in re- gard to him by an infusion of theological odium." In the *New Englander,* the New Haven minister E. O. Dunning accused the *North American* of making pusillanimous excuses for "the voluptuary of Monticello." "Over confident in hasty conclusions, and disposed to cast 'theological odium' upon the religion of New England fifty years ago, [the *North American*] has stepped forth with the alacrity of an accepted champion to vindicate the private character of a man, who, whatever may be said of his intellectual emi- nence or distinguished public services, has, certainly, never been esteemed for moral purity or practical piety." Most of Dunning's article rehearsed the familiar litany of Jefferson's impieties, but the minister also took aim at Randall. Not only had he misrepresented Jefferson; he had also violated basic rules of evidentiary truth. How could a grandchild's general recollec- tions of Jefferson's conversational style outweigh Daniel Webster's specific testimony about a particular conversation? And what sort of answers did Randall expect when he asked Jefferson's acquaintances "what were his pri- vate virtues"? According to Dunning, Randall had produced yet another mutual-admiration-society biography, designed above all to please Jeffer- son's relatives and friends.[112]

Deeper divisions followed the Mason-Dixon line. Northern reviewers criticized Randall's style and especially his Democratic bias. Even though the *Atlantic Monthly* gave Randall credit for industry, accuracy, abundant new material, and "quite unusual perception of character," it faulted him severely for prolixity and digression. Worse, it argued that Randall's artistry lapsed over into artifice: "[t]he tropes and metaphors, the tawdry tinsel, the common tricks of feeble rhetoricians." Both the *Atlantic* and the *North American* disputed Randall's claim that many Federalists were covert monarchists. The *Life of Jefferson* had too much "one-sidedness and exaggeration," according to the *North American,* and Randall had treated his subject's opponents with more rancor than Jefferson ever displayed. The *Atlantic* wished for the day when biographers would "cease to be advocates." Horace Greeley, who admired much about Randall's work, nevertheless refused to countenance his excuse that Federalist biographers had attacked first; Marshall's *Life of Washington* was a half century old and was written in the midst of partisan wars long since over, and of course John Hamilton's life of his father would "never rise above the dignity of a party pamphlet." Randall aspired to "a higher rank" and had to be "judged accordingly." [113]

Conversely, southern reviewers adopted Randall's book as their own. The *Southern Literary Messenger* called it the best biography since Boswell's *Life of Johnson.* Southern reviews offered virtually no criticism of Randall's style; instead they praised his "vigour and perspicuity" and his "clear and bold" writing. They also found Randall eminently fair, indeed a long-overdue counterweight to the New England, Federalist bias of most previous American biographies and histories. Randall himself complained about this bias, writing to his friend Grigsby that "New England slanders against Mr. J." and denouncing Charles Francis Adams as a "little twopenny *Boston* cliquist" who had defamed Jefferson in order to glorify his grandfather. In turn, Grigsby reviewed Randall's work for the *Richmond Enquirer:* "So many misrepresentations of our leading statesmen . . . have been made by Northern writers, that we have long ceased to look even for justice from Northern pens." The southern acclaim for Randall's book stemmed in part from Jefferson's position as Virginia's greatest and most maligned son. It also resulted from how Randall interpreted Jefferson's attitude toward slavery. Letting Jefferson appear "*in his own words*" and claiming to express "no opinion of my own on the subject," Randall argued that Jefferson had opposed slavery personally but had also opposed any agitation to eliminate it or to bar its westward extension. Randall knew that this view, founded in the "truth" of Jefferson's own words, would "offend all the Northern fanatics" who believed Jefferson "the Great

Apostle of Anti Slavery," and he hoped that southern praise would balance northern criticism. He was not disappointed. Grigsby, whose *Richmond Enquirer* reviews were widely reprinted, recommended the work to "every Virginian who is proud of the great son of the Old Dominion." Randall would "be hunted . . . by all the *filial* biographers of Federalism, by the whole New England literary clan!" But even that testified to his honesty: in southerners' eyes Randall's work was not partisan, and the fact that "it was not written by a Virginian" gave it additional credence. Randall's *Life of Jefferson* became fodder for the growing sectional crisis, and specifically for the increasingly assertive southern attack on northern history writing.[114]

At the same time, Randall espoused another conception of biography writing—one that Jared Sparks barely recognized. In the 1850s Randall and Grigsby conducted a running debate over a forty-year-old biography: *Sketches of the Life and Character of Patrick Henry*. Randall called William Wirt's book "the least life-like biog. I ever read" and "the very worst & most smothering & extinguishing biography *to the Subject of it* that was ever written!" Wirt's elaborate prose and depiction of Henry as Greco-Roman statesman had obscured Henry's own characteristics. "It is all Wirt, Wirt, Wirt,—ornate Wirt—not a bit of native Henry a man of more than 50 times the real genius of his biographer." By presenting a "*public* model of Henry . . . dressed up & untrue to the original," Wirt had diminished his subject. Grigsby, in their day the foremost historian of Virginia, did not deny "that there is much bad taste in the writing, that the work was hastily and imperfectly executed, and that the fame of Henry deserves a better record." But Grigsby believed Wirt's book—which, he reminded Randall, presumed modestly to be only "Sketches"—"a most worthy and particular contribution to our biographical literature. It has done much good, and will do great good for years to come." As "a Virginian," Grigsby considered "the effect of [Wirt's] book on our young men" and praised it as "the tribute of an adopted son to the memory of our great orator." Besides, Wirt had preserved numerous anecdotes and facts that would otherwise "have perished altogether."[115]

As Grigsby wrote to Randall, "We regard the book from different points of view."[116] Of the two, Grigsby better understood and sympathized with Wirt's motives and purposes. For classically educated men in the early republic, biography writing commemorated a worthy ancestor, educated the rising generation, and demonstrated the republican virtue of the author. The man who wrote biography earned noble fame for his civic service. Grigsby perceived Wirt's place in that culture of biography, not to mention his specific status as an "adopted" Virginian all the more desirous of praising the commonwealth's favorite son. A leader in the Virginia Historical Society, Grigsby also appreciated that Wirt had belonged to the last generation capable of saving Revolutionary memories from oblivion. Randall was less generous, and he employed another set of standards entirely. He, too, believed Henry deserved a fitting monument, but his terms had little to do with usefulness to a rising generation and nothing to do with neoclassical ideas of fame, virtue, or biography. He saw the biographer as more than a moralistic or antiquarian conduit between past and present. Rather, Randall asked this question: was Wirt's Henry "life-like"? Randall's language implied that he was not and that a biographer's portrayal could "smother" or "extinguish" a subject as easily as bring him to life. Truth to life required two characteristics in a biographer: the literary talent to depict a subject, and the sympathy with that subject necessary to avoid imposing (for instance) an overly metaphorical writing style upon a plain-speaking orator. Whereas Grigsby's vision of biography looked backward, taking Wirt on his own republican terms, Randall's was firmly grounded in the present. It echoed the emergent romantic view, critically current in 1857, that biography was a form of literary art.

As such, the biographer shared as much with the portraitist as with the historian. After stating the importance of the individualizing foible (even if he claimed not to find any in Jefferson), Randall went further: he cited novelists as practitioners of the truth to life that biographers needed more of. "Do the great masters of fiction, untrammeled by the biographer's *facts,* free to choose both their traits and their incidents, represent their favorite characters—those they mean to render most attractive to their readers— either as icicles or prudes?" Biographers could take a lesson from fiction. And from portraiture: "The artist knows that shadows are necessary to throw out what should be prominent and give expression to his picture; and, consequently, he throws the light so on his subject as to *make shadows.* Without this all is flat and tame. Minor faults, in biography, are the painter's shadows!" The danger was that "pure art" could be mistaken for "candor"—that the novelist's or the artist's tricks could enable a biographer to make lies more believable. What would happen if the biographer's "truth to life" became purely a literary artifice, employed to lead readers to suspend their suspicions about the actual truth of the biography?[117]

Randall valued truth as much as did Sparks, but he defined it more subjectively. Randall repeatedly told Grigsby that he intended to write "the naked *truth*" no matter what partisans on either side might say. In his first volume he explained what truth meant. "We conceive there is one plain rule to follow in all cases; and that is to be truthful in the expression of

opinions formed on fair, and what is believed to be sufficiently full investigation. In other words, the writer should be fearlessly true to himself,
to *his own* mind and conscience." Randall needed, he told Grigsby, to envision "my *whole* subject" before he began writing, because "No painter or
sculptor ever wrought a *great* work, without having a perfect & vivid ideal
before him." He acknowledged that the biographer's "high art" lay in constructing, not just revealing, character, for "no two pair of eyes will see
any man or thing just alike." Research was essential: the biographer had to
conduct "sufficiently full investigation." But it was not enough. When the
biographer at last decided his "opinion," the eyes through which he saw
his subject would inevitably be his own.[118]

For Henry Randall in 1857, then, truth to fact, truth to life, and truth
to himself all mattered. Critics might contest all three truths. Some would
challenge the particular biographer's facts, depictions, and conceptions; in
the 1850s, those challenges often grew out of the widening sectional divide.
Others might question the very transformations in biography that the new
"truths" implied. If biography would be the vehicle to add women, Native
Americans, or African Americans to the nation's historical imagination,
new kinds of evidence might need to be accepted as "authentic." Writing
with a sympathetic understanding of one's subject—which might require a
sympathetic understanding of that subject's region—could subject the biographer to tensions between fact and feeling. Above all, if biography was
literary artistry, the biographer had a more creative role to play than Jared
Sparks, the biographer as historian, might have admitted.

Hawthorne, Sparks, and Biography at Midcentury

In September 1852, the Democratic party's magazine ranked Jared Sparks with "those whom the God of the Jews accursed as the movers and destroyers of landmarks." Equally astonishing, these words appeared in a celebratory article about a new book that hardly resembled anything Sparks ever wrote: Nathaniel Hawthorne's *Life of Franklin Pierce*, the authorized biography of the party's standard bearer.[1] It is all too easy to separate biographies into categories with distinct terms of analysis: to speak of campaign lives in terms of political ideologies and visions of manhood and historical biographies in connection with the New England Unitarian Whigs and their detractors. This tendency becomes more tempting when we remember that biographies emanated from different realms of America's literary culture — the political-communications network of newspapers and local editors, the benevolent empire of the Evangelical United Front and the American Tract Society, the literary publishers of Boston and New York. Even readers like Michael Floy and Julia

Parker distinguished varieties of biographies and held them to different standards — religious, patriotic, artistic. Still, they read across the lines we use to talk about genres: not just the boundaries between biography and fiction, but also those within biography itself. How can we reconstruct a world in which some people probably read lives of William Henry Harrison, Ann Judson, *and* Cotton Mather? Noting these readers' own multiple standards, we might leave our categories intact and distinct. Conversely, we can also look for moments when somebody juxtaposed seemingly incongruous biographies, blurred the lines between biographical forms — and ask why. Such a moment occurred in September 1852, when Jared Sparks faced authorial disgrace and Nathaniel Hawthorne turned his pen to the campaign biography of his college friend.

Sparks's troubles began on February 12, 1851, when a correspondent to the New York *Evening Post* challenged how he had edited George Washington's letters. This writer had compared Sparks's versions of several letters (in his *Life and Writings of Washington*) against the same letters as recently published in William B. Reed's biography of his grandfather, Pennsylvania's Revolutionary president Joseph Reed. Apparently Sparks had omitted certain passages of the letters and "dignified" the language in other places, for instance substituting "General Putnam" for Washington's "Old Put." The British historian Lord Mahon soon intensified the charges. Researching in England's State Papers, Mahon happened to read the originals of several Washington letters that Sparks had reprinted. In his *History of England,* Mahon reported more discrepancies, notably alterations in letters where Washington had criticized New England. A pamphlet war ensued. Sparks responded that he had considered grammatical correction the editor's duty: indeed, he had only corrected what Washington himself would have, given the time. He had not favored one region over another, nor had he added passages as Mahon claimed. Sparks also challenged Reed's versions of several documents. Reed, it turned out, had accidentally left passages out of a few letters, thus nurturing the impression that Sparks had added those passages. Mahon accepted Sparks's reply to this last charge but insisted that Sparks's editing had been inexcusable. On one level this controversy concerned only the accuracy of documents and the rules of editing. Sparks edited Washington's writings as he would have edited an article for the *North American Review,* and the *Evening Post* and Lord Mahon challenged this practice.[2]

As played out in American magazines, the dispute ran deeper. It was about editorial honesty, according to the *Literary World.* Republishing the *Evening Post* article along with a commentary of its own in March 1851, the *World* argued that Sparks's excessive license had suppressed the truth and thereby misrepresented Washington. The *North American* defended Sparks (one of its own) and attacked Mahon, largely over the issue of editorial prerogative. After Sparks's first pamphlet response, *Harper's* took his side in September 1852: Sparks had refuted Mahon's "hasty" charges "clearly, calmly, and convincingly." Following Mahon's response the same month, the *Literary World* changed its emphasis. Sparks's editing remained inexcusable ("we must desire the evidence, the whole evidence, and nothing but the evidence"), but now Mahon deserved censure on nationalistic grounds. In his latest pamphlet, the English historian had warned young American historians to give the unvarnished truth. "You are far too great a nation, and have far too high a destiny before you, for these little devices of suppression and concealment. Be less vain and more proud! Show yourselves as you really are!

Publish your State Papers as you find them! Do not in the West treat the characters of your great men as in the East they treat the persons of their Harem slaves!" The *Literary World* told Mahon to mind his own backyard first. American writers had shown no "particular want of truthfulness," so why "arrogantly confine his lecture to young *American* historians"? This was the context in which the *Democratic Review* published its article in September 1852—but its critique of Sparks would shift the issues of debate, back to biography.[3]

Meanwhile, in June 1852 the Democrats nominated the little-known Franklin Pierce for president, and Hawthorne offered to write his friend's biography. Hawthorne originally professed reluctance to write Pierce's life and disinterest in any patronage post that might result from the service, but by early fall he produced a competent campaign biography and began to consider the consulship at Liverpool a desirable reward. He arranged for his publishers, Ticknor, Reed, and Fields of Boston, to produce the book even though campaign literature lay outside their usual activities (and even though Ticknor was "a bitter whig," according to Hawthorne). The *Life of Franklin Pierce* came out on September 11, just seven weeks before the election but in time for the *Democratic Review* to devote an article to it in that month's issue and for the *Literary*

World to review it in the September 25 issue that also contained its article on Sparks and Mahon. To its publishers, Hawthorne's *Life of Franklin Pierce* was more than a campaign biography. Ticknor, Reed, and Fields produced more copies of it than of any previous book in the firm's history, and every copy contained copious advertisements. The paperback edition, which comprised three quarters of the copies printed, had advertisements for "HAWTHORNE'S WRITINGS" on and inside the back cover, and an entire page of reviews of the just-published *Blithedale Romance* inside the front cover. The publishers' packaging and Hawthorne's name linked the *Life of Franklin Pierce* commercially to the literary world.[4]

The book's contents lay squarely within the conventions of campaign biography. Hawthorne knew those conventions precisely, as a July letter to Pierce revealed: "There will be ample stuff, I think, for this [the military] part of the work—which, though it should be made prominent, ought not to be so much as to overshadow you as a man of peaceful pursuits. 'Cedant arma togae.' A statesman in your proper life— a gallant soldier in the hour of your country's need—such, in the circumstances, is the best mode of presenting you." Hawthorne molded his friend's life to the well-tested, popular images of Cincinnatus and Union man. Like every campaign

Price 37½ cents.

LIFE

OF

FRANKLIN PIERCE.

BY

NATHANIEL HAWTHORNE.

With an Authentic Portrait.

BOSTON:
TICKNOR, REED, AND FIELDS.
MDCCCLII.

The Boston publishers Ticknor and Fields printed more copies of Nathaniel Hawthorne's *Life of Franklin Pierce*—most of them paperbound, like this one—than of any previous book in the firm's history. This paperbound edition contained several pages of advertisement for Hawthorne's more "literary" works. (Courtesy American Antiquarian Society) biographer before him, he also gave his subject a patriotic ancestry. Like previous Democratic biographers, he made Pierce an ardent exponent of Jacksonian democracy and heir to Old Hickory (including an implausible scene in which the dying Jackson suggests that Pierce would be just the man to lead the nation!), as well as a man of the people in his native New Hampshire. Hawthorne did depart from convention in describing Pierce's growth over time. In earlier campaign lives (and several pamphlet biographies of Pierce), candidates needed not develop great qualities, for they seemed born with them. Experiences served to reveal character not to instill or enhance it. Hawthorne's Pierce developed: an initially indolent collegian, he found industrious habits later. Perhaps this was the Pierce Hawthorne had known, but such a portrayal served political ends too: squaring early difficulties with later success, making a virtue of Pierce's failures, and suggesting that the 48-year-old Pierce could similarly grow into the presidency.[5]

This was not the first time Hawthorne had ventured into formulaic biography. His 1842 book *Biographical Stories for Children* resembled other volumes of juvenile biography, complete with framing narrative (little Edward Temple is losing his eyesight, and his father tells biographical anecdotes to exercise his imagination and raise his spirits) and moralistic resolutions (little Prince Charlie will not understand why little "Noll" Cromwell refuses to defer to him; Charles's antidemocratic arrogance lasts into adulthood, costs him his head, and elevates his juvenile antagonist to power).[6] The difference between these *Biographical Stories* and the *Life of Franklin Pierce* was not that Hawthorne had learned how to transcend formula, for he knew that success in these ventures lay in adherence to formula. However, between the children's book and the campaign biography he made his literary reputation with *The Scarlet Letter, The House of the Seven Gables,* and *The Blithedale Romance.* This reputation made the *Life of Franklin Pierce* a literary event, despite its conventionality. Hawthorne's *Life of Franklin Pierce* received far more attention than any previous campaign biography because Hawthorne had written it.

Predictably, the reviews split along partisan lines. Democratic and Whig newspapers agreed that the biography was "as pleasant reading as the best of the author's romances" but interpreted this remark differently. Democrats meant that Hawthorne had transcended the ordinarily workmanlike qualities of the genre, while Whigs meant that he had outdone himself in creating an entirely fictional character. The debate centered on how "the distinguished novelist" had used his unquestionably "splendid talents":

by telling Pierce's life "in language as eloquent as it is truthful," or by countering "the barrenness" of that life with "a few incidents manufactured for the purposes of this campaign." The parties' national organs extended the debate begun in local newspapers. The *American Whig Review* upbraided Hawthorne for prostituting his talents for "the vivid inspiration of some promised office." Concluding its favorable notice of *The Blithedale Romance* with a few paragraphs on the *Life of Franklin Pierce,* the *Whig Review* lamented that Hawthorne had produced a book likely to "bring him neither fame nor credit." The Whig magazine reminded him that the present was an age of democratic literature, not "servile" literary patronage. "There are 'hacks' enough, Heaven knows, infesting every city, who would be right glad and well fitted to perform such filthy work. . . . [L]et your rare genius soar for ever above the atmosphere of mushroom heroes and penny biographies."[7] The *Democratic Review,* of course, told a different story—at the same time it attacked Jared Sparks.

Two ideas underlay the *Democratic Review*'s critique of Sparks: that he had replaced the real Washington with a lifeless "Puritan" substitute, and that he embodied the "Old Fogy" school of biography writing all too common in contemporary America. Sparks

has despoiled all our great men, and more particularly our greatest men, of their characteristics; has destroyed their individuality; removed because it was offensive to him, every peculiar mark and token by which we love to recognise—by which we can only recognise—the eccentricities of a noble manhood; spoiled Washington's bad grammar, and robbed dear old Putnam of his curses; . . . and reduced all things we worship, our great men, our heroes, our Penates, to a vulgar low rank of first-class Puritan college propriety. Mr. Jared Sparks has made biography what it never was before—the lie to history.

In securing the historical "dignity" of his subjects, Sparks had abandoned truth, but truth of a different definition than his own. The *Democratic Review* meant specifically *biographical* truth, the sort of portrayal that allowed readers to "recognise" subjects in their humanity and "individuality." Sparks had replaced individuality with archetypal virtue, indeed Puritan (and Whig) New England virtue. He was not alone: the *Democratic Review* found most American political biography equally lacking. Reading Marshall's *Life of Washington* resembled a medieval form of torture, and most volumes of American leaders' works were the products of "paper-makers, speech-collectors, fragment-editors." Worse, "the biographies of our great men have all been thrown into the hands of lawyers." These "Old Fogy persons" who "imagined they could write!" produced biographical legal briefs instead. They pleaded their subjects' cases to the world, covering up and apologizing for exactly the human touches that made biographies true to life. America had produced great subjects for biography, especially Jefferson and Jackson, but never the biographer to do them justice.[8]

Enter Hawthorne, the "literary character" American biography needed. Pierce was fortunate to have "attracted the attention of a proved and elegant writer . . . respected abroad and beloved at home." Hawthorne had indulged in no "rhodomontade," had not perverted the facts, had not covered up or apologized for his subject's humanity. Unlike most biographers, he possessed a sense of "proportion," giving each part of Pierce's life proper weight and never becoming tediously verbose. Hawthorne's success resulted also from his long acquaintance with Pierce. The biography was "the simple statement of a man's life, by a schoolfellow and friend, who is anxious that the world should duly estimate the most marked characteristics of a retiring yet great career." Whereas Old Fogy biographers adulated their subjects, Hawthorne *knew* his.[9]

Politics certainly helps explain the

Democratic Review's stance and language. The Old Fogy biographers were mostly New England Whigs, the "legatees" of their New England subjects. The unabashedly Federalist John Marshall, though a Virginian, had attacked Jefferson and the Republicans in his *Life of Washington.* And Sparks seemed to represent the New England, "Puritan" moralism that Democrats reviled (despite the critique of Puritanism prevalent in Sparks's Library of American Biography). In a sense, the *Democratic Review*'s notion of biography squared with its political ideology. The previous year, in an article entitled "The Duty of a Biographer," the magazine had argued against the familiar notion "de mortuis nil, nisi bonum" and in favor of complete truth telling in biography. Now it criticized biographers for touching up and covering up their subjects. Here was a biographical version of Democrats' social laissez-faire: freed from righteous biographers, George Washington should appear as himself, just as Americans ought to be free from New England, Whig moral reformism. The phrase "Old Fogy" also had political connotations. Old Fogies were the rhetorical foil of the Young America movement of the early 1850s, whose periodical champion was the *Democratic Review.* By the fall campaign of 1852, the language of youth and newness battling Old Fogies appeared more frequently than any ideology specific to the movement. The *Literary World,* the other national magazine that discussed Hawthorne's *Life of Pierce* and Sparks's editing in a single issue in September 1852 (though in separate articles), had connections to Young America's earlier, literary incarnation. Its editor (and Hawthorne's friend) Evert A. Duyckinck had been a leader in that movement, which had also championed New York as the center of a newly energetic, truly American literature. The Young America connection helps explain the *Literary World*'s simultaneous critiques of Sparks and Mahon. Sparks seemed to personify New England's stodginess and self-importance, while Mahon had imperiously offered unsolicited advice to *young* American historians.[10]

Embedded in the politics, the *Democratic Review* and *Literary World* were describing a new idea of biography, however incongruously they attached it to Hawthorne's *Life of Franklin Pierce.* Hawthorne did provide two useful elements. First, his preface emphasized his own authorship and suggested a kind of biographical truth unusual for campaign biographies and historical-political biographies. Claiming unfamiliarity with campaign biography, describing his closeness to Pierce, and resting on his reputation as a literary man, Hawthorne rhetorically (and disingenuously) replaced one notion of biography writing with another. "Conven-

tional" images would disappear, supplanted by the knowledge of an intimate, apolitical friend above the fray of politics. Such a friend could offer a "truer" portrait, more reliable than another formulaic biography: "misrepresented by indiscriminate abuse, on the one hand, and by aimless praise, on the other," Pierce deserved to "be sketched by one who had had opportunities of knowing him well, and who is certainly inclined to tell the truth." Between Whigs' indiscriminate abuse and Democrats' aimless praise — the praise common to biographies of all sorts, not just campaign lives — lay Hawthorne and "the truth."[11] Second, by focusing on Pierce's late but steady maturation, Hawthorne suggested the possibilities of biography as bildungsroman. Noting this recurring theme, Democratic reviewers hailed the *Life of Franklin Pierce* as an example of campaign biography as literary art.

The concept of biography as an artistic pursuit stood at odds with both Sparks's historical vision and the didactic approach. The "true" biographer, as the *Democratic Review* put it, had to suit the biography to the subject, not the other way around. Writing an "exact and full representation of a great man" required first the imagination to inhabit a subject's "being" and then the literary ability to set it "down on paper for the comprehension of the crowd" — as difficult a task as playing one of Shakespeare's heroes well. Because Sparksian biography always maintained the "dignity of history," it could never excel in what defined biography: the sense that the individual life had a human story. Even in its overtly partisan discussion of Sparks and Hawthorne, the *Democratic Review* reconfigured the relationship between biography and history. Biography was not a branch of history. Rather, the two were distinct, and sometimes the dignity of history had to be sacrificed for the truth of biography, that is, the truth of human life. Moreover, because every subject possessed "individuality," cookie-cutter didacticism and biographical moralism alike — from Hawthorne's 1842 *Biographical Stories* to Washington getting "Sparked" — undermined biographical truth.[12] This concept of biography would flower in America in the 1850s.

By decade's end, it would also produce the biographer whose absence the *Democratic Review* lamented in September 1852: not Nathaniel Hawthorne but James Parton. In 1858 Horace Greeley recommended a new book to Henry Stephens Randall, who had just finished writing his *Life of Thomas Jefferson*: Parton's *Life of Aaron Burr.* Randall liked what he read. "It *is* a work of ability and has the interest of a novel throughout. There is one point I especially like about it — his getting down from the historic stilts. If biography is mere history, why keep on the stilts if you like them, and be as dry as Judge Marshall. But no man on earth can write *personal* biography, and tell *little incidents* and *anecdotes* in that style, without making himself and his anecdotes ridiculous." Perhaps, as one editor told Randall, a book like his *Life of Jefferson* or Parton's *Life of Burr* would not "run away from the counters of the stores like Fanny Fern's bad-in-grain volumes, or Uncle Tom's Cabin, or the 'Wide World' and a hundred other equally perishable productions."[13] Against a "damned mob of scribbling women," biographies stood as little chance of bestsellerdom as *The Scarlet Letter* did, and biographers could evince their jealousy or anxiety just as Hawthorne could. But new, literary notions of biography, and Parton's style of writing it, would bring biography closer to the novel than anyone since Parson Weems had imagined.

The Inner Man in
the Literary Market,
1850–1880

From early in life, I have wondered why such men as Dickens and Thackeray should
choose to expend themselves upon fiction, when they could find true stories to tell so much
more interesting, & I often used to say: Some day, a man will come along who will
create a new branch of the fine arts—Biography. But it never crossed my mind, that I
should attempt anything of the kind, for I knew very well that to make a real & vivid
biography would require an amount and minuteness of investigation which could never
be repaid in money, nor done without money. —James Parton to Charles Eliot Norton,
February 5, 1867

From the 1850s on, American critics sought to do what James Parton described: make biography a branch of the fine arts, not a handmaiden to
history or a handbook of virtues. As art, biography would assume new
characteristics. It would capture subjects' inner lives, or, in the words of
the *New York Times,* "show precisely what manner of men they were."[1] A
romantic conception, the quest for the inner man distinguished the biographer from the historian. It would redefine character as individuality: not
the archetypal virtues of self-made men's biographies and pious women's
memoirs, not the little foibles of Samuel Johnson's "domestic privacies,"
but the elements of mind and soul that made a subject unique. And it
would read like a novel, even as it told only truth. This new biography
might thrive in the literary marketplace, but it would always remain above
it. Like true romantic poetry and prose, its authors would draw inspiration
from their subjects, not their pocketbooks.

James Parton drew his inspiration from both. He was the first American to make biography his literary career, a choice that became possible
only when biography came to be defined as a *literary* endeavor distinct
from didactic and historical writing. Like the critics, Parton infused biog-

raphy with a romantic spirit: the *Times* characterized him as a seeker of subjects' "inner lives." At the same time, he continued to evoke the two kinds of biography that had prevailed for half a century. He always emphasized the minuteness of his investigation, and he believed that readers could draw lessons from biography. In working with multiple visions of the genre, Parton created his own, a distinct biographical style and ideology that critics and readers recognized as contemporary and particularly American. The style blended elements from the very popular fiction and journalism that some critics derided as commercial. The ideology emphasized American freedom and ingenuity, not romantic genius. Parton created this new "American biography" at a moment when new notions of hierarchy entered American literary culture and publishing. To earn a living in biography, he published his work with a variety of magazines and firms: with not only the nation's leading literary publisher but also subscription-publishing houses whose productions were widely considered of lower literary quality; with not only the highbrow *North American Review* but also New York's most famous middle-class story paper and the *Youth's Companion*. Every site of publication demanded a distinct kind of biography, and Parton knew how to meet their demands. He built a career as "biographer" because he understood the American literary universe of the 1860s and 1870s—its multiple genres and its multiple markets.

Parton's fan letters indicated that his career strategy succeeded. Some viewed his work as a window into his subjects' character; others commented on it as history; still others valued it for its didactic uses. By the late 1860s, Parton's readers (and most reviewers and numerous publishers and magazine editors) saw him as America's foremost biographer. Because many of them understood "biographer" to be his career, Parton received requests to write biographies of all sorts: lives of Lincoln, but also campaign biographies and obituaries of readers' beloved relatives. More generally, Americans who discussed their biographical reading in the 1860s and 1870s increasingly expressed romantic sensibilities like those the critics prescribed, even if they interpreted biographies far more diversely than the critics, with their subtle and overt assaults on common readers' tastes, might have preferred.

The Critics, the Public, and the Romantic Transformation of Biographical Theory

No distinctively American biographical theory developed in periodical criticism between 1830 and 1860. Unlike in the first quarter of the century, when critical concepts drawn from Samuel Johnson's essays had vied with notions of biography derived from American republicanism, calls for specifically "American" biography dwindled after 1820. Reviewers praised Sparks and other authors for contributing to Americans' knowledge of their past, but few critics considered "American biography" an endeavor with its own properties. Instead, American periodicals' critical discussions of biography came to reflect English romantic concepts, without the earlier tension between English literary models and American political-cultural imperatives. This transformation separated American criticism of biography from most of the actual biographies written in America during these years. Articles about the genre *as a genre* tended not to discuss the forms of biography that proliferated most: religious memoirs, didactic lives of self-made men, or campaign biographies. With the important exceptions of Ralph Waldo Emerson and Henry Theodore Tuckerman, virtually no American writer produced biographies and biographical sketches along the romantic model. The emerging biographical theory also gave critics, especially those who wrote for self-consciously high-literary magazines, literary grounds for defining most biographies as bad. By 1860, a number of American periodicals created an implicit hierarchy that cast not only most biographies, but also the authors and readers of those biographies, as "low." Because the new criticism defined biography as a literary art distinct from both didactic writing and history, it suggested a new literary career: "biographer."

As early as 1817, American critics began to consider the sanctity of private life and the protection of heroes from petty scandal-mongers. The *Port Folio* claimed that biographers should not indulge in "idle, indecent, or impertinent anecdotes" *unless* publishing such incidents "can be shown, positively, to be conducive to some proper purpose, moral or intellectual." The doctrine of privacy was at this point incomplete (indecent anecdotes were still acceptable if they served a proper purpose), and it was still a matter for critical dispute. In its 1830 article "Biographical Mania," the *New-York Mirror* noted that some critics ridiculed the desire to see public figures "arrayed in their 'dressing gown and slippers.'" However, the *Mirror* welcomed this desire as a symptom of enlightenment and democracy. If people wanted public men to appear in their "private character, to stand the scrutiny of their fellow men," this was because the "march of intellect" had made "nearly every man of only limited accomplishments a thinker and an observer." It was also peculiarly appropriate in a nation with a "republican government, where the ruling men of the times should be known as they really are." This argument inverted the earlier idea that republican biographies should focus on subjects' public character—but it nonetheless suggested that American political ideology dictated distinct characteristics in American biographies. Changing definitions of "republican" help account for the inversion. Especially in the hands of Jacksonians, American republicanism assumed a far more democratic cast than in the first decades of the century. By 1830, too, campaign biographies were part of political campaigns, offering citizens knowledge (however partisan) about "the ruling men of the times."[2]

Over the next thirty years, the qualifications dropped away and the doctrine of privacy came to dominate American biographical criticism. The *Christian Examiner* wrote categorically in 1840 that publicizing private foibles "is very much like disinterring the dead, in order to gratify a perverse curiosity." The *North American Review* decried the abuse of biography for the sake of "paltry gossip." Satisfying the "prurient curiosity" of contemporary readers would produce "ephemeral" works. If Plutarch had concentrated on his subjects' private habits, would anyone still read his *Lives*? "Delicacy" also hung in the balance when biographers invaded subjects' privacy. Why, asked the *North American,* "should death remove the seal with which in life the most obtrusive inquisitiveness would not dare to tamper?" The subject's property extended to "[c]onfidential interviews, communications designed for no third person, . . . [f]oibles that were veiled from open view," and "[p]rivate correspondence." Only someone who would "rifle a dead man's purse or wardrobe" would seek and publish any of these. Mixing metaphors furiously, Evert A. Duyckinck called scandal-mongers "biographical assassins," "foul cellar-rats who gnaw at the foundations of mighty edifices," and vultures with a "scent for carrion and decay." The blemishes they unearthed were like "motes placed in the object-glass of a telescope, which, magnified a thousand-fold, become spots on the sun." In 1857, the Boston *Evening Gazette* published an article with the same title as the *New-York Mirror*'s twenty-seven years before. But now the "Biographical Mania" was a literary disorder, not a happy by-product of democratic intelligence. Biographers were "a species of harpies" who either worshipped subjects mindlessly or dredged up private immoralities to besmirch the reputations of the great. No special rules applied to American biographers; the *Gazette* cited cases of biographical indecency on both sides of the Atlantic to make its point.[3]

The doctrine of privacy reflected evolving notions about the separation between public and private life and about the sanctity of the domestic sphere *and* the private document. In the United States and England, the genteel middle class increasingly defined itself by partitioning life into "spheres": a public and presumably masculine world of commerce and politics, a domestic and feminized world of child-raising and family. We have seen how didactic biographies participated in promulgating this cultural ideology, by placing presidential candidates in entirely masculine public "families" and depicting the female subjects of many religious memoirs in their homes and through their diaries and correspondence with other women. The concept of "separate spheres" was not solely an issue of gender; it also became an equally powerful marker of place and class. Farm families and working-class families generally could not divide work from home. Nor did working-class families live in enclosed domestic spaces, for the tenements of New York offered little of the privacy that defined the middle-class household. The concept of privacy—keeping others, particularly those below one's own class, out of one's home and personal affairs—extended to personal documents, as critics of biography saw it. Readers who wanted to see the intimate letters of the great and genteel, and authors who supplied such documents, were like interloping guests who did not belong in the parlor at all.[4]

Propriety was not the only objection to publishing private documents. Although it would seem that correspondence, diaries, and other such sources could only help reveal a subject's character, the *North American* and other journals were not so certain. Too many so-called biographies were really tedious, multivolume heaps of documents, and it was no wonder that they remained "uncut on the shelves of private and public libraries." Mere piles of correspondence and memoranda placed an unfair burden on the reader, who "has embarked with his author as a cabin-passenger, and finds himself, before he is fairly out to sea, compelled to work his passage," organizing for himself the materials that the author had failed to digest. Worse, as the *Christian Review* pointed out in 1856, such sources could easily "mislead" the biographer. Humility or meekness expressed in a diary or letter could have been written in a moment of "retirement or reflection" or in deference to convention, and thus would not show a subject's characteristics in actual social relations. Still more dangerous, biographers could misuse documents. A hack biographer could take a single unrepresentative letter as a measure of "character," just as an inept scientist would mistake a "mote" on the telescope for a sunspot. The *Atlantic Monthly* drew an analogy between bad biographers and entomologists. If the writer minutely and dispassionately documented his subject the way the scientist would dissect an insect, he would miss something more fundamental than any fact or foible could reveal.[5]

The repeated image of motes misread as sunspots underscored something deeper: complaints about misusing documents and invading privacy were also statements about what counted as "truth." When the *Christian Examiner* argued against biographically "disinterring the dead" for curiosity's sake, it cautioned those who "pretend an uncommon concern for the truth, and who are exceedingly anxious that the whole truth be told, to remember that there is more than one species of truth. There is a truth of *sentiment* as well as of *facts*."[6] This might seem a critique of Sparksian truth, in which documentary evidence was paramount. More accurately, it was a critique of the rationality behind Sparks's definition, of the idea that truth could emerge solely from documents and "facts." (It was no accident that critics compared bad biographers to scientists.) Most critics who championed the doctrine of privacy did not take aim at narrative biographies of second-rank historical figures like most of the ones in Sparks's Library of American Biography. After all, Sparks and the authors who followed his lead discussed only the barest "domestic privacies." The problem arose with biographies that claimed to illustrate their subjects' thought processes, inner motives, and unique characteristics—and with biographical subjects for whom such topics seemed central. Two kinds of subjects particularly inhabited this category: intellectual figures (especially authors of some originality) and public men like Napoleon whose actions had made a significant mark upon their societies and world history. These were the subjects whom nineteenth-century critics, authors, and readers called men of "genius." For such men, different rules of "truth" applied.

Those rules, as well as most of the concepts of biography in midcentury American periodicals, had roots in English romantic biographical criticism. Sometimes that criticism was defensive. In the wake of Boswell's *Life of Johnson,* tell-all biographies of still-living and recently deceased writers became popular mainstream fare. No longer confined to admittedly scandalous Grub Street productions, they came in numerous forms: "lives and letters" containing masses of correspondence, volumes of "table talk" with anecdotes of the great man's conversation, expositions of private life. Such Boswellian biographies swelled into large volumes or multivolume sets (John Gibson Lockhart's *Life of Sir Walter Scott* ran seven volumes). Thanks to new publishing technologies and an expanding reading public, these biographical works proliferated and sold. Despite objections that surviving acquaintances and relatives would suffer from biographers' inappropriate revelations, authors were now public figures as the pilgrimages to Scott's home and the publicity around Byron showed. Some authors, notably the leading romantics Wordsworth and Coleridge, balked at this development and worried about being "Boswellized" themselves.

Hastily compiled lives of just-deceased authors, Coleridge wrote in 1810, encouraged "worthless curiosity" rather than "useful knowledge" or fair assessment of a subject's worth. Wordsworth famously shunned the public eye, other writers appointed literary executors or authorized biographers to write their lives and preempt scandal-hunters, and still others simply burned their papers. The desire for privacy, then, was not merely an abstract concept arising from the living arrangements of an urban middle class; it was also the romantic authors' response to their increasingly nosy public.[7]

The aversion to biographical revelation had another, more positive side: it was intimately connected to larger ideas about truth and the role of the biographer. Even though the romantics disputed many of Samuel Johnson's literary judgments, they found an alternative to Boswellian biography in Johnson's *Lives of the Poets.* The Boswellian model, which inspired works like Thomas Moore's *Life of Byron* and Lockhart's *Life of Scott,* emphasized uncovering material and letting the subject "speak for himself" through it. Boswell and his successors repeatedly described the work of ascertaining facts because they believed that recording objective facts led to successful presentation of a subject. Johnson's *Lives of the Poets* offered a radically different method. Most important, Johnson composed where Boswell compiled. Johnson generally did not recount the poets' lives chronologically from birth to death, with a sketch of the "character" at the end. Using anecdotes and incidents selectively, he interpreted and assessed their lives and their poetry, thus employing biography as literary criticism. Far from being the subject's sycophant or an obsessive fact checker, Johnson as biographer became an important literary figure in his own right, empowered to evaluate his subject's life and works. Also unlike Boswell, Johnson did not believe a subject's character emerged from unmediated letters, transcribed conversations, and detailed information about what happened when. Johnson rejected the notion that facts revealed truth. For him, the biographer's perception of human character determined whether he would record and assess a subject's life accurately. When Johnson advised biographers to seek subjects in their "domestic privacies," he did not mean that they should dredge up scandal. He wanted them to seek the little-known habit or anecdote that could illuminate a subject's whole character—and knowing which habit or anecdote to use took a perceptive biographer indeed.[8]

The romantics inflected Johnson's ideas with their own. Wordsworth, Coleridge, and others agreed that purely factual narratives might not be "true to life," that an author's life and works were connected, and that literary biography was an important vehicle of literary criticism. When romantic authors wrote literary biography, they tended to prefer the form Johnson had made popular: series of short, interpretive sketches, not long lives-and-letters. This choice resulted partly from the business of publishing, where many biographical series initially appeared as magazine serials, lucrative endeavors in an age of rising periodical circulation. More than this, the preference for analytical collective biography stemmed from the romantic conviction that biography was itself a form of literary artistry. Because art was not science, compilation alone did not suffice; biography's truths were based as much on the biographer's perceptions as on external facts. As art, biography shared a central characteristic with poetry—the need for creative inspiration. The phrase *con amore,* which the romantics frequently used to describe a poet's relationship to his subject, applied equally to biographers. (Recall that the American romantic historian William H. Prescott protested that he could not write Charles Brockden Brown's biography "con amore.") A biographer did not have to love his subject, but without some inspiration the biography would be as lifeless as formulaic poetry.[9]

Within romantic biographies, several questions recurred frequently: Was the subject a man of "genius"—original in thought and action? How did he triumph over the obstacles society placed in his path? Did he embody the "spirit of the age," the essential ideas or characteristics of his place and period? By the time Thomas Carlyle wrote *On Heroes and Hero-Worship* (1840), the "romantic theory of the genius" had already permeated English biography and English attitudes toward public figures. Pantheons of heroes, "secular saints' calendars," and organizations devoted to classifying heroes all attested to the popularity of hero-worship, whether the hero be Nelson or Scott, Napoleon or Byron. In a much-quoted passage, Carlyle summarized the creed of romantic biography: "If an individual is really of consequence enough to have his life and character recorded for public remembrance, . . . the public ought to be made acquainted with all the inward springs and relations of his character. . . . In one word, what and how produced was the effect of society on him? and what and how produced was his effect on society?" The issues here were interpretive, not didactic; the romantic biographer sought to understand the subject's "character" and relationship to his society.[10]

Echoing their English counterparts, American critics also emphasized the biographer's delineation of character. Romanticism, not republicanism, dominated how they defined "character." A synonymous term, the "inner man," appeared in the *American Monthly Magazine* in 1829 (and elsewhere thereafter): biography's appeal lay in its "panoramic view of the inner man—the budding and blossoming and maturation of the intellect, the dawn of the moral being . . . the mode of disciplining the intellectual forces, and marshalling them for combat." The terms "character," "inner man," and "genius" all implied uniqueness. Central to this concept of character was *individuality:* a great man's character distinguished him from all other men. The *North American Review* explained in 1859 that biographers should discuss how a subject "towered *toto capite* above his contemporaries, . . . the *specific* grounds for his success or his reputation." If the reader could "recognize" the subject "in all its individuality," the biographer had achieved his aim. In contrast, the contemporaneous didactic works of William Makepeace Thayer took "character" as a set of characteristics that the biographer exhibited in living form to instill in the reader. The biographies of self-made men stressed *individualism,* the role of individual effort in success or failure, but not *individuality,* the particular constellation of traits that distinguished the subject from all others. The central message of Thayer's *The Bobbin Boy,* for example, was that each reader could emulate young Nathaniel Banks's virtues, and thereby perhaps follow him into the governor's mansion. But the *Atlantic Monthly* ridiculed Thayer's works as cheap didacticism, which made truly great and original subjects into examples of everyday virtues for young readers to imitate. If biographies like this—"Pop, goes the unerring rifle of some biographical sharp-shooter"— were what happened to people who became famous, nobody would seek distinction. According to these critics, the principal objective of biography was "truth to life," not promulgating a set of cookie-cutter virtues.[11]

This idea of character resolved a paradox in the new criticism: the simultaneous attack on eulogy (telling too little of the subject) *and* intrusiveness (telling too much). For all the complaints about invasion of privacy, the critique of eulogistic biography continued unabated. The *Christian Examiner* recognized that "Biographies, like monumental inscriptions, have been somewhat noted for what lawyers call suppression of the truth; a defect, not much to be preferred to deliberate misstatement." In the same 1857 article that diagnosed intrusive biographers' and their overeager readers' "Biographical Mania," the *Evening Gazette* faulted biographers for "apotheosising" George Washington. In fact, this critic argued that deifying Washington and violating the "private lives of public people" were kindred pitfalls—a stance that makes sense when connected to the romantic conception of "truth to life." Eulogy obscured inner and individual character in abstract praise and overt didacticism; the reader saw the biographer's adulation of the subject, not the subject himself. And excessive revelation could drown truly distinctive features in a sea of trivia. As the *Evening Gazette* put it, all men grumbled at cold mutton and preferred hot coffee, but the biographer needed to reach beyond the ordinary. All the "details of pedigree, the pranks and follies and whippings of childhood, the minutiae of courtship and housekeeping" obscured the deeper leading traits of character. The "private" man was not necessarily the "inner" man.[12]

To encourage "the more or less vivid reflection of character," reviewers and critics in the 1850s explicitly defined what made a biographer successful. Above all, he had to be an artist, as metaphors from painting and sculpting suggested. Truth to nature demanded that biographers present their subjects in "sunlight and shadow," bad as well as good. The *Southern Literary Messenger* compared writing biography with Michelangelo's decoration of the Sistine Chapel, and observed that the "biographer should be as truly an artist as the sculptor, the painter, or the novelist, for his works are just as susceptible of criticism according to the rules of art as are the works of the others." In the *North American Review* Evert A. Duyckinck quoted Wordsworth's 1816 essay calling biography writing an art, whose "critical and moral laws" had too frequently been broken. Anyone who inherited a relative's or acquaintance's papers now considered himself a biographer, much as if an ordinary citizen found a quarry and carpenter's tools and set out without training to build a church or statehouse. The accidental carpenter would be more likely to succeed than the accidental biographer, because "in the economy of the world a thousand may fittingly use their hands where one is permitted . . . profitably to use his brains." The artistic rules of biography thus responded to the perceived abuses of the genre: biographers eulogizing their subjects, throwing masses of undigested documents at their readers, using biography to show off their own rhetoric, or making extraneous authorial pronouncements.[13]

Successful biographical artistry began with literary craftsmanship. The *Southern Literary Messenger* described the first step, arranging materials, as the province of "reason." This intellectual faculty enabled the biographer to connect events with their causes, "to discriminate between fact and fiction," and ultimately to "select, from the mass of materials in his possession, such only as are true, and such as are adapted to his purpose." Mixing scientific and artistic metaphors, one critic wrote that the biographer "should take a microscopic survey of the character he designs to portray, and transfer to his canvas a faithful likeness."[14] In biography as in science, however, mere collection and arrangement of materials did not explain the larger meaning of a life or the roots of individual genius. Further, treating biography as science instead of art fostered "a lack of reverence [that] is especially damaging to the reputation of men of genius." A purely dispassionate relationship with one's subject made writing *con amore* impossible by definition. Like Transcendentalists who criticized the Baconian scientific paradigm of their day for classifying and observing things but not addressing "principles, causes, and essences," these critics believed that collection and arrangement marked only the beginning of a biographer's quest for the inner man.[15]

Having arranged the materials, the biographer next had to sketch scenes and portray characters vividly. The *Southern Literary Messenger* described "imagination" as the biographer's second prerequisite. "The great antagonist faculty to reason," imagination enchanted everything it touched, enlivening "bare narration." Imagination produced "[h]appy delineations of character, individual and national; pictorial descriptions of men and scenery, of manners and customs, of events and their accessories, of battles, sieges, marches, of great assemblies, and of the calm delights of domestic life." In emphasizing literariness, critics moved biography closer to the novel than their predecessors of the early republic would have dared. The elements of imagination, the *Messenger* acknowledged, were the hallmarks of the novel. But biography remained "far more instructive than the most powerful modern novel" because it told the life of a real person. Even though the *Messenger* hinted at the "meretricious and dangerous qualities" of fiction, however, it recommended that the biographer borrow from the novelist's art. In the early republic, novels like *Charlotte Temple* had assumed the guise of biography in order to answer moral critics of fiction. Now biographers were encouraged to write more like novelists— never forsaking "truth," of course—in order to satisfy critics and please readers.[16]

The true biographer's most important characteristic, in the view of the *North American,* was "a subtile moral and intellectual element" that resembled a romantic understanding of "genius." This "sober judgment and imaginative sympathy" enabled the biographer to understand his subject's true character and achievements. To write the lives of literary figures, with whom the *North American* was most concerned, a biographer had to understand the inspiration that had produced the subject's literary works. The biographer without a "high aesthetic standard" could not accurately delineate the relationship between an author's life and works—especially the relationship between ostensibly eccentric behavior and literary originality. Only the rare biographer could understand that Wordsworth's seclusions in nature and "absorption of mind in his own poetic creations" were "sacrifices, so to speak, made for our advantage in the perfection of the verse to which they gave birth." The ordinary, unenlightened biographer would paint Wordsworth's "moral grandeur" instead as "the awkwardness, the rusticity, the egotism, or the vanity, of the man." This aesthetic understanding of character explains the "reverence" for genius that animated the *North American*'s criticism, as well as the Boston *Evening Gazette*'s distinction between ordinary "human nature" and the "God-gifted poet" whose biographers should "embalm the good, forget the bad."[17]

Two Americans before 1860—Ralph Waldo Emerson and Henry Theodore Tuckerman—produced the sort of biographies that this romantic criticism implied. Emerson had known the power of biography since reading Plutarch as a boy. While biography remained a constant theme through his life and various careers, his uses of it changed over time. In 1829, early in his ministry of Boston's Second (Unitarian) Church, Emerson told his congregation that "there are biographies of great and good men, and bad men, by which you can hardly help being made better": a didactic conception not unlike that found in numerous other sermons, articles, and lectures of the period. Given his profession, it is not surprising that he recommended following the lives of the great and good for spiritual improvement. More surprising—to his congregants in the early 1830s, if not to twentieth-century historians and literary critics who know the contours of his later career—was the transformation within his sermons as he moved toward his break with the ministry. By 1832 Emerson was preaching that a "greater self" inhered within each individual, and that biography's power lay in its ability to unlock that self, not to suggest that the reader mimic the virtues of the superior biographical "hero." Written as Emerson yearned for greatness beyond the ministry, these sermons edged him toward the romantic vision he would express in *Representative Men* eighteen years later. After he left the Second Church and began work as a lyceum lecturer, Emerson planned a series of lectures called "Biography." Delivered in 1835 before the Society for the Diffusion of Useful Knowledge in Boston, these lectures revealed his early debt to Plutarch as well as his incipient romanticism: he spoke on men (John Milton, Michelangelo, Martin Luther, the Quaker George Fox, and Edmund Burke) who had served him as exemplars of "integrity and self-reliance," and he rejected subjects of greater moral ambiguity, such as Goethe and Napoleon. All his subjects were in some sense "artists" (with the brush or with the pen) who had resisted the authorities of their day. Biography helped Emerson navigate his own crisis of vocation. The lives of men like Luther and Fox inspired him to leave the established ministry and envision a career as "scholar," and his biographical lectures helped him establish a new career as a lecturer and prophet of individuality.[18]

By the time Emerson wrote *Representative Men,* that career had made him famous across the United States and in England. The book was not biography in any sense that most nineteenth-century readers would have recognized. It was nothing like the bulk of lives—didactic, religious, or historical—published in the first half of the century. As several reviewers noted, the book revealed more of Emerson and his ideas than of the Representative Men themselves. Reviewers did not describe *Representative Men* as biography at all. They identified its genre from the book's subtitle, "Seven Lectures."[19] (Emerson had delivered the lectures in America and England in 1845–46.) However, Emerson clearly considered *Representative Men* a form of biography. In the first lecture, "Uses of Great Men," he wrote that the "moral of biography" lay in its power to strengthen a reader's "resolution." Each subject represented the ideal of a character type, as the chapter titles indicated—"Plato: Or, the Philosopher," "Swedenborg: Or, the Mystic," and so on. More than this, each was "representative" in that he embodied some aspect of "the genius of humanity," "the real subject whose biography is written in our annals." Imaginative communion or "sympathy" with such men liberated the reader from everyday existence, an idea that had been in Emerson's mind since his lecture series on "Biography" in 1835. Then he had written in his journal that "The great value of Biography consists in the perfect symmetry that exists between like minds. Space & time are an absolute nullity to this principle. . . . We are imprisoned in life in the company of persons painfully unlike us or so little congenial to our highest tendencies & so congenial to our lowest that their influence is noxious." The influence of Plato, Swedenborg, or Goethe was different: it inspired, awakened, elevated. "Representative men" were not to be hero-worshiped in some passive way (hence Emerson's title, which rejected even his friend Carlyle's word "hero"). Unlike "vulgar talent" that sought to "dazzle and blind the beholder," "true genius . . . will liberate, and add new senses."[20]

Because the "use" of great men lay in liberating the reader rather than providing factual knowledge or a series of steps to emulate, the chapters of *Representative Men,* like many English romantic biographical sketches, did not follow chronological narrative form. As a whole, the book moved from the ancients (Plato) to the moderns (Bonaparte and Goethe).[21] Within individual sketches, facts and dates mattered little. These were Emersonian essays on the meanings of different character types, with the particulars of individual lives subordinate. Like other romantics, Emerson found standard biographical narrative confining and unrevealing. As he wrote in his journal while still a minister, "I would draw characters, not write lives. I would evoke the spirit of each and their relics might rot."[22]

"Great geniuses have the shortest biographies," he wrote of Plato, if one meant the "external biography" that included wives and children, domestic life and tastes. These men's biographies were "interior." The chapter on Swedenborg took its subject from birth to death (complete with dates) in four pages midway through the essay; the other forty-eight pages were devoted to Swedenborg's ideas and their reception. "Napoleon: Or, the Man of the World" never stated when Bonaparte was born or died—because the "million readers of anecdotes or memoirs or lives of Napoleon" already knew that "thoroughly modern" information. Instead, citing incidents throughout Bonaparte's career, Emerson focused on Napoleon as representative of the democratic spirit and the shopkeeping middle class unique to the nineteenth century. Napoleon's egotism ultimately brought him down, but only because the "democrat" party and the "conservative" party represented different stages of the same movement: "The democrat is a young conservative; the conservative is an old democrat," and Napoleon "may be said to represent the whole history of this party, its youth and its age."[23] *Representative Men* defined "biography" as meditation upon the significance of great men. Little wonder, then, that reviewers treated it largely as Emersonian philosophical essays.

Although less imaginative than *Representative Men*, the biographical essays of Henry Theodore Tuckerman more clearly followed the romantic interpretation of the genre. Tuckerman used biography as literary criticism, subordinated factuality to intuitive truth, and delineated the sources and effects of "genius." His essays sought to recognize genius but displayed little of the individuality that romantic critics prized in Emerson's. Born in 1813, a decade after Emerson, Tuckerman contributed to various literary magazines in the 1840s and 1850s. An adoptive New Yorker, he befriended prominent Gotham figures in the Young America movement, which championed the idea of an American literature: Rufus Wilmot Griswold, whose anthologies *The Poets and Poetry of America* (1842), *The Prose Writers of America* (1847), and *The Female Poets of America* (1848) attached biographical sketches to selections from leading writers, and Evert A. Duyckinck, who edited the first biographical dictionary of American literati, the *Cyclopaedia of American Literature* (1855). Tuckerman himself produced one of the first critical studies of American art, *Artist Life, or Sketches of American Painters,* in 1847. A modern scholar has described Tuckerman as "one of those vague, sentimental, romantic critics of the nineteenth century whom Poe so detested," and he used the language of romanticism freely—notably in two volumes entitled *Characteristics of Literature, Illustrated by the Genius of Distinguished Men* (1849 and 1851).[24]

In the 1850s Tuckerman wrote eleven biographical articles for the *North American Review*. The subjects included English, French, and American authors (from Defoe to Montaigne to Cooper), and four American statesmen (Washington, Franklin, Hamilton, and DeWitt Clinton).[25] Tuckerman recognized that different subjects required different sorts of biographies, for "Biography is an art that demands a peculiar sense of the appropriate." Three English examples made his point: only a superb conversationalist could receive a biography like Boswell's *Life of Johnson;* a simple, "authentic" chronicle of actions suited a man of "deeds rather than words," as Robert Southey demonstrated in his *Life of Nelson;* a subject more distinguished for "inward resources" than outward actions required the "sympathetic intelligence and moral insight" of Carlyle's *Life of John Sterling.* In every case, "the more or less vivid reflection of character" should be the biographer's goal—but where and how character appeared depended on the subject. Accordingly, Tuckerman concentrated on public accomplishments in articles about political figures, literary style and substance in the lives of authors, and domestic kindnesses in the life of the clergyman author Sydney Smith. Like Emerson, Tuckerman was concerned less about precise dates of birth and death and other such "external facts" than about writings, anecdotes, struggles, and achievements that illustrated character.[26]

Through all of Tuckerman's essays ran common romantic concerns and phrases. Above all, did the subject possess "genius"? Tuckerman measured each man against this standard, which he generally took to mean "individuality" (a word he used in seven of the eleven essays) and force of will, especially in the face of social resistance. Clearly drawing on Carlyle, Tuckerman found evidence of genius in five subjects: Defoe (in whose sketch the word appeared five times, twice in the same sentence with "individuality"), Sterne (five mentions of his "genius"), Cooper (eight), Clinton (six), and Hamilton (five). Addison was not a genius. His work "illustrates the amenities, and not the heroism, of literature"; "Taste, and not enthusiasm" inspired him. In these phrases Tuckerman juxtaposed opposites. Heroism and enthusiasm were signs of genius, while taste and amenities, though attractive, were not. Tuckerman looked for genius in political as well as literary figures. He found it especially in Clinton, whose biography read strikingly like Defoe's (perhaps because Tuckerman reviewed James Renwick's *Life of DeWitt Clinton* shortly after he reviewed Defoe's life and works). Clinton's genius was "executive" or "administrative," but it displayed the same characteristics as Defoe's: originality of vision (planning the Erie Canal and championing internal improvements before his society envisioned them), determination to carry out that vision, and struggle against short-sighted opponents. "It is fortunate," Tuckerman explained, "that in men of true genius the will is usually as strong as the aim is original, and that perseverance goes hand in hand with invention."[27]

Tuckerman shaped romantic biography to an American audience. Defoe's "liberal principles" and social reform work "anticipated the colonial revolt and the triumph of freedom in America," and his "Essay on Projects" had "quickened the mental enterprise of Franklin." Franklin's practical traits, above all, Tuckerman recognized as American. Cooper, "our national representative in letters," displayed authentically American strengths *and* weaknesses in his writing: unrefined style but also "bold invention," "the force of will and the incompleteness of insight, the natural energy and truth, and the artistic inadequacy." Beyond the obvious connection to Tocqueville's characterization of Americans as ever restless, practical but inartistic, this description also fit America's own new heroes of romance, nature's noblemen like Zachary Taylor who embodied "chivalric and frontier ideals" and who began to have their biographies written even before the Mexican War ended. Men of genius could plan canals across a continent or create a national bank, not just write original poetry or prose.[28]

In addition to romantic concepts of genius and American ideas of national character, Tuckerman also borrowed the language (though not the meaning) of "representative men" directly from Emerson. He described Defoe, Berkeley, Smith, and Cooper each as "a representative man," and sprinkled the word "representative" through many of the essays. Sometimes Tuckerman used the term without any clear meaning—perhaps merely to invoke Emerson.[29] Unlike Emerson, however, Tuckerman never implied that the representative man embodied the greatness inherent in all humanity. When Tuckerman used the term meaningfully, representative men were specific to time and place. Every group of Europeans who first explored America contained "a representative man, around whom the colony or roving band is grouped on the uncrowded canvas of our early history." Here the biography of an individual could encapsulate the history—the "nation, aim, and faith"—of his larger group. Pairing English colonizers with representatives of the Spanish, Dutch, and French explorations, Tuckerman marveled at "What varied associations and opposite elements of character are suggested by the figures thus delineated of De Soto and Penn, Lord Baltimore and Hendrick Hudson, Roger Williams and Father Marquette!" These pairs also revealed the importance of ancestry for Tuckerman: nationality and ethnicity helped forge a representative man's character, a belief that many romantic historians shared. For instance, Hamilton's "chief inherited traits" were not just "Scotch and French" but specifically French Huguenot and "Scotch noble," the most "desirable combination."[30] Tuckerman's biographical essays marked the acme of American biography along romantic lines. No "genius" himself—the essays offered little new interpretation—Tuckerman was nonetheless the sort of author the *North American* meant when it called for men with "sober judgment and imaginative sympathy" and a "high aesthetic standard" to raise the level of biography writing.

In fact, the *North American*'s 1857 call for "a new school of biographers" appeared in a review of Tuckerman's own *Essays, Biographical and Critical*, a review written by his friend Evert Duyckinck. Important literary and social divisions lay beneath the *North American*'s concept (expressed here and again in 1859) that successful life-writing required a rare aesthetic spirit—and Duyckinck's language revealed them.

> There is one paramount quality, a characteristic which runs throughout the volume, which is peculiarly Mr. Tuckerman's own,—a certain sympathy, breadth, and generosity of treatment. A good subject may be safely left with him. It is the curse of much writing of this description, that it falls into the hands of literary hacks and jobbers, with more of the scandal-monger than the gentleman in their composition,—the valets of letters, to whom no worth or eminence, however well tried or exalted, is heroic. With the small revilers and detractors, the "minute philosophers" of the ridiculous, the foul cellar-rats who gnaw at the foundations of mighty edifices, Mr. Tuckerman has no sympathy.

In redefining biography principally as an art—whose rules too few practitioners understood or obeyed—the *North American* shifted the terms of debate over biography. Earlier criticism had emphasized the reader's instruction above all else: biography was seen in functional rather than literary or artistic terms. Now, for the *North American* and for other literary magazines of the late 1850s, the issue was construction (how a biographer composed his work) rather than instruction. Moreover, the central figure in the biographical process became not the reader but the subject, whose reputation and lasting fame could be destroyed by a "literary hack" or "jobber." The first division, then, pitted hack biographers against true artists, who included both aesthetically enlightened biographers like Tuckerman and the men of "genius, talent, high position" who deserved better than the hacks gave them. The second division pitted a public all too willing to buy scandalous, intrusive biographies against an enlightened criticism (like the *North American*'s own) that could explain the difference. "It is high time for our critical journals to take severe cognizance of such outrages" against the reputations and privacy of the great, wrote the *North American* in 1859. This stance placed the magazine in opposition not only to the intrusive biographer but also to the common reader—much as the Boston *Evening Gazette* did when it said that "It is the public's crime that the most trifling details are so eagerly sought after of the private lives of public people." The didactic criticism of the early republic, of course, had also divided critics from readers: earlier critics prescribed biography for presumably malleable readers who mistakenly read novels. But while earlier critics had argued that novels harmed readers, the *North American* and like-minded journals suggested in the 1850s that readers (and the writers who pandered to them) degraded biography. The *North American*'s critique can be understood, at least in part, as the reaction of a relatively little-read magazine against the popular literary market that neglected it. But the *North American* was not alone.[31]

The critique of biography reflected the fluidity of American literary culture around midcentury. As American urban society expanded and American cities offered dwellers increasing anonymity, a public sphere developed in which it was increasingly difficult to tell who was virtuous, sincere, and "genteel." (Remember that the *North American* described Tuckerman as a "gentleman" in a world of "scandal-mongers" and "valets.") A similar fluidity existed within American literature, as the rise of mass printing and publishing helped introduce new literary genres and forms. The penny press offered a vision of "objectivity" based on sensationalism, in contrast to the overtly partisan papers that had heretofore dominated the news. The sensational was not confined to newspapers. Novels like George Lippard's *The Quaker City* and books that explored the seamier side of cities sold prodigiously—especially to the urban working class, a relatively new social phenomenon in America and certainly a new segment of the reading population. In sensational literature, as in the big cities themselves, anonymity reigned. The "hacks and jobbers" who worked for the papers and wrote the cheap fiction often went by pseudonyms, and within a decade "fiction factories" would be churning out dime novels without identifiable authors. The nineteenth-century reading population also grew with the rise in female literacy; women's reading in the new, urban middle class was largely responsible for the popularity of sentimental literature, in the form of novels, magazines, and gift books. *Godey's Lady's Book* sold better than any other magazine of the 1850s, and the biggest bestsellers of the decade (*Uncle Tom's Cabin, The Wide, Wide World,* and Maria Cummins's *The Lamp-*

lighter) all belonged to the category of sentimental fiction. Authors moved from one genre and publishing site to another; Louisa May Alcott, for example, began her career writing articles for sensationalist magazines *and* the genteel *Atlantic Monthly*.[32]

These various new genres and forms coexisted and mixed in the literary marketplace of Jacksonian America, and their rhetoric infused many of the new biographies. Lives of pious Christians (particularly women) drew on the same language as sentimental fiction; lives of rogues traded in the rhetoric of sensation. Even campaign biographies were not immune. One life of Franklin Pierce—not Hawthorne's—quoted a legal argument in which Pierce supposedly appealed to a jury on behalf of suffering women and children and called another witness a strumpet—invoking the languages of tear-stained domesticity and tawdry crime to elect a president. Hawthorne offered a rhetoric of truth more consonant with romantic sensibilities. As one who had known the candidate since college, he could write *con amore,* without artificial rhetoric lifted from sentimental novels and penny papers.[33] But when mass-market languages intruded upon the lives of "great men" or "men of genius," making supposedly unique individuals into more specimens of piety or exposing their vices as one would write a felon's life, something had gone amiss. The severe biographical criticism of the 1850s, then, represented a quest for order amid the apparent chaos of the literary market.

Creating a Career as "Biographer": The Literary Worlds of James Parton

James Parton, the first American writer to be identified above all by the term "biographer," was a creature of the popular literary market that the romantic critics deplored, indeed of its most suspect manifestation—journalism. By 1866, however, the nation's leading literary publisher had bought the rights to his works, a mark of his popular appeal *and* his respectability. Parton's commercial and critical success raises these questions: how could any biographer attain the status of a "literary" figure in the 1860s, and why was he the biographer who did? Parton capitalized on the possibility that romantic ideas of biography created: the potential for biography to be envisioned as literary art, not just a branch of history or a form of didacticism, and thus for the biographer to be seen (and to see himself) as a literary artist. More specific, readers and critics alike considered Parton a uniquely American biographer. The variety of American subjects he chose—Horace Greeley, Aaron Burr, Andrew Jackson, Benjamin Franklin—help account for this reputation. Most biographers of Americans were identified with one subject, as Henry Randall was with Jefferson; Parton was identified with the genre. His selection of subjects told only part of the story. Parton did not simply explore, as Henry Tuckerman might have, how Franklin or Jackson or Greeley exemplified the "spirit of his age" or of the United States. In the eyes of his contemporaries, for good or ill, Parton's ideology and writing style themselves embodied the spirit of *his* age. Parton used biography to examine and ultimately celebrate democratizing, entrepreneurial, modernizing America in the era of the Civil War. Moreover, he wrote his biographies by drawing on conventions and stylistic devices from America's most popular reading fare, the newspaper and the novel.

By the time Ticknor and Fields acquired the rights to his work, Parton had achieved a remarkable combination: a critical reputation for writing biographies artistically and a lucrative career as a popular biographer. This combination might have confounded some of the romantic critics, who believed artistic accomplishment incompatible with broad appeal in the literary (or, as they saw it, unliterary) market. Parton succeeded because the reputation and the career were not entirely synonymous. Each came to reinforce the other, but the two were distinct. As early as 1857 when he was completing the life of Burr and already planning to write about Jackson, Parton envisioned a career in biography writing. That is, he saw biography as the source of his own authorial identity and of some (though certainly not all) of his income. But critics of his *Burr* remained to be persuaded that he was anything more than a journalist, bringing that profession's insufficient insight and troublingly free-wheeling writing style to a genre where they did not belong. Over the next decade, the career took shape and the reputation changed. Parton made a living in biography by interpreting the genre broadly and writing it in diverse ways for different sites of publication: full-length historical biographies of Jackson and Franklin, interpretive biographical articles for the *North American Review,* and short didactic pieces for Robert Bonner's story-paper, the *New York Ledger.* Parton's career consisted of the entirety of these. His reputation, at least among critics, came from the historical biographies and the *North American* pieces. It did not come from what Parton himself called his "Ledger Lines," although those paid his bills as he worked on more "literary" biographical productions. As biographical hierarchy emerged (a development the romantic criticism implied), Parton made a career by working at multiple levels within the genre. He could do so, in large part, because the fluidity

James Parton

Parton's *Triumphs of Enterprise, Ingenuity, and Public Spirit* announced his status as celebrity biographer: the publishers placed the biographer's own portrait (complete with autograph) in the frontispiece, rather than the image and signature of one of the book's subjects. (Courtesy American Antiquarian Society) within the genre and within American literary culture allowed—indeed, encouraged—him to define the very concept of "biographer" for himself.

Whereas Jared Sparks's career centered in Boston, Harvard, and the scholarly world of the *North American Review,* James Parton's began a generation later in New York, the profession of journalism, and the literary marketplace. Born in England in 1822, Parton came to America as a boy of five when his widowed mother brought the family across the Atlantic. Of Ann Parton's five children, James was singled out for extensive education: seven years in New York's public schools, then an academy in White Plains. Like other men inclined to make themselves, he spent his early twenties searching for a vocation, spending several years as a schoolteacher in White Plains and Philadelphia. Back in New York in 1848, Parton wrote an essay about *Jane Eyre* and delivered it to the house of Nathaniel Parker Willis, the well-known poet and essayist and editor of the *Home Journal,* a New York weekly newspaper. Willis published Parton's piece, and within months the young man was a regular contributor to Willis's paper. In 1852 he became its editorial assistant and first encountered the work of "Fanny Fern"—who turned out to be Willis's estranged sister Sara Eldredge. The Willis connection led Parton into book authorship and marriage. Nathaniel introduced him to the publishers Lowell and Daniel Mason, who encouraged him to write a life of Horace Greeley, and Sara married him in January 1856.[34]

Parton's emergence as a writer coincided with the emergence of a new medium: the middle-class urban newspaper. Journalism had changed substantially since the 1810s. Then, virtually every newspaper had unabashed partisan sympathies, and editors sought governmental printing contracts when their allies won office. The partisan press did not disappear in the 1830s and 1840s—witness how newspaper editors wrote and printed and sold campaign biographies and promoted candidates in their papers—but a new phenomenon came to exist beside it in America's largest cities. In New York, now too segmented by class and neighborhood for citizens to know the city intimately, a variety of newspapers competed to tell the stories of modern urban life. Those known collectively as the penny press became popular for sensationalistic accounts of crime and corruption. Others, like Willis's *Home Journal,* eschewed scenes of urban vice in favor of articles about the theater, fashion, and middle-class customs. Both varieties differed from the partisan press. Rather than long transcripts of political speeches and descriptions of governmental debate and activity, they preferred shorter pieces about local happenings, curiosities, and individuals. Now James Gordon Bennett's *New York Herald* and Benjamin Day's *New York Sun* employed reporters to track down stories and tell them in ways that would sell papers. A journalistic style developed, complete with racy narratives and vivid descriptions. Middle-class papers like Willis's adopted that style as well, even if the scenes they depicted were less grimy and self-fashioned literati like Willis looked down at the sensationalism of the penny dailies. The distinction between penny papers and middle-class weeklies is important for understanding Parton's choices and reception. Parton would write for a variety of magazines and papers, but never for the sensationalist penny press. However, to some critics outside the newspaper world, all newspaper writing seemed like hackwork. Because the journalistic styles of the penny papers and the middle-class papers resembled each other and departed from the sedate "literary" style of many monthly and quarterly magazines, an author like Parton could be mistaken for a generic "journalist."[35]

The Life of Horace Greeley, published by Mason Brothers in 1855, attested to Parton's middle-class, journalistic roots. The book resembled the biographies of the self-made men whom Freeman Hunt profiled in his *Merchant's Magazine.* Like Hunt, Parton recommended his subject's honesty, temperance, and perseverance to striving young men. Franklinian echoes abounded. Greeley was a newspaperman, Parton cited Franklin's *Autobiography,* and a frontispiece entitled "Young Greeley's Arrival in New York" depicted the friendless youth (in ragged hat and pants too short, his possessions tied to a stick he carried over his shoulder) the way Franklin had described his own entry into Philadelphia. Parton's Greeley embodied self-made manhood, and other young men might follow his path. Parton dedicated the book "To the Young Men of the Free States," as did other biographers of self-made men in these years. As one reviewer put it, the "bit of 'sectionalism'" in this dedication was "not without its significance." Greeley's antislavery views, which Parton shared, made him anathema to southerners. More important, his rise could exemplify northern free-labor ideology: middle-class self-making was possible only in a society where young men had to work to rise, and where work itself was celebrated; a slave society and economy stigmatized work. Also like Hunt's mercantile biographies, Parton's book celebrated a relatively new profession, in this case journalism. *The Life of Horace Greeley* told the story of the *New York Tribune:* its founding, its reformist stands, its everyday operations. Far from a degraded endeavor, "The Cheap Press" was America's exemplary profession. "[T]he great leveller, elevator, and democraticizer," it provided all citizens access to information and gave honest, literate young men a noble calling. Biographer and subject were intertwined. In celebrating Greeley, Parton was celebrating the northern, urban, middle-class, democratic, free-soil society where he had found opportunity and the specific vocation in which he was beginning to make his own mark.[36]

Another issue concerned Parton and reviewers: to what extent was the *Life of Greeley* itself, like Greeley's *Tribune,* an ephemeral product of current-day life? Biographies of living figures in 1854 consisted mostly of newspaper and magazine sketches (whose subjects ranged from authors and politicians to criminals) and campaign biographies. Their subjects' distinction might or might not last, and the biographies themselves were published in forms (newspapers, pamphlets, cheap books) not designed for permanence. Most lives of the living worked to promote their subjects. Was Parton's book simply another version of the campaign biography, even if Greeley was not running for anything? Parton said no: "If the lives of politicians like Tyler, Pierce, and others, may be written in their life-time, with a view to subserve the interests of party, why may not the life of Horace Greeley, in the hope of subserving the interests of the country?" Was it as impermanent as other lives written by journalists? Again Parton said no, aligning his work with historical biography as well as journalistic reporting. As he explained in the preface, he had consulted historical works, perused thousands of issues of Greeley's papers, and traveled to New Hampshire and Massachusetts to interview Greeley's associates and acquaintances. The *North American Review* agreed with Parton: this "is not an ephemeral book,—like the lives of many men more or less distinguished," nor "like a campaign life of Clay, of Taylor, of Jackson; it is a piece of standard English literature." The *North American* announced Parton as a new discovery in the literary world of "title-pages"—a world distinct from "newspaper-work"—and hoped that he would appear "as a *book*-author once more." The *Christian Examiner* also praised the *Life of Greeley,* but suggested several ways Parton had not transcended his journalistic roots: too many "trivial details," frequently careless use of language, and "*slang* expressions." Conversely, the *Examiner* applauded Parton's vivid descriptions of New England life and scenery—another by-product of journalistic experience, or at least of familiarity with popular literature. The skills of the journalist, it seemed, could help make a discerning writer into a literary author.[37]

The same skills could also raise doubts about his abilities and motives—which is precisely what happened with Parton's next project, *The Life and Times of Aaron Burr* (1857). Once again, Parton chose a controversial subject (as he would continue to do throughout his career). Despite

Parton's *The Life of Horace Greeley* made the publisher of the *New York Tribune* into the consummate Franklinian self-made man, as this frontispiece image of Greeley's arrival in New York suggested. (Book in author's collection; photograph by Ted Cook)

two biographies written in the 1830s, Parton exclaimed that even in 1857 Burr remained "a baffling enigma!"[38] Parton set out to solve the mystery, and in significant ways he wrote *The Life and Times of Aaron Burr* just as romantic critics prescribed. First he collected newspapers and literature of Burr's day, dozens of books, and countless primary documents. He made a list of twenty "persons to be consulted" and interviewed at least six of them. These interviews made "Aaron Burr himself" Parton's most valuable source. According to Parton, Burr had delighted in talking about his life, and his "surviving friends and connections" provided "just the needed light upon his character and conduct, which ransacked libraries had failed to shed." (Sparksian reliance on the printed document led only part way in the search for character.) Arranging the materials into a unified, interpretive portrait came next. Parton ultimately wanted to explain "what manner of man he was, and what, in the great crises of his life, he either did or meant to do"—a virtual paraphrase of the questions that romantic critics thought a biographer should answer. Throughout the book Parton answered Carlyle's key biographical questions: how did the subject influence society, and how did society influence the subject? Burr, Parton argued, pioneered the tactics that later political parties would use and anticipated America's westward progress in his scheme for southwestern empire (and perhaps gave Jackson ideas). He was also a creature of his own milieu: a period when a "Man of the World" practiced "gallantry" with the ladies and when dueling survived because "Honor" ranked above "Honesty"; an army life that taught men to place ends above means and laid the seeds for an unprincipled man to act totally without scruple. Parton's Burr never embodied pure good or pure evil, and he changed over time. American politics, no place for a man oblivious to the public good, proved Burr's downfall; he might have succeeded in Napoleonic France. Even after Burr became the most notorious man in America, he retained admirable qualities (especially a love of children).[39]

Parton also employed and reshaped familiar notions of didacticism in biography. Several times in the book, he challenged the way most biographers moralized. "To suppress the good qualities and deeds of a Burr is only less immoral than to suppress the faults of a Washington. In either case, the practical use of the Example is lost." In a passage that admiringly cited Carlyle's treatment of Robespierre, Parton explained his own view. When the characters of bad men

> are *truly* drawn, we are more likely to be surprised at the number of good
> qualities they possessed, than horrified at their bad ones. And this is, in
> truth, of all the facts in the case, the most appalling! That a man may be
> *so* good, and yet not good; that he may come so near excellence, and yet
> so fatally miss it; that he may be so little removed in moral quality from
> many who pass the ordeal of life with little reproach, and yet incur so
> deep a damnation—these are the facts which move and scare us when

we know aright and fully the men who figure in history as atrocious characters.

This paragraph suggested how Parton fused romantic and didactic impulses. Emulating history's great men elevated the youthful reader. But any "sensible" reader would understand that character—his own and any man's—contained sunlight and shadow, virtues and faults. At the same time, the last sentence of Burr's story did impart a lesson. No matter how long past the specific conditions of turn-of-the-century politics, Burr's and Hamilton's "graver errors" and "radical vices . . . belong to human nature, and will always exist to be shunned and battled."[40]

Parton also modified the methods of historical biography. Parton's research signaled his intention to write Burr's life historically, and within the text he occasionally cited his sources. Like Sparks and other historical biographers, Parton sometimes took issue with previous interpretations; several of the "mysteries" he attempted to solve through documentary evidence concerned historical fact, not Burr's character.[41] Stylistically, however, Parton departed from the historical biographers. Casting historical controversies as mysteries to be unraveled, he employed the journalist's language, not the historian's. He entered the narrative frequently with first-person interpretations and thoughts addressed to the reader, as in this introduction to the story of Burr's alleged treason: the American people's distrust of Burr in 1805 "is a clew which may guide us through the labyrinth we are about to attempt. I have groped in it long, as others have before me. It is tortuous and heaped with falsehoods, as surely no other 'passage' of history ever was before. I invite the reader to enter, and follow the path which lead [sic] me to—what looks like daylight." This passage read more like a scene from the journalist George Foster's *New York by Gas-Light* or contemporary "mysteries of the city" books than like anything Jared Sparks ever wrote. Here biographical investigation resembled seeking hidden passageways off dark streets, with the biographer (like the sensational journalist) leading his reader along.

Striking descriptions of scenery and vivid storytelling rendered other passages unabashedly novelistic, as in the first paragraph of the book when Parton introduced Jonathan Edwards:

In the autumn of 1722, when New York was a town of eight thousand inhabitants, and possessed some of the characteristics of a Dutch city, an English sea-port, a new settlement, a garrisoned town, and a vice-royal residence, there used to walk about its narrow, winding streets, among the crowd of Dutch traders, English merchants, Indians, officers and soldiers, a young man whose appearance was in marked contrast with that of the passers-by. His tall, slender, slightly stooping figure, was clad in homespun parson's gray. His face, very pale, and somewhat wasted, wore an aspect of singular refinement, and though but nineteen years of age, there was in his air and manner the dignity of the mature and cultivated man.

When the *New York Times* criticized Parton's style a decade later, it had passages like this—stylistically more fictional than factual—in mind. All of Parton's biographies opened this way, and all of them contained novelistic devices, including conversations in dialogue and foreshadowings of future developments. Unlike novels, of course, biographies had predefined endings, and historically informed readers already knew how the stories would turn out. Parton seems to have accentuated the mysteries of his subjects in order to provide (or at least promise) fresh twists in familiar tales.[42]

Even as Parton adopted some techniques from other popular literary genres, he reminded his readers of the boundaries biographers could not cross. After mentioning that the Revolution disrupted many domestic lives, he wrote that "The future Scott of America will know how to make all this very familiar to the American people by the romantic and pathetic fiction which it will suggest to him." In other words, he, James Parton, was *not* writing fiction, despite employing some of its conventions. Parton also set himself apart from "the writers of biographical gossip," those hacks whom critics accused of invading subjects' privacy. Parton devoted great attention to Burr's happy marriage and his "relations with women" late in life, but only to refute the charges of Burr's lechery. These he attributed to unsubstantiated gossip and to Matthew Davis's flaws as Burr's literary executor and biographer. "Where is . . . a book that shall deal the death-blow to that fell destroyer of reputations, THEY SAY?" he asked. Parton's documents and interviews enabled him to claim that "I have ascertained the *truth* respecting this matter, and all the truth." The insistence on truth, above all, distinguished him from the nation's future Scott and from the scandal-mongers.[43]

In advertising *The Life and Times of Aaron Burr,* Parton's publishers emphasized both its attention to fact and its resemblance to fiction. "A Brilliant Success!!! Four Editions in Six Weeks!!" Mason Brothers exclaimed, just as they billed the popular novels of Fanny Fern (for they were her publishers, too). Publishers were just beginning in the 1850s to trumpet a book's popularity in order to generate more popularity, usually for the biggest sellers, novels. They were also starting to quote favorable reviews in their advertisements, and here, too, Parton's *Burr* benefited from the latest advertising methods: one ad quoted fifteen reviews. The *New York Tribune* wrote that Parton had "performed his task with the zeal of an antiquary and the taste of an artist," just the mixture of science and art that the *Southern Literary Messenger* prescribed for biographers. Three of the quoted reviews commented that Parton had "sifted" his materials, testimony that he was far more than a compiler. *Mrs. Stephens' Illustrated New Monthly* called the book the most "honest and able" biography since Boswell's *Life of Johnson* and noted that Parton, "almost severe in his truthfulness," gave "both the sunshine and the shadow of a conspicuous man." A number of the squibs in Mason Brothers' ad compared Parton's work favorably with novels: "More exciting than romance"; "the attractiveness of the most exciting fiction"; "The most popular biography of the day, and seems likely to run a race with Uncle Tom." Like a good novel, *The Life and Times of Aaron Burr* could not be put down once begun. Forty years earlier, John Adams criticized William Wirt's *Sketches of the Life and Character of Patrick Henry* by comparing it to Jane Porter's novels. Now, comparing Parton's work to *Uncle Tom's Cabin* in literary value or in popularity was high praise.[44]

Many literary periodicals disagreed with the glowing reviews (mostly from newspapers) that Mason Brothers quoted. The most common complaints evidenced the continued intermingling of didactic, historical, and romantic standards. Parton had not censured Burr adequately, argued the *New Englander* and the *Atlantic Monthly*—a sign that he was "not fit to teach his young countrymen." These magazines and the *Southern Literary Messenger* listed dozens of historical inaccuracies large and small. The *Messenger* called Burr's surviving friends and turn-of-the-century newspapers, Parton's most valuable sources, unreliable witnesses. Above all, none of these reviewers believed Parton an insightful or accurate "delineator of character." He simultaneously apologized for Burr and cited materials that indicted Burr; he refused to admit Burr's flaws even when his own evidence revealed them; he failed to understand Burr's essential artificiality, duplicity, and lack of intellectual depth. In part, these critiques suggested unwillingness to see a complex Burr: both the *Atlantic* and the *Messenger* summed Burr up with far less "sunlight" than Parton had. All of these reviews took issue with Parton's *emphasis*. Burr's hollow gentility and shallow intellect seemed to pale in length and authorial fervor beside Parton's animated accounts of his lurid adventures.[45]

Herein lay the fundamental critique: James Parton, journalist, wanted to make a lucrative best-seller more than an accurate biography. The *Christian Examiner* lamented that "The life of Burr, who deserves justice and nothing more, is admirably told, made as attractive as a novel, and will be read everywhere." The *New Englander* congratulated Parton for his "great skill in the art of book-making"—no compliment—and speculated that he wrote the life of Burr only because it "would sell well, and yield large returns." The *Atlantic* noted Parton's use of "the slang usually confined to sporting papers." Most damning, the *Messenger* drew a line between journalism and biography and placed Parton on the wrong side:

> We suppose the author's main object was to make a readable book, and that rather than spoil a good story, he would err on the side of conjecture. This tendency to sacrifice absolute truth to immediate effect, is the almost unavoidable habit of journalists; but the tact which makes popular selections or weaves amusing comments for a newspaper, is out of place in describing a life which, whatever be its intrinsic value, has a relative historic importance. Herein scrupulous adherence to authenticity is indispensable, and led Mr. Sparks to establish the rule for his series of American Biography, that every event of historical interest should be sustained by documentary evidence.

In the winter and spring of 1857–58, it thus remained unclear if Parton had found a new, popular, *and* reliable approach to biography (as his publishers advertised) or if he was simply another hack with insufficient insight and a degraded writing style. Parton had chosen biography as his chief literary pursuit—by the time the life of Burr appeared, he was already planning a biography of Jackson—but critics did not yet define him as a "biographer."[46]

With his three-volume *Life of Andrew Jackson* (1860–61), Parton succeeded in winning critical acclaim. Recalling their negative reviews of *Burr*, several magazines (including the *Atlantic Monthly* and the *New Englander*) voiced pleasure at now being able to praise Parton's work. What had changed? The reviews of *The Life and Times of Aaron Burr* seem to have chastened Parton somewhat regarding historical documentation. The first volume of *Jackson* opened with a thirteen-page, heavily annotated bibliography of more than two hundred items: memoirs and biographies of Jackson and his enemies and associates, campaign biographies (which Parton noted as such), histories of Tennessee, newspapers, magazines, speeches in pamphlet form, and governmental records. By not just including a bibliography but placing it before the table of contents, Parton foregrounded his research—perhaps for those who had doubted his documentation in the life of Burr. Parton also used long quotations and footnotes far more generously in the *Life of Jackson*. As Parton highlighted his claims to historical rigor, he dropped any pretense of didacticism. He compared his endeavor to the restoration of an old church whose imperfections had been covered with "WHITEWASH!" With the whitewash removed, what remained was "honest, curious, interesting, real. Not a model to copy, but a specimen to study." [47] These differences notwithstanding, the *Life of Jackson* resembled the *Life and Times of Burr* in most respects. A preface that began, " 'Oh, hang General Jackson!' exclaimed Fanny Kemble one day," indicated that Parton's penchant for animated prose had survived the critics' barbs intact. So had his essential source of information, especially regarding Jackson's early years: acquaintances and descendants. In Washington, Raleigh, and Nashville, as well as South Carolina and Alabama, Parton listened to "men and women, bond and free, who knew him well, knew him at all periods of his life, lived near him, and with him, served him and were served by him. . . . I listened, also, to many who were always opposed to the man, and still like him not." These interviews and hundreds of books, newspapers, and documents allowed Parton to announce, as he had in *Burr,* "thus it was that contradictions were reconciled, that mysteries were revealed, and that the truth was made apparent." The novelistic touches, the journalistic free-dom with language, and the use of information Sparks might have called "tradition" all remained constant from Parton's *Burr* to his *Jackson.*[48]

The newly positive critical response resulted primarily from Parton's choice of subject, not any change of style. *De Bow's Review* summarized the change perfectly: "Mr. Parton's first biographical work, the life of Burr, was a great success. He was not praised by the critics — quite the reverse. *He* appeared to think that Burr was not a devil incarnate, and *they* had inherited and loved the notion that he was. The critics were indignant, but the 'Life' was interesting, and the people read the book and cared nothing about the critics. The 'Life of Jackson' has no such prejudices to encounter." Jackson was controversial but not scandalous. Reviewers who found no legitimate reason for another life of Aaron Burr could all agree on the importance of a biography of Jackson. Twenty-three years had elapsed since Jackson's presidency, and fifteen since his death; a biographer possessed both the temporal distance to write impartially and the ability to learn from Jackson's acquaintances who would be dead a generation hence. By focusing on Jackson as an historical and not an exemplary figure, Parton did dispel one line of attack he had encountered before. Critics who hated Jackson could not complain that Parton recommended an unworthy man for the emulation of American youth.[49] Once Parton chose an "acceptable" sub-ject, reviewers praised much of what they had criticized in his life of Burr. According to the *Atlantic Monthly,* the same "sympathy with his subject" that had led Parton to "palliate" Burr's faults had given "vigor and spirit to his delineation of a character in most respects so different as that of Jackson." (Writing *con amore* was fine as long as the subject was not as bad as Burr.) Magazines that had challenged Parton's reliance on Burr's surviving acquaintances applauded him for seeking out people who had known Jackson intimately. After having questioned Parton's motives and his fitness for writing *Burr,* the *Atlantic* came around completely, praising his "decided talent for biography" and his "thoroughness of research and honesty of purpose." Reviewers unanimously described Parton's style as "easy, bold, dashing" or as "animated, almost impetuous." This time, however, almost none linked that style to the degradation of the popular literary market or suggested that it rendered Parton's work suspect as biography. The style "of a successful newspaper reporter," as the *New Englander* put it, was no longer cause for criticism. On the contrary, Parton's ability "to arrest and keep the attention of the reader" became a virtue when linked to a worthy subject.[50]

One new comment began to appear in these reviews: Parton was creating a kind of biography specific and appropriate to the modern United States. The *Christian Review* moved in this direction: "The author never cramps himself to the requirements of any model of biographical literature with which we are acquainted, but pushes on his narrative with a geniality and freshness of spirit, a frankness of utterance, and a profusion in the grouping of contemporaneous persons and scenes, that admit of no flagging in the curiosity and interest of the reader." The *Atlantic* offered an example of Parton's innovation: "Mr. Parton begins his book with a new kind of genealogy, and one suited to our Western hemisphere, where men are valued more for what they are than for what their grandfathers were." (Parton opened the book with a description and history of the Scots-Irish and their migration to America, rather than with generations of Jackson's lineage.) To this critic, Jackson was not simply a better man than Burr. He was a more American biographical subject. Burr modeled his demeanor on European courtliness, but Jackson embodied the American frontier and the spirit that had settled it. And Parton had found the way to tell an *American* life.[51]

The *Life of Andrew Jackson* began the most productive period of Parton's career, a decade when his biographical work took numerous forms, appeared in a variety of publications, and confirmed his status as America's "prince of biographers." In an 1867 letter to Charles Eliot Norton, editor of the *North American Review,* Parton explained his vision of the genre and his conception of his own work. Since early life he had wondered why Dickens, Thackeray, and other eminent novelists wrote fiction when so many true stories were more interesting. He had not imagined that he could be the person to make biography "a new branch of the fine arts," because the research to "make a real and vivid biography" required too much money. To his surprise, Mason Brothers had advanced him the money to research Greeley's life, the book had sold thirty thousand copies, and with his proceeds ($2,000) he had been able to begin his next project. Still, Parton believed that he had never "produced something excellent" because of his constant need to make a living. To work on a *North American* piece he had to give up work for the *New York Ledger* that paid twice as much. This tension between earning a living and writing "something excellent" characterized his career in the 1860s.[52]

In fact, in the early 1860s the two sides of Parton's biographical work existed in symbiosis. His full-length historical lives established the reputation that gave his brief biographical articles in Robert Bonner's *New York Ledger* credibility as the work of a scholar, even if their content and tone were not scholarly. The income from these pieces and other mass-market work bought the time and travel necessary to write books like his *Franklin*. Only when Ticknor and Fields, a publisher more "literary" than Bonner or Mason Brothers, solicited Parton's work in mid-decade would tensions surface within this symbiosis. Bonner congratulated Parton on Ticknor and Fields's offer but feared losing a principal contributor and offered Parton a raise to keep writing *Ledger* articles. One critic saw Parton's endeavors as competing with each other, expressed disappointment that "haste of composition" marred Parton's "best work," and called it "a pity that his talents should be employed in providing monthly entertainments." Most telling were Parton's own words to his new publisher. On January 29, 1867, Parton thanked James Fields for sending the new edition of his books "bound in green cloth": "Nothing could be more elegant. Work so beautifully clad has a kind of merit and dignity." Eleven months later, Parton told Fields that a subscription-publishing firm in Hartford wanted "a large octavo of my Ledger Lines." Parton asked whether Ticknor and Fields would want such a book, but presumed that "the stuff they want is beneath you." Fields must have agreed, for Parton's *People's Book of Biography* appeared from the Hartford presses of A. S. Hale in 1868. Here were two literary worlds, which Parton, his "literary" publisher, and critics saw as hierarchically situated: one characterized by material elegance, textual merit of some sort, and Ticknor and Fields; the other by large octavo volumes, "Ledger

Lines," and subscription publishing.[53] Each was identified with a different vision of biography, too—and a distinct way of portraying "character."

Parton's major work of the Civil War years, the *Life and Times of Benjamin Franklin* (1864), completed what his *Jackson* had begun: it made him unquestionably the foremost American associated with the genre of biography. Once more Parton selected a subject thoroughly identified with American national character, in this case ingenuity and self-making. Although he drew heavily on Franklin's *Autobiography,* he also used the Franklin papers compiled by Sparks in the 1830s, conducted extensive research in documents of Franklin's day, and read nineteenth-century histories of the Revolution. The *Atlantic Monthly,* now Parton's champion, marveled at the scope and difficulty of the undertaking and awarded Parton the highest compliment contemporary critics could give: he was at once scholar and literary artist. "He is a good delver, a good sifter, and, what is equally important, a good interpreter,—not merely bringing facts to the light, but compelling them to give out, like Coreggio's pictures, a light of their own." The *North American Review* wrote that at last "Mr. Parton had a subject peculiarly fitted for his genius": the prototypical American Yankee. In moving from journalist to biographer, Parton had come full circle, from the Franklinesque Greeley to Franklin himself. But in the decade since that first biography, Parton had won a "well-established reputation as an historical biographer." In critics' eyes, Parton had risen above the exemplary lives of self-made men (as his contemporary William Makepeace Thayer never would) and put the label of "hack" behind him.[54]

As if to confirm Parton's literary standing, in August 1864 Charles Eliot Norton invited him to contribute to the *North American Review.* Overjoyed, Parton accepted in a letter that revealed his sense of the magazine's place in American literary culture. "Having been brought up in the fear and admiration of the North American Review, I read the letter of one of its editors with gratification and awe. Your approval of my writings does me very great honor." In order to understand Norton's invitation fully, it is important to know one other fact about the *North American* in 1864: the venerable quarterly was under new management. In the late 1850s, when it published Henry Tuckerman's derivatively romantic biographical articles and condemned popular tastes, a style like Parton's would have been wholly out of place. But in 1864 the Boston publishing house of Ticknor and Fields bought the *North American.* The firm's managing partner, James T. Fields, had for several years infused the *Atlantic Monthly* with contemporary issues and articles in the emerging realist style (such as Rebecca Harding Davis's

"Life in the Iron Mills"). Fields and the *North American*'s editors, Norton and James Russell Lowell, sought similarly to modernize their stodgy new acquisition. Soliciting Parton's contributions was part of this project.[55]

Parton's eight biographical essays for the *North American* (1864–67) revealed how far he, the magazine, and the United States had come since 1857. Here more than ever before in his career, Parton wrote as the English romantics did and prescribed: interpretively, subordinating facts to analysis, his own assessments in the forefront. Unlike the derivative American criticism of the 1850s, however, Parton's romanticism—if it can be called romanticism at all—never attempted to transcend or condemn its present-day, American context. Parton chose relatively recent, and mostly American, subjects: the Congressional triumvirate of Henry Clay, Daniel Webster, and John C. Calhoun, the inventor Charles Goodyear, the philanthropist Stephen Girard, and the newspaper publisher James Gordon Bennett. Only John Randolph and Voltaire hailed from earlier eras, and Voltaire was the only non-American. This selection contrasted markedly with Henry Tuckerman's in the 1850s. Tuckerman had chosen mostly English and European literary figures, and all of his American subjects save Cooper had died by 1828. By 1865, Parton could describe Clay, Webster, Calhoun, and Randolph as figures of a bygone era. States' rights and slavery, the issues that had animated politics between 1820 and 1860, had "perished" along with these men, and even the men of that era still alive (like James Buchanan) had faded into insignificance. Parton's stance in these articles, however, was not the historian's. Nor did it resemble Tuckerman's. In seeking to identify subjects' "genius," the transcendent quality that often pitted the individual against his age, Tuckerman had affected distance from mundane, contemporary concerns. By contrast, Parton's critical analyses always emphasized their own context in postwar America. Sometimes he drew analogies between past and present, for instance likening Webster's loyal opposition to the War of 1812 to that of "patriotic 'War Democrats' . . . during the late Rebellion." On other occasions, Parton traced change over time, like the shift from a partisan-centered press to independent journalism. Postwar hindsight also enabled him to make harsh assessments like this one: "While slavery existed no statesmanship was possible, except that which was temporary and temporizing."[56]

As brief biographies, these essays sought to reveal the "inner man" truthfully: in all complexities, no matter what partisans might think of Parton's assessments. Parton worked his way through each subject's life, noting where eulogists or campaign biographers had oversimplified the picture. The narrative highlighted Parton's own observations, made by drawing vivid analogies and describing his subjects' revealing habits and traits. Like a "Marshfield elm" with "dry and crumbling pith" beneath what seems "solid wood," Webster remained outwardly grand and heroic while his character deteriorated in his last decades, a casualty of too much wine and adulation. Parton's references to Webster's drinking aroused controversy; several critics considered it unseemly, just as the *North American* itself probably would have a decade earlier. But Parton would not deny essential characteristics, whether Webster's dissolution or Burr's virtues, just because the public or the critics wished not to hear them. In "James Gordon Bennett and the New York Herald," he lamented the fact that New York's newspapers suppressed information that contradicted their political views. "The final pre-eminent newspaper of America will soar far above such needless limitations as these, and present the truth in *all* its aspects, regardless of its effects upon theories, parties, factions, and Presidential campaigns." Parton's vision of biographical truth mirrored this statement. The preeminent biographer of America had to present the truth in all its aspects, regardless of its effects on the subject's reputation or on the biographer's own popularity. A decade earlier, the *North American* had published the most strident critiques of present-day biographical practice. By publishing Parton, the magazine enshrined that new practice, including its fascination with contemporary figures and willingness to discuss a subject's flaws.[57]

When Ticknor and Fields bought the rights to publish Parton's books in April 1866, it solidified his status as the foremost American biographer—the man who made biography "American" in ideology and style and who, alone among Americans, practiced biography as literary art. In some ways, the shift was unremarkable. Parton's longtime publishers, the Mason brothers of New York, had decided to leave the book trade. Authors often changed publishers in midcentury America when their publishing houses went out of business (as many did in a boom-and-bust economy), and Fields had become well acquainted with Parton through his contributions to the *North American*. Parton was a proven moneymaker: his books sold, and his *Ledger* articles had made his a familiar name in hundreds of thousands of households. In other respects, this move had literary significance. For over a decade Ticknor and Fields had promoted itself as the publisher of America's most important literary figures, whose work it published in well-known uniform editions designed to create a literary canon through material appearance (the "Blue and Gold" editions) as well as textual quality. Before 1866 Ticknor and Fields had rarely published biographies this way. Immediately after acquiring the rights to Parton's works, however, Fields planned a uniform edition of them to showcase the firm's new author. To be sure the edition would get reviewed, Ticknor and Fields added a new volume, *Famous Americans of Recent Times,* a compilation of eleven Parton articles. The publisher advertised "James Parton's Works" aggressively in the *Atlantic Advertiser and Miscellany,* the house supplement attached to its flagship *Atlantic Monthly.* Not coincidentally, a laudatory article on "Parton's Biographical Writings" appeared in the *North American* in April 1867, just months after the Parton edition appeared. Parton had not simply switched publishers; he had become a "Ticknor and Fields author."[58]

While the *Life and Times of Benjamin Franklin,* his *North American* essays, and his new publisher staked Parton's claim to a literary reputation, he made his living with biographical work designed for a wider audience — and less interested in the "inner man" than in celebrity and didacticism. From the late 1850s on, his steadiest income came from short, didactic articles for Bonner's *New York Ledger.* Bonner had built America's most popular weekly story-paper through one simple strategy: buy original pieces from famous authors, pay them well, give them bylines, and advertise the acquisitions aggressively. Signing Fanny Fern to an exclusive contract was Bonner's first great triumph. When he bought the paper in 1851, its circulation was 2,500; a year after Fern started writing weekly columns, it was 180,000; by 1860 it had more than doubled again. The *Ledger* made writers like Fern even more popular than they had been before. It ran single stories and articles from Harriet Beecher Stowe and Charles Dickens. And it made household names of writers who had been only moderately known — like James Parton (whose presence in the *Ledger* may have had something to do with Fern, by 1856 his wife and Bonner's biggest star). The subjects of Parton's articles ranged from George Washington to Blaise Pascal, but his style remained constant: anecdotal, often explicitly didactic, and direct in engaging his audience (through addresses to "our readers" and rhetorical questions). In these pieces, "character" was not synonymous with the "inner man," a complex mix of habits and traits, virtues and vices for the biographer to reveal or interpret. Rather, "character" appeared the way it had in the *Life of Greeley* and William Thayer's books, as a trait or set of traits presented for the reader's emulation. A sketch of Cornelius Vanderbilt exemplified Parton's *Ledger* pieces. It contained anecdotes with invented dialogue (" 'Well,' said Davis, 'don't you know why we have given the contract to you?' 'No.' 'Why, it is because we want this business *done,* and we know you'll do it.' "). And it offered clear morals, not complexities of character. As Parton concluded it, Vanderbilt's "character is one which young men who aspire to lead in practical affairs may study with profit."[59]

Parton also cashed in on the rage for lives of the Civil War commanders. In a few months' respite from the Franklin project in 1863, he wrote *General Butler in New Orleans,* a life of one of the Union's most controversial generals. As a defense of Butler and a biography of a living subject, Parton's book aroused debate. Although Parton maintained that Butler had not played any role in the book's creation, some critics were skeptical. Conversely, Butler's adherents read the book as a virtual campaign biography and wrote Parton that they hoped Butler would seek the White House.[60] As biography, *General Butler in New Orleans* belonged to a class of works that emerged during the war. The dime-novel publishers Beadle and Adams produced "Dime Biographies" of Lincoln, Grant, Fremont, and McClellan as well as the safely deceased Anthony Wayne, Lafayette, Washington, and Crockett. For the Appleton publishing firm, the Rev. Phineas Camp Headley, previously the author of lives of Josephine, Lafayette, and Mary Queen of Scots, imitated William Thayer's books for boys with a trilogy called "Lives of Modern American Heroes": *The Hero Boy* (on Grant), *The Patriot Boy* (Major-General O. M. Mitchel), and *The Miner Boy and His Monitor* (Captain John Ericsson, inventor of the ironclad). After the war Headley penned biographies of Generals Grant, Sherman, and Sheridan — all to capitalize on these instant heroes in the aftermath of victory. The Civil War did not just create a new legion of heroes. It also helped legitimize biographies of living subjects. Parton would soon become a central figure when publishers sought to promote volumes on the "men of our time."[61]

Because of Parton's established literary *and* commercial cachet, subscription publishing firms also sought his work from 1867 on. After the war dozens of new publishers, many in Hartford, sold books exclusively by subscription. Their productions had a look all their own. They were big: octavos, not the duodecimos more common in trade publishing. They were ornate: often in green bindings with elaborate, heavy gold or black stamping. (Eye-catching appearance was critical to salesmen who had only the bindings and a few dozen pages of proposed contents to show potential subscribers.) These books were made to look at, not just to read. A disproportionate number were biographies, of exactly the sort Parton wrote for the money: lives of contemporary (including living) figures, collections of short biographical sketches and anecdotes. Parton's *People's Book of Biography,* the book of "Ledger Lines" he thought "beneath" Ticknor and Fields, appeared within two years of Harriet Beecher Stowe's *Men of Our Times,* L. P. Brockett's *Men of Our Day,* and *Eminent Women of the Age*

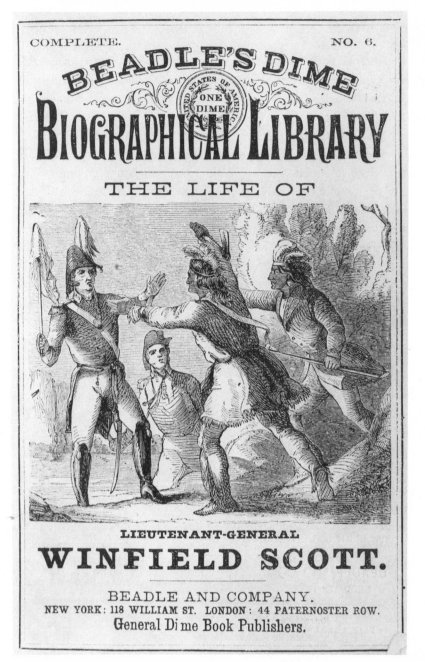

COMPLETE.

NO. 6.

BEADLE'S DIME

ONE
DIME

BIOGRAPHICAL LIBRARY

THE LIFE OF

LIEUTENANT-GENERAL

WINFIELD SCOTT.

BEADLE AND COMPANY.
NEW YORK: 118 WILLIAM ST. LONDON: 44 PATERNOSTER ROW.
General Dime Book Publishers.

The dime-novel publishers Beadle and Company began a Dime Biographical Library in 1860 that included Orville J. Victor's *Life and Military and Civic Service of Lt. Gen. Winfield Scott* (1861). Beadle's biographies, which soon covered many of the Union generals, fueled interest in the lives of "men of our time." (Courtesy American Antiquarian Society) (to which Parton contributed).[62] *People's Book of Biography* was only the first of many subscription books that bore Parton's name. Sometimes these books' actual connection to him was tenuous; one 1870 volume announced sketches "by James Parton and other Prominent Writers" on its spine but contained only one piece by him (out of eighty-six). Parton's name alone became an asset, a device to engage other contributors and win subscribers.[63]

Parton's contributions to subscription-house books differed significantly from the works that Ticknor and Fields published, particularly in how they defined "character." "Ledger Lines" of course did not possess the narrative sweep of the *Life and Times of Burr* or the *Life of Jackson*, but differences are clear even when we compare *People's Book of Biography* with *Famous Americans of Recent Times*, the Ticknor and Fields collection of Parton's articles. The articles in *Famous Americans* were historical or analytical lives of their subjects. In them Parton adopted a scholarly or critical tone, distinguished his work from the puffery of campaign biographies and eulogies, and aimed to illuminate a subject's individuality. Since most had originally appeared in the *North American*, they were long: forty-three pages, on average. In contrast, the *People's Book* contained didactic thumbnail sketches of eminent figures, often recounting one episode, not a whole life. Mostly five to seven pages long, they described famous men's characteristics for the purpose of a reader's emulation. Parton's *Eminent Women of the Age*, also a subscription book, sought to do for women "of the present day" what the *People's Book* did for men: "to make an impression for good upon the young women of our land" by offering examples of "individual excellence or eminence" and "a proper representation of the various professions in which women have distinguished themselves" (education, medicine, women's rights, the theater). But of Parton's four articles in this book, only his biography of Florence Nightingale worked toward this purpose. His other three pieces recounted anecdotes about Frances Kemble's appearance on the stage and unhappy marriage to a slaveholder, Jenny Lind's work to become a world-renowned singer, and Queen Victoria's kindness and simplicity. In sketches like these (and all the sketches in his later subscription book, *Some Noted Princes, Authors, and Statesmen of Our Time*), we can see the emerging interest in "personality" and celebrity—not "character" in either the romantic or the didactic sense.[64]

When Parton wrote that the "stuff" A. S. Hale and Company wanted was "beneath" Ticknor and Fields, he was thus talking about hierarchical relationships between different sorts of biography, not just different sorts of publishers. His implication, that historical and analytical lives ranked above didactic and celebrity ones, reflected the critical standards that had emerged in England and America over the previous two decades. Now biography's central purpose was not "amusement and instruction" (the stock phrase of the early republic) but artistic presentation of inner character, the qualities of mind and action that made the subject unique and thus impossible to emulate. Parton's *Burr, Jackson,* and *Franklin* and the shorter pieces he wrote for the *North American Review* sought to meet this standard. Even if some critics still faulted Parton's literary execution, they applauded him for revealing his subjects as living figures, not demigods. Significantly, when Ticknor and Fields published its edition of Parton's works in 1867, it did not include the *Life of Horace Greeley*—Parton's first biography, and the explicitly didactic life of a self-made man. Like the "Ledger Lines," this book was beneath Ticknor and Fields.[65]

According to several recent historians and literary critics, a bifurcation occurred within American culture between 1850 and 1900. Critics, cultural entrepreneurs, and scholars sought to sacralize Shakespeare, orchestral music, and fine art, to remove them from mass appeal and popular consumption and create cultural hierarchy. Within literature and literary publishing, an analogous shift seems to have occurred as firms like Ticknor and Fields and magazines like the *Atlantic Monthly* represented themselves as the purveyors of "high" culture, distinct from and above middle-class story papers like the *New York Ledger* and far above dime novels. James Parton's career complicates this "highbrow/lowbrow" narrative in several ways. Unlike Louisa May Alcott, who found a "middle" world of domestic writing when the *Atlantic* began rejecting her stories and when she decided to stop writing sensationalistic stories for *Frank Leslie's Illustrated Newspaper,* Parton straddled whatever gap existed. He recognized that his diverse biographical productions were differently and hierarchically situated within the genre, and that different sites of publication inhabited different strata within American literary culture. Yet Parton was able to construct a critically successful *and* popular career in biography—the first American author to do so—because, for him, each stratum made the other possible. Commercial and critical success writing "high" biography, his historical biographies and his *North American* articles, made possible his appeal to subscription firms and lecture bureaus, which sent him around the country in the 1870s. And Parton's less critically prestigious endeavors financed his more time-consuming historical lives, including the *Life of Voltaire* (1881), which took nearly fifteen years and became his magnum opus.[66]

In other words, if different sorts of biographies inhabited unequal positions in the biographical universe of the 1860s, Parton's career shows that hierarchy did not necessarily imply bifurcation. The "merit and dignity" of Ticknor and Fields's volumes was not as far removed from the Ledger Lines as their different appearances, contents, and sites of publication might superficially suggest. Intriguingly, in his *Atlantic Monthly* article "Henry Ward Beecher and His Church" (republished in *Famous Americans*), Parton identified the strata of American churchgoers with their reading habits. Fashionable New York churches, decorated in expensive wood and stained glass, discouraged "Bridget, who cannot read" and "the man whose only literary recreation is the dime novel" while welcoming Bridget's "mistress, who comes to church cloyed with the dainties of half a dozen literatures" and "the man saturated with Buckle, Mill, Spencer, Thackeray, Emerson, Humboldt, and Agassiz." But Beecher's Brooklyn church, "adapted to the needs as well as to the tastes, of the people frequenting it" and therefore unadorned with the finery of the Manhattan one, was home to "the sort of people who take the 'Tribune,' and get up courses of lectures in the country towns." In connecting Beecher to the readers of Greeley's *New York Tribune,* Parton was celebrating his own ideal readers: the broad, literate middle class, whose tastes lay somewhere above dime novels and somewhere beneath fancy European literatures and esoteric science and philosophy. Different reading preferences existed within this middle class. The *New York Ledger* was not the *Atlantic Monthly,* for instance, even if some families probably subscribed to both. And in different periodicals Parton offered different definitions of "character." These distinctions notwithstanding, Parton's work always aimed at the reader's improvement—whether he was dedicating the *Life of Greeley* to "The Young Men of the Free States" in 1855 or delineating the complexities of modernity a dozen years later.[67]

This was the "Americanism" that a critic in the *Nation* detected in Parton's work, and it indeed united his various endeavors. *Famous Americans of Recent Times* pulled Parton's ideology of American progress, expressed piecemeal in his essays, into a unified whole. The *Nation* summarized that ideology in reviewing the book: a belief in

> the superiority of goodness to talents, of principle to will, and the dependence of serviceableness of character and of right principles of action upon the enlightenment of the understanding. His aim is to make this plain not by direct enforcing or technical moralizing, but by a straightforward narrative of the lives of men conspicuous enough to serve as examples, and by the honest statement of the results of those lives, so far as they can be estimated, to the men themselves and to their

generation. Mr. Parton's creed is essentially utilitarian, and "the greatest good of the greatest number" is the formula of his religion. Hence, all that limits the free and just action of the natural faculties of man is hateful to him.

Parton's essays on Girard, Bennett, Goodyear, and Beecher epitomized his philosophy. What made these men relevant for Parton and, he argued, for his postwar readers was their lasting influence on the present. Each had left a more useful legacy than any antebellum politician had: Girard's college, Goodyear's process of vulcanizing India rubber, Bennett's newspaper, Beecher's liberal Christianity. Further, each exemplified a form of virtue specific to modern society: philanthropy and the encouragement of education (Girard), the spirit of invention pursued despite repeated failures and financial ruin (Goodyear), the quest for truth in defiance of political interests (Bennett), and a religious vision that banished "cant and sanctimoniousness" (Beecher). In describing what distinguished Beecher's religion, Parton equally described the principles on which he sought to write biography. "Without formally rejecting time-honored forms and usages, he has infused into his teachings more and more of the modern spirit, drawn more and more from science and life, less and less from tradition." The "modern spirit" in biography, Parton's work implied, animated both substance and style: the substance arising from the question, "What can we, in democratic, enterprising, postwar America, learn from this subject's life?"; the style suited to a nation of newspaper and novel readers.[68]

The real bifurcation within biography cannot be glimpsed within Parton's works as much as *between* the kinds of biography he wrote and another kind he never wrote: scandal-mongering lives of the great and famous. When critics of the 1850s and 1860s argued for perceptive sketches of character composed with literary ability, they reserved their harshest words for biographers who dredged up dirt in order to sell books. Recounting private indiscretions sullied reputations but did not reveal character. This was the bottom of the biographical hierarchy, associated with the sensationalism of mass journalism and dime novels. Parton's journalistic origins, even if they were in middle-class papers, rendered him especially susceptible to charges of scandal-mongering and crass "book-making," just as those origins gave critics an explanation for his stylistic defects (as he learned with his *Life and Times of Aaron Burr*). Had Parton been accused and critically convicted of such practice—for instance, had critics unanimously believed that his references to Webster's drinking served solely to demean Webster's reputation, not to illuminate his character—the career he had built could have collapsed, a personal and professional calamity that subscription volumes of Ledger Lines could not bring about.[69]

James Parton constructed a career as "biographer" at the moment when such a construction became possible in the United States. The critical redefinition of the genre around midcentury reconceived biography as distinct from both the didactic mission and the Sparksian creation of scholarly American history. In those earlier models, authors of biographies defined themselves primarily as moralists, ministers, or historians. An author might be "the biographer of Washington" or of some other particular figure, but his or her authorial stance emerged from the function that the biography served (to instruct, to commemorate, to gather facts for national history). In the newer concept—which came to coexist with the earlier two, not replace them—biography writing was fundamentally a project of literary artistry and character analysis, a different endeavor that made "biographer" a distinct literary choice. The books that Parton wrote between 1857 and 1867, the ones that Ticknor and Fields published in elegant green bindings, provide the first American illustration of that choice. The work he deemed "beneath" America's foremost literary publisher reminds us that other kinds of biographical work envisioned biography differently, paid better, and continued to flourish no matter what romantic critics wanted. And Parton's career itself demonstrates the continuing connections between those multiple biographical worlds.

Romantic Reading and the Celebrated Biographer

Well before the 1850s, as we have seen, some Americans read biographies in romantic terms. When thinking about Napoleon or certain other figures, Michael Floy asked himself whether they possessed "genius." Schoolteacher Julia Parker hoped that Madame de Staël's unique talents could inspire and elevate her. Both Floy and Parker, as well as most other readers whose recorded thoughts about biography survive, tempered such romantic inflections with the didactic notions that prevailed before midcentury. They read biographies for their own moral, intellectual, and spiritual improvement, not for Emersonian transcendence of everyday existence. Three decades later, at least one American reader found it possible to reject the didactic conception outright. On January 12, 1874, Espy Williams of New Orleans took issue with critics of the "excessive-moral school" who had attacked Thomas Moore's *Life of Lord Byron* for offering no "good . . . to the reading world." Williams challenged their premise: what "*good*" had biography ever done?

Of all the kinds of literature[,] that which *aims* at the highest usefulness is often of the least; and in regard to biography, it is not nor can
it ever be of more use than something to while away time. No one yet
fashioned his life after that of another, first because of an innate pride
which repels the thought of his being a copyist, and second, and principally, because he cannot. A man is himself alone, and he can never so
overreach the "selfness" of his nature as to mark out a course upon the
experience of another and abide by it. So biographies, although perhaps
being intended as mirrors of example from which others may profit, are
not made use of as such.

Besides, continued Williams, only "personal friends, and admirers of the
subject" read a biography, and such readers would not learn from it, only
"feed their admiration." Here was a thoroughly romantic attitude toward
biography, complete with a belief in human individuality and the hero-
worshiping impulse.[70]

This attitude emerged from a reader of romantic propensities, a twenty-
one-year-old playwright and poet immersed in the literary culture of New
Orleans. Born in January 1852, Espy Williams was the son of transplanted
northerners, a Cincinnatian father who had given up law to become an
engineer and surveyor and a Philadelphian mother well educated in classical languages and literature. In addition to the literary education he
probably received at home, Espy attended public schools in New Orleans
for several years. According to one account written during his lifetime,
"he was familiar with Shakespeare, the other Elizabethan dramatists, and
dramatic literature in general" by the age of sixteen.[71] In 1869, financial
difficulties at home and in the city forced him to leave school and take a
job as clerk in an insurance firm. Business became his career: he ultimately
became a wealthy, prominent banker. Literature remained his deeper passion. Before his twenty-first birthday, Williams had already submitted
poetry to papers in and outside New Orleans and copyrighted several
plays. He belonged to a local theatrical group, read his work before the
Philomethean Literary Society, and borrowed books regularly from the
city's lyceum library. Perusing the book reviews in literary magazines, he
sometimes took issue with critics and applied his own romantic standards
to his reading. His diary, the record of a cocky young man, attested to his
"craving ambition" to "make myself a place among those whose names are
in the mouths of living men long after *they* have been taken away from this
earth." When he began the diary in 1874, he explained that it would not
record "the common events that I pass through" or "the trivial thoughts on

the trivial things which come under my observation." Nor would it trace his strivings toward moral improvement as so many other young men's diaries did. Its purpose was solely "to keep a record of the books, etc., which I read, and other things which appertain to literature and literati."[72]

Williams described reading three biographies in the thirteen months he intermittently kept his diary: Moore's *Life of Byron: with his Letters and Journals,* James Rees's *The Life of Edwin Forrest, with Reminiscences and Personal Recollections,* and John Forster's *The Life of Charles Dickens.* These choices were all consonant with his paramount interest in literature and the theater, but significant differences existed among the three. Moore's *Byron* was a life and letters, compiled by a literary executor; *Forrest* told of the theatrical life that Rees, a dramatic critic better known as Colley Cibber, shared with his subject; Forster's *Dickens* came closest to a life-and-times narrative, written by one who had known its subject well. By 1874, Moore's work was over forty years old, and had been republished more than a dozen times. The other two were contemporary lives (published within the previous two years) of contemporary men (Dickens died in 1870, Forrest in 1872). All of these facts made a difference in Williams's experience. He commented, for instance, on how *Byron* sometimes made him "forget it [is] written by Moore" and how he had read each of Forster's three volumes just after it appeared.[73]

Other differences stemmed from why Espy Williams read the books and what he made of them and their subjects. Williams read Moore's *Life of Byron* for the same reason he said most people read biographies: he had loved Byron since boyhood and wanted to know more about the "genius" behind the poetry. He considered Moore "a good biographer" for neither succumbing to the "excessive-moral school" nor intruding "into the readers notice where it is not absolutely necessary to explain the text." Best of all, Moore's work revealed "Byron as a man." Too commonly, Williams explained, "great men" were "spoken of, not as *men* but as mythical somethings known by those names" or as *"gods."* This mistake devalued genius. If readers thought Byron omnipotent, they would not appreciate the genius that distinguished him *among* men. Williams praised Forster for a biographical practice ostensibly the opposite of Moore's: Forster made himself "a very important character" in the *Life of Dickens.* Because Dickens and Forster were intimately acquainted, "it is *not* surprising that the life of one should contain much of the life of the other." (No indication exists that Williams read Boswell, but this comment suggests appreciation for a Boswellian approach.) "Besides," he continued, "Biography should be not only a picture of one man's life, but at the same time a picture of the times themselves, and to do this more lives than one must be embraced." He may have read the *Life of Dickens* to learn about a celebrated author within the context of recent British literary culture, not primarily to understand a genius. Strikingly, Williams never wrote anything about Dickens himself, as he did about Byron and Edwin Forrest.[74]

After reading Rees's *Life of Edwin Forrest,* Williams wrote that the book "is not deserving the honor of being published *as* a Biography," and Rees "is nothing of an author, and *especially* not a Biographer." Elaborating upon this negative assessment, Williams expressed what a biography ought to be and to do. Whereas Moore's writing style was "a pleasure," Rees used "very common-place" language and made linguistic errors—elements that reviewers of biographies also commonly noticed. Rees also repeated himself too often, "which is terrible, especial[ly] when what he repeats thus is something about himself." Here an "intrusive" biographer was unwelcome because his intrusions served his ego rather than his subject or his reader. "After reading [Rees] you do not feel that you think anything more of Forrest; Either personally or as an actor than you did before." Rees might have given a sense of the man offstage ("personally"), explained Forrest's method onstage ("as an actor"), or sought Forrest's inner character in order to analyze his acting. Williams enjoyed comparing the styles of different actors who appeared on the New Orleans stage—including Forrest, whom he saw in *Richelieu* in 1871. Perhaps the young playwright and theatergoer read Rees's book in order to understand better an actor he admired. No matter why he read it, he closed it disappointed. The successful biographer had to reveal something that "enlightened" the reader, a term Williams used to describe the effect of Forster's *Life of Dickens.*[75]

This desire for biographical enlightenment—not to mention the use of biography merely to "while away time"—differed markedly from the emphasis on improvement found in so many other readers' diaries, especially earlier in the century. Williams did not read biographies to find models for his own action; indeed, he denied this was possible. Nor did he read biographies, it seems, to gain inspiration for his own improvement. He certainly did not read them (at least the ones he described in his literary diary) out of national pride. Living far from America's artistic centers, he envisioned himself part of the transatlantic culture of letters and theater and placed himself into it by reading *Blackwood's Magazine* and *Godey's* and the *Atlantic Monthly* and by learning about the Philadelphia stage and the English literary world through biographies. Celebrity biographies and lives of immediately deceased actors and authors imaginatively brought readers like Williams closer to worlds they would never visit. Ideally, those biographies brought their subjects closer, too. When they worked, they enabled the reader to "know" Byron or Dickens in some way, not to improve his own character.

If Espy Williams's diary offers a glimpse into biographical reading influenced by literary romanticism, James Parton's fan mail presents a more diverse picture. Parton kept dozens of letters from readers, spanning the late 1850s into the 1880s. Readers told him about the pleasure derived from his most recent book, thanked him for the enjoyment he had provided them for years, and recommended diverse new subjects for his pen. This variety notwithstanding, Parton's letters from readers suggest two general observations. First, numerous readers saw Parton as a literary artist; as one wrote, "you 'swing' our English Language more vigorously and powerfully than any person now living in America."[76] The concept of "fan mail" itself implies a reader's recognition of the author, which had earlier seemed anomalous for biography. If a biography aimed to present its subject as a model for emulation or to narrate authentic historical facts, the biographer's most appropriate stance was effacement of creative authorship. But readers recognized Parton as more than a transparent conduit to the subject or a historian telling the "truth." They gave him credit for making biographies fascinating, enlightening, engaging. Second, by making a famous name in biography writing, Parton became public property in many readers' eyes. Readers suggested he had certain responsibilities to the American public; several even questioned his choices of subjects if they seemed to violate his duty. Readers' expectations of a "Biographer" varied. Some considered his responsibility an exalted one, while others saw him as a biographer for hire. In all of these cases, Parton's readers confirmed not only his status but also the essential tenet of both Samuel Johnson and the romantics: the biographer mattered.

This notion was literally visible in William Menzies's copy of the *Life and Times of Aaron Burr.* In the late 1850s, Parton had just completed the *Life and Times of Burr,* was beginning work on the *Life of Jackson,* and asked Menzies to lend him some Jacksonian pamphlets for his research. Menzies complied, and asked in return for some relic of Aaron Burr—not an uncommon request in an era when historians clipped the signatures off manuscript letters for autograph collectors. Parton sent Menzies a lock of Burr's hair, along with a letter explaining how he had procured it from a relative of the Burrs. Menzies created his own, unique edition of the *Life and Times of Aaron Burr:* he bought the book in sheets (that is, unbound), interleaved letters signed by Burr and Parton and numerous engravings, and had the new whole bound in rich green leather. Inside the front cover, he pasted an envelope containing the lock of Burr's hair and Parton's letter authenticating it. Menzies was not the only reader who grangerized (added illustrations to and thus individualized) one of Parton's books. One Boston book collector transformed the two volumes of the *Life and Times of Franklin* into six with dozens of engraved plates. Menzies's interaction with Parton, however, was particularly suggestive. For Menzies, getting to "know" Aaron Burr took two forms: reading Parton's biography and seeking a relic of the subject himself. In both, the biographer was the intermediary. But far from an invisible author who performed best if seen least, Parton had his own presence in Menzies's book: not just a distinct authorial voice and literary style, but also the autographed letters from him pasted in along with Burr's. This book bears witness to the tangible as well as the literary connections between subject, biographer, and reader, and it demonstrates how the biographer himself could share center stage with his subject.[77]

Catharine Sedgwick, the well-known author of domestic novels like *Hope Leslie* and *The Linwoods* as well as of Lucretia Maria Davidson's memoir in Sparks's Library of American Biography, was in her seventies when she read Parton's *Franklin* in 1865. She wrote him two letters, gushing in praise and wavering in hand. She was infirm; she wished the book came in a smaller edition that would be easier to read in bed; her maid kept telling her, "Miss Sedgwick, you know what a headache you got reading so much of that book yesterday," "Miss S—do put up that book!"—"Miss S I must take away that book." But she could not put it down, because "I snatch it as I did at a novel." For Sedgwick, a biography that read like a Walter Scott novel was not simply enjoyable; it was right for the times. Having "painfully crawled thro'" George Ticknor's *Life of William Hickling Prescott,* she believed that "Scholarly lives by feudal writers are not exactly adapted to these vitalized times." Parton's style better suited a vigorous age, and Sedgwick looked forward to reading his *Jackson* next. Parton had achieved something more: he had revealed his subject in new ways for this aged reader. Sedgwick had thought she "knew all about" Franklin, but "I now feel as though I had known nothing about him." Now, too, she could apply Franklin's life to contemporary problems. Writing to Parton the day after Lee's surrender, she wished, "Oh that we had a Franklin to bring order out of chaos."[78]

With stylistic power and literary accomplishment came responsibility to the nation and its readers: according to Sedgwick, Parton still had enormous work to do. She speculated that his mixed reputation, to this point, resulted from writing books like the *Life of Greeley.* Even she had been predisposed against Greeley before reading Parton's biography, and one of her "enlightened" friends believed that the biographer of Greeley and Bennett "could not elevate any other by his pen." To Sedgwick, this friend's comment explained why Parton's books had not "produced the *sensation* they are yet destined to." The secret lay in picking the right subjects. Biographies like the *Franklin* were a "rich gift to your country," and she asked him to keep using "your time & health as you have done for your country." Therefore, his plan to write Voltaire's life next seemed a waste of time on an unworthy subject: "Shall we not kneel to the memory of Washington when the thought of Voltaire will excite only a flippant smile?" In an age when authors' personas as well as their works were packaged for public consumption, Parton was the Biographer, a public figure no less than his subjects. With this publicity came demands and expectations: for instance, to write Washington's biography rather than Voltaire's.[79]

In the mid-1860s when *General Butler in New Orleans* and the *Life and Times of Franklin* appeared within a year of each other, Parton received mail from a variety of readers, not just noted authors like Sedgwick. A soldier in the 18th Army Corps wrote from Fortress Monroe in Virginia. A defeated member of the British Parliament wrote from London. A woman whose father wrote for a New York German paper had recommended *General Butler* to her acquaintances and would "do every thing further in my power to promote its circulation." The former diplomat Nicholas P. Trist, who had negotiated the peace treaty that ended the Mexican War, reported that the *Franklin* became "more and more delicious at every page" to his bedridden sister-in-law. Several readers offered slight corrections to Parton's facts. Underscoring the dangers of writing contemporary biographies, Reverdy Johnson complained that nearly every reference to himself in *General Butler* was "wholly incorrect" and hoped Parton would correct "the injustice you have done me (I am sure undesignedly)." George William Curtis, editor of *Harper's Monthly,* noted that Parton had gotten the sculptor of Franklin's statue wrong: it was Richard S., not Horatio, Greenough. In general, though, even readers' corrections came in laudatory letters. Curtis wrote, "Every sincere American owes you great thanks for your masterly Life of Franklin, which, I am sure, will become very precious in our literature."[80]

What, exactly, did readers enjoy about Parton's books and expect from him? Sedgwick implied four elements, all of which appeared in other readers' letters too. First, Parton entertained. Correspondents most commonly thanked him for providing them "pleasure." One reader reported that his sister found the *Life of Franklin* more fascinating than anything else she had read recently, "and she is a pretty sharp critic of these works." Jesse Furlong, a New York lawyer, used language equally applicable to novels: "I have read and re-read your charming biography of Aaron Burr so often that most of the characters are firmly fixed in my memory." Harriet Beecher Stowe thanked Parton "for the pleasure you have given me in biographical works which you have had the faculty of making more interesting than romance — (let me trust it is not by making them in part works of imagination)." Second, as Stowe's parenthetical addition suggested, readers trusted Parton to portray subjects faithfully and adhere to historical truth, no matter how novelistic his style. Several readers employed the language of portraiture to describe Parton's achievement. Others emphasized the historical "instruction" he had given them. Envisioning Parton as earlier readers had seen Jared Sparks, correspondents told him about manuscript materials related to his subjects, asked him to verify facts, and sought advice for historical works they were writing. Third, Parton's work offered Americans a usable past. Just as Sedgwick wished for "a Franklin" in modern, chaotic times, Chauncey F. Black praised Parton for "giving us both Jefferson and his philosophy in such admirable simplicity, and in a form so well suited to the popular digestion." Like George William Curtis, William Bigelow thanked Parton on patriotic grounds: "We do so little in this country to do honor to the memory of those who have illustrated it, that I feel disposed to encourage foreigners if they will do it for us. You have done already so much to repair this national defect. . . ."[81]

Finally, what Sedgwick and other readers expected of Parton was more biography. Having established his reputation, he received a cacophony of requests from periodicals, readers, and people who may have known his name better than his work. These requests revealed how many ways it was possible to think about him. To literary magazines such as *Galaxy* and *Scribner's*, he was Parton of the *Life of Franklin* and the *North American Review*, author of interpretive pieces on historical and contemporary topics. To *Frank Leslie's Illustrated Weekly*, which asked him for a series on "The Boyhood of Noble Men," he was the celebrity scribbler of "Ledger Lines" best known for didactic sketches à la William Makepeace Thayer. To readers who wanted memoirs of their relatives and friends, Parton's name offered the possibility of larger circulation than such books might otherwise command. Asking Parton to write the memoirs and assuring him the necessary materials were readily available, they appealed to his morality, his sense of charity, and especially his pocketbook. Because abolitionist Owen Lovejoy had left no inheritance, his widow "had an idea that something might be made for the children by the sale of the book, if well written." She knew Parton only as "a successful writer of that kind of books," but that reputation sufficed. And since Lovejoy's many friends and admirers around the

United States were "reading people," the biography would "sell well" if written soon. Requests like these suggested their writers' conception of Parton: America's national biographer could be hired.[82] To other readers, he was something more than a celebrity author, a famous name to increase a book's or magazine's circulation. In the weeks after Lincoln's assassination, two readers—a thirty-two-year-old newspaperman and a schoolgirl—inquired hoping he would write Lincoln's biography. Whether for immortalizing and humanizing America's heroes or for championing the American ideology of self-making, Parton won American readers' gratitude for serving the nation.[83]

Now recognized as a benefactor of "every sincere American," Parton seems to have confounded his public by choosing Voltaire as his next major subject. Parton inquired whether *Harper's* might be interested in a serial biography like the one of Napoleon by John S. C. Abbott that had first popularized the magazine. No such serial ever materialized, and the editor of another magazine tried to dissuade Parton from the project altogether. But for Parton, Voltaire's life would be the climax of a career writing biographies of men who represented freedom and equality: Greeley, Jackson, Franklin. Voltaire espoused the most radical freedom of all, emancipation from religious doctrine. He fascinated Parton because the biographer's own religious views echoed the philosopher's; as a Free Religionist, Parton considered even the belief in God to be an enslaving superstition. For fifteen years from 1865 to 1880, Parton's articles, lectures, and subscription-house books all worked toward the same end: to make money for his Voltaire research. The project was public knowledge, for a reader in Fort Wayne, who called himself "an admirer of all your works" and "looked forward" to the Voltaire book, wrote to Parton in 1873 to ask when it would appear. (This reader also unwittingly attested to Parton's own celebrity: he asked for an autographed response.) The two-volume, 1,200-page *Life of Voltaire* appeared at last in 1881.[84]

Readers' letters about the *Life of Voltaire* emphasized Parton's literary style, the insight he provided into Voltaire's character, and the service he had done by writing the book. According to James Redpath, Parton had skillfully handled all the facts and tactfully dealt with Voltaire's controversial private life. Another reader wrote that the biography had enhanced his previous interest in Voltaire, for "How could it be otherwise in the hands of so brilliant a writer as Parton?" Joseph Henry Allen encouraged Parton to take up Napoleon or Lafayette next, in order "to carry your knowledge, judgment, & art of telling a story over into revolutionary times." These letters praised all the elements that critics prescribed in a biographer: expert sifting of materials and facts, literary ability, and insight into character. This combination had given Redpath "my first clear view of Voltaire." For these readers, Parton had accomplished what critics thought romantic biographers should. He had thrown light on the character of a "most extraordinary genius" and cast his subject as "a great man," not just "a great text." Moreover, with this "masterpiece" he had rendered service to "the cause of liberty." Thanking Parton for the pleasure he had provided and wishing for more Parton biographies, Elizur Wright wrote, "Please don't die, if you can help it." Another reader hoped "the book will sell well, & bring you compensation for the long labor upon it."[85]

It did not. Only 1,822 copies sold in its first three years of publication. Why did Parton's public fail to appreciate what he considered his greatest work? Partly because Parton always had multiple publics. Those who knew him primarily from his *Ledger* pieces and from subscription volumes like the *People's Book of Biography* might not be interested in a massive, two-volume work on a single subject. (And a massive work with myriad quotations in French, at that.) One reader who admired the *Voltaire* recommended a condensed "people's edition," implying that Parton's full-length work was too daunting for the "people." Those who had read his previous scholarly works might have been more receptive, but seventeen years had elapsed since *Franklin*. Although no sales records survive from Parton's years with Mason Brothers, Parton's own anecdotal recollections suggested that his *Greeley* and *Butler*, lives of contemporary figures, fared better in the literary marketplace than *Jackson* or *Franklin*. Thus if the potential audience for *Voltaire* consisted largely of those who had read his earlier historical lives, this was already a small fraction of James Parton's fans.[86]

Most of all, Parton's readers deserted him because he deserted them when he chose to write the life of Voltaire. When Parton became "dangerously enamored" of this project in the 1860s, he foresaw "the immensity of the labor and the odiousness of his name." Over sixteen years he performed the labor, but the other problem remained. Would readers in the mid-nineteenth century take to the life of a man identified with atheism and radical Enlightenment thought? Parton strayed doubly from his readers' expectations. He chose a subject neither American nor contemporary, possibly jarring readers who associated him with Franklin and Jackson, Greeley and Butler. Further, in choosing Voltaire he revealed the ways his philosophy lay outside the American, Gilded Age mainstream. Parton believed Voltaire's championship of intellectual freedom was relevant to the present day, the logical culmination of the newspaper revolution and the abolition of slavery. This belief extended the notion of freedom beyond where most of Parton's contemporaries would have, just as Parton's rejection of Christianity put him at odds with mainstream society. All the readers' correspondence Parton preserved about the *Life of Voltaire* came from men with similarly strong reformist tendencies: Joseph Henry Allen, the Unitarian publisher and author of a three-volume history of Christianity that culminated in the modern liberal movement; James Redpath, manager of the Boston Lyceum Bureau (in which Parton was a popular lecturer) and onetime fiery abolitionist and defender of John Brown; Jonathan Baxter Harrison, soon to write in support of the Indian-reform, conservationist, and labor movements. As long as Parton's subjects comported with middle-class definitions of American freedom (that is, freedom to rise in capitalist society through industry and ingenuity), he continued to win readers. Even a modest reformist spirit won popularity. Parton's new *Captains of Enterprise* (1884), which he subtitled "Men of Business who have done something besides make money" and intended as "an antidote to Wall Street and Jay-Gouldism," sold extremely well. When he strayed into territory temporally, nationally, and ideologically beyond his readers' interests, his audience narrowed.[87]

Around 1880, three episodes in Parton's biographical career exemplified the different worlds—of biographies, of publishers, *and* of readerly expectations—he inhabited, or was thought to inhabit. One, of course, was the publication of his *Life of Voltaire:* the culmination of his career as a scholarly, historical biographer, published by the literary firm of Houghton Mifflin, and appealing to a rarefied audience. The second began with an 1879 letter from Perry Mason and Company, publishers of the *Youth's Companion.* On behalf of the company, Hezekiah Butterworth asked Parton "for articles of special value to young men—graphic pictures of the turning points in life's moral history, such as Samuel Smiles gives, with an influence of incalculable value, to young people in his life of George Moore and industrial biographies." Smiles, the foremost English writer to promote self-making through biography, had achieved transatlantic fame with books like *Self-Help.* Butterworth wanted similar articles especially suited to American boys, and whom better to ask than Parton? "The finest episodes in the lives of the best Americans all stand out in your mind like hills in the sunlight." For a hundred dollars a column, Parton could "furnish from time to time some striking, telling incidents of the best American biography; not *biographies,* but the strong stereoscopic *incident* that made the subject of it worthy of a biography." To demonstrate his magazine's literary reputability, Butterworth informed Parton that Rebecca Harding

Davis, James T. Fields, and others had already provided articles. The *Youth's Companion,* in other words, appealed to Parton on grounds of middlebrow, didactic respectability. It was not high literature, but noted literary men and women wrote for it, and it sought a lofty purpose, "influence . . . with our large audience of readers." Like the *Life of Voltaire,* the *Youth's Companion* fit into Parton's authorial strategy; for years he had written the sort of articles Butterworth wanted in his *Ledger* pieces and lectures. Parton agreed, and for the rest of his life he contributed regularly to the *Youth's Companion,* making his name familiar to a new generation of readers.[88]

The third episode involved a request Parton refused. On May 14, 1880, the Democratic financier and politician William Collins Whitney wrote confidentially to Parton. Whitney's father-in-law, Henry B. Payne, might become a candidate for the Democratic presidential nomination, and it was "of importance under these circumstances that the incidents of his life should be written up by a competent hand," in case it were needed. Whitney was handling the arrangements because Payne was "extremely modest & unambitious" (what better stance for a potential candidate?) and he wanted Parton to write the campaign biography. Whitney would pay Parton's way to New York to discuss the proposal. The whole project had to be accomplished "quietly" and would be "of no commercial value" if Payne were not nominated. Whitney would pay all the expenses himself, presumably to a subscription publisher, the sort of firm that would assume such a risk and that increasingly by 1880 was the source of campaign biographies. This letter offered no clues whether William C. Whitney had ever read one of James Parton's biographies. To him, Parton may simply have been a well-known author of biographies and a "competent hand" who would write anything for "proper compensation," a celebrity author but a hack nonetheless.[89] Not surprisingly, Parton never wrote Henry Payne's biography. A quarter century earlier, Parton had distinguished his *Life of Horace Greeley* from campaign biographies. In his *Life of Jackson* and his *North American* articles on Clay and Webster, he had noted how superficial and inaccurate campaign biographies tended to be, given their purpose. Multiple biographical worlds existed in the years of James Parton's career, and he worked in several of them. But some types of biography, no matter what the potential financial rewards, remained beneath the Biographer.

James A. Garfield, Biography Reader
and Biographical Subject

"From the Cradle to the Grave: Scenes and Incidents in the Life of Gen. James A. Garfield." President Garfield's assassination occasioned a variety of biographies, including this 1882 poster version of his life and death. (Poster in author's collection; photograph by Ted Cook)

Two deaths help explain why James A. Garfield became the foremost exemplar of self-made manhood in 1880s America. His father's, when James was not yet two, gave biographers the beginning of their story and strengthened their claim that the young man had had to make himself. Garfield's own, by an assassin's bullet after half a year in the White House, provided a relatively blank slate upon which biographers could draw. Thanks to the mass production of engraved images, pictures could now tell a life story nearly as well as words, a fact not lost on the publishers J. W. Sheehy and Company of New York. Sheehy's visual biography, a memorial poster tracing Garfield's life "From the Cradle to the Grave," appeared shortly after the president's death. Composed of twenty-three engravings, plus the "Derivation of Our Martyr's Name" and a three-line poem, the poster offered three images of Garfield. The self-made man was born in a log cabin, read by the age of three, worked along the "tow path" as a teenaged canalboat driver, attended college, and "won his spurs" at the Battle of Chickamauga. The family man supported a wife, an aged mother, and five children, whose portraits surrounded the central image of the president. The assassin's victim, depicted in seven scenes, was the focus of America's most dramatic event since Lincoln's murder: Charles

Guiteau firing the shots in Union Station, railroad workers laying tracks to the New Jersey seaside so that Garfield could convalesce away from humid Washington, his mother anticipating news, his wife encouraging him "when the crisis came" and finally "bewailing her loss" over the casket in the Capitol Rotunda. Absent entirely was the respected, powerful congressman, lawyer, and orator: the poster did *not* show the eighteen years between Chickamauga and Union Station.[1] In memorializing Garfield, J. W. Sheehy and Company effaced his career—a facet of modern life with no dramatic pictorial equivalent, or perhaps a middle period out of place in a story of beginnings and endings, fatherless self-making and senseless martyrdom.

James A. Garfield read biographies for more than a quarter century before he became their subject, and his biography reading offers another window into his life story. In childhood Garfield loved nautical stories, especially *The Pirate's Own Book,* an enormously popular volume of sensational tales about famous pirates and seafarers. These stories whetted his desire to go to sea, even if he never got farther than canaling near Cleveland. More serious biographies came later. As a student at Williams College in February 1856, Garfield read Robert Southey's *Life and Correspondence of Henry Kirke White,* the first volume of Washington Irving's *Life of George Washington,* and Sir Walter Scott's novel *Heart of Midlothian.* Not unlike Michael Floy two decades earlier, Garfield responded in his diary as an impressionable young man seeking models to inspire him. He identified with White, whose "ambitions and plans . . . I have felt as something peculiar to me." White's life exemplified "the affectionate son and brother, the persevering scholar, the noble man and above all the true Christian"—all of which Garfield himself hoped to be at that moment of his life. Garfield ended this diary entry with a prayer that God fortify his resolution, just as Floy had after reading the life of Thomas Halyburton. Reading Irving's *Washington* a few weeks later, Garfield found himself awash in "deep and fervent emotions of patriotic feeling." He compared Irving's biography favorably against Scott's novel. *Heart of Midlothian* contained interesting characters and portrayed Scottish life "beautifully," but Irving's book "touched cords in my heart that thrill with far greater intensity than anything I have ever read from the Poet of Abbotsford." "Peculiar to me," "cords in my heart," "thrill": Garfield was reading biographies *con amore,* much as contemporary critics encouraged biographers to write them. Far from inhabiting opposing moral poles, biography and fiction were now literary converses, biography giving "the facts to find

the spirit" and novels giving "the spirit to find the fact."[2] Discussing biographies and genre in the same years he sought to define his character and career, Garfield revealed both the changes in biographical discourse and his own piety, patriotism, *and* romanticism.

Garfield's biography reading took new directions when politics became his career. Antislavery politics helped him reconcile his desires to achieve something of moral purpose and to play an active role in the world rather than devote his life to teaching or the ministry. Garfield's choice exemplified another sort of romanticism: the "transformation in consciousness" that characterized prosperous, middle-class Americans of his generation, who "moved away from inherited religious definitions of meaning"—definitions that had seemed natural in the 1830s—and sought to devise their own answers to life's questions. At the core of those answers lay experience, engagement with the world through war, career, and leisure. The citizens of Garfield's Ohio district elected him to Congress in 1862, while he was still in the army. For eighteen years he served in the House of Representatives and supplemented his income with occasional legal work. His leisure activities befitted an increasingly cosmopolitan, professional man. The Garfield family traveled to Italy, France, Switzerland, and Germany in the late 1860s, partaking in the "imaginative acquisition" of foreign cultures that middle-class Americans found increasingly affordable in the Gilded Age. Literature offered another form of worldly engagement. As an adult, Garfield particularly enjoyed the lives of literary or intellectual subjects far removed from his own experiences and public concerns. Garfield, who often read with his wife Lucretia in the evenings, was "almost envious" of the publisher George Ticknor's literary life (depicted in an 1876 life-and-letters biography), and he remarked several times that he could not hate as heartily as had Thomas Babington Macaulay (portrayed in George Trevelyan's two volumes). Reading the lives of Ticknor, Macaulay, and the Prussian diplomat and scholar Baron von Bunsen became a form of vicarious travel, bringing foreign people and worlds into the Garfields' own domestic circle. Biography reading could forge new bonds of intimacy outside that circle, too. When visiting George Bancroft's wife (who had known Ticknor well) or General Robert Schenck and his daughter (who had known Macaulay's sister), the Garfields could now "reminisce" about common friends whom James and Lucretia knew only through biography.[3]

In other cases, Congressman Garfield read biography for professional reasons. He read his friend William Dean Howells's campaign biography of his party's candidate, Rutherford B. Hayes, in September 1876. Three months later, when the outcome of the election was disputed, he perused the chapters of Parton's *Life of Aaron Burr* pertaining to the disputed Jefferson-Burr election of 1800—perhaps to prepare for his role on the Electoral Commission that would determine Hayes's fate, perhaps simply to gain historical perspective on the current dilemma. He read William V. Wells's *The Life and Public Services of Samuel Adams* to prepare a speech for the dedication of Adams's statue in the House of Representatives, and referred to a biography of Margaret Fuller when writing an address on the life of Almeda Booth, an Ohioan friend who had recently died and whom he considered the Fuller of the West. Biographies offered the mature Garfield confirmation of his own beliefs rather than lessons to shape those beliefs. Parton's book showed how every political crisis whether in 1800 or 1876 had led observers to "prophesy the failure of the Republic," a "theory of ruin" Garfield rejected. Adams's biography renewed "my faith in radicalism. Nobody but radicals have ever accomplished anything in a great crisis."[4]

Now that he knew many of the major figures of the day, Garfield also read biographies of his contemporaries—not for the inspiration or self-modeling he had sought in youth, but for reminders of his own experiences. When he called on President Grant in 1876, the two veterans fell into conversation about General Sherman's newly published *Memoirs,* which both men had enjoyed. In his diary Garfield defended Sherman against those who criticized soldiers for writing their memoirs so soon after the war — participating privately in the critical debate about whether the abundance of biographies of "men of our time" was a good thing. For a week in late spring 1874, Garfield struggled with Robert Bruce Warden's *Account of the Private Life and Public Services of Salmon Portland Chase,* the recently deceased chief justice of the Supreme Court. Garfield, who had met Chase in Washington during the war, received an advance copy of the book, probably because he represented Chase's native Ohio in Congress. Garfield hated Warden's style even as he relished retracing Chase's life. Warden violated the dictum that the biographer stay "behind his canvas entirely," for his work was the "absurdest piece of egotism and biographic indecency I have ever met": "Warden is what Jane Austen would call a '*Strong, Natural, Sterling' Ass.*" (Garfield had just read *Pride and Prejudice* and *Sense and Sensibility.*) Congressman Garfield detested Warden for a more specific reason. By 1874 Garfield was himself a "man of our time," whose career Chase described in his diary — in an entry that found its way into Warden's book.

Warden followed the quotation with his own opinion, doubtless the biographic indecency Garfield hated most: "Garfield is an orator, and he seems to have been also a good soldier; but he never seemed to me a worthy of the finest type; and this is the most favorable judgment I could possibly pronounce respecting him were I required to judge him on my present information and belief." [5]

Despite Warden, Garfield enjoyed "that part [of the book] that is biographical" and identified with Chase's early experiences — which he tested against the narrative of his own life. Garfield suggested, somewhat enviously, that Chase had had an easier beginning than he. Where Garfield faced poverty and the challenge of making himself, Chase "had powerful friends" to shape his education and "give him culture" from an early age. "Before he was sixteen he was delivering a Greek Oration at Worthington, Ohio, in the presence of his uncle, the Bishop. At sixteen I had never seen a Greek book." Garfield's response to Chase's life demonstrated his faith in the ethic of the self-made man. He "was almost alarmed" to learn that Chase had applied to an uncle for a clerkship, "delighted" that the uncle had refused the young man, and certain that Chase "afterwards blessed the memory of his Uncle" for forcing him to make his own way. [6] The Garfield reading Chase's life in 1874 was not the young student seeking inspiration from the lives of the pious and great. Rather, this Garfield was the successful, middle-class politician crafting the narrative of his own origins at the same time he read the story of Chase's.

And from the mid-1870s on, Garfield actively constructed the story of his own past, as the biography reader became a biographical subject in his own right. Among the biographical innovations of the Gilded Age were county and state histories—a local sort of "men of our time" volume. These books included biographical sketches of the early pioneers and prominent living citizens, who also formed the most obvious clientele for the books. (Like modern-day publishers of *Who's Who* volumes, their publishers appealed to civic leaders simultaneously as subjects and potential subscribers.) In July 1878 "a Mr. M. P. Jones . . . came to get materials for a sketch of my life, for Cleave's Cyclopedia of Ohio," Garfield wrote in his diary. In this case the book agent achieved only half his mission, for Garfield "spent an hour with him, giving him the main facts, but declined to subscribe for the book." Within the week, the Washington journalist Albert G. Riddle came calling, "to write a sketch of my life for the history of Lake County." The two men discussed "the history of my father and mother, and of my own early life." [7]

In encounters like these, Garfield seized the opportunity to shape the public, printed presentation of himself. A surviving manuscript of an interview (probably Riddle's) with Garfield reveals how the congressman described his early years—and how much of his subsequent biographers' portrayals came originally from his own telling. Describing himself as "one of the few younger men of this generation who had the valuable experience of having taught in a log school house," he identified himself with the privations that had strengthened an earlier generation. Recalling how he chopped a hundred cords of wood as a fifteen-year-old farmhand, he continued: "I think of my boy Hal of about the same age chopping that amount of wood. Why if he should chop a cord I would consider him deserving of great credit and he would feel doubtless that he had accomplished a great feat." He portrayed himself as one who had risen from the bottom, on his own work alone. Because he lacked the experience to serve as a sailor, he chose to begin a rung lower, on a canal boat. When the only available place on the canal boat was as a driver, "This was as I would have it. As canaling was at the bottom of sailing so driving was at the bottom of canaling. I took the job." After his canal-boat days ended, Garfield returned to school on his own: "Let me say right here that that $17, which mother and brother Thomas gave me, was the only help (money) I ever had given me in getting through college and started in life."[8]

Even as Garfield supplied the master narrative for his biographers, he also provided its language, drawing from popular stories of self-made men. In this interview he sketched scenes from his canaling days, complete with dialogue and dialect, vivid descriptions of fights and near-skirmishes, and lessons:

As Dave rushed toward me, with his head down, muttering his oaths, he reminded me of nothing so much as a mad bull and I determined to treat him accordingly. Remaining perfectly still until he was almost before me, I suddenly jumped aside and as he passed I dealt him a terrible blow just back of and under the left ear.

With great force he fell with his head between two beams in the bottom of the boat.

In an instant I was upon him with one hand at his throat and the other clenched, up lifted to strike.

"Pound the damn fool to death, Jim," called out the voice of the Captain. "If he haint no more sense not to git mad at an accident he had orten die. Why don't you strike, damn me if I will interfere."

But I didn't strike. I couldn't, some way. It seemed to me that it would be wrong and besides my anger had subsided when I saw Dave wholly in my power. I remembered our friendship, too, and so released my hold.

"Sorry, Jim, I was such a fool as to git mad," said Dave, rising, "but that cussed old pole did hurt my shoulder so. Give me yer hand. Good frin's, now?" and he walked off to his post rubbing his side.

This scene, complete with the "mad bull" image and much of the recollected dialogue, appeared in Riddle's sketch of Garfield in the *History of Geauga and Lake Counties, Ohio, with Illustrative and Biographical Sketches of Its Pioneers and Most Prominent Men* (1878), and again in Riddle's campaign biography in 1880. Other biographers embellished the anecdote, but it originated with Garfield himself—a practical politician long past his rustic, adventurous, brief summer on the canal boat.[9]

Riddle summed Garfield up in 1878 as a work in progress, a man still lacking something. Riddle called that something "egoism," the assertiveness of the self-seeker. Nothing Garfield had done, except his early adventures on the canal, seemed born of a passion. He "became a teacher because it was there to be done." He never plunged into legal practice. He seemed always ready to retire from public life. "In short, to a superficial observer, his life, rich and varied, seems rather the result of his surroundings." Garfield had always demonstrated an ability to grow, Riddle wrote; perhaps he would find this missing passion as he had achieved so much else. Garfield recognized himself in Riddle's sketch, which he called "the best [of myself] that has yet been written." "His criticisms of my character are revelations of myself to myself, and I think in the main are correct."[10] At this point Garfield's biography remained the province of county and state histories, where a perceptive reporter could record the ambiguities as well as the strengths of his character.

All of this changed on June 8, 1880, when the Republican party nominated Garfield for the presidency. Potential biographers and their publishing firms wired and wrote immediately about their plans. One Boston firm introduced Colonel Russell H. Conwell as the "best man for writing a book on the Public Services of General Garfield," because Conwell—"one of the best biographical writers in the country"—had been active in previous campaigns but always refused office, had had acquaintance "with public men & affairs," had served in the war, and had written best-selling books before. In addition, his campaign life of Rutherford Hayes had pleased Hayes's family and friends as well as the public. Other biographers had known Garfield longer, including

the popular novelist and journalist James R. Gilmore (who wrote under the pseudonym Edmund Kirke) and Garfield's longtime friends Albert Riddle and Burke Hinsdale. Some things had not changed: the candidate still could not seem to have been involved in producing his own biography. Gilmore wrote Garfield that only one editor at Harper and Brothers would know the candidate had furnished materials and read proofs. And the fact that Harper's was publishing the book echoed Ticknor and Fields's publication of Hawthorne's *Life of Pierce* twenty-eight years earlier. Once again, enlisting a well-respected, traditionally apolitical firm could place a campaign biography above the fray: "This mode of publishing will do you a vast deal of good, for, as you know, the Harpers are outside of politics, and have an uncounted clientage."[11]

These professions notwithstanding, the candidate was anything but uninvolved. To prepare for the biographical rush, Garfield dictated a sixty-page document labeled "Notes for the Benefit of Biographers" that picked up his life story where his previous interview transcript had left off, at the end of his collegiate days. Much of this new document (also in the form of an interview) detailed Garfield's positions on public issues, explained legal cases in which he had been involved, and answered the potential accusations of his political opponents. As in the earlier interview, however, Garfield demonstrated a keen awareness of his audience, even prescribing which of his speeches biographers should excerpt. Although much of his auto-biographical document explained the public actions and positions of a nine-term congressman, as professional a politician as any in Washington, Garfield took pains to portray himself differently. Defending himself against the charge that his Washington home had been an extravagance financed from questionable sources, Garfield presented the episode as an example of his familial devotion: he would not leave his fast-growing family behind in Ohio. Explaining how he had argued cases before the Supreme Court without an extensive legal career, he made a point of describing how he had studied law "in my own room at Hiram." People "who have been very anxious to belittle me as a lawyer" complained because "all professions are exceedingly jealous of anybody that comes up to the profession through any other than the regular channels." Perhaps a "culture of professionalism" was taking hold in Gilded Age America, but this professional man did all he could to obscure his participation in it. He preferred instead that biographers array him with another set of middle-class virtues, domesticity and self-made manhood.[12]

By 1880, campaign biographies had become luxury books for middle-class parlors. Commercial firms, especially subscription publishers (Harper's was the exception), had supplanted the old political-publishing network where campaign biographies had been cheap books or pamphlets published by newspaper editors. Some campaign lives rivaled the finest subscription-house wares in ornamentation. James S. Brisbin's biography of Garfield, published simultaneously by firms in Philadelphia, Chicago, Cincinnati, Atlanta, St. Louis, San Francisco, Springfield (Massachusetts), and Emporia (Kansas), was bound in maroon cloth, embossed in gold and black, and illustrated with twenty-five engravings. Its front cover showed a ladder—with rungs labeled Canal Hand, Student, Teacher, S. Senator, Soldier, Maj. General, U.S. Senator—stretching from the canal boy tugging his boat at the bottom to the gold-embossed White House and "Candidate for President" at the top. The contents of these campaign biographies, too, suggested their place in the parlor. James Gilmore asked Garfield for "a good photograph of your wife, and a photographic copy of the crayon of your mother which hangs in yr Reception-rooms at Washington." Brisbin's book contained two chapters on Garfield's house in Mentor and his family, in which the biographer abandoned "the impersonal style hitherto employed" in favor of the first-person. Thus the biographer, and vicariously the reader, visited the Garfields at home. Domestic space was now also the hub of a presidential campaign. Sitting at dinner next to Mrs. Garfield, Brisbin shared the table with "Hon. A. G. Riddle, of Washington, and Major [Jonas] Bundy, of the *New York Mail;* both these gentlemen, like myself, engaged in writing a history of Garfield's life." The home that Brisbin described mirrored the homes where his book would be read: bustling sites of middle-class comfort and companionate marriage.[13]

What had become of the campaign-life formulas of the 1840s, when candidates' masculine public "families" were more visible than their wives and children at home? The new circumstances of publication partly accounted for the difference. For a subscription firm to make money on a book, it had to appeal to readers who could afford to spend several dollars. For that audience to buy the book, the firm had to make it attractive, not just informative. Images of the candidate at home, like anecdotes of the candidate as a youth or a soldier, could increase the book's appeal to a whole reading family. Without portraits of Garfield's wife and mother, Harper and Brothers would be "behind their competitors." One biography of Garfield's opponent Winfield Scott Hancock contained biographical sketches of all the first ladies from Martha Washington to Mrs. Hancock, "who in all probability will preside in the establishment of the next President of the United States." Partly, too, depicting the candidate at home with his family reflected new ways of looking at public figures. Books on the homes of American authors and statesmen, which had appeared since the 1850s, suggested that domestic space revealed its inhabitants' character (an idea that domestic novels helped propagate). Like the three biographers at Mentor in June 1880, reporters increasingly sat in their subjects' parlors and dining rooms for interviews. This blurring of the boundary between public and private made it all the more important that certain proprieties be observed. Hancock's biographer never mentioned Mrs. Hancock's first name, and descriptions of Lucretia Garfield remained short and largely stereotypical. James R. Gilmore wanted to describe "the influences which yr wife and mother have had upon your career" but took pains to assure the candidate that, even if Mrs. Garfield's portrait must be included, the publishers were "gentlemen & not disposed to intrude upon the privacies of private life."[14] In the 1830s and 1840s, campaign biographies themselves had helped delineate a masculine zone of public, political action. By 1880, any reluctance to discuss candidates' wives stemmed from Victorian notions of genteel

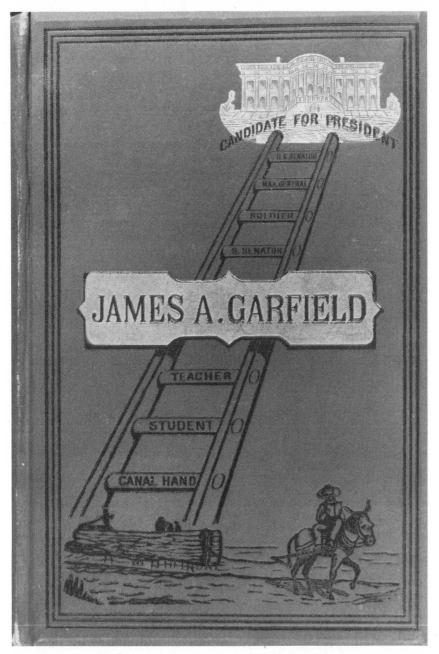

Cover design from James S. Brisbin, *From the Tow-Path to the White House*. Many of James A. Garfield's campaign biographies were ornately bound, including this one—which mimicked the spine of William Makepeace Thayer's *The Bobbin Boy*. (Book in author's collection; photograph by Ted Cook)

propriety, not republican tenets of political culture.

Gentleman publishers did know their market, however—a fact brought home in the weeks and months after Garfield's assassination. Once again, biographies proliferated. Some were republications of the campaign lives, with a few chapters added on the shooting, the president's eleven-week struggle for life, and the nation's mourning. (Those eleven weeks gave publishers time to prepare their new biographies, so that the books began to appear almost immediately after Garfield finally died on September 19.) In these appended chapters, and in entirely new works like John Clark Ridpath's *Life and Work of James A. Garfield,* Mrs. Garfield assumed added prominence as the symbol of national hope and mourning: "The purity of character and heroism of the wife were so touching, so sublime, that she became a loved sister or daughter to all the people. She was enshrined in their hearts by her saintly fortitude, until day by day her every movement and every word was treasured as a revelation." Ridpath's book contained two frontispiece portraits, of President Garfield *and* of "Mrs. James A. Garfield." If the Harpers felt the need to reassure Lucretia Garfield of their honorable intentions when she was the candidate's wife, no such compunctions applied when she became America's First Widow. The ubiquitous images of Mrs. Garfield in 1881 were uniformly ethereal and often symbolic: she represented not only a recently divided nation united in mourning, but also ideal female character, in finest display when in deepest suffering. Three years later, Republicans would use Lucretia Garfield for more partisan ends. One biography of candidate James G. Blaine was dedicated to her and the Garfield children, while another published a congratulatory telegram she sent Mrs. Blaine upon her husband's nomination.[15]

What of the fallen president himself? Within a year of his death and increasingly as the years passed, James A. Garfield became what his own 1878 interview highlighted: a model of self-made manhood for young, male readers. Campaign biographies, of course, had long prescribed themselves to America's young men, and this rhetoric continued well into the 1880s. As outgoing President Rutherford Hayes recognized, Garfield's origins were particularly conducive to this treatment, and the 1880 election—the first largely issueless one in decades, with Reconstruction over and the bloody shirt fading to pink—was the perfect moment for a campaign based on personalities. The elaborate binding of Brisbin's book echoed the spine of Thayer's *The Bobbin Boy,* which depicted its young subject at the bottom of a ladder leading to the Massachusetts statehouse at the top. Several titles of Garfield's campaign biographies also revealed a debt to Thayer, by now the foremost author of self-made men's biographies for middle-class boys: "From the Tow-Path to the White House" (Brisbin); "From the Farm to the Presidential Chair" (James Dabney McCabe). Russell Conwell, among others, hoped that his book would "benefit . . . the thousands of young men in America who need the encouragement which the success of General Garfield gives." Garfield's death created a new opportunity—to empty his biography of the political debates, the speeches, all the substance of politics essential to a campaign biography (and to the notes Garfield dictated in 1880 for the benefit of biographers). In *From Canal Boy to President: Or, the Boyhood and Manhood of James A. Garfield,* Horatio Alger gave Garfield the Ragged-Dick treatment. Dedicated to the president's sons Harry and James, "whose private sorrow is the public grief," the book appealed directly to boys and young men, often referring to "my young readers." Alger made "no claim to originality," only to instructiveness. Like didactic biographies since the 1830s, this one found the roots of adult success in early life (governing a classroom foreshadowed governing a nation, for instance). It devoted just ten pages to Garfield's congressional career, mostly to show his "pluck." Like

Alger's novels, it told its story with copious dialogue, simple language, and clear lessons. The principal lesson was this: "this homespun boy, with his poor array of frying-pan and dishes, was years after to strive in legislative halls, and win the highest post in the gift of his fellow-citizens. And none of these things would have been his, in all likelihood, but for his early struggle with poverty." [16]

Fittingly, the most enduring biography of Garfield came from the pen of William Makepeace Thayer. Thayer first considered writing Garfield's biography during the campaign. He told the candidate that he could write a paperbound biography to sell to "the masses" for "fifty cents or less," unlike the two-dollar biographies that most Americans would not buy. Although this campaign life never appeared, Thayer described a second project to Garfield: "a book for boys on your early life, like what I wrote on Lincoln, viz, 'The Pioneer Boy or How Abe Became President,' not to appear in the book market, however, until your inauguration." This project became *From Log-Cabin to the White House,* Thayer's most successful work since *The Pioneer Boy.* Thayer described the obvious parallels between Lincoln and Garfield: birth in log cabins, self-education, election as president, assassination. Because he never focused much on what his subjects actually did in their political careers, the vast difference between their presidential records mattered little. As always, Thayer's story lay in "how it was done," the virtues that led the canal-boy to the White House. It was in Thayer's stories, many of them taken indirectly from Garfield's own telling, that Garfield became most widely known in the decades after his death. Other memorial biographies went through a printing or two in 1881 and 1882, but *From Log-Cabin to the White House* remained in print in the United States as late as 1908. Even more remarkably, it was translated into Swedish for an 1895 Stockholm edition and into Russian for an 1888 Russian edition—a useful reminder that self-made manhood was never a uniquely American preoccupation. It was already in its thirty-fourth London edition by 1890; three different English publishers produced editions. In England, *From Log-Cabin to White House* seems to have found a use that Thayer, and Garfield himself, would have appreciated: boys' schools and trusts awarded copies of the book for good conduct and regular attendance.[17] An American biography had made its way back across the Atlantic to serve in constructing English lives.

CHAPTER 5

Publishers, Pantheons, and the Public, 1880–1900

American Men of Letters *is the very best title.* . . . *"Lives of Eminent Americans" strikes me as disagreeable, commonplace, pretentious, just the sort of title for a bogus subscription book. Besides, it would include all creatures. You want to confine the series to a choice and rather charmed circle.* — Charles Dudley Warner to Henry Oscar Houghton, January 14, 1881

[O]ur corps of writers have gone to the people, the men and women who have, by their enterprise and industry, brought the county to a rank second to none among those comprising this great and noble State, and from their lips have the story of their life struggles. —Portrait and Biographical Album of Lancaster County, Nebraska, *1888*

In the winter of 1880–81, two New Englanders proposed American biographical series to the Boston publisher Houghton, Mifflin and Company. John Torrey Morse Jr., a Harvard graduate who had abandoned legal practice to pursue a literary career, suggested a series called "American Statesmen." Charles Dudley Warner, Mark Twain's friend and coauthor of *The Gilded Age,* proposed "American Men of Letters." Over the next twenty years, these two series became America's preeminent biographical projects, dominating the biographical landscape as had Jared Sparks in the 1830s and 1840s and James Parton in the 1860s. They also helped inspire other publishers to launch similar series: American Reformers, Beacon Biographies, Famous Women, and more. Together, Houghton Mifflin believed, the American Statesmen and American Men of Letters would create a national pantheon, a "choice and charmed circle" of the most important American political and literary figures. Publicly Houghton Mifflin implied that its pantheon was wholly self-evident and that the series themselves were coordinated projects of cultural production. Nothing could have been further from the truth. Houghton Mifflin, Morse, and Warner found themselves dependent on the schedules and desires of their potential authors—some of whom had difficulty accepting the manufactured uniformity of a biographical series at all. Readers had their say, too. The impression of coherent, unassailable canons belied the way the series took shape. Internal difficulties notwithstanding, the American Statesmen and American Men of Letters did construct biographical visions of the American past. Overwhelmingly populated by northeastern subjects and biographers, these series represented their New England publisher's, editors', and authors' conception of the reconstructed United States and its great men less than a generation after the Civil War. Their American past also offered cautionary lessons for the present: ambivalence about literary realism, outright horror at excessive democracy.

These visions stood at odds with another sort of contemporary biographical pantheon: the local history or "mug book." In the first place, mug books, filled with short biographies of local notables, were not northeastern. Emerging around the Centennial and proliferating over the next quarter century, they told the stories of midwesterners, westerners, and even southerners. In the second, they were optimistic and profoundly democratic. Their biographical sketches—and the national picture they created when considered as a whole—stressed pioneering and prosperity, not the dangers of democracy. They extended the range of biographical subjects far beyond anything previously imagined, certainly beyond the Houghton Mifflin "circle." Mug books' specialized, regional subscription publishers knew their audience and market more directly than Houghton Mifflin. Their traveling canvassers solicited biographies from the same local professionals, solid farmers, and self-made businessmen who would subscribe to buy the books. This process encouraged ordinary Americans to think autobiographically about themselves and biographically about their relatives, whose lives would find their way into print for the first time. At the same time, mug books' anonymous writers, headquartered in metropolitan centers like Chicago and San Francisco, epitomized how the rhetoric of individualism could be manufactured by large-scale, faceless corporations, the publishing analogue to Gilded Age factories.

Even as publishers' series, mug books, and periodicals' series of eminent "men of our time" made this an age of biographical pantheons, academics and critics raised deeper questions about the centrality and depiction of great men. The developing academic profession of history enshrined objectivity as its creed, and with it a scientific (or, more accurately, scientistic) method and ideology. The method descended from Jared Sparks, though without the pruning of documents that continued to tarnish Sparks's reputation. Drawn from evolutionary theory and the social sciences' emphasis on environment, the ideology was more novel. Some historians came to challenge the idea that great men were the central force in history, that individuality and genius shaped events. They thus questioned the very significance of biography. Literary realism also helped reshape critical notions about biography by the end of the century. In particular, it encouraged the rejection of Victorian suppressions in depicting character. Critics increasingly argued for truth telling, even at the expense of "discretion." Some even suggested that readers had a right to know the "whole truth" about famous people, a stance that sounded like the motto of contemporary mass journalism. However, "the whole truth" was a slippery phrase. It meant different things to different critics, and for many critics it depended on the right sort of reading public: one that knew how to reject journalistic excesses and read biographies *con amore*.

Biography as a Literary Publisher's Enterprise

Houghton, Mifflin and Company was only months old when John Torrey Morse and Charles Dudley Warner proposed their biographical series. When Henry Oscar Houghton dissolved his partnership with James R. Osgood in May 1880, his newly incorporated Houghton Mifflin acquired the rights to most of the American literary stars once in the Ticknor and Fields firmament: Emerson, Hawthorne, Longfellow, Stowe, Parton. By then Houghton had owned the *Atlantic Monthly,* the Gilded-Age standard-bearer of American "high" literature, for seven years. Thus in January 1881 Houghton had reason to imagine his firm as the champion of America's literary reputation, the worthy successor to the mantle of Ticknor and Fields. Perhaps this vision made him the more receptive to Morse's and Warner's ideas: the two series might stand alongside Houghton Mifflin's canon of American literature. As the publisher advertised them, the American Statesmen would present "a thorough sketch of the whole history of the period covered by it"; the American Men of Letters, "a fair view of the different phases of our literature."[1] The two series were connected ventures for Houghton. He published them in volumes of identical size, typography, and editorial details. He advertised the volumes of each in the back pages of both. He conjoined them when thinking about their sales, too. Why, he wondered by mid-decade, was the American Statesmen far outselling the American Men of Letters? Packaging each series as a unified, uniform whole and envisioning the two series as similar and connected did not make them so.

Like so much else in American biography, the proliferation of biographical series toward century's end, and the Houghton Mifflin series in particular, had a British antecedent. The English Men of Letters series, edited by John Morley, began in 1878 and quickly became a literary institution in late-Victorian England, with thirty-six volumes by 1884. Because Morley like Samuel Johnson envisioned literary biography as a form of literary criticism, he recruited noted literati to write the biographies, among them Anthony Trollope and Leslie Stephen. Brief, analytical biographies, the English Men of Letters volumes were conceived partly in reaction against the trend toward compendious, uncritical lives-and-letters and partly to teach a mass audience about prominent literary men and their work. By explaining to the relatively unschooled what constituted literary value, the series performed a conservative function in a time of social unrest and cultural crisis. Authors' lives became models of the bourgeois success ethic: according to the biographer-critics, literature succeeded to the extent that it balanced realism with respectability, eschewing coarseness and excessive polemic. The series treated writers who addressed "universal" themes and excluded those who dealt in the transitory and the domestic. No woman of letters appeared in the first series of volumes, and the biographers commonly praised works for "manliness." Widely disseminated in the United States, the English Men of Letters showed American publishers and authors how to define a national pantheon through concise, analytical biography.[2]

Both of Houghton Mifflin's series could trace their origins directly to the English Men of Letters. Morse wrote decades later that he had envisioned the American Statesmen after "reading a volume of Morley's *English Men of Letters* Series." Warner's connection was more complicated and less happy. In 1879 Warner wrote an article on Washington Irving for the *Atlantic Monthly*. At the suggestion of *Atlantic* editor William Dean Howells, Warner offered the book to Morley, whose series already had a transatlantic reputation. When Morley rejected it, Howells was "more disgusted than I know how to say." Howells believed that if Warner had "cut up" his American literary predecessor and "mishandled" the United States, then the presumably Anglocentric Morley might have taken his book. What Howells saw as an issue of national chauvinism, Warner interpreted on literary grounds: the book was "too biographical and too little critical" for Morley. Thus in November 1880 Warner suggested to Henry Houghton a series of "biographies of American Men of Letters," which took both shape and name from the English series.[3]

Getting started meant selecting subjects and biographers — choices that would define the series. For Morse, the "obvious question of fundamental principle" was whether or not his series would enhance American historical scholarship. He wanted to do what Jared Sparks had in the Library of American Biography a half century earlier: add to Americans' historical knowledge by treating "names less hackneyed in the popular mind, concerning which more that is fresh & novel can be said." To achieve this end, he sought "competent hands," often professors of history, to write the volumes and proposed to give them some latitude in choosing their subjects. Thus Gouverneur Morris became part of Morse's list when "two persons competed eagerly to write about him," and Patrick Henry won a place because Cornell's Moses Coit Tyler "was quite 'set' upon" him. When Morse submitted his list of potential subjects in April 1881, Houghton Mifflin objected to many of them. Probably for commercial reasons, the publishers wanted the American Statesmen to include "the dozen, or thereabouts, most distinguished names in our history without regard to the amount of attention any one of them may have already rec[eive]d from previous writers, & the amount of knowledge which the public generally have." The underlying issue, as Morse saw it, was "for whom the series is intended." "If for school-boys & school-girls, we should have Washington, Franklin, John Adams, Jefferson, Hamilton, Madison & that ilk; but if for general & adult readers, it is probable that in such brief biographies as we propose to furnish we could add little to their knowledge concerning these men; & should have to depend for success upon a degree of brilliancy & originality in thought & treatment . . . which it is highly improbable that we shall secure in more than two or three instances."[4]

Morse and Houghton both got most of what they wanted. They agreed on Jefferson, John Quincy Adams, Madison, Calhoun, Clay, and Daniel Webster. Of the subjects Houghton objected to most strenuously, Morse got Morris and John Randolph included. Morse also won agreement to James Monroe, whom he conceded "was certainly not 'a statesman of great calibre'" but defended on the grounds that "*nothing* has ever been written of him." Houghton Mifflin suggested three names not on Morse's list: Franklin, Hamilton, and John Adams. Morse acceded but worried that Franklin and Adams would be difficult to do in new ways. "[A]ll Americans over 20 years of age imagine, at least, that they know all about [Franklin] . . . & certainly they are as sick of hearing his name as the Athenians were that of Aristides the Just." Morse himself was sick of reading of Adams. All three, however, could be admitted if "good writers" could be secured. Editor and publisher agreed to eliminate Aaron Burr. Houghton Mifflin seems to have doubted the merit of including Andrew Jackson, perhaps on political grounds, but Morse defended the choice. "He was of limited intellect & did more mischief than all other presidents & statesmen put together, but his influence was immense & lasting; he is a most brilliant topic." Equally important, "his life, if well done, would be the most popular & valuable of the series." In this case, political importance and potential commercial success both justified inclusion.

When the publishers announced the American Statesmen series in the summer of 1881, they described two purposes that combined their original vision with Morse's: "First, of avoiding the traversing of ground already sufficiently familiar. Second, of presenting in the complete series a thorough sketch of the whole history of the period covered by it." In order to make the series "a valuable and permanent addition to historical literature," all the authors would be "persons who have made the study of our history a chief pursuit, who are familiar with all its facts, thoroughly instinct with its spirit, and able to trace hidden connections and to draw from the great undigested mass of material its true significance and philosophy." Here was the vision of the emerging profession of history, which eschewed antiquarianism (fascination with the undigested mass of material) for a broader vision of historical progress. Houghton Mifflin promised to bring the fruits of such "profound study" to "the general reader" who might not read Hermann Von Holst's *Constitutional History of the United States* but could certainly appreciate his life of John C. Calhoun.[5]

Charles Dudley Warner and Houghton Mifflin formulated their list of American Men of Letters on historical as much as literary grounds. Warner and the publisher haggled a bit over what the series should be called: "American Men of Letters" (Warner's preference) or "Lives of Eminent Americans" or "Warner's Biographies" (the firm's ideas). These disputes reflected Houghton Mifflin's concern that there were not enough "American Men of Letters" to make a whole series, but Warner assured the firm that his title could encompass "historians, and even some statesmen . . . novelists, poets, etc." while remaining a "choice and rather charmed circle."[6] In contrast to the initial disputes between Morse and Houghton over potential Statesmen subjects, Warner and the publisher seem to have settled easily on a list of men (and women) of letters: Irving, Cooper, Hawthorne, Theodore Parker, Thoreau, William Ellery Channing, George Sumner, Washington Allston, Margaret Fuller, Lydia Maria Child, and "others subject, of course, to modifications that may arise." In addition,

James T. Fields, the former publishing titan who edited the series briefly in its planning stage, hoped to include "the Life of some southern author, if we could find one of sufficient eminence" — an attempt to restore the South to the Union of letters just four years after Reconstruction had ended, or perhaps to attract southern buyers to the series.[7]

This series, then, would tell "the history of American literature in the Lives of those who have been its representative authors," not just the stories of idiosyncratic men of genius. Not only was a southern author (eventually William Gilmore Simms) to be included, but also an author from the antislavery movement (Edmund Quincy was eventually chosen over Child). Noah Webster represented the literature of the early republic. After reading Horace Scudder's manuscript, Warner recommended that he "interject into the first part something more about the literary, intellectual and social conditions of the New England community in which Webster was born, the state of culture, what the people read, what they learned at school and from the pulpit, their recreations &c, so as to give the genesis of such a man as Noah," and that he include something about the Hartford Wits, even though Webster was not one of them, "as I do not intend to give a volume to any of them separately." (Scudder took Warner's advice.) When a life of the Hartford Wit Joel Barlow was proposed for the series several years later, Warner counseled rejection because Barlow "was in letters less representative" than others and Scudder had already covered the Wits' milieu. Like Webster, Nathaniel Parker Willis, the influential antebellum magazine writer and editor, merited inclusion for literary-historical reasons rather than for the value of his writings: "He represented a phase of our literature which we cannot leave out. For over twenty years the reading public fed a good deal in such sort of stuff as he furnished, and the development of which he was a type is important in our literary history. . . . However thin Willis and his literature was, they really stand for something. We want the series to represent the development of our literature in all its phases." Some subjects (like Emerson, Poe, and Hawthorne) belonged in the "charmed circle" for their individuality; others, for their representativeness. And "our literature" consisted both of unique individuals and of literary cultures like the magazine world of Willis and the antislavery movement of Quincy.[8]

As the two series became American literary institutions by the late 1880s, potential biographers and readers alike proposed more subjects. Eugene L. Didier of Baltimore offered to write the life of the Southern novelist John Pendleton Kennedy for the Men of Letters. J. Brander Matthews wondered whether John Howard Payne, the early American dramatist and author of "Home, Sweet Home," might "be made the vehicle of an interesting account of the stage in these United States in the first quarter of this century." Without any intention of writing the book, James Parton suggested Thomas Paine, "the first of his class in North America, the first to live by his pen." Warner seems to have rejected all of these ideas, as well as Francis Lieber (merely "a scholar, and a publicist") and Barlow (whose inclusion "would seem to imply the possibility of including a great many second-rate men"). Morse received two inquiries about Thomas Hart Benton, whom he eventually added to the American Statesmen. But he rejected William H. Seward (too recent in 1887, but later acceptable for the "second series" in 1898), Richard Henry Lee, and DeWitt Clinton ("outside of New York State he would now excite little interest"). Bemusedly he "sent a similar response to a young lady who thought that Millard Fillmore! was entitled to a place among 'American Statesmen.'"[9]

Like the discussions about subjects, the choices of biographers suggested what each editor wanted his series to become. Morse recruited a substantial number of academic historians to write American Statesmen volumes. Holst, Tyler, William Graham Sumner (who wrote *Andrew Jackson*), and James K. Hosmer (*Samuel Adams*) all taught in universities. Daniel Coit Gilman (*James Monroe*) was the first president of Johns Hopkins University, which had initiated American higher education along the German model. In all, nearly half of the American Statesmen authors were professors. The other half included journalists, attorneys, and political figures, many of them Harvard-educated men of affairs like Morse himself, Henry Cabot Lodge, and Theodore Roosevelt (who wrote *Thomas Hart Benton* and *Gouverneur Morris*).[10] Whether professors or nonacademic Harvard men, Morse's authors shared a long study of American history: they were "competent hands" in a scholarly sense. Academics were not Warner's first choices for the American Men of Letters. The "right" literary biographer needed some familiarity with the subject in question, ideally through personal acquaintance. More important, he needed the proper "sympathy" to represent the subject's works fairly. The romantic vision of literary biography continued to prevail here; the men who wrote the lives of literati had to be "men of letters" themselves, able to write *con amore*. At the same time, romanticism now went hand in hand with the demands of the market. A biographer of renown could boost sales and enhance the reputation of the entire series. Thus Warner and Houghton rejoiced when Oliver Wendell Holmes agreed to write the Emerson volume, and they sought in vain for years to induce James Russell Lowell to write Hawthorne and William Dean Howells to write Longfellow.[11] Warner's original authors were mostly New England men of letters in their fifties and sixties, many of them affiliated with abolitionism and the antebellum New England literary community: Franklin B. Sanborn (who wrote *Henry David Thoreau*), Octavius Brooks Frothingham (*George Ripley*), Thomas Wentworth Higginson (*Margaret Fuller Ossoli*). In all, the Men of Letters authors resembled the gentleman of letters more than the academic critic, perhaps also because the academic study of American literature barely existed in the 1880s.[12]

Whether scholarly rigor or literary sympathy was at a premium, biographers for the American Statesmen and American Men of Letters required one more characteristic: the willingness to write within the constraints of a publisher's series. Carl Schurz, the prominent reformer and former secretary of the interior, infuriated Morse first by his delays and then by submitting two volumes on Henry Clay and refusing to shorten them. William Everett refused Warner's invitation to write the life of William Hickling Prescott. He did not like the compensation Houghton Mifflin offered, a standard ten percent royalty, but the pay was only symptomatic of a larger problem. A royalty agreement based on copies sold implied creative authorship, and indeed the publishers claimed to engage "men of letters" to write the volumes for the series. However, Houghton Mifflin treated the authors as laborers performing "task-work"—much like the pressmen who printed the books, but without any guarantee of compensation. His book's "design" could not possibly be his own, complained Everett, "when it is a publisher's scheme, under an editor's care . . . an assigned task, with countless limitations fencing it in." Among those limitations Everett counted the very notion that a series of literary biographies could narrate American literary progress. Warner's plan

> does not correspond to my way of looking at distinguished authors. The development of American Literature is to me an absolutely intangible thing. I can understand that there may be such a thing, but I do not see how you can write about an individual with reference to it. . . . I know what *men* are; I have not the least conception of *developments*. I could perhaps tell the story of Prescott's life and works; but himself as the centre of a group,—like the fancy pictures called Irving and his friends,—is not only beyond my execution, but even my understanding. He wrote with no such consciousness,—and hence to me the thing did not exist.[13]

Warner had great difficulty getting his contributors to complete—and in some cases even to begin—their work. Perhaps the men of letters he had engaged found the work as unappealing or as alien to their familiar endeavors as Everett did. Nine American Men of Letters volumes appeared by the end of 1885, but over the next eight years only three more came out. Lowell had agreed to write Hawthorne's life but made no progress. George Washington Cable had agreed to do William Gilmore Simms but sent nothing. About half of the originally announced authors failed to complete their books. Some were replaced, while other volumes (including those on Hawthorne and Longfellow) went unwritten until after Warner's death in 1900. By June 1885 the publisher was prodding Warner to move his authors along, a refrain that would become familiar. Houghton Mifflin encouraged "discarding books which have no chance of life, or securing authors who can take hold of them with resolution." At least to the publisher, resolution had become as important as sympathy. Meanwhile the American Statesmen series proceeded rapidly: nine volumes in the first two years, eighteen by 1888, twenty-three by 1893. Some of Morse's original contributors dropped out but most completed their agreed works within a few years. Henry Houghton congratulated Morse for the fact that "your series has gone on more regularly than any other that we remember being connected with."[14]

At first, Houghton blamed the delinquency of the Men of Letters volumes for a problem that emerged by 1885: "This Series has not done nearly as well as the Statesmen Series." Except for Warner's own *Washington Irving* and Holmes's *Ralph Waldo Emerson* (1884), the Men of Letters books were not breaking even. From 1887 on, sales of American Statesmen volumes more than doubled those of the Men of Letters in all but two years. Several books in Warner's series virtually disappeared from sales after their first few years in print. Significantly, readers were making choices not just *between* the series, but also *within* them. The least popular volumes in the Men of Letters series were precisely those that reflected the publisher's and editors' desire for representativeness: now-forgotten magazinist Willis and southerner Simms. Similarly, political figures now forgotten or deemed ephemeral sold worst among the Statesmen volumes: Gouverneur Morris, Martin Van Buren, Lewis Cass, John Jay. In both series, the most popular subjects were the ones still familiar to a late-century audience: Emerson, Irving, and Franklin in the Men of Letters; Hamilton, Jefferson, and Washington in the Statesmen. The publisher had been right from the beginning. Previously neglected subjects might possess historical novelty, but familiar favorites would sell better. Despite these internal variations, Houghton emphasized the commercial disparity between the two series and blamed "the halting way" the American Men of Letters volumes had appeared. He thought "we could do much better with it if the volumes should succeed each other faster, and with more regularity."[15] In other words, the American Men of Letters "Series" would sell better if readers perceived it *as* a series (as the bindings, title pages, and the rest indicated they should)—a perception that long delays made difficult.

Several other explanations may help account for the commercial failure of the American Men of Letters. Quite possibly, American readers were more interested in the lives of political figures than in those of literary men. As one American periodical noted in the 1890s, the best biography of a great literary man—the surest way to understand him—lay in his work.[16] Biography provided the best way for readers to "know" political figures like Jefferson or Clay, but not the straightest route to the heart of Fuller or Poe. Then again, the *English* Men of Letters series won enough popularity in the United States to encourage Houghton Mifflin to pursue its American series in the first place. Perhaps it was *American* men of letters whose lives American audiences had little interest in reading. The American Statesmen series ratified a political pantheon and a distinctly American political history that American readers already knew. The American Men of Letters series charted new territory, even if biographical dictionaries of American authors and books on American authors' homes had appeared since before the Civil War. When Houghton Mifflin advertised the series as "a fair view of the different phases of our literature," American audiences had little sense of a national literary history from which to start. "Our literature" may have meant something else to Americans who read Shakespeare and Dickens alongside Emerson and Stowe. Maybe the literary tradition in which Americans envisioned themselves was the English one, broadly conceived as the tradition of literature in the English language. John Morley, whose English Men of Letters included Hawthorne, shared this conception. When viewed this way, Americans did read the biographies of America's literary pantheon: the English Men of Letters volumes, plus the lives of Emerson and Irving and Franklin in the American Men of Letters. Faced with the success of one series and the failure of the other, Houghton Mifflin responded to what it recognized as readers' demand. In 1897 it planned a new "Standard Library Edition" of just the Statesmen series, and soon it was marketing this edition together with the works, not the lives, of Longfellow, Emerson, Whittier, Lowell, Hawthorne, *and* Dickens, Thackeray, and Macaulay.

This new edition of the American Statesmen created an explicit textual coherence previously lacking. Formerly the volumes had shared only appearance: they looked the same but appeared whenever authors completed them, in no particular order. Advertisements after 1897 listed the volumes in order of their subjects' lives, rather than continuing to list them by date

WHITTIER. 9 vols.

LOWELL. 11 vols.

EMERSON. 14 vols.

LONGFELLOW. 14 vols.

HOLMES. 15 vols.

HAWTHORNE. 15 vols.

HARTE. 16 vols.

MACAULAY. 20 vols.

THACKERAY. 22 vols.

AMERICAN STATESMEN. 32 vols.

DICKENS. 32 vols.

HOUGHTON, MIFFLIN & CO.'S

STANDARD LIBRARY EDITIONS

THE ENTIRE SERIES, 11 SETS
200 VOLUMES, $16 A MONTH

SINGLE SETS, $2 — $3 A MONTH
TWO SETS $3 — $5 A MONTH, ETC.

INSTALLMENT PRICE SAME
AS CASH PRICE. NO CHARGE
FOR OPENING AN ACCOUNT

OVER 3000 ILLUSTRATIONS
IN THE SERIES

FINE BOOKS
AT LOW PRICES

EVERY SET COMPLETE
AND WELL EDITED

SETS SENT ON APPROVAL
IF DESIRED

NOT SOLD BY
BOOK STORES

ADDRESS
THE
PUBLISHERS
DIRECT

By the time Houghton Mifflin produced this advertisement for "Our Special Offer Beginning the Twentieth Century" in February 1901, the American Men of Letters series had proven a commercial failure. Thus the publishers advertised the successful American Statesmen series alongside the works, not the biographies, of its prominent authors. (Courtesy Houghton Library, Harvard University) of publication. Now numbered, the volumes became in Houghton Mifflin's words "a political history of the United States, antedating the Revolution and extending through the Civil War and Reconstruction period" (with five new volumes written at the end of the century). Morse wrote a general introduction and introductions to each of five chronological sections. The publisher also added a "topical index," which appeared as the thirty-second and final volume and likewise provided readers with connections between the volumes in the series. As the publisher now explained, the series contained not just "a complete and perfect picture of the growth and development of the United States" but also the "intelligent understanding of all the great political questions of the day" that citizens of a republic needed.[17]

In his general introduction, Morse now claimed that a "principle of selection" had shaped the series from the outset. According to Morse, several subjects had been chosen not primarily because they were great statesmen, but because they embodied elements of American political development essential for a complete history: Patrick Henry, "the South in the period preceding the Revolution"; Thomas Hart Benton, "the character of the Southwest"; and Lewis Cass, "the Northwest—or what used to be called the Northwest not so very long ago." As the publishers advertised, these were "representative men."[18] This vision, in fact, resembled Warner's original plan for the Men of Letters series, which used figures like Willis to represent particular literary cultures. Morse's "principle" also included a notion of American progress.

> It has been the editor's intention to deal with the advancement of the country. When the people have moved steadily along any road, the men who have led them on that road have been selected as subjects. When the people have refused to enter upon a road, or, having entered, have soon turned back from it, the leaders upon such inchoate or abandoned excursions have for the most part been rejected. Those who have been exponents of ideas and principles which have entered into the progress and have developed in a positive way the history of the nation have been chosen; those who have unfortunately linked themselves with rejected ideas and principles have themselves also been rejected.

Thus Governor Hutchinson of colonial Massachusetts (who opposed the Revolution) and Andrew Johnson (whose vision of Reconstruction lost to that of Thaddeus Stevens and Charles Sumner) did not merit places. Nor did Burr, whose "name would have been a degradation of the series" and whose "career was strictly selfish and personal," or James Buchanan, whose "wrong-headed blundering is sufficiently depicted for the purposes of this series by the lives of those who foiled him." The one exception, Calhoun, was included "for reasons so obvious that they need not be rehearsed," and Holst's volume on Calhoun argued that its subject had led the deluded and inevitably doomed opposition to progress.[19] The series, thus organized, introduced, and indexed in the Standard Library Edition, presented a history of American democratic (but not Democratic) progress. Morse's references to "the people" suggested that the paths the nation followed were popularly sanctioned, and that "American Statesmen" earned inclusion by leading the way.

This narrative of orderly selection—which, as we will soon see, mirrored the series' own emphasis on social and political order—became possible only *after* the volumes had been originally published. As we have observed, the process by which subjects entered the American Statesmen series in the 1880s and early 1890s was far more haphazard. Publisher, editor, and authors all had their say in who "belonged." The existence of the series did not simply create a commonly shared image of the national pantheon but instead encouraged readers and authors to propose their own additions to it. The series included Patrick Henry not because Morse or the publishers believed that a colonial Virginian was necessary. They wanted Moses Coit Tyler to write a volume, and Tyler chose Henry. Thomas Hart Benton was added to the list only after several correspondents suggested his name to Morse in the mid-1880s. And the recreation of the series in a Standard Library Edition occurred only because the American Statesmen volumes had proven commercially successful in their first, less textually ordered, incarnation. Had the American Statesmen fared as poorly as the American Men of Letters, it would not have appeared in Houghton Mifflin's "Offer Beginning the Twentieth Century" alongside the works of Emerson, Hawthorne, and Dickens. The firm was making a commercial decision, and at the same time implicitly acknowledging that its readers had made their choice.

Pantheons, National and Local

Judge Matthew Deady of Oregon, one of those readers, represented that choice perfectly. Deady read four of the American Statesmen biographies soon after they appeared. Having read John Torrey Morse's *Life of Alexander Hamilton* a few years earlier, he knew the name on the cover of the American Statesmen volumes and understood them as part of a larger whole, writing in July 1883 that he had finished "the life of Monroe in Morse's series." However, Deady never mentioned reading any volume of the American Men of Letters. If his sense of political history was American, his sense of literary history was English: he read the lives of Bunyan and Pope in the English Men of Letters, as well as a biography of George Eliot.[20]

Matthew Deady's own life story offers clues to how he read the American Statesmen books. Born in 1824, son of an Irish Catholic itinerant schoolmaster, Deady lived in Maryland, western Virginia, Mississippi, and Ohio as a boy. He left his father's home at seventeen, apprenticed himself for four years in Ohio, taught school, read law, and moved to the Oregon Territory in 1849. In short, at twenty-five Deady had lived in every region of the United States except New England. Once in Oregon, he quickly involved himself in politics. He became a territorial supreme-court justice and president of the territory's constitutional convention, where he opposed an abolitionist clause for Oregon's constitution. In 1859 he was appointed United States district judge for Oregon. He supported Kentuckian John C. Breckinridge, the southern Democratic candidate, for president in 1860 but switched his allegiance to the Republicans when the Civil War broke out. These origins help explain what Deady wrote in his diary when he finished reading Carl Schurz's *Henry Clay* a quarter century later: "A pleasant and suggestive book, with a strong anti slavery bias and a disposition to judge men on the Slavery question by the circumstances of today rather than then." He also considered Sydney Howard Gay's *James Madison* "very lopsided on the slavery question. Fifty years will have to roll by before the popular mind recovers its equilibrium on this question. The war and the result of it have made a man who owned Negroes or obeyed and respected the injunctions of the Constitution on this subject, look like a criminal by this generation." Deady identified another theme running through the series: its Whig bias. Morse's *John Quincy Adams* seemed to him "a judicious and friendly defense of an able, patriotic, and industrious man without tact or sympathy." Schurz's *Clay,* by contrast, led him to note "What an irascible, ignorant, prejudiced old savage history is making out of the political and military hero of my boyish days—Andrew Jackson. More and more it grows on me that his strength with the people, after the luck of New Orleans, arose from the fact that he was socially on their plane—good and common—as compared with his contemporaries." Matthew Deady was noticing coherent interpretive threads in the American Statesmen series: not just pro-Whig but hostile to the spirit of American democracy; not just antislavery but abusive toward those who had not embraced abolition; not just seeking a contemporary audience but unfairly present-minded in its judgments about the past.[21]

Both Houghton Mifflin series interpreted the American past and present. The American Statesmen and American Men of Letters aimed to provide general readers with the outlines of American literary and political history, in volumes concise and inexpensive enough to gain a popular readership yet written by men with literary skill and historical knowledge. Given the variety of authors, it was not surprising that the volumes differed within each series. Some (including Woodberry's *Edgar Allan Poe* and Gilman's *James Monroe*) were based on extensive research in primary documents. Others drew primarily on previously published biographies. A few (including Edward Cary's *George William Curtis*) resembled "lives and letters" with copious extracts from subjects' correspondence. Some authors emphasized the value of distance for critical biography, while others, especially in the Men of Letters, had been selected precisely because they had known their subjects or lived in their subjects' milieu and could write *con amore*.[22] This variety notwithstanding, coherent ideological strands recurred within each series, usually linked to the relationship between the Revolutionary or antebellum past and the Gilded Age present. In each case, the question involved the nature of progress. Many biographers in the American Men of Letters shared an ambivalence toward literary realism, which by the 1880s had supplanted romanticism in critical and popular estimation. Numerous American Statesmen writers advanced the mugwump philosophy of political reform and critique of excessive democracy that Matthew Deady observed.

The American Men of Letters series offered individual portraits in American literary history and a vision of that history itself. Most of the individual portraits placed the subject into his or her milieu, for better or worse. Cooper's upbringing along the Hudson, Noah Webster's childhood in vestigially Puritan Connecticut, and Fuller's sternly academic girlhood home shaped their conceptions of authorship. In some cases, family traits became central to the author's own character. Fuller, for instance, possessed her ancestors' "New England vigor—which was a Roman vigor, touched by Christianity." In others, the connection seemed born of revolt: Nathaniel Parker Willis emerged as something of a dandy and as a sentimental writer in part as a reaction against his Calvinist parents. In one instance that revealed the series' sectional bias, William P. Trent, a professor of history at the University of the South, argued that the feudal Old South—which Warner himself had described as uncongenial to literature—had stifled William Gilmore Simms's true creativity: "While chivalry was a good thing, modern civilization is a much higher thing." Conservative southern reviewers, already fuming at the ascendancy of New South politicians and editors who sought to bring the region into capitalist, "modern"—northern—culture, raged against Trent and his book even as northern magazines praised it.[23]

While Trent's *Simms* exposed the series' sectional bias, numerous volumes revealed its literary-critical sensibility: a reaction against contemporary realism. The American Men of Letters version of American literary history began in the republic's first years, when the conditions of literary production were relatively primitive and when authors asserted America's literary independence from England. Some writers in the series (like those in Jared Sparks's Library of American Biography fifty years before) described the hardships of the past as a source of strength, a contrast to the more prosperous but less hardy present. If the ordinary colonist's access to books in Webster's Connecticut "was poverty-stricken as compared with the abundant resources of our own day, . . . in the very sterility of that life there was a certain iron which entered into the constitution of the people who lived it. If there were not the leisure and culture of the present day, neither were there the mental indolence and dissipation." According to Warner, in modern society "the standard works of approved literature" —including Irving—went unread thanks to the proliferation of cheap, ephemeral, new books. In the schema of the American Men of Letters, the earliest figures were the most clearly American. Webster's idiosyncratic but clearly patriotic grammar, speller, and dictionary sought to give the United States a national culture to match its political institutions. Scudder's Webster represented not just Federalism but also an individualism now superseded by more corporate, national forms of endeavor. By the 1880s projects like dictionaries and Bible revisions—and biographical series— were the work of groups of men, churches, and publishers, not individuals like Webster. In a time "when our literature was still essentially colonial," Fuller became "a literary pioneer," launching "the first thoroughly American literary enterprise," for "whatever else it was," Transcendentalism "was indigenous."[24] Between this past and the Gilded Age present lay a chasm.

In political terms, this chasm was the Civil War; in literary terms, the movement to realism, repeatedly cited as an antithesis to America's literary past. Warner argued that the vogue for realism had led readers to discount Irving and Sir Walter Scott and replace them with the transitory and journalistic. Irving "belonged to the idealists," which for Warner was a positive trait: "he escaped the desperate realism of this generation, which has no outcome, and is likely to produce little that is noble." Trent attributed the decline of Simms's reputation to the same source—and similarly emphasized the "ennobling qualities of great romances," which had to be upheld "against the attacks of the realists." Henry A. Beers stated the point most directly. Nathaniel Parker Willis had "sunk into comparative oblivion" because "Every generation begins by imitating the literary fashions of the last, and ends with a reaction against them. At present 'realism' has the floor, sentiment is at a discount, and Willis's glittering, high-colored pictures of society, with their easy optimism and their unlikeness to hard fact, have little to say to the readers of Zola and Henry James." By the time Willis died in 1867, "a new literature had grown up in America. The bells of morning tinkled faintly and far off, lost in the noise of fife and drum, and the war opened its chasm between the present and the past."[25] If realism was the philosophical and literary force that had eclipsed much of America's literary past, the authors of the American Men of Letters volumes called for recognition of, if not return to, the earlier romanticism.

They were quick to distinguish romanticism from sentimentalism—and to criticize the latter in gendered terms. Warner pointedly refuted the charge that the Knickerbocker school had given birth to sentimentalism, a "surface disease" with a "bathetic tone." Irving's "manly sentiment and true tenderness" had not brought about "the sentimental gush." Those who succeeded him lost his "corrective humor [and] his literary art." Still, despite Irving's charm his work lacked "intellectual virility," in Warner's words. Beers faced a greater challenge, since Willis clearly belonged to the sentimentalists. He offered his subject no quarter, calling most of Willis's productions ephemeral effusions, even though Willis himself had criticized annual sentimental gift books as "yearly flotillas of trash." Higginson, of course, dealt with the question of gender most directly in *Margaret Fuller Ossoli*. Higginson combined Fuller's public activity with the traits of Victorian womanhood to create a portrait of a woman who pushed but ultimately did not exceed the limits of her gender. This Fuller was predominantly a woman of public action. She initiated the Conversations (which fueled the reform activity of women listeners), founded and edited the *Dial*, and wrote for New York newspapers, in an era when such attainments generally lay outside woman's province. But "with all her Roman ambition," she remained "'a very woman' at heart," who married for love and died in a shipwreck with her husband and child. Higginson included a whole chapter of letters between Fuller and her husband to reinforce this impression. For a woman author, this sentimental denouement made sense. For a man like Irving or Willis, sentimentalism betrayed weakness.[26] Warner's title had been right from the start: the series asserted an "American" literary history, offered a vision of literary manliness that denigrated the sentimental, and suggested a progression of "letters" that moved from colonial antecedents to the idealistic past to the realistic world of the 1880s.

The American Statesmen series displayed a Whiggish orientation that celebrated the orderly progress of America, in particular the American North, and attacked the philosophy and policy of Jefferson and Jackson.[27] Morse, the series' most frequent author, praised Benjamin Franklin's "genuine . . . faith in man" over the "exaggerated gospel of the people" preached by "Democrats of the revolutionary school in France and the Jeffersonian school in the United States." In Lodge's *George Washington,* Jefferson appeared as a plotter who sought to undermine his rival Hamilton and to discredit his enemies with charges of monarchism. The Federalists' faults here tended to be personal, not philosophical: John Adams's "vanity," his son's "uncharitable" nature. Their very unpopularity became a badge of honor. John Quincy Adams, "hardly abused and cruelly misappreciated in his own day," was honored by "subsequent generations . . . as one of the greatest of American statesmen" for his accomplishments and his character.[28] The antithesis of the Adamses was Andrew Jackson. Morse, who believed Jackson politically dangerous and "of limited intellect," must have been pleased by Sumner's volume, which criticized many of Jackson's policies and depicted Old Hickory as immensely popular but equally reckless. As Henry Clay's antagonist, Jackson also made his way into Carl Schurz's volumes. Schurz portrayed the intense drama of Jackson's and Clay's rivalry: Jackson, though "very ignorant," possessed the genius of command and a bravery that inspired those around him; Clay, though occasionally inclined toward "peremptory command" and intolerant of "adverse opinion," possessed "the leadership of a statesman zealously striving to promote great principles." Schurz quickly made clear which titan represented evil. Immediately after taking office, Jackson swept out his predecessor's appointees, cloaking the spoils system in the name of reform. For civil-service crusader Schurz, "Never was the word 'reform' uttered with a more sinister meaning." On one side stood John Quincy Adams and Clay, who supported a nationalist economic philosophy and a strong union—and whom Morse and Schurz pointedly called "statesmen." On the other stood the forces of disorder (Jackson and, to a lesser extent, Jefferson) and slavery (Calhoun).[29]

This vision connected the biographers with the political reformers of the 1880s, the northern, upper-middle-class "mugwumps" who stood for civil-service reform and against the rowdy partisanship that had built the nation's major parties. Indeed, many of the men who wrote for Morse were political reformers. The oldest of them, like Schurz and Sydney Howard Gay (who claimed to write *James Madison* "from the Federalist point of view"), had been abolitionists. The younger men like Theodore Roosevelt and Lodge were their successors: aristocratic in background, generally college educated and Republican. Not surprisingly, they criticized in the past what they perceived as the antecedents of contemporary ills; the spoils system of Jackson had presaged the Gilded Age urban political machines that mugwumps condemned. Not all of the authors shared this outlook. Edward Shepard, for example, defended Jefferson against "partisan" historians who saw Jeffersonian democracy as the forerunner of Jacksonian corruption, and he praised Van Buren—the premier spoilsman, in the Whig view—as a master of *both* the "exalted art of the politician" and the "consummate art of the statesman."[30] More frequently, the tone and philosophy of northern, late-Victorian genteel reform permeated the American Statesmen volumes. Little wonder that Matthew Deady, who spent much of his childhood in the South and came to Republican politics only after early allegiance to the Jacksonian Democracy, found their interpretation difficult to swallow whole.

As he read the American Statesmen biographies, Matthew Deady also participated in another biographical phenomenon of his day, one that seemed more democratic and closer to home. Three months before he picked up Morse's *John Quincy Adams,* Deady made this entry in his diary: "Friday I received 25 copies of Hodge & Galvin's *Pen Pictures of representative men* for which I am taxed $25 and furnished with three pages of biography written by John W. Whalley and pruned and purged by myself. It is full of good average people and some great scallowags and petty rogues, all done up in the same high colors and utter disregard for 'the blistering facts.'"[31] Like the *Cyclopedia of Ohio* that included James A. Garfield's biography several years before his election as president, Frank E. Hodgkin's *Pen Pictures of Representative Men of Oregon* was a book of state history and biography. It was published locally, by the Farmer and Dairyman Publishing House of Portland. It treated contemporary subjects, the local analogues to the nationally prominent "men of our time" profiled in numerous subscription volumes of the late 1860s and 1870s. Most significant, it connected biographer to subject and literature to commerce. Matthew Deady paid not only for the book but also for the three pages of biography he received in it. Whalley interviewed the subjects, who had the opportunity to prune and purge their sketches. That opportunity, and the fact that the biographical subjects were also the book's subscribers, explained why the sketches presented few "blistering facts." Over the next decade Deady would become involved in several more "mug books" (so nicknamed for their engraved portraits of subjects willing to pay for them). In the process, he would participate in a biographical endeavor that was the mirror image of Houghton Mifflin's series: local or regional rather than national, focused on everyplace except the Northeast, filled with "good average people" instead of a "choice and rather charmed circle," and confident about the American future rather than worried about the excesses of democracy and realism.

Books with titles like *Portrait and Biographical Album of Otoe and Cass Counties, Nebraska* and *Biographical and Historical Memoirs of Northeast Arkansas* abounded in the last quarter of the nineteenth century. One immediate impetus was the nation's centennial celebration. In his May 1876 Centennial proclamation, President Grant endorsed the congressional resolution recommending that every county and town produce "an historical sketch of said county or town from its formation." However, most county and state histories and biographical albums were published not by local companies like the Farmer and Dairyman Publishing House but by metropolitan firms organized especially to produce them. These firms were the descendants of Midwestern county-atlas publishers of the 1860s and 1870s, who sent surveyors and subscription agents out to the counties to map the land and take orders for the books. Publishers like Alfred T. Andreas made county atlases into heirlooms for rural and small-town families, permanent evidence of their achievements in cultivating the land and establishing social institutions in formerly frontier places. By the mid-1870s in the Midwest, atlases gave way to county histories—which from the start contained biographies of local citizens.[32]

These biographies sold the books. In some cases, subjects of biographical sketches were required to subscribe for the volumes. Even when they were not, the prospect of having one's biography preserved for future generations apparently led most to subscribe. Thus the "Portrait and Biographical Album" or "Biographical Record" version of the genre emerged by the late 1880s, with county history relegated to brief chapters or eliminated altogether. This progression from county atlas to history to biographical album ("mug book") made commercial sense for publishers: once a county had an atlas, another would be superfluous; the same was true of a county history. Thus citizens of Berrien County, Michigan, could buy their county's atlas in 1873, the *History of Berrien and Van Buren Counties, with Biographical Sketches of Its Prominent Men and Pioneers* seven years later, and the *Portrait and Biographical Record of Berrien and Cass Counties* in 1893. In many places outside the Midwest, the county-atlas phase never occurred at all. Dozens of California county histories appeared in the 1880s, replete with "Biographical Sketches of Early and Prominent Settlers and Representative Men." States like Nevada, too sparsely populated for county histories to be profitable, got a state history instead. Several publishers took names to suggest their new mission. After 1878 books appeared from the Western Biographical Publishing Company in Cincinnati, the Biographical Publishing Company in Philadelphia, and the United States Biographical Publishing Company of Marshall, Texas. Chicago, center of the county-history and mug-book trade as far west as Colorado, was home to the Biographical Publishing Company, A. W. Bowen and Company, Lake City Publishing Company, and the especially prolific Chapman Brothers. On the Pacific coast a handful of firms in San Francisco and Oakland dominated the trade.

To produce county histories and mug books, publishers developed a combination of localized and centralized effort. Chapman Brothers might dispatch its employees—a subscription agent and a writer, or one person in both roles—to Lancaster County, Nebraska. The Chicago publishers would already have made a local contact: a leading businessperson, newspaper editor, or town officer. This Lancaster notable introduced Chapman Brothers' employees to other keepers of local history and suggested that local citizens cooperate with the visitors from Chicago. The traveling writer might produce a draft of the county history while in residence, so that the local contact could check it on the spot for accuracy. Writer and subscription agent would take the biographies, much as a traveling photographer might take people's pictures. In some counties the writer went out to farmsteads and businesses to speak with the potential subjects. Elsewhere he set up headquarters in a newspaper or business office or tavern and citizens came to him. Sometimes the citizens supplied their own biographies; sometimes they dictated and the writer took notes; sometimes the publisher provided a questionnaire to guide subjects' self-reporting. Publishers might send an artist along, too, to sketch portraits of those who paid for the privilege. As they took biographies, the Chapman employees also took subscriptions. They told potential patrons that every subject would have his name in the book's index. They showed samples of Chapman Brothers' work: a previously published history of another county, or a salesman's dummy displaying the binding to be used and the quality of typeface and engravings that subscribers could expect. They explained how much different lengths of biographical sketch cost. And they collected orders, with payment for book and sketch due upon delivery of the books. Their work completed, the Chapman employees returned to Chicago, or sent in the written material and orders and moved on to the next county to start anew.[33]

Back in Chicago, the publisher's writers, engravers, and printers swung into action. Every firm that specialized in county histories and mug books employed writers who converted the material written by the traveling employees or the subjects themselves into biographical sketches of three hundred to more than three thousand words. Publishers like Chapman Brothers were the biographical equivalent of the contemporary "fiction factories" like Beadle and Adams, which turned out dime novels by the hundreds. Their writers remained anonymous, valued for producing formulaic sketches. The books' prefaces were signed "Chapman Brothers" or "The Publishers." With five hundred or more sketches in a book, creativity hardly mattered. William Everett may have complained to Houghton Mifflin about the "countless limitations" of writing for the American Men of Letters series, but writing for mug books was truly assembly-line authorship. Besides full-page portraits, engravings often included views of subjects' imprint on the landscape (farmsteads, houses, or offices in the case of small-town luminaries), which occupied anywhere from a third of a page to two full pages depending on how much the subject had paid. The binding equaled the writing and engraving in importance. After all, these books were heirlooms to be displayed in the parlor and passed to one's children and grandchildren. When the book was finished, the publisher sent an agent back to the county to deliver it and collect the money.[34]

Mug books' prefaces retold the story of their creation, usually with the financial transactions left out. Each publisher's stock prefaces appeared again and again, a repetition that might have proven humorous or embarrassing had readers in Lancaster County looked at mug books from neighboring Otoe and Cass Counties and learned that those places also had "a rank second to none among those comprising this great and noble state." Publishers described how difficult their labors had been. They had made every effort to contact potential subjects and ensure the accuracy of the sketches. It was not their fault if a subscriber found someone missing from the book: some local citizens had refused to provide information, others had been indifferent, and a few "could never be found, though repeated calls were made at their residence or place of business." Instead of dwelling on the indifferent or antagonistic, publishers generally ended on a positive note by thanking "the public" or the local citizens whose "information, advice and cordial support, have aided them in their efforts."[35]

Rather than place their products within the context of Gilded Age,

If Houghton Mifflin's series were packaged to be seen on the bookshelf, mug books like this *Portrait and Biographical Album of Midland County, Michigan* (Chicago, 1884) were designed for the parlor table. This ornately embossed front cover appeared on numerous mug books of the 1880s; only a line on the spine indicated which county's luminaries populated the book. (Courtesy American Antiquarian Society)

middle-class consumer culture—of which they were undoubtedly a part—publishers situated the books within the more venerable, less commercial history of biography itself. Several quoted Macaulay or Carlyle on biography as the most appealing form of history. The *Biographical Souvenir of the State of Texas* noted that "one of our greatest Americans has said that the history of any country resolves itself into the biographies of its stout, earnest, progressive and representative citizens." The biographical sketches in these books served multiple purposes: preserving "biography and family genealogy," recording history that would otherwise be lost, even providing inspiration and models for the rising generation. If there was a "popular demand," it was for "the preservation of local history and biography" rather than for the "beautiful volume" to adorn a parlor (although the appearance of the volumes was a primary selling point). Chapman Brothers took its readers as far back as the Egyptian pyramids, which had sought to answer "the greatest dread of mankind from remotest ages," the fear of being forgotten. The advent of printing in "modern ages" had created a more enduring form of memorial. At last "the present generation" had pioneered the most effective form of all. In this "admirable system of local biography," "every man, though he has not achieved what the world calls greatness, has the means to perpetuate his life, his history, through the coming ages."[36]

Here was publishers' strongest rhetorical point: mug books democratized biography. The publishers had not simply gone to the potential subjects for biographical information. They had expanded the range of biographical subjects far beyond any previous conception of the genre. According to O. L. Baskin and Company, its biographical sketches were short because "it was thought better to present the prominent points in the lives of a larger number than fulsome eulogies of a few." F. A. Battey and Company made the point more overtly in its Texas *Biographical Souvenir:* "Until quite recently but little attention has been given to the preservation of biography, except in so far as it pertained to the preferred classes — persons who had been prominent in governmental affairs, or distinguished in their profession or calling, or in some way made conspicuous before the public. Within the past decade, however, there has been a growing demand from the popular classes for the preservation, not only of biography, but of family genealogy." The publishers of mug books claimed to answer this new demand. The Goodspeed Publishing Company, for instance, argued that its *Biographical and Historical Memoirs of Northeast Arkansas* drew subjects from "the most illustrious families of the state — all worthy citizens from the upper, middle, and lower classes."[37] The demand undoubtedly fed itself: the publishers' employees who visited thousands of counties and towns, and the mug books purchased at the end of the process, encouraged "worthy citizens" to think of themselves, their relatives, and their acquaintances as biographical subjects.

The biographical sketches in these books indeed encompassed a wide variety of subjects, from ordinary citizens with eighty-acre farms all the way to railroad executives. They were concerned primarily with agriculture, secondarily with commerce. For instance, Goodspeed's book identified approximately 120 residents of Clay County, Arkansas, by occupation. Just over two-fifths were described as "farmer" or "farmer and stockman." About a third were engaged in small-town commerce as "manufacturer," "merchant," or simply "business man." The rest included local officeholders (sheriffs, justices of the peace, postmasters) and professional men (ten "physicians" or "surgeons," two lawyers, a newspaper editor). Mug books often emphasized a county's business sector. Probably far more than 40 percent of Clay County's residents were farmers, but local businesspeople may have been more interested in having themselves included. To the seven hotel proprietors, the biographical sketch may have seemed a form of advertising. Chapman Brothers' 1888 *Portrait and Biographical Album of Lancaster County, Nebraska* similarly included a variety of businessmen and governmental officials, but it represented farming far more heavily. Most of the biographies told of men who had come to the county (mostly since the war) and established farms ranging from eighty-acre homestead claims to expanses of more than a thousand acres.

The variety of sketches in the Lancaster County volume is revealing in several additional ways. First, the book vastly underrepresented urban population. Lancaster County included the booming city of Lincoln, which grew from 13,000 to more than 55,000 residents during the 1880s. Population in the county's twenty-five mostly rural precincts grew only from about 15,000 to about 21,000 in that decade. But although Lincoln dwellers comprised more than two-thirds of the county's population when the Chapman team came to Nebraska, only about a fifth of the biographies treated Lincoln residents. Like urban dwellers elsewhere, most ordinary Lincolnites had not (or not yet) distinguished themselves in business or in agriculture. And mug books did not seek primarily to record urban history; they were records of rural and small-town accomplishment. Second, undercurrents of social stratification were evident. Biographies of prominent, urban subjects might note that they and their wives "enjoy the acquaintance and friendship of the cultivated people of Lincoln." People of wealth or influence displayed their standing by paying for the longest sketches, the engraved portraits, and the views of their farmsteads. Joel Newton Converse—physician, former president of the Union and Logansport Railroad Company, member of several fraternal orders, and owner of a 1,280-acre farm, 300 cattle, and more than 100 fine horses— got a three-page biography, full-page engravings of himself and his wife, and a two-page collage of views of his Cottage Hill Farm. Third, however, the book did justify its publishers' democratic rhetoric. More than half the subjects farmed 160 acres or fewer, a clear but also a modest achievement. The county appeared to be a true melting pot: German, Irish, and Scandinavian immigrants appeared beside New Englanders, southerners, and longtime midwesterners. Migration histories were a staple of the biographies, often accompanied by platitudes about the virtues of whatever culture the subjects came from. Rank played little role in how the sketches were ordered. The first three biographies told of Turner M. Marquett, general attorney for the Burlington and Missouri River Railroad Company; Charles Buelow, an immigrant from Germany who had come to America just two decades earlier, fought in the war, and bought an eighty-acre farm; and Thomas F. Chenoweth, superintendent of the county poor farm.[38]

When subscribers got their books, they could happily contemplate images of self-made success: counties raised to prosperity by the work of industrious farmers, businessmen, and local officials; businesses testifying to the solidity and gentility of their communities; individuals in possession of fertile fields they or their parents had cultivated. Six elements comprised the standard biography: occupation and place of residence or business ("one of the leading farmers of Lancaster County . . . owns a large and valuable farm in Saltillo Precinct, a part of it being on section 12"); ancestry; migration history; military service; marriage, wife's family, and children if any; and religious, voluntary, and political affiliations. Self-made men were the norm. Biographies described one man as "a fair sample of what can be accomplished by industry and perseverance" and another as "an example that might well be imitated by the young men of to-day, for at the early age of fourteen years he left the home place, without means, to battle his own way in the world, and his endeavors have been resultful of good, and he is now a well-to-do farmer of Clay County." No matter how fully genealogy appeared in the biographies, it did not determine destiny. Above all, the subject prospered from his own handiwork. Many biographical sketches defined subjects as "representative men," but not in the Emersonian sense. In mug books, to be "representative" most often meant that the subject resembled many other people in the county who lived and succeeded similarly. A representative man was "representative" in his individualism, but not for individuality.[39]

On a larger scale, these representative men symbolized the progress the county—and by extension the American frontier—had made in a few short decades. The sketch of Charles Buelow, the German immigrant turned "representative" Nebraska farmer, was not atypical. After his homeland education, immigration to the United States, work as a farm hand outside Chicago, service in the Civil War, and establishment of his own family, Buelow arrived in Nebraska:

> He came to this county in the spring of 1877, and bought the land where he now resides, which comprises a farm of eighty acres, which has well repaid all the energies and care devoted to it. Whether we turn to the fields and mark the superior agricultural efforts, to the barns and stables with their improved stock, or to the house with its pleasant rooms, which reflect in their arrangement and order the well-directed, cheerful lives of the inmates, we are satisfied that Nebraska must go on rapidly toward the grand future which is hers, and which must come to any country possessing such homes. In the beginning Mr. Buelow had many difficulties to contend with. . . .

This passage moved seamlessly from Buelow's own life story to the larger saga of Nebraska and back to Buelow's personal hardships. Buelow's fields, barn, and house became microcosms of the entire state and its "grand future." Such life stories were allegories of middle-class, rural progress on land that had once been "uncivilized," unimproved "wilderness."[40]

Even as these stories expressed individuals' pride in their achievements, they also combined to tell a national history. It is noteworthy that the *Portrait and Biographical Album of Lancaster County* and many other mug books opened with biographies and portraits of America's presidents and the state's governors. This beginning implied that the subsequent local biographies were part of a larger national epic. Civil War veterans earned their country's debt again in turning "what was known as the 'Great American Desert' into magnificent harvest fields, and in planting opulent cities and busy towns where before there were wild, silent, untrodden wastes, thus showing, as the great and glorious Milton wrote, that 'Peace hath her victories, no less renowned than war.'" Americans from disparate places had "improved" the frontier, carving farms and forging communities from wilderness; the rhetoric of improvement applied to more than the making of selves. County histories and mug books extended this saga beyond Nebraska. "Any country possessing such homes" could be virtually anywhere in the Midwest or along the Pacific Coast where the early travails of the "pioneer generation" had led inexorably to cheerful order: well-arranged, middle-class farmhouses, fields laid out in perfect rectangles. Presumably the newest immigrants too (and there were many in Nebraska) could achieve their own place in the county's, state's, and nation's history and in future mug books. That accomplishment would occur if they followed the path of self-making, but not if they made themselves objects of pity and reform: "Instead of sitting down in weakness and complaint, as so many have done, Mr. Buelow rose and gave battle to the unfavorable surroundings of adversity." If this national history celebrated immigrants' contributions at a high-water point of American xenophobia, it did so within the melting-pot ideology of individualism that biographies like William Makepeace Thayer's had helped create in the same years the Buelows were improving their lands. And it quite naturally omitted the newest arrivals whom many established Americans scorned, for they had not yet created the farmsteads of which Miltonic epics were made. Willa Cather would tell their stories a generation later.[41]

A different American epic brought forth another sort of mug book in the aftermath of Reconstruction. African American volumes of collective biography, which began to appear in the last quarter of the century and multiplied after 1900, celebrated the expansion of black churches and the establishment of schools and colleges, North and South. Some of these books were national in scope, ranging across occupations, religious denominations, and regions. Others, such as W. H. Mixon's *History of the African Methodist Episcopal Church in Alabama, with Biographical Sketches* (1902), treated more geographically or denominationally specific groups of subjects. All sought to show African American men's and women's accomplishments to the rising generation—and to white Americans. As William J. Simmons wrote, "I have noticed in my long experience as a teacher, that many of my students were wofully ignorant of the work of our great colored men—even ignorant of their names." His *Men of Mark: Eminent, Progressive, and Rising* (1887) therefore belonged in "the hands of intelligent, aspiring young people everywhere, that they might see the means and manners of men's elevation, and by this be led to undertake the task of going through high schools and colleges." Many of the subjects had been slaves, but slavery had not crushed "the life and manhood of the race. I wish the book to show to the world—to our oppressors and even our friends—that the Negro race is still alive," vigorous enough to have withstood two and a half centuries of bondage. Education and spirituality were these books' paramount themes. Most were written by ministers or educators. The subjects exemplified both self-making and institutional development. Each demonstrated the potential of African Americans, no less than Euro-Americans, for intellectual achievement (even more than worldly success), while at the same time their biographies championed the churches and especially the schools which had nurtured them and in which many of them made their careers.[42]

Unlike midwestern county mug books, African American biographical compendia made their authors as prominent as their subjects. Many opened with a sketch of the author-compiler, who became an exemplar of black progress as well as a benefactor of the race. For instance, Charles W. Purce, president of Selma University in Alabama, wrote the introduction to Albert W. Pegues's *Our Baptist Ministers and Schools* (1892) as a biographical sketch of Pegues himself. Born in 1859, Pegues had attended a Freedmen's Aid Society school "near his cabin" in 1867, working night and day with "the same grit that his liberator, Abraham Lincoln, had." He had proceeded to higher education, graduating third in his class at Bucknell University (as the only black man in the class)—and taking both "the regular classical course" and an extra course in ancient and modern philosophy. Now he was both an ordained minister and dean and professor of Latin and philosophy at Shaw University, "one of the greatest universities established for the education of colored youth." At every stage, he set "an example to youth in lowly circumstances that there is no obstacle, however difficult, hard, and embarrassing, that cannot be overcome by a determined mind and a fixed purpose." Sketches like this one did not simply celebrate racial progress and offer examples to young people. They also entered into a contemporary curricular debate among African Americans, squarely taking the side of classical education (and what W. E. B. Du Bois would soon call the "talented tenth") over the technical education emphasized at schools like Hampton Institute and by leaders like Booker T. Washington.[43] Black mug books championed the emergence of an African American professional class of educators, ministers, journalists—and biographers.

From the Pacific Coast came another kind of subscription volume without any pretensions to democracy. Hubert Howe Bancroft's *Chronicles of the Builders of the Commonwealth* (1891) was the most conscious biographical assertion of regional improvement as national epic. "During the last half-century," Bancroft wrote in his preface, "this western world has unfolded from a primeval wilderness into a garden of the fairest civilization. . . . a single glance at the existing state of affairs before this epoch, and at what followed it, overwhelms us with a sense of the marvels which have been accomplished within this short period of time by men most of whom are yet among the living." Surely those men deserved their biographical due. No ordinary mug book, the seven-volume *Chronicles* was the biographical sequel to Bancroft's thirty-nine-volume *Works* (1874–90), the first comprehensive history of the American West from the Pacific to the Continental Divide and from Central America to Alaska. One of California's first great book dealers and publishers, Bancroft sold the *Works* by subscription throughout the West. Meanwhile, throughout the 1880s other publishers in San Francisco and Oakland were making a lucrative business in California county histories, whose chief attraction was their biographical sketches and portraits. By 1888, as Bancroft was completing the *Works,* he saw a new opportunity: a regional biographical album. Biographical sketches in the *Works* had appeared only in footnotes, without portraits—and for those, people had subscribed for thirty-nine volumes at a total cost of $175.50 to $390 (depending on the binding). How much would they pay for much longer biographies and handsome engravings? At least a thousand dollars, Bancroft decided, and that for only a modest portrait and four pages of biography. The most elegant portrait and a thirty-page biography would cost $10,000. Bancroft's original title for the project, "Chronicles of the Kings," reflected its price: only the wealthiest men in the West would be able to subscribe. The capstone to both Bancroft's histories and the California county-history craze, *Chronicles of the Builders of the Commonwealth* earned over $200,000 from 106 subscribers. It also exposed the financial foundation on which it was built. Newspapers reported that Bancroft's agents virtually extorted subscriptions by threatening to write people's lives up if they declined (but with what details and tone?) and playing on personal vanities ("Would you want a shorter biography than a millionaire oyster canner's, Senator?").[44]

Chronicles of the Builders appealed baldly to the emergent stratification of Western society. At a moment of labor unrest, Chinese immigration, and massive westward migration, a biography in the *Chronicles* attested to the supremacy of railroad titans, land barons, and assorted other millionaires. This was nearly as choice and charmed a circle as Houghton Mifflin's Statesmen and Men of Letters, but here the primary criterion for inclusion was money. Bancroft's prospectus and introduction offered subscribers a Social-Darwinist pat on the back. "To be a great benefactor of the race it is not necessary that a man . . . be what is commonly called a good man, or specially benevolent, or amiable, or charitable, or a person who professedly puts forth all his powers for the benefit of others. . . . Fortunately, in the economy of political and social affairs, things are so arranged that those results which are highest and best for the individual are highest and best for the community." These books told of "the makers and the rulers of the commonwealth, the political and social dominators, the embodiment of the power, wealth, and intelligence of the community, . . . the builders of empire." In the now-classic language of biographical didacticism, Bancroft explained that "To study the lives of great men is natural and beneficial . . . elevating and improving." In this context, though, such language aimed mainly to flatter the subjects since only they and their families and acquaintances were likely to read these biographies.[45]

One of Bancroft's "builders" was Judge Matthew Deady, whose fifty-one-page biography appeared in the second volume of the *Chronicles*. Along with two other judges and a few other subjects, Deady received his biography and portrait free for services rendered: he wrote commendatory letters about the forthcoming *Chronicles,* which Bancroft sent to potential subscribers and had printed in the *San Francisco Examiner* to advertise the project. Deady had helped Bancroft for years. He publicly endorsed the *Works* and served as the publisher-historian's primary local expert for its two *Oregon* volumes, in which he also received a free biographical footnote (and prevailed upon Bancroft to include Mrs. Deady's parents, too). However, that biographical treatment dissatisfied him. A footnote, however long, did not suffice. Other patrons of the *Works* undoubtedly agreed, a sentiment that helped persuade Bancroft to undertake the *Chronicles*. Thus by September 1888 Matthew Deady was revising Oregon biographies for Bancroft's new project, noting in his diary that they contained "all the good that can be said of their subjects with their faults left out." Dictating his own biography proved harder: "It puzzles me what to say and what to leave out." Soon the publishers' mishandling had Deady wondering whether to "draw out of the enterprise." The portrait displeased him ("the head is too narrow"), and Bancroft's "bright clever" writer David Sessions did not understand legal or judicial work. Deady wished he had "employed a prominent Oregonian" to write the biography. (A publisher's employee was not paid to write *con amore,* after all.) Since the customer-subject's satisfaction was guaranteed, Bancroft had the engraving redone and Deady edited Sessions's "loose and undiscriminating" draft until it satisfied him. At Christmas 1890, Matthew Deady gave his portrait and biography as presents.[46]

The biography Deady finally approved struck a balance between mug-book sketch, historical character study, and life-and-speeches. Its first ten pages were autobiography from the judge's own dictation. As Deady explained in his diary, "As it would be evident that I furnished this information, I thought it better to speak in the first person." Autobiographical narrative ended when Deady's "public career" as a legislator began in December 1850. The next twenty pages narrated his career as a public servant, with occasional references to his "characteristic" attributes: "moral courage . . . in voting as his conscience dictated"; a swift "administration of justice, . . . firmly enforced for both the high and the low"; a "sound, calm, and philosophical spirit"; "prodigious industry, profound learning, and great ability." The last section included extracts from his legal decisions, public addresses, and occasional speeches. Along the way, the biographer described Deady's personal appearance, his political views, and his wife's life story. Deady's biography above all linked the judge's accomplishments with the development of Oregon, as befitted Bancroft's larger purpose.

> . . . it was fortunate for Oregon that a man of so much native strength and largeness of character should have become so important a factor in her history in the critical formative period. It is easy for the most casual observer to see how his strong personality has been directly instrumental in shaping the career of his adopted state. And while he already is seen to stand head and shoulders above his contemporaries, there can be no question but that he will become more and more prominent as the smaller men of his day fade away into oblivion with the lapse of time.

This passage showed how compatible mug-book democracy and the biography of great men could be, and yet how different the two modes remained. The first sentences echoed mug-book sketches. Deady had helped transform a frontier place (in this case an entire state) into its present, civilized condition. The man both made and symbolized his milieu. But the last line created a hierarchy of achievement, exactly as John Torrey Morse, Charles Dudley Warner, and Henry Houghton did when they decided who did and did not belong in their series.[47] Mug books sought to ensure that "representative men" would never "fade away into oblivion with the lapse of time." Lives of extraordinary characters—whether Houghton Mifflin's Statesmen and Men of Letters or Bancroft's Kings—cast "smaller men" into the shade, offering a different picture of who made American history and which American history mattered most.

True Lives at Century's End

Thanks to their subjects' self-reported family history and their publishers' ideology, mug books unquestionably enshrined as "true" much that Jared Sparks would have called "tradition." However, neither academics nor critics—the most active commentators on biographical truth late in the century—took much notice of mug books. Their notions of truth emerged with the rise of realism in American literature and thought. Like romanticism or republicanism, the term "realism" denoted a broad variety of ideas and approaches. In the most general sense, realism represented a revolt against the idealism of the romantic and transcendental movements, a revolt with two sets of implications for biography.[48] Practitioners of the emerging academic profession of history emphasized "objective" truth, gathered through a quasi-scientific method. Heavily influenced by evolutionist theory, many of them also espoused an quasi-Darwinian ideology, arguing that environmental influences shaped human character and action. This ideology could threaten the very underpinnings of biography. If individual "genius" could always be explained by larger historical conditions, what distinguished biography from analytical history? For critics, the "whole truth" increasingly became the watchword. These critics, whose magazines sought a wide middle-class audience interested in contemporary life and society, argued that readers had a right to know about the lives of the great and the famous. Their doctrine of frankness superficially resembled Samuel Johnson's idea about showing subjects in their domestic privacies, and it stood at odds with Victorian suppressions of individual personality. Its immediate roots were late-nineteenth-century literary realism and journalistic revelation—which were not synonyms. In critics' view, telling the whole truth depended on the right sorts of biographers and readers: biographers who truly understood their subjects, not hacks or detractors seeking only the dirt; judicious readers who wanted to understand subjects as rounded human beings, not to salivate over gossip.

These continuing debates over biography can be glimpsed within the editorial rooms of Houghton, Mifflin and Company. The American Men of Letters and American Statesmen series were the publisher's preeminent biographical undertakings of the 1880s and 1890s, but hardly its only efforts. Every year the firm received manuscript biographies, solicited and unsolicited. Several contemporary critics noted that the current age produced a wider range of biographies than ever before, and Houghton Mifflin's manuscripts reflected this variety. They included lives of authors, reformers, scientists, war heroes, an architect, and a merchant, plus collective biographies of self-made men, the signers of the Declaration of Independence, and Spanish and Spanish-American women writers. Houghton Mifflin's editors read and evaluated the manuscripts, writing up reports that remain uncatalogued in the publisher's archives to this day. The editors met, apparently weekly, in "powwows" to discuss their decisions. They discussed two distinct clusters of issues: the relationship between the biographical subject and his milieu (and between individuality and environmental influence), and the questions of what to tell and who should tell it.

When evaluating biographies of the "lives-and-times" model, Houghton Mifflin's editors wondered exactly what was the proper relationship between "life" and "times" in biography. This issue arose as well in the American Statesmen and American Men of Letters series, when publishers and editors included "representatives" of particular periods or movements and when authors described subjects as products of their milieus (or, like William Everett, refused to do so). Reading a manuscript biography of Bishop Lancelot Andrews, two Houghton Mifflin editors disagreed. One praised the work for illuminating the historical Anglican-Puritan clashes of the seventeenth century. The other complained that the book was more concerned "with what Andrews did than with what he was. His individuality is not brought out." In other words, was the "life" important only as a window onto the "times," or should the biographer reveal Andrews's character as well as recount his deeds and milieu? Historical interest alone got General Beauregard's Civil War memoirs and the *Memoirs and Letters of Dolly Madison* accepted. The life of the Louisiana jurist François Xavier Martin was *not* worth publishing on historical grounds (its material on the "*Times* of Martin . . . would be available in a monograph on Louisiana"), but Martin himself "was so thoroughly peculiar . . . at once so virtuous and so despically mean, so honorable and so filthy—that this biography is very interesting." Even if the biographer had not written the book "artistically," she had avoided painting Martin either "a monster" or "a demigod." Revealing Martin's human complexity and "great individuality" was this book's chief merit.[49]

While reading lives-and-letters and journalistic depictions of famous people, the editors considered what properly constituted the "whole truth." Houghton Mifflin received lives-and-letters of subjects as disparate as reformer Lucretia Mott, astronomer Ormsby M. Mitchel, poet John Greenleaf Whittier, and scientist Louis Agassiz. Horace Scudder's editorial report on Elizabeth Agassiz's life and correspondence of her husband typified the positive responses: "an admirable scientific biography of Agassiz with just so much personal detail as will serve to lighten the work. The material is mainly in Agassiz's correspondence, and the connecting passages are clearly and vivaciously written." Scudder considered the balance between the professional and the personal, the inclusion of important documentary material, and the literary ability of the compiler-biographer. Such books were clearly the "official" lives of their subjects, replete with the subject's letters and written or compiled by someone he or she would have trusted with those documents. In Houghton Mifflin's view, an authorized or official biography deserved to appear first—whether it was written by a close relative or literary executor (like Samuel T. Pickard, whose "official Life of Whittier" the publisher accepted in 1894) or it was a product of its subject's own pen. Hence the firm rejected W. S. Kennedy's *John Ruskin: A Portrait and a Study* because Ruskin had "already announced a forthcoming autobiography." Kennedy's book seemed to belong to "the rather ignoble class of premature biographies": journalistic works about still-living subjects, often prepared without their consent. To Houghton Mifflin's editors, a journalistic or celebrity biography reeked of tawdriness even if it was "less objectionable than some of its class" (like Henry J. Jennings's *Lord Tennyson: A Biographical Sketch*). This class included the unauthorized publication of letters, a contemporary phenomenon decried by many critics and satirized in Edith Wharton's 1900 novella *The Touchstone*.[50]

We can get deeper into these debates over biography by examining what happened to the reputations of two biographers we have encountered before. Elizabeth Ellet's *The Women of the American Revolution,* republished in 1900 as part of the colonial revival, received a scathing review in the *New York Times* exactly fifty years after *Sartain's Union Magazine* had accorded her a "niche in the enduring temple of American literature." The *Times*'s review, which shared much with the academic vision of history, underscored the bifurcation between sentiment and scholarship that had occurred since Ellet's day. In contrast, James Parton came to be hailed in the 1880s and 1890s as a champion of truth telling. Parton's reputation survived well after he stopped writing major biographical works—and despite the fact that Houghton Mifflin's editors actually rejected several volumes of his biographical sketches in the mid-1880s as "slovenly . . . hopelessly commonplace and inelegant."[51] The late-century estimation of Parton's and Ellet's work, indeed, reveals what mattered to academics and critics in the 1890s.

Elizabeth Ellet's *The Women of the American Revolution* seemed to embody the antithesis of modern scholarly biography in 1900. Back in the late 1840s Ellet had seen herself as part of a circle of historians whose leader was Jared Sparks. Despite that self-perception, her work was lumped with amateur history by century's end. The *New York Times* wrote that *The Women of the American Revolution* "should have added interest just at this time, when a revival of Revolutionary days is the fashion in fiction. Herself a daughter of the Revolution, who, as the story goes, flirted with Alexander Hamilton himself, many of the sketches are pen pictures drawn from her own memory. The two volumes . . . should prove of exceeding interest to present-day Colonial Dames and Societies of the Daughters of the American Revolution." What a difference fifty years made. In 1850 Ellet's "industry and talents" won wide acclaim; in 1900 her work was reduced to "pen portraits" that ranked with fiction. Literary anthologists dismissed her as yet another forgettable author, "whose productions as a whole have little of the quality of permanence" and whose midcentury popularity was "difficult at the present day to account for."[52]

Ellet's reputation declined in part because romanticism had altered the definition of "serious biography." Even in her own day, the *North American Review* had complained that *The Women of the American Revolution* lacked the "graces of fancy" that elevated the raconteur's anecdotes to the biographer's narrative. Ellet had avoided the trappings of fiction to set herself apart from women novelists and win the esteem of the historical community. But already by the 1850s critics saw—and Parton began to practice—biography as art and the biographer's task as artistic production. Moreover, when critics reconceived biography's purpose as the revelation of the "inner man," Ellet's largely archetypal biographies seemed thin. Romantics redefined biographical instruction, too, from presenting examples to be imitated to portraying people whose very individuality could inspire the reader to cultivate his or her own. When in 1900 the *Times* called Ellet's sketches "no attempt at serious biography," it drew on this notion of what biography was supposed to be and do.

Classifying *The Women of the American Revolution* as merely "a volume of reference as to 'who was who'" and suggesting that societies of Revolutionary descendants were its most likely readers, the *Times* also lumped it with a type of biography that had not even existed in Ellet's day: the mug book. In fact, in an 1892 address to the Daughters of the American Revolution titled "Heroic Women of the Revolution," Janet Elizabeth Richards drew anecdotes and even phrases and sentences directly from *The Women of the American Revolution* even though she never mentioned Ellet by name. Richards echoed Ellet's theme: "To the *women* of '76, no less than to its men, belongs the honor of achieving this great gain for liberty. And to us, the daughters of these honored dames, does it particularly pertain to gather and preserve the records, honor the deeds, and cherish the memory of the Women of the American Revolution!" However, Richards and the D.A.R. severed Ellet's link between the community of historians and the world of female readers. Ellet had sought to reach beyond the eyes of *Godey's* readers and the interest of antiquarians; she had suggested a new conception of American history itself. The D.A.R. aimed instead to preserve the foremothers' memory among their female descendants, who showered the speech with applause at the first D.A.R. convention.[53] In compiling family and local lore, Ellet had made filiopiety into national history. Richards and the D.A.R. reversed this move, returning the Revolutionary women to genealogical interest (of a more elite sort than midwestern mug books). The D.A.R. abandoned Ellet's emphasis on the Revolutionary women as figures of national history or models for contemporary women.

Given Ellet's ideology, women's-rights advocates of 1900 were far less likely than the D.A.R. to claim her as an intellectual foremother. To them Ellet's model of female "influence" over husbands and sons was not the progressive force that it had seemed to *Godey's Lady's Book* in 1848, and Ellet's work came to be seen as the sentimental "tradition" or lore that she had eschewed.[54] Women academic historians and women's-rights activists were apt to prefer more recent biographies of women who had earned a name for their public achievements. The Boston publisher Roberts Brothers published a Famous Women series in the 1880s of more than twenty such biographies: book-length lives (not short sketches) of Margaret Fuller, Harriet Martineau, Jane Austen, George Eliot, the Quaker philanthropist Elizabeth Fry, the English actress Sarah Siddons, and others. New books of biography for girls and young women also appeared, containing short lives of eminent women of action from Florence Nightingale to Jenny Lind. One of these, *Women Who Win* (1896), was the final book of William Makepeace Thayer's forty-year career. Ellet's late-century successors were writers like Anne Hollingsworth Wharton, who wrote numerous volumes of "domestic history" and the introduction to the 1900 edition of *The Women of the American Revolution*. In contrast, many of the women in the academic profession of history were committed to the women's-rights movement, women's activism in society—and a new model of scholarship.

That model enshrined the "objective" detachment between historian and subject. The developing academic historical profession distanced itself from amateur historians, descendants, and writers who sought to revive or instill emotional connection between past and present.[55] Echoing the professional stance, the *New York Times* review demonstrated how the new division of historical understanding involved author, genre, and audience. Its simplest and most amusing mistake, that Ellet "flirted with Alexander Hamilton himself," revealed how deeply the *Times* misread Ellet's goals. Ellet could not have known, much less flirted with, Hamilton: his fatal duel with Aaron Burr occurred in 1804, eight years before her birth. In linking Hamilton with Ellet and calling Ellet's sketches "pen pictures drawn from the author's own memory," the *Times* collapsed the seventy years between the Revolution and *The Women of the American Revolution* and therefore dismissed Ellet as a historian engaged in research. To the *Times*, the past could be divided for particular, narrow audiences. Ellet's volumes would interest "present-day Colonial Dames and Societies of the Daughters of the American Revolution" but not "serious" historians. By connecting Ellet's work with "the fashion in fiction," the *Times* relegated Ellet, her work, and its readers to the "sub-historical" level suggested by only one British magazine a half century before.

This division implied hierarchy. Unlike the new segmentation of theater and music into "highbrow" and "lowbrow" worlds, the professionalization of history did not cut along lines of social class. Academic historians and the D.A.R. women "generally came from the same social and ethnic background." But the result was similar: a formerly unifiable audience divided into two fundamentally different kinds of audiences, defined by their level of expertise and their relationship to what they watched or read. Professional historians, like the newly calm and genteel audiences for opera and theater, emphasized "cool detachment" from their subjects. "Popular" history made emotional or physical contact with the past (for instance, in visits to historical sites). Moreover, the division between "serious" history and "the fashion in fiction" was significant for how scholars and critics portrayed it: the highbrow was male, the lowbrow female. Certainly the revised, professional understanding of history relegated men's as well as women's writings to "amateur" status, and certainly the academic ranks included some women historians. But the *Times* used the D.A.R. and Colonial Dames as representatives of all that "serious" biography was not— much as J. Franklin Jameson, the early champion of history's professionalization, characterized the field of local history as "the poke bonnets and spinning wheels of all garrets."[56] The D.A.R. became a convenient feminine symbol for the amateur, the fond descendant dabbling in history.

The distinction between academics and descendants found its way into the American Statesmen series, notably in Moses Coit Tyler's *Patrick Henry*. As Tyler, the foremost academic historian of colonial America, saw it, his book superseded William Wirt's. Because so much authentic evidence "lay buried in inaccessible documents, Wirt had to trust largely to the somewhat imaginative traditions concerning Patrick Henry which he found floating in the air of Virginia; and especially to the supposed recollections of old people." Wirt had made as good a book as he could, but Tyler had more "disinterested" sources at his disposal—"facts" fixed on the page, not "emotional impressions" floating in the air. He thanked Henry's grandson, a Virginia historian appropriately named William Wirt Henry, for providing access to myriad documents but never trying "to hamper my judgment, or to sway it from the natural conclusions to which my studies might lead." The key words here were "judgment" and "natural." Their professional "judgment" set professional historians apart from amateurs, even as they couched those judgments in a language of objectivity.[57] Tyler's words implied both symbiosis and tension between two sorts of biographer. On the one hand, he and William Wirt Henry, who would soon publish the three-volume *Life, Correspondence, and Speeches of Patrick Henry,* assisted each other. Both acknowledged that assistance in their books. On the other, the academic professional saw the descendant as a potential threat, who could seek to hamper professional judgment and deserved applause for not doing so. At the very worst, the descendant could withhold or condition access to the manuscripts so dear to the "professional" biographer who was to make some estimation of the subject. This fear, translated into contemporary fiction in Henry James's "The Aspern Papers," was borne out in numerous cases dating back two generations. Gouverneur Morris's widow attached strings to Jared Sparks's use of her husband's papers in the 1830s. Half a century later, James Fenimore Cooper's daughter refused Thomas R. Lounsbury of Yale access to manuscripts as he prepared Cooper's biography for the American Men of Letters series.[58] The tension between biographers and descendants heightened as men within academic disciplines saw themselves as members of distinct professional communities, created by their training and ratified by their positions within institutions.

The tension rose further because academic historians pursued biography differently than descendants did. Lives-and-letters, compiled by descendants or authorized biographers, effaced the biographer: the subject was preeminent throughout, his own words provided the core of his biography, and the biographer served primarily to thread a narrative through the letters and speeches. Academic historical biographers cast themselves as interpreters of the past. Often they explained the relationship between the man and his times. Several biographers in the American Men of Letters series, particularly history professor William P. Trent, presented their subjects as products of their environments. In his *George Washington* for the American Statesmen series, Henry Cabot Lodge (although not an academic) made a similar point. "To know George Washington," he began, "we must first of all understand the society in which he was born and brought up." Lodge's description of family influence was especially revealing:

> before we approach the man we must know his ancestors. The greatest leader of scientific thought in this century has come to the aid of the genealogist, and given to the results of the latter's somewhat discred-

ited labors a vitality and meaning which it seemed impossible that dry and dusty pedigrees and barren tables of descent should ever possess. We have always selected our race-horses according to the doctrines of evolution, and we now study the character of a great man by examining first the history of his forefathers.[59]

Was Washington, in these clearly Darwinian terms, mainly the product of surroundings and heredity? If he was, would the uniqueness of great men fall before modern, scientific notions of the individual? Lodge was not ready to go that far. Despite his language, he ultimately reaffirmed the individuality of greatness: Washington had transcended his Virginian, aristocratic environment and upbringing to become the first true "American," a man of genius for his ability to conceive of America in national terms.

Justin Winsor took the implications of environmental determinism farther than Lodge or most contemporary biographers would have dared. Winsor, one of the founders of the American Historical Association and the academic profession of history, wrote the first "academic" life of Christopher Columbus, published in 1891 by Houghton Mifflin. To establish that he, the professional historian, had taken account of all extant evidence, Winsor spent his first two chapters describing the scanty documents of Columbus's life and evaluating the previous biographies. His title — *Christopher Columbus, and How He Received and Imparted the Spirit of Discovery* — gave away his interpretation: Columbus was simply a product of his age. Far from Washington Irving's visionary discoverer, Winsor's Columbus merely embodied "the ripened aspirations of his time." He had no particular genius, just the "courage and constancy" needed to demonstrate a pre-existing theory. If Columbus had not existed, some other explorer would have filled his place. In the four-hundredth anniversary of Columbus's arrival in America, Winsor's argument fell on hostile ears. Reviewing the book for the *Dial,* C. A. L. Richards noted that Winsor had written with "all fulness of knowledge" and "probable fairness of judgment, seeing things in the cold light of critical history." But cold light made bad biography; Winsor lacked "much imaginative insight or personal sympathy for his hero." John A. Mooney attacked Winsor's pretensions to "scientific" history in the *American Catholic Quarterly Review.* "The assumption of superiority, the claims to learning, to critical ability, to comprehensive study, to acquaintance with 'original' sources, while they evidence the childishness of his mind, are at the same time a proof that, if he be in real earnest, he hopes to have only ignorant readers, and to carry them by his want of modesty." Columbus was "a genius; a man of high mind, of great soul, of extraordinary sensibility, gifted with quick perception, with the imagination of a poet, with rare patience, with splendid courage"—but "Centuries will come and go before Mr. Winsor shall have evoluted into an original authority." Vehement critique from a Catholic periodical was predictable, given that Columbus was Catholic Americans' greatest hero. At the same time, Richards and Mooney both suggested that scientific history diverged from biography, and that historians made bad biographers when they denied individual genius.[60]

In 1893, just a year after the debates over Winsor's *Columbus*, *McClure's Magazine* published "James Parton's Rules of Biography," consisting of nine letters the famous biographer had written in 1888 and 1889. The publication of this article showed that Parton, who had died in 1891, remained the preeminent name in American biography. So did the origin of the letters: a potential biographer asking to "consult [Parton] *professionally*." In December 1888 Alfred R. Conkling was planning the biography of his uncle, New York's notorious, recently deceased political leader Roscoe Conkling. "Inasmuch as you have had so much experience in biographical writing, I should highly value any suggestions from you," Conkling wrote. Parton wrote back that biography's "great charm" was also the biographer's "great difficulty": telling "the truth . . . simply, directly, boldly, charitably." Human beings were complicated, often self-contradictory. Parton offered six rules for how to "make the book really correspond with the man, and make the same impression upon the reader that the man did upon those who knew him best." Some of them—doing research, avoiding eulogy, organizing material with a sense of proportion—were quite conventional by 1888. However, the sixth—"to hold back nothing which the reader has a right to know"—implied a new relationship between biographer, subject, and reader. Throughout his career Parton had defied any critical disdain for popular biography and its audience. Now he implied that biographies owed most to their readers: not providing instruction, but satisfying interest in prominent figures. If Conkling's book was to have "value" and "interest," it had to "present fairly his less favorable side," a difficult task given that Conkling wanted "*to set my uncle right* before a busy & an ungrateful people." Overly eager to burnish his ancestor's reputation, and less willing to show all sides, Conkling was the sort of descendant contemporary critics complained about. When *The Life and Letters of Roscoe Conkling, Orator, Statesman, and Advocate* appeared in December 1889, Parton warned Conkling, "You must not expect the public to remain satisfied with the omissions and suppressions of your book. Sooner or later, somebody will supply them, and you might just as well have told the whole story."[61]

"James Parton's Rules of Biography" expressed a critical stance that various periodicals were coming to espouse by the 1890s: biographers should tell the whole truth and stop suppressing anecdotes and traits of character that might reflect badly on their subjects. Certainly the argument for suppression continued to flourish, notably in conservative periodicals. In an 1883 piece in *Littell's Living Age,* a religious magazine that specialized in reprinting articles from English periodicals, Margaret Oliphant decried both biographers who "ransacked" the private cabinets and "very hearts" of great men and "the unthinking satisfaction of the common public in such revelations of domestic privacy." Now, unlike in the 1850s, other critics fought back. "Overrefined," "Bowdlerized" biographies, not excessive revelations, were the problem. The English biographer Edmund Gosse wrote in *Cosmopolitan* in 1903 that "the first theoretical object of the biographer should be indiscretion, not discretion." In his "Easy Chair" column in *Harper's,* editor George William Curtis explained the new dictum most forcefully in 1884. Apparently a celebrated American author had once criticized Parton for discussing Daniel Webster's drinking. This author had argued "that the public interest in Webster was based wholly on his great intellectual powers and his public services, and that it was most impertinent to speak of his personal habits." Why not talk about how often Webster "changed his linen or washed his hands," too? "Respectable writers" should not tolerate such stories, which led biography down the path to "contemptible gossip." Curtis disagreed. To be sure, the attack on Parton's portrayal of Webster was "not unnatural . . . in an age when interviewing has developed a taste for mere personal details and scandal to which unscrupulous journalism does not hesitate to pander." But the author who criticized Parton "forgot the universal and instinctive interest which attaches to the personality of eminent men." Curtis then took his readers back thirty years, to the controversy over Jared Sparks's editing of Washington's letters. By not telling "the truth," Sparks had mistreated both Washington and his readers. Had Parton *not* presented Webster wine and all, he would have been as guilty of "falsehood" and "gross misrepresentation" as Sparks. "[I]f a biographer assumes to tell us of the man, he must tell the truth; and if his life was loose, irregular, immoral, or noble, unselfish, and well-ordered, he must treat us as men able to hear the truth. He must neither smooth the wrinkles nor correct the spelling, but tell the truth."[62]

Critics like Gosse did not endorse scandal-mongering biographies; precisely the opposite. They argued that sensationalistic lives of famous people, written by journalists and other hacks out for money, were the direct by-product of eulogistic biographies. No man was a hero to his valet, and valets were now writing more biographies than ever. Those biographies sold because subjects' wives and sons and nephews and disciples had not supplied "the whole story." If official biographers presented their subjects as rounded personalities complete with flaws and foibles, their books would preempt the valets'. Moreover, a sympathetic biographer could place the flaws and foibles in their proper proportion, as minor elements within a larger character rather than as the focal points they became when trumpeted by mercenary sensationalists. The argument against suppression, then, aimed not to undermine the reputations of the great but to steer a middle course between equally one-sided extremes.

It was no coincidence that Gosse's article appeared in *Cosmopolitan* and "James Parton's Rules of Biography" in *McClure's,* for these new magazines used journalistic themes and techniques to seek a popular audience. One scholar has called their approach—emphasizing "timeliness," treating current issues, using photography—"dignified sensationalism," a label that certainly fits their notion of biographical truth telling.[63] Some popular magazines' biographical pronouncements also now championed the reader's "right to know," a far cry from both the didactically oriented criticism of the early republic and the *North American's* concern for the reputations of the great. The debate between George William Curtis and Parton's unnamed critic superficially resembled the clash between Charles Caldwell and Samuel Stanhope Smith nearly seventy years before: should the biographer present his subject in public dignity or in domestic privacies? However, the terms had shifted fundamentally. In 1816 Caldwell and Smith had shared the premise that biography ought above all to improve or instruct the reader. In the 1880s the reader's improvement was not at issue. In fact, several critics lambasted didacticism and moralism as perversions of biography's "primal purpose." The conflict was now between the subject's dignity and the reader's curiosity, between the right to privacy and the right to know. The biographer's first obligation, in Curtis's view, was to tell the truth: for the subject's sake, to be sure (because if the descendant-biographer suppressed the truth someone else would supply it and undermine the descendant's credibility), but especially for the reader's. Of course there were limits. But in a contest between Victorian suppression of "personality" and the reader's interest, truth and the reader became allies.[64]

By 1884 critics like Curtis could allow more to the reader precisely because that reader was more clearly defined than in the 1850s. Then the *North American* had worried about hacks invading and debasing the world of literature. Now the middle-class reader of *Harper's*, like its genteel critic, was presumed to know the proper boundaries between his rights and the subject's privacy, and between biography and "unscrupulous journalism." The biographer still required the "sympathy, intelligence, and proportion" that earlier critics had stressed. Parton reiterated these in his "Rules of Biography." But now the readers of biographies were assumed to have those same characteristics. As Annie Russell Marble wrote in *The Dial* in 1901, "The readers of Froude's Carlyle, Kingsley's Memoirs, or the Love-Letters of the Brownings or Victor Hugo, do not rank among the sensation-loving public that scans the personal gossip of the yellow journals or gloats over the latest erotic novel. The readers of biography, as a rule, bring a reverential spirit." Biographers could be honest because their readers were "men able to hear the truth" without succumbing to Biographical Mania.[65]

As the century closed, a new sort of biographies used exactly this rhetoric. Paul Leicester Ford's *The True George Washington* (1896) came first, and its popularity prompted its publisher to inaugurate a series called The "True" Biographies. By 1908 there were *The True Thomas Jefferson, The True Benjamin Franklin, The True William Penn,* and *The True Andrew Jackson,* all claiming "to present in entertaining form, free from glamour, some of the greatest epochs and characters in our national history, and with as close fidelity to the truth as could be gleaned from the conflicting record of events." These books differed markedly from biographies with "Real" in their titles — *The Real Bismarck, The Real Lincoln.* The "Real" biographer, as a wag in *Puck* put it, "sees things at a discount of sixty per cent." "Real" biographers tended to be their subjects' detractors, seeking to deflate reputations. (In *The Real Lincoln,* southerner Charles L. C. Minor condemned his subject as a coward, infidel, despot, extremist, and worse.) The "True" biographers did not question their subjects' greatness but objected to the lifelessness of previous biographies. Ford wrote that "we have well-nigh discarded from the lives of our greatest men all human faults and feelings; have enclosed their greatness in glass of the clearest crystal, and hung up a sign, 'Do not touch.' . . . But with this process of canonization have we not lost more than we have gained, both in example and in interest?" He and the other "True" biographers wanted to "humanize" their subjects, to depict them as men rather than museum pieces. *The True George Washington,* for instance, contained chapters on Washington's family relations, physique, education, relations with the fair sex, work as farmer and master, social life, tastes and amusements, friends, enemies, and status as soldier and citizen.

These biographers did not merely emphasize character—or, more accurately, "personality" in the sense that contemporary journalists portrayed famous people—over history. By organizing chapters topically rather than chronologically, they also discarded the narrative form that had made great men's lives into sequences of deeds and events.[66]

Ironically, a realist novel offered the most insightful look at contemporary biographical forms and approaches. William Dean Howells's *The Rise of Silas Lapham* (1885) took the form of a biography itself: it narrated the life and character of a Gilded Age "Paint King." As he planned the book (originally called "The Rise of Silas Needham"), Howells might as well have been planning a biography along the lines that George William Curtis and Edmund Gosse prescribed. "Nothing is spared, good or bad, as to the truth of Needham's life and character; the vulgarity of his nature in some respects is shown; his family troubles are dealt with; and the man's essential goodness and patience and moral strength are only covertly indicated." Even the novel's title evoked biography. Biographies for young men, campaign lives of presidential candidates, and the myriad newspaper and magazine sketches of "men of our time" all focused on their subjects' rise to wealth, power, or community esteem. Howells reversed this familiar narrative. Silas Lapham accidentally burns down his gaudy new Back Bay house, loses his fortune, and ends up beginning again in the rural Vermont town of his origins. His "rise" is purely moral and is never rewarded: deciding to redress a perceived wrong he did to a partner decades earlier, he instigates his own ruin. Howells saw "this adversity, consciously and deliberately chosen," as Lapham's "rise"—but of course popular contemporary biographies (like Horatio Alger stories) always painted early adversity as the prologue and path to self-made success. *The Rise of Silas Lapham* was the sort of character portrayal that contemporary critics like Howells himself wished biographers would adopt.[67]

Within the novel, Howells illustrated several sorts of biography at odds with his ideal. He had recognized the formulaic qualities of biographies for at least a quarter century. In his 1860 campaign life of Lincoln, he had poked fun at the convention that all candidates needed "an indisputable grandfather" who had served in the Revolution. Now he made the point more satirically. As *The Rise of Silas Lapham* opens, journalist Bartley Hubbard is interviewing Lapham for the "Solid Men of Boston" series in the newspaper *Boston Events*. Slightly nervous, Lapham begins by asking Hubbard, "So you want my life, death, and Christian sufferings, do you, young man?" Of course, the Paint King knows that this is not to be a pious

Christian memoir—and that his life hardly fits that model. Overt moralizing has little relevance for Howells anyway. At the novel's end the minister Mr. Sewell, who expresses Howells's own realist critique of sentimentalism and desire that novelists paint "life as it is," notes that "the operation of evil . . . in the moral world . . . is often so very obscure; and it often seems to involve, so far as we can see, no penalty whatever." Bartley Hubbard's article belongs to the "men of our time" narratives of solid, capitalist, American self-making into which Lapham can easily place himself. But Hubbard has a hard time taking the formula seriously as Lapham starts his life story.

> ". . . I was born in the state of Vermont, pretty well up under the Canada line—so well up, in fact, that I came very near being an adoptive citizen; for I was bound to be an American of *some* sort, from the word Go! That was about—well, let me see!—pretty near sixty years ago: this is '75, and that was '20. Well, say I'm fifty-five years old; and I've *lived* 'em, too; not an hour of waste time about *me,* anywheres! I was born on a farm, and—"
>
> "Worked in the fields summers and went to school winters; regulation thing?" Bartley cut in.
>
> "Regulation thing," said Lapham, accepting this irreverent version of his history somewhat dryly.
>
> "Parents poor, of course," suggested the journalist. "Any barefoot business? Early deprivations of any kind, that would encourage the youthful reader to go and do likewise? Orphan myself, you know," said Bartley, with a smile of cynical good comradery.
>
> Lapham looked at him silently, and then said with quiet self-respect, "I guess if you see these things as a joke, my life wont inter*est* you." [68]

Howells had little more patience for the formulaic narrative than his journalist character did, but neither did he condone Hubbard's blatant disrespect for Silas Lapham. Howells's contemporary readers already knew Bartley Hubbard as the protagonist of *A Modern Instance* (1882). Originally from a rural New England background not unlike Lapham's, Hubbard is now Howells's quintessential urban journalist, a hack who writes formula sketches for the money but would rather expose the underside of city life and famous men. *A Modern Instance* reveals him as rotten to the core. He cheats on and deserts his wife, sues for divorce in Indiana to conceal the action from her, and finally meets his demise in a tawdry scuffle in the Southwest. (Howells thus resurrected him for *Silas Lapham,* which took place early in the period covered by *A Modern Instance.*) In *Silas Lapham* Bartley goes well past mocking biographical formula. He mocks Lapham himself, whose very conception of the self-made-man narrative comes from newspaper sketches like the "Solid Men of Boston." He inserts snide remarks in Lapham's biography, balancing them with exaggerated passages of "high reverence." His wife Marcia, whose basic goodness and strength Howells depicted in *A Modern Instance,* hopes Bartley "*wont* make fun of him, as you do of some of those people." "Nothing that *he'll* ever find out," Bartley replies. Bartley wishes he could "let myself loose on him. . . . Confound the limitations of decency, anyway!" The journalist's creed, as he explains to Silas Lapham, is that the subject should not be modest because "What we want is the whole truth, and more; we've got so much modesty of our own that we can temper almost any statement." Bartley's "whole truth," however, was not Howells's just as it was not George William Curtis's. If allowed to confound the limitations of decency, Bartley would have descended to the realm of "unscrupulous journalism." The dominant voice in *The Rise of Silas Lapham,* Howells's own, was a sympathetic realism different from both Lapham's rustic, sometimes boorish self-confidence and Hubbard's jaded cynicism.[69] In Howells's hands the subject emerged as a rounded, multifaceted character with whom readers could sympathize—not a whitewashed exemplar of virtue, not a formulaic self-made man, and not a journalistic caricature. This was just what contemporary critics wanted from a good biographer.

CONCLUSION

The Dawn of Biography Is Breaking

At the turn of the twentieth century, American critics began to sketch a history of the genre—a history that left nineteenth-century American biographies out. Not coincidentally, many of the same critics argued that a modern age demanded and would produce new sorts of biographies. These new biographies would far surpass any that had come before in their attention to individuality, now defined in psychological, not romantic terms. As the Boston critic and biographer William Roscoe Thayer put it in 1905, "The dawn of Biography is breaking." This dawning would cast not just nineteenth-century American biographies, but also their primary purposes, into the shadows. The cultural work those biographies had sought to perform gave way to psychological work: twentieth-century critics dismissed biographies written for didactic, political, or moral purposes as "impure." Instead they championed ones that revealed the subject's innermost self, the unconscious realm hidden beneath even the domestic privacies that Samuel Johnson had urged biographers to explore.[1] Meanwhile academic literary critics ignored biography almost entirely as a form of literature, and professional historians came to denigrate biography in general as insufficiently analytical and most nineteenth-century biographies as simply hagiographical. The dawn of the new, in criticism and in the academy, meant the eclipse of nineteenth-century American biography. Nonetheless, the story of nineteenth-century American biography—not just the now-forgotten texts but also the writing, publication, and reading of them—remains significant, for it illuminates the ways nineteenth-century American culture worked: how people explained, disseminated, debated, and transformed the meanings of individual character and national identity.

The turn-of-the-century critics' history of biography went like this: biography began in ancient and medieval hagiography, reached its apex in Boswell's *Life of Johnson,* and endured troubled times in the nineteenth century. The earliest histories had been the stories of great men, chanted by bards to tribesmen around the campfire. These biographical sagas had helped mold tribal character and solidarity, much as lives of the saints in the Middle Ages later served to strengthen Christians' character and faith. The lives of ancient heroes, Roman caesars, and medieval churchmen alike had been told collectively, fitting subjects into archetypal models rather than portraying unique individuals. Boswell marked a potential turning point. As Annie Russell Marble wrote in 1901, his *Life of Johnson* heralded "a new portrayal of man's life in its entirety, interpreted by loving insight." Boswell's book also prefigured other biographies made "vital and thrilling" by their use of subjects' letters and conversation and biographers' personal reminiscences. But the nineteenth century had not proven a biographical golden age. Even before Boswell, historians and philosophers had begun to argue that larger trends of ideas and affairs, not great men, shaped history. Evolutionary theory intensified this interpretation in the nineteenth century. Meanwhile, the ancient tendency to portray notables only as exalted, public figures continued unabated. Victorian suppressions only exacerbated the problem. In short, biography's past offered little reason for optimism about its future.[2]

Nineteenth-century American biographies were virtually absent from these critics' history of the genre, and the *development* of biography in America was missing altogether. Addressing the young men of Exeter in 1886 on the topic of biography, the Episcopal bishop Phillips Brooks recommended no fewer than thirty-nine biographies, ranging from Plato's *Pictures of Socrates* and Augustine's *Confessions* to Johnson's *Lives of the Poets* and Boswell's *Johnson* to about a dozen books published in just the past five years. Only eight of Brooks's thirty-nine had American subjects, and five of those were brand new: Grant's *Memoirs,* Mrs. Louis Agassiz's biography of her husband, lives of Hawthorne and William Lloyd Garrison written by their children, and Holmes's *Ralph Waldo Emerson* in the American Men of Letters series. All were official biographies, mostly of New England subjects, decidedly not didactic or historical or journalistic. Although William Roscoe Thayer did include Jared Sparks in the story of the genre, it was not in praise: Sparks's puritanical editing had "made a mummy of" George Washington.[3] Most American critics left American biographies out entirely. Certainly the paucity of American biographies on their lists indicated that biography remained a transatlantic genre at century's end. Americans were as likely to read lives of English and European subjects as of American ones. Lives of English men of letters were more popular in America than biographies of native literati. The discourse about biography also remained transatlantic. Much biographical criticism in American periodicals was still reprinted from English work, and American critics and reviewers frequently cited English discussions of the genre.

More important, nineteenth-century American biographies disappeared from the turn-of-the-century retrospectives because most of those biographies failed to meet the transatlantic critical standards enshrined since the 1850s. When Annie Russell Marble noted that ancient and medieval collective biographies had been written not to reveal individuality but to demonstrate subjects' "kingly ecclesiastical or pietistic traits" for readers' admiration or emulation, she could easily have added Joseph Delaplaine's *Repository of the Lives and Portraits of Distinguished Americans* and other early-republican biographical collections to her list.[4] Republican ideology, as much as Christian belief, encouraged the presentation of patterned virtues. When Sadie Simons, a teacher at Central High School in Washington, D.C., wrote that ancient peoples had used biographies to shape and reinforce tribal spirit, she might as well have placed Weems's *Life of Washington* and countless campaign biographies in the same functional category. Of course, doing so would have meant identifying early American biography with the "primitive" biographical traditions, deficient in depicting individual character and suspect as history, from which the European literary world had separated itself at least since Boswell. Early American biographies could not square with the conception that America represented the acme of the world's progress—a conception, ironically, that those very biographies had trumpeted—and so they fell from even American critics' history of the genre.

Even as they wrote a story of biography's past that erased nineteenth-century American biographies, turn-of-the-century critics also suggested what biography's present and future might look like. Indeed, modernity mattered more to them than antiquity. The titles of their articles were revealing: "Popular Forms of Modern Biography"; "The Biography of To-Day." In just two pages of her 1901 article, Annie Marble described the beginning of the twentieth century as "this complex age of realism, science, and romance," "the crowded days of the present," "the clever, rushing age," "this mercantile age," and "this composite age which exacts vitality, accuracy, and literary judgment." Writers like Marble raised two sorts of questions. What should modern readers get from biography? And how had modernity in its various manifestations reshaped biography itself?[5]

To the first question, older and newer answers coexisted. Phillips Brooks prescribed biographical romanticism as an antidote to the rush and routine of modern life. His premise was simple. "I want to speak to you about the subjects of biographies, and the writers of biographies, and the readers of biographies. A life must first be lived, and then it must be written, and then it must be read, before the power of a biography is complete." This triangular biographical experience, Brooks explained, had existed when John Stuart Mill read Condorcet's *Life of Turgot,* when the dying Benjamin Franklin read Johnson's *Lives of the Poets,* and when his listeners—the students at Exeter—themselves read Boswell's *Life of Johnson.* Biography brought subject, biographer, and reader into imaginary communion. This acquaintance across place and time seemed all the more relevant to Brooks in an era of professionalization, when even academic life was being divided and subdivided into disciplines, each espousing its own "cheap little standards" and none considering its larger "divine meaning and motive." Ralph Waldo Emerson could have written this sentiment fifty years earlier, but this was precisely the point: biography provided a universal bulwark against the ephemera of everyday life. If anyone was in danger of losing his larger perspective in the whirl of modern life, it was the young men of Exeter, on their way to colleges and professions. Drawing directly from Emerson, Brooks argued that the good biography reader needed "a true life of his own." He offered this advice: "summon the inspiration of the greatest and most vital men whom you can find to touch your life with their fire, and make you not what they are, but more thoroughly and energetically yourself." With this statement Brooks repudiated simplistic biographical didacticism (relegated by now to children's books) and the "feeble repetition" inherent in a culture of professionalism, specialization, and fashion.[6]

Others responded that biography could help readers answer, not just escape, the central questions of modern life. Like a century of other commentators, Sadie Simons believed that biography had an educational mission. Unlike them, she conceived of education and therefore of biography in modern, social-scientific terms, and she asked social-scientific rather than romantic questions. Although a schoolteacher, Simons was no latter-day Julia Parker, the young Philadelphia woman of the 1840s who used biographies as models of women's accomplishments and American patriotism for her female students. Nor did Simons's 1899 article, "Educational Value of Biography," begin as a lecture summoning elite prep-schoolers into romantic communion with the great. It appeared in the *Educational Review,* a professional journal for educators who perceived their work as science and professionalized it with just such journals in the same years historians, economists, and political scientists did. Simons's biographical prescription was less universal than Phillips Brooks's. She divided biographies into three categories and explained which ones best suited children of different ages. In particular, Simons defined "Sociological" biographies as the product of the modern age. Exemplified by Winsor's *Columbus,* these biographies explained their subjects' actions as the results of environment. Critical and interpretive, sociological biographies helped "undo the evil work of the hero-worshipers," but they also tended to distort fact and ignore individuality "to suit general principles." Hence they should be reserved for the older student who could "sift and distinguish for himself." At all ages, however, students could benefit from biography. It did not merely bring history alive and inspire "noble emulation." Now it also shed light on "the relation of the man to the group and the influence of individual endeavor upon the destiny of societies," sociological issues especially relevant to "the mature minds of to-day." Simons sought a balance between two nineteenth-century extremes: the romantic glorification of great men and the evolutionist subordination of human agency to larger forces. Biography could help readers find that balance. It could reveal what importance the individual possessed in particular contexts, a pivotal problem of the new social sciences.[7]

To answer the question of how modernity had affected biography, critics cited the literature of realism and the science of psychology as the modern biographer's potential allies. The pendulum was already swinging back from the Victorian mummification of great men, Thayer wrote. Even if occasionally "sleazy," the publication of "memoirs, letters, *chroniques scandaleuses*" bespoke life instead of death and humanized famous people. Now other developments could benefit biography, too. Novels, which had once seemed the morally suspect, all-too-popular antithesis of biographies, were "teaching us to distinguish the most minute variations of character, and to trace the rack-and-pinion interaction of cause and effect." The useful trend in the novelist's art was the realism of Howells, not the romanticism of Scott. Psychology and physiology were inventing "new instruments for measuring human faculty more accurately." Other critics went further than Thayer, who (with a tinge of romanticism) warned biographers and readers not to trust science alone to capture human character. Psychologists were just beginning to use the biographical case study as an analytical tool; thus it was predictable that psychologist H. Addington Bruce (soon to write books on *Scientific Mental Healing* and *The Riddle of Personality*) criticized "The Biography of To-Day" for not giving "a studied presentation of causes and effects." By 1900, too, G. Stanley Hall had popularized the notion of adolescence as a distinct stage of development and Freudian psychology was permeating American scholarly circles (though not yet gaining popular readership). In this "age of child-study," wrote Annie Marble, biographers should give more "psychologic emphasis" to subjects' adolescence and early adulthood. Doing so would make biographies more like modern fiction and thus more appealing to readers, and it would "proclaim the scientific perspective."[8]

Not until after the First World War would biographers fulfill the implications of this criticism. The Englishman Lytton Strachey, the American Gamaliel Bradford, and other experimenters "aestheticized and psychologized" biography between the world wars. Rejecting Victorian hero-worship, compendiousness, and "moral earnestness," they artistically revealed contradictions the subject would not have discussed—or did not consciously know. No longer were actions, words, or even domestic privacies presumed to be transparent windows into character. Instead, they became both clues to and veils over the deeper psyche. Freudian psychology profoundly influenced this new biography; indeed, Bradford called his short sketches of leading men and women "psychographs." The psychoanalyst was a biographer of sorts. He accumulated evidence from the subject's own words and sifted it into an interpretation of motives. This form of biography served new purposes. It was fundamentally self-referential because the biographer-analyst's "reader" was the patient himself or herself. And the reader-patient read the story (or heard the analyst's interpretation) as a cure for deep, unseen problems that had manifested themselves in everyday actions. If the analyst published his case studies, he did so for his own professional community. Psychoanalysis as biography, then, was linked to an emerging therapeutic culture and embedded in the new scientific professions. Biography as psychoanalysis (including Freud's own 1910 biography of Leonardo da Vinci) used Freud's analytical categories to interpret—diagnose—the life of a deceased subject. The evidence might or might not be as direct as the psychoanalyst's, but the purpose was the same: to get beneath not just public actions but even conscious motives.[9]

This new focus redefined biography away from its nineteenth-century purposes. Nineteenth-century biographers (and many readers and critics) had emphasized biography's social and cultural work: its power to shape individuals' moral and civic lives and to insert individuals' lives into the nation's history. When biographers came to emphasize the psychological, they suggested that biography above all performed personal work. Psychological biographies could interpret lives in purely personal context: without the doctrinal underpinnings of Christian memoirs, without the democratic ideology of campaign biographies, without the historical framework of the Library of American Biography or the American Statesmen series.

Curiosity, not morality or patriotism, defined these new biographies' appeal to readers. Americans had long enjoyed biography out of simple curiosity about other people's lives. However, this new biography—and its very assumptions about what motivated people's actions—emptied out any semblance of a larger social purpose. And this occurred at the same time academic historians, devaluing the centrality of great men, began also to devalue biography as a useful vehicle for historical analysis. Biography was on its way to losing both of its nineteenth-century missions, the didactic and the historical. Little wonder, then, that twentieth-century historians of biography continued what the turn-of-the-century critics started: the obliteration of most nineteenth-century American biographies from historical or literary memory.

Of course, the critics' story was not everyone's story. Biographers still espoused didactic purposes, and making "self-made" men and women remained a fundamental goal of countless biographies. At least one biography yoked together old and new, romantic and didactic, English and American. In Silas Xavier Floyd's *Life of Charles T. Walker, D.D.* (1902), an African American Baptist clergyman, multiple languages of biography intertwined. The introduction, written by the Rev. Robert Stuart MacArthur, opened as numerous nineteenth-century lives had, discussing the importance and difficulty of writing biography. Not unlike Phillips Brooks, MacArthur cited Carlyle, Boswell's *Life of Johnson,* Lockhart's *Life of Scott,* and more recent biographies of Macaulay and Tennyson. He then placed Floyd's life of Walker into their biographical tradition: "a life nobly lived, and a writer competent to describe it in fitting terms." Floyd's own preface, however, added Walker himself to the list of America's self-made men—Lincoln, Garfield, Franklin, Greeley, and even Frederick Douglass—who "have left an undying influence, whose early life was without friends, and whose heritage was void of patrimony." For Floyd, the purpose of Walker's biography was "to encourage, inspire, and incite to new endeavor thousands of young colored men all over the land." [10]

That biography did not lose its older missions entirely has had more to do with educators and ordinary readers than with academics or critics. The lives of eminent figures continue to offer children moral and historical lessons and to build their patriotism, ethnic identity, and concepts of gender roles. For many adults, biography is the preferred form of history. David McCullough's biographies climb the nonfiction best-seller lists, and "Biography"—including its segments on historical figures, not just those on contemporary celebrities—is the most popular program on the A&E network and has spawned a monthly magazine. Just as clearly, however, these purposes of biography command little academic or critical respect. Biography has become a tool in many academic fields. Anthropologists, sociologists, and oral historians use life stories as data in the reconstruction of cultures.[11] Literary critics use authors' biographies (now inflected with psychological overtones) to help explain their works, an approach that dates back at least to Samuel Johnson. But as a distinct literary genre, biography is expected to rise above such utilitarian purposes—a notion quite different from that of the early nineteenth century, when the purposes helped define the genre.

If the advent of the psychological redefined how writers and critics saw biography, it also reshaped how ordinary people saw themselves. Undoubtedly psychological ideas have helped change the ways people read biographies, not just the ways authors write them. Freud and his contemporaries and disciples intensified people's interest in their own psychological selves. In the process, they may well have fostered a culture of *auto*biography: one in which telling one's own story becomes a form of therapy, and in which hearing the self-told stories of others (not just hearing the stories of self-made others) offers examples in how to tell one's own story (not just how to make one's own self). The individual psyche, after all, differs fundamentally from the "character" Parson Weems or William Makepeace Thayer wanted readers to develop. In the twentieth century, autobiography assumed a very different status than it had in the nineteenth. Then, autobiography was a subset of biography. To some critics and authors it was the truest form of biography, but it was nonetheless a form of biography. Now, autobiography inhabits its own category. At the rarefied end of the spectrum, academic critics treat it as Literature, lavishing scholarly attention on this genre that did not exist *as* a genre a hundred years ago. At the tabloid end, readers and viewers devour celebrities' "own stories" and the confessions of ordinary people on afternoon talk shows.

If we have a "culture of biography" today, it is a culture that autobiography has reshaped. The "biographical" information that millions of readers want is the stuff of the first-person interview and the psychologist's couch. Second-hand dish suffices, but the subject's own story is better. Even biographers get in on the autobiographical act. Dozens of them have written articles and delivered lectures on "how I came to write a biography." They confess how immersing themselves in someone else's life helped them understand their own, as if self-diagnosis were a benefit of writing biography, not just of reading it. Nineteenth-century American biographers certainly had personal motivations. William Wirt wanted to solidify his place in a Virginian elite he had not joined by birth. Elizabeth Ellet hoped to make a reputation among historians after the New York literary community had disowned her. James Parton wanted to make a literary living as something more than a hack journalist. They would never have dreamed of publishing such motives, however. They described preserving the histories of people who would otherwise be forgotten, instilling virtue in a rising generation, imparting glory to their state or nation, defining the national character. Their explanations—like their readers' descriptions of why they read and what they enjoyed, and like their critics' standards— were grounded in their particular nineteenth-century contexts of life and print. The personal terms in which many present-day biographers describe their endeavors are no less rooted in our own culture. The critical differences are these: Today's biographers believe that they, not the subjects themselves and certainly not God, "make" individual lives into biographies. Some of them happily confess how writing biography has changed their own lives.[12] But very few argue that biography has the power to mold its readers' lives.

What, finally, do we gain by studying biographies and concepts of biography that served cultural purposes over a century ago and seem outmoded today? The debates about individual character and national identity, in which biographies and conflicts over biography became staging grounds, remain with us. Proponents of "character education" in public schools imply that "character" is a bundle of characteristics and values that can be inculcated and imbibed. To their opponents, emphasizing one constellation of values and virtues over others threatens to stifle true individuality under the guise of teaching students to make their own moral choices. In a conservative era, one premise of the entire debate over character education is that the nation's strength, perhaps even its survival, depends on the virtue of its citizens—the very rationale on which nineteenth-century moralists, critics, and biographers championed biography reading. We still ask, too, how much of famous people's private lives ought to be made public. If a person's true character emerges only in private life, how far into that life is it fair to look (or pry)? If, instead, public character and private morality are distinct, is examination of private morality anything more than salacious scandal-mongering? Most prominent, Americans still debate who and what belongs in our national history. Some argue that America's history is fundamentally the story of its great men and their accomplishments, the sort of story that a Library of American Biography or a series called American Statesmen could tell. Others interpret history more broadly and cast the biographical net more widely, much as Elizabeth Ellet did a century and a half ago. The process of widening the bio-

biography
an interdisciplinary quarterly

Volume 20   Number 2   Spring 1997

Two faces of today's *Biography*. The quarterly journal published by the Biographical Research Center in Honolulu (*left*) includes scholarly articles on the practice of biography and case studies of biographical approaches. The monthly magazine published by the Arts and Entertainment cable network (*right*) appeals to the continuing popular fascination with famous people, historical and contemporary.

Jack Nicholson | Sarah McLachlan | Audrey Hepburn

Every life has a story.

Biography

**Just Shoot Me's
David Spade**

AUGUST 1998 / $2.99 IN USA, $3.99 IN CANADA

Donald Foster
On the Trail of JonBenét Ramsey's Killer

Fashion Designer
Isaac Mizrahi
on Success, Style, and His Insecurities

Jamie Lee Curtis
Down-to-Earth Mom Battles Aliens

The Bright Wit and Dark Soul of
Dorothy Parker

Rosie O'Donnell
and the Childhood Pain that Haunts Her Today

08>

0 74820 08140 2

graphical net encourages us to reassess both the methods we use to tell historical "truth" and the larger narrative of American history itself. We may think of this expansion as a phenomenon of the last thirty years, brought about by the decline of the American century and of consensus history, by recent social movements, or by the emergence of new studies within the academy. But even mug books of the late nineteenth century used biography to reframe the basic narrative of America's past. By collecting the lives of ordinary, self-made citizens, these books placed the agricultural settlement of former frontiers, not the Puritans or the politicians, at the heart of the national epic.

Even if we take nineteenth-century American biography on its own terms (as this book has done), it has much to tell us. Biographies and the myriad published discussions of the genre illuminate nineteenth-century American culture: what words like "character" and "individuality" meant, how individual lives fit into the larger national history, and where (or whether) life-writing belonged in the realm called "literature." As we have seen, these were not discrete issues. The 1816 battle over Delaplaine's *Repository* simultaneously concerned America's international literary reputation and the appropriate sphere in which to find a man's character. Elizabeth Ellet sought at midcentury to add Revolutionary women to an American history that had ignored them, to redefine what sorts of evidence counted as truth, *and* to instill foremothers' virtues in a new generation of women. James Parton's diverse biographical productions of the 1860s and 1870s had different literary cachet, in large part, because of how they defined character: didactic sketches fell somewhere below "literature," while lengthier depictions of subjects in all their uniqueness staked his claim to a literary reputation.

While exploring the relationships between character formation, the American historical narrative, and the development of a literary genre, this book has also posed the question of nineteenth-century American biography's importance more broadly. Let us return to Phillips Brooks's conception of biography as a triangular process: "A life must first be lived, and then it must be written, and then it must be read, before the power of a biography is quite complete." Even if not all Americans shared Brooks's romantic interpretation of what gave biography power, many agreed that biography was far more than words on the page, books about eminent men and women. Twentieth-century scholars and critics missed the story of biography in nineteenth-century America because they saw biographies solely as texts, and most nineteenth-century ones as bad literature or inaccurate history. We would continue to miss this story if we merely interpreted biographical texts rather than exploring the diverse ways in which biographers and publishers, critics and readers made biography a part of nineteenth-century American life.

By envisioning biography in nineteenth-century America as an active process, not just a genre of books, we can glimpse how nineteenth-century American culture actually worked. Phillips Brooks imagined a wholly intellectual process, a meeting of three minds liberated from their everyday cares and even their own historical moments. It would be easy to discuss biographies themselves on the same rarefied level: as purveyors of grand concepts like republicanism, nationalism, and romanticism. Yet specific personal circumstances and precise contexts of society, politics, and publishing framed exactly *how* these concepts looked—and were transformed and debated—as they traveled from biographers to readers. William Wirt began his biographical odyssey in 1805 with a Johnsonian "itch" but produced a historical biography a decade later for reasons that were practical and ideologically specific to that moment. Depending on their own circumstances, readers approached Wirt's book differently: as a tribute to the Old Dominion's favorite son and bygone golden age, as a dangerously Virginia-centered version of national history that demanded a Massachusetts antidote, or as a primer of virtuous character and a warning against indolence. A reader like Michael Floy, the young Methodist in 1830s New York, used biographies to shape his life. He wanted to emulate the faith and good works of the men whose lives he read in print. But his youth, his Methodism, and his metropolitan access to books also influenced which biographies he read and the ways he read them. Animated by personal objectives, cultural missions, and regional, national, or transatlantic notions of biography itself, biographers and critics used the lives of eminent men and women to create and propagate meaning: moral values, patriotic beliefs, understandings of American history. Reading those printed lives, Americans with their own objectives, missions, and notions made meanings for themselves.

NOTES

ABBREVIATIONS USED IN THE NOTES

AAS	American Antiquarian Society, Worcester, Mass.
AM	*Atlantic Monthly*
AQ	*American Quarterly*
CDW-WL	Charles Dudley Warner Collection, Watkinson Library, Trinity College, Hartford, Conn.
CHS	Connecticut Historical Society, Hartford
HL	Houghton Library, Harvard University, Cambridge, Mass.
HMC-HL	Houghton Mifflin Collection (bMS Am 1925), Houghton Library, Harvard University, Cambridge, Mass.
JAH	*Journal of American History*
JER	*Journal of the Early Republic*
JP-HL	James Parton Papers (bMS Am 1248), Houghton Library, Harvard University, Cambridge, Mass.
JS-HL	Jared Sparks Papers (MS Sparks), Houghton Library, Harvard University, Cambridge, Mass.
LAB	Library of American Biography, ed. Jared Sparks
NAR	*North American Review*
NYHS	New-York Historical Society
NYPL	New York Public Library
PAAS	*Proceedings of the American Antiquarian Society*
TJ-UVa	Thomas Jefferson Papers, Manuscripts Division, University of Virginia Library, Charlottesville
UNC	Southern Historical Collection, University of North Carolina, Chapel Hill
WMQ	*William and Mary Quarterly*
WW-LC	William Wirt Papers, Library of Congress, Washington, D.C.
WW-MdHS	William Wirt Papers (MS. 1011), Maryland Historical Society, Baltimore

Throughout the notes, primary sources are cited in complete form on the first reference in each chapter, as they are in the bibliography. (Brief citations are used subsequently.) Titles of some additional nineteenth-century sources, which are peripheral to this study, are listed in the notes to acknowledge their place in the literature, but full citations are not given. For secondary sources, brief citations are used throughout the notes; full citations for these works can be found in the bibliography.

1. Kaser, *Books and Libraries in Camp and Battle,* 16–17; *Catalogue of Books in the Jail and House of Correction, in Worcester* (Worcester, Mass., 1860); *Catalogue of the Library in Rhode Island State Prison* (Providence, 1867); both in Public Library Catalogues Collection, AAS. "Biographical Mania," *New-York Mirror, and Ladies' Literary Gazette* 7 (May 15, 1830): 359; "The Biographical Mania," *Evening Gazette* (Boston), July 4, 1857, 8.

2. On the ways classical conceptions of civic character became central to republican thought in eighteenth-century America, see Adair, "Fame and the Founding Fathers," 3–26; and Gordon S. Wood, *Creation of the American Republic,* 65–70. Daniel Walker Howe emphasizes faculty psychology, with its notions of the "balanced character," in defining ideas about American selfhood from the Great Awakening through republicanism to nineteenth-century liberalism; see *Making the American Self.* Because eighteenth-century Anglo-Americans took the theatrical metaphor quite literally, a third meaning of "character" was also possible: one *was* (or played) a character on the very stage where performance revealed one's true self and fixed one's reputation. On this metaphor, see Agnew, *Worlds Apart.*

3. I will not be examining the theological details of how different Christian sects used biography to highlight their particular versions of the conversion experience or the relationship between grace and Christian nurture in the life of the convert. (Nor do I address how groups outside the Protestant mainstream used biography.) Despite these differences, we can speak in general about "evangelical biographies." As mentioned above, like the lives of self-made men, they focused on individual experience and self-improvement. Unlike them, however, evangelical biographies emphasized the role of regenerating grace in character formation. Before conversion, simply trying to imitate the life of a saint would backfire: the reader would realize that virtuous self-making was impossible without supernatural grace. Religious memoirs that focused on subjects' preconversion lives offered inspiration to religious strivers, but not models to follow directly. When evangelical biographies offered more imitable models, they were generally for postconversion cultivation of Christian character.

   On nineteenth-century notions of character and the self, see Rabinowitz, *The Spiritual Self in Everyday Life,* esp. 108–17; Daniel Walker Howe, *Making the American Self,* esp. 122–28; Cmiel, *Democratic Eloquence;* and Reinier, *From Virtue to Character.* On the concerns that could arise from the newly fluid notions of self-formation, see Halttunen, *Confidence Men and Painted Women.*

4. Phillips Brooks, "The Phillips Exeter Lectures: Biography" (Boston: Ginn and Co., 1893). Brooks originally delivered the lecture in 1886. On late-century conflicts over the notion of "professional" character, see especially Cmiel, *Democratic Eloquence,* chaps. 5 and 8.

5. Noah Webster, *A Compendious Dictionary of the English Language* (New Haven: Increase Cooke and Co., and Hartford: Hudson and Goodwin, 1806), 30; Webster, *An American Dictionary of the English Language,* 6th ed. (New York: S. Converse, 1830), 89. This latter definition remained the same in the 1837, 1842, 1848, and 1861 editions of Webster's dictionary.

6. James Parton, ed., *Some Noted Princes, Authors, and Statesmen of Our Time* (New York: Thomas Y. Crowell and Co., 1885), v.

7. The neglect of nineteenth-century biography stems, in large measure, from a central principle of twentieth-century biographical criticism: the distinction between "pure" and "impure" biography. Originally formulated by Harold Nicolson in 1928, this distinction rests on the dictum that "biography must be a truthful record of an individual . . . composed as a work of art; it thus excludes narratives which are unhistorical, which do not deal primarily with individuals, or which are not composed with a conscious artistic purpose." Whereas pure biographies record "personality" faithfully and aesthetically, impure ones are generally written for purposes "extraneous to the art itself": celebrating the dead, teaching moral lessons, promoting a political candidate or religious belief. As we will see, the seeds of this distinction were sown much earlier. Since Nicolson, virtually all critical attention to biography has been devoted to those deemed pure. Even though critics in the 1980s began to argue that biographies were ultimately "fictions," authorial constructions rather than objectively true narratives, they have continued to avoid those biographies previously labeled impure, shifting the terms of analysis but perpetuating the old divisions. See Nicolson, *Development of English Biography*, 8, 10; Garraty, *Nature of Biography;* O'Neill, *History of American Biography;* and Joseph W. Reed, *English Biography in the Early Nineteenth Century.* Recent work that examines biography for tropes, narrative structures, and metaphors—but still focuses on "pure" biographies (generally lives of authors) —includes Phyllis Rose, "Biography as Fiction"; Nadel, *Biography: Fact, Fiction, and Form;* Nadel, "Biography and Four Master Tropes"; Petrie, *Ultimately Fiction;* Epstein, *Recognizing Biography;* and much of the contents of the journal *Biography,* founded in the late 1970s.

   Scholars who have recovered, and explored the "cultural work" of, nineteenth-century literature include Tompkins, *Sensational Designs,* esp. xii–xix; Baym, *Woman's Fiction;* Daniel A. Cohen, *Pillars of Salt, Monuments of Grace;* Davidson, *Revolution and the Word;* Denning, *Mechanic Accents;* Reynolds, *Beneath the American Renaissance;* and Schiller, *Objectivity and the News.*

8. Walt Whitman, "When I Read the Book" (1867), in Whitman, *Walt Whitman: Complete Poetry and Selected Prose and Letters,* 9; Henry Wadsworth Longfellow, "What Is Autobiography," in *Final Memorials of Henry Wadsworth Longfellow,* ed. Samuel Longfellow (Boston: Ticknor and Co., 1887).

9. In addition to circulation records, which survive for only a very few libraries, library catalogs indicate what books were available to readers who might not have been able to afford to buy books or who chose to borrow rather than buy certain books. Libraries large and small, urban and rural, in all regions of the country had these catalogs printed, and many survive (notably in the Public Library Catalogues Collection at AAS). Especially in the first half of the century, social libraries were established by groups of individuals who bought shares in them (and sometimes paid annual fees as well). These libraries' catalogs may well have reflected members' tastes, since they chose what books to purchase and were probably unlikely to use their funds to purchase works of little or no interest to the membership. The same was true of circulating libraries—libraries usually run by a bookseller or printer that loaned works for a fee. These libraries were business ventures, not collective endeavors. But their proprietors, too, had an interest in stocking works that patrons would borrow. By contrast, the public library movement that gathered force in the last quarter of the century was less directly responsive to readers' desires and more connected to "improvement" movements of the time that attempted to shape those desires. Recent studies that examine nineteenth-century library records to suggest reading

patterns include Gross, "Much Instruction from Little Reading"; and Ronald J. Zboray, "Reading Patterns in Antebellum America."

10. On Americans' increasing proclivity to envision lives, especially their own, as stories, see Appleby, "New Cultural Heroes in the Early National Period," 163–88; Appleby, "Introduction" in her *Recollections of the Early Republic*, xix–xxi; Bushman, *Refinement of America*, 288–89; and Anne C. Rose, *Victorian America and the Civil War*, esp. 245–55.

11. Brodhead, *Cultures of Letters*. Both the new historicism and the history of the book contain multiple and diverse approaches; each label has become a catch phrase for a wide range of work. New historicism includes works that tether textual analysis rather loosely to large economic developments (for example, Walter Benn Michaels's "Romance and Real Estate," in his *Gold Standard and the Logic of Naturalism*, 87–112) and studies that examine texts in relation to their authors' specific experiences of publishing, education, or politics (see Richard Brodhead's analysis of Louisa May Alcott and Charles Chesnutt in *Cultures of Letters*, chaps. 3 and 6). Similarly, some historians examine local or regional reading cultures using county records and quantitative methods, while others look at individual authors' relationships with publishers and readers using correspondence and sales records. William J. Gilmore, *Reading Becomes a Necessity of Life*, is a rich example of a regional study; Kelley, *Private Woman, Public Stage*, offers a collective portrait of twelve women novelists' negotiations between authorship and prevailing concepts of women's roles. For a brief overview of some assumptions and questions that new historicists tend to share, see Veeser, "The New Historicism," in his edited collection *The New Historicism Reader*, 1–32. Darnton, "What Is the History of Books?," provides a useful overview of the concerns of historians of the book.

12. This is not meant to single out Davidson's or Denning's work as uniquely problematic. Indeed, Davidson's *Revolution and the Word* and Denning's *Mechanic Accents* are among the most sophisticated studies to date of the relationships between critics, texts, and actual readers—a fact that makes their ultimate failure to introduce readers into the discussions of genre all the more noteworthy. Susan K. Harris goes further than either Davidson or Denning, using several women's diaries in her study of nineteenth-century women's fiction and her analysis of the late-nineteenth-century debates over women's education and reading. See her *19th-Century American Women's Novels* and "Responding to the Text(s)."

13. Machor, "Introduction: Readers/Texts/Contexts," in *Readers in History*, x. Machor's collection contains only two essays—Harris's on women readers and Marva Banks's "*Uncle Tom's Cabin* and Antebellum Black Response"—that deal directly with ordinary readers, as opposed to literary figures who read other writers' literary works. Amy M. Thomas's analysis of Ella Gertrude Clanton Thomas's reading (in "Who Makes the Text? Reading in Nineteenth-Century America"), based on this nineteenth-century southerner's voluminous journals, is an excellent example of the possibilities of an individual case study. Barbara Sicherman's essays, notably "Reading *Little Women*," and the recent work of Ronald J. Zboray and Mary Saracino Zboray, especially "Have You Read . . . ?" and "Reading and Everyday Life in Antebellum Boston," also explore the ways readers' circumstances affected their interpretations of texts.

14. Biography would look even less monolithically middle class if one were to include the biographies of criminals and working-class figures that appeared regularly in the penny press from the second quarter of the century on. My study focuses primarily on biographies published in book form and thus does not treat types of biographies that appeared

mostly or entirely in periodicals. Perhaps this decision skews my analysis toward the lives of successful Americans. Then again, it also leads me to omit thousands of biographies of the great and famous and of middle-class entrepreneurs—which far outnumbered criminal and lower-class biographies in American periodicals. The connection between criminal biography and working-class ideas is explored in Schiller, *Objectivity and the News;* the development of criminal biography as a genre is a major element in Daniel A. Cohen, *Pillars of Salt, Monuments of Grace.* Cohen's book is also one of the few works to deal with the development of a genre (actually, the several genres that made up New England crime literature) over a long period.

CHAPTER ONE

1. Samuel Miller, *A Brief Retrospect of the Eighteenth Century . . . Containing a Sketch of the Revolutions and Improvements in Science, Arts, and Literature, during That Period,* 2 vols. (New York: T. and J. Swords, 1803), 2:149–54, 478.

2. "Biography," *American Law Journal* 1 (January 1808): 121; review of Joseph Delaplaine's *Repository of the Lives and Portraits of Distinguished Americans, Portico* 2 (October 1816): 282; John Maxwell, *The American Patriot and Hero: A Brief Memoir of the Illustrious Conduct and Character of His Excellency George Washington, the Chief Commander, and Successful Leader of the Armies of the United States of America, during Their Late War with Great Britain* (Lancaster, Pa.?: printed for the author, 1795).

3. William Allen, *An American Biographical and Historical Dictionary, Containing an Account of the Lives, Characters, and Writings of the Most Eminent Persons in North America from Its First Discovery to the Present Time* (Cambridge: W. Hilliard, 1809). Entries in other biographical dictionaries of the period were similarly concentrated in religious and political figures. See, for example, John Eliot, *A Biographical Dictionary, Containing a Brief Account of the First Settlers, and Other Eminent Characters among the Magistrates, Ministers, Literary and Worthy Men in New-England* (Salem: Cushing and Appleton; Boston: Edward Oliver, 1809); [James Jones Wilmer], *The American Nepos: A Collection of the Lives of the Most Remarkable and the Most Eminent Men, Who Have Contributed to Discovery, the Settlement, and the Independence of America* (Baltimore: John Vance and Co., 1805). Other biographical dictionaries, like James Hardie's *New Universal Biographical Dictionary, and American Remembrancer of Departed Merit* (New York: Johnson and Stryker, 1801), included entries on American and European subjects; still others, such as *Public Characters, or Contemporary Biography* (Baltimore: Bonsal and Niles, 1803), were largely drawn from British works of the same sort, with American figures appended. On the prevalence of biography in magazines of the 1810s, see Edgar, *A History and Bibliography of American Magazines,* 31.

4. Information on the subscriptions to Marshall's *Life of Washington* is derived from *The Life of George Washington: Maps and Subscribers' Names* (Philadelphia: C. P. Wayne, 1807), 1–22; on the work's creation, publication, and reception, see Teute, "*Life of George Washington:* Editorial Note." Morse's work was *A True and Authentic History of His Excellency George Washington, Commander in Chief of the American Army during the Late War, and Present President of the United States* (Philadelphia: Printed by Peter Stewart for Robert Steward, 1790). Other biographies published in the decade after Washington's death include Thomas Condie, *Biographical Memoirs of the Illustrious Gen. Geo. Washington, Late President of the United States of America* (Philadelphia: Charless and Ralston, 1800); David Ramsay, *The Life of George*

Washington (New York: Hopkins and Seymour, 1807); Mason Locke Weems, *A History, of the Life and Death, Virtues and Exploits, of General George Washington* (Georgetown, D.C.: Green and English, 1800); John Marshall, *The Life of George Washington* (Philadelphia: C. P. Wayne, 1807); John Corry, *Biographical Memoirs of the Illustrious Gen. Geo. Washington, Late President of the United States of America, and Commander in Chief of Their Armies* (Philadelphia: Printed by Joseph Charless for H. and P. Rice and James Rice and Co., 1801; also New York, 1807; Philadelphia, 1808; New Haven, Conn., 1809; later editions include Wilmington, Del., 1810; Trenton, N.J., 1811; Poughkeepsie, N.Y., 1812; Baltimore, 1812; Pittsburgh, 1813; Barnard, Vt., 1813; Boston, 1815; Bridgeport, Conn., 1815; Lebanon, Pa. [German edition], 1815).

5. Weems's correspondence with Wayne is found in Skeel, *Mason Locke Weems*, 2:256 and passim; the letter about Wayne's disappointment with the Marshall biography, dated May 24, 1807, appears in 2:362. On the problems of selling Belknap's *American Biography*, see David Ramsay to Jeremy Belknap, March 14, 1794, quoted in *Belknap Papers*, Collections of the Massachusetts Historical Society, 6th ser., 4 (Boston: Massachusetts Historical Society, 1891): 568–69. See also "American Biography," *American Quarterly Review* 1 (March 1827): 6; Gilreath, "Weems, Carey, and the Southern Booktrade"; and "Names of Subscribers," in Eleazar Lord, *Lempriere's Universal Biography* (New York: R. Lockwood, 1825), back of vol. 2. Only thirty-seven of the subscriptions to the Lempriere work came from south of Pennsylvania.

6. For a superb, concise overview of early-national publishing, see Davidson, *Revolution and the Word*, 15–37. For another, locally focused examination, see William J. Gilmore, *Reading Becomes a Necessity of Life*, 157–222. For Smith's quotation, see Ruland and Bradbury, *From Puritanism to Postmodernism*, 91.

7. Davidson, *Revolution and the Word*, 18. On publishers' willingness or unwillingness to take risks on literary works, see William J. Gilmore, *Reading Becomes a Necessity of Life*, 198; and Davidson, 18–21. This issue is central to the differentiation between job printers and publishers (a nascent occupational category around 1800 in cities like Philadelphia), described in Remer, *Printers and Men of Capital*. Editions of *Charlotte Temple* in these years issued from Poughkeepsie, N.Y., Brookfield, Mass., Brattleboro, Vt., Alexandria, Va., and Danbury, Conn., as well as from Carey in Philadelphia.

8. Anthony Haswell, *Memoirs and Adventures of Captain Matthew Phelps, Formerly of Harwington in Connecticut, now Resident in Newhaven in Vermont* (Bennington, Vt.: Anthony Haswell, 1802).

9. Gilreath, "American Book Distribution," 527–28; Nord, "A Republican Literature"; Gilreath, "Weems, Carey, and the Southern Booktrade."

10. Posey's collection, inventoried in 1818, is described in Michael Hope Harris, "The Availability of Books and the Nature of Book Ownership on the Southern Indiana Frontier," 153. Jefferson's is detailed in Gilreath and Wilson, *Thomas Jefferson's Library: A Catalog with the Entries in His Own Order*, esp. 17–34. On other personal collections, see Richard Beale Davis, *Intellectual Life in Jefferson's Virginia*, 88–118. Fewer than one-fifth of the biographies in the Charleston Library Society and the Library Company of Philadelphia were published in the United States. *A Catalogue of Books Belonging to the Charleston Library Society, January, 1811* (Charleston, 1811), 15–34; *A Catalogue of the Books Belonging to the Library Company of Philadelphia* (Philadelphia, 1807), 375–87. For smaller Indiana collections, see Harris, "Availability of Books," 144–45. On libraries, see Jesse H. Shera, "The Beginnings

of Systematic Bibliography in America, 1642–1799," in *Essays Honoring Lawrence C. Wroth,* ed. Frederick Richmond Goff et al. (Portland, Maine: Anthoensen Press, 1951), 274, cited in Davidson, *Revolution and the Word,* 27. The libraries whose catalogs were examined include Brentwood Social Library, Vt. (Exeter, N.H., 1806), Dated Pamphlets Collection, AAS; and the following, all in Public Library Catalogues Collection, AAS: Williams College Library (Bennington, Vt., 1794); Hartford Library Company (Hartford, Conn., 1797); Nathaniel Coverly Circulating Library (Newbury, Vt., 1797); Lexington Library (Lexington, Ky., 1804); Mechanic Library Society (New Haven, Conn., 1804–11?); Youth's Library (Salisbury, Conn., 1806); Dorchester Library (Dorchester, Mass., 1807); Middlebury College Library (Middlebury, Vt., 1811); Boscawen Social Library (Concord, N.H., 1811); Charlestown [N.H.] Society Library (Bellows Falls, Vt., 1818); Albany Apprentices' Library (Albany, N.Y., 1822); Salem Mechanics' Library (Salem, Mass., 1823); Charlotte Social Library (Chittenden City, Vt., 1826); and Library of the University of Virginia (Charlottesville, Va., 1828). On the limited selection of books in rural communities before 1830, see David D. Hall, "Uses of Literacy in New England," 1–2.

11. Farmers and Mechanicks Library Records, Washington County, N.Y., 1816–68, AAS. All references to the library are from this collection.

12. Advertisements for Dodd and Stevenson's circulating library and bookstore appear in *Washington County Post* (Salem, N.Y.), May 14, 1823, March 29 and April 5, 1826. Little is known about the members of the Washington County Farmers and Mechanicks Library. Lists of the county's wills to 1850 include just nine of the sixty-nine renters in the circulation records. Although some members' wills may not be listed because those members died after 1850 or because they moved out of the county, county histories published in the late nineteenth century mention just one of the individuals in the library's records. This lack of information suggests that the Washington County farmers and mechanics were rural citizens of relatively low economic and social standing. Gertrude A. Barber, comp., *Abstracts of Wills of Washington County, New York, from 1788–1825* (n.p., 1937); Barber, comp., *Washington County, New York: Index of Wills from 1825–1850* (n.p., 1937); *History and Biography of Washington County and the Town of Queensbury, New York* (Chicago: Gresham Publishing Co., 1894); *History of Washington County, New York* (Philadelphia: Everts and Ensign, 1878).

13. Multiple charging does not necessarily indicate multiple reading of the same works by the same individuals. For example, a member who had borrowed the *Life of Franklin* might borrow it again for another family member. Alternatively, an individual might not read a work the first time he or she borrowed it, and thus might borrow it again in order to read it. However, the multiple chargings of Marshall's *Washington,* which show that members did move through the series, volume by volume, usually before borrowing individual volumes again, suggest that members were reading the works they checked out. On the concept of "intensive reading," see David D. Hall, "Uses of Literacy in New England," 31–34. In "Religious Reading and Readers in Antebellum America," David Paul Nord has recently complicated the image of preindustrial "intensive" readers, suggesting that rural New Jerseyites in the early republic actually read in a variety of ways that combined "intensive" patterns with other sensibilities connected to a market system of capitalist book distribution.

14. The controversy over Weems's and Horry's life of Marion is described more fully in "Fables of Parson Weems," following this chapter.

15. For a typical English preface dealing with biography's instructive power, see Philip Dod-

dridge, *Some Remarkable Passages in the Life of Hon. Col. James Gardiner, Who Was Slain at the Battle of Preston Pans, September 21, 1745* (Boston: I. Thomas and E. T. Andrews, 1792), 15. For similar statements in other American-imprinted English works, see Benjamin Say, *A Short Compilation of the Life and Writings of Thomas Say . . .* (Philadelphia: Budd and Bartram, 1796), 3; and *Some Account of the Life and Religious Labours of Sarah Grubb* (Trenton, N.J.: Isaac Collins, 1795), v.

16. Wilmer, *American Nepos*, v; S. Backus, "An Oration on Biography, Spoken the First Anniversary of the Themean Society, April 5, 1811," *Floriad* 1 (June 21, 1811): 33; "On Biography," *New England Quarterly Magazine: Comprehending Literature, Morals, and Amusement* 1 (April/May/June 1802): 46; "Biography," *American Law Journal* 1 (January 1808): 121; "Biography: The Life of William Cowper," *Portico* 1 (January 1816): 53; "On Biography," *Weekly Visitant* 1 (March 22, 1806): 89; "The Biography of Illustrious Men," *Christian Philanthropist* 1 (September 3, 1822): 67. Young people were especially encouraged to read biography, for "the youthful aspirer" could learn from the contrasting fates of the virtuous and the base. "Publisher's Address," *Boston Weekly Magazine* 1 (October 12, 1816): 1.

17. Morse, *A True and Authentic History of His Excellency George Washington*, 7. On Tyler and the issue of republican art and literature, see Shalhope, *Roots of Democracy*, 53–82; and Ellis, *After the Revolution*.

18. On seventeenth- and eighteenth-century models of character sketches, see Brownley, "Johnson's *Lives of the English Poets*" (quotation on p. 36–37). On the Theophrastan character, see Smeed, *The Theophrastan "Character."* The standard works on English biography in this period remain Donald A. Stauffer's *English Biography before 1700* and *The Art of Biography in Eighteenth-Century England*. Also useful is Longaker, *English Biography in the Eighteenth Century*. More recent examinations include Wendorf, *Elements of Life;* Anderson, *Biographical Truth;* and the essays in Browning, *Biography in the 18th Century*, especially those by James Noxon, Glen Bowersock, and Robert Halsband; and in Daghlian, *Essays in Eighteenth-Century Biography*, especially those by Donald Greene and James L. Clifford. Michael McKeon examines the relationship between the contemporaneous development of the novel and of more rounded biographies of literary figures in "Writer as Hero," 17–41.

19. Tichi, "Spiritual Biography and the 'Lords Remembrancers,'" 57; Eberwein, "'Indistinct Lustre,'" 205. The most influential interpretation of the Puritan typological imagination is Bercovitch, *Puritan Origins of the American Self*. On Mather's biographies, see also Van Cromphout, "Cotton Mather as Plutarchan Biographer"; Watters, "Biographical Technique in Cotton Mather's *Magnalia*"; Manierre, "Cotton Mather and the Biographical Parallel"; and Gay, *A Loss of Mastery*, 53–87. On the English roots of the genre, see Haller, *Rise of Puritanism*, 100–108; on the tradition of saints' lives, see Heffernan, *Sacred Biography*.

20. Miller, *Brief Retrospect*, 2:150; Samuel Johnson, *The Rambler*, no. 60 (October 13, 1750), in *The Works of Samuel Johnson* (Oxford: Talboys and Wheeler, 1825), 2:287–88. In *The Idler*, no. 84 (Saturday, November 24, 1759), Johnson compared biography to romance and history—much as would later American critics—and argued that autobiography was the truest form of biography. These essays first appeared as American imprints in 1803, but were widely available in America before then in London imprints and newspaper excerpts. The psychological element of Johnson's biographical theory—the notion that a faithful biography would accurately reveal the inner workings of its subject's mind— was less prevalent among American critics than the moral element, at least in the first

decades of the nineteenth century. On Johnson's concept of biography, see especially Brownley, "Johnson's *Lives of the English Poets*"; Altick, *Lives and Letters,* 46–57; Nicolson, *Development of English Biography,* 80–83; Stauffer, *Art of Biography in Eighteenth-Century England,* 386–402; and Parke, *Samuel Johnson and Biographical Thinking.*

21. "Biography," *Monthly Register, Magazine, and Review of the United States* 2 (December 1806): 33–37. A similar statement appeared in the *Portico* a decade later: review of William Dunlap, *The Life of the Late Charles Brockden Brown, The Portico* 1 (May 1816): 382. Dryden's introduction was quoted in "American Biography," *American Quarterly Review,* 1–2. Johnson was not the only British source of early American biographical criticism. Boswell's *Life of Johnson* (1791) provided a controversial model full of "domestick privacies," and critics also drew on Dryden's introduction to Plutarch's *Lives* and on Vicesimus Knox's *Essays, Moral and Literary.* Knox's essay "Cursory Thoughts on Biography" formed the bulk of an article in *New-England Galaxy and Masonic Magazine* 1 (October 10, 1817): 1. Boswell won mixed reviews: some critics found his work "unrivalled and inimitable," but others rejected his methods either as overly intrusive or as merely dull when applied to less intriguing subjects than Johnson. See "American Biography," *American Quarterly Review* 1 (March 1827): 6; *Monthly Anthology, and Boston Review* 4 (May 1807): 277; Miller, *Brief Retrospect,* 2:152–53. In addition, several magazines published a parody of Boswell called "Lesson in Biography; or How to Write the Life of One's Friend": *New-York Magazine; or, Literary Repository* 4 (November 1793): 667–71; *Companion and Weekly Miscellany* 1 (November 3, 1804): 36–38; *Literary Magazine and American Register* 6 (August 1806): 99–103.

22. Backus, "An Oration on Biography," 21; "On the Utility of Biography," *Literary and Philosophical Repertory* 1 (April 1812): 46–47. Early American novels routinely identified their narratives as "founded on fact" or as "tales of truth"; the original title of the best-selling *Charlotte Temple* was *Charlotte: A Tale of Truth.* The critique of novel reading is discussed in Davidson, *Revolution and the Word,* esp. chap. 3, and Kerber, *Women of the Republic,* 236–45.

23. Michael T. Gilmore, "Eulogy as Symbolic Biography," 131; "Biography," *Literary Tablet* 1 (August 6, 1803): 2; "On Biography," *Weekly Visitant,* 89; "American Biographical Works," *Analectic Magazine* 4 (August 1814): 174; review of *Delaplaine's Repository, Portico* 2 (October 1816): 286; see also "On Biography," *Athenaeum* 1 (1814): 78. Because biographical critics in the early republic tended to define "truth" negatively, against the flaws of novels and eulogies, it should be noted that novels and eulogies violated "truth" differently. In a novel, the entire story sprang from an author's imagination. In eulogy, the foundation—the life being commemorated—was real, even if the eulogist idealized it. But these complaints rarely moved toward a positive conception of "truth," based on the biographer's method of gathering or authenticating evidence; that would emerge later. If critics of this period wanted biographers to portray subjects as they truly were, their only hints of method were the inclusion of domestic habits and minor blemishes, and a depiction of character founded on actual acquaintance with the subject.

24. "Biography," *Monthly Register, Magazine, and Review of the United States* 2 (December 1806): 34; Backus, "Oration on Biography," 19; "Biography," *Monthly Register* 2 (December 1806): 35.

25. Even a favorable commentator in the *General Repository and Review* blamed Marshall's deficiencies as a historian on the fact that he had inaccurately deemed it a biography: "His work is styled biographical, but is in fact historical; and the author, by assuming for it

only the former modest character, which it does not in fact deserve, appears to have been less careful to perfect it in the latter." "Life of Judge Marshall," *Port Folio* 5 (January 1815): 5; *Monthly Anthology, and Boston Review* 5 (June 1808): 261; "Biography," *New-England Galaxy, and Masonic Magazine* 1 (October 10, 1817): 1; *General Repository and Review* 3 (January 1813): 109; "American Biography," *American Quarterly Review*, 4–5.

26. "Biography," *New-England Galaxy and Masonic Magazine* 1 (October 10, 1817): 1; review of *Delaplaine's Repository, Portico* 2 (October 1816): 282; "Memoirs of the Late George Wythe, Esquire," *American Gleaner and Virginia Magazine* 1 (January 24, 1807): 1.

27. Thomas Woodward, *The Columbian Plutarch: Or, an Exemplification of Several Distinguished American Characters* (Philadelphia: Clark and Raser, 1819), iv–v; Thomas J. Rogers, *A New American Biographical Dictionary: Or, Remembrancer of the Departed Heroes and Statesmen of America* (Easton, Pa.: T. J. Rogers, 1813). A similar combination of biographical theory and national assertiveness appeared in Wilmer, *American Nepos*, v–vi.

28. Review of *Life of Brown, Portico* 1 (May 1816): 383; Samuel Stanhope Smith, review of *Delaplaine's Repository, Analectic* 8 (September 1816): 208–9.

29. David Humphreys, *An Essay on the Life of the Honorable Major-General Israel Putnam: Addressed to the State Society of the Cincinnati in Connecticut* (Middletown, Conn.: Printed by Moses H. Woodward, for Hudson and Goodwin, Hartford, 1794), 7, 18; Samuel L. Knapp, *Memoirs of General Lafayette: With an Account of His Visit to America* (Boston: E. G. House, 1824), iv; "American Biographical Works," *Analectic Magazine* 4 (August 1814): 174; Thomas Wilson, *The Biography of the Principal American Military and Naval Heroes: Comprehending Details of Their Achievements during the Revolutionary and Late Wars* (New York: John Low, 1817), 9.

30. Greene, *America's Heroes*, 35–56; Gould, "Representative Men," 89; Buell, *New England Literary Culture*, 225. On the cultural entrepreneurs of the early republic and their multiple purposes, see Ellis, *After the Revolution*.

31. [Henry James Pye], *The Democrat: Or, Intrigues and Adventures of Jean Le Noir* (New York: James Rivington, 1795), v–vi; James Cheetham, *The Life of Thomas Paine, Author of Common Sense, the Crisis, Rights of Man, &c.&c.&c.* (New York: Southwick and Pelsue, 1809); Fruchtman, *Thomas Paine, Apostle of Freedom*, 395. On the Cheetham-Paine feud, see Fruchtman, 394–95, 428–33. On Jefferson's response to Marshall's biography, see Freeman, "Slander, Poison, Whispers, and Fame," 25–28.

32. Cheetham, *Life of Thomas Paine*, xxiii; Fruchtman, *Thomas Paine*, 395. The lawsuit received considerable coverage in the newspapers, and at least three pamphlets reprinted the speech made by Madame Bonneville's attorney: *Speech of Counsellor Sampson, on the Trial of James Cheetham, for Libelling Madame Bonneville, in His Life of Thomas Paine, with a Short Sketch of the Trial* (New York: Charles Holt, 1810); *Speech of Counsellor Sampson, on the Trial of James Cheetham, for Libelling Madame Bonneville, in His Life of Thomas Paine, with a Short Sketch of the Trial* (Portsmouth [N.H.]: William Weeks, 1810); *Speech of Counsellor Sampson: With an Introduction, to the Trial of James Cheetham, Esq. for a Libel on Mrs. Margaret Brazier Bonneville, in His Memoirs of Thomas Paine* (Philadelphia: John Sweeny, 1810).

33. Wilmer, *American Nepos*, 298–303. For the notion that collective recognition was a particularly republican form of commemoration, see Fortune, "Portraits of Virtue and Genius," which offers a similar interpretation of the collective portrait pantheons.

34. Also, many of the periodicals that championed Johnsonian ideas about biography (like periodicals generally in this era) ceased publication within their first years, so that it is

difficult to know whether they would have mounted sustained critiques of American biographies.

35. For information on Delaplaine's early career and difficulties in publishing the *Repository,* see Marshall, "Golden Age of Illustrated Biographies," 32–45.

36. *Poulson's American Daily Advertiser* (Philadelphia), July 26, 1816; *Southern Patriot, and Commercial Advertiser* (Charleston), July 26, 1816, reprinted from *Philadelphia True American.*

37. *Port Folio* 4th ser., 2 (September 1816): 259; *Portico* 2 (October 1816), 286, 293, and passim. See also *Analectic Magazine and Naval Chronicle* 8 (September 1816): 193–209.

38. S. [Samuel Stanhope Smith], review of *Delaplaine's Repository, Analectic* 8 (September 1816): 193–209 and passim. Smith had been Caldwell's antagonist since at least 1811, when Caldwell had written a book attacking Smith's view of racial differences. The conflict was so heated that when Smith died in 1819, some of his friends blamed Caldwell. See Horsman, *Race and Manifest Destiny,* 99, 116–17.

39. C. [Charles Caldwell], *The Author Turned Critic: Or, the Reviewer Reviewed, Being a Reply to a Feeble and Unfounded Attack on Delaplaine's Repository, in the Analectic Magazine and Naval Chronicle, for the Month of September 1816* (Philadelphia, 1816), 5–7, 12, 15. The attribution of the review to Smith and the response to Caldwell appear in Marshall, "Golden Age of Illustrated Biographies," 39, 42. Although twenty-two years Smith's junior, Caldwell addressed Smith as an immature and inexperienced critic throughout the pamphlet.

40. Smith, review of Delaplaine, 199; Caldwell, *Author Turned Critic,* 6.

41. *Portico* 2 (December 1816): 514.

42. *Analectic* 10 (September 1817): 485–88.

43. The criticisms appeared in *United States Gazette* 52 (November 6, 1817): 1–2, in an article reprinted from the *New-York Evening Post* that also appeared in *Boston Weekly Messenger* 7 (November 13, 1817); *Boston Daily Advertiser* 19 (November 6, 1817); and *New-York Evening Post,* December 20, 1817. Defenses of the *Repository* included another article in *United States Gazette* 52 (November 6, 1817): 3–4; *New York Daily Advertiser,* October 28, 1817; and *Weekly Aurora* (Philadelphia) 8 (November 3, 1817): 294.

44. *New-York Evening Post,* December 20, 1817; *Weekly Aurora* (Philadelphia) 8 (November 3, 1817): 294; *Democratic Press,* ca. November 1817, reprinted in *United States Gazette* 52 (November 6, 1817). The other article that offered point-by-point refutations of periodical critics' charges was the one reprinted from the *Democratic Press* by the *United States Gazette* 52 (November 6, 1817).

45. Delaplaine's project expired after its third installment in early 1819, but not because of critical censure. High production costs, slow sales, an inadequate distribution network beyond Philadelphia, and ultimately the depression of 1819 killed the *Repository;* see Marshall, "Golden Age of Illustrated Biographies," 44. Almost no literary magazines ever reviewed Weems's work, and the parson's volume inhabited a literary world quite different from that of the Philadelphia literati. It is thus perhaps ironic that the *Portico* wrote this in its scathing 1816 review of the *Repository:* "The 'Life of Washington,' written 'by the Rev. M. L. Weems,' and to be found in almost every school-room, a plain, unaspiring duodecimo, will be regarded, by every lover of true biography, with ten times more veneration, than the pompous quarto pages, which bear that title in the *Repository.*" *Portico* 2 (October 1816): 292.

46. The best short biography of Wirt is Robert, "William Wirt, Virginian." Discussions of his biography of Henry appear in Hankins, "Puritans, Patriots, and Panegyric," 106–9;

Cash, "Biography and Southern Culture," 14–22; William Robert Taylor, "William Wirt and the Legend of the Old South," 477–93; and William R. Taylor, *Cavalier and Yankee*, 67–94. The most famous part of Wirt's book, Henry's "liberty or death" speech, has been the subject of continuing debate and derision among historians; see, for instance, McCants, "The Authenticity of William Wirt's Version of Patrick Henry's 'Liberty or Death' Speech," 387–402. The standard full-length biography remains John P. Kennedy, *Memoirs of the Life of William Wirt, Attorney General of the United States*, 2 vols. (Philadelphia: Lea and Blanchard, 1849). Kennedy's biography is largely a compilation of Wirt's letters, which Kennedy edited from the originals now at the Maryland Historical Society and the Library of Congress. Whenever possible, I quote from the original letters; quotations may therefore deviate from Kennedy.

47. Wirt's oratorical vision is summarized well in Hample, "William Wirt's Familiar Essays," 25–41.

48. On the composition, views, and Virginian consciousness of this elite, see Richard Beale Davis, *Intellectual Life in Jefferson's Virginia*, esp. 77–118, 257–94. Davis places Wirt squarely within this group here and in *A Colonial Southern Bookshelf*.

49. Wirt to St. George Tucker, January 31, 1805; Wirt to Benjamin Edwards, March 17, 1805; Wirt to Elizabeth Gamble Wirt, May 19, 1805; all in WW-MdHS, reel 1. See also Wirt to Elizabeth Gamble Wirt, April 16, 1805, WW-MdHS, reel 1. On his absences from home for research, see Wirt to Elizabeth Gamble Wirt, August 9, 1805, WW-MdHS, reel 1. Wirt also, however, told a fellow professional man that he did not "mean to play the Plutarch to the injury of my professional pursuits," suggesting that he knew authorship brought limited returns. Wirt to Benjamin Edwards, March 17, 1805, WW-MdHS, reel 1. Collective biographies that employed similar rhetoric included Wilmer, *American Nepos*, and Woodward, *Columbian Plutarch*. See also Shaffer, *Politics of History*, 2, 8–9, 14–22. On the laudable passion for fame, see Adair, "Fame and the Founding Fathers," 3–26; Stourzh, *Alexander Hamilton and the Idea of Republican Government*, chap. 3. Adair describes the particularly desirable sort of fame achieved by the historian who would "praise virtuous behavior that deserves immortal remembrance and . . . damn infamous actions"—a concept of fame Wirt may have known from his reading of Tacitus (22).

50. The voluminous literature of the "republican synthesis" and its critics is summarized well in Rodgers, "Republicanism: the Career of a Concept." The definition of "The sacrifice of individual interests to the greater good of the whole" as "the essence of republicanism" and of citizens' public virtue as indispensable for maintaining that essence is Gordon Wood's; see *Creation of the American Republic*, 53, 65–70. Two central historiographical questions have involved whether "republicanism" indeed lay at the heart of American revolutionary and postrevolutionary ideology (a contention disputed by Joyce Appleby and others) and when republicanism gave way to "liberal" notions of the American state and society. The latter question is more important here: I agree with Steven Watts that the years when William Wirt planned his life of Henry were the period in which the definitions and language of republicanism were being recast into forms resembling liberalism. See Watts, *Republic Reborn*.

51. On the development of political parties in Virginia in the 1790s, see Beeman, *The Old Dominion and the New Nation;* for Wirt's appointment to replace the Federalist clerk of the house, see 212. Kathryn R. Malone, "Revolutionary Republicanism in Early National

Virginia," focuses largely on issues of banking and states' rights, rather than on partisan development or cultural change.

52. Isaac, *Transformation of Virginia,* esp. 243–69; for Henry's connection to evangelicalism, see also Charles L. Cohen, "The 'Liberty or Death' Speech." On other challenges to the existing social order on "republican" grounds, see Shalhope, *Roots of Democracy,* chap. 6. On Tyler's *The Contrast,* see Shalhope, 77–79; on Brackenridge's *Modern Chivalry,* see Watts, *Republic Reborn, 42–58.*

53. Wirt to Thomas Jefferson, July 23, 1805, TJ-UVa, reel 5; Wirt to St. George Tucker, January 31, 1805, WW-MdHS, reel 1.

54. St. George Tucker to Wirt, April 4, 1813, in Kennedy, *Life of Wirt,* 1:353–55.

55. William Wirt, "Memoirs of Patrick Henry," Manuscripts Division, University of Virginia Library, Charlottesville, typescript pp. 1–3. Further references are to pages in the typescript.

56. Ibid., 6, 14–21.

57. Ibid., 6. Several historians have noted the connection between Wirt's humble beginnings and his portrayal of Henry's; see Robert, "William Wirt, Virginian," 433, and Taylor, "William Wirt and the Legend of the Old South," 482–83. It is worth noting that Henry's origins were not as humble as Wirt's: Henry's father, John, had married a wealthy widow and become a plantation owner and member of the backcountry gentry. By exaggerating the poverty of Henry's origins, Wirt may have been suggesting the potential for men like himself to reach the elite through their own achievement. (Of course, Wirt married into the elite, much as John Henry had.) On the Henry family, see Mayer, *Son of Thunder,* 19–31.

58. In a letter likely written to St. George Tucker in early 1813, Wirt explained why he had laid the Henry biography aside for several years. Even though he consulted every reliable source, he was unable to reconcile conflicting statements about Henry's character (and even about the basic facts of public events). Tucker implored him in 1813 to complete the project before the surviving Revolutionary figures and their acquaintances, the principal sources of information, died. Wirt agreed, and took up the work again because he had acquired new factual information and believed that not writing the biography would wrong Henry's memory and injure the "rising generation"—which, as he expressed in his *Old Bachelor* essays, now more than ever needed the instruction derived from the lives of their early leaders. Wirt, fragment of letter, WW-LC; St. George Tucker to Wirt, April 4, 1813, in Kennedy, *Life of Wirt,* 1:353–55. Because the issues in Wirt's letter are connected with those in Tucker's to him, and because Tucker there refers to a letter from Wirt not otherwise extant in WW-LC or WW-MdHS, it is quite possible that the fragment is Wirt's letter to Tucker of early 1813. On Wirt's philosophy in the *Old Bachelor* essays, see Richard Beale Davis, *Intellectual Life in Jefferson's Virginia,* 284.

59. Wirt continued to ask Henry's acquaintances to describe Henry's appearance and speaking style, and he tried to determine whether Henry had read Livy every year as he had claimed. Jefferson denied that this was possible, given Henry's intellectual indolence. Jefferson to Wirt, September 4, 1816, TJ-UVa, reel 5; Wirt to Jefferson, WW-MdHS, reel 3.

60. Jefferson to Wirt, September 29, 1816, TJ-UVa, reel 5.

61. Wirt to Jefferson, September 10, October 23, 1816, WW-MdHS, reel 3.

62. William Wirt, *Sketches of the Life and Character of Patrick Henry* (orig. 1817), 7th ed. (New York: M'Elrath, Bangs, and Co., 1834), 207.

63. Wirt to Dabney Carr, September 13, 1817, WW-MdHS, reel 3; Robert, "William Wirt, Virginian," 425. Advance announcements of Wirt's work included *Port Folio* 4th ser., 6 (August 1815): 183–84, which included the publisher's announcement; "Domestic Literary Intelligence," *Analectic* 6 (July 1815): 83; "Remarks on the Character of Patrick Henry: To the Editor of the Analectic Magazine," *Analectic* 6 (November 1815): 376–82.

64. As Michael Warner has pointed out, anonymity and pseudonymity were at the heart of the republican public sphere of eighteenth-century America, for these forms of authorship served to distance views from the particular individuals who espoused them, to represent those views as public sentiments distinct from their authors' private interests. Warner argues that the eighteenth-century public sphere frayed by century's end with the advent of the novel, which suggested new forms of discourse, whether "liberal" or "mass-cultural," that lay outside the "civic arena" and were thus difficult for the republican conception to accommodate. See *Letters of the Republic,* 150–51. The issue of biographical anonymity suggests another source of tension in the earlier public sphere: the bitterly partisan debates of the early republic, in which writing history and biography could assume an overtly Federalist or Republican cast. Marshall's *Life of Washington,* whose Federalist bias spurred Jefferson to consider a response, was the most controversial case; see Freeman, "Slander, Poison, Whispers, and Fame."

65. Wirt, *Sketches,* v.

66. Ibid., 25. For Wirt's continued consideration of what his friend Tucker called "the epistolary stile," see Tucker's notes in response to a letter from Wirt dated August 16, 1815, in "William Wirt's Life of Patrick Henry," *WMQ,* 1st ser., 22 (April 1914): 250–57.

67. Wirt to Joseph Delaplaine, November 5, 1818, William Wirt Collection, Barrett Library, Special Collections Department, University of Virginia; Wirt to Jefferson, October 23, 1816, WW-MdHS, reel 3; Wirt, *Sketches,* 404–12, 418–21, 443.

68. Wirt, *Sketches,* 33, 83, 312. Wirt employed flowery language in part because this was his wont, a tendency he discouraged in his protégés and tried to correct in himself. At the same time, his metaphorical language answered a biographical problem: very few transcripts of Henry's speeches survived, and even written transcripts could not do justice to the feelings that Henry's oratory *as spoken language* evoked in listeners. Wirt may have sought to substitute a form of written language designed to evoke feeling for an unrecoverable spoken presence. On Wirt's tendency toward flowery language and his attempts to "curb" it in his own legal oratory, see Richard Beale Davis, *Intellectual Life in Jefferson's Virginia,* 383. Wirt wrote repeatedly that written words could not capture Henry's oratorical power; see *Sketches,* 281–82, 298–99, 331. It is worth noting, too, that Henry was accused in his own day of using artifice to convince and persuade—although his artifice was the impression of being "natural," while Wirt's was the proliferation of metaphors and allusions. Quite possibly, what was unrecoverable about Henry's oratory was as much its context as its peculiar power: as Charles L. Cohen and Rhys Isaac suggest, its religious references linked it to the evangelical awakening in Revolutionary-era Virginia; its plain style was the emerging language of evangelical religion. Cohen, "The 'Liberty or Death' Speech"; Isaac, *Transformation of Virginia,* 267–69.

69. Wirt, *Sketches,* 52–53, 72–73, 433. The image of Henry as man of the people begins in the discussion of the parsons' controversy, 45.

70. Wirt's comparisons of Henry and Demosthenes appear, for instance, in *Sketches,* 54, 125.

For discussions of the early-national proclivity to model American heroes as "Idols of Order" in classical garb, see Greene, *America's Heroes*, 35–56.

71. Wirt, *Sketches*, 131. Wirt's portrayal of Henry on this score may have owed something to Edmund Randolph's unpublished manuscript history of Virginia, which Wirt consulted. Randolph described Henry's assaults against the older Virginia aristocracy—but suggested that Henry represented "the real Virginian planter": "He was respectable in his parentage, but the patrimony of his ancestors and of himself was too scanty to feed ostentation or luxury." Thus a firebrand of the 1760s and 1770s need not remain so once the traditional aristocracy, dependent on "the favor of the king," had been displaced by "real" planters. Edmund Randolph, *History of Virginia*, 178. For Wirt's consultation of Randolph's work, see *Sketches*, xi.

72. Wirt, *Sketches*, 399. On the fears that parties could destroy the republic, see John R. Howe Jr., "Republican Thought and the Political Violence of the 1790s."

73. Wirt, *Sketches*, 30, 243–44, 396.

74. Ibid., 280. Wirt's position might usefully be contrasted with that of another cultural producer of these years, the painter Charles Willson Peale. Peale's 1822 self-portrait *The Artist in His Museum* depicted the aging artist lifting the curtain to reveal visitors, young and old, observing specimens of American heroism and wildlife in the frames and cases that lined his museum's walls. In this museum generations could presumably unite, but on the orderly, Enlightenment terms that Peale—the oldest figure in the picture—prescribed. Wirt's position was different. The men who provided him with information and whose approval of his book he most coveted, like Jefferson and Adams and Tucker, all reached adulthood before the Revolutionary War. Most Americans alive in 1817 had been born well after the war; indeed, the "rising generation" of young Virginians to whom Wirt dedicated his book was the one born after the adoption of the Constitution. Wirt belonged to the generation between. Even if he like Peale hoped to stem Americans' declension from classical and republican ideals, he did so from a more difficult position, for he recognized the problem of bridging generationally disparate audiences.

75. Charles Caldwell, *Memoirs of the Life and Campaigns of the Hon. Nathaniel Greene* (Philadelphia: Robert Desilver, 1819), ix, xv, 400.

76. "Remarks on the Character of Patrick Henry," 381. Jefferson to Wirt, November 12, 1816, TJ-UVa, reel 5; Wirt to Dabney Carr, September 13, 1817, August 20, 1815, January 12, 1816; all in WW-MdHS, reel 3. Intriguingly, both Jefferson and Wirt used the word "tomahawk" to describe how European critics would treat the book.

77. Richard Morris Jr. to Wirt, January 17, 1817, WW-LC, reel 1; William Brockenbrough to Wirt, February 10, 1817, WW-LC, reel 1; Wirt to Richard Morris Jr., January 19, 1817, in Kennedy, *Life of Wirt*, 1:367–68. The book itself implied that Wirt wanted readers inside *and* outside Virginia: he both referred specifically to Virginian readers and suggested a more national audience. See Wirt, *Sketches*, 245, 275, 280–81n, 412.

78. The quoted letter from a subscriber appeared in *Poulson's American Daily Advertiser* 46 (November 13, 1817). The other subscriber's letter appeared four days later. James Webster's first advertisement in the *United States Gazette* appeared in volume 52 (November 4, 1817); it ran for the next two days as well. Another short article in the same paper on November 12 described Webster's donation of books, including Wirt's, to the Philadelphia Athenaeum—another form of publicity. Library catalogs containing Wirt's *Sketches*

include *Charter, Bye-Laws, and Catalogue of Books, of the Charlestown [N.H.] Social Library, January 1, 1818* (Bellows Falls, Vt., 1818); *A Catalogue of the Books Belonging to the Charleston [S.C.] Library Society* (Charleston, 1826), 260; and *A Catalogue of the Books Belonging to Charlotte Social Library, January 1, 1826* (Chittenden City, Vt., 1826). For reviews of and excerpts from Wirt's life of Henry, see *Richmond Enquirer* 14 (November 18, 21, 25, and 28, 1817); *Alexandria* (Va.) *Gazette,* November 21, 22, 24, 25, 26, 28, and 29, December 8, 10, and 11, 1817 (much of this reprinted the material from the *Richmond Enquirer*); *National Intelligencer* (Washington, D.C.), December 10, 1817 (reprinting a review from the *National Advocate*); *Independent Chronicle and Boston Patriot,* December 3, 1817 (reprinting the same review); *Albany Argus,* November 28, December 2, 1817 (reprinting review and extracts from the *Richmond Enquirer*); *Southern Patriot, and Commercial Advertiser* (Charleston), November 22, 25, 26, and 28, December 18, 19, 1817 (the newspaper's own review, followed by extracts from the *Richmond Enquirer*); *Boston Weekly Messenger,* December 4, 1817 (extract from the *Richmond Enquirer*); *Boston Daily Advertiser,* November 28 (the same extract) and 29, 1817; *Commercial Advertiser* (New York), November 25, 1817; *New York Daily Advertiser,* November 27, 1817; and *Portico* 4 (December 1817): 428–40.

Joseph Delaplaine himself also praised Wirt's work, in a letter in November 1818. In some ways, Wirt's and Delaplaine's circles overlapped: a Philadelphia publisher produced Wirt's book; many magazines reviewed both the *Repository* and the life of Henry, using the same set of standards. However, while Delaplaine was a printer never without new schemes for making money, Wirt was a self-consciously genteel Virginia lawyer, who masked his economic concerns with the trappings of hospitality and classical education. Delaplaine wanted Wirt, now attorney general of the United States, to participate—for a small fee—in a portrait gallery of distinguished Americans that he grandly called "Delaplaine's Panzographia." Wirt turned Delaplaine down. Wirt may well not have wanted his portrait on a wall, visible to any curiosity-seeker willing to pay an admission fee. The fame associated with Delaplaine's scheme was of entirely the wrong sort. Justifiable, republican fame arose out of one's actions and writings: serving the people well, or commemorating a Revolutionary worthy in biography. Certainly Wirt hoped his book would sell widely—witness his longing descriptions of how well novels sold—and expressed annoyance with his publisher for not making enough copies of the initial edition available to Virginia towns where it would sell best. But the reputation that mattered most to him depended on authenticity, not popularity. Wirt to Delaplaine, November 5, 1818, William Wirt Collection, Barrett Library, Special Collections Department, University of Virginia.

79. Several reviewers echoed Jefferson's criticism on this issue: one stated that "there is too much paint, and ornament, and—we must add,—not a little glitter"; another wrote that Wirt's "attempts to dazzle have more generally the effect of confusing." Jefferson to Wirt, November 16, 1816, and September 29, 1816, both in TJ-UVa, reel 5. The account of Jefferson's harsher comments about the book appeared in George Ticknor Curtis, *Life of Daniel Webster* (Boston, 1870), 1:585, cited in William R. Taylor, *Cavalier and Yankee,* 68. Criticism of Wirt's literary ornamentation appeared in *Port Folio,* 5th ser., 4 (December 1817): 521; and *American Monthly Magazine and Critical Review* 2 (April 1818): 422.

80. Wirt to Dabney Carr, August 20, 1815, WW-MdHS, reel 3.

81. Jay B. Hubbell, *The South in American Literature, 1607–1900* (Durham, N.C.: Duke University Press, 1954), quoted in William R. Taylor, *Cavalier and Yankee,* 69. On September 24, 1816,

Wirt wrote to William Pope, "As to Johnny Taylor, I shall do my duty, and let him do his worst" (WW-MdHS, reel 3).

82. Wirt to Francis W. Gilmer, January 26, 1817, quoted in Kennedy, *Life of Wirt,* 2:15. For an example of the Virginia gentry's disdain of Weems, see St. George Tucker to Wirt, April 4, 1813, quoted in ibid., 1:316.

83. Wirt to James Webster, January 13, 1818, WW-LC, reel 4. Adams to Wirt, January 5, 1818; Wirt to Adams, January 12, 1818; Adams to Wirt, March 7, 1818; Adams, n.d.; all quoted in Kennedy, *Life of Wirt,* 2:44–54.

84. John Adams to William Tudor, n.d., quoted in Kennedy, *Life of Wirt,* 2:53.

85. Two recent historians have described the shifts in Virginia society between the pre-Revolutionary era and the early nineteenth century. Isaac's *Transformation of Virginia* sketches how a gentry-dominated society became permeated by evangelical religion and revolutionary politics in the 1760s and 1770s, and how by the 1790s those forces had made even the elite itself less culturally assertive and more introspective. In *The Pursuit of Happiness,* Jan Lewis traces changing elite ideas about family, love, and success from the immediate post-Revolutionary period into the 1830s, finding Virginians of a younger generation increasingly forced to work for their living, more uncertain of their future prospects than their parents had been, and turning for comfort toward familial love rather than older forms of political, economic, and social assertion. Both Isaac and Lewis hint at the development of a "private sphere" often associated with the nineteenth-century northern middle class. Lewis's version especially suggests why Virginians of a younger generation might seek tales of the state's "age of glory": such myths could become another source of comfort in an uncertain world. Conversely, they might just as easily remind nineteenth-century Virginians of their own distance from that world, and reinforce the very insecurities that Lewis describes.

86. [Jared Sparks], "Mr. Wirt's Life of Patrick Henry," *NAR* 6 (March 1818): 296, 309.

FABLES OF PARSON WEEMS

1. Kennedy, *Life of Wirt,* 1:352–53.

2. *Monthly Magazine and American Review* 3 (September 1800): 210; *Monthly Anthology, and Boston Review* 9 (1810): 414–19; both quoted in Skeel, *Mason Locke Weems,* 1:14, 55.

3. Weems to C. P. Wayne, December 14, 1802; Weems to Carey, May 24, 1807; both printed in Skeel, *Mason Locke Weems,* 2:256, 362.

4. Weems to Carey, January 12 or 13, 1800, printed in Skeel, *Mason Locke Weems,* 2:126; M. L. Weems, *A History, of the Life and Death, Virtues and Exploits, of General George Washington* (Georgetown: Green and English, 1800), dedication page.

5. Crawford, "Images of Authority, Strategies of Control," 61–74; Fliegelman, *Prodigals and Pilgrims,* 201; Watts, *Republic Reborn,* 142–44.

6. Weems to Carey, May 24, 1807, printed in Skeel, *Mason Locke Weems,* 2:362.

7. Mason L. Weems, *The Life of Washington,* ed. Marcus Cunliffe (Cambridge, Mass.: Belknap Press of Harvard University Press, 1962), 1–3. This edition is a reprinting of Weems's ninth edition (Philadelphia: Mathew Carey, 1809).

8. Weems, *Life of Washington,* 7, 9, 19, 21, 104, 180.

9. Skeel, *Mason Locke Weems,* 1:100–101, 2:427; Marcus Cunliffe, "Introduction," in Weems, *Life of Washington,* xxvii–xxviii. The South Carolinian author William Gilmore Simms

was the observer who had read Horry's manuscript as well as Weems's biography; see Simms, *Views and Reviews, Second Series* (New York: Wiley and Putnam, 1845), 123–41. On Weems's desire to see his works used as schoolbooks, see Christopher Harris, "Mason Locke Weems's *Life of George Washington*," 92–101; and Harris, "Character Portraits of American Military Heroes of the Revolution." See also Weems to Thomas Jefferson, February 1, 1809, asking for a recommendation of his life of Washington as a schoolbook, and Weems to Horry, February 5, 1809, expressing a similar hope that the life of Marion would "become a school book in South Carolina" (Skeel, *Mason Locke Weems*, 2:389–90).

10. Abraham Lincoln, *The Collected Works of Abraham Lincoln*, 4:235–36.

11. Susan Warner, *The Wide, Wide World* (orig. 1850), ed. Jane Tompkins (New York: Feminist Press, 1987), 329–30.

12. Warner, *Wide, Wide World*, 329, 506, 516.

CHAPTER TWO

1. "Romance Biographies," *Christian Examiner* 73 (September 1862): 175; Evert A. Duyckinck, "Biography" (review of *Essays, Biographical and Critical*, by Henry T. Tuckerman), *NAR* 84 (April 1857): 406. Explanations of the interest in biography that emphasize individualism, particularly the romantic individualism of the 1830s, include Haselton, "The Fairest Meed: Biography in America before 1865." Scholars who link the development of American biography to nationalism and national history include Callcott, *History in the United States*, 97–101; and Kammen, *A Season of Youth*, 40–43.

   Information on the proliferation of biographies after 1820 is drawn from O'Neill, *Biography by Americans*. According to O'Neill's bibliography—which he admitted was "incomplete" (particularly in recording "only the important books in the case of famous men"), which listed only biographies written by Americans and not American editions of European works, and which did not distinguish between nationally produced works that went through numerous editions and local memorial volumes printed just once— approximately 40 biographies by Americans appeared before 1800, approximately 60 between 1800 and 1820, approximately 240 between 1821 and 1840, and approximately 630 between 1841 and 1860. While the rate of increase in biographies was not as great as that in novels, it was nonetheless substantial—and likely more substantial than O'Neill's listings indicate—far outpacing the growth of the American population. On the number of American-written novels, see Zboray, "A Fictive People," 4–5. On the development of the novel in the United States, see Davidson, *Revolution and the Word;* and Winans, "Novel-Reading Public," 267–75.

2. The role of nineteenth-century developments in publishing and distribution in creating a national reading population has long been recognized. The classic statement of this view is Charvat, *Literary Publishing in America,* chap. 1. Changes in publication technology are described in Lawrence C. Wroth and Rollo G. Silver, "Book Production and Distribution from the American Revolution to the War between the States," in Lehmann-Haupt, *The Book in America,* esp. 71–85, 119–29; and Tebbel, *A History of Book Publishing in the United States,* 203–61. Ronald J. Zboray, *A Fictive People,* explores the distribution of books and offers useful correctives to the earlier views. Gilreath, "American Book Distribution," 538–53, provides an overview of both the history of book distribution from the Revolution to the Civil War and the historiography of book distribution.

3. Established in 1830, the Family Library contained 52 volumes by 1833 and 187 (representing 127 titles) a dozen years later. Part of its allure lay in its price: each volume cost forty-five cents, the entire series eighty dollars. This low cost was possible because most of the early volumes were reprints of European works, which Harper could republish free of copyright fees. The series' appeal also lay in the chronological and geographical breadth of its subjects. See Exman, *The Brothers Harper*, 33; "Harper's Popular Libraries: Harper's Family Library," in *Harper's Illustrated Catalogue of Valuable Standard Works, in the Several Departments of General Literature* (New York: Harper and Brothers, 1848). Harper called its products "standard works" not just because they hoped to sell them but also because their works *were* standard fixtures in social and circulating libraries by 1848.

4. *Catalogue of the Mercantile Library of San Francisco* (San Francisco, 1854); "Catalogue of Books Belonging to Calais Circulating Library," Calais, Vermont (unpublished ledger, 1832–51), Vermont Historical Society, Montpelier, Vermont. The Calais catalog demonstrates how a small rural library (308 volumes) acquired its collection over time. The library began with 70 volumes in 1832, added an average of 30 books a year for the next four years, then averaged just 8 new books a year from 1837 to 1851, with an especially large number of acquisitions in 1845. Thirty-six of the libraries surveyed included some edition of Irving's *Columbus,* which seems to have been the work most common to the libraries. The Mercantile Library of Philadelphia owned five copies, including four different editions. *A Catalogue of the Mercantile Library Company of Philadelphia. Published April, 1850* (Philadelphia, 1850), 254. The information in this paragraph is based primarily on research in the Public Library Catalogues Collection, AAS. On the development of various classes of libraries in this period, see Kaser, *A Book for a Sixpence,* and William Douglas Boyd Jr., "Books for Young Businessmen," both of which suggest that mercantile libraries, established as mutual-improvement societies for young men, possessed proportionally more biographies than did circulating libraries, whose clientele was often heavily female. This may indicate the pervasiveness of the idea (discussed below) that biography could help to form the character of the "self-made man."

5. The 1849 catalog of the American Sunday-School Union, for example, included more than one hundred biographies in its various library series, from the "Very Cheap Library" to a series of books bound in muslin. A few of the Union's biographies dealt with political figures such as Napoleon and Washington, but most were lives of ministers, women, and children. *Catalogue of Books and Other Publications of the American Sunday-School Union, Designed for Sunday-Schools, Juvenile, Family, and Parish Libraries, and for General Reading. No. 36. July, 1849* (Philadelphia: American Sunday-School Union, 1849). On the American Tract Society and American Sunday-School Union, see Thompson, "Printing and Publishing Activities," 81–114. On the dissemination of the societies' works, see Michael H. Harris, " 'Spiritual Cakes upon the Waters,' " 98–120. The locally produced biographies whose places of publication are mentioned are Eli W. Caruthers, *A Sketch of the Life and Character of the Rev. David Caldwell, D.D.* (Greensborough, N.C.: Swaim and Sherwood, 1842); Michael Diehl, *Biography of Rev. Ezra Keller, Founder and First President of Wittenberg College* (Springfield, Ohio: Ruralist Publishing Co., 1859); Philetus Roberts, *Memoir of Mrs. Abigail Roberts: An Account of Her Birth, Early Education, Call to the Ministry* (Irvington, N.J.: Moses Cummings, 1858); and James Wood, *Memoir of Sylvester Scovel, D.D., Late President of Hanover College, Ia.* (New Albany, Ind.: J. B. Anderson, 1851). Other sites of biographical publication outside the major publishing centers (New York, Philadelphia, Boston, and

Cincinnati) included Nashville, Richmond, Utica, Pittsburgh, Savannah, and Hopedale, Massachusetts.

6. *Log Cabin Farmer* (Steubenville, Ohio), July 2, 1840, p. 2, Campaign Newspapers Collection, AAS. On political publishing and newspapers, see Smith, *The Press, Politics, and Patronage.*

7. Worcester County Atheneum Records, 1830–48, Manuscript Collection, AAS. In addition to those mentioned above, the Atheneum's members included future governor John Davis and future mayor Peter Bacon, lawyers Emory Washburn, Thomas Kinnicutt, and others, and ministers Alonzo Hill and George Allen. Most of the members are included in Charles Nutt, *History of Worcester and Its People,* 4 vols. (New York: Lewis Historical Publishing Co., 1919).

8. Constitution and Circulation Records, Benson Female Lending Library, Windsor County, Vermont, Vermont Historical Society, Montpelier, Vermont.

9. *Diary of Christopher Columbus Baldwin, Librarian of the American Antiquarian Society, 1829–1835,* Transactions and Collections of the American Antiquarian Society, no. 8 (Worcester: American Antiquarian Society, 1901), 81, 169.

10. Records of the Female Reading Class, Colchester [Connecticut], February 21, May 22, 1816, CHS. Based on the names mentioned in these records, it is possible to conclude that these women were reading in Samuel Burder's *Memoirs of Eminently Pious Women,* originally published in London in 1815, the year before the Reading Class convened.

11. Centre Missionary Sewing Circle, August 11, 1843, Central Church Records, Octavo Volumes 23 and 24, Manuscript Collection, AAS.

12. Launcelot Minor Blackford diary, ca. 1850, quoted in Cantrell, "The Reading Habits of Ante-Bellum Southerners," 210.

13. Rena L. Vassar, ed., "The Life or Biography of Silas Felton Written by Himself," *PAAS* 69 (October 1959): 129. Blackford diary, 1855, and Mercer diary, August 8, 1858, both quoted in Cantrell, "Reading Habits of Ante-Bellum Southerners," 216–17. John Montgomery Gordon diary, July 14, 1835, quoted in Douglas Gordon, ed., "A Virginian and His Baltimore Diary: Part III," *Maryland Historical Magazine* 51 (September 1956): 226. Felton's other reading included the life of Baron Trenck, Burrough's memoirs, and Lee's memoirs (Vassar, 152–53).

14. Harriet B. Cooke, *Memoirs of My Life Work: The Autobiography of Mrs. Harriet B. Cooke* (New York: Robert Carter, 1858), excerpted in Appleby, *Recollections of the Early Republic,* 236; Lousia May Alcott Journal, June 1857, *The Journals of Louisa May Alcott,* ed. Joel Myerson and Daniel Shealy (Boston: Little, Brown and Co., 1989), 85; David Schenck diary, August 30, 1854, quoted in Cantrell, "Reading Habits of Ante-Bellum Southerners," 216; Maria Mitchell diary, February 15, 1853, quoted in Phebe Mitchell Kendall, comp., *Maria Mitchell: Life, Letters, and Journals* (Boston: Lee and Shepard, 1896), 25–26. According to Susan K. Harris, "One consistent pattern among women who recorded their reading is an intense interest in biographies of heroic women." Harris, *19th-Century American Women's Novels,* 24.

15. Martha Foster Crawford diary, January 25, 1850; George Gilman Smith diary, April 3, 1856, and "Autobiography," both quoted in Cantrell, "Reading Habits of Ante-Bellum Southerners," 209. Samuel Rodman diary, December 12, 1839, in Zephaniah W. Pease, ed., *The Diary of Samuel Rodman: A New Bedford Chronicle of Thirty-Seven Years, 1821–1859* (New Bedford, Mass.: Reynolds Printing, 1927), 200.

16. Hannah Davis Gale Journal, February 28, 1838, 132, Gale Family Papers, AAS. William Johnson diary, June 9, 1850; Benjamin L. C. Wailes diary, March 22, 1860; Blackford diary, June 1855, July 23, 1852, and July 24, 1850; Alexander Beaufort Meek diary, January 1848; all quoted in Cantrell, "Reading Habits of Ante-Bellum Southerners," 212–21.

The lives of criminals were a popular genre in this period; see, for instance, *The Lives and Exploits of the Banditti and Robbers of All Nations*, 2 vols. (Philadelphia: R. W. Pomeroy, 1839), 10. Like the sensational fiction that rivaled contemporary sentimental literature in popularity, these works substituted a journalistic voyeurism for the moralism of earlier "lives and confessions." See Schiller, *Objectivity and the News;* and Daniel A. Cohen, *Pillars of Salt, Monuments of Grace*. On the nature of sensational fiction, see Reynolds, *Beneath the American Renaissance*. On the tradition of eccentric and criminal biography, see Stauffer, *The Art of Biography in Eighteenth Century England,* 196–231.

17. Horace Mann to Henry Barnard, July 27, 1852, quoted in Mary Tyler Peabody Mann, *Life of Horace Mann,* 2d ed. (Boston: Lee and Shepard, 1865), 376.

18. "Civis," "Art. XII.—Biography," *American Annals of Education and Instruction, and Journal of Literary Institutions* 1 (June 1831): 281; Joel Hawes, *Lectures to Young Men, on the Formation of Character, &c.* (Hartford: Cooke and Co., 1829), 147–48; *The Young Man's Own Book: A Manual of Politeness, Intellectual Improvement, and Moral Deportment* (Philadelphia: Key and Biddle, 1833), 99. Similar messages appear in Henry Ward Beecher, *Seven Lectures to Young Men, on Various Important Subjects* (Indianapolis: T. B. Cutler; Cincinnati: W. H. Moore and Co., 1844), and Isaac Taylor, *Youth's Own Book: Character Essential to Success in Life* (Hartford: Canfield and Robins, 1836). The phrase "confidence men and painted women" is derived from Halttunen's book of that title. The mission of these advice manuals was transatlantic: the biographical work of Samuel Smiles (*Life of George Stephenson, Lives of the Engineers*) and Edwin Paxton Hood represented the same developments in Great Britain. Smiles, whose works were reprinted in the United States, might be considered the British parallel of the American William Makepeace Thayer, discussed below. On Smiles, see Cockshut, *Truth to Life,* 105–24; and Nadel, *Biography: Fiction, Fact, and Form,* 21–30. On Hood, see Maidment, "Popular Exemplary Biography in the Nineteenth Century," 148–67.

19. Halttunen, *Confidence Men and Painted Women,* chaps. 1–3; Watts, *The Republic Reborn,* 113–14; Ryan, *Cradle of the Middle Class,* esp. chap. 4; Kett, *Rites of Passage,* esp. chap. 4; Blumin, *The Emergence of the Middle Class.*

20. Henry Howe, *Memoirs of the Most Eminent American Mechanics: Also, Lives of Distinguished European Mechanics* (New York, 1842), 37–38. Steven Watts locates the origins of the interest in "self-made manhood" earlier, in the late eighteenth century and the first decades of the nineteenth; see *Republic Reborn,* 64–70, 289–92. But the idea reached its apex later. See Wyllie, *The Self-Made Man in America;* and Cawelti, *Apostles of the Self-Made Man.* Cawelti identifies Franklin as "the model for the tradition of the self-made man . . . a new hero, different in character from traditional military, religious, and aristocratic conceptions of human excellence and virtue" (9).

21. *Merchant's Magazine, and Commercial Review* 1 (August 1839): 135; and ibid. 2 (May 1840): 414–15.

22. The development of liberal capitalism, the decline of Revolutionary republicanism, and the relationship between the two have received immense attention from historians over the past two decades. In broadest terms, between the 1790s and 1840s American

society increasingly became dominated by regional markets, which loosened the organic bonds of farming communities and household economies and reinforced the impersonal nature of urban life. The changing patterns of social life encouraged and were reinforced by new cultural ideologies that redefined the concepts of "virtue" and "independence." Virtue, once seen in civic terms as the sacrifice of private interest for the public good, was refocused as self-interest in a society where individual pursuit of self-interest was considered the highest public good. In republican theory, independence denoted each citizen's freedom from economic subservience to another and consequent ability to exercise his own mind in service of the public. Republican theory stipulated that independence was necessary for citizen virtue. In liberal theory, independence was freedom from the bonds of community, the unfettered ability to pursue self-interest. The timing of this transformation in American society and culture is extremely difficult to pinpoint, in large measure because of the shifting meanings of terms and regional and generational differences. A useful synthesis is Rodgers, "Republicanism: The Career of a Concept."

23. [John Frost], *Lives of American Merchants, Eminent for Integrity, Enterprise, and Public Spirit* (New York, 1844), 5–6.

24. "Mercantile Biography: Life and Character of Gideon Lee," *Merchant's Magazine, and Commercial Review* 8 (January 1843): 63; "Mercantile Biography: John Grigg, of Philadelphia," *Merchant's Magazine, and Commercial Review* 25 (July 1851): 37. Joseph F. Kett has noted the increasing presence of childhood in biographies, particularly as "a positive thrust for, rather than merely an indication of, later development." "Adolescence and Youth in Nineteenth-Century America," 98.

25. *Lives of Distinguished Shoemakers* (Portland: Davis and Southworth, 1849), title page and iii.

26. Ibid., iii–iv. In exploring the origins of artisanal biographies in England, Brian Maidment has described a debate among the middle-class moralists who usually wrote such works. The "decisive book in the definition of the genre," G. L. Craik's *The Pursuit of Knowledge Under Difficulties* (1830–31) was the joint project of Craik and the chairman of the Society for the Diffusion of Useful Knowledge, Lord Brougham. In an era when intellectual self-education did not assure financial gain and many self-taught men lived in poverty, Craik hoped to present artisans' pursuit of knowledge as "a socially and politically disinterested activity which provided a reward in itself." Brougham argued for presenting a more direct connection between intellectual and material improvement. Brougham won the debate—and his victory set the stage for more complacently middle-class biographies that made the same connection. "Popular Exemplary Biography in the Nineteenth Century," 154–56.

27. *Lives of Distinguished Shoemakers,* iv, 44–45, 272. Another collection of shoemakers' lives suggested just how close these "artisanal" biographies were to the other varieties of self-made biography. This second collection stressed reading itself as a principal value and argued for shoemakers' biography because shoemakers were "a reading class"—perhaps more so than artisans in other trades. J. Prince, *A Wreath for St. Crispin: Being Sketches of Eminent Shoemakers* (Boston: Bela Marsh, 1848), v.

28. MacGregor, " 'Lords of the Ascendant,' " 15–30.

29. On antebellum political culture, and particularly its dissemination through institutions besides parties, see Baker, *Affairs of Party;* and Daniel Walker Howe, *The Political Culture of the American Whigs.* For an overview of Jacksonian political culture and recent histo-

riography that defines it broadly, see Howe, "The Evangelical Movement and Political Culture."

30. John Henry Eaton, *The Life of Andrew Jackson, Major-General in the Service of the United States: Comprising a History of the War in the South, from the Commencement of the Creek Campaign, to the Termination of Hostilities before New Orleans* (Philadelphia: Samuel F. Bradford, 1824); Eaton, *The Letters of Wyoming, to the People of the United States, on the Presidential Election, and in Favor of Andrew Jackson* (Philadelphia: S. Simpson and J. Conrad, 1824). Anti-Jackson biographies included *Sketch of the Life of John Quincy Adams; Taken from the Port Folio of April, 1819* (n.p., 1824); and [Benjamin Franklin Butler], *Sketches of the Life and Character of William H. Crawford, by Americanus* (Albany, N.Y., 1824). On the prevalence of the Cincinnatus image from the colonial period to the American Renaissance, see Schramer, "The Myth of Cincinnatus."

31. *Baltimore Republican and Commercial Advertiser,* December 7, 1835, 2; Eaton, *Life of Andrew Jackson,* v; see also Edward Everett [Ttereve Sudravde], *Sketch of the Life of John Quincy Adams* (n.p., 1827), 3; *Events and Incidents in the History of Gen. Winfield Scott* (Washington, 1852), 2.

32. See Tompkins, *Sensational Designs,* 122–46.

33. George D. Prentice, *Biography of Henry Clay* (Hartford: Samuel Hanmer Jr. and John Jay Phelps, 1831), iii; James B. Swain, *The Life and Speeches of Henry Clay* (New York: Greeley and McElrath, 1844), 1:iii; *Life of General Lewis Cass: Comprising an Account of His Military Services in the North-West during the War with Great Britain, His Diplomatic Career and Civil History* (Philadelphia: G. B. Zieber and Co., 1848), 11–14; see also Isaac Rand Jackson, *Narrative of the Civil and Military Services of William H. Harrison: Compiled from the Most Authentic Authorities* (Philadelphia, 1836), 3.

34. William M. Holland, *The Life and Opinions of Martin Van Buren, Vice President of the United States* (Hartford: Belknap and Hamersley, 1835), vii, 79–80; George H. Hickman, *The Life and Services of the Hon. James Knox Polk, with a Compendium of His Speeches on Various Public Measures* (Baltimore: N. Hickman, 1844), 6. On the partisan archetypes, see Heale, *The Presidential Quest,* 170–85. The development of the "second party system" has long been the subject of historiographical debate; for a useful review of the field, see Feller, "Politics and Society."

35. James Hall, *A Memoir of the Public Services of William Henry Harrison, of Ohio* (Philadelphia: Key and Biddle, 1836), 29; Junius, *Life of Henry Clay* (New York: Greeley and McElrath, 1844); *The Clay Minstrel: Or, National Songster* (New York: Greeley and McElrath et al., 1844), 10–11, 25. Whigs drew on faculty psychology to envision society as a hierarchy of functions much like the individual body. As a body's rational faculties must control its animal and mechanical ones in order to maintain harmonious balance, so must a society's most talented men govern those not endowed with natural abilities. See Daniel Walker Howe, *The Political Culture of the American Whigs,* 29–31. For a similar interpretation of how this philosophy expressed itself in social relations, see Ashworth, *"Agrarians" and "Aristocrats,"* 62–73. On the Whigs' use of evangelical rhetoric, see Carwardine, "Evangelicals, Whigs, and the Election of William Henry Harrison," 47–75. Lawrence Frederick Kohl has recently interpreted the distinctions between Whigs and Democrats psychologically, using David Riesman's typology: "Inner-directed" Americans, comfortable with the more impersonal relationships of modern society, tended to become Whigs;

"tradition-directed" Americans, "who still felt bound to others in more personal ways, became Jacksonians." However, campaign biographers most often tended to fuse the social visions that Kohl identifies as traditional and modern. *Politics of Individualism,* 6.

36. Hickman, *Life of Polk,* 6; Henry Rowe Schoolcraft, *Outlines of the Life and Character of Gen. Lewis Cass* (Albany: Joel Munsell, 1848), 4, 47–48, 61; see also Heale, *The Presidential Quest,* 162–68. Sometimes the candidates' links to the archetypal characteristics were tenuous: William Henry Harrison, scion of a prominent Virginia family, was said to have been left with no inheritance but his father's integrity, while Franklin Pierce's sole connection with the frontier lay in his father's settlement in New Hampshire after the Revolution.

37. See Howe, "The Evangelical Movement and Political Culture," 1232–39.

38. For Whig adoption of "feminine political symbols," see Ryan, *Women in Public,* 137; also Varon, "Tippecanoe and the Ladies, Too." Stories of Whig women leaving Democratic fiancés appeared in "A Change," *The Weekly Pilot* (Baltimore), October 10, 1840, 263; "Matrimony and Politics," *The Weekly Pilot,* October 24, 1840, 299; and "Another Conversion," *The Yeoman* (Richmond), September 10, 1840, 4. The dialogue between the mechanic and his wife, drawn from a speech by Samuel G. Goodrich, apparently first appeared in the *Boston Atlas* and was reprinted in *The Weekly Pilot,* October 10, 1840, 269; *Harrison Democrat* (Roxbury, Mass.), October 6, 1840, 2–3; and *Harrison Eagle* (Taunton, Mass.), October 10, 1840, 88. Other descriptions of Whig women's efforts include "The Ladies Coming to the Rescue," *Spirit of '76* (Indianapolis), August 8, 1840, 4; *Weekly Pilot,* August 22, 1840, 156; *The Republican* (Springfield, Mass.), August 7, 1840, 2; *The North Bend* (Worcester, Mass.), October 3, 1840; *Extra Ohio Statesman* (Columbus, Ohio), October 10, 1840, 4; and *The Democratic Rasp* (Whig paper, Utica, N.Y.), October 2, 1840, 2. The Democratic warning about "feminine Tippecanoes" appeared in *The Castigator* (Middletown, Conn.), October 23, 1840, 3. All of these newspapers are in the Campaign Newspapers Collection, AAS.

John Ashworth's analysis of the parties' larger social visions suggests another potential division between Democratic and Whig portrayals of candidates' families. According to Ashworth, the Democrats viewed society as fundamentally egalitarian (but for white men only), while Whigs envisioned society as a hierarchy and thus did not have to admit the equality of nonwhites in order to admit them into society: blacks and Indians were simply inferior beings, whose status called for the paternalism of their superiors. Although women hardly occupied the same degraded social status as blacks or Indians, the contrasting models of egalitarianism and hierarchy might have suggested different places for women in the public portrayal of candidates' lives. Democrats might see no place for women: their candidates were self-made men. But Whigs could portray their standard-bearers as paternalistic figures at home as well as in society. Anecdotes about Harrison's mercy for a treacherous slave and Clay's benevolence in his community could find parallels at home, where candidates became caring heads of households, exerting the same rational faculties that made them leaders in public life. But no biographer portrayed his subject in this way (*"Agrarians" and "Aristocrats,"* 221–23).

39. Eaton, *Life of Andrew Jackson;* Swain, *Life and Speeches of Clay,* 1:8; Nathan Sargent [Oliver Oldschool], *Brief Outline of the Life of Henry Clay* (Washington, D.C.: John T. Towers, 1844), 4; see also William Emmons, *A Biography of Martin Van Buren, Vice President of the United States* (Washington: Jacob Gideon Jr., 1835), 1.

40. Holland, *Life and Opinions of Van Buren*, 74; James Hall, *Memoir of William Henry Harrison*, 55; Charles S. Todd and Benjamin Drake, *Sketches of the Civil and Military Services of William Henry Harrison* (Cincinnati: U. P. James, 1840), 18. Henry Schoolcraft's relatively full description of Lewis Cass's wife was, in fact, atypical: "Mrs. Cass is a Virginian, a daughter of the late Gen. Philip Spencer, and a lady of piety, high moral worth, and decision of character, who found full exercise for her exertions, in rearing a young family, on so exposed a frontier, and thronged as her daily dwelling was, with parties of chiefs and warriors, whose wants taxed her benevolence, and were not easily satisfied." In addition to the standard identification of Mrs. Cass by her father and omission of her first name, this paragraph encompasses the four traits modern scholars have defined as the "cult of true womanhood": piety, purity, benevolence, and domesticity. Schoolcraft, *Outlines of the Life of Cass*, 16; Welter, "Cult of True Womanhood," 151–74.

41. Holland, *Life and Opinions of Van Buren*, vii, 361; Swain, *Life and Speeches of Clay*, 195; Junius, *Life of Clay*, 2.

42. Schoolcraft, *Outlines of the Life of Cass*, 4; James Hall, *Memoir of William Henry Harrison*, 10; Holland, *Life and Opinions of Van Buren*, 23; Daniel Mallory, *The Life and Speeches of the Hon. Henry Clay, in Two Volumes* (New York: Robert P. Bixby and Co., 1843), 9.

43. Swain, *Life and Speeches of Clay*, 9–10; Schoolcraft, *Outlines of the Life of Cass*, 5. Harrison's enlistment appeared in many of his biographies, including *A Biographical Sketch of the Life and Services of Gen. William Henry Harrison, Together with His Letter to Simon Bolivar* (Montpelier, Vt., 1836), 4.

44. The one exception to the rule of filial reverence occurs in biographies of Harrison: young Harrison leaves the medical career for which his father had hoped in order to join the army. On generational tensions in the early republic, see Fliegelman, *Prodigals and Pilgrims;* Watts, *Republic Reborn;* and Forgie, *Patricide in the House Divided.* Wallach, *Obedient Sons,* suggests that young men in antebellum America sought to reconcile reverence for the past with their own action and innovation, an argument that parallels the treatment of fathers in campaign biographies.

45. James Hall, *Memoir of William Henry Harrison*, 189; *Sketches of the Life and Public Services of Gen. Lewis Cass* (Boston, 1848), 10. On the rise of new disciplinary structures in the middle-class family of the mid-nineteenth century, see Brodhead, "Sparing the Rod," 67–96; and Wishy, *The Child and the Republic*, chap. 5.

46. For an example of this use of "private," see Mallory, *Life and Speeches of Clay*, 191–92; and Byars, "The Making of the Self-Made Man," 35. Campaign biographies' dichotomy between "public services" and "private life" roughly corresponds to the modern concept of the public and private "sectors." Until recently, when historians spoke of "public" and "private" in relationship to nineteenth-century politics, they, too, meant this division between the realms of masculine endeavor. For a recent example, see Kohl, *Politics of Individualism*, 108–15. Mary Ryan's work suggests the need to consider both meanings of "public/private" together: the division between government and the people (usually viewed as men), and the emerging definition of economic/political and domestic/familial "spheres" in Victorian America. Biography differed from other genres (such as novels and children's literature) in the omission of wives and children.

47. Susan Warner, *The Wide, Wide World* (orig. 1850), ed. Jane Tompkins (New York: Feminist Press, 1987). Catharine Sedgwick's *Home* (Boston: James Munroe and Co., 1835) offers an example of a domestic novel in which mother and father govern the home together.

48. Holland, *Life and Opinions of Van Buren*, 16; *Clay Minstrel*, 14–15; see also James Hall, *Memoir of William Henry Harrison*, 9.

49. Holland, *Life and Opinions of Van Buren*, 20.

50. William Dean Howells, *Life of Abraham Lincoln* (orig. 1860; Springfield, Ill.: Abraham Lincoln Association, 1938), 50–51.

51. Howells, *Life of Abraham Lincoln*, 17.

52. Ryan, *Cradle of the Middle Class*, chap. 4; Ryan, *Women in Public*.

53. "An American Lady," *Sketches of the Lives of Distinguished Females, Written for Girls, with a View to Their Mental and Moral Improvement* (New York: J. and J. Harper, 1833), xiv–xv.

54. Arabella Stuart Wilson, *The Lives of Mrs. Ann H. Judson and Mrs. Sarah B. Judson, with a Biographical Sketch of Mrs. Emily C. Judson, Missionaries to Burmah* (Auburn, N.Y.: Derby and Miller, 1851), ii.

55. *Biographium Faemineum. The Female Worthies: Or, Memoirs of the Most Illustrious Ladies, of All Ages and Nations* (London: S. Crowder, 1766), iv–v; Samuel L. Knapp, *Female Biography: Containing Notices of Distinguished Women, in Different Nations and Ages* (Philadelphia: Thomas Wardle, 1836), x. For a discussion of a compilation similar to the 1766 London book, see Ruth Perry, "George Ballard's Biographies of Learned Ladies," in Browning, *Biography in the 18th Century*, 85–111. On republican motherhood and Enlightenment ideas of women's education, see Kerber, *Women of the Republic*, esp. chaps. 7–9; Solomon, *In the Company of Educated Women*, 1–26; and Cott, *Bonds of Womanhood*, chap. 3.

56. Mary Hays, *Female Biography* (Philadelphia: Birch and Small, 1807), iii; John Bennet, "Letters to a Young Lady: Letter X," *The American Museum* 10 (October 1791): 202.

57. An American Lady, *Sketches of the Lives of Distinguished Females*, xi, 17–18.

58. Ibid., 216, 227.

59. *Christian Examiner* 65 (September 1858): 293. On the records of the Benson Female Library Society, see note 8, above. On the New York Society Library, see Ronald J. Zboray, "Reading Patterns in Antebellum America," 310. Zboray's study is a sample of two three-year periods (1847–49 and 1854–56) from the charge records.

60. *Godey's Lady's Book* 26 (March 1843): 155; *Harper's* 10 (April 1855): 715; *Christian Examiner* 65 (September 1858): 293. Although Queen Victoria was not the subject of these biographies, the fascination with queens' lives may have been enhanced by her presence on the British throne. Beginning in the late 1840s, the Massachusetts ministers Jacob Abbott and John S. C. Abbott produced a series of historical biographies of monarchs from ancient times, Tudor and Stuart England, and Napoleonic France; these became staples of social libraries from the 1850s on. See also Greenhouse, "The American Portrayal of Tudor and Stuart History, 1835–1865," 29. Greenhouse's study focuses primarily on visual representations but also discusses magazine sketches and full-length biographies and histories.

61. An American Lady, *Sketches of the Lives of Distinguished Females*, 42; Greenhouse, "The American Portrayal of Tudor and Stuart History," chap. 4. Nina Baym has also discussed portrayals of the queens in *American Women Writers and the Work of History*, 218–22. Baym distinguishes between two sets of portrayals of Elizabeth: earlier women historians, inspired by the Enlightenment idea that intellect had no sex, praised Elizabeth's intelligence, while women historians around midcentury, with a more Victorian worldview, condemned Elizabeth for sacrificing her femininity.

62. The classic formulation is Welter, "The Cult of True Womanhood." Since Welter's article, historians and literary critics have qualified and reassessed her claim that this was

the prominent feminine ideal in Jacksonian America, including Baym, *Woman's Fiction;* McCall, " 'The Reign of Brute Force Is Now Over,' " 217–36.

63. For a discussion of the hagiography of the Judsons, see Brumberg, *Mission for Life,* esp. chap. 1.

64. Sarah Sleeper, *Memoir of the Late Martha Hazeltine Smith* (Boston: Freeman and Bolles, 1843), 79; [Francis Wayland], *A Memoir of Harriet Ware, First Superintendent of the Children's Home, in the City of Providence* (Providence: George H. Whitney, 1850), 126, 150.

65. Sleeper, *Memoir of Martha Hazeltine Smith,* 22, 54, 141, 143, 210.

66. Brumberg, *Mission for Life,* 81. On Beecher's domestic ideology, see Sklar, *Catharine Beecher,* 157–67. On Hale's work, particularly *Woman's Record,* see Baym, "Onward Christian Women," 249–70.

67. Arabella Stuart Wilson, *The Lives of Mrs. Judson . . . ,* iii–iv, 6.

68. John A. Clark, *The Young Disciple: Or, a Memoir of Anzonetta R. Peters* (Philadelphia: William Marshall and Co., 1837), 4. On the sentimentalization of ministers' memoirs, see Douglas, *The Feminization of American Culture,* 188–99.

69. Clark, *The Young Disciple,* 3; Andrew Reed, *Martha: A Memorial of an Only and Beloved Sister* (New York: Harper and Brothers, 1835), 9–10; Robert Baird, *Memoir of Anna Jane Linnard* (Philadelphia: Henry Perkins; Boston: Perkins, Marvin, and Co., 1835), 29. The most important scholarship on female memoirs in the early republic is Gillespie, " 'The Clear Leadings of Providence,' " 197–221. The idea of "authorship in the service of God" was the principal convention of Victorian religious biography. In a sense, this justification for authorship paralleled campaign biographers' explanation for writing candidates' lives: not to glorify the candidate, but to serve democracy by making citizens aware of those for whom they might vote. Similarly, religious biographies often denied any intention to cast glory on their subjects; rather, the glory was God's, the power that had led the subject to Christianity and could do the same for the reader. Many female memoirs resembled the lives of pious children, similarly undistinguished for anything but their piety. Focusing on conversions and happy deaths witnessed by other children, family members, and clergymen, child biographies were manuals of life and death for parents and children alike: parents needed to instill piety in children early in life, just as children needed to understand and rejoice in their subordination to God. On the origins of these biographies, see MacDonald, *Literature for Children in England and America,* 22–28.

70. Douglas, *The Feminization of American Culture,* 195; James I. Helm, *Memoir of Martha Thomson Sharp, by Her Pastor* (New York: American Tract Society, 1848), 8; Charles Lester, *The Mountain Wild Flower: Or, Memoirs of Mrs. Mary Ann Bise* (New York: E. French, 1838), 9–10, 16. On the difference between male historians' and female memoirists' sense of "history," see Douglas, chap. 5. Douglas correctly notes how memoirs of women (and increasingly of ministers) operated independently of external historical events and even omitted specific dates and sites of personal events. Yet she slights the reason contemporary compilers might have offered for these omissions: in the evangelical vision, the crucial narratives were the progress toward a Christian world and the progress of individuals toward conversion.

71. Contemporary dictionaries and encyclopedias suggested this difference in their definitions of "memoirs." Although most described "historical" memoirs, dealing with prominent public figures, the distinction was clear: the authors of memoirs "have either taken part, personally, in the scenes described, or have been connected with the actors so inti-

mately as to have derived their information from the most trust-worthy sources." Francis
Lieber, *Encyclopaedia Americana* (Philadelphia: Carey and Lea, 1830), 8:399–401. "Biography" was usually defined simply as "the life and character of a particular person,"
suggesting none of this intimacy. Noah Webster, *An American Dictionary of the English
Language,* 6th ed. (New York: S. Converse, 1830), 89; see also *Encyclopaedia: Or, a Dictionary of Arts, Sciences, and Miscellaneous Literature* (Philadelphia, 1798), 3:232. Intriguingly, an
1864 dictionary for women defined "biography" as "personal history," perhaps implying
a closeness akin to that of the "memoir." William Grimshaw, *The Ladies' Lexicon, and Parlour Companion* (Philadelphia: J. B. Lippincott Co., 1864), 41. This definition may also have
reflected changes in what "biography" was thought to be, in particular the movement
toward seeking the "inner man" described in Chapter 4 below.

72. Reed, *Martha,* 13; Lot Jones, *Memoir of Mrs. Sarah Louisa Taylor: Or, an Illustration of the
Work of the Holy Spirit, in Awakening, Renewing, and Sanctifying the Heart,* 5th ed. (New York:
D. Fanshawe, 1847), 157–58.

73. [Sophia Linsley], *Memoirs of Miss Mary Lyon, of New Haven, Conn.* (New Haven: A. H.
Maltby, 1837), 143–44; Jones, *Memoir of Mrs. Sarah Louisa Taylor,* 111, 146; Lester, *The Mountain Wild Flower,* 33.

74. Brodhead, "Sparing the Rod," sets forth the notion of the "disciplinary intimacy" of sentimental fiction. Davidson, *Revolution and the Word,* esp. chap. 6, discusses early-republican
women's fiction as subversive.

75. See Gillespie, " 'The Clear Leadings of Providence,' " 203. This argument resembles
Karen Halttunen's about the transformation of sentimental culture in Victorian America.
According to Halttunen, etiquette books and forms of "sincere" dress originally aimed
to make "character" transparent in an increasingly impersonal urban society. Soon, however, hypocritical "confidence men" who sought to enter genteel society adopted the
forms recommended by the very manuals written to keep them out of middle-class parlors. Similarly, religious memoirs may in some cases have taught readers the appropriate
feelings to display, rather than guide fellow evangelical Christians along the path to "sincere" conversion. See *Confidence Men and Painted Women,* esp. 186–90.

76. Clark, *The Young Disciple,* 4–5. Other sorts of pressure may also have been involved: possibly, for example, the women whose memoirs the ministers wrote—or the surviving
families of those women—were among the ministers' financial supporters in a congregation, or the prominent families in a community. More work on the social history of
congregations and memoirs would be required to test such a hypothesis.

77. Biographical information appears in Verne Lockwood Samson, "William Makepeace
Thayer," *Dictionary of American Biography,* 18:412–13. William M. Thayer, *The Poor Boy and
Merchant Prince: Or, Elements of Success Drawn from the Life and Character of the Late Amos
Lawrence* (Boston: Gould and Lincoln, 1857), vi; Thayer, *The Poor Girl and True Woman: Or,
Elements of Woman's Success Drawn from the Life of Mary Lyon and Others* (Boston: Gould and
Lincoln, 1859), 1.

78. The "how it was done" motto appears in Thayer's *The Poor Boy and Merchant Prince,* v; *From
Poor-House to Pulpit: Or, the Triumphs of the Late Dr. John Kitto, from Boyhood to Manhood, a
Book for Youth* (Boston: E. O. Libby and Co., 1859), v; and *The Pioneer Boy, and How He Be-
came President* (Boston: Walker, Wise, and Co., 1863), iii. Thayer described his childhood
biographical desires in *The Unfinished Autobiography of William M. Thayer* (Boston: Barta
Press, [1898]), 13. In this autobiography, Thayer described his childhood experience of

reading to his mother, whose love of learning guided him toward his career as minister and author. "Both mother and son loved biography" above all else. But Thayer wished then that all biography could be written in the "colloquial style," a desire that moved him to write as he did. Like earlier American critics, Thayer condemned fiction and worried about the "new-fangled notions of our day, which really exalt fiction above truth" (15). A similar critique of fiction appeared in *The Poor Girl and True Woman*, 140–41.

79. *The Bobbin Boy: Or, How Nat Got His Learning, an Example for Youth* (Boston: J. E. Tilton and Co., 1860), 97–98, 125.

80. Ibid., 11–12, 26–27, 151–52, 310.

81. Thayer, *Unfinished Autobiography*, 54–55.

TWO READERS' WORLDS

1. The two diaries were published as *The Diary of Michael Floy Jr., Bowery Village, 1833–1837*, ed. Richard Albert Edward Brooks (New Haven: Yale University Press, 1941); and *Life and Thought: Or, Cherished Memorials of the Late Julia A. Parker Dyson*, ed. E. Latimer (2d ed., Philadelphia: Claxton, Remsen, Hafflefinger and Co., 1871). Because *Life and Thought* was published as a memorial volume, nearly two decades after Parker's death in 1852, it contains only excerpts from her diary and letters. It is therefore impossible to know how complete the entries are, or even whether Latimer excised portions that would present Parker in a light other than the one described here. As Latimer wrote, the extracts were only such "as are necessary to this biographical sketch" and were "delicately and carefully made; restricted to such as shall illustrate character, mode of thought and expression, presenting to view, in some degree, her high intellectual attainments, and that unobtrusive moral worth for which she was distinguished" (8). In short, *Life and Thought* was itself a female memoir, designed to display its subject's excellences for the benefit of readers. Susan K. Harris, *Nineteenth-Century American Women's Novels*, uses Parker's diary as an example (24), as does Mary Kelley, in her article "Reading Women/Women Reading," 411, 416.

2. Richard Albert Edward Brooks, "Preface," in *The Diary of Michael Floy Jr.*, vi–vii.

3. Floy diary, October 20, 1833, March 27, 1835, in *The Diary of Michael Floy Jr.*, 6, 147.

4. On the concept of "steady sellers," see David D. Hall, "The Uses of Literacy in New England," 24.

5. The development of denominational authority during the Second Great Awakening is well described in Butler, *Awash in a Sea of Faith*, chap. 9.

6. *The Diary of Michael Floy Jr.*, 59 n. 70.

7. Floy diary, September 30, August 22, 1834, in *The Diary of Michael Floy Jr.*, 102, 108.

8. Floy diary, April 21, 1836, October 22, 1833, in *The Diary of Michael Floy Jr.*, 7, 232. For Harper's promotion of its Family Library, see "Harper's Popular Libraries: Harper's Family Library," in *Harper's Illustrated Catalogue of Valuable Standard Works, in the Several Departments of General Literature* (New York: Harper and Brothers, 1848).

9. Floy diary, September 25, 1834, January 23, 1836, in *The Diary of Michael Floy Jr.*, 106–7, 215.

10. Floy diary, November 23, 1834, May 2, 1836, in ibid., 120, 233.

11. Floy diary, May 30, 1836, in ibid., 239.

12. Parker to "My dear E.," March 9, 1837, in Latimer, *Life and Thought*, 11–12.

13. Parker letter, dated August 1840; Parker diary, July 31, 1841; Parker letter, dated Janu-

ary 1840; Parker, "William Ellery Channing" (probably written shortly after Channing's death in 1842); all in Latimer, *Life and Thought,* 43, 45, 63, 252.

14. Parker diary, June 28, July 24, July 25, August 9, December 10, 1841, in Latimer, *Life and Thought,* 59, 62, 66, 77. Other educated women of the era shared Parker's fascination with intellectual women, notably de Staël; see Kelley, "Reading Women," 409–21.

15. Parker diary, August 22, August 7, July 5, October 23, July 29, 1841, in Latimer, *Life and Thought,* 60–66, 73. Meeting Sarah Josepha Hale was a highlight of Parker's first year in Pennsylvania: on September 21, 1841, she recorded the meeting in her diary with the addendum, "She is a woman for whose character I have much admiration" (71).

16. Parker diary, July 10, 1841, in Latimer, *Life and Thought,* 60. For Longfellow's "A Psalm of Life," see Hollander, *American Poetry, the Nineteenth Century,* 1:370–71.

CHAPTER THREE

1. Review of *Lempriere's Universal Biography, Atlantic Magazine* 2 (April 1825): 468.

2. On the historical-society movement, see Callcott, *History in the United States,* 35–45; and Van Tassel, *Recording America's Past,* 59–66, 95–110.

3. The phrase is Van Tassel's (*Recording America's Past,* 103).

4. Sheidley, "Sectional Nationalism"; Buell, *New England Literary Culture,* 214–38.

5. [Jared Sparks], review of William Wirt, *Sketches of the Life and Character of Patrick Henry, NAR* 6 (March 1818): 294–98.

6. Hilliard and Brown advertisement in Sparks, *The Life of John Ledyard, the American Traveller: Comprising Selections from His Journals and Correspondence* (Cambridge: Hilliard and Brown, 1828), 5; see also p. v.

7. Jared Sparks, *The Life of Gouverneur Morris, with Selections from His Correspondence and Miscellaneous Papers* (Boston: Gray and Bowen, 1832), 1:vi; Sparks to Mrs. Morris, August 27, 1831, quoted in Adams, *Life and Writings of Sparks,* 2:168–69; Sparks to Alexander Slidell Mackenzie, October 28, 1839, JS-HL 147g; *NAR* 34 (April 1832): 465. For evidence of the positive reception of Sparks's early work, see, for instance, *Christian Examiner* 13 (September 1832): 124.

8. Adams, *Life and Writings of Sparks,* 2:189.

9. Sparks to George Bancroft, November 22, 1832; Sparks to John Quincy Adams, November 22, 1832; both in JS-HL 147f. On the same date, Sparks's copied-letter book states that he wrote to several other possible authors, presumably in the same or similar language. Among those Sparks requested to write for the library was Robert Walsh, a Philadelphia journalist and editor who was already preparing an American biographical dictionary. Sparks took pains to assure him that the library would be a different sort of work entirely. Sparks to Robert Walsh, December 26, 1832, JS-HL 147f.

10. Sparks to John Quincy Adams, November 22, 1832; Sparks to John McVickar, November 22, 1832; both in JS-HL 147f. Many letters to potential authors explained the financial terms (the publishers had agreed to pay a dollar per printed page), and once the series became successful at least one author asked Sparks for a loan to be repaid with biographies for the library. See Sparks to Charles Wentworth Upham, November 27, 1832, JS-HL 147f; Sparks to Alexander Slidell Mackenzie, October 28, 1839, JS-HL 147g; Alexander H. Everett to Sparks, December 21, 1836, JS-HL 153.

11. Thornbrough and Riker, *The Diary of Calvin Fletcher*, 2:547–52, 3:13–14, 177, 188; *Knicker-bocker Magazine* 25 (April 1845): 355; *American Whig Review* 2 (November 1845): 545.

12. *Catalogue of Books in the Keene Circulating Library, Kept by George Tilden, September, 1834* (Keene, N.H., 1834); *Catalogue of the Mercantile Library of San Francisco* (San Francisco, 1854); *A Catalogue of Books in the Ladies' Library, in Lebanon (South Society) Conn. November 1st, 1844* (Norwich, Conn., 1844); *Catalogue of the Public School Library of New Orleans* (New Orleans, 1848); Young Men's Association of the City of Milwaukee, *Charter, Rules and Regulations of the Association, and Board of Directors, with a Catalogue of the Library and List of Members* (Milwaukee, 1855). The entire collection of library catalogs surveyed, including those cited here, is in the Public Library Catalogues Collection, AAS.

13. "Sparks' American Biography," *Methodist Quarterly Review* 30 (October 1848): 513–14.

14. Sparks to George Bancroft, December 1, 1832; Sparks to Adams, November 22, 1832; Sparks to Samuel Gilman (memorandum in letterbook describing letter), December 7, 1832; all JS-HL 147f. Sparks to Gulian C. Verplanck, November 29, 1832, W. Hugh Peal Collection, Special Collections and Archives, University of Kentucky Library, Lexington, Ky.

15. Charles Wentworth Upham to Sparks, April 12, 1833, and June 5, 1833, JS-HL 153. In some cases, documents were readily available, thanks to the older historical societies; see Sparks to Bancroft, November 22, 1832, JS-HL 147f; Francis Bowen to Sparks, July 14, 1836, and William B. O. Peabody to Sparks, June 8, 1836, both in JS-HL 153. In the case of Henry Vane, Upham admitted that some of the papers probably remained in England and some of Vane's speeches were impossible to find in the United States. Charles Wentworth Upham, *Life of Sir Henry Vane, Fourth Governor of Massachusetts,* LAB 4:87. For many biographers, Sparks himself was an important resource; see Alexander H. Everett to Sparks, August 10, 1843; Edward Everett to Sparks, April 23, 1833, both in JS-HL 153.

16. Henry Ware, a Unitarian clergyman and professor at Harvard Divinity School, suggested in rhyme how insular Sparks's early volumes were. In an after-dinner poem delivered to the men of Phi Beta Kappa on August 29, 1839, Ware spoke of the society's divines, lawyers, poets, and historians. Eventually "Our Society's Authors" reached Sparks and company: "Then the many fair writers in Sparks's Biography, / First trying their hands in small historiography; / As Upham, the eloquent champion of Vane; / And Peabody, guessing the matter out plain; / And Francis, portraying, as true pen should paint, / The career of the Indians' apostle and saint." Of course Ware focused on the Phi Beta Kappa contributors to the Library of American Biography, but he had plenty such men to mention. His lines also revealed these New Englanders' notion of the library and of biography more generally: "small historiography" that could be an early effort and prelude to greater authorial accomplishments. "Our Society's Authors. Read to the Ph. B. K. after the Annual Dinner, August 29, 1839," in *The Miscellaneous Writings of Henry Ware* (Boston: James Munroe, 1846), 256.

17. William B. O. Peabody, *Life of Cotton Mather,* LAB 6:268–69, 196; Francis Bowen, *Life of William Phips,* LAB 7:3, 81; Convers Francis, *Life of John Eliot, Apostle to the Indians,* LAB 5:5.

18. Reviews of the LAB in the *North American Review* include *NAR* 38 (April 1834): 466–86; *NAR* 42 (January 1836): 116–48; and *NAR* 43 (October 1836): 516–25. On the sectarian controversies, see Buell, *New England Literary Culture,* 226. The Massachusetts Sabbath

School Society's series, entitled *Lives of the Chief Fathers of New England,* appeared in six volumes between 1846 and 1849.

19. "Sparks' American Biography," *Methodist Quarterly Review* 30 (October 1848): 513–14.

20. Oliver W. B. Peabody, *Life of Israel Putnam,* LAB 7:128–29; Francis, *Life of John Eliot,* 31; George S. Hillard, *The Life and Adventures of Captain John Smith,* LAB 2:216, 234.

21. Edward Everett, *Life of John Stark,* LAB 1:5–6, 9; Jared Sparks, *Life of Ethan Allen,* LAB 1:229–30; Peabody, *Life of Israel Putnam,* 105–6.

22. Hillard, *Life and Adventures of Captain John Smith,* 396; Henry Wheaton, *Life of William Pinkney,* LAB 6:83–84.

23. Sparks cautioned authors not to elaborate on events that other volumes treated at length, and his own life of Benedict Arnold avoided discussing the battle of Ticonderoga, with a footnote instructing the reader to see his life of Ethan Allen two volumes earlier. Jared Sparks, *The Life and Treason of Benedict Arnold,* LAB 3:24n; Sparks to Upham, November 27, 1832, JS-HL 147f.

24. Numerous biographers catalogued their sources of information—whether family papers, state papers, or previously published works. See, for instance, Francis, *Life of John Eliot, the Apostle to the Indians,* LAB 5:vi; and Bowen, *Life of Sir William Phips,* LAB 7:3. Some of the biographies were also replete with footnotes weighing different historians' accounts. A few biographies for the library were drawn primarily from previous accounts: Prescott's life of Charles Brockden Brown drew heavily on William Dunlap's extensive 1815 biography, and Oliver W. B. Peabody used David Humphreys's essay on Israel Putnam for his depiction of Putnam's character and various incidents.

25. Upham to Sparks, December [?], 1834; Prescott to Sparks, August 1, 1833, both in JS-HL 153. By 1836, when Sparks contacted James Luce Kingsbury about writing a life of Timothy Dwight, he had come to agree that "In the case of authors, criticisms on their writings will of course have a place"; see Sparks to Kingsbury, January 25, 1836, Kingsbury Collection, Box 2, Folder 115, Manuscripts and Archives, Yale University. Catharine Sedgwick, *A Memoir of Lucretia Maria Davidson,* LAB 7:221. The title page of the Davidson memoir identified Sedgwick not by name but only as "The author of 'Redwood,' 'Hope Leslie,' &c., &c.," a common attribution for female-authored fiction.

26. Harper and Brothers bought the stereotype plates of the first ten volumes from Hilliard and Gray in 1838 and encouraged Sparks to continue the series. But Harper did not meet Sparks's terms, and negotiations fell through. Little and Brown acquired the plates from Harper and published the second series. In 1848 they reissued the entire series (ten volumes of the 1830s and fifteen of the 1840s). For the publishing correspondence and history, see Adams, *Life and Writings of Jared Sparks* 2:194–205.

27. *Knickerbocker Magazine* 25 (April 1845): 355.

28. Henry Reed, *Life of Joseph Reed,* LAB 18:212. A similar statement appears in Samuel K. Lothrop, *Life of Samuel Kirkland, Missionary to the Indians,* LAB 25:362. Two of the four biographies written by their subjects' grandsons (those of Joseph Reed and Nathanael Greene) identified that relationship on their title pages—suggesting that the authors had requested that designation. (If Sparks had considered that relationship an advertisement for the authenticity of these biographies, after all, why would it not have appeared on the title pages of all lives written by grandsons?)

29. William Gammell to Sparks, November 23, 1843; George W. Burnap to Sparks, February 7, 1845; Gammell to Sparks, March 30, 1846; all in JS-HL 153.

30. Charles F. Hoffman, *The Administration of Jacob Leisler: A Chapter in American History,* LAB 13:182–84, 187. Hoffman clearly wrote in the spirit of his contemporaries Washington Irving and James Fenimore Cooper, whose fictional works portrayed the Dutch settlers of New York fondly in the face of New England migration to the state since the Revolution (see 184, 188). Burnap made a similar claim for Maryland against historians who would emphasize Massachusetts *and* Virginia: Maryland, not either of those first colonies, had pioneered religious freedom. Burnap, *Life of Leonard Calvert,* LAB 19:14–15.

31. See, for instance, the concluding paragraph of Fordyce Hubbard, *Life of William Richardson Davie,* LAB 25:135. William Peabody—one of Sparks's Massachusetts contributors—made a similar point in his *Life of James Oglethorpe,* LAB 12:203.

32. See, for instance, Peabody, *Life of Oglethorpe,* 203; Burnap, *Life of Calvert,* 3–4.

33. See, for instance, Sparks to Cyrus P. Bradley, January 30, 1837, JS-HL 147f, declining a biography of Nathan Hale because the first series of the LAB already had its full complement of lives.

34. John M. Peck to Sparks, September 20, 1845, February 21, 1846, October 15, 1846, JS-HL 153. See also Theodore C. Pease, "John Mason Peck," in *Dictionary of American Biography,* 14:381–82.

35. Henry Whiting to Sparks, December 23, 1844; Lorenzo Sabine to Sparks, November 18, 1845, December 31, 1845; all in JS-HL 153. Sparks to Sabine, July 28, 1848, JS-HL 147h. See also Sparks to William Reed, October 3, 1842, JS-HL 147g; Alexander Slidell Mackenzie to Sparks, October 18, 1839, JS-HL 153.

36. I. W. Stuart, *Life of Jonathan Trumbull, Sen., Governor of Connecticut* (Boston: Crocker and Brewster, 1859), iii; William Cutter, *The Life of Israel Putnam, Major-General in the Army of the American Revolution* (New York: George F. Cooledge and Brother, 1848), iv; Ashbel Steele, *Chief of the Pilgrims: Or the Life and Times of William Brewster* (Philadelphia: J. B. Lippincott, 1857), x–xi.

37. *Christian Examiner* 44 (May 1848): 330; *Christian Examiner* 67 (July 1859): 148; *Harper's* 11 (August 1855): 405. Dozens of other reviews contained similar plaudits for biographers who had done primary research.

38. B. B. Thatcher, *Indian Biography* (orig. 1832; New York: Harper and Brothers, 1842), preface. On the McKenney-Hall project, see Horan, *Portrait Gallery of American Indians,* 105–11; and Drinnon, *Facing West,* 165–202. Drinnon interprets the impulse behind the portfolio as one side of imperialism: a dominant culture's anthropological desire to preserve relics of the peoples it destroys. McKenney, according to Drinnon, was a Quaker philanthropist gone bad, a one-time proponent of benevolent "civilization" who turned fleetingly to Indian removal (perhaps in a vain effort to keep his job) and ultimately to mercenary motives.

39. William L. Stone, *Life of Joseph Brant-Thayendanegea, Including the Indian Wars of the American Revolution* (New York: Alexander V. Blake, 1838), xiii–xvi. For biographical information, see Julian P. Boyd, "William Leete Stone," in *Dictionary of American Biography,* 18:89–90.

40. Stone, *Life of Joseph Brant-Thayendanegea,* xvi–xix, xxii, xxvi–xxvii. Stone's sequel did not allow the method he had used in the life of Brant. Red-Jacket "could speak but very little English, and could not write at all. He could therefore maintain no written correspondence, and consequently left no letters, or other written memorials, to aid his biographer. Such was not the fact in the case of Brant, whose papers were of vast assistance. It must also be kept in mind that Brant was a man of war, and Red-Jacket a man of

peace. Hence in a memoir of the latter a far smaller amount of stirring and bloody incident is to be anticipated, than in one of the former." William L. Stone, *The Life and Times of Red-Jacket, or Sa-Go-Ye-Wat-Ha: Being the Sequel to the History of the Six Nations* (New York: Wiley and Putnam, 1841), v.

41. On the genre of first-person narratives and their rhetoric of truth, see Fabian, *Plain Unvarnished Tales.*

42. Herman Melville, "Bartleby" (orig. 1853; New York: Dover, 1990), 3; Melville, *Israel Potter: His Fifty Years of Exile* (New York: G. P. Putnam, 1855), 3–5.

43. Melville, *Israel Potter,* 4. For a similar interpretation of Melville's use of biography, see Reagan, "Melville's *Israel Potter* and the Nature of Biography"; see also Bellis, "*Israel Potter:* Autobiography as History as Fiction."

44. William C. Nell, *The Colored Patriots of the American Revolution, with Sketches of Several Distinguished Colored Persons* (Boston: Robert F. Wallcut, 1855), 9; William Wells Brown, *The Black Man, His Antecedents, His Genius, and His Achievements* (New York: Thomas Hamilton, 1863), 6. Brown updated and republished his book several times after the Civil War, including as *The Rising Son: Or, the Antecedents and Advancement of the Colored Race* (New York: Thomas Hamilton, 1876).

45. For the purposes of this chapter, the phrases "scholarly" and "professional" refer to men like Sparks who established standards for biography and history in their own works and in magazines such as the *NAR.* In fact, as Nina Baym's *American Women Writers and the Work of History* reveals, many women did write history before the Civil War, including books designed for schools and home lessons and lives of European queens. But most of these women, unlike Ellet, either accepted the concept of American history as the study of battles and men or placed women in the alternative progression of Christian history. And virtually none sought to write history on Sparks's terms.

46. Ellet's work has received almost no attention from twentieth-century scholars. Exceptions include Conrad, *Perish the Thought,* 116–22; Gelles, "The Abigail Industry," 660–61; and Kerber, "'History Can Do It No Justice,'" 3–9.

47. Elizabeth F. Ellet to Carey and Hart, January 17, 1848, Miscellaneous MSS E, NYHS.

48. On the tensions that women novelists faced, see Kelley, *Private Woman, Public Stage,* x–xii, 164–79. Even if Ellet never won their popularity, her articles shared the pages of *Godey's* and other popular magazines with the stories of the "literary domestics," and her letters reveal that she knew several of them personally. The best discussion of intellectual women's dilemmas is Conrad, *Perish the Thought,* 11–44, 116–22. However, Conrad does not explore how Ellet's move to scholarly biography compounded this tension. Ellet might be viewed as what Bell Gale Chevigny has called a "daughter writing," a woman trying to recover her foremothers in the hope of understanding herself. Chevigny suggests that "the act of daughters writing about [foremothers] is likely to be, on some level, an act of retrieval which is experienced as rescue." This theory deals most closely with women biographers in the second half of the twentieth century, recovering "our history and ourselves, each at least partly in terms of the other." Yet it also helps to illuminate the project of this nineteenth-century woman biographer. See "Daughters Writing," 98–99.

49. Biographical sketches of Ellet include Alma Lutz, "Elizabeth Fries Lummis Ellet," in *Notable American Women, 1607–1950: A Biographical Dictionary,* 1:569–70; Clyde N. Wilson, "Elizabeth F. Ellet," in *Dictionary of Literary Biography,* 30:84–88; and Lina Mainiero, *American Women Writers: A Critical Reference Guide from Colonial Times to the Present,* 1:581–83.

50. Ellet's anonymous version of the Italian play *Euphemio of Messina* was published in 1834, and her tragedy *Teresa Contarini* was performed at New York's Park Theatre the following year. In 1837 the *Oasis* reprinted a laudatory biographical sketch of her from Sarah Josepha Hale's *Lady's Book;* three years later *Graham's Magazine* mentioned that "Mrs. Ellet is well known as a writer of considerable merit, though perhaps she can scarcely be ranked among our more popular authors." *Godey's* listed her among its regular contributors; *The Ladies' Magazine* printed her work almost monthly until its demise in 1843; annual gift books also carried her work. "Sketch of Mrs. Ellet," *Oasis* (Oswego, N.Y.) 1 (October 21, 1837): 36–37; "Review of *Scenes in the Life of Joanna of Sicily,*" *Graham's Magazine* 16 (July 1840): 48.

51. Her husband wrote in 1838 that "Mrs. E. is so exceedingly anxious to quit the South that I have promised her to accept the first good situation which may offer at the North." The following year, Elizabeth wrote hopefully of a possible position for William at Columbia College in New York. Apparently no such position opened, for the Ellets remained in South Carolina until 1848. While there, Ellet attempted to interest a Boston publisher in a parlor game devised by the Charleston writer and editor Caroline Gilman; it was in this context that she wrote of knowing nothing about financial business. William Henry Ellet to Timothy R. Green, December 27, 1838, South Caroliniana Library, University of South Carolina, Columbia; Elizabeth F. Ellet to Cornelia da Ponte, March 8, 1839, Overbury Collection, Barnard College Library, New York; Ellet to Samuel Colman, February 28 [no year], Overbury Collection.

The animosity between Poe and Ellet led to her exclusion from his "The Literati of New York" (*Godey's,* 1846), but he wrote a scathing paragraph on her that remained unpublished until after his death. In it he contended that her articles had "the disadvantage of *looking* as if hashed up for just so much money as they will bring" and described her as "short and much inclined to *embonpoint*." The change in Poe's attitude toward Ellet is exemplified by his additional implication that she was guilty of a "wholesale charge of plagiarism." In February 1845, little more than a year earlier, Poe had *defended* Ellet against this charge, blaming the lack of a citation on a printer. He later wrote that Ellet's provocations had murdered his young wife, and called Ellet "the most malignant and pertinacious of all fiends—[a woman whose loathsome love I could do nothing but repel with scorn]." Ellet to Osgood, July 8, 1846, Rufus Wilmot Griswold Collection, Boston Public Library. Charles Briggs [Harry Franco, pseud.] used Ellet as the model for the bluestocking Lizzy Gilson in *The Trippings of Tom Pepper: Or, the Results of Romancing* (New York: Mirror Library, 1847). *The Literati,* vol. 3 of *The Works of the Late Edgar Allan Poe,* ed. Rufus Wilmot Griswold (New York: Redfield, 1855), 202–3; *Broadway Journal* 1 (February 15, 1845): 109; Poe to Sarah Helen Whitman, October 18, 1848, in *The Letters of Edgar Allan Poe,* 2:393. On the incident, see DeJong, "Lines from a Partly Published Drama," 31–58; Moss, *Poe's Literary Battles* and *Poe's Major Crisis.* Walsh, *Plumes in the Dust,* presents the story as romantic drama with Ellet as the villainess. These studies rely heavily on Poe's and Osgood's letters; see *The Letters of Edgar Allan Poe,* 2:393–94, 406–9, 430–32; and letters by Poe, Osgood, and Rufus Wilmot Griswold in the Griswold Collection, Boston Public Library.

52. Also significant for her work on the Revolutionary women, Ellet revealed in *Evenings at Woodlawn* how oral traditions entered print culture. Oral storytelling, dependent on the memory and imagination of the individual teller, remains a popular evening's entertain-

ment for Professor Azêle and the Woodlawn group. Unlike this coterie, Ellet's readers would find the legends fixed on the page, even if they chose to read the "evenings" aloud in their own homes. This transformation becomes explicit in the book's conclusion, when Professor Azêle consents to have the tales published. The professor's references to other authorities, notably the German author J. P. Lyser, complicate matters further: if the legends are an oral tradition, they have already been mediated by other tellers and perhaps other written accounts. And that tradition is not a common folk heritage. It is the legend of foreign lands, which must be translated by a highly educated, well-traveled teller. The audience, a genteel, leisured group that substitutes these stories for cardplaying and music, can know the stories only because of the translator's work. Woodlawn's physical and emotional warmth and seclusion identify the setting as the midcentury middle-class household, which achieves control over a foreign, unknown world by translating its legends into English and absorbing them into the parlor. This was the audience for *Godey's,* where Ellet first published many of the legends and, in 1847 and 1848, a number of her biographical sketches of Revolutionary women. Elizabeth F. Ellet, *Evenings at Woodlawn* (New York: Baker and Scribner, 1849), iii, 11, 212, 348.

53. Elizabeth F. Ellet, "Letter to M.D.S.," *Godey's Lady's Book* 38 (January 1849): 3; Ellet to Lydia Huntley Sigourney, March 21, 1848, CHS. For virtually identical statements, see Ellet to James Fenimore Cooper, March 11, 1848, Yale Collection of American Literature, Beinecke Rare Book and Manuscript Library, Yale University; to Thomas Robbins, March 14, 1848, CHS; to Col. Webb, March 21, 1848, Miscellaneous Papers (Ellet, Elizabeth F.), Rare Books and Manuscripts Division, NYPL; and to Gulian C. Verplanck, May 13, 1848, Verplanck Papers, Box 4 E #6, NYHS.

54. Ellet to Cooper, March 11, July 6, 1848, Beinecke Library; to Sparks, December 7, 1847, and May 23, September 19, November 4, 1848, JS-HL 153. Ellet apparently hoped to show Cooper letters she had received from descendants and to talk with him about her project. He saw Ellet at least twice; she "Talked a great deal of her book." Cooper, diary entry, March 30, 1848, in *Correspondence of James Fenimore Cooper,* ed. James Fenimore Cooper (New Haven: Yale University Press, 1922), 2:748. Two days later Cooper wrote to his wife that Ellet was "Ardent and hard working, but with a husband and no children, which lessens one's interest in her labours." *Correspondence of Cooper,* 2:587. See Ellet to Cooper, March 21, April 4, 1848, Beinecke Library.

55. Ellet to Sparks, December 7, 1847, JS-HL 153; to Israel K. Tefft, January 10, [1848], Miscellaneous Papers (Ellet, Elizabeth F.), Rare Books and Manuscripts Division, NYPL; to Thomas Robbins, March 14, 1848, CHS. On Ellet's desire to teach contemporary Americans about their foremothers, see also Ellet to Lydia Sigourney, March 21, 1848, CHS; to Cooper, March 11, 1848, Beinecke Library; and to Col. Webb, March 21, 1848, NYPL. Ellet's appeals to correspondents' patriotism were similarly numerous: see Ellet to Verplanck, May 13, 1848, Verplanck Papers, Box 4 E-#6, NYHS; to Mrs. Wilkes, February 14, 1848, Charles Roberts Autograph Collection, Quaker Collection, Haverford College Library; to Sigourney, March 21, 1848, CHS; to Israel Tefft, December 14, 1847, Miscellaneous Papers (Ellet, Elizabeth F.), NYPL.

56. Ellet to Robbins, March 14, 1848, CHS; to Cooper, March 11, 1848, Beinecke Library; to Sigourney, March 21, 1848, CHS.

57. Ellet to Carey and Hart, January 17, 1848, Miscellaneous MSS E, NYHS; to Carey and Hart, February 8, 1848, Rare Books and Manuscripts Division, NYPL. Carey and Hart

must not have met Ellet's price. Baker and Scribner published *The Women of the American Revolution* in two duodecimo volumes in the fall of 1848; any documents or contracts specifying Ellet's "bargain" have been lost. The publisher's cards of Baker and Scribner, which remain in the Princeton University Library, list only the copyright date and price of each book the firm printed, as well as the subsequent printings and prices.

58. Elizabeth F. Ellet, *The Women of the American Revolution* (New York: Baker and Scribner, 1848), 1:iii.

59. Ibid., 2:133.

60. Ibid., 2:18. To describe Ellet as an exponent of the "cult of domesticity" or "cult of true womanhood" is too simple, both because of the multiple interpretations and facets of those terms and because of Ellet's own emphasis on particular virtues and traits. Ellet's presentation of the Revolutionary women, while it certainly promoted domestic roles and characteristics, should not be seen as a tribute to "piety, purity, submissiveness, and domesticity." Ellet attributed piety to several characters, including Dorcas Richardson (1:273), Elizabeth Steele (1:300), Martha Wilson (2:67), and Jane Campbell (2:189). But religion never served as a motivating factor in Ellet's narratives; piety appeared only in lists of the women's traits. Purity was never an issue. "Domesticity," the trickiest of the four terms, represented a broad spectrum of responsibilities and traits. Ellet did advance the belief that woman's "proper" sphere lay in the home, but also important were the ways Ellet's subjects differed from stereotypical "true women," particularly in their intellectual abilities.

61. Ibid., 1:52, 2:34–35.

62. For every biography that began "Esther De Berdt was born in the city of London . . . ," another started with a sentence like this: "When Major Henry Knox, then a resident of Boston, was parading the company . . . he was seen, among many who admired the young officer, by Miss Lucia Flucker, the daughter of the Secretary of the Province of Massachusetts." Like Ellet's mother in the dedication, Lucia Flucker immediately appeared as the sum of her familial roles, in a prepositional phrase between her future husband and her father. Ibid., 2:22, 1:36, 1:107.

63. Ibid., 2:125–26.

64. Ibid., 2:123–27, 135.

65. Ibid., 2:18–24.

66. Ibid., 2:22, 1:281, 2:35, 2:160, 1:53, 1:384–86.

67. This interpretation should not be pushed too far; after all, many of the sketches described unlearned farm wives rather than scholarly gentlewomen. But it is important to consider Ellet's personal position while reading certain chapters. Ibid., 1:220, 2:32, 1:76, 2:102.

68. On *Godey's* as advocate of active womanhood, see McCall, " 'The Reign of Brute Force Is Now Over.' " Also like *Godey's,* Ellet studiously avoided contentious political issues, particularly that of slavery (see Baym, *American Women Writers and the Work of History,* 238). A few sketches in *The Women of the American Revolution* mentioned slaves' presence in southern households, but African-American women were not among Ellet's heroines. Although Ellet lived in South Carolina for a dozen years, slavery and African Americans appeared infrequently in her published works, and not at all in her extant letters. One notable exception was her 1840 *Rambles About the Country,* a travel volume designed especially for children, endorsed by the Massachusetts Board of Education, and reprinted three times during the next thirty years. In this book Ellet described southern society,

African American and white, and suggested that poor whites had the worst lot because masters were bound by American laws and social customs to treat slaves humanely. Ellet, *Rambles About the Country* (Boston: Marsh, Capen, Lyon, and Webb, 1840). Race was more often a factor in Ellet's usually (but not exclusively) stereotypical portrayals of Native Americans as savage betrayers of whites and threats to white women.

The characteristics and roles with which Ellet associated her subjects were not the only link between *The Women of the American Revolution* and the domestic literature that sold so well. Ellet occasionally employed sentimental language, whose literary purpose was to create bonds of empathy between subject and reader (for instance, see 2:174).

69. The clearest example of Ellet's entry into historiographical debates concerned the wife of Benedict Arnold. Discussing Margaret Arnold's role in her husband's treachery, Ellet compared historians' views (was she a Lady Macbeth or simply an unconscious instrument of Benedict's schemes?) and ultimately concurred with Sparks that Margaret knew nothing of his plans. Ellet also argued that Margaret, "fond of display and admiration, and used to luxury," offered "nothing in her influence or associations to countervail the persuasions to which he ultimately yielded." In other words, Ellet demonstrated the historian's fidelity by evaluating conflicting interpretations and ended with an interpretation of her own, one consonant with her emphasis on "influence." *Women of the American Revolution,* 1:xii, 2:216.

70. Ibid., 1:110, 1:145, 2:298.

71. For example, Ellet included the story of Mary Philipse because "Mr. Sparks assures me" that a confidential friend of George Washington thought the young soldier interested in Mary (1:203); see also 2:221. Given that Ellet sought Sparks's opinion of her work immediately after its publication, her "confidence" in his facts and interpretations may have been influenced by a desire for his approval, as well as genuine respect for his work and prominence.

72. Ibid., 1:ix–xi, 1:15, 2:96.

73. Ibid., 1:15. Jane Tompkins has most forcefully argued for the revolutionary power of domestic ideology, with its typology of sacrifice and language of sentiment (*Sensational Designs,* 122–47). The entire spectrum of domestic writing associated women's responsibility and influence within the home with national advancement and patriotic duty. In her introductory chapter Ellet intertwined the language of sentiment and female influence with national metaphors, notably the idea that "Patriotic mothers nursed the infancy of freedom" (1:14). The "home-sentiment" that women nurtured in their husbands and sons included both the feelings taught within the domestic sphere and the love of a larger "home," the newly independent nation. The metaphor of the nation as a child to be nurtured was hardly new; it had gained currency in the days of the Revolution itself. But Ellet altered the familiar metaphor to emphasize the contribution of "foremothers." Women's role in nurturing the nation as well as the child was a constant theme of domestic handbooks, novels, and women's magazines; the idealization of Mary Washington represented only the most visible personification of this theme. Ellet extended the imagery backward in time, giving a history to the fundamental argument of domestic ideology.

74. Ellet, *Women of the American Revolution,* 1:110, 3:51; Ellet to Sparks, September 19, 1848, JS-HL 153. "Almost the same thing happened with the sketch of Mrs. Greene," Ellet wrote to Sparks, "but fortunately I became wise before the publication of the book—and had only to destroy the stereotype plates and rewrite the sketch." Sabine's account of Mrs.

Knox apparently emphasized her masculine interests even more strongly than Ellet did, for Ellet wrote of "softening" his information.

75. Analyzing Ellet's depiction of Abigail Adams, Edith B. Gelles has placed Ellet's work squarely within this vision. Gelles correctly notes Ellet's use of her subjects as figures for emulation, a tendency especially pronounced in Abigail's sketch (2:31), but Ellet also implied several other understandings or constructions of the past. Gelles, "The Abigail Industry," 660–61.

76. Ellet, *Women of the American Revolution*, 2:96.

77. Ibid., 1:x, 2:259, 1:43. Expressions of how the present cannot understand the past filled Ellet's pages (see also 1:21). Ellet juxtaposed not only present with past but also contentment or luxury with anxiety or difficulty. Here the second and third visions of the past intersected: *because* the Revolutionary generation endured and survived its "ancient times of trial," the present generation could enjoy prosperity and tranquility—and read about its foremothers from a distance of experience as well as time. At the same time, Ellet implied that present-day prosperity was itself responsible for the destruction of the past. General Putnam's headquarters, after all, gave way to "a new and elegant mansion . . . a more costly edifice." Although Ellet never explicitly connected her references to prosperity, taken together they suggested that the prosperous present's debt to the "troublous" past was memory and preservation (2:95).

78. Ellet to Thomas Robbins, March 14, 1848, CHS.

79. Ellet, *Women of the American Revolution*, 2:189, 2:117, 2:31. As Ellet wrote of Mrs. Motte's house, "I have stood upon the spot, and felt that it was indeed classic ground, and consecrated by memories which should thrill the heart of every American" (2:72). Many readers could not stand upon these historic spots, and most could not read the unpublished letters Ellet had seen; Ellet and her writing connected these readers with the Revolutionary past.

80. Ibid., 2:149, 2:141.

81. Review of *The Women of the American Revolution*, *Godey's Lady's Book* 38 (January 1849): 66; *NAR* 68 (April 1849): 364–65, 387–88. Reviews in *Godey's* seldom criticized books, but this review headed the book notices and ran twenty-three lines, longer than most other reviews. The following month, *Godey's* again recommended the purchase of *The Women of the American Revolution*—this time as a Valentine's Day present, in an article arguing that books rather than commercially produced cards made sincere Valentine's gifts. "A New Fashion for Valentines," *Godey's Lady's Book* 38 (February 1849): 74. Few articles in *NAR* were written by women; the editors may have categorized Ellet's work as a "woman's book" and offered the review to Kirkland. But the lack of any author's name on the piece placed *The Women of the American Revolution* into the same public category as any other book the magazine reviewed. Kirkland also edited the *Union Magazine of Art and Literature*—which reviewed *The Women of the American Revolution* more enthusiastically and less critically than did the *NAR*. Even if Kirkland did not write the *Union's* review, she presumably read and approved it; the difference between these reviews thus mirrors the magazines' standards, rather than particular reviewers' preferences.

82. Writers identified with the "domestic" who also wrote historical works included Caroline Kirkland, Catharine Sedgwick, and Harriet Beecher Stowe; see Baym, *American Women Writers and the Work of History*. Some of the best-known historical works of the period were the products of novelists, including Washington Irving, William Gilmore Simms,

and James Fenimore Cooper. See also Douglas, *The Feminization of American Culture*, 184–86; and Callcott, *History in the United States*, 35–45, 110–13.

83. "The Women of the American Revolution: To Mrs. E. F. Ellet" (poem by "Caroline C"), *Godey's Lady's Book* 38 (January 1849): 64–65; "The Women of the American Revolution," *Chambers' Edinburgh Journal* 10 (November 25, 1848): 349.

84. "Letter to M.D.S.," 3–6.

85. Ibid., 6; Ellet to Sparks, November 4, 1848, JS-HL 153. *Godey's* and the *Union Magazine* had noted early in 1848 that Ellet was preparing a work on the Revolutionary women and would appreciate details and anecdotes from any who might have them. Her apology, didactic in its explanation of what did not constitute history, may also have been a sincere response to the readers who found their submissions unprinted. *Godey's* 36 (January 1848): 72–73; *Union Magazine* 2 (April 1848): 190.

86. Ellet, *Women of the American Revolution*, 1:145–47.

87. "Declaration of Sentiments and Resolutions, Seneca Falls Convention (1848)," in Kraditor, *Up from the Pedestal*, 184; Ellet, *Women of the American Revolution*, 1:13–15.

88. Robinson, "Restoring Domestic Order." This movement into public can be usefully compared with the other public activities of antebellum women recently discussed by Mary Ryan: women's preservationist work was essentially socially conservative, unlike the woman's-rights movement and perhaps more akin to reform movements. In this way the work of Ellet and the Mount Vernon Ladies' Association can be linked with the vision of Catharine Beecher, who similarly merged women's importance in the home with their public presence, whether as author and teacher (her own public roles) or as schoolteachers civilizing the American West. Like Beecher, Ellet took on "the contradictory task of both nationalizing and personalizing the American domestic environment" in translating individual memory of domestic scenes into national history. Sklar, *Catharine Beecher*, xii; see also Ryan, *Women in Public*.

89. The rest of Simms's review discussed Ellet's southern subjects, reprinting several sketches verbatim. Such long extracts, a staple of literary reviews in both the North and the South, told readers what to expect in a book. In this case, Simms may have hoped the review would entice his readers to buy Ellet's work: after all, he took credit (and Ellet gave him credit, in her "Letter to M.D.S." in *Godey's*) for having encouraged her to write it. Simms, "Ellet's *Women of the American Revolution*," *Southern Quarterly Review* 17 (July 1850): 334. On Simms's and his intellectual circle's conception of writing history and biography, see Wakelyn, *The Politics of a Literary Man*, 115–36, 200; Faust, *A Sacred Circle*, esp. 73–80; and McCardell, *The Idea of a Southern Nation*, 141–76. On romantic history as practiced by four prominent northern historians, see Levin, *History as Romantic Art*. Simms complained a decade later that Ellet had not shown proper gratitude for his encouragement, "though I gave her the subject of the women of the Revolution and counselled her in what quarters to seek her materials." Simms to Henry Barton Dawson, April 23, [1859], in Simms, *The Letters of William Gilmore Simms*, 4:148.

90. Simms's book-length biographies were *The Life of Francis Marion* (New York: Henry G. Langley, 1844), *The Life of Captain John Smith, the Founder of Virginia* (New York: George F. Cooledge and Brother, 1846), *The Life of the Chevalier Bayard* (New York: Harper and Brothers, 1847), and *The Life of Nathanael Greene, Major-General in the Army of the Revolution* (New York: George F. Cooledge and Brother, 1849). The first two of these appeared in Cooledge's "Illustrated Library" series in 1847, along with a biography of Israel Putnam.

Simms also contributed eight biographical sketches to Rufus Wilmot Griswold's *Washington and the Generals of the Revolution* (Philadelphia: Carey and Hart, 1847), a competitor to Joel Tyler Headley's *Washington and His Generals,* one of the most popular works of the 1840s on the American Revolution. Simms arranged with Griswold to receive $25 for each biography he furnished — a sum he later considered too small for some of the longer sketches, since he could have made more money by submitting them to *Godey's* or *Graham's.* Simms to Carey and Hart, December 13, [1847], in *Letters of Simms,* 2:380–81.

91. "Life of William Richardson Davie, Governor of North Carolina" (review article), *Southern Literary Messenger* 14 (August 1848): 512. The *Messenger,* which viewed itself (at least until the mid-1850s) as a national magazine designed to promote literature in the South, also praised Jared Sparks as "confessedly better acquainted with the history of the country than any other living man" and stated that the inclusion of Hubbard's *Life of Davie* in Sparks's Library of American Biography was the best "recommendation" a biography could have (510). The point that southern magazines generally did not run biographies comes from an examination of the entire runs of five periodicals: the *Southern Literary Journal* (Charleston, 1835–38), the *Southern Literary Messenger* (Richmond, 1834–64), the *Southern Quarterly Review* (New Orleans, 1842–57), the *Southern Review* (Charleston, 1828–32), and the *Virginia Historical Register* (Richmond, 1848–53). Of the five, only the *Messenger* published biographical sketches occasionally: a series on "Living American Poets and Novelists" (including Simms, Cooper, and several others) and several sketches of political figures, mostly southern, in the late 1830s, and scattered sketches over the next quarter century. The *Virginia Historical Register,* affiliated with the state's historical society, promised in its first issue to "pay due attention to [Virginia's] Biography" but never published biographies, except for an extract from Ellet's sketch of Mary Washington. *Virginia Historical Register* 1 (1848): iii.

92. "Life of Davie," *Southern Literary Messenger,* 511–12; Simms, "Kennedy's *Life of Wirt,*" *Southern Quarterly Review* 17 (April 1850): 197.

93. Simms, "Kennedy's *Life of Wirt,*" 197–98.

94. Simms to James Lawson, April 25, [1840], in *Letters of Simms,* 1:171.

95. Simms, *The Life of Francis Marion,* vii.

96. Ibid., 13, 334. A useful discussion of Simms's presentation of southern subjects as models of chivalry and southern notions of honor is Cash, "Biography and Southern Culture, 1800–1940," 22–28. Cash notes that Simms describes various subjects in medieval or feudal terms (see *Life of Marion,* 327). The distinction between southern "sectionalism" and southern "nationalism" is explained in McCardell, *The Idea of a Southern Nation.* McCardell traces the idea of a southern nation from 1830 to the eve of civil war, and contends that southern "sectionalism" in fact was transformed around 1850. McCardell distinguishes *sectionalism* — the perception of "a common interest in a specific issue or set of issues," which need not preclude American nationalism — from *nationalism* — the belief that the South's interests were "incompatible with those of the rest of the Union and were, in fact, being threatened."

97. Simms took issue with southern biographers, too, when he opposed their politics or their presentation of subjects' lives. For instance, he confessed to Kennedy that he was "no great admirer" of Wirt, whose "Whiggism" (like Kennedy's) conflicted with Simms's own Democratic loyalties. Simms's laudatory review admitted his mixed opinions of Wirt but praised Kennedy as a "Southron" writing southern biography. Yet it also attacked

Kennedy's "confident speculations on the permanence and integrity of the Union." If the majority worked "to the dishonor and perhaps destruction of the minority," should not the minority resort to "secession"? Simms was not criticizing Kennedy's portrayal of Wirt so much as Kennedy's own political views as they crept into the portrayal of Wirt. Simms to John Pendleton Kennedy, May 1, [1850], in *Letters of Simms,* 3:37; Simms, "Kennedy's Life of Wirt," 228–29.

98. Simms to Nathaniel Beverly Tucker, August 7, September 11, November 27, [1850], in *Letters of Simms,* 3:57–58, 64–65, 77; [Nathaniel Beverly Tucker], "Garland's *Life of Randolph,*" *Southern Quarterly Review* 20 (July 1851): 41–61; Hugh A. Garland, "Letter from Hugh A. Garland, Esq.," *Southern Quarterly Review* 21 (January 1852): 220–23.

99. Simms to Tucker, August 7, [1850], in *Letters of Simms,* 3:57–58. On southern intellectuals' frustration with their unappreciative fellow southerners, see Faust, *A Sacred Circle,* esp. 17–24; and McCardell, *The Idea of a Southern Nation,* 155.

100. For an overview of McRee's life and literary career, see Clyde Wilson, "Griffith John McRee," 1–23.

101. Griffith J. McRee to David Lowry Swain, January [?], April 28, 1856, October 21, 1855, David Lowry Swain Papers, UNC.

102. Griffith J. McRee, *Life and Correspondence of James Iredell, One of the Associate Justices of the Supreme Court of the United States* (New York: D. Appleton and Co., 1857), 2:588–89; McRee to Swain, April 28, 1856; see also McRee to Swain, August 27, [1856], Swain Papers, UNC.

103. McRee to Swain, August 27, [1856]; March 12, 1857, Swain Papers, UNC.

104. Eli W. Caruthers to McRee, August 29, November 3, 1856, Griffith John McRee Papers, UNC; see also McRee to Swain, July 8, [1856], Swain Papers, UNC.

105. McRee to Swain, March 12, 1857, Swain Papers, UNC.

106. Perhaps, too, the type of biography that the *Life of Iredell* was—a "life and letters," two fat volumes replete with transcripts of correspondence—helps explain why only the "liberal and educated few" read it. A quarter century earlier Jared Sparks had learned the same lesson with his *Life of Gouverneur Morris,* and he separated the "Life" volume of his *Life and Writings of Washington* from the volumes of correspondence so that it could be sold separately. Unwittingly, McRee's friend Caruthers also suggested the limited market for lives and letters: "every lawyer & every man of education who feels an interest in our revolutionary history will want a copy." Caruthers to McRee, November 3, 1856, McRee Papers, UNC.

107. W. Hooper to McRee, June 15, 1858; Medino Kindley [?] to McRee, December 10, 1857; Cadwallader Jones to McRee, March 27, 1858; all in McRee Papers, UNC. Other letters praising McRee's contribution to North Carolinian or southern history and literature included Thomas H. Might to McRee, March 11, 1858, and J. A. Miller to McRee, March [?], 1858, in McRee Papers, UNC. McRee received letters from North Carolinians in Raleigh, Wilmington, Murfreesboro, Fayetteville, Greensboro, and Hillsboro.

108. Randall to Horace Greeley, March 17, 1858, in Henry S. Randall Correspondence (M-1321-P), Manuscripts Department, Alderman Library, University of Virginia, Charlottesville; "Introduction," in Klingberg and Klingberg, *Randall and Grigsby.*

109. Randall to Grigsby, December 4, 1856, November 3, 1857, Klingberg and Klingberg, *Randall and Grigsby,* 71, 111; Henry S. Randall, *The Life of Thomas Jefferson* (New York: Derby and Jackson, 1857–58), 1:160–62; Randall to Jared Sparks, April 16, 1856, JS-HL.

110. For Randall's tenacity in research, see Randall to Grigsby, June 18, 1856, Klingberg and

Klingberg, *Randall and Grigsby,* 57; for consultation with Sparks as an authority on facts, see Randall to Sparks, April 16 and June 7, 1856, JS-HL; for Randall's attitude toward family lore, see Randall to Grigsby, February 15 and December 4, 1856, Klingberg and Klingberg, *Randall and Grigsby,* 30, 72. Randall shared "Dusky Sally's" paternity in letters to Sparks (February 28, 1859, JS-HL) and to James Parton (June 1, 1868, JP-HL).

111. Randall, *Life of Jefferson,* 1:162, 3:506–8.

112. [Thomas Bulfinch], "Jefferson's Private Character," *NAR* 91 (July 1860): 108, 112; [E. O. Dunning], "Private Character of Thomas Jefferson," *New Englander* 19 (July 1861): 648–52, 668. On the sectarian split within New England's literary magazines, see Buell, *New England Literary Culture,* esp. chap. 9.

113. [W. Dorsheimer], "Thomas Jefferson," *AM* 2 (November 1858): 706; [W. Dorsheimer], "Thomas Jefferson," *AM* 2 (December 1858): 794; *NAR* 87 (October 1858): 563; Horace Greeley to Randall, March 18, 1858, Accession #4507, Box CF, Manuscripts Department, Alderman Library. Similarly, the New York *Herald* (December 20, 1857) believed that "The reverence which Dr. Randall feels for the character of Jefferson has blinded him in a measure to the impartiality required in his literary task."

114. Randall to Grigsby, June 18, 1856, Klingberg and Klingberg, *Randall and Grigsby,* 58, 60; *Southern Literary Messenger* 26 (April 1858): 319; [Hugh Blair Grigsby], reviews of *Life of Jefferson, Richmond Enquirer,* December 29, 1857, January 14 and June 26, 1858. Randall also complained to Sparks about Charles Francis Adams's treatment of Jefferson. However, knowing that the New Englander Sparks would have a different view of the Adamses than the Virginian Grigsby, Randall did not use phrases like "twopenny Boston cliquist," and he made sure to mention his admiration for John Adams. Randall to Sparks, November 26, 1858, JS-HL.

115. Henry Stephens Randall to Hugh Blair Grigsby, September [?] 1857, April 25, 1859; Grigsby to Randall, October 6, 1857, July 25, 1858; all in Klingberg and Klingberg, *Randall and Grigsby,* 105–7, 135, 164–65.

116. Grigsby to Randall, July 25, 1858, Klingberg and Klingberg, *Randall and Grigsby,* 135.

117. Randall, *Life of Jefferson,* 1:162–63.

118. Randall to Grigsby, November 14, February 15, May 25, 1856, Klingberg and Klingberg, *Randall and Grigsby,* 65, 30, 51; Randall, *Life of Jefferson,* 1:161.

HAWTHORNE, SPARKS, AND BIOGRAPHY AT MIDCENTURY

1. "Hawthorne's Life of Pierce.—Perspective," *Democratic Review* 31 (September 1852): 276.

2. For the original accusations, see "Nuces Literariae, by Friar Lubin," New York *Evening Post,* February 12, 1851, reprinted in *Literary World* 8 (March 1, 1851): 170. Sparks's statements appeared originally in newspapers and were reprinted as pamphlets: *A Reply to the Strictures of Lord Mahon and Others, on the Mode of Editing the Writings of Washington* (Cambridge, Mass.: John Bartlett, 1852); *Letter to Lord Mahon, Being an Answer to His Letter Addressed to the Editor of Washington's Writings* (Boston: Little, Brown, 1852); *Remarks on a "Reprint of the Original Letters from Washington to Joseph Reed, during the American Revolution, Referred to in the Pamphlets of Lord Mahon and Mr. Sparks"* (Boston: Little, Brown, 1853). Mahon's original criticisms appeared in his *History of England from the Peace of Utrecht to the Peace of Versailles* (London: J. Murray, 1836–54), 6: appendix. Mahon responded to Sparks's first pamphlet in *A Letter from Lord Mahon to Mr. Sparks, Being a Rejoinder to His*

"*Reply . . .*" (London: J. Murray, 1852). The Sparks-Mahon controversy is discussed at length in Adams, *Life and Writings of Sparks,* 2:479–506; and Bassett, *The Middle Group of American Historians,* 100–113.

3. "Mr. Jared Sparks's Liberties with George Washington," *Literary World* 8 (March 1, 1851): 165–66; *Harper's New Monthly Magazine* 5 (September 1852): 566; "Lord Mahon's Rejoinder to Mr. Sparks," *Literary World* 11 (September 25, 1852): 199–200. See also "Marks and Remarks," *Literary World* 11 (July 17, 1852): 40; *Harper's* 5 (November 1852): 860; "Lord Mahon and Mr. Sparks," *Living Age* no. 440 (October 23, 1852): 189–90.

4. For a more extended discussion of the political and publishing machinations behind Hawthorne's *Life of Franklin Pierce,* see Casper, "The Two Lives of Franklin Pierce," 203–30. For Ticknor as "bitter whig," see Hawthorne to Ticknor, June 13, 1852, in Hawthorne, *The Letters, 1843–1853,* 547. The paperback copy of the *Life of Franklin Pierce* is at AAS.

5. Hawthorne to Pierce, July 5, 1852, Hawthorne, *The Letters, 1843–1853,* 560–61. Several scholars have analyzed Hawthorne's *Life of Franklin Pierce* in terms of the author's other work. Lee H. Warner argues that, faced with a dearth of material and an unavoidably mediocre subject, "Hawthorne created his own, fictional Frank Pierce," using his other characters as models. Yet most of the characteristics Warner sees in terms of Hawthorne's earlier characters were conventions of campaign biography by 1852. Richard Boyd offers a more probing analysis of the biography's inner politics, particularly the way Hawthorne excluded "all those disturbing elements which might disrupt his utopian scene of social harmony," such as the slavery issue. Useful as this argument is for contrasting the *Life of Franklin Pierce* with the darker social vision of Hawthorne's most famous fiction, much of what Boyd describes was also quite common to the campaign life, especially by the 1850s: its emphasis on Union and avoidance of divisive issues like slavery. Lee H. Warner, "Nathaniel Hawthorne and the Making of the President," 20–36; Boyd, "The Politics of Exclusion," 337–51. See also Bercovitch, *The Office of the Scarlet Letter,* 86–88.

6. Nathaniel Hawthorne, *Biographical Stories for Children* (Boston: Tappan and Dennet, 1842), 211–84. For analysis of this book in the contexts of Hawthorne's other juvenile writing and his personal struggles, see Laffrado, *Hawthorne's Literature for Children,* 41–65.

7. "As pleasant reading as the author's romances" appeared in several reviews, including the pro-Pierce *Washington Union* (September 14, 1852) and *The Campaign* (September 18, 1852) and the anti-Pierce *Arkansas Whig* (October 7, 1852). Other reviews quoted in this paragraph include [Alex Bickerstaff, pseud.], "Review of the Attempt on the Life of Frank Pierce," *Concord Tribune* (October 15, 1852): 1–2; *Daily Cincinnati Gazette* (July 8, 1852); and "The Blithedale Romance," *American Whig Review* 16 (November 1852): 417–24.

8. "Hawthorne's Life of Pierce.—Perspective," 276–77.

9. Ibid., 278.

10. Ibid., 277; "The Duty of a Biographer," *Democratic Review* 28 (March 1851): 254–58. On the multiple incarnations of "Young America" and its use as a phrase that could mean many things to many people, see Wallach, *Obedient Sons,* 116–50.

11. Nathaniel Hawthorne, *Life of Franklin Pierce* (Boston: Ticknor, Reed, and Fields, 1852), 3–4. The *Literary World* made several of the same points as the *Democratic Review;* see "Hawthorne's Life of Franklin Pierce," *Literary World* 11 (September 25, 1852): 195–96.

12. "Hawthorne's Life of Pierce.—Perspective," 277; for "Sparked," see "Nuces Literariae," 170.

13. Henry Stephens Randall to Horace Greeley, March 29, 1858; Robert A. West to Randall,

January 8, 1855; both in Henry S. Randall Correspondence, Manuscripts Department, Alderman Library, University of Virginia, Charlottesville.

CHAPTER FOUR

1. The quotations here and in the next paragraph are from *New York Times* (March 25, 1867): 2.
2. "Biography," *Port Folio* n.s. 3 (January 1817): 29–30; "Biographical Mania," *New-York Mirror, and Ladies' Literary Gazette* 7 (May 15, 1830): 359.
3. *Christian Examiner* 27 (January 1840): 344; [William H. Prescott], "Lockhart's Life of Scott," *NAR* 46 (April 1838): 431–32; "Biography—Plutarch's Lives," *NAR* 89 (October 1859): 533, 535; [Evert A. Duyckinck], "Biography" (review of *Essays, Biographical and Critical,* by Henry T. Tuckerman), *NAR* 84 (April 1857): 407, 411, 416, 418; "The Biographical Mania," *Evening Gazette* (Boston), July 4, 1857, 8.
4. On the development of the middle class and the ideology of "separate spheres" in Victorian England, see Davidoff and Hall, *Family Fortunes;* for the American version, see Ryan, *Cradle of the Middle Class;* on American working-class families, see Stansell, *City of Women.*
5. Duyckinck, "Biography," 408; "Biographical Literature," *Christian Review* 21 (October 1856): 567; [Mary Abigail Dodge], "The New School of Biography," *AM* 14 (November 1864): 580.
6. *Christian Examiner* 27 (January 1840): 344.
7. The outstanding study of romanticism in English biography is Cafarelli, *Prose in the Age of Poets.* The bulk of this and the two subsequent paragraphs is derived from Cafarelli's work, which sensitively analyzes both the romantic biographical texts and their contexts of publishing, authorship, and reception. On romantic authors' concern about being "Boswellized" in the literary market of the early nineteenth century, see 70–71. The best analysis of the Boswellian long biographies is Joseph W. Reed, *English Biography in the Early Nineteenth Century, 1800–1838.* Coleridge's statement on biography originally appeared in "A Prefatory Observation on Modern Biography," *The Friend* 21 (January 25, 1810): 338, quoted in Reed, *English Biography,* 41. Wordsworth's similar statement appeared in his "Letter to a Friend of Burns" (1816), reprinted in *Wordsworth's Literary Criticism,* ed. Nowell C. Smith (London: C. Frowde, 1905), 210. On the influences of Boswell and romanticism on American biography and biographical criticism, see also Haselton, "The Fairest Meed: Biography in America before 1865."
8. Cafarelli, *Prose in the Age of Poets,* 1–27, 47.
9. Ibid., 1, 16–19, 50–51.
10. Carlyle's essay on Burns was quoted in at least two American articles: "A Biographer at Work," *New Englander* 25 (April 1866): 222; "Biography," *Penn Monthly* 6 (April 1875): 276–77. On the rise of hero-worship as an English Victorian fashion, see Altick, *Lives and Letters,* 82–86. Altick suggests that hero-worship met Victorian Britons' need for "reassurance" in an industrial and commercial society that appeared to elevate impersonal forces over individual agency.
11. "Loose Thoughts on Biography," *American Monthly Magazine* 1 (July 1829): 255; "Biography—Plutarch's Lives," 534; [Henry T. Tuckerman], "The Character of Washington," *NAR* 83 (July 1856): 1; [Mary Abigail Dodge], "The New School of Biography," 580. All of these critics called for biographers to reveal their subjects' individuality, but they dis-

agreed about whether every human being was animated by "one great central principle, one predominant characteristic, one ruling passion" (the Plutarchan view), or whether most individuals, especially men of "genius," had complex combinations of traits. The former view appeared in *Christian Examiner* 22 (July 1837): 344; the latter throughout most of the other articles cited here.

12. *Christian Examiner* 39 (September 1845): 171–72; "The Biographical Mania," *Evening Gazette*, 8. The strongest statement against eulogy and whitewashing was "The Duty of a Biographer," *Democratic Review* 28 (March 1851): 255–58.

13. "Biographical Studies," *American Quarterly Church Review* 18 (January 1867): 624–25; "Biography," *Southern Literary Messenger* 23 (October 1856): 286–87; Duyckinck, "Biography," 406–7. Writing in the *NAR*, William H. Prescott had used the "sunlight and shadow" metaphor in 1838; see "Lockhart's Life of Scott," 432. Criticisms of biographers who merely compiled documents include *Christian Examiner* 26 (May 1839): 192–93; *Christian Examiner* 50 (March 1851): 228–29. One source of the problem was the desire of children to commemorate their parents, a worthy objective that could lead mistakenly to eulogy and "book-making," the publication of biographies for the sake of publishing something quickly rather than revealing inner character. Some reviewers gave "compilers" credit for giving materials to the future biographer, but the *NAR* was not so generous; see "Biography—Plutarch's Lives," 535. For a defense of those who wrote the lives of acquaintances and relatives, see "Life and Writings of Dr. Follen," *Christian Examiner* 33 (September 1842): 34–35. For a critic's attack on biographers' showing off, see *Harper's* 1 (October 1850): 70, as well as Henry Randall's opinion that *Sketches of the Life and Character of Patrick Henry* was all "Wirt, Wirt, Wirt, ornate Wirt." The preference for a style that did not interfere with the "plot" (in this case the subject's life story) was common to criticism of biography and the novel in this period. On contemporary criticism of fiction, see Baym, *Novels, Readers, and Reviewers*.

14. Duyckinck, "Biography," 407; "Biography," *Southern Literary Messenger,* 286; "Loose Thoughts on Biography," 257. The *Christian Review* somewhat humorously offered a prescription for collecting the "modern memoir": advertise for the subject's letters, gather his diaries and journals, "invite the personal recollections and reminiscences of intimate friends," collect "the records of schools, academies, and colleges" to tell of his youth, and consult "nurses, watchers, physicians, clergymen, and other attendants and friends" to tell of his death. "Biographical Literature," 560–61.

15. "The New School of Biography," 580; Duyckinck, "Biography," 411. For a similar statement, see *Harper's* 1 (October 1850): 715. The *New Englander* wrote in 1866 that cold analysis "could endanger the life of the subject, making the real man seem only a corpse under the knife of the dissecting surgeon." "A Biographer at Work," 224. On Transcendentalism and science, see Dahlstrand, "Science, Religion, and the Transcendentalist Response to a Changing America," 1, 7–8.

16. "Biography," *Southern Literary Messenger,* 286–87. See also the *New Englander,* which recommended that biographers "study for their task by writing novels"; "A Biographer at Work," 221. This shift resulted in great measure from the American popularity of Sir Walter Scott's novels, which were less susceptible to moralists' critiques than early seduction tales had been. The rage for Scott's works encouraged not just romantic biography but also the colorful romantic histories of Parkman, Prescott, Bancroft, and others. See Levin, *History as Romantic Art,* 9.

17. Duyckinck, "Biography," 407, 411–12; "The Biographical Mania," *Evening Gazette,* 8.

18. Sermon 36, 1829, in Emerson, *The Complete Sermons of Ralph Waldo Emerson,* 1:282; Roberson, "Young Emerson and the Mantle of Biography," 163. Roberson effectively places the biographical elements of Emerson's sermons within the context of early-national didactic biography. She argues that the sort of biography against which Emerson rebelled in his sermons represented the same social order against which he rebelled when he left the church: the world of his father, in which ministers were figures of conservative stability and biographies presented "Idols of Order" for emulation. Emerson's lecture series, "Biography," appears in *The Early Lectures of Ralph Waldo Emerson,* 1:93–201. Unfortunately, the first lecture in Emerson's series, which apparently discussed the value of biography, has been lost. The commentary by editors Whicher and Spiller (93–96) describes the impetus for the lectures and links them to Emerson's early education in Plutarch. Emerson's selection and treatment of subjects reflected his own struggle to create a vocation for himself in which he could continue to be a public man, without the constraints of the ministerial life and with the freedom to criticize an increasingly capitalist, commodified society. All the subjects of these lectures were "thinkers and artists who translated their thought into a reforming impulse" and "found [their] own age wanting." Cayton, *Emerson's Emergence,* 147–48.

19. For examples of magazines identifying *Representative Men* with Emerson's essay style, see *Graham's Magazine* 36 (March 1850): 221; *NAR* 70 (April 1850): 522; and *American Whig Review* 11 (February 1850): 216.

20. Emerson, *Representative Men: Seven Lectures* (orig. 1850; Boston: Houghton, Mifflin, 1903), 13–14, 18, 32. "Perfect Symmetry," Emerson journal, January 13, 1835, in *The Journals and Miscellaneous Notebooks of Ralph Waldo Emerson,* 5:11. The relationship between Emerson's *Representative Men* and Carlyle's *On Heroes and Hero-Worship* has attracted much scholarly attention. Emerson and Carlyle, of course, were friends who maintained a long correspondence; both, too, were Transcendentalists (although Carlyle's Transcendentalism waned as Emerson's was beginning). Summarizing the various arguments about connections between the books, Kenneth Marc Harris (in "Transcendental Biography: Carlyle and Emerson") rejects the idea that Emerson's language of "representativeness" implies a more democratic spirit than Carlyle's. Instead, Harris emphasizes a different contrast: whereas Carlyle placed the roots of heroes' ideas squarely within the heroes themselves, Emerson argued that his "representative men" both drew their ideas from their contexts and drew on ideas that existed in nature.

21. Emerson, *Representative Men,* 270.

22. Emerson journal, August 12, 1832, in *Journals and Miscellaneous Notebooks of Emerson,* 4:35. "Vulgar" biographies, he explained in 1840, searched for "the genesis of a man's thought" not intellectually but "externally in his parentage, in his country, climate, college, election by his fellow citizens, & the like." Emerson journal, May 6, 1840, in ibid., 7:347.

23. Emerson, *Representative Men,* 43–44, 225, 256. On Emerson's essay on Napoleon, see Patterson, "Emerson, Napoleon, and the Concept of the Representative." Other discussions of *Representative Men*—which scholars have approached in various ways—include Richardson, "Emerson on History"; Berry, *Emerson's Plutarch;* Yang, "Emerson as a Biographer"; Harris, "Transcendental Biography."

24. Janice L. Edens, "Henry Theodore Tuckerman," in *Dictionary of Literary Biography,* 64:237. Edens's profile (236–41) is the best modern sketch of Tuckerman's career.

25. Tuckerman's biographical-critical articles for the *North American Review* included "Daniel De Foe," *NAR* 78 (April 1854): 265–83; "Joseph Addison," *NAR* 79 (July 1854): 90–109; "Life of De Witt Clinton," *NAR* 79 (October 1854): 485–502; "George Berkeley," *NAR* 80 (January 1855): 171–98; "Laurence Sterne," *NAR* 81 (October 1855): 361–89; "Sydney Smith," *NAR* 82 (January 1856): 100–111; "The Character of Washington," *NAR* 83 (July 1856): 1–30; "The Character of Franklin," *NAR* 83 (October 1856): 402–22; "Alexander Hamilton," *NAR* 86 (April 1858): 368–411; "Michael De Montaigne," *NAR* 87 (October 1858): 356–88; and "James Fenimore Cooper," *NAR* 89 (October 1859): 289–316. The articles on Washington and Clinton were ostensibly reviews of new biographies of those men (by Washington Irving and Samuel Smucker, respectively). Several pieces responded to new editions of an author's oeuvre; however, Tuckerman never gave much attention to the new publication itself. Several of Tuckerman's shorter character sketches also appeared in the *Southern Literary Messenger* in the late 1850s—a fact that suggests caution when considering sectional divisions in American literature. The *NAR* and the *Messenger,* the foremost intellectual periodicals of their regions, shared much intellectually (a sense of bringing higher culture to readers, for instance).

26. Tuckerman, "The Character of Washington," 1–2; and "Montaigne," 359.

27. Tuckerman, "Daniel De Foe," 275, 279; "Joseph Addison," 107, 95; and "Life of DeWitt Clinton," 485, 492, 501, 490. Tuckerman identified Washington as something different, but no less than a man of genius: "a great moral unity, and not an erratic and marvellous genius" ("The Character of Washington," 2).

28. Tuckerman, "Daniel De Foe," 272; and "James Fenimore Cooper," 289–90. The idea that American romantic heroes came from events like the Mexican War and were portrayed as nature's noblemen (in contrast to aristocrats) is drawn from Robert W. Johannsen, *To the Halls of the Montezumas,* 108–12; and James D. Wilson, *The Romantic Heroic Ideal,* 2–3, 193.

29. Tuckerman, "Daniel De Foe," 265; "George Berkeley," 172; "Sydney Smith," 104; and "James Fenimore Cooper," 307. The apparently meaningless use of the phrase appears in sentences like this one: "As a representative man, Sydney Smith was more endeared for his liberal, frank, and mirthful nature than for its refinements."

30. Tuckerman, "George Berkeley," 172; and "Alexander Hamilton," 372.

31. Duyckinck, "Biography," 418; "Biography—Plutarch's Lives," 535; "The Biographical Mania," *Evening Gazette,* 8. The *NAR*'s circulation actually declined in the three decades before the Civil War from its 1830 peak of 3,200 subscribers (in the days when Jared Sparks had edited it). These thirty years were the very period during which books and magazines were appearing in ever-increasing numbers, when the *Christian Examiner* attributed the phenomenal increase in biographies to "these days of book-making and of publishing." *Harper's,* which became the flagship magazine of New York's leading publishing house, and by extension of the Gotham-centered publishing culture and middle-class readers, enjoyed a circulation of 50,000 within six months of its founding in 1850 and 200,000 by 1860. Not surprisingly, *Harper's* was far less critical of readers' tastes. When it faulted a biography (which it rarely did, since its reviews were virtual publishers' advertisements), it never did so on the grounds that the author had tried to satisfy the longings of a misguided, scandal-hungry public. See Mott, *History of American Magazines,* 231–32, 391.

32. On the fluidity of urban society, see Halttunen, *Confidence Men and Painted Women.* On

sensational literature, see Schiller, *Objectivity and the News;* Denning, *Mechanic Accents;* and Tucher, *Froth and Scum.* On Alcott, see Brodhead, *Cultures of Letters,* 74–89.

33. The full story of the battle over the Pierce biographies appears in my "Two Lives of Franklin Pierce."

34. The only biography of Parton is Flower, *James Parton: The Father of Modern Biography;* on Parton's upbringing and early career, see 7–24. Joyce W. Warren speculates that Fanny Fern (Sara Willis Eldredge) played some role in the Mason Brothers' offer to Parton, as she was one of the firm's popular authors in the mid-1850s; on their relationship, see Warren, *Fanny Fern,* 150–59.

35. On the transformation of the press's earlier political role, see, for instance, Dicken-Garcia, *Journalistic Standards in Nineteenth-Century America,* 30–51. The relationship between different New York papers and the city's emerging social classes has occasioned considerable scholarly disagreement. Alexander Saxton and Dan Schiller have argued that the penny press appealed especially to the working classes, with whom its ideology of egalitarianism resonated most loudly. Michael Schudson suggests a closer connection between the papers and the rising middle class. As Andie Tucher perceptively explains, much of the argument depends on which paper one examines. The fluidity of New York's society in the 1830s and 1840s militates against any rigid identification between papers and classes. It is clearer, based on its emphasis on belles lettres, theater, and middle-class leisure, that Willis's *Home Journal* did not seek a working-class readership. Saxton, "Problems of Class and Race in the Origins of the Mass Circulation Press," 211–34; Schiller, *Objectivity and the News;* Schudson, *Discovering the News,* 12–60; Tucher, *Froth and Scum,* 211–12. For a debate in which Willis's paper clearly opposed the working-class penny press, see Klein, "Art and Authority in Antebellum New York City," 1549–57. See also Crouthamel, *Bennett's New York Herald and the Rise of the Popular Press.*

36. James Parton, *The Life of Horace Greeley, Editor of the New York Tribune* (New York: Mason Brothers, 1855), iii, viii, 138; "Barnum's and Greeley's Biographies," *Christian Examiner* 58 (March 1855): 260.

37. Parton, *Life of Greeley,* viii–x; *NAR* 80 (April 1855): 547–48; "Barnum's and Greeley's Biographies," 260–61.

38. James Parton, *The Life and Times of Aaron Burr* (New York: Mason Brothers, 1858), vii. Not only had Burr's life been filled with controversies, but biographies of him had also long been a litmus test of ideas about biography itself. The first two biographies, by Samuel L. Knapp (published in 1835, when Burr was still alive) and Matthew L. Davis (1837, just after Burr's death), both claimed the virtue of time: decades had elapsed since Burr's alleged treason, presumably long enough for more balanced assessments of his worth. Criticism of these books illustrated concepts of biography in transition. Running throughout the reviews was the didactic, republican notion that had existed since the turn of the century: biographies of Burr had a political-cultural obligation to warn against antirepublican self-aggrandizement and unprincipled demagoguery. Against this standard, Davis and Knapp failed because they did not censure Burr appropriately. Simultaneously, some reviewers echoed the newer generation of historical biographers: it was now time to write balanced historical accounts of America's early political leaders. Still other criticism voiced romantic sensibilities. Taking Burr's character as an enigma to be unraveled — what perversions of character had led a brilliant and promising man, the son of Prince-

ton's second president and grandson of Jonathan Edwards, astray?—these critics commented on whether the biographers had revealed the inner Burr. Most believed they had not, that Knapp and Davis had either obscured Burr's character in eulogy or unwittingly reinforced his notoriety but not lifted the clouds of "mystery" surrounding him. The previous lives of Burr were Samuel L. Knapp, *The Life of Aaron Burr* (New York: Wiley and Long, 1835); and Matthew L. Davis, *Memoirs of Aaron Burr: With Selections from His Correspondence*, 2 vols. (New York: Harper and Brothers, 1837). Notable criticism—most of which blended the various reasons for attacking the biographies—included *Cincinnati Mirror and Chronicle* 4 (May 2, 1835): 218; "Davis's *Memoirs and Journal of Burr*," *NAR* 49 (July 1839): 155–206; "Memoirs of Aaron Burr," *American Quarterly Review* 21 (March 1837): 74–111; *New York Review* 2 (January 1838): 173–213; and *Southern Literary Journal* 3 (May 1838): 364–77. On American images of Burr over time (particularly in drama and fiction rather than biography), see Nolan, *Aaron Burr and the American Literary Imagination.*

39. Parton, *Life of Burr*, vii–viii, 371, 649; Flower, *James Parton*, 215–18.

40. Parton, *Life of Burr*, x, 140, 696.

41. Ibid., 179, 294, 510.

42. Ibid., 25, 380; on the "mysteries of the city" genre, see Blumin, "Introduction: George G. Foster and the Emerging Metropolis," 19–27.

43. Parton, *Life of Burr*, 88, 134–35, 636. Elsewhere in the book, Parton wrote that the facts of Burr's alleged treason "were as different from [prosecutor William] Wirt's version of them as fact ever is from romantic fiction" (506).

44. Mason Brothers, advertisement for Parton's *Life and Times of Aaron Burr*, *American Publishers' Circular* 4 (January 30, 1858): 60. The same ad appeared in the February 6 and February 13 issues. On publishers' use of sales figures to sell more books, see Geary, "The Domestic Novel as a Commercial Commodity," 375–88.

45. "Aaron Burr," *AM* 1 (March 1858): 600, 614; *New Englander* 16 (February 1858): 215; "Aaron Burr," *Southern Literary Messenger* 26 (May 1858): 322; "Aaron Burr," *New Englander* 16 (May 1858): 299. Some critiques also resulted partly from particular magazines' hostility to Parton's views. His portrayal of Puritanism as somber and repressive alienated the orthodox *New Englander*, and his glowing biography of abolitionist Greeley may have stuck in the *Southern Literary Messenger*'s craw. Not all reviews were so harsh. *Harper's* applauded Parton's "genuine talent for historical research and biographic delineation" and specifically the chapter on Jonathan Edwards—the same chapter the *New Englander* hated. The *Ladies' Repository* commended Parton for "a Boswellian fullness of details" without a hint of "Boswellian toadyism." Both *Harper's* and the *Ladies' Repository* considered Parton impartial. *Harper's* 16 (February 1858): 402–3; *Ladies' Repository* 18 (February 1858): 122.

46. *Christian Examiner* 64 (May 1858): 454; "Aaron Burr," *New Englander* 16 (May 1858): 291, 295; "Aaron Burr," *AM* 1 (March 1858): 597; "Aaron Burr," *Southern Literary Messenger* 26 (May 1858): 322–23.

47. James Parton, *Life of Andrew Jackson* (orig. 1860; Boston: James R. Osgood and Co., 1876), 1:x–xi.

48. Ibid., 1:v, viii–ix; Parton to Mrs. Van Cleve, April 20, 1858, quoted in Flower, *James Parton*, 51. A fuller description of Parton's southern trip and search for evidence of Jackson appears in Flower, *James Parton*, 47–58.

49. "Life of Andrew Jackson, by James Parton," *De Bow's Review* 29 (September 1860): 342.

Testimony to the importance of Jackson's biography appeared in *AM* 7 (March 1861): 381; and *New Englander* 18 (February 1860): 234.

50. *AM* 7 (March 1861): 381–82; *New Englander* 19 (January 1861): 213; *Harper's* 20 (January 1860): 262; *New Englander* 18 (May 1860): 539.

51. *Christian Review* 26 (January 1861): 165; *AM* 7 (March 1861): 381.

52. Frances E. Willard, "A Noble Life: Mrs. Lillie Hayes Waugh," *Ladies' Repository* 11 (May 1873): 321; James Parton (hereafter JP) to Charles Eliot Norton, February 5, 1867, Charles Eliot Norton Papers (b MS Am 1088), HL.

53. Robert Bonner to JP, August 4, 1866, JP-HL; JP to Norton, September 12, 1865, Norton Papers; "Mr. Parton's New Volume," *Nation* 4 (April 11, 1867): 291; JP to James T. Fields, January 29 (FI 3262), December 22 (FI 3270), December 27 (FI 3259), 1867, all in James T. Fields Papers, Manuscripts Department, Henry E. Huntington Library, San Marino, Calif.

54. James Parton, *Life and Times of Benjamin Franklin* (orig. 1864; Boston: James R. Osgood and Co., n.d.), 1:7; *AM* 14 (September 1864): 384; *Harper's* 29 (August 1864): 404; *NAR* 99 (July 1864): 302–3.

55. JP to Charles Eliot Norton, August 19, 1864, Norton Papers; Flower, *James Parton*, 78. On Fields's attention to new literary trends and his editorship of the *Atlantic*, see Ellery Sedgwick, *A History of the Atlantic Monthly*, 69–111.

56. James Parton, *Famous Americans of Recent Times* (orig. 1867; Boston: Houghton, Mifflin, 1881), 51, 81. *Famous Americans* contained all but one of Parton's *North American* essays, as well as four pieces he had published in other periodicals.

57. Parton, *Famous Americans*, 105, 298.

58. See "James Parton's Writings," *Atlantic Advertiser and Miscellany*, No. 113 (March 1867): 2, as well as squibs and advertisements in No. 115 (May 1867) and No. 116 (June 1867); and "Parton's Biographical Writings," *NAR* 104 (April 1867): 597–602. On Ticknor and Fields's self-construction as America's premier literary publishing firm, see Brodhead, *Cultures of Letters*, 82, 153; and especially Jeffrey D. Groves's essays, "Ticknor-and-Fields-ism of All Kinds" and "Judging Literary Books by Their Covers."

59. Parton, *Famous Americans*, 382, 390. On Bonner and the *Ledger*, see Warren, *Fanny Fern*, 143–49.

60. In praise of Butler and in hopes that he might run for president, see Joseph M. Bell to JP, November 22, 1863; Charles Nordhoff to JP, February 18, 1864; and Thomas Perronet Thompson to JP, March 15, 1864; all in JP-HL. Nordhoff used "run" in its multiple meanings: "I am glad to hear the book is having a great run. I know of nothing that would run better, except the General himself—I think if he were put up, he would run straight into the White House, wh[ich] would perhaps be for him what a fifteenth or twentieth Edition is for you—a sure thing from the beginning." Parton's letter to the editor of the *Springfield Republican* (November 30, 1863, JP-HL) accused the paper of personal attacks against him, and denied the charge that Butler had "employed" him to write the book.

61. Beadle and Adams' dime biographies are catalogued and described in Albert Johannsen, *The House of Beadle and Adams and Its Dime and Nickel Novels*, 1:364–72. Beadle and Adams produced three sets of biographical booklets: Beadle's Dime Biographical Library (1860–65), Men of the Time (1862), and Lives of Great Americans (1876–77). Lives of Great Americans included a number of titles from the earlier Dime Biographical Library. In

1864 another publisher, James Redpath, wrote Parton that he wanted to base a "Dime Book for the Camp Fire" on Parton's life of Butler. Redpath to JP, January 16, 1864, JP-HL. On Headley's trilogy, see the Wm. H. Appleton advertisement in *American Literary Gazette and Publishers' Circular*, n.s. 4 (December 15, 1864): 140.

62. Harriet Beecher Stowe, *Men of Our Times: Or, Leading Patriots of the Day* (Hartford: Hartford Publishing Co., 1868); L. P. Brockett, *Men of Our Day: Or, Biographical Sketches of Patriots, Orators, Statesmen, Generals, Reformers, Financiers and Merchants, Now on the Stage of Action* (Philadelphia: Ziegler, McCurdy and Co., 1869); James Parton et al., *Eminent Women of the Age: Being Narratives of the Lives and Deeds of the Most Prominent Women of the Present Generation* (Hartford: S. M. Betts and Co., 1869).

63. James Parton, Bayard Taylor, Amos Kendall, E. D. Mayo, J. Alexander Patten, and Other Writers, *Sketches of Men of Progress* (New York and Hartford: New York and Hartford Publishing Co., 1870–71). Apparently Parton's only contribution to the volumes (besides his name) was a sketch of George W. Childs. Similarly, Bayard Taylor's name—the most famous besides Parton's—appeared second on the title page, but Taylor wrote only one sketch. The book was probably compiled by an editor at the publishing firm. At least one potential contributor doubted whether the company was authorized to use Parton's name in soliciting articles; see Frederick Augustus Porter Barnard to JP, November 12, 1870, JP-HL. Parton's fame also propelled him to the lecture circuit, where he gave talks on America's forefathers. In a *Harper's Weekly* cartoon entitled "Celebrities of the Platform," he appeared with a piece of paper that read "Lives of Dead Men Parton."

64. Parton et al., *Eminent Women of the Age*, v, 37; James Parton, ed., *Some Noted Princes, Authors, and Statesmen of Our Time* (Norwich, Conn.: Henry Bill Publishing Co., 1885).

65. The *Nation*'s review of *Famous Americans* offers a striking, though not the only, example of the continued comments about Parton's flawed style despite general praise for his work and its spirit. The *Nation*, though, faulted "our more fastidious critics" for concentrating too heavily on his stylistic defects at the expense of "the essential merits of his books" and praised "the uncritical public" for giving his works the "popularity which, on the whole, they well deserve." The *Nation* could well have been talking about the critical review in the *New York Times* (March 25, 1867), 2, that had appeared a few weeks earlier ("Mr. Parton's New Volume," 290). Only when Greeley ran for the presidency in 1872 did the firm (now Fields and Osgood) republish Parton's life of him—for its potential sale as a campaign biography, not as part of Parton's "literary" oeuvre.

66. In *Highbrow/Lowbrow*, Lawrence Levine has made the strongest argument for cultural bifurcation in late-nineteenth-century America. For the same paradigm applied to literary culture, see Brodhead, *Cultures of Letters*, 69–89. If Parton had written only "Ledger Lines," his career might have taken the shape of J. Alexander Patten's: Patten wrote short lives of businessmen, "Self-Made Men of Our Times," for *Frank Leslie's Chimney Corner*, and may have been the actual, uncredited compiler and main author of *Sketches of Men of Progress*—the subscription book whose publisher placed James Parton's famous name on the spine. My speculation that J. Alexander Patten may have actually edited the volume that bore Parton's name on the spine is based on several facts. Patten, not Parton, wrote the largest number of pieces in the book (eight, as opposed to Parton's one). Johannsen, *The House of Beadle and Adams and Its Dime and Nickel Novels* (2:221–22), identifies Patten as a New York journalist and columnist who wrote dozens of short biographical sketches, as well as several dime novels. He was part of the new phenomenon in dime-novel pub-

lishing, in which authors became little more than factory workers, turning out books at astounding speed and without any bylines (or under stock company pseudonyms).

67. Parton, *Famous Americans,* 354–56.

68. "Mr. Parton's New Volume," 290; Parton, *Famous Americans,* 370. The essays in *Famous Americans* themselves attested to how Parton adopted different biographical styles for different magazines. The seven *North American* pieces, as we have seen, were analytical and interpretive. The article on Beecher read differently. Parton began in the first-person plural, by taking his readers on a visit to one of the new, fashionable New York churches. This style, unfitted to the *North American* even in the 1860s, suited Fields's *Atlantic Monthly* perfectly, by suggesting realism, the vicarious journey to contemporary American places as they truly were. (Fields would next engage Parton to travel to the major midwestern cities, in order to prepare similar reports for the *Atlantic*'s readers.) The article on Cornelius Vanderbilt, which at sixteen pages was far shorter than any other essay in the book (the others averaged forty-four), resembled Parton's other didactic, anecdotal *Ledger* pieces. *Famous Americans of Recent Times* testified to Parton's ability to bring his diverse work together—by juxtaposition, if not by style.

69. On the growing belief among contemporary critics of journalism that scandal-mongering was an evil, see Dicken-Garcia, *Journalistic Standards in Nineteenth-Century America,* 110.

70. Espy Williams diary, January 12, 1874, in Paul T. Nolan, "Journal of a Young Southern Playwright," 1st installment, 40–41.

71. May W. Mount, *Some Notables of New Orleans* (New Orleans: privately published, 1896), 57, quoted in Rickels, "The Literary Career of Espy Williams," 15. Rickels's dissertation, esp. 1–43, provides a useful narrative of Williams's life to the point (1874–75) when he kept his diary.

72. Williams diary, January 30, 1875, in Nolan, "Journal of a Young Southern Playwright," 2d installment, 48; January 11, 1874, 1st installment, 39–40.

73. Ibid., January 12, 1874, 1st installment, 40; March 12, 1874, 2d installment, 41.

74. Ibid., January 12, 1874, 1st installment, 40–42; March 12, 1874, 2d installment, 41.

75. Ibid., March 12, 1874, 2d installment, 40–41.

76. Webster B. Samphere to JP, October 21, 1873, JP-HL.

77. William Menzies copy of James Parton, *Life and Times of Aaron Burr,* AAS. Parton's letter and the lock of Burr's hair are pasted inside the front cover. For other examples of readers individualizing Parton's works, see Curtis Guild to JP, December 14, 1880; Charles Nordhoff to JP, February 18, 1864, both JP-HL. Like Menzies, Nordhoff intended "to fasten the General's [Butler's] note, & yours, together in my copy of the *Life,* & thus I shall have gained a double prize."

78. Catharine Maria Sedgwick to JP, February 28 and April 9, 1865, JP-HL.

79. Sedgwick to JP, April 9, 1865, JP-HL.

80. Joseph M. Bell to JP, November 22, 1863; Thomas Perronet Thompson to JP, March 15, 1864; Gertrude Blade to JP, May 26, 1864; Nicholas P. Trist to JP, November 16, 1864; Reverdy Johnson to JP, March 17, 1864; George William Curtis to JP, July 12, 1864; all in JP-HL.

81. E. L. Youmans to JP, July 13, [1864?]; George Alfred Townsend to JP, March 18, 1880; Jesse K. Furlong to JP, March 29, 1878; Harriet Beecher Stowe to JP, n.d.; Samuel Hilliard Bowman to JP, March 24, 1866; Robert Shelton Mackenzie to JP, October 26, 1864;

Chauncey Forward Black to JP, February 7, 1882; William Bigelow to JP, May 8, 1868; all in JP-HL. For readers consulting Parton about historical evidence, see Fred[erick] Chase to JP, January 16, 1869; William Warland Clapp to JP, January 22, 1886, both in JP-HL, as well as the aforecited letters from Jesse K. Furlong and George Alfred Townsend.

82. Requests from periodicals for Parton's contributions included William Conant Church to JP (for the *Galaxy*), May 14, 1866; Scribner and Co. to JP (for *Scribner's Monthly*), July 24, 1872; John G. Shea to JP (for *Frank Leslie's*), January 14, 1874; also E. L. Godkin to JP (probably for the *Nation*), June 6, [n.y.]; Ford, Olmsted to JP (for the Boston *Watchman and Reflector*), March 1, [n.y.]; Bartley T. Campbell to JP (for the Pittsburgh *Evening Mail*), October 22, 1868; William Warland Clapp to JP (for the Boston *Journal*), October 2, 1869; W. Walter to JP (for *Great Western Monthly! The People's Magazine*), December 6, 1873; all in JP-HL. Individuals' requests to write biographies of friends and relatives include John Howard Bryant to William Cullen Bryant, April 12, 1864 (asking Cullen Bryant to forward Mrs. Lovejoy's wish to Parton); and Charles Tappan to JP, August 4, 1867; both in JP-HL.

83. Albert Deane Richardson to JP, April 25, 1865, JP-HL; JP to Fanny (Hodges) Shaver, May 11, 1865, Autograph File, HL.

84. JP to George William Curtis, July 15, 1864, Curtis Papers (bMS Am 1124.9), HL; JP to "Mr. Clark," March 25, 1867, Rogers Room, HL; Robert Shelton Mackenzie to JP, November 1, 1864, JP-HL; H. C. Moderwell to JP, April 28, 1873, JP-HL. Ticknor and Fields wrote Parton in 1866 that the proposed volume of his *North American* essays (which became *Famous Americans of Recent Times*) would earn him nearly enough money "to carry on your Voltaire project." Ticknor and Fields to JP, April 11, 1866, JP-HL. Parton wrote to Charles Eliot Norton, "Publishers and friends all say, Don't do it. But the subject has caught me with a grip that I cannot escape from, and I feel that I must do it or die" (JP to Norton, August 27, 1864, Norton Papers, HL).

85. James Redpath to JP, n.d. [likely late 1881 or early 1882]; Jesse W. [Stell?] to Robert Green Ingersoll, February 20, 1882; Joseph Henry Allen to JP, October 30, 1883; Redpath to JP, February 27, 1882; Elizur Wright to JP, May 23, 1881; Jonathan Baxter Harrison to JP, November 3, 1881; all in JP-HL.

86. On the sales of Parton's *Life of Voltaire,* see Sales Book 6, HMC-HL. Stell to Ingersoll, February 20, 1882; Redpath to JP, n.d., both in JP-HL. For Parton's perception of his sales, see Julius H. Ward, "James Parton," *New England Magazine* 13 (January 1893): 631–32; JP to Curtis, July 15, 1864, Curtis Papers, HL, in which Parton explained that the "recent inflation and panic have checked the sale of Franklin."

87. JP to Curtis, July 15, 1864; JP to Houghton, Mifflin, and Company, January 15, March 22, 1884; both in HMC-HL. On Parton's religious views and general reformist beliefs, see Flower, *James Parton,* 155–63. Parton denied any desire to promote Voltaire in his work; he wrote Curtis that he wanted to write Voltaire's life "in the pure spirit of investigation, without vituperation or eulogy." Nevertheless, simply taking on this project may have struck some readers as an act of partisanship.

88. Perry Mason and Company to JP, January 9, 1879, JP-HL.

89. William Collins Whitney to JP, May 14, 1880, JP-HL.

1. "From the Cradle to the Grave: Scenes and Incidents in the Life of Gen. James A. Garfield" (poster; New York: J. W. Sheehy and Co., 1882).

2. James A. Garfield, biographical interview ca. 1878, in *Papers of James A. Garfield*, Series 17D, scrapbook p. 102, interview p. 5. Entries for February 3 and 28, 1856, and December 9, 1857, in *The Diary of James A. Garfield*, 1:278–79, 307. The standard modern biography is Peskin, *Garfield;* on Garfield's years as student and teacher, see pp. 33–59. Garfield's praise of Irving's style—"The artist staid behind his canvas entirely out of sight"—resembled the romantic notion that biography was a literary art akin to portraiture and fiction. Like contemporary critics, he couched his comparison in literary terms, marking a break from the condemnation of novels evident in most early-republican criticism. For Garfield, staying out of sight meant avoiding moralistic interruptions of the literary narrative. We cannot know whether Garfield was reading Emerson, Tuckerman, or the contemporary articles about biography, but in the late 1850s he was writing literary essays and occasional poetry.

3. Entry for March 26, 1876, *Diary of James A. Garfield*, 3:260. Anne C. Rose, *Victorian America and the Civil War*, 4. Rose's analysis of middle-class "consciousness" in the era of the Civil War is based on the lives of seventy-five Americans, representing every region of the nation. Garfield is one of her subjects. On his conversion and career choice, see pp. 216–17; on middle-class leisure as a search for "imaginative acquisition" and self-definition, see chap. 3. Garfield's romantic tendencies did not disappear in the 1870s: as he read Goethe's *Autobiography* and George Henry Lewes's biography of Goethe, he remarked that "The development of the Poet's mind is among the most wonderful things I have seen." Entry for November 8, 1874, *Diary of James A. Garfield*, 2:387. Garfield's modern biographer has suggested that Garfield's own "intellectual objectivity" and "capacity for detachment and self-doubt" help explain his admiration for figures of greater will and "emotional intensity," such as Macaulay and James G. Blaine. Peskin, *Garfield*, 396.

4. Entries for April 9, May 19, September 18, and December 15–17, 1876, *Diary of James A. Garfield*, 3:268, 293, 354, 395–96.

5. Entries for May 29, 1874, and January 16, 1876, *Diary of James A. Garfield*, 2:328, 3:216; Robert B. Warden, *An Account of the Private Life and Public Services of Salmon Portland Chase* (Cincinnati: Wilstach, Baldwin and Co., 1874), 489. Garfield complained privately to Warden of his treatment; Warden promised to delete the offending passage if a second edition appeared. (It did not.) See Warden to Garfield, August 25, September 7 [?], 1876, *Papers of Garfield*, ser. 4, vol. 34, #159, and vol. 35, #240. Warden, a former judge and Chase's authorized biographer, had access to the chief justice's personal papers and served as his personal secretary in Chase's last years. The title of his biography indicates what he wanted to write—and what Chase wanted: a full, objective biography that included private as well as public life. Chase's daughter, more protective of her father's reputation than Chase was himself, arranged with another author to write Chase's biography (or hagiography), and tried to get that biography out before Warden's. When this strategy failed, she had unfavorable reviews of Warden's work placed in sympathetic newspapers. For the episode, see Frederick Blue, "Kate's Paper Chase," 353–63.

6. Entries for May 30 and 31, 1874, *Diary of James A. Garfield*, 2:329.

7. Entries for July 15 and 20, 1878, ibid., 4:93–95.

8. James A. Garfield, biographical interview ca. 1878, *Papers of Garfield,* interview pp. 4, 6, 8, 23.

9. Ibid., interview pp. 10–12; A. G. Riddle, *The Life, Character and Public Services of Jas. A. Garfield* (Cleveland: W. W. Williams, 1880), 30–31.

10. Riddle, *Life of Jas. A. Garfield,* 72–78. This character sketch, and much of the entire first section of Riddle's campaign biography of Garfield, appeared originally as "General James A. Garfield: A Study," in Riddle, *History of Geauga and Lake Counties, Ohio, with Illustrative and Biographical Sketches of Its Pioneers and Most Prominent Men* (Philadelphia: Williams Brothers, 1878), 64–73.

11. On Conwell's biography, see the following letters in *Papers of Garfield,* ser. 4: George A. Foxcroft to B. B. Russell and Co., June 9, 1880, vol. 73, #305; B. B. Russell and Co. to Garfield, June 9, 1880, vol. 73, #306; Nathaniel P. Banks to Russell H. Conwell, June 9, 1880, vol. 73, #311; Banks to Garfield, June 9, 1880, vol. 73, #312; Conwell to Garfield, June 28, 1880, vol. 78, #152. For the discussion of Harper and Brothers' publication of Garfield's life, see James R. Gilmore to Garfield, June 14, 1880, *Papers of Garfield,* ser. 4, vol. 75, #162. Campaign biographies of Garfield included Conwell, *The Life, Speeches and Public Services of Gen. James A. Garfield of Ohio* (Boston: B. B. Russell and Co., 1880; with other publishers listed in Philadelphia, New York, Portland, Chicago, and Indianapolis); Riddle, *Life of Jas. A. Garfield;* James S. Brisbin, *From the Tow-Path to the White House: The Early Life and Public Career of James A. Garfield, Maj. Gen'l U.S.A.* (Philadelphia, Springfield, Mass., Chicago, Cincinnati, Atlanta: Hubbard Bros., 1880; with other publishers in St. Louis, Emporia, Kans., and San Francisco); Jonas M. Bundy, *The Life of Gen. James A. Garfield* (New York: A. S. Barnes and Co., 1880); James Roberts Gilmore [Edmund Kirke, pseud.], *The Life of James A. Garfield, Republican Candidate for the Presidency: With Extracts from His Speeches* (New York: Harper and Brothers, 1880; also published by Harper in German); Charles C. Coffin, *The Life of James A. Garfield* (Boston: J. H. Earle, 1880); and James Dabney McCabe, *From the Farm to the Presidential Chair: Being an Accurate and Comprehensive Account of the Life and Public Services of Gen. James A. Garfield* (Philadelphia: National Publishing Co., 1880). Many of these books also contained brief biographies of Garfield's running mate, Chester A. Arthur.

An excellent discussion of how Garfield's biographers got their material on his early years—from the candidate's own speeches and writings—appears in Booraem, *The Road to Respectability,* 207–16. Booraem also speculates that James Brisbin's book was the compiled effort of several different writers.

12. This document, labeled "Notes for the Benefit of Biographers at Mentor during Summer 1880," is in *Papers of Garfield,* ser. 17D, scrapbook p. 106 (the entire sixty-page document is apparently inserted at that page of the scrapbook). Within the document (whose unnumbered pages I have numbered for citation), Garfield's reference to the Almeda Booth speech is on p. 40, and his description of his legal training is on pp. 16–17. Explicit instructions to biographers about speeches, incidents, or points to include appear on pp. 2, 5, 7, 16, 23, 27, and 37. The argument that a culture of professionalism took hold in "late-Victorian" America is most fully developed in Bledstein, *The Culture of Professionalism,* and is implicit throughout Rose, *Victorian America and the Civil War,* which suggests that the emphasis on career represented one answer to the post-romantic search for meaning.

13. Brisbin, *From the Tow-Path to the White House,* binding and 310, 345; James R. Gilmore to Garfield, June 14, 1880, *Papers of Garfield,* ser. 4, vol. 75, #162.

14. James R. Gilmore to Garfield, June 28, 1880, *Papers of Garfield,* ser. 4, vol. 78, #198; John W. Forney, *Life and Military Career of Winfield Scott Hancock* (Philadelphia: R. B. Morris and Co., 1880), 476–77.

15. Russell H. Conwell, *The Life, Speeches, and Public Services of James A. Garfield, Twentieth President of the United States. Including an Account of His Assassination, Lingering Pain, Death, and Burial* (Portland, Maine: George Stinson and Co., 1881), 352; John Clark Ridpath, *The Life and Work of James A. Garfield, Twentieth President of the United States . . . and the Tragic Story of His Death,* memorial ed. (Cincinnati, Philadelphia, Chicago, Kansas City: Jones Brothers and Co., 1881; with other publishers in Indianapolis, Detroit, and Des Moines), frontispieces; Hugh Craig, *The Biography and Public Services of Hon. James G. Blaine* (New York: H. S. Goodspeed and Co., 1884), dedication; Russell H. Conwell, *The Life and Public Services of James G. Blaine* (Augusta, Maine: E. C. Allen and Co., 1884), 433. Like Conwell's volume, McCabe's, Bundy's, and Brisbin's biographies were republished with new chapters after Garfield's death. However, Brisbin's name was replaced with that of William Ralston Balch, the newspaper editor who presumably wrote the new chapters. James Baird McClure, of the Chicago publishing firm of Rhodes and McClure, had written both a campaign biography of Hancock and *Stories and Sketches of Gen. Garfield* during the 1880 campaign—a sign of how publishers now tried to cover all bases in election years. Capitalizing on current affairs again, he edited a Garfield memorial volume the next year.

16. Conwell, *Life, Speeches and Public Services of Garfield,* [5]; Horatio Alger, Jr., *From Canal Boy to President, or the Boyhood and Manhood of James A. Garfield* (New York: John R. Anderson and Co., 1881), [3], 5–6, 74, 247. Like Brisbin's campaign biography, Alger's book announced its message on its front cover: embossed on the green binding were illustrations of Garfield towing his canal boat and taking the oath of office. For Hayes's comments, see Peskin, *Garfield,* 493.

17. William M. Thayer to Garfield, June 15, 1880, *Papers of Garfield,* ser. 4, vol. 75, #316. An unsigned, undated manuscript in the *Papers of Garfield* (ser. 4, vol. 84, #42), also in Thayer's hand, asks Garfield for the names and addresses of people who could provide information about his "Early Life," "College Life," life "Between Graduation and War Record," "War Record," and "Life in Congress." *From Log-Cabin to the White House: Life of James A. Garfield—Boyhood, Youth, Manhood, Assassination, Death, Funeral* (Boston: James H. Earle, 1885) first appeared in 1881. The first London edition appeared the same year, from the firm of Hodder and Stoughton, which published many of Thayer's books. Several London copies of the book, in my possession, contain bookplates that identify their use: the Hope Trust presented Hodder and Stoughton's fortieth edition (1905) "to William Wright for regular attendance and good conduct at Arthur Street Senior Abstinence Meeting" in 1906–7; and an unidentified school awarded another edition (London: Frederick Warne and Co., n.d.) "to Christopher Tompkins for Attendance" at Christmas 1894.

CHAPTER FIVE

1. Houghton, Mifflin and Company (hereafter HM&C), announcement for "American Statesmen," ca. 1881, HMC-HL. HM&C, proof announcement for "American Men of Letters," enclosed with HM&C to Charles Dudley Warner (hereafter CDW), August 6, 1881, CDW-WL.

2. Kijinski, "John Morley's 'English Men of Letters' Series and the Politics of Reading,"

216, 220–21. Several scholars have recently written about the English Men of Letters series. According to F. J. M. Korsten, whose " 'English Men of Letters' Series" offers a useful overview, "after a number of years the series was on the market in a bewildering variety of formats, covers, colours, and titles" (569, 512). See also Amigoni, *Victorian Biography*, esp. 120–56.

3. I have described the origins of the Houghton Mifflin series at greater length in "Defining the National Pantheon," 185–96. For Morse's reference to reading an English Men of Letters volume, see John T. Morse Jr., "Incidents Connected with the American Statesmen Series," *Proceedings of the Massachusetts Historical Society* 64 (Boston: Massachusetts Historical Society, 1932): 371. This article offers Morse's recollections of editing the series, including his difficulties with Carl Schurz (who wrote *Henry Clay*) and the plagiarism of Allan Magruder (who wrote *John Marshall*). Morse's memory of the series' origins was colored somewhat by the 1898 reordering of the series and the fifty years that had passed between its inception and this article. From the extant correspondence, it is clear that his vision was less coherent in 1880–81 than it became over the course of the series' publication. See Oscar Handlin, "John Torrey Morse," in *Dictionary of American Biography*, 22:475–76.

The original idea for Warner to turn his article on Irving into a full-length biography came from the publisher G. P. Putnam's Sons, which wanted the biography as a volume in its new series of Irving's works. But shortly after Morley rejected Warner's manuscript, Putnam's also withdrew its offer—citing one recent and one forthcoming biography of Irving and arguing that the market could not sustain three lives of Irving. Warner was thus free to make other arrangements, and approached Houghton. Putnam to CDW, July 7, 1880, CDW-WL. Howells expressed his disgust to CDW in a letter of March 12, 1880, CDW-WL; for the response, see CDW to Howells, March 15, 1880, William Dean Howells Collection (bMS Am 1784 [521]), HL. See also Howells to CDW, December 27, 1879; Putnam to CDW, January 5, 1880; John Morley to Howells (telegraph message), n.d. (but almost certainly January 20, 1881); all in CDW-WL.

4. John Torrey Morse (hereafter JTM) to HM&C, April 30, 1881, HMC-HL. All quotations in this and the next paragraph are from this letter.

5. Advertisement for "American Statesmen" series, Advertising scrapbook, HMC-HL.

6. The discussion of the series' title revealed much about Warner's and Houghton's concepts of the enterprise. Warner sought to create an American counterpart, maybe even a rival, to John Morley's English Men of Letters. Houghton's idea, "Warner's Biographies," left open the opportunity to group Warner's biography of Irving with his other books "if we do not publish the series"—thus creating a standard edition of Warner like the firm's editions of Hawthorne, Dickens, and others. Houghton suggested "Lives of Eminent Americans" next, but to Warner that title resembled "a bogus subscription book," a compendious volume of biographical sketches in gaudy green binding. Warner, who had written subscription books and whose friend Mark Twain had become famous in large part through subscription publishing, wanted books similar to Houghton's editions of the literature itself: small volumes with a minimum of show. Houghton acceded to Warner's general idea but still ventured that it "would also include women." For six months the firm's letters to Warner consistently called the series "American Men and Women of Letters." However, Houghton Mifflin's proof announcement read simply "American Men of Letters," "a generic term that may include both sexes." Henry O. Houghton to CDW, January 22, 1881; November 22, 1880; November 24, 1880; January 28,

1881; all in CDW-WL; CDW to Houghton, January 14, 1881, HMC-HL. For references to the "American Men and Women of Letters," see Houghton to CDW, February 5, 1881; HM&C to CDW, April 11, April 18, April 25, April 30, May 17, July 13, July 19, 1881, all in CDW-WL. For the proof announcement, see HM&C to CDW, August 6, 1881, CDW-WL. On the bindings associated with subscription firms and with Ticknor and Fields, see Groves, "Judging Literary Books by Their Covers."

7. H. O. Houghton to CDW, February 5, 1881; HM&C to CDW, April 25, 1881; both in CDW-WL. As the project took shape, Houghton asked James T. Fields, who had been a partner in Ticknor and Fields and its successor Fields, Osgood and Company, to serve as general editor of the series. (Apparently Warner at first declined this task.) But Fields withdrew in mid-April and died on April 24, and the firm approached Warner once again. On the editorship of the series, see H. O. Houghton to CDW, January 17, January 22, February 5, April 20, May 17, July 5, 1881, all in CDW-WL; HM&C to CDW, April 18, April 25, April 30, May 17, and June 2, 1881, all in CDW-WL; CDW to HM&C, June 1, 1881, HMC-HL.

8. HM&C to CDW, April 25, 1881, CDW-WL; CDW to Horace E. Scudder, September 15, 1881, Scudder Papers (MS Am 1124.9 [27]), HL. CDW to HM&C, January 14 and 22, 1885; H. O. Houghton to CDW, January 23, 1885, HMC-HL. Warner's most forceful statement of who did *not* belong came in 1898, when Houghton Mifflin proposed Walt Whitman for the series because of "a continuous and permanent interest in him." Warner asked, "Whatever he is, would you in any way call him a Man of Letters?" Even if Whitman's work displayed "genius in places," he was "an awful *poser.*" "If he must go into our Series," concluded Warner, "I should not wish to have him treated by one of his abject worshipers, who repudiates our whole idea of the difference between poetry and prose, in order to admit him among the poets." HM&C to CDW, March 26, 1898, CDW-WL; CDW to HM&C, May 15, 1898, HMC-HL. See Monteiro, "Whitman, Warner, and the American Men of Letters Series," 26–27.

9. Suggestions for the American Men of Letters appear in Eugene L. Didier to HM&C, January 27, 1885; HM&C to CDW, January 30, 1885; James Parton to HM&C, April 21, 1885; HM&C to CDW, April 22, 1885; and J. Brander Matthews to CDW, October 23, 1882; all in CDW-WL. Rejections are described in CDW to HM&C, November 22, 1895; and H. O. Houghton to CDW, January 23, 1885; both in HMC-HL. Morse described proposals for the American Statesmen in letters to HM&C, August 12, 1884; October 12, 1887; November 30, 1887; and December 22, 1887, all in HMC-HL.

10. As Morse recalled, Lodge had asked him to include Roosevelt because "Theodore has nothing to do—in a word, *he needs the money.*" Morse, "Incidents Connected with the American Statesmen Series," 381.

11. See, for instance, CDW to HM&C, November 8, 1895, HMC-HL, in which Warner described why Howells would be the ideal author for Longfellow's biography.

12. When Warner commenced the American Men of Letters series, Moses Coit Tyler had begun his work on colonial and Revolutionary American literature. But few other scholars had studied American literature, even fewer universities offered courses in it, and the Modern Language Association, founded in 1883, rarely heard papers on American writings. The one academic among the initial Men of Letters authors, Thomas R. Lounsbury of Yale, was a personal friend of Warner who wrote *James Fenimore Cooper.* George E. Woodberry (*Edgar Allan Poe*), the youngest author, later became a noted literary critic.

Over time two history professors, John Bach McMaster of the University of Pennsylvania and William P. Trent of the University of the South, joined Warner's contributors—but only after Higginson gave up Benjamin Franklin for Fuller and the Louisiana novelist George Washington Cable failed to produce a life of Simms. On the lack of academic attention to American literature in this period, see Vanderbilt, *American Literature and the Academy,* chaps. 6–7, esp. 108–9.

13. William Everett to CDW, May 14, 1888, CDW-WL. Other authors in the series complained about aspects of the editing, particularly the general prescription that volumes should run approximately three hundred pages. To keep Lounsbury's *James Fenimore Cooper* to 306 pages, the publishers used a smaller typeface and more lines to the page. Other authors' complaints involved particulars that were not specific to the series form, such as the permitted number of galley corrections and the terms of the royalty. For Morse's annoyance with Schurz, see Morse, "Incidents Connected with the American Statesmen Series," 378–80.

14. Houghton's displeasure at the delays in the American Men of Letters can be seen in HM&C to CDW, June 5, 1885; October 24, 1885; January 19, 1886; March 2, 1888; all in CDW-WL. His praise for Morse's steadier production of books appears in H. O. Houghton to JTM, April 9, 1884, HMC-HL.

15. H. O. Houghton to CDW, February 17, 1885, HMC-HL. For more detailed discussion of sales in the two series, see Casper, "Defining the National Pantheon," 206–9. Sales figures are derived from HM&C, Sales Books, vols. 31–32, HMC-HL.

16. "A New Theory of Biography," *The Dial* 24 (May 1, 1898): 281–83.

17. The new edition of the American Statesmen offered buyers the material quality associated with Houghton Mifflin's well-known Standard Library Editions of its authors' work: heavier paper, more elegant bindings, engravings of the statesmen and their homes. HM&C, "Standard Library Edition/American Statesmen" (advertisement), October 6, 1898; "Our Special Offer Beginning the Twentieth Century" (advertisement), February 21, 1901; Advertising scrapbooks, HMC-HL. Binding details taken from Daniel C. Gilman, *James Monroe* (orig. 1883; Boston: Houghton, Mifflin, 1899).

At the same time Houghton Mifflin created the Standard Library Edition of the American Statesmen series, the firm also created a "Large Paper Edition," limited to five hundred copies. This edition, "printed on a very fine antique laid paper, deckle edges," could be purchased in "polished buckram" for $3.50 per volume or in "the finest French levant" for $7.50 per volume. The Standard Library Edition sold for $1.50 per volume in cloth or $3.50 per volume in half morocco. The numbered edition, made from another new set of plates, sold out within the first year. See "American Statesmen/Large-Paper Edition" (advertisement), May 31, 1898, Advertising scrapbooks, HMC-HL.

18. HM&C, "Standard Library Edition/American Statesmen Series," 2; John T. Morse Jr., "Editor's Introduction," in Morse, *Benjamin Franklin* (Boston: Houghton, Mifflin, 1898), v–vii.

19. Ibid., vii–x.

20. Matthew Deady diary, July 7, 1883, in *Pharisee among Philistines: The Diary of Judge Matthew P. Deady, 1871–1892,* 2:416. Deady mentioned reading in the English Men of Letters in 1880 (1:324, 325) and in the life of Eliot four years later (2:449).

21. Deady diary, October 22, 1887, November 1, 1884, February 24, 1883, October 15, 1887, in *Pharisee among Philistines,* 2:410, 455, 524. Biographical information on Deady appears in

Malcolm Clark's introduction to the diary and in Hubert Howe Bancroft, *Chronicles of the Builders of the Commonwealth: Historical Character Study* (San Francisco: The History Company, 1891), 2:465–515.

22. For examples of authors describing the value of distance for critical assessment, see Charles Dudley Warner, *Washington Irving* (Boston: Houghton, Mifflin, 1881), 2; and Edward M. Shepard, *Martin Van Buren* (Boston: Houghton, Mifflin, 1888), 3.

23. Warner, *Washington Irving,* 297; Thomas Wentworth Higginson, *Margaret Fuller Ossoli* (Boston: Houghton, Mifflin, 1884), 8. Simms's friends and descendants had been aghast when Warner and Houghton first engaged George Washington Cable to write the biography. Though a prominent and popular southern novelist, Cable was allied with the "New South" movement. How could he possibly write a sympathetic biography? One of Simms's closest friends thought that Warner just wanted a book "for the Yankee market, a book to *sell.*" When Cable relinquished the project, Warner enlisted Trent, a young professor of history at the University of the South in Sewanee. On the controversy, see McCardell, "Trent's *Simms:* The Making of a Biography," 179–203.

John Kijinski has suggested that writers in the English Men of Letters series generally presented their subjects as models of middle-class respectability ("Morley's 'English Men of Letters' Series," 213–15). No such overarching model applies to the American series, especially because the series sought to show the various literary cultures of the United States. The volumes that appeared during Warner's editorship (1881–1900) fall roughly into two categories: books commissioned especially for the series and those prepared originally for other purposes that found a home in the American Men of Letters. For example, Octavius Brooks Frothingham wrote his biography of George Ripley soon after Ripley's death in 1880 as a memorial volume, and agreed to "adapt" it for inclusion in the series. Frothingham's *Ripley* and Edward Cary's *George William Curtis* (also a memorial volume) contained far more extracts from their subjects' letters than the typical volume in the series; they lay somewhere between the "life and letters" and the more concise analytical biography envisioned by Warner and the publishers. The works commissioned for the series—which are the ones discussed here—were more clearly works of composition and interpretation rather than compilation. See HM&C to CDW, December 21, 1881; and Frothingham to CDW, December 21, 1881; both in CDW-WL.

24. Horace E. Scudder, *Noah Webster* (Boston: Houghton, Mifflin, 1881), 26, 293–94; Warner, *Washington Irving,* 8; Higginson, *Margaret Fuller Ossoli,* 130–32.

25. Warner, *Washington Irving,* 293; William P. Trent, *William Gilmore Simms* (Boston: Houghton, Mifflin, 1892), 328; Henry A. Beers, *Nathaniel Parker Willis* (Boston: Houghton, Mifflin, 1885), 2–3, 351. See also Gougeon, "Holmes's Emerson and the Conservative Critique of Realism," 107–25.

26. Warner, *Washington Irving,* 19–20, 300; Beers, *Nathaniel Parker Willis,* 82; Higginson, *Margaret Fuller Ossoli,* 233.

27. It is important to note that within the American Statesmen series, distinct authorial visions clearly existed. For example, Hermann Von Holst's *John C. Calhoun* (orig. 1882; Boston: Houghton, Mifflin, 1899) repeated for the popular audience of the American Statesmen series the central argument of his *Constitutional History of the United States,* which one scholar has characterized as "one long legal barrage at the doctrine of states' rights." Though Holst did narrate Calhoun's political career, Calhoun appeared primarily as "the representative of an *idea*" (7) and ultimately as "the greatest and purest of proslavery

fanatics" (351). Henry Adams's *John Randolph* reflected its author's lifelong "ambivalence about personal power and its relation to accomplishment," also a theme of his contemporaneous biography of Albert Gallatin and his *History of the United States of America during the Administrations of Thomas Jefferson and James Madison*. Adams also described Randolph's political experience as an "education" (although one that the headstrong Virginian ultimately ignored), a model not unlike what would appear in *The Education of Henry Adams*. William Graham Sumner's *Andrew Jackson* (Boston: Houghton, Mifflin, 1882) lauded the Supreme Court's ascendancy under John Marshall as the bulwark against the abuses of "a surging democracy," a view that reflected Sumner's own Gilded Age belief in the judiciary as the guardian of stability (362). On Holst's *Constitutional History*, see Novick, *That Noble Dream*, 76. On the relation between Adams's *Randolph* and his other works, see Hughson, *From Biography to History*, 30–46.

28. John T. Morse Jr., *Benjamin Franklin* (Boston: Houghton, Mifflin, 1889), 415; Henry Cabot Lodge, *George Washington* (Boston: Houghton, Mifflin, 1889), 2:219–25; Morse, *John Adams* (Boston: Houghton, Mifflin, 1884), 264; Morse, *John Quincy Adams* (orig. 1882; Boston: Houghton, Mifflin, 1899), 12; see also Sumner, *Andrew Jackson*, 11–12.

29. Sumner, *Andrew Jackson*, 359; Carl Schurz, *Henry Clay* (Boston: Houghton, Mifflin, 1889), 1:321, 324–25, 333.

30. Shepard, *Martin Van Buren*, 5, 397. On Gay's career as reformer, see Frank Monaghan, "Sydney Howard Gay," *Dictionary of American Biography*, 7:195.

31. Deady diary, December 2, 1882, in *Pharisee among Philistines*, 2:403.

32. Grant's proclamation, dated May 25, 1876, appears in *A Compilation of the Messages and Papers of the Presidents, 1789–1902*, ed. James D. Richardson (Washington: Bureau of National Literature and Art, 1903), 7:391. On the emergence of county-atlas publishing and its mutation into county histories and mug books, see Conzen, "The County Landownership Map in America," 17–23. When county histories and mug books took the atlases' place as profitable family heirlooms, atlases became tailored to "real estate and business interests and the needs of local civil administration," rather than to ordinary families (23). On Andreas's checkered career, see Conzen, "Maps for the Masses," 47–63.

33. For an entertaining description of how the mug-book trade worked, see Oscar Lewis, "Mug Books: A Dissertation Concerning the Origins of a Certain Familiar Division of Americana." Further information is found in Hanna, "Every Man His Own Biographer," 291–98; and Conzen, "Maps for the Masses," 58–60.

34. On dime-novel publishers as "fiction factories," see Denning, *Mechanic Accents*, 17–26. Historian Earl Pomeroy has written that people accumulated wealth first, bric-a-brac for the parlor next, and finally local history and biography. See Pomeroy, "Old Lamps for New," 118.

35. The identical reference to different counties as being foremost in Nebraska appeared in the prefaces of *Portrait and Biographical Album of Lancaster County, Nebraska, Containing Full Page Portraits and Biographical Sketches of Prominent and Representative Citizens of the County, Together with Portraits and Biographies of All the Governors of the State, and of the Presidents of the United States* (Chicago: Chapman Brothers, 1888) and *Portrait and Biographical Album of Otoe and Cass Counties, Nebraska* (Chicago: Chapman Brothers, 1889). Descriptions of the difficulty of making mug books appeared in these volumes (from which is drawn the quotation about indifference and opposition), as well as in *Biographical Souvenir of the State of Texas* (Chicago: F. A. Battey and Co., 1889), *History of the City of Denver, Arapahoe County,*

and Colorado: Containing . . . Biographical Sketches (Chicago: O. L. Baskin and Co., 1880), and various other books. *Biographical and Historical Memoirs of Northeast Arkansas* (Chicago, Nashville, and St. Louis: Goodspeed Publishing Co., 1889) and *History of the City of Denver* are among the many books whose prefaces acknowledged the assistance of local citizens.

36. Prefaces to *Biographical Souvenir of the State of Texas, Biographical and Historical Memoirs of Northeast Arkansas,* and *Portrait and Biographical Album of Lancaster County, Nebraska*—which were the products of three different publishers, all concerned with placing mug books into a larger tradition of preserving lives and histories from oblivion.

37. Prefaces to *History of the City of Denver, Biographical Souvenir of the State of Texas,* and *Biographical and Historical Memoirs of Northeast Arkansas.*

38. Population statistics for Lancaster County appear in *Report of the Population of the United States at the Eleventh Census: 1890* (Washington, D.C.: Government Printing Office, 1895), 1:231. For the example of Lincoln gentility quoted, see *Portrait and Biographical Album of Lancaster County,* 146.

39. *Portrait and Biographical Album of Lancaster County,* 154; *Biographical and Historical Memoirs of Northeast Arkansas,* 198, 216. In just the first sixty pages of biographical sketches in the Lancaster County book, seven different men are described as "representative."

40. *Portrait and Biographical Album of Lancaster County,* 147.

41. Ibid., 147–48, 205.

42. William J. Simmons, *Men of Mark: Eminent, Progressive, and Rising* (orig. 1887; Cleveland and Baltimore: Geo. M. Rewell and Co., 1890), 6–7; W. H. Mixon, *History of the African Methodist Episcopal Church in Alabama, with Biographical Sketches* (Nashville: A.M.E. Church Sunday School Union, 1902). See also M. A. Majors, *Noted Negro Women: Their Triumphs and Activities* (Chicago: Donohue and Henneberry, 1893).

43. A. W. Pegues, *Our Baptist Ministers and Schools* (Springfield, Mass.: Willey and Co., 1892), 10–15. Similarly, Mixon's *History of the African Methodist Episcopal Church in Alabama* opened with a "Sketch of the Author." On the debate over African-American education, see Brodhead, *Cultures of Letters,* 184–89.

44. Bancroft, *Chronicles of the Builders of the Commonwealth,* 1:v–vi. For an excellent history of the publication of Bancroft's *Works* and *Chronicles,* see Clark, *A Venture in History,* esp. 121–42. See also Caughey, *Hubert Howe Bancroft,* 313–29.

45. Bancroft, "Prospectus" for *Chronicles of the Kings,* quoted in Clark, *A Venture in History,* 126; Bancroft, *Chronicles of the Builders of the Commonwealth,* 1:x–xi.

46. Deady diary, September 11 and 14, October 20, 1888; March 19, August 9, 1890; all in *Pharisee among Philistines,* 2:539–40, 591, 598.

47. Ibid., August 9, 1890, 2:598; Bancroft, *Chronicles of the Builders of the Commonwealth,* 2:465, 475, 478, 481, 490, 494–95, 509.

48. A particularly useful overview of the varieties of realism is Shi, *Facing Facts.*

49. Houghton Mifflin editorial manuscript reports, #4665 (April 10, 1894); #103 (January 2, 1883); #1041 (December 4, 1885); #1939 (ca. March 1888). The editors' reports on manuscripts submitted to Houghton Mifflin are housed in the Houghton Library, MS Storage 245. Those reports are numbered chronologically. For this study, reports numbered 1–2000 and 4001–4800 (covering October 1882 through April 1888 and October 1892 through September 1894) were examined.

50. Houghton Mifflin editorial reports #741 (December 31, 1884); #1613 (June 7, 1887); #647 (September 30, 1884); #739 (December 19, 1884); #4684 (April 24, 1894). Biographies

made up quite a small proportion of the manuscripts received, for several possible reasons. Imaginative literature (fiction, poetry) required less research to write. Given the effort required, people who wrote biographies may have sought publishers before beginning their projects, reducing the number of unsolicited manuscripts a firm like Houghton Mifflin would receive. Also, many biographies, especially of the life-and-letters variety, were published by subscription firms.

51. Morse to Parton, February 16, 1883, JP-HL; Houghton Mifflin editorial manuscript reports, #1358 (August 25, 1886) and #1709 (July 26, 1887).

52. *New York Times,* October 20, 1900, 725; Oscar Fay Adams, *A Dictionary of American Authors* (Cambridge, Mass.: Riverside Press, 1897), 117; *The National Cyclopaedia of American Biography* (New York: James T. White and Co., 1909), 11:38. All subsequent references to the *Times* review are from the same page.

53. Janet Elizabeth Richards, "Heroic Women of the Revolution," *American Monthly Magazine* 1 (September 1892): 292. The published version of the address includes parenthetical notes about the audience's reception, including five interruptions of "Applause" and "Great Applause" at the end.

54. Sklar, "American Female Historians in Context," 181. Similarly, modern historians of women qualify their recognition of Ellet's pioneering efforts with the caveat that she was locked into the "domestic model" in which women were saintly ideals, not distinctive individuals (Gelles, "The Abigail Industry," 661). Linda Kerber has offered the most balanced assessment to date, though she ultimately suggests that modern historians "cannot rely" on Ellet's history because she "ignored themes that we now find indispensable." Kerber, " 'History Can Do It No Justice,' " 4–5, 7, 9.

55. Novick, *That Noble Dream,* 1–2, 52–53.

56. On the class and ethnic identity of the historians and the D.A.R. women, see Veysey, "The Plural Organized Worlds of the Humanities," 69; on the "cool detachment" that academic historians emphasized, see Novick, *That Noble Dream,* 53; for Jameson's denigration of local history as feminine, see David Brumberg, "The Case for Reunion: Academic Historians, Public Historical Agencies, and the New York Historians-in-Residence Program," *The Public Historian* 4 (Spring 1982): 74, quoted in *That Noble Dream,* 519–20. The best overview of cultural bifurcation in the late nineteenth century is Levine, *Highbrow/Lowbrow.*

57. Moses Coit Tyler, *Patrick Henry* (Boston: Houghton, Mifflin, 1887), v–vii.

58. For Sparks's negotiations with Mrs. Morris, see chapter 3. For Lounsbury's frustration with Susan Cooper's unwillingness to grant access, see Lounsbury to CDW, January 28, 1882, CDW-WL.

59. Lodge, *George Washington,* 1:15, 30.

60. Justin Winsor, *Christopher Columbus and How He Received and Imparted the Spirit of Discovery* (Boston: Houghton, Mifflin, 1891), 496–97; C. A. L. Richards, "A Pessimistic Biography of Columbus," *Dial* 12 (December 1891): 267; John A. Mooney, "Columbus and the 'Scientific' School," *American Catholic Quarterly Review* 17 (October 1892), 836–37. Four months after publishing Richards's critical review of Winsor's *Columbus,* the *Dial* published a second, favorable article on the book. The author of this article, William Frederick Poole, was Winsor's colleague: both were prominent in professionalizing librarianship, and Poole had contributed articles to Winsor's *Narrative and Critical History of America* (1888) and *Memorial History of Boston* (1881). Not surprisingly, Poole wrote that "Dr. Winsor's

attractive work embodies the latest and most authoritative conclusions on the subject which the best European and American research and scholarship have reached." W. F. Poole, "Christopher Columbus," *Dial* 12 (April 1892): 421–23. On Winsor's career and writings, see L. Moody Simms, "Justin Winsor," in *Dictionary of Literary Biography*, 47:358–64; on Poole, see Carl B. Roden, "William Frederick Poole," in *Dictionary of American Biography*, 15:66–67.

61. "James Parton's Rules of Biography," *McClure's Magazine* 1 (June 1893): 59–62; Alfred R. Conkling to James Parton, December 7, 21, 1888, January 1, March 24, 1889, JP-HL.

62. [George William Curtis], "Editor's Easy Chair," *Harper's New Monthly Magazine* 68 (March 1884): 639–40.

63. Margaret Oliphant, "The Ethics of Biography," *Littell's Living Age* 158 (August 11, 1883), 333; Edmund Gosse, "The Ethics of Biography," *Cosmopolitan* 35 (July 1903): 318, 322; Walter Lewin, "Bowdlerized Biography," *The Forum* 10 (February 1891), esp. 660–63; "Aspects of Biography," *Nation* 73 (December 5, 1901), 431; Schneirov, *The Dream of a New Social Order*, 81.

64. On moralizing as perversion of biography's proper purpose, see Annie Russell Marble, "Popular Forms of Modern Biography," *Dial* 31 (September 1, 1901), 126; and Gosse, "The Ethics of Biography," 319.

65. [Curtis], "Editor's Easy Chair," 639; Marble, "Popular Forms of Modern Biography," 127.

66. J. B. Lippincott Company, advertisement for "The 'True' Biographies Series," in the back of William Eleroy Curtis, *The True Thomas Jefferson* (Philadelphia: J. B. Lippincott Co., 1908); A. B. Keeler, "The 'Real' Biographer," *Puck* 46 (September 20, 1899): [5]; Charles L. C. Minor, *The Real Lincoln, from the Testimony of His Contemporaries* (Richmond, Va.: Everett Waddey Co., 1904); Paul Leicester Ford, *The True George Washington* (Philadelphia: J. B. Lippincott Co., 1896), 5–6.

67. William Dean Howells, "The Rise of Silas Needham" (synopsis for projected book, MS in the Huntington Library, San Marino, California), published in William Dean Howells, *The Rise of Silas Lapham* (orig. 1885; New York: Norton Critical Edition, 1982), 328.

68. Howells, *The Rise of Silas Lapham*, 3–4, 175, 320.

69. Ibid., 11, 18, 21. Amy Kaplan has explained Howells's realism as a reaction against not just sentimentalism but also the emerging culture of conspicuous consumption, celebrity, and journalism; see *The Social Construction of American Realism*, 15–43.

CONCLUSION

1. William Roscoe Thayer, "Biography," *NAR* 180 (February 1905): 263; Nicolson, *The Development of English Biography*, 8, 10. This Thayer was no relation to William Makepeace Thayer, of *The Bobbin Boy* fame.

2. Sadie E. Simons, "Educational Value of Biography," *Educational Review* 17 (January 1899): 70; Edmund Gosse, "The Ethics of Biography," *Cosmopolitan* 35 (July 1903): 318–19; Annie Russell Marble, "Popular Forms of Modern Biography," *The Dial* 31 (September 1, 1901): 126.

3. Phillips Brooks, *The Phillips Exeter Lectures: Biography* (Boston: Ginn and Co., 1893), 181–82; Thayer, "Biography," 264. Originally delivered and copyrighted in 1886, Brooks's lecture was published in pamphlet form, perhaps for classroom use.

4. Marble, "Popular Forms of Modern Biography," 126.

5. Ibid., 128–29; H. Addington Bruce, "The Biography of To-Day," *The Outlook* 77 (May 28, 1904): 235–37.

6. Brooks, *The Phillips Exeter Lectures,* 181–82, 200–202, 206. Brooks's lecture circulated beyond the bounds of Exeter: Annie Marble cited it in 1901 ("Popular Forms of Modern Biography," 128). T. J. Jackson Lears has described Brooks as a clergyman of the late-century, liberal-Protestant, therapeutic variety, less interested in moral absolutes than in wedding moral to material progress. These clergymen and contemporary "secular moralists" "blunted all the sharp edges in Protestant tradition and produced a bland religion of reassurance." That religion extended the romanticism that Anne C. Rose identifies with the generation of middle-class Americans whose seminal experience was the Civil War and who rejected the moral absolutes of their parents' Second Great Awakening. Born in 1835, Brooks clearly belonged to this generation. Lears notes also that Brooks and his circle had little interest in the social problems of the working classes—which helps explain which issues his lecture on biography did and did not address. Lears, *No Place of Grace,* 23–24; Rose, *Victorian America and the Civil War.* See also Bledstein, *The Culture of Professionalism;* on the ways professionalization promoted distinct vocabularies and helped undermine shared senses of language, see Cmiel, *Democratic Eloquence.*

7. Simons, "Educational Value of Biography," 70–79.

8. Thayer, "Biography," 261–65, 272, 277; Marble, "Popular Forms of Modern Biography," 128–29; Bruce, "The Biography of To-Day," 236; see also Walter Lewin, "Bowdlerized Biography," *The Forum* (February 1891): 662–63. Thayer had come late to his acceptance of realism: in 1889 he charged "the apostles of realism" with threatening to "abolish our idols and our ideals." And as his article on "Biography" illustrates, romanticism remained his dominant chord. William Roscoe Thayer, "Realism," unpublished manuscript, n.d., in William Roscoe Thayer Papers, HL; also quoted in Shi, *Facing Facts,* 10. On the development of psychology in turn-of-the-century America, see Hale, *Freud and the Americans.*

9. Hoberman, *Modernizing Lives,* 5, 13; Hutch, "Explorations in Character," 312–25.

10. Silas Xavier Floyd, *Life of Charles T. Walker, D.D.* (Nashville: National Baptist Publishing Board, 1902), 6, 12–13.

11. See Bertaux, *Biography and Society;* Langness and Frank, *Lives: An Anthropological Approach to Biography.*

12. For examples of biographers describing their craft and its effect on their own lives, see Mandell, *Life into Art;* Christianson, *Writing Lives Is the Devil!;* and Bowen, *Adventures of a Biographer.* For a critique of this tendency, particularly as practiced by recent feminist biographers, see Brightman, "Character in Biography," 206–10.

BIBLIOGRAPHY

Manuscripts and Other Unpublished Sources

Baltimore, Maryland
Maryland Historical Society Library
  Manuscripts Department
    William Wirt Papers (MS 1011)

Boston, Massachusetts
Boston Public Library
  Rufus Wilmot Griswold Papers

Cambridge, Massachusetts
Houghton Library, Harvard University
  Autograph File
  Charles Eliot Norton Papers (bMS Am 1088)
  Editorial Reports (MS Storage 245)
  George William Curtis Papers (bMS Am 1124.9)
  Horace E. Scudder Papers (MS Am 1124.9 [27])
  Houghton Mifflin Collection (bMS Am 1925)
  James Parton Papers (bMS Am 1248)
  Jared Sparks Papers (MS Sparks)
  William Dean Howells Collection (b MS Am 1784 [521])
  William Roscoe Thayer Papers

Chapel Hill, North Carolina
Southern Historical Collection, Wilson Library, University of North Carolina at Chapel Hill
  David Lowry Swain Papers
  Griffith John McRee Papers

Charlottesville, Virginia
Alderman Library, University of Virginia
  Special Collections Department
    Henry S. Randall Correspondence (#6891)
    Papers of Thomas Jefferson
    Clifton Waller Barrett Library of American Literature
      William Wirt Collection (#9599)
    Wirt, William, "Memoirs of Patrick Henry: In a Series of Letters to a Young Gentleman at William and Mary College in Williamsburg — Letter I" (#3490) (manuscript and typescript, microfilm)

Columbia, South Carolina
South Caroliniana Library, University of South Carolina
  Manuscripts Division
    William Henry Ellet Correspondence

Hartford, Connecticut
Connecticut Historical Society
  Elizabeth F. Ellet Correspondence
  Female Reading Class (Colchester) Records
Watkinson Library, Trinity College
  Charles Dudley Warner Papers

Haverford, Pennsylvania
Haverford College Library
  Charles Roberts Autograph Collection, Quaker Collection
    Elizabeth F. Ellet Correspondence

Lexington, Kentucky
University of Kentucky Library
  Special Collections and Archives
    W. Hugh Peal Collection
      Jared Sparks Correspondence

Montpelier, Vermont
Vermont Historical Society
  Benson Female Lending Library, Windsor County
    Constitution and Circulation Records
  Calais Circulating Library
    "Catalogue of Books Belonging to Calais Circulating Library" (ledger)

New Haven, Connecticut
Beinecke Rare Book and Manuscript Library, Yale University
  Yale Collection of American Literature
    Elizabeth F. Ellet Correspondence
Manuscripts and Archives, Yale University
  Kingsbury Collection

New York, New York
Barnard College Library
  Overbury Collection
    Elizabeth F. Ellet Correspondence
New-York Historical Society
  Manuscripts Division
    Elizabeth F. Ellet Correspondence (Misc. MSS, Ellet)
    Gulian Verplanck Papers
New York Public Library
  Rare Books and Manuscripts Division
    Elizabeth F. Ellet Correspondence

San Marino, California
Henry E. Huntington Library
  Manuscripts Department
    James T. Fields Papers

Washington, D.C.
Library of Congress
  Manuscript Division
    William Wirt Papers

Worcester, Massachusetts
American Antiquarian Society
  Campaign Newspapers Collection
  Dated Pamphlets Collection
  Manuscript Collection
    Central Church Records, Octavo Vols. 23 and 24
      Centre Missionary Sewing Circle
    Gale Family Papers
      Hannah Davis Gale Journal
    Washington County, N.Y., Farmers and Mechanicks Library Records
    Worcester County Atheneum Records
  Public Library Catalogues Collection

Biographies, Diaries, and Literary Works

Adams, Oscar Fay. *A Dictionary of American Authors*. Cambridge, Mass.: Riverside Press, 1897.

Alger, Horatio, Jr. *From Canal Boy to President, or the Boyhood and Manhood of James A. Garfield*. New York: John R. Anderson and Co., 1881.

Allen, William. *An American Biographical and Historical Dictionary, Containing an Account of the Lives, Characters, and Writings of the Most Eminent Persons in North America from Its First Discovery to the Present Time*. Cambridge, Mass.: W. Hilliard, 1809.

An American Lady. *Sketches of the Lives of Distinguished Females, Written for Girls, with a View to Their Mental and Moral Improvement*. New York: J. and J. Harper, 1833.

Baird, Robert. *Memoir of Anna Jane Linnard*. Philadelphia: Henry Perkins, 1835.

Baldwin, Christopher Columbus. *Diary of Christopher Columbus Baldwin, Librarian of the American Antiquarian Society, 1829–1835*. Transactions and Collections of the American Antiquarian Society, no. 8. Worcester: American Antiquarian Society, 1901.

Bancroft, Hubert Howe. *Chronicles of the Builders of the Commonwealth: Historical Character Study*. 7 vols. San Francisco: The History Company, 1891.

Beecher, Henry Ward. *Seven Lectures to Young Men, on Various Important Subjects*. Indianapolis: T. B. Cutler, 1844.

Beers, Henry A. *Nathaniel Parker Willis*. Boston: Houghton, Mifflin, 1885.

Belknap, Jeremy. *Belknap Papers*. Collections of the Massachusetts Historical Society, 5th ser., 2–3; 6th ser., 4. Boston: Massachusetts Historical Society, 1877–91.

Biographical and Historical Memoirs of Northeast Arkansas. Chicago, etc.: Goodspeed Publishing Co., 1889.

A Biographical Sketch of the Life and Services of Gen. William Henry Harrison, Together with His Letter to Simon Bolivar. Montpelier, Vt.: N.p., 1836.

Biographical Souvenir of the State of Texas. Chicago: F. A. Battey and Co., 1889.

Biographium Faemineum. The Female Worthies: Or, Memoirs of the Most Illustrious Ladies, of All Ages and Nations. London: S. Crowder, 1766.

Briggs, Charles F. [Harry Franco, pseud.]. *The Trippings of Tom Pepper: Or, the Results of Romancing.* New York: Mirror Library, 1847.

Brisbin, James S. *From the Tow-Path to the White House: The Early Life and Public Career of James A. Garfield, Maj. Gen'l U.S.A.* Philadelphia, etc.: Hubbard Bros., 1880.

Brockett, L. P. *Men of Our Day: Or, Biographical Sketches of Patriots, Orators, Statesmen, Generals, Reformers, Financiers and Merchants, Now on the Stage of Action.* Philadelphia: Ziegler, McCurdy and Co., 1869.

Brooks, Phillips. *The Phillips Exeter Lectures: Biography.* Boston: Ginn and Co., 1893.

Brown, William Wells. *The Black Man, His Antecedents, His Genius, and His Achievements.* New York: Thomas Hamilton, 1863.

Bundy, Jonas M. *The Life of Gen. James A. Garfield.* New York: A. S. Barnes and Co., 1880.

[Butler, Benjamin Franklin]. *Sketches of the Life and Character of William H. Crawford, by Americanus.* Albany, N.Y., 1824.

C[aldwell, Charles]. *The Author Turned Critic: Or, the Reviewer Reviewed, Being a Reply to a Feeble and Unfounded Attack on Delaplaine's Repository, in the Analectic Magazine and Naval Chronicle, for the Month of September 1816.* Philadelphia, 1816.

Caldwell, Charles. *Memoirs of the Life and Campaigns of the Hon. Nathaniel Greene.* Philadelphia: Robert Desilver, 1819.

Caruthers, Eli W. *A Sketch of the Life and Character of the Rev. David Caldwell, D.D.* Greensborough, N.C.: Swaim and Sherwood, 1842.

Catalogue of Books and Other Publications of the American Sunday-School Union, Designed for Sunday-Schools, Juvenile, Family, and Parish Libraries, and for General Reading. Philadelphia: American Sunday-School Union, 1849.

Cheetham, James. *The Life of Thomas Paine, Author of Common Sense, The Crisis, Rights of Man, &c. &c. &c.* New York: Southwick and Pelsue, 1809.

Clark, John A. *The Young Disciple: Or, a Memoir of Anzonetta R. Peters.* Philadelphia: William Marshall and Co., 1837.

The Clay Minstrel: Or, National Songster. New York: Greeley and McElrath et al., 1844.

Coffin, Charles C. *The Life of James A. Garfield.* Boston: J. H. Earle, 1880.

Condie, Thomas. *Biographical Memoirs of the Illustrious Gen. Geo. Washington, Late President of the United States of America.* Philadelphia: Charless and Ralston, 1800.

Conwell, Russell H. *The Life and Public Services of James G. Blaine.* Augusta, Maine: E. C. Allen and Co., 1884.

――――. *The Life, Speeches, and Public Services of Gen. James A. Garfield of Ohio.* Boston: B. B. Russell and Co., 1880.

――――. *The Life, Speeches, and Public Services of James A. Garfield, Twentieth President of the United States: Including an Account of His Assassination, Lingering Pain, Death, and Burial.* Portland, Maine: George Stinson and Co., 1881.

Cooper, James Fenimore. *Correspondence of James Fenimore Cooper.* Edited by James Fenimore Cooper. 2 vols. New Haven: Yale University Press, 1922.

Corry, John. *Biographical Memoirs of the Illustrious Gen. Geo. Washington, Late President of the United*

States of America and Commander in Chief of Their Armies. Philadelphia: Printed by Joseph Charless for H. and P. Rice and James Rice and Co., 1807.

Craig, Hugh. *The Biography and Public Services of Hon. James G. Blaine*. New York: H. S. Goodspeed and Co., 1884.

Curtis, William Eleroy. *The True Thomas Jefferson*. Philadelphia: J. B. Lippincott Company, 1908.

Cutter, William. *The Life of Israel Putnam, Major-General in the Army of the American Revolution*. New York: George F. Cooledge and Brother, 1848.

Davis, Matthew L. *Memoirs of Aaron Burr: With Selections from His Correspondence*. 2 vols. New York: Harper and Brothers, 1837.

Deady, Matthew P. *Pharisee among Philistines: The Diary of Judge Matthew P. Deady, 1871–1892*. Edited by Malcolm Clark. 2 vols. Portland: Oregon Historical Society, 1975.

Delaplaine, Joseph. *Delaplaine's Repository of the Lives and Portraits of Distinguished Americans*. 3 vols. Philadelphia: Joseph Delaplaine, 1816–19.

Diehl, Michael. *Biography of Rev. Ezra Keller, Founder and First President of Wittenberg College*. Springfield, Ohio: Ruralist Publishing Co., 1859.

Doddridge, Philip. *Some Remarkable Passages in the Life of Hon. Col. James Gardiner, Who Was Slain at the Battle of Preston Pans, September 21, 1745*. Boston: I. Thomas and E. T. Andrews, 1792.

Eaton, John Henry. *The Letters of Wyoming, to the People of the United States, on the Presidential Election, and in Favor of Andrew Jackson*. Philadelphia: S. Simpson and J. Conrad, 1824.

———. *The Life of Andrew Jackson, Major-General in the Service of the United States: Comprising a History of the War in the South, from the Commencement of the Creek Campaign, to the Termination of Hostilities before New Orleans*. Philadelphia: Samuel F. Bradford, 1824.

Eliot, John. *A Biographical Dictionary, Containing a Brief Account of the First Settlers, and Other Eminent Characters among the Magistrates, Ministers, Literary and Worthy Men in New England*. Salem, Mass.: Cushing and Appleton, 1809.

Ellet, Elizabeth F. *Evenings at Woodlawn*. New York: Baker and Scribner, 1849.

———. *Rambles About the Country*. Boston: Marsh, Capen, Lyon, and Webb, 1840.

———. *The Women of the American Revolution*. 3 vols. New York: Baker and Scribner, 1848–50.

Emerson, Ralph Waldo. *The Complete Sermons of Ralph Waldo Emerson*. Edited by Albert J. von Frank. 4 vols. Columbia: University of Missouri Press, 1989.

———. *The Early Lectures of Ralph Waldo Emerson*. Edited by Stephen E. Whicher and Robert E. Spiller. Cambridge, Mass.: Harvard University Press, 1959.

———. *The Journals and Miscellaneous Notebooks of Ralph Waldo Emerson*. Edited by William H. Gilman et al. 16 vols. Cambridge, Mass.: Belknap Press of Harvard University Press, 1960–82.

———. *Representative Men: Seven Lectures*. 1850. Reprint. Boston: Houghton, Mifflin, 1903.

Emmons, William. *A Biography of Martin Van Buren, Vice President of the United States*. Washington, D.C.: Jacob Gideon Jr., 1835.

Encyclopaedia: Or, a Dictionary of Arts, Sciences, and Miscellaneous Literature. Philadelphia: Thomas Dobson, 1798.

Events and Incidents in the History of Gen. Winfield Scott. Washington, D.C.: Kirkwood and McGill, 1852.

Everett, Edward [Ttereve Sudravde, pseud.]. *Sketch of the Life of John Quincy Adams*, 1827.

Floy, Michael, Jr. *The Diary of Michael Floy Jr., Bowery Village, 1833–1837*. Edited by Richard Albert Edward Brooks. New Haven: Yale University Press, 1941.

Floyd, Silas Xavier. *Life of Charles T. Walker, D.D. ("The Black Spurgeon"), Pastor Mt. Olivet Baptist Church, New York City*. Nashville: National Baptist Publishing Board, 1902.

Ford, Paul Leicester. *The True George Washington*. Philadelphia: J. B. Lippincott Company, 1896.

Forney, John W. *Life and Military Career of Winfield Scott Hancock*. Philadelphia: R. B. Morris and Co., 1880.

[Frost, John]. *Lives of American Merchants, Eminent for Integrity, Enterprise, and Public Spirit*. New York: Saxton and Miles, 1844.

Garfield, James A. *The Diary of James A. Garfield*. Edited by Harry J. Brown and Frederick D. Williams. 4 vols. East Lansing: Michigan State University Press, 1967–81.

———. *The Papers of James A. Garfield*. Microfilm ed. Washington, D.C.: Library of Congress, 1970.

Gilman, Daniel C. *James Monroe*. 1883. Reprint. Boston: Houghton, Mifflin, 1899.

Gilmore, James Roberts [Edmund Kirke, pseud.]. *The Life of James A. Garfield, Republican Candidate for the Presidency, with Extracts from His Speeches*. New York: Harper and Brothers, 1880.

Gordon, Douglas, ed. "A Virginian and His Baltimore Diary: Part III." *Maryland Historical Magazine* 51 (September 1956): 224–36.

Grimshaw, William. *The Ladies' Lexicon, and Parlour Companion*. Philadelphia: J. B. Lippincott Co., 1864.

Griswold, Rufus Wilmot. *Washington and the Generals of the Revolution*. Philadelphia: Carey and Hart, 1847.

Hall, James. *A Memoir of the Public Services of William Henry Harrison, of Ohio*. Philadelphia: Key and Biddle, 1836.

Hardie, James. *The New Universal Biographical Dictionary and American Remembrancer of Departed Merit*. New York: Johnson and Stryker, 1801.

Harper's Illustrated Catalogue of Valuable Standard Works, in the Several Departments of General Literature. New York: Harper and Brothers, 1848.

Haswell, Anthony. *Memoirs and Adventures of Captain Matthew Phelps, Formerly of Harwington in Connecticut, now Resident in Newhaven in Vermont*. Bennington, Vt.: Anthony Haswell, 1802.

Hawes, Joel. *Lectures to Young Men, on the Formation of Character, &c.* 3d ed. Hartford, Conn.: Cooke and Co., 1829.

Hawthorne, Nathaniel. *Biographical Stories for Children*. Boston: Tappan and Dennet, 1842.

———. *The Letters, 1843–1853*. Edited by William Charvat et al. Vol. 16, *Centenary Edition of the Works of Nathaniel Hawthorne*. Columbus: Ohio State University Press, 1985.

———. *Life of Franklin Pierce*. Boston: Ticknor, Reed, and Fields, 1852.

"Hawthorne's Life of Pierce.—Perspective." *Democratic Review* 31 (September 1852): 276–88.

Hays, Mary. *Female Biography*. Philadelphia: Birch and Small, 1807.

Helm, James I. *Memoir of Martha Thompson Sharp, by Her Pastor*. New York: American Tract Society, 1848.

Hickman, George H. *The Life and Services of the Hon. James Knox Polk, with a Compendium of His Speeches on Various Public Measures*. Baltimore: N. Hickman, 1844.

Higginson, Thomas Wentworth. *Margaret Fuller Ossoli*. Boston: Houghton, Mifflin, 1884.

History and Biography of Washington County and the Town of Queensbury, New York. Chicago: Gresham Publishing Co., 1894.

History of the City of Denver, Arapahoe County, and Colorado: Containing . . . Biographical Sketches. Chicago: O. L. Baskin and Co., 1880.

History of Washington County, New York. Philadelphia: Everts and Ensign, 1878.

Holland, William M. *The Life and Opinions of Martin Van Buren, Vice President of the United States.* Hartford, Conn.: Belknap and Hamersley, 1835.

Hollander, John, ed. *American Poetry: The Nineteenth Century.* 2 vols. New York: Library of America, 1993.

Holst, Hermann Von. *John C. Calhoun.* 1882. Reprint. Boston: Houghton, Mifflin, 1899.

Howe, Henry. *Memoirs of the Most Eminent American Mechanics: Also, Lives of Distinguished European Mechanics.* New York: A. V. Blake, 1842.

Howells, William Dean. *Life of Abraham Lincoln.* 1860. Reprint. Springfield, Ill.: Abraham Lincoln Association, 1938.

———. *The Rise of Silas Lapham.* 1885. Reprint, ed. Don L. Cook. New York: Norton Critical Edition, 1982.

Humphreys, David. *An Essay on the Life of the Honorable Major-General Israel Putnam: Addressed to the State Society of the Cincinnati in Connecticut.* Middletown, Conn.: Printed by Moses H. Woodward, for Hudson and Goodwin, Hartford, 1794.

Jackson, Isaac Rand. *Narrative of the Civil and Military Services of William H. Harrison. Compiled from the Most Authentic Authorities.* Philadelphia, 1836.

Johnson, Samuel. *The Works of Samuel Johnson, LL.D.* Oxford: Talboys and Wheeler, 1825.

Jones, Lot. *Memoir of Mrs. Sarah Louisa Taylor: Or, an Illustration of the Work of the Holy Spirit, in Awakening, Renewing, and Sanctifying the Heart.* 5th ed. New York: D. Fanshawe, 1847.

Junius. *Life of Henry Clay.* New York: Greeley and McElrath, 1844.

Kennedy, John P. *Memoirs of the Life of William Wirt, Attorney General of the United States.* 2 vols. Philadelphia: Lea and Blanchard, 1849.

Klingberg, Frank J., and Frank W. Klingberg, ed. *The Correspondence between Henry Stephens Randall and Hugh Blair Grigsby, 1856–1861.* University of California Publications in History, no. 43. Berkeley: University of California Press, 1952.

Knapp, Samuel L. *Female Biography: Containing Notices of Distinguished Women, in Different Nations and Ages.* Philadelphia: Thomas Wardle, 1836.

———. *The Life of Aaron Burr.* New York: Wiley and Long, 1835.

———. *Memoirs of General Lafayette: With an Account of His Visit to America.* Boston: E. G. House, 1824.

Kraditor, Aileen S., ed. *Up from the Pedestal: Selected Writings in the History of American Feminism.* New York: Quadrangle, 1968.

Latimer, E. *Life and Thought: Or, Cherished Memorials of the Late Julia A. Parker Dyson.* 2d ed. Philadelphia: Claxton, Remsen, Hafflefinger and Co., 1871.

Lester, Charles. *The Mountain Wild Flower: Or, Memoirs of Mrs. Mary Ann Bise.* New York: E. French, 1838.

Lieber, Francis. *Encyclopaedia Americana.* Philadelphia: Carey and Lea, 1830.

Life of General Lewis Cass: Comprising an Account of His Military Services in the North-West during the War with Great Britain, His Diplomatic Career and Civil History. Philadelphia: G. B. Zieber and Co., 1848.

Lincoln, Abraham. *The Collected Works of Abraham Lincoln.* Edited by Roy P. Basler. New Brunswick, N.J.: Rutgers University Press for the Abraham Lincoln Association, 1953.

[Linsley, Sophia]. *Memoirs of Miss Mary Lyon, of New Haven, Conn.* New Haven: A. H. Maltby, 1837.

The Lives and Exploits of the Banditti and Robbers of All Nations. 2 vols. Philadelphia: R. W. Pomeroy, 1839.

Lives of Distinguished Shoemakers. Portland, Maine: Davis and Southworth, 1849.

Lodge, Henry Cabot. *George Washington.* 2 vols. Boston: Houghton, Mifflin, 1889.

Longfellow, Henry Wadsworth. *Final Memorials of Henry Wadsworth Longfellow.* Edited by Samuel Longfellow. Boston: Ticknor and Co., 1887.

Lord, Eleazar. *Lempriere's Universal Biography.* 2 vols. New York: R. Lockwood, 1825.

McCabe, James Dabney. *From the Farm to the Presidential Chair: Being an Accurate and Comprehensive Account of the Life and Public Services of Gen. James A. Garfield.* Philadelphia: National Publishing Company, 1880.

McRee, Griffith J. *Life and Correspondence of James Iredell, One of the Associate Justices of the Supreme Court of the United States.* 2 vols. New York: D. Appleton and Co., 1857.

Majors, M. A. *Noted Negro Women: Their Triumphs and Activities.* Chicago: Donohue and Henneberry, 1893.

Mallory, Daniel. *The Life and Speeches of the Hon. Henry Clay, in Two Volumes.* 2 vols. New York: Robert P. Bixby and Co., 1843.

Mann, Mary Tyler Peabody. *Life of Horace Mann.* Boston: Lee and Shepard, 1865.

Marshall, John. *The Life of George Washington.* 5 vols. Philadelphia: C. P. Wayne, 1804–7.

———. *The Life of George Washington: Maps and Subscribers' Names.* Philadelphia: C. P. Wayne, 1807.

Maxwell, John. *The American Patriot and Hero: A Brief Memoir of the Illustrious Conduct and Character of His Excellency George Washington, the Chief Commander, and Successful Leader of the Armies of the United States of America, during Their Late War with Great Britain.* [Lancaster, Pa.?]: Printed for the author, 1795.

Melville, Herman. "Bartleby." 1853. Reprint. New York: Dover, 1990.

———. *Israel Potter: His Fifty Years of Exile.* New York: G. P. Putnam and Co., 1855.

Miller, Samuel. *A Brief Retrospect of the Eighteenth Century . . . Containing a Sketch of the Revolutions and Improvements in Science, Arts, and Literature, during That Period.* 2 vols. New York: T. and J. Swords, 1803.

Minor, Charles L. C. *The Real Lincoln, from the Testimony of His Contemporaries.* Richmond, Va.: Everett Waddey Co., 1904.

Mitchell, Phebe, comp. *Maria Mitchell: Life, Letters, and Journals.* Boston: Lee and Shepard, 1896.

Mixon, W. H. *History of the African Methodist Episcopal Church in Alabama, with Biographical Sketches.* Nashville: A.M.E. Church Sunday School Union, 1902.

Morse, Jedidiah. *A True and Authentic History of His Excellency George Washington, Commander in Chief of the American Army during the Late War, and Present President of the United States.* Philadelphia: Printed by Peter Stewart for Robert Stewart, 1790.

Morse, John T., Jr. *Benjamin Franklin.* Boston: Houghton, Mifflin, 1898.

———. "Incidents Connected with the American Statesmen Series." *Proceedings of the Massachusetts Historical Society* 64 (1932): 370–88.

———. *John Adams.* Boston: Houghton, Mifflin, 1884.

———. *John Quincy Adams.* 1882. Reprint. Boston: Houghton, Mifflin, 1899.

Myerson, Joel, and Daniel Shealy, eds. *The Journals of Louisa May Alcott.* Boston: Little, Brown and Co., 1989.

The National Cyclopaedia of American Biography. New York: James T. White and Co., 1909.

Nell, William C. *The Colored Patriots of the American Revolution, with Sketches of Several Distinguished Colored Persons.* Boston: Robert F. Wallcut, 1855.

Nolan, Paul T. "The Journal of a Young Southern Playwright, Espy Williams of New Orleans, 1874–75." *Louisiana Studies* 1 (Fall, Winter 1962): no. 3, 30–50; no. 4, 33–54.

Parton, James. *Famous Americans of Recent Times.* 1867. Reprint. Boston: Houghton, Mifflin, 1881.

———. "James Parton's Rules of Biography." *McClure's Magazine* 1 (June 1893): 59–62.

———. *The Life and Times of Aaron Burr.* New York: Mason Brothers, 1858.

———. *Life and Times of Benjamin Franklin.* 2 vols. Boston: Ticknor and Fields, 1864.

———. *Life of Andrew Jackson.* 3 vols. 1860. Reprint. Boston: James R. Osgood and Co., 1876.

———. *The Life of Horace Greeley, Editor of the New York Tribune.* New York: Mason Brothers, 1855.

———. *People's Book of Biography: Or, Short Lives of the Most Interesting Persons of All Ages and Countries.* Hartford: A. S. Hale, 1868.

Parton, James, et al. *Eminent Women of the Age: Being Narratives of the Lives and Deeds of the Most Prominent Women of the Present Generation.* Hartford, Conn.: S. M. Betts and Co., 1869.

———. *Sketches of Men of Progress.* New York and Hartford, Conn.: New York and Hartford Publishing Company, 1870–71.

Parton, James, ed. *Some Noted Princes, Authors, and Statesmen of Our Time.* New York: Thomas Y. Crowell and Co., 1885.

Pease, Zephaniah, ed. *The Diary of Samuel Rodman: A New Bedford Chronicle of Thirty-Seven Years, 1821–1859.* New Bedford, Mass.: Reynolds Printing, 1927.

Pegues, A. W. *Our Baptist Ministers and Schools.* Springfield, Mass.: Willey and Co., 1892.

Poe, Edgar Allan. *The Letters of Edgar Allan Poe.* Edited by John Ward Ostrom. 2 vols. New York: Gordian Press, 1966.

———. *The Works of the Late Edgar Allan Poe.* Edited by Rufus Wilmot Griswold. New York: Redfield, 1855.

Portrait and Biographical Album of Lancaster County, Nebraska, Containing Full Page Portraits and Biographical Sketches of Prominent and Representative Citizens of the County, Together with Portraits and Biographies of All the Governors of the State, and of the Presidents of the United States. Chicago: Chapman Brothers, 1888.

Portrait and Biographical Album of Otoe and Cass Counties, Nebraska. Chicago: Chapman Brothers, 1889.

Prentice, George D. *Biography of Henry Clay.* Hartford: Samuel Hanmer Jr. and John Jay Phelps, 1831.

Prince, J. *A Wreath for St. Crispin: Being Sketches of Eminent Shoemakers.* Boston: Bela Marsh, 1848.

Public Characters: Or, Contemporary Biography. Baltimore: Bonsal and Niles, 1803.

[Pye, Henry James]. *The Democrat: Or, Intrigues and Adventures of Jean Le Noir.* New York: James Rivington, 1795.

Ramsay, David. *The Life of George Washington.* New York: Hopkins and Seymour, 1807.

Randolph, Edmund. *History of Virginia.* Edited by Arthur H. Shaffer. Charlottesville: University Press of Virginia, 1970.

Reed, Andrew. *Martha: A Memorial of an Only and Beloved Sister.* New York: Harper and Brothers, 1835.

Report of the Population of the United States at the Eleventh Census: 1890. Part 1. Washington, D.C.: Government Printing Office, 1895.

Richards, Janet Elizabeth. "Heroic Women of the Revolution." *American Monthly Magazine* 1 (September 1892): 278–92.

Richardson, James D., ed. *A Compilation of the Messages and Papers of the Presidents, 1789–1902.* 10 vols. Washington, D.C.: Bureau of National Literature and Art, 1903.

Riddle, A. G. *History of Geauga and Lake Counties, Ohio, with Illustrations and Biographical Sketches of Its Pioneers and Most Prominent Men.* Philadelphia: Williams Brothers, 1878.

———. *The Life, Character, and Public Services of Jas. A. Garfield.* Cleveland, Ohio: W. W. Williams, 1880.

Ridpath, John Clark. *The Life and Work of James A. Garfield, Twentieth President of the United States . . . and the Tragic Story of His Death.* Memorial ed. Cincinnati: Jones Brothers and Co., 1881.

Roberts, Philetus. *Memoir of Mrs. Abigail Roberts: An Account of Her Birth, Early Education, Call to the Ministry.* Irvington, N.J.: Moses Cummings, 1858.

Rogers, Thomas J. *A New American Biographical Dictionary: Or, Remembrancer of the Departed Heroes and Statesmen of America.* Easton, Pa.: T. J. Rogers, 1813.

Sargent, Nathan [Oliver Oldschool, pseud.]. *Brief Outline of the Life of Henry Clay.* Washington, D.C.: John T. Towers, 1844.

Schoolcraft, Henry Rowe. *Outlines of the Life and Character of Gen. Lewis Cass.* Albany, N.Y.: Joel Munsell, 1848.

Schurz, Carl. *Henry Clay.* 2 vols. Boston: Houghton, Mifflin, 1889.

Scudder, Horace E. *Noah Webster.* Boston: Houghton, Mifflin, 1881.

Sedgwick, Catharine. *Home.* New York: James Munroe and Co., 1835.

Shepard, Edward M. *Martin Van Buren.* Boston: Houghton, Mifflin, 1888.

Simmons, William J. *Men of Mark: Eminent, Progressive, and Rising.* 1887. Reprint. Cleveland and Baltimore: Geo. M. Rewell and Co., 1890.

Simms, William Gilmore. *The Letters of William Gilmore Simms.* Edited by Mary C. Simms Oliphant, Alfred Taylor Odell, and T. C. Duncan Eaves. 6 vols. Columbia: University of South Carolina Press, 1952–82.

———. *The Life of Captain John Smith, the Founder of Virginia.* New York: George F. Cooledge and Brother, 1846.

———. *The Life of Francis Marion.* New York: Henry G. Langley, 1844.

———. *The Life of Nathanael Greene, Major-General in the Army of the Revolution.* New York: George F. Cooledge and Brother, 1849.

———. *The Life of the Chevalier Bayard.* New York: Harper and Brothers, 1847.

———. *Views and Reviews, Second Series.* New York, 1845.

Sketches of the Life and Public Services of Gen. Lewis Cass. Boston: Boston Daily Times, 1848.

Sketch of the Life of John Quincy Adams: Taken from the Port Folio of April, 1819, 1824.

Sleeper, Sarah. *Memoir of the Late Martha Hazeltine Smith.* Boston: Freeman and Bolles, 1843.

Sparks, Jared. *The Life of Gouverneur Morris, with Selections from His Correspondence and Miscellaneous Papers.* 2 vols. Boston: Gray and Bowen, 1832.

———. *The Life of John Ledyard, the American Traveller: Comprising Selections from His Journals and Correspondence.* Cambridge, Mass.: Hilliard and Brown, 1828.

[———]. "Mr. Wirt's Life of Patrick Henry." *North American Review* 6 (March 1818): 293–324.

———, ed. *The Library of American Biography.* 25 vols. Boston: Little and Brown, 1834–48.

Steele, Ashbel. *Chief of the Pilgrims: Or, the Life and Times of William Brewster.* Philadelphia: J. B. Lippincott, 1857.

Stone, William L. *The Life and Times of Red-Jacket, or Sa-Go-Ye-Wat-Ha: Being the Sequel to the History of the Six Nations.* New York: Wiley and Putnam, 1841.

———. *Life of Joseph Brant-Thayendanegea, Including the Indian Wars of the American Revolution.* New York: Alexander V. Blake, 1838.

Stowe, Harriet Beecher. *Men of Our Times: Or, Leading Patriots of the Day.* Hartford, Conn.: Hartford Publishing Co., 1868.

Stuart, I. W. *Life of Jonathan Trumbull, Sen., Governor of Connecticut.* Boston: Crocker and Brewster, 1859.

Sumner, William Graham. *Andrew Jackson.* Boston: Houghton, Mifflin, 1882.

Swain, James B. *The Life and Speeches of Henry Clay.* 2 vols. New York: Greeley and McElrath, 1844.

Taylor, Isaac. *Youth's Own Book: Character Essential to Success in Life.* Hartford, Conn.: Canfield and Robins, 1836.

Thatcher, B. B. *Indian Biography.* 1832. Reprint. New York: Harper and Brothers, 1842.

Thayer, William M. *The Bobbin Boy: Or, How Nat Got His Learning: An Example for Youth.* Boston: J. E. Tilton and Co., 1860.

———. *From Log-Cabin to the White House: Life of James A. Garfield: Boyhood, Youth, Manhood, Assassination, Death, Funeral.* Boston: James H. Earle, 1885.

———. *From Poor-House to Pulpit: Or, the Triumphs of the Late Dr. John Kitto, from Boyhood to Manhood: A Book for Youth.* Boston: E. O. Libby and Co., 1859.

———. *The Pioneer Boy, and How He Became President.* Boston: Walker, Wise, and Co., 1863.

———. *The Poor Boy and Merchant Prince: Or, Elements of Success Drawn from the Life and Character of the Late Amos Lawrence.* Boston: Gould and Lincoln, 1857.

———. *The Poor Girl and True Woman: Or, Elements of Woman's Success Drawn from the Life of Mary Lyon and Others.* Boston: Gould and Lincoln, 1859.

———. *The Unfinished Autobiography of William M. Thayer.* Boston: Barta Press, [1898].

Thornbrough, Gayle, and Dorothy L. Riker, eds. *The Diary of Calvin Fletcher.* 9 vols. Indianapolis: Indiana Historical Society, 1972–83.

Todd, Charles S., and Benjamin Drake. *Sketches of the Civil and Military Services of William Henry Harrison.* Cincinnati: U. P. James, 1840.

Trent, William P. *William Gilmore Simms.* Boston: Houghton, Mifflin, 1892.

Tuckerman, Henry Theodore. "Alexander Hamilton." *North American Review* 86 (April 1858): 368–411.

———. "The Character of Franklin." *North American Review* 83 (October 1856): 402–22.

———. "The Character of Washington." *North American Review* 83 (July 1856): 1–30.

———. "Daniel De Foe." *North American Review* 78 (April 1854): 265–83.

———. "George Berkeley." *North American Review* 80 (January 1855): 171–98.

———. "James Fenimore Cooper." *North American Review* 89 (October 1859): 289–316.

———. "Joseph Addison." *North American Review* 79 (July 1854): 90–109.

———. "Laurence Sterne." *North American Review* 81 (October 1855): 361–89.

———. "Life of DeWitt Clinton." *North American Review* 79 (October 1854): 485–502.

———. "Michael De Montaigne." *North American Review* 87 (October 1858): 356–88.

———. "Sydney Smith." *North American Review* 82 (January 1856): 100–111.

Tyler, Moses Coit. *Patrick Henry.* Boston: Houghton, Mifflin, 1887.

Vassar, Rena L., ed. "The Life or Biography of Silas Felton Written by Himself." *Proceedings of the American Antiquarian Society* 69 (October 1959): 119–54.

Ward, Julius H. "James Parton." *New England Magazine* 13 (January 1893): 627–39.

Warden, Robert B. *An Account of the Private Life and Public Services of Salmon Portland Chase.* Cincinnati: Wilstach, Baldwin and Co., 1874.

Ware, Henry. *The Miscellaneous Writings of Henry Ware.* 4 vols. Boston: James Munroe, 1846.

Warner, Charles Dudley. *Washington Irving.* Boston: Houghton, Mifflin, 1881.

Warner, Susan. *The Wide, Wide World.* 1850. Reprint, ed. Jane Tompkins. New York: Feminist Press, 1987.

[Wayland, Francis]. *A Memoir of Harriet Ware, First Superintendent of the Children's Home, in the City of Providence.* Providence, R.I.: George H. Whitney, 1850.

Webster, Noah. *A Compendious Dictionary of the English Language.* New Haven: Increase Cooke and Co.; Hartford: Hudson and Goodwin, 1806.

———. *An American Dictionary of the English Language.* 6th ed. New York: S. Converse, 1830.

Weems, Mason L. *A History, of the Life and Death, Virtues and Exploits, of General George Washington.* Georgetown, D.C.: Green and English, 1800.

———. *The Life of Washington.* 9th ed. Philadelphia: Mathew Carey, 1809. Reprint, ed. Marcus Cunliffe. Cambridge, Mass.: Belknap Press of Harvard University Press, 1962.

Whitman, Walt. *Walt Whitman: Complete Poetry and Selected Prose.* Edited by Emory Holloway. London: Nonesuch Press, 1971.

Willard, Frances E. "A Noble Life: Mrs. Lillie Hayes Waugh." *Ladies' Repository* 11 (May 1873): 321–26.

"William Wirt's Life of Patrick Henry." *William and Mary Quarterly* 1st ser., 22 (April 1914): 250–57.

[Wilmer, James Jones]. *The American Nepos: A Collection of the Lives of the Most Remarkable and the Most Eminent Men, Who Have Contributed to Discovery, the Settlement, and the Independence of America.* Baltimore: John Vance, 1805.

Wilson, Arabella Stuart. *The Lives of Mrs. Ann H. Judson and Mrs. Sarah B. Judson, with a Biographical Sketch of Mrs. Emily C. Judson, Missionaries to Burmah.* Auburn, N.Y.: Derby and Miller, 1851.

Wilson, Thomas. *The Biography of the Principal American Military and Naval Heroes: Comprehending Details of Their Achievements during the Revolutionary and Late Wars.* New York: John Low, 1817.

Winsor, Justin. *Christopher Columbus and How He Received and Imparted the Spirit of Discovery.* Boston: Houghton, Mifflin, 1891.

Wirt, William. *Sketches of the Life and Character of Patrick Henry.* Philadelphia: James Webster, 1817. Reprint. 7th ed. New York: M'Elrath, Bangs and Co., 1834.

Wood, James. *Memoir of Sylvester Scovel, D.D., Late President of Hanover College, Ia.* New Albany, Ind.: J. B. Anderson, 1851.

Woodward, Thomas. *The Columbian Plutarch: Or, an Exemplification of Several Distinguished American Characters.* Philadelphia: Clark and Raser, 1819.

Wordsworth, William. *Wordsworth's Literary Criticism.* Edited by Nowell C. Smith. London: C. Frowde, 1905.

The Young Man's Own Book: A Manual of Politeness, Intellectual Improvement, and Moral Deportment. Philadelphia: Key and Biddle, 1833.

Articles on Biography as a Genre

Note: This list includes neither reviews of individual works nor biographical articles about particular subjects. Newspapers and magazines consulted for reviews are listed under Periodicals; biographical articles discussed in this book are included under the section "Biographies, Published Diaries, and Literary Works."

"American Biographical Works." *Analectic Magazine* 4 (August 1814): 174.

"American Biography." *American Quarterly Review* 1 (March 1827): 1–37.

"Aspects of Biography." *Nation* 73 (December 5, 1901): 431–32.

Backus, S. "An Oration on Biography, Spoken the First Anniversary of the Themean Society, April 5, 1811." *Floriad* 1 (June 7 and 21, 1811): 17–21, 33–35.

"A Biographer at Work." *New Englander* 25 (April 1866): 218–27.

"Biographical Literature." *Christian Review* 21 (October 1856): 552–70.

"Biographical Mania." *New-York Mirror, and Ladies' Literary Gazette* 7 (May 15, 1830): 359.

"The Biographical Mania." *Evening Gazette* (Boston) (July 4, 1857): 8.

"Biographical Studies." *American Quarterly Church Review* 18 (January 1867): 622–27.

"Biography." *American Law Journal* 1 (January 1808): 121.

"Biography." *Literary Tablet* 1 (August 6, 1803): 2.

"Biography." *Monthly Register, Magazine, and Review of the United States* 2 (December 1806): 33–37.

"Biography." *Penn Monthly* 6 (April 1875): 274–86.

"Biography." *Port Folio* n.s., 3 (January 1817): 29–30.

"Biography." *Southern Literary Messenger* 23 (October 1856): 282–88.

"Biography." *Yale Literary Magazine* 10 (June 1845): 331–33.

"The Biography of Illustrious Men." *Christian Philanthropist* 1 (September 3, 1822): 67.

"Biography—Plutarch's Lives." *North American Review* 89 (October 1859): 521–35.

Bruce, H. Addington. "The Biography of To-Day." *The Outlook* 77 (May 28, 1904): 235–37.

[Civis.] "Art. XII.—Biography." *American Annals of Education and Instruction, and Journal of Literary Institutions* 1 (June 1831): 281.

[Curtis, George William]. "Editor's Easy Chair." *Harper's New Monthly Magazine* 68 (March 1884): 639–40.

[Dodge, Mary Abigail]. "The New School of Biography." *Atlantic Monthly* 14 (November 1864): 579–89.

"The Duty of a Biographer." *Democratic Review* 28 (March 1851): 254–58.

[Duyckinck, Evert A.]. "Biography" (Review of Henry T. Tuckerman, *Essays, Biographical and Critical*). *North American Review* 84 (April 1857): 406–25.

Gosse, Edmund. "The Ethics of Biography." *Cosmopolitan* 35 (July 1903): 317–23.

Keeler, A. B. "The 'Real' Biographer." *Puck* 46 (September 20, 1899): [5].

[Knapp, Samuel L.]. "On Biography." *New-England Galaxy and Masonic Magazine* 1 (October 10, 1817): 1.

"Lesson in Biography: Or, How to Write the Life of One's Friend." *New-York Magazine: Or, Literary Repository* 4 (November 1793): 667–71; *Companion and Weekly Miscellany* 1 (November 3, 1804): 36–38; *Literary Magazine and American Register* 6 (August 1806): 99–103.

Lewin, Walter. "Bowdlerized Biography." *The Forum* 10 (February 1891): 658–66.

"Loose Thoughts on Biography." *American Monthly Magazine* 1 (July 1829): 251–63.

Marble, Annie Russell. "Popular Forms of Modern Biography." *Dial* 31 (September 1, 1901): 125–29.

Oliphant, Margaret. "The Ethics of Biography." *Littell's Living Age* 158 (August 11, 1883): 323–33.

"On Biography." *Athenaeum* 1 (1814): 78–79.

"On Biography." *New England Quarterly Magazine: Comprehending Literature, Morals, Amusement* 1 (April/May/June 1802): 46–47.

"On Biography." *Weekly Visitant* 1 (March 22, 1806): 89–90.

"On the Utility of Biography." *Literary and Philosophical Repertory* 1 (April 1812): 39–46.

"Parton's Biographical Writings." *North American Review* 104 (April 1867): 597–602.

"Romance Biographies." *Christian Examiner* 73 (September 1862): 175–86.

Simons, Sadie E. "Educational Value of Biography." *Educational Review* 17 (January 1899): 70–79.

Thayer, William Roscoe. "Biography." *North American Review* 180 (February 1905): 261–79.

Periodicals

Albany (N.Y.) Argus, 1817

Alexandria (Va.) Gazette, 1817

American Catholic Quarterly Review, Philadelphia

The American Museum, Philadelphia, 1791

American Publisher's Circular (*American Literary Gazette and Publisher's Circular*), New York and Philadelphia

American Quarterly Review, Philadelphia

American Whig Review, New York

Analectic Magazine, Philadelphia

Arkansas Whig, Little Rock, 1852

Atlantic Advertiser and Miscellany, Boston

Atlantic Magazine, New York

Atlantic Monthly, Boston

Baltimore Republican and Commercial Advertiser, 1835

Boston Daily Advertiser, 1817

Boston Weekly Messenger, 1817

The Campaign, Washington, D.C., 1852

Chambers' Edinburgh Journal

Christian Examiner, Boston and New York

Christian Review, Boston

Cincinnati Mirror and Chronicle

Commercial Advertiser, New York, 1817

Concord (N.H.) Tribune, 1852

Daily Cincinnati Gazette, 1852

De Bow's Review, New Orleans

Democratic Review (*United States Magazine and Democratic Review*), New York

General Repository and Review, Cambridge, Mass.

Godey's Lady's Book, Philadelphia

Graham's Magazine, Philadelphia

Harper's New Monthly Magazine, New York

Independent Chronicle and Boston Patriot, 1817

Knickerbocker Magazine, New York

The Ladies' Magazine

Ladies' Repository, Cincinnati and New York

Literary World, New York

Living Age (Littell's Living Age), Boston

Merchant's Magazine, and Commercial Review, New York

Methodist Quarterly Review, New York

Monthly Anthology, and Boston Review

Nation, New York

National Intelligencer, Washington, D.C., 1817

New Englander, New Haven, Conn.

New York Daily Advertiser, 1817

New-York Evening Post, 1817

New York Review

New York Times, March 1867, October 1900

North American Review, Boston

The Oasis, Oswego, N.Y.

Port Folio, Philadelphia

Portico, Baltimore

Poulson's American Daily Advertiser, Philadelphia, 1816–17

Richmond (Va.) Enquirer, 1817, 1857–58

Southern Literary Journal, Charleston

Southern Literary Messenger, Richmond

Southern Patriot, and Commercial Advertiser, Charleston, 1816–17

Southern Quarterly Review, New Orleans

Union Magazine of Art and Literature, New York and Philadelphia

United States Gazette, Philadelphia, 1817

Virginia Historical Register, Richmond

Washington County Post, Salem, N.Y., 1823–26

Washington (D.C.) Union, 1852

Weekly Aurora, Philadelphia, 1817

Secondary Sources

Adair, Douglass. "Fame and the Founding Fathers." In *Fame and the Founding Fathers: Essays by Douglass Adair*, edited by Trevor Colbourn, 3–26. New York: Norton, 1974.

Adams, Herbert Baxter. *The Life and Writings of Jared Sparks*. 2 vols. Boston: Houghton, Mifflin, 1893.

Agnew, Jean-Christophe. *Worlds Apart: The Market and the Theater in Anglo-American Thought, 1550–1750*. Cambridge: Cambridge University Press, 1986.

Altick, Richard D. *Lives and Letters: A History of Literary Biography in England and America*. New York: Knopf, 1969.

Amigoni, David. *Victorian Biography: Intellectuals and the Ordering of Discourse.* New York: St. Martin's Press, 1993.

Anderson, Judith H. *Biographical Truth: The Representation of Historical Persons in Tudor-Stuart Writing.* New Haven: Yale University Press, 1984.

Appleby, Joyce. "New Cultural Heroes in the Early National Period." In *The Culture of the Market: Historical Essays,* edited by Thomas L. Haskell and Richard F. Teichgraeber III, 163–88. Cambridge: Cambridge University Press, 1993.

———, ed. *Recollections of the Early Republic: Selected Autobiographies.* Boston: Northeastern University Press, 1997.

Ashworth, John. *"Agrarians" and "Aristocrats": Party Political Ideology in the United States, 1837–1846.* Cambridge: Cambridge University Press, 1983.

Baker, Jean H. *Affairs of Party: The Political Culture of Northern Democrats in the Mid-Nineteenth Century.* Ithaca, N.Y.: Cornell University Press, 1983.

Barber, Gertrude A., comp. *Abstracts of Wills of Washington County, New York, from 1788–1825.* N.p., 1937.

———. *Washington County, New York: Index of Wills from 1825–1850.* N.p., 1937.

Bassett, John Spencer. *The Middle Group of American Historians.* New York: Macmillan, 1917.

Baym, Nina. *American Women Writers and the Work of History.* New Brunswick, N.J.: Rutgers University Press, 1995.

———. *Novels, Readers, and Reviewers: Responses to Fiction in Antebellum America.* Ithaca, N.Y.: Cornell University Press, 1984.

———. "Onward Christian Women: Sarah J. Hale's History of the World." *New England Quarterly* 63 (June 1990): 249–70.

———. *Woman's Fiction: A Guide to Novels by and about Women in America, 1820–1870.* Ithaca, N.Y.: Cornell University Press, 1978.

Beeman, Richard R. *The Old Dominion and the New Nation, 1788–1801.* Lexington: University Press of Kentucky, 1972.

Bellis, Peter J. "Israel Potter: Autobiography as History as Fiction." *American Literary History* 2 (Winter 1990): 607–26.

Bercovitch, Sacvan. *The Office of the Scarlet Letter.* Baltimore: Johns Hopkins University Press, 1991.

———. *The Puritan Origins of the American Self.* New Haven: Yale University Press, 1975.

Berry, Edmund G. *Emerson's Plutarch.* Cambridge, Mass.: Harvard University Press, 1961.

Bertaux, Daniel, ed. *Biography and Society: The Life History Approach in the Social Sciences.* Sage Studies in International Sociology, no. 23. Beverly Hills: Sage Publications, 1981.

Bledstein, Burton. *The Culture of Professionalism: The Middle Class and the Development of Higher Education in America.* New York: Norton, 1976.

Blue, Frederick. "Kate's Paper Chase: The Race to Publish the First Biography of Salmon P. Chase." *The Old Northwest* 8 (Winter 1982–83): 353–63.

Blumin, Stuart. *The Emergence of the Middle Class: Social Experience in the American City, 1760–1900.* Cambridge: Cambridge University Press, 1989.

———. "Introduction: George G. Foster and the Emerging Metropolis." In *New York by Gas-Light and Other Urban Sketches,* edited by Stuart M. Blumin, 1–61. Berkeley: University of California Press, 1990.

Booraem, Hendrik, V. *The Road to Respectability: James A. Garfield and His World, 1844–1852.* Lewisburg, Pa.: Bucknell University Press, 1988.

Bowen, Catherine Drinker. *Adventures of a Biographer.* Boston: Atlantic–Little, Brown, 1959.

Boyd, Richard. "The Politics of Exclusion: Hawthorne's *Life of Franklin Pierce.*" *American Transcendental Quarterly* n.s., 3 (1989): 337–51.

Boyd, William Douglas, Jr. "Books for Young Businessmen: Mercantile Libraries in the United States, 1820–1865." Ph.D. diss., Indiana University, 1975.

Brightman, Carol. "Character in Biography." *Nation* 260 (February 13, 1995): 206–10.

Brodhead, Richard. *Cultures of Letters: Scenes of Reading and Writing in Nineteenth-Century America.* Chicago: University of Chicago Press, 1993.

————. "Sparing the Rod: Discipline and Fiction in Antebellum America." *Representations* 21 (Winter 1988): 67–96.

Browning, J. D., ed. *Biography in the 18th Century.* New York: Garland Publishing, 1980.

Brownley, Martine Watson. "Johnson's *Lives of the English Poets* and Earlier Traditions of the Character Sketch in England." In *Johnson and His Age,* edited by James Engell, 29–53. Cambridge, Mass.: Harvard University Press, 1984.

Brumberg, Joan Jacobs. *Mission for Life: The Story of the Family of Adoniram Judson, the Dramatic Events of the First American Foreign Mission, and the Course of Evangelical Religion in the Nineteenth Century.* New York: Free Press, 1980.

Buell, Lawrence. *New England Literary Culture: From Revolution through Renaissance.* Cambridge: Cambridge University Press, 1986.

Bushman, Richard. *The Refinement of America: Persons, Houses, Cities.* New York: Knopf, 1992.

Butler, Jon. *Awash in a Sea of Faith: Christianizing the American People.* Cambridge, Mass.: Harvard University Press, 1990.

Byars, Ronald Preston. "The Making of the Self-Made Man: The Development of Masculine Roles and Images in Ante-Bellum America." Ph.D. diss., Michigan State University, 1979.

Cafarelli, Annette Wheeler. *Prose in the Age of Poets: Romanticism and Biographical Narrative from Johnson to DeQuincey.* Philadelphia: University of Pennsylvania Press, 1990.

Callcott, George H. *History in the United States, 1800–1860: Its Practice and Purpose.* Baltimore: Johns Hopkins University Press, 1970.

Cantrell, Clyde H. "The Reading Habits of Ante-Bellum Southerners." Ph.D. diss., University of Illinois, 1960.

Carwardine, Richard. "Evangelicals, Whigs, and the Election of William Henry Harrison." *American Studies* 17, no. 1 (1983): 47–75.

Cash, William Francis. "Biography and Southern Culture, 1800–1940." Ph.D. diss., University of Texas, 1990.

Casper, Scott E. "Defining the National Pantheon: The Making of Houghton Mifflin's Biographical Series, 1880–1900." In *Reading Books: Essays on the Material Text and Literature in America,* edited by Michele Moylan and Lane Stiles, 179–222. Amherst: University of Massachusetts Press, 1996.

————. "The Two Lives of Franklin Pierce: Hawthorne, Political Culture, and the Literary Market." *American Literary History* 5 (Summer 1993): 203–30.

Caughey, John Walton. *Hubert Howe Bancroft: Historian of the West.* Berkeley and Los Angeles: University of California Press, 1946.

Cawelti, John G. *Apostles of the Self-Made Man.* Chicago: University of Chicago Press, 1965.

Cayton, Mary Kupiec. *Emerson's Emergence: Self and Society in the Transformation of New England, 1800–1845.* Chapel Hill: University of North Carolina Press, 1989.

Charvat, William. *Literary Publishing in America, 1790–1850.* Philadelphia: University of Pennsylvania Press, 1959.

Chevigny, Bell Gale. "Daughters Writing: Toward a Theory of Women's Biography." *Feminist Studies* 9 (Spring 1983): 357–79.

Christianson, Gale E. *Writing Lives Is the Devil! Essays of a Biographer at Work.* Hamden, Conn.: Archon Books, 1993.

Clark, Harry. *A Venture in History: The Production, Publication, and Sale of the Works of Hubert Howe Bancroft.* University of California Publications, Librarianship, no. 19. Berkeley: University of California Press, 1973.

Cmiel, Kenneth. *Democratic Eloquence: The Fight over Popular Speech in Nineteenth-Century America.* Berkeley: University of California Press, 1990.

Cockshut, A. O. J. *Truth to Life: The Art of Biography in the Nineteenth Century.* New York: Harcourt Brace Jovanovich, 1974.

Cohen, Charles L. "The 'Liberty or Death' Speech: A Note on Religion and Revolutionary Rhetoric." *William and Mary Quarterly* 3d ser., 38 (October 1981): 702–17.

Cohen, Daniel A. *Pillars of Salt, Monuments of Grace: New England Crime Literature and the Origins of American Popular Culture, 1674–1860.* New York: Oxford University Press, 1993.

Conrad, Susan P. *Perish the Thought: Intellectual Women in Romantic America, 1830–1860.* Secaucus, N.J.: Citadel Press, 1978.

Conzen, Michael P. "The County Landownership Map in America: Its Commercial Development and Social Transformation, 1814–1939." *Imago Mundi* 36 (1984): 17–23.

———. "Maps for the Masses: Alfred T. Andreas and the Midwestern County Atlas Trade." In *Chicago Mapmakers: Essays on the Rise of the City's Map Trade,* edited by Michael P. Conzen, 47–63. Chicago: Chicago Historical Society for the Chicago Map Society, 1984.

Cott, Nancy F. *The Bonds of Womanhood: "Woman's Sphere" in New England, 1780–1835.* New Haven: Yale University Press, 1977.

Crawford, T. Hugh. "Images of Authority, Strategies of Control: Cooper, Weems, and George Washington." *South Central Review* 11 (Spring 1994): 61–74.

Crouthamel, James L. *Bennett's New York Herald and the Rise of the Popular Press.* Syracuse: Syracuse University Press, 1989.

Daghlian, Philip B., ed. *Essays in Eighteenth-Century Biography.* Bloomington: Indiana University Press, 1968.

Dahlstrand, Frederick C. "Science, Religion, and the Transcendentalist Response to a Changing America." In *Studies in the American Renaissance, 1988,* edited by Joel Myerson. Charlottesville: University Press of Virginia, 1988.

Darnton, Robert. "What Is the History of Books?" In *Reading in America: Literature and Social History,* edited by Cathy N. Davidson, 27–52. Baltimore: Johns Hopkins University Press, 1989.

Davidoff, Leonore, and Catherine Hall. *Family Fortunes: Men and Women of the English Middle Class, 1780–1850.* London: Hutchinson, 1987.

Davidson, Cathy N. *Revolution and the Word: The Rise of the Novel in America.* New York: Oxford University Press, 1986.

———, ed. *Reading in America: Literature and Social History.* Baltimore: Johns Hopkins University Press, 1989.

Davis, Richard Beale. *A Colonial Southern Bookshelf: Reading in the Eighteenth Century.* Mercer University, Lamar Memorial Lectures, no. 21. Athens: University of Georgia Press, 1979.

———. *Intellectual Life in Jefferson's Virginia, 1790–1830*. Knoxville: University of Tennessee Press, 1964.

DeJong, Mary G. "Lines from a Partly Published Drama: The Romance of Frances Sargent Osgood and Edgar Allan Poe." In *Patrons and Protégées: Gender, Friendship, and Writing in Nineteenth-Century America,* edited by Shirley Marchalonis, 31–58. New Brunswick, N.J.: Rutgers University Press, 1988.

Denning, Michael. *Mechanic Accents: Dime Novels and Working-Class Culture in America.* London: Verso, 1987.

Dicken-Garcia, Hazel. *Journalistic Standards in Nineteenth-Century America.* Madison: University of Wisconsin Press, 1989.

Douglas, Ann. *The Feminization of American Culture.* New York: Knopf, 1977.

Drinnon, Richard. *Facing West: The Metaphysics of Indian-Hating and Empire-Building.* Minneapolis: University of Minnesota Press, 1980.

Eberwein, Jane Donahue. "'Indistinct Lustre': Biographical Miniatures in the *Magnalia Christi Americana.*" *Biography* 4 (Summer 1981): 195–207.

Edgar, Neal L. *A History and Bibliography of American Magazines, 1810–1820.* Metuchen, N.J.: Scarecrow Press, 1975.

Ellis, Joseph J. *After the Revolution: Profiles of Early American Culture.* New York: Norton, 1979.

Epstein, William L. *Recognizing Biography.* Philadelphia: University of Pennsylvania Press, 1987.

Exman, Eugene. *The Brothers Harper: A Unique Publishing Partnership and Its Impact on the Cultural Life of America from 1817 to 1853.* New York: Harper and Row, 1965.

Fabian, Ann. *Plain Unvarnished Tales: Americans and True Stories.* Berkeley: University of California Press, 1999.

Faust, Drew Gilpin. *A Sacred Circle: The Dilemma of the Intellectual in the Old South, 1840–1860.* Philadelphia: University of Pennsylvania Press, 1977.

Feller, Daniel. "Politics and Society: Toward a Jacksonian Synthesis." *Journal of the Early Republic* 10 (Summer 1990): 135–62.

Fliegelman, Jay. *Prodigals and Pilgrims: The American Revolution against Patriarchal Authority, 1750–1800.* Cambridge: Cambridge University Press, 1982.

Flower, Milton E. *James Parton: The Father of Modern Biography.* Durham, N.C.: Duke University Press, 1951.

Forgie, George B. *Patricide in the House Divided: A Psychological Interpretation of Lincoln and His Age.* New York: Norton, 1979.

Fortune, Brandon Brame. "Portraits of Virtue and Genius: Pantheons of Worthies and Public Portraiture in the Early Republic, 1780–1820." Ph.D. diss., University of North Carolina, 1986.

Freeman, Joanne B. "Slander, Poison, Whispers, and Fame: Jefferson's 'Anas' and Political Gossip in the Early Republic." *Journal of the Early Republic* 15 (Spring 1995): 25–57.

Fruchtman, Jack, Jr. *Thomas Paine, Apostle of Freedom.* New York: Four Walls Eight Windows, 1994.

Garraty, John A. *The Nature of Biography.* New York: Knopf, 1957.

Gay, Peter. *A Loss of Mastery: Puritan Historians in Colonial New England.* Berkeley: University of California Press, 1966.

Geary, Susan. "The Domestic Novel as a Commercial Commodity: Making a Best Seller in the 1850s." *Papers of the Bibliographical Society of America* 70 (Third Quarter, 1976): 365–93.

Gelles, Edith B. "The Abigail Industry." *William and Mary Quarterly* 3d ser., 45 (October 1988): 656–83.

Gillespie, Joanna Bowen. " 'The Clear Leadings of Providence': Pious Memoirs and the Problems of Self-Realization for Women in the Early Nineteenth Century." *Journal of the Early Republic* 5 (Summer 1985): 197–221.

Gilmore, Michael T. "Eulogy as Symbolic Biography: The Iconography of Revolutionary Leadership, 1776–1826." In *Studies in Biography,* edited by Daniel Aaron, 131–57. Cambridge, Mass.: Harvard University Press, 1978.

Gilmore, William J. *Reading Becomes a Necessity of Life: Material and Cultural Life in Rural New England, 1780–1835.* Knoxville: University of Tennessee Press, 1989.

Gilreath, James. "American Book Distribution." *Proceedings of the American Antiquarian Society* 95 (October 1985): 501–83.

———. "Mason Weems, Mathew Carey, and the Southern Booktrade, 1794–1810." *Publishing History* 10 (1981): 27–49.

Gilreath, James, and Douglas L. Wilson. *Thomas Jefferson's Library: A Catalog with the Entries in His Own Order.* Washington, D.C.: Library of Congress, 1989.

Gougeon, Len. "Holmes's Emerson and the Conservative Critique of Realism." *South Atlantic Review* 59 (January 1994): 107–25.

Gould, Philip. "Representative Men: Jeremy Belknap's *American Biography* and the Political Culture of the Early Republic." *a/b: Auto/Biography Studies* 9 (Spring 1994): 83–97.

Greene, Theodore P. *America's Heroes: The Changing Models of Success in American Magazines.* New York: Oxford University Press, 1970.

Greenhouse, Wendy. "The American Portrayal of Tudor and Stuart History, 1835–1865." Ph.D. diss., Yale University, 1989.

Gross, Robert. "Much Instruction from Little Reading: Books and Libraries in Thoreau's Concord." *Proceedings of the American Antiquarian Society* 97 (April 1987): 129–88.

Groves, Jeffrey D. "Judging Literary Books by Their Covers: House Styles, Ticknor and Fields, and Literary Promotion." In *Reading Books: Essays on the Material Text and Literature in America,* edited by Michele Moylan and Lane Stiles, 75–100. Amherst: University of Massachusetts Press, 1996.

———. " 'Ticknor-and-Fields-ism of All Kinds': Thomas Starr King, Literary Promotion, and Canon Formation." *New England Quarterly* 68 (June 1995): 206–22.

Hale, Nathan G., Jr. *Freud and the Americans: The Beginnings of Psychoanalysis in America, 1876–1917.* New York: Oxford University Press, 1971.

Hall, David D. "Introduction: The Uses of Literacy in New England, 1600–1850." In *Printing and Society in Early America,* edited by William L. Joyce et al., 1–47. Worcester, Mass.: American Antiquarian Society, 1983.

Haller, William. *The Rise of Puritanism.* New York: Columbia University Press, 1938.

Halttunen, Karen. *Confidence Men and Painted Women: A Study of Victorian Culture in America, 1830–1870.* New Haven: Yale University Press, 1982.

Hample, Judy. "William Wirt's Familiar Essays: Criticism of Virginia Oratory." *Southern Speech Communication Journal* 44 (1978): 25–41.

Hankins, Richard. "Puritans, Patriots, and Panegyric: The Beginnings of American Biography." *Studies in the Literary Imagination* 9 (Fall 1976): 95–109.

Hanna, Archibald, Jr. "Every Man His Own Biographer." *Proceedings of the American Antiquarian Society* 80 (October 1970): 291–98.

Harris, Christopher. "Character Portraits of American Military Heroes of the Revolution, 1782–1832." Ph.D. diss., Brown University, 1985.

———. "Mason Locke Weems's *Life of George Washington:* The Making of a Bestseller." *Southern Literary Journal* 19 (Spring 1987): 92–101.

Harris, Kenneth Marc. "Transcendental Biography: Carlyle and Emerson." In *Emerson: Retrospect and Prospect,* edited by Daniel Aaron, 95–112. Cambridge, Mass.: Harvard University Press, 1982.

Harris, Michael H. " 'Spiritual Cakes upon the Waters': The Church as a Disseminator of the Printed Word on the Ohio Valley Frontier to 1850." In *Getting the Books Out: Papers of the Chicago Conference on the Book in 19th-Century America,* edited by Michael Hackenberg, 98–120. Washington, D.C.: The Center for the Book, Library of Congress, 1987.

Harris, Michael Hope. "The Availability of Books and the Nature of Book Ownership on the Southern Indiana Frontier, 1800–1850." Ph.D. diss., Indiana University, 1971.

Harris, Susan K. *19th-Century American Women's Novels: Interpretative Strategies.* Cambridge: Cambridge University Press, 1990.

———. "Responding to the Text(s): Women Readers and the Quest for Higher Education." In *Readers in History: American Literature and the Contexts of Response,* edited by James L. Machor, 259–82. Baltimore: Johns Hopkins University Press, 1993.

Haselton, Stephen J. "The Fairest Meed: Biography in America before 1865." Ph.D. diss., Columbia University, 1959.

Heale, M. J. *The Presidential Quest: Candidates and Images in American Political Culture, 1787–1852.* London: Longman, 1982.

Heffernan, Thomas J. *Sacred Biography: Saints and Their Biographers in the Middle Ages.* New York: Oxford University Press, 1988.

Hoberman, Ruth. *Modernizing Lives: Experiments in English Biography, 1918–1939.* Carbondale: Southern Illinois University Press, 1987.

Horan, James D. *The McKenney-Hall Portrait Gallery of American Indians.* New York: Crown Publishers, 1972.

Horsman, Reginald. *Race and Manifest Destiny: The Origins of American Racial Anglo-Saxonism.* Cambridge, Mass.: Harvard University Press, 1981.

Howe, Daniel Walker. "The Evangelical Movement and Political Culture in the North during the Second Party System." *Journal of American History* 77 (March 1991): 1216–39.

———. *Making the American Self: Jonathan Edwards to Abraham Lincoln.* Cambridge, Mass.: Harvard University Press, 1997.

———. *The Political Culture of the American Whigs.* Chicago: University of Chicago Press, 1979.

Howe, John R., Jr. "Republican Thought and the Political Violence of the 1790s." *American Quarterly* 19 (Summer 1967): 147–65.

Hughson, Lois. *From Biography to History: The Historical Imagination and American Fiction, 1880–1940.* Charlottesville: University Press of Virginia, 1988.

Hutch, Richard A. "Explorations in Character: Gamaliel Bradford and Henry Murray as Psychobiographers." *Biography* 4 (1981): 312–25.

Isaac, Rhys. *The Transformation of Virginia, 1740–1790.* Chapel Hill: University of North Carolina Press, 1982.

Johannsen, Albert. *The House of Beadle and Adams and Its Dime and Nickel Novels: The Story of a Vanished Literature.* 2 vols. Norman: University of Oklahoma Press, 1950.

Johannsen, Robert W. *To the Halls of the Montezumas: The Mexican War in the American Imagination.* New York: Oxford University Press, 1985.

Kammen, Michael. *A Season of Youth: The American Revolution and the Historical Imagination.* New York: Knopf, 1978.

Kaplan, Amy. *The Social Construction of American Realism.* Chicago: University of Chicago Press, 1988.

Kaplan, Justin. "A Culture of Biography." *Yale Review* 82 (October 1994): 1–12.

Kaser, David. *A Book for a Sixpence: The Circulating Library in America.* Pittsburgh: Phi Beta Mu, 1980.

———. *Books and Libraries in Camp and Battle: The Civil War Experience.* Westport, Conn.: Greenwood Press, 1984.

Kelley, Mary. *Private Woman, Public Stage: Literary Domesticity in Nineteenth-Century America.* New York: Oxford University Press, 1984.

———. "Reading Women/Women Reading: The Making of Learned Women in Antebellum America." *Journal of American History* 83 (September 1996): 401–24.

Kerber, Linda K. " 'History Can Do It No Justice': Women and the Reinterpretation of the American Revolution." In *Women in the Age of the American Revolution,* edited by Ronald Hoffman and Peter J. Albert, 3–42. Charlottesville: University Press of Virginia, 1989.

———. *Women of the Republic: Intellect and Ideology in Revolutionary America.* Chapel Hill: University of North Carolina Press, 1980.

Kett, Joseph F. "Adolescence and Youth in Nineteenth-Century America." In *The Family in History: Interdisciplinary Essays,* edited by Theodore K. Rabb and Robert I. Rotberg, 95–110. New York: Harper Torchbooks, 1973.

———. *Rites of Passage: Adolescence in America, 1790 to the Present.* New York: Basic Books, 1977.

Kijinski, John L. "John Morley's 'English Men of Letters' Series and the Politics of Reading." *Victorian Studies* 34 (Winter 1991): 205–25.

Klein, Rachel N. "Art and Authority in Antebellum New York City: The Rise and Fall of the American Art-Union." *Journal of American History* 81 (March 1995): 1534–61.

Kohl, Lawrence Frederick. *The Politics of Individualism: Parties and the American Character in the Jacksonian Era.* New York: Oxford University Press, 1989.

Korsten, F. J. M. "The 'English Men of Letters' Series: A Monument of Late-Victorian Literary Criticism." *English Studies* 6 (1992): 503–16.

Laffrado, Laura. *Hawthorne's Literature for Children.* Athens: University of Georgia Press, 1992.

Langness, L. L., and Gelya Frank. *Lives: An Anthropological Approach to Biography.* Novato, Calif.: Chandler and Sharp, 1981.

Lears, T. J. Jackson. *No Place of Grace: Antimodernism and the Transformation of American Culture, 1880–1920.* New York: Pantheon Books, 1981.

Lehmann-Haupt, Hellmut. *The Book in America: A History of the Making and Selling of Books in the United States.* New York: R. R. Bowker, 1951.

Levin, David. *History as Romantic Art: Bancroft, Prescott, Motley, and Parkman.* Stanford, Calif.: Stanford University Press, 1959.

Levine, Lawrence W. *Highbrow/Lowbrow: The Emergence of Cultural Hierarchy in America.* Cambridge, Mass.: Harvard University Press, 1988.

Lewis, Jan. *The Pursuit of Happiness: Family and Values in Jefferson's Virginia.* Cambridge: Cambridge University Press, 1983.

Lewis, Oscar. "Mug Books: A Dissertation Concerning the Origins of a Certain Familiar Division of Americana." *The Colophon* 17 (1934).

Longaker, Mark. *English Biography in the Eighteenth Century.* Philadelphia: University of Pennsylvania Press, 1931.

McCall, Laura. " 'The Reign of Brute Force Is Now Over': A Content Analysis of *Godey's Lady's Book,* 1830–1860." *Journal of the Early Republic* 9 (Summer 1989): 217–36.

McCants, David A. "The Authenticity of William Wirt's Version of Patrick Henry's 'Liberty or Death' Speech." *Virginia Magazine of History and Biography* 87 (October 1979): 387–402.

McCardell, John. *The Idea of a Southern Nation: Southern Nationalists and Southern Nationalism, 1830–1860.* New York: Norton, 1979.

———. "Trent's *Simms:* The Making of a Biography." In *A Master's Due: Essays in Honor of David Herbert Donald,* edited by William J. Cooper Jr., Michael F. Holt, and John McCardell, 179–203. Baton Rouge: Louisiana State University Press, 1985.

MacDonald, Ruth K. *Literature for Children in England and America from 1646 to 1774.* Troy, N.Y.: Whitston Publishing Company, 1982.

MacGregor, Alan Leander. " 'Lords of the Ascendant': Mercantile Biography and Irving's *Astoria.*" *Canadian Review of American Studies* 21 (Summer 1990): 15–30.

Machor, James L., ed. *Readers in History: Nineteenth-Century American Literature and the Contexts of Response.* Baltimore: Johns Hopkins University Press, 1993.

McKeon, Michael. "Writer as Hero: Novelistic Prefigurations and the Emergence of Literary Biography." In *Contesting the Subject: Essays in the Postmodern Theory and Practice of Biography and Biographical Criticism,* edited by William H. Epstein, 17–41. West Lafayette, Ind.: Purdue University Press, 1991.

Maidment, Brian. "Popular Exemplary Biography in the Nineteenth Century: Edward Paxton Hood and His Books." *Prose Studies* 7 (September 1984): 148–67.

Malone, Kathryn R. "The Fate of Revolutionary Republicanism in Early National Virginia." *Journal of the Early Republic* 7 (Spring 1987): 27–51.

Mandell, Gail Porter. *Life into Art: Conversations with Seven Contemporary Biographers.* Fayetteville: University of Arkansas Press, 1991.

Manierre, William R., II. "Cotton Mather and the Biographical Parallel." *American Quarterly* 13 (Summer 1981): 153–60.

Marshall, Gordon. "The Golden Age of Illustrated Biographies: Three Case Studies." In *American Portrait Prints: Proceedings of the Tenth Annual American Print Conference,* edited by Wendy Wick Reaves, 29–71. Charlottesville: University Press of Virginia, 1984.

Mayer, Henry. *A Son of Thunder: Patrick Henry and the American Republic.* New York: F. Watts, 1986.

Michaels, Walter Benn. *The Gold Standard and the Logic of Naturalism.* Berkeley: University of California Press, 1987.

Monteiro, George. "Whitman, Warner, and the American Men of Letters Series." *Walt Whitman Quarterly Review* 1 (1984): 26–27.

Moss, Sidney P. *Poe's Literary Battles: The Critic in the Context of His Literary Milieu.* Durham, N.C.: Duke University Press, 1963.

———. *Poe's Major Crisis: His Libel Suit and New York's Literary World.* Durham, N.C.: Duke University Press, 1970.

Mott, Frank Luther. *A History of American Magazines, 1850–1865.* Cambridge, Mass.: Harvard University Press, 1938.

Moylan, Michele, and Lane Stiles, eds. *Reading Books: Essays on the Material Text and Literature in America*. Amherst: University of Massachusetts Press, 1996.

Nadel, Ira Bruce. "Biography and Four Master Tropes." *Biography* 6 (Fall 1983): 307–15.

———. *Biography: Fact, Fiction, and Form*. New York: St. Martin's Press, 1984.

Nicolson, Harold. *The Development of English Biography*. 1928. Reprint. London: Hogarth Press, 1968.

Nolan, Charles J. *Aaron Burr and the American Literary Imagination*. Westport, Conn.: Greenwood Press, 1980.

Nord, David Paul. "Religious Reading and Readers in Antebellum America." *Journal of the Early Republic* 15 (Summer 1995): 241–72.

———. "A Republican Literature: A Study of Magazine Reading and Readers in Late Eighteenth-Century New York." *American Quarterly* 40 (March 1988): 42–64.

Novick, Peter. *That Noble Dream: The "Objectivity Question" and the American Historical Profession*. Cambridge: Cambridge University Press, 1988.

Nutt, Charles. *History of Worcester and Its People*. 4 vols. New York: Lewis Historical Publishing Co., 1919.

O'Neill, Edward H. *Biography by Americans, 1658–1936: A Subject Bibliography*. Philadelphia: University of Pennsylvania Press, 1939.

———. *A History of American Biography*. Philadelphia: University of Pennsylvania Press, 1935.

Parke, Catherine N. *Samuel Johnson and Biographical Thinking*. Columbia: University of Missouri Press, 1991.

Patterson, Mark. "Emerson, Napoleon, and the Concept of the Representative." *ESQ* 31 (Fourth Quarter 1985): 230–42.

Peskin, Allan. *Garfield*. Kent: Ohio State University Press, 1978.

Petrie, Dennis W. *Ultimately Fiction: Design in Modern American Literary Biography*. West Lafayette, Ind.: Purdue University Press, 1981.

Pomeroy, Earl. "Old Lamps for New: The Cultural Lag in Pacific Coast Historiography." *Arizona and the West* 2 (Summer 1960): 107–26.

Rabinowitz, Richard. *The Spiritual Self in Everyday Life: The Transformation of Personal Religious Experience in Nineteenth-Century New England*. Boston: Northeastern University Press, 1989.

Reagan, Daniel. "Melville's *Israel Potter* and the Nature of Biography." *American Transcendental Quarterly* 3 (September 1989): 257–76.

Reed, Joseph W. *English Biography in the Early Nineteenth Century, 1801–1838*. New Haven: Yale University Press, 1966.

Reinier, Jacqueline S. *From Virtue to Character: American Childhood, 1775–1850*. New York: Twayne, 1996.

Remer, Rosalind. *Printers and Men of Capital: Philadelphia Book Publishers in the New Republic*. Philadelphia: University of Pennsylvania Press, 1996.

Reynolds, David S. *Beneath the American Renaissance: The Subversive Imagination in the Age of Emerson and Melville*. Cambridge, Mass.: Harvard University Press, 1989.

Richardson, Robert D. "Emerson on History." In *Emerson: Retrospect and Prospect,* edited by Daniel Aaron, 49–64. Cambridge, Mass.: Harvard University Press, 1982.

Rickels, Patricia Kennedy. "The Literary Career of Espy Williams: New Orleans Poet and Playwright." Ph.D. diss., Louisiana State University, 1961.

Roberson, Susan L. "Young Emerson and the Mantle of Biography." *ATQ* n.s., 5 (September 1991): 151–68.

Robert, Joseph C. "William Wirt, Virginian." *Virginia Magazine of History and Biography* 80 (October 1972): 387–441.

Robinson, Kristin H. "Restoring Domestic Order: Sectional Crisis and the Preservation of Mount Vernon." Unpublished paper, 1991.

Rodgers, Daniel T. "Republicanism: The Career of a Concept." *Journal of American History* 79 (June 1992): 11–38.

Rose, Anne C. *Victorian America and the Civil War.* Cambridge: Cambridge University Press, 1992.

Rose, Phyllis. "Biography as Fiction." *TriQuarterly* 55 (Fall 1982): 111–24.

Ruland, Richard, and Malcolm Bradbury. *From Puritanism to Postmodernism: A History of American Literature.* New York: Viking, 1991.

Ryan, Mary P. *Cradle of the Middle Class: The Family in Oneida County, New York, 1790–1865.* Cambridge: Cambridge University Press, 1981.

———. *Women in Public: Between Banners and Ballots.* Baltimore: Johns Hopkins University Press, 1990.

Saxton, Alexander. "Problems of Class and Race in the Origins of the Mass Circulation Press." *American Quarterly* 36 (1984): 211–34.

Schiller, Dan. *Objectivity and the News: The Public and the Rise of Commercial Journalism.* Philadelphia: University of Pennsylvania Press, 1981.

Schneirov, Matthew. *The Dream of a New Social Order: Popular Magazines in America, 1893–1914.* New York: Columbia University Press, 1994.

Schramer, James Joseph. "The Myth of Cincinnatus: The Citizen-Soldier in Early American Literature." Ph.D. diss., University of Minnesota, 1987.

Schudson, Michael. *Discovering the News: A Social History of American Newspapers.* New York: Basic Books, 1978.

Sedgwick, Ellery. *A History of the Atlantic Monthly, 1857–1909: Yankee Humanism at High Tide and Ebb.* Amherst: University of Massachusetts Press, 1994.

Shaffer, Arthur H. *The Politics of History: Writing the History of the American Revolution, 1783–1815.* Chicago: University of Chicago Press, 1975.

Shalhope, Robert E. *The Roots of Democracy: American Thought and Culture, 1760–1800.* Boston: Twayne, 1990.

Sheidley, Harlow Elizabeth Walker. "Sectional Nationalism: The Culture and Politics of the Massachusetts Conservative Elite, 1815–1836." Ph.D. diss., University of Connecticut, 1990.

Shi, David E. *Facing Facts: Realism in American Thought and Culture, 1850–1920.* New York: Oxford University Press, 1995.

Sicherman, Barbara. "Reading *Little Women:* The Many Lives of a Text." In *U.S. History as Women's History: New Feminist Essays,* edited by Linda K. Kerber, Alice Kessler-Harris, and Kathryn Kish Sklar, 245–66. Chapel Hill: University of North Carolina Press, 1995.

Skeel, Emily Ellsworth Ford. *Mason Locke Weems: His Works and Ways.* 3 vols. New York: Plimpton Press, 1929.

Sklar, Kathryn Kish. "American Female Historians in Context, 1770–1930." *Feminist Studies* 3 (Fall 1975): 171–84.

———. *Catharine Beecher: A Study in American Domesticity.* New York: Norton, 1976.

Smeed, J. W. *The Theophrastan "Character": The History of the Literary Genre.* Oxford: Oxford University Press, 1985.

Smith, Culver H. *The Press, Politics, and Patronage: The American Government's Use of Newspapers, 1789–1875.* Athens: University of Georgia Press, 1977.

Solomon, Barbara Miller. *In the Company of Educated Women: A History of Women and Higher Education in America.* New Haven: Yale University Press, 1985.

Stansell, Christine. *City of Women: Sex and Class in New York, 1789–1860.* Urbana: University of Illinois Press, 1986.

Stauffer, Donald A. *The Art of Biography in Eighteenth-Century England.* Princeton: Princeton University Press, 1941.

———. *English Biography before 1700.* Cambridge, Mass.: Harvard University Press, 1930.

Stourzh, Gerald. *Alexander Hamilton and the Idea of Republican Government.* Stanford: Stanford University Press, 1970.

Taylor, William Robert. *Cavalier and Yankee: The Old South and American National Character.* 1957. Reprint. New York: Oxford University Press, 1993.

———. "William Wirt and the Legend of the Old South." *William and Mary Quarterly* 3d ser., 14 (1957): 477–93.

Tebbel, John. *A History of Book Publishing in the United States.* New York: Bowker, 1972.

Teute, Fredrika. "*The Life of George Washington:* Editorial Note." In *The Papers of John Marshall,* vol. 6, edited by Charles F. Hobson. Chapel Hill: University of North Carolina Press, 1990.

Thomas, Amy M. "Who Makes the Text? Reading in Nineteenth-Century America." Ph.D. diss., Duke University, 1992.

Thompson, Lawrence Roger. "The Printing and Publishing Activities of the American Tract Society from 1825 to 1850." *Papers of the Bibliographical Society of America* 35 (Second Quarter, 1941): 81–114.

Tichi, Cecelia. "Spiritual Biography and the 'Lords Remembrancers.'" In *The American Puritan Imagination: Essays in Revaluation,* edited by Sacvan Bercovitch, 56–73. Cambridge: Cambridge University Press, 1974.

Tompkins, Jane. *Sensational Designs: The Cultural Work of American Fiction, 1790–1860.* New York: Oxford University Press, 1985.

Tucher, Andie. *Froth and Scum: Truth, Beauty, Goodness, and the Ax Murder in America's First Mass Medium.* Chapel Hill: University of North Carolina Press, 1994.

Van Cromphout, Gustaaf. "Cotton Mather as Plutarchan Biographer." *American Literature* 46 (January 1975): 465–81.

Vanderbilt, Kermit L. *American Literature and the Academy: The Growth, Roots, and Maturity of a Profession.* Philadelphia: University of Pennsylvania Press, 1986.

Van Tassel, David D. *Recording America's Past: An Interpretation of the Development of Historical Societies in America, 1607–1884.* Chicago: University of Chicago Press, 1960.

Varon, Elizabeth R. "Tippecanoe and the Ladies, Too: White Women and Party Politics in Antebellum Virginia." *Journal of American History* 82 (September 1995): 494–521.

Veeser, H. Aram, ed. *The New Historicism Reader.* London: Routledge, 1994.

Veysey, Laurence. "The Plural Organized Worlds of the Humanities." In *The Organization of Knowledge in Modern America, 1860–1920,* edited by Alexandra Oleson and John Voss, 51–106. Baltimore: Johns Hopkins University Press, 1979.

Wakelyn, Jon L. *The Politics of a Literary Man: William Gilmore Simms.* Westport, Conn.: Greenwood Press, 1973.

Wallach, Glenn. *Obedient Sons: The Discourse of Youth and Generations in American Culture, 1630–1860*. Amherst: University of Massachusetts Press, 1997.

Walsh, John Evangelist. *Plumes in the Dust: The Love Affair of Edgar Allan Poe and Fanny Osgood*. Chicago: Nelson-Hall, 1980.

Warner, Lee H. "Nathaniel Hawthorne and the Making of the President—1852." *Historical New Hampshire* 28 (1973): 20–36.

Warner, Michael. *The Letters of the Republic: Publication and the Public Sphere in Eighteenth-Century America*. Cambridge, Mass.: Harvard University Press, 1990.

Warren, Joyce W. *Fanny Fern: An Independent Woman*. New Brunswick, N.J.: Rutgers University Press, 1994.

Watters, R. E. "Biographical Technique in Cotton Mather's *Magnalia*." *William and Mary Quarterly*, 3d ser., 2 (April 1945): 154–63.

Watts, Steven. *The Republic Reborn: War and the Making of Liberal America, 1790–1820*. Baltimore: Johns Hopkins University Press, 1987.

Welter, Barbara. "The Cult of True Womanhood, 1820–1860." *American Quarterly* 18 (Summer 1966): 151–74.

Wendorf, Richard. *The Elements of Life: Biography and Portrait-Painting in Stuart and Georgian England*. Oxford: Clarendon Press, 1990.

Wilson, Clyde. "Griffith John McRee: An Unromantic Historian of the Old South." *North Carolina Historical Review* 47 (January 1970): 1–23.

Wilson, James D. *The Romantic Heroic Ideal*. Baton Rouge: Louisiana State University Press, 1982.

Winans, Robert B. "The Growth of a Novel-Reading Public in Eighteenth-Century America." *Early American Literature* 9 (1975): 267–75.

Wishy, Bernard. *The Child and the Republic: The Dawn of Modern American Child Nurture*. Philadelphia: University of Pennsylvania Press, 1968.

Wood, Gordon S. *The Creation of the American Republic, 1776–1787*. Chapel Hill: University of North Carolina Press, 1969.

Wyllie, Irvin G. *The Self-Made Man in America: The Myth of Rags to Riches*. New Brunswick, N.J.: Rutgers University Press, 1954.

Yang, James Min-Ching. "Emerson as a Biographer." Ph.D. diss., Indiana University, 1985.

Zboray, Ronald J. *A Fictive People: Antebellum Economic Development and the American Reading Public*. New York: Oxford University Press, 1993.

———. "A Fictive People: Antebellum Economic Development and the Reading Public for American Novels, 1837–1857." Ph.D. diss., Columbia University, 1984.

———. "Reading Patterns in Antebellum America: Evidence in the Charge Records of the New York Library Society." *Libraries and Culture: A Journal of Library History* 26 (Spring 1991): 301–33.

Zboray, Ronald J., and Mary Saracino Zboray. " 'Have You Read . . . ?' Real Readers and Their Responses in Antebellum Boston and Its Region." *Nineteenth-Century Literature* 52 (September 1997): 139–70.

———. "Reading and Everyday Life in Antebellum Boston: The Diary of Daniel F. and Mary D. Child." *Libraries and Culture* 32 (Summer 1997): 285–323.

Builders of the Commonwealth; *Works*),
300–303

Banks, Nathaniel, 121, 123

Barlow, Joel, 38, 277–78

Barnard, Henry, 87

Beadle and Adams (publishers), 239, 293

Beecher, Catharine, 114

Beecher, Henry Ward, 243–44

Beers, Henry A. (*Nathaniel Parker Willis*),
288

Belknap, Jeremy (*American Biography*; "American Plutarch"), 21–23, 38, 138

Bennet, John, 108

Bennett, James Gordon, 224, 236, 237, 244,
251

Benson Female Lending Library (Vt.),
83–84, 110

Benton, Thomas Hart, 278, 283–84

Berkeley, George, 217

Best-sellers, 10, 18, 201, 219

Bildungsroman, 14, 29, 75, 200

Biographers:

—anonymous, 44, 56–57, 91, 96, 272, 293

—as compilers, 92, 115–18, 206–9, 300,
305

—descendants as, 115, 150–51, 186, 189,
211, 309–14

—detachment from subjects (objectivity), 8,
272–73, 308–10

—as historians, 60–62, 135–36, 140–41,
171–72, 245, 278, 305, 311–12

—and identification with subjects, 48, 54,
168, 224–25, 243–44, 326–27

—as literary artists or composers, 96, 191–
92, 199, 202–3, 208, 211–13, 218–19, 230,
235–37, 245, 249, 253–54, 307

—as moralists, 72, 119–24, 171, 227–28, 245,
325

—as mythmakers, 66, 68–69

—as partisans, 38, 145–46, 189–90, 199,
285–86, 289–90

—personal motives of, 48–50, 159–62, 164,
254–55, 326–27

—and psychoanalysts, 324

—readers' awareness of, 86–87, 127–30,
247–56, 261

—as scandal-mongers, 38–39, 204–8, 218–
20, 244–45, 304, 313–15, 323

—as subjects, 300

—subjects' assistance to, 264–66, 292, 302

—sympathy with subjects (*con amore*), 9,
137, 146, 148–49, 163–64, 180, 182–83,
186, 192, 200, 209, 212–13, 220, 232–33,
278–79, 302

—writing for series, 143–45, 148–51, 272,
275–80, 284

"Biographical Mania," 2, 10, 15, 78–80, 101,
204–5, 210, 315

Biographical Souvenir of the State of Texas,
294–95

Biographies:

—advertisements for, 81, 229–30, 238, 273

—as alternative to history, 8, 35, 157–58,
169–70, 176–77, 184

—and character, 6–7, 32–34, 42–43, 51–53,
57–60, 74, 88–90, 123–24, 206–12, 214–
16, 227–28, 238–45, 326–27

—critics' ideas about, 30–37, 40–45, 141,
143, 146, 173–75, 178–80, 188–90,
193–201, 204–13, 218–20, 225, 229–35,
243–44, 304, 311–15, 318–25

—didactic role of, 4–5, 31–32, 43, 54,
57–58, 73–74, 86–87, 88–124, 128, 134,
166–69, 197, 200–201, 204, 206, 209–10,
213–14, 219, 227–28, 238–42, 325

—English models for American, 4–5,
19–20, 33–37, 203–4, 207–9, 255, 274–75

—evidence in, 51–52, 54–55, 66, 73, 115–19,
135–36, 139–41, 149–55, 162–64, 170–
71, 183, 187–88, 208, 214–15, 225–27,
231, 305, 309–10

—and gender, 75–76, 77–78, 82–87, 88–119,
121–23, 158–78, 288–89, 309

—generic characteristics of, 95–96, 128–30,
141, 148–49, 186–87, 211–12

—"great man" emphasis in, 4–5, 8, 158–59,
169–71, 207, 295–96, 300–303, 310–12

—as history, 4, 7–9, 57, 60–62, 135–92, 228,
231, 286–90, 298–99, 310–12, 325, 327,
330

—as inspiration, 85–86, 129, 131–33, 213–
15, 259

284–86; as documents for biographers, 116–18, 206

Dickens, Charles, 234, 238, 247–49, 281, 284

Dictionaries, biographical, 1, 21, 23, 36, 38, 142

Didier, Eugene, 277

Doddridge, Philip (*Life of Col. James Gardiner*), 25, 126

Douglass, Frederick, 158, 325

Du Bois, W. E. B., 300

Dunlap, William (*Life of Charles Brockden Brown*), 36–37

Duyckinck, Evert A., 205, 211, 215, 218

Eaton, John (*Life of Andrew Jackson*), 87, 95

Educational Review, 322

Edwards, Jonathan, 146, 228–29

Eliot, John (*Biographical Dictionary*), 38

Eliot, John (apostle to the Indians), 144–46

Elizabeth I, 82, 111–12

Ellet, Elizabeth Fries, 8, 13; and Jared Sparks, 135–36, 163–64, 169, 175–76; and tradition, 136, 158–59, 162–63, 169, 172, 175–76, 181, 187; research methods of, 136, 158–59, 162–66, 169–73, 175–77, 183; self-conception and self-promotion of, 159–64, 168–69, 172, 175–76, 306, 326–27, 330; early life and career, 159–64, 179; and male historians, 159–65, 169, 178; turn-of-the-century reevaluation of, 306–8

—works: *The Women of the American Revolution*, 135–36, 158–80, 306–8; *Evenings at Woodlawn*, 161–62, 172; "Letter to M. D. S.," 175–76

Emerson, Ralph Waldo, 131, 204, 213–15, 243, 245, 273, 277–78, 280–81, 284, 297, 322; *Representative Men*, 213–15, 217

English Men of Letters series, 274, 281, 285, 320

Eulogy, 34–36, 41, 44, 53, 64, 137, 142, 150, 186, 210–11

Evangelical Christianity, 6, 14, 25, 74, 78, 97, 107, 113, 118, 130, 193

Everett, Edward (*Life of John Stark*), 143, 147

Everett, William, 279, 293, 305

Evolutionary theory, 5, 273, 301, 303, 311, 320

F. A. Battey and Company, 295

Famous Women series, 271, 308

Farmer and Dairyman Publishing House, 290–91

Fatherhood, 72, 75, 100–102

Fay, Theodore S. (*Norman Leslie*), 131

Female Reading Class (Colchester, Conn.), 84

Female Worthies, The, 107–8

Fern, Fanny. *See* Parton, Sara Willis Eldredge

Fiction. *See* Novels

Fields, James T., 234–36, 256, 277

Finney, Charles Grandison, 88

Fletcher, Calvin, 143

Flint, Timothy, 144, 151

Floriad, 40

Floy, Michael, 125–34, 193, 245, 259, 331

Floyd, Silas Xavier (*Life of Charles T. Walker*), 325

Ford, Paul Leicester (*True George Washington*), 315–16

Forster, John (*Life of Charles Dickens*), 247–49

Foster, George (*New York by Gas-Light*), 228

Foxe, John (*Book of Martyrs*), 33

Francis, Convers (*Life of John Eliot*), 144, 145–46

Frank Leslie's Illustrated Weekly, 252

Franklin, Benjamin, 14, 26–28, 36, 77, 82, 85, 90, 91, 105–6, 119, 122–23, 144–45, 216–17, 221, 234–35, 238–39, 242, 250–54, 275, 280, 322, 325; *Autobiography*, 77, 89, 91, 102, 105, 224, 235

French and Indian War, 146

French Revolution, 38

Freud, Sigmund, 3, 323–24

Frost, John (*Lives of American Merchants*), 90

Frothingham, Octavius Brooks (*George Ripley*), 279

Fuller, Margaret, 85, 131, 260, 276, 281, 286–88, 308

Holst, Hermann von (*John C. Calhoun*), 276, 278, 284

Horry, Peter, 29–30, 73–74

Houghton, Henry Oscar, 271, 273–74, 278, 280, 303

Houghton, Mifflin and Company, 5, 8, 10, 13, 255, 271–76, 279–84, 286, 293, 304–5

Howe, Henry (*Memoirs of the Most Eminent American Mechanics*), 89

Howells, William Dean (*Life of Abraham Lincoln; The Rise of Silas Lapham*), 105–6, 260, 274, 278, 316–18, 323

Hubbard, Fordyce (*Life of William Robertson Davie*), 149, 179

Humphreys, David (*Life of Israel Putnam*), 19, 37

Hunt, Freeman (*Merchant's Magazine and Commercial Review*), 89–91, 93, 104, 224

Hunter, Henry (*Sacred Biography*), 25

Hutchinson, Anne, 149

Indians. *See* Native Americans

Individualism, 7, 18, 90, 94, 210, 287, 297

Individuality, 7, 90, 198, 201, 210, 246, 273, 277, 297, 305, 307, 321, 330

Iredell, James, 183–85

Irving, Washington (*Life and Voyages of Christopher Columbus; Life of George Washington; Memoir of Margaret Miller Davidson*), 22, 80, 133, 259, 274, 276, 279, 280–81, 287–88, 311

Jackson, Andrew, 87, 95, 97–100, 122, 146, 153–54, 197, 199, 221, 227, 231, 232–33, 235, 241–42, 249–51, 253, 256, 275, 276, 278, 285, 289–90

James, Henry (*The Aspern Papers*), 288, 310

Jameson, Anna (*Lives of Female Sovereigns*), 110

Jameson, J. Franklin, 309

Jefferson, Thomas, 26–27, 38, 48–49, 55, 58, 62, 64–65, 95, 133, 153–54, 199, 260, 289–90; Jeffersonian republicanism, 48–49, 95, 97; as biographical subject, 122, 186–90, 199, 275, 280–81

Johnson, Samuel, 3, 6, 31, 33–35, 39–40, 43–44, 46, 51–54, 57, 60, 62, 72–74, 109, 132, 135, 139, 141, 203, 208–9, 274; and "domestic privacies," 4–5, 20, 34–35, 39–40, 42–44, 51–52, 60, 74, 109, 202, 207–8, 249, 304, 313, 319, 326, 331; *Lives of the English Poets*, 10, 19, 25, 34, 51, 57, 148, 182, 208, 320, 322

Josephine (empress of France), 79, 82–83, 86, 131, 239

Judson, Adoniram, 112

Judson, Ann Hasseltine, 107, 110, 112–14, 117, 119, 145

J. W. Sheehy and Company, 258

Kaplan, Justin, 2, 17–18

Kennedy, John Pendleton (*Life of William Wirt*), 179–80, 182, 183, 277

Kennedy, W. S. (*John Ruskin*), 305–6

Kirkland, Caroline, 173

Knapp, Samuel L. (*Female Biography; Memoirs of General Lafayette*), 37, 108–10

Knickerbocker, 143, 156

Knowles, James (*Life of Roger Williams; Memoir of Mrs. Ann Judson*), 82, 112, 145

Knox, Lucia, 169, 171

Larry Locke, Man of Iron, 16

Lawrence, Amos, 121

Lee, Gideon, 91

Lester, Charles (*The Mountain Wild Flower*), 117

Letters: as evidence of reading, 13, 117, 203, 249–56; as documents for biographers, 116–18, 169–71, 176, 184–86, 205–8, 306, 310

Liberalism, 6–7, 11, 38, 59, 74–75, 78, 90–91, 94, 99, 105–6

Libraries, 12–13, 26–30, 43–44, 63, 70, 81–84, 110, 143, 206, 246

Library of American Biography, 8, 13, 80, 136–37, 141–52, 156, 163, 173, 179, 181, 183, 207, 231, 250, 275, 287, 324, 327; as national biography, 141–43, 147–51; New England bias of early volumes, 144–48; frontier biography in, 146–47, 151–52;

BELMONT UNIVERSITY LIBRARY